The Bare Facts
Video Guide

Craig Hosoda

Additional copies (volume purchases also available) can be
purchased from:

The Bare Facts
P.O. Box 3255
Santa Clara, CA 95055-3255

ISBN 0-9625474-1-7

INTRODUCTION

Why The Bare Facts Video Guide?

It used to be that people did nude scenes in films at the beginning of their careers trying to get their "big break." Once they established themselves, they announced they would not be doing any more nudity and hoped that everybody would forget their earlier performances. Daryl Hannah and Phoebe Cates for example. But more and more actors and actresses are surprising us and doing nudity in films much later in their careers (Sigourney Weaver and Julie Andrews). Fortunately, there are a few who do nudity in just about every film they are in. Bo Derek and Sylvia Kristel for example. This book compiles all of these unbashful actors and actresses into one reference to help you locate their nude scenes on video tape to save you time and money. I have listed a few close calls like Geena Davis in "Earth Girls are Easy" or Christina Applegate in "Streets."

Some actresses that have done *Playboy* and *Penthouse* pictorials are included because not all actresses do nude scenes in films. Unrevealing pictorials that would be rated PG are not listed (Janet Jones and Jayne Kennedy for example). Only pictorials from *Playboy* and *Penthouse* are listed since they are the easiest men's magazines to find. I haven't finished reviewing all of the back issues in this edition but I will for the next edition.

Actresses that **look** like they have done nudity in films, but have used body doubles instead, are also noted. A body double is a stand-in that is used for nude shots when an actor or actress is too modest. You can usually spot a body double being used when there is a nude body without seeing a face.

How you can help:

I have spent my time concentrating on getting the greatest *number* of celebrities into this book as possible. Therefore, you'll find the entries for some people like Natassja Kinski or Claudia Jennings, rather sparsely documented since it's relatively easy to locate films they have nude scenes in. Obviously, I haven't been able to view all the movies ever made (yet), so there will be films with nude scenes that I have missed. If you find any mistakes or have additions, please write to me and they will be corrected in the next edition. I only look at video tapes, not the theatrical release in movie theaters, so you won't see times for *The Guardian* or *Wild Orchid* listed in this edition because they weren't on video tape when this book was printed. But you can be assured that they will be in the next edition! Future editions will also be cross referenced by film title.

Enjoy!

HOW TO USE THIS BOOK

The book is divided into two sections: Actresses and Actors. In each section, the people are listed alphabetically by last name. Under each name are films, TV shows and magazines that the person has appeared in. The non-nudity titles are listed to help you remember who a particular person is. If they have appeared nude in a film or magazine, the title is in **bold face**. Following the title is the year the film was released, then the character name or article title. Under the title is the time or the page number the nudity occurs. Then there is a brief description of how the person appears in the scene followed by a one to three star rating.

Time definitions
Very, very brief: Need to use PAUSE to see one frame
Very brief: Use SLOW MOTION to see under 1 second
Brief: About 1 second
No comment: 2 to 15 seconds
Long scene: Longer than 15 seconds

Rating definitions
*   Yawn. Usually too brief or hard to see for some reason.
**   Okay. Check it out if you are interested in the person.
***   Wow! Don't miss it. The scene usually lasts for a while.

The ratings are approximate guides to how much nudity an actor or actress has in a scene. More weight is given on how famous a person is, how well lit and clear the scene is, if it's a close shot and the length of time they stay still so you can see clearly. So if someone has an erotic love scene but they don't show any skin or they are topless but their backs are toward the camera, it won't get rated.

To help you find the nude scenes quickly and accurately, the location on video tape is specified in minutes rather than counter numbers since different VCR's have different counters. The time starts at 0:00 minutes after the film's company logo disappears (Universal, Vestron Video, etc.).

Actresses that have appeared nude in only one film and are never seen anywhere else are not included because this book helps you locate someone you've seen somewhere else before, unclothed on another video tape. "One timer" actors are listed though, without them, the Actors section would be woefully thin!

Some film titles have bold type with no descriptions and others have bold type with descriptions and no minutes. These are video tapes that readers have sent as additions that aren't on video tape or I haven't had time to verify. These titles are listed so as not to waste people's time sending me duplicate additions.

THANKS, THANKS AND MORE THANKS!

First of all, I need to thank my wife, Marie, for her help and patience putting up with all my video tape viewing. I also need to thank my children, Christopher and Melanie, for taking their naps so I can watch video tapes. Thanks also to my parents and parents in-laws and the rest of my family for all their help and support.

A special thanks to Video Mania in San Jose, California. Video Mania is the best reason for a video tape fanatic to move to the Bay Area (if you don't mind an occasional earthquake). With over 18,000 different titles, they are probably the most well stocked rental store in the world. Thanks to George and Nickee Amado and their staff: Sharon, Peter, Mike, Jeff, Kevin, Scott, and Robert. This book would have been a lot harder to make without your help!

Thanks to all my friends and the media people who have enabled me to spread word about The Bare Facts through newspapers, magazines, radio and television: Steve Advokat, Marsha Armstrong/Evening Magazine, Martha Babcock/ Entertainment Weekly, Paul Bannister, Julie Bennet, Nance Brandhorst, Joe Bob Briggs, S. C. Dacy, GraceAnne DeCandido, Sharon Dizenhuz, Paul Donnelley/ British Penthouse, Deborah Fernandez, Cheryl Geroch/Magnum Entertainment, Leslie Guttman/San Francisco Chronicle, Richard Hart, Andrea Hill, Ron Iden/ Video-Star, Bruce Kluger/Playboy Magazine, Michelle Lee (not the actress), Liz McNeil, James Marlowe, Dan O'Day, Chuck O'Dell/San Jose Honda-Sony, Mark Ouimet, Jim Pehling, Dawn Reshen/Media Management, Neil Reshen/Celebrity Sleuth, Bonnie Rothman/MTV, Roselyn Royce, Mike Santomauro, Bella Shaw/CNN, Matt Siegel/HBO, Irv Slifkin, Valerie Smith, John Storey, Carolyn Turek and T. Michael Turney.

Thanks to all the people who have sent me additions and corrections: Vince Antonicelli, Shane Arron, Tim Bamford, Matt Bear, J. Bepko, Jim Bereza, Laurance P. Black, Glenn Chivens, Wallace C. Clopton, Bill Jack Kitaen Dallianis, James M. Demsey, Bill Dieffenbach, Bob Dolsay, Michael Duck, Thomas R. Ebersole, J. K. Embree, Joseph Falco, Ray Finocchiaro, R. A. Fowler, Steven J. Frey, Ward Gambrell, Charles Gray, René Hernandez, Dale A. Hesler, F. Hillman, Martin Hudley, Richard Huggins, Chris Khalaf, Wayne & Jodie Kingsley, Philip Long, Tom Martella, John Noble Masi, Greg McCaughey, David McLellan, Mark Merenda, Gary Mullings, Chris Munson, Matt Pachosa, Richard S. Paisley, Alan S. Palmer, Troy Pensley, Doug Preston, J. R. (Bob) Ramp, John Reeks, T. R. Rouff, George M. St. George, Ernest Seddon, E. Z. Smith, G. B. Van Tuyle, Jason J. Vincente, Frank Volpe, Larry Allen Webb, Dick Williams, Steve Williams and Earl Workman.

Actresses

A

AAMES, ANGELA

Films:
Fairytales (1979)..................Little Bo Peep
  0:14 - Nude with "The Prince" in the woods. ***
H.O.T.S. (1979).....................Boom-Boom Bangs
  0:21 - Topless parachuting into pool. *
  0:39 - Topless in bathtub playing with a seal. *
  1:33 - Topless playing football. *
...All the Marbles (1981)..................Louise
  a.k.a. The California Dolls
  0:20 - Topless in Peter Falk's motel room talking
   with "Iris," then sitting on the bed. **
Famous T & A (1982)...................herself
  0:50 - Topless scene from "Fairytales." **
The Lost Empire (1983)..............Heather McClure
  0:31 - Topless and buns taking a shower while
   "Angel" and "White Star" talk to her. ***
Scarface (1983)...........Woman at the Babylon Club
Basic Training (1984)...................Cheryl
  0:19 - Brief topless in bathtub. *
Bachelor Party (1984).......................Mrs. Klupner
Chopping Mall (1986).....................Miss Vanders

ABRIL, VICTORIA

Films:
Comin' At Ya! (1982)...................Abilene
The Moon in the Gutter (1983; French/Italian) Bella
On the Line (1984; Spanish).....................Engracia
  0:16 - Topless getting undressed to have sex with
   "Mitch." ***
  0:29 - Very brief topless, making love in bed with
   "Mitch." *
  0:54 - In white lingerie getting dressed.
L'Addition (1985; French)..........................
The Caged Heart (1985; French).........................
Padre Nuestro (1987)................................
  Topless in bed.
Tie Me Up! Tie Me Down! (1990; Spain)..............
Magazines:
Playboy (Nov 1987)............."Sex in Cinema 1987"
  Page 143: Topless in bed. *

ACKERMAN, LESLIE

Films:
The First Nudie Musical (1976).......................Susie
Hardcore (1979)..............................Felice
  0:44 - Topless in porno house with George C.
   Scott. *
Blame it on the Night (1984)..........................Shelly
TV:
  Skag (1980).....................Barbara Skagska

ADAMS, BROOKE

Films:
James Dean-A Legend in His Own Time (1976)......
Shock Waves (Death Corps) (1977)..................Rose
Days of Heaven (1978)....................................Abby
A Man, A Woman and a Bank (1979)...........Stacey
Cuba (1979).................................Alexandra Pulido
Tell Me a Riddle (1980)..................................Jeannie
Utilities (1983).....................................Marion
The Dead Zone (1983)....................................Sarah
Almost You (1985).......................................
Key Exchange (1985)........................Lisa
  0:10 - Nude on bicycle with her boyfriend, but you
   can't see anything because of his strategically
   placed arms.
  0:45 - Very brief right breast getting into the
   shower with her boyfriend, then hard to see
   behind the shower curtain. *
Invasion of the Body Snatchers (1986)
  ....Elizabeth Driscoll
  0:49 - All covered in pod gunk in her bedroom
   when Donald Sutherland discovers her. Don't
   really see anything
  1:43 - Brief topless behind plants when Sutherland
   sees her change into a pod person. Hard to see
   because plants are in the way. **
  1:48 - Topless walking through the pod factory
   pointing out Sutherland to everybody. Long
   shot, hard to see. *
Made for HBO:
  The Lion of Africa (1987)..
Miniseries:
  Lace..Pagan
  Lace II (1985)..Pagan
Made for TV Movies:
  Murder on Flight 502 (1975)................................
  Bridesmaids (1989)...Pat
TV:
  O.K. Crackerby (1965-66)..........Cynthia Crackerby

ADAMS, MAUD

Films:
The Christian Licorice Store (1971)
  ....Cynthia Vicstrom
The Girl in Blue (1973; Canada)..........Paula/Tracy
  a.k.a. U-turn
  1:19 - In two piece swimsuit getting out of lake.
  1:16 - Side view of right breast sitting on bed with
   "Scott." *
Mahoney Estate (1973; Canadian)...........................
The Man with the Golden Gun (1974; British)
  ....Andrea Anders
Killer Force (1975; Switzerland/Ireland)
  ....Claire Chambers
Rollerball (1975)...Ella
Laura (1979)...Sarah
The Hostage Tower (1980)...............Sabrina Carver

Tattoo (1981)..Maddy
  0:22 - Very brief topless taking off clothes and putting a bathrobe on. *
  0:23 - Topless opening bathrobe so Bruce Dern can start painting. **
  0:25 - Brief topless getting into the shower to take off body paint. **
  0:58 - Brief topless and buns getting out of bed. **
  1:04 - Topless, knocked out on table before Dern starts tattooing her. **
  1:07 - Topless looking at herself in the mirror with a few tattoos on. ***
  1:24 - Topless lying on table masturbating while Dern watches through peep hole in the door. **
  1:36 - Full frontal nudity taking off robe then making love with Dern (her body is covered with tattoos). ***
Octopussy (1983; British).........................Octopussy
  1:06 - Very brief nude getting out of swimming pool while "Bond" watches. Long, long shot.
Target Eagle (1982).......................................Carmen
Playing for Time (1984)..
Hell Hunters (1985).....................Amanda Hoffman
Nairobi Affair (1986)..........................Anne Malone
Jane and the Lost City (1987; British)...Lola Pagola
The Women's Club (1987)..................... Angie Blake
  0:17 - In black panties, garter belt and stockings making out with Michael Paré.
Angel III: The Final Chapter (1987).............Nadine
Deadly Intent (1988)...
Intimate Power (1989)..........................Sineperver
TV:
Big Bob Johnson & His Fantastic Speed Circus
  (1978)..................................Vickie Lee Sanchez
Playing for Time (1980)....................................Mala
Chicago Story (1982)...............Dr. Judith Bergstrom
Emerald Point N.A.S. (1983-1984)...Maggie Farrell
Magazines:
Playboy (Oct 1981)....................."Tattooed Woman"
  Pages 100-107: Topless photos from "Tattoo." ***
Playboy (Dec 1981).................. "Sex Stars of 1981"
  Page 238: Right breast, holding pink robe against herself.
Playboy (Aug 1983)
  ...."The Spy They Love To Love"
  Page 92: Topless on pier.
Playboy (Sep 1987)........."25 Years of James Bond"
  Page 131: Left breast. **

ADJANI, ISABELLE
Films:
Story of Adele H. (1975; French)..........Adele Hugo
Barocco (1976; French)..................................Laure
The Tenant (1976; French)............................Stella
The Driver (1978)................................ The Player
The Bronte Sisters (1979; French)..................Emily
Nosferatu, The Vampire (1979; French/German)
  .... Lucy Harker

Possession (1981; French/German)...... Anna/Helen
  0:04 - Topless in bed. *
  0:16 - Topless lying in bed when Sam Neill pulls the covers over her. *
  0:47 - Right breast, then topless lying in bed with Neill. ***
  1:08 - Right breast lying on floor with Neill, then sitting up. *
Quartet (1981; British/French)............. Marya Zelli
  1:06 - Topless in bed with Alan Bates. **
Next Year if All Goes Well (1983; French)
  ....Isabelle
  0:27 - Brief right breast, lying in bed with "Maxime." *
One Deadly Summer (1984; French)............Eliane
  0:21 - Brief topless changing in the window for "Florimond." **
  0:32 - Nude, walking in and out of the barn. ***
  0:36 - Brief left breast lying in bed when "Florimond" gets up. *
  0:40 - Buns and topless taking a bath. *
  1:41 - Part of right breast, getting felt up by an old buy, then right breast then brief topless. *
  1:47 - Topless in bedroom with "Florimond." **
  1:49 - In white bra and panties talking with "Florimond."
Subway (1985)..Helena
Ishtar (1987)................................ Shirra Assel
  0:27 - Very brief left breast flashing herself to Dustin Hoffman at the airport while wearing sunglasses. *
Camille Claudel (1990; French)..............................

AGBAYANI, TETCHIE
Films:
The Emerald Forest (1985)............................Caya
  1:48 - Topless in the river when "Kachiri" is match making all the couples together. *
Gymkata (1985) ....Princess Rubali
Rikky & Pete (1988; Australia)................... Flossie
  0:58 - Brief upper half of left breast in bed with "Pete" when "Rikky" accidentally sees them in bed. *
  1:30 - Topless in black panties dancing outside the jail while "Pete" watches from inside. ***
Mission Manila (1989)..............................Maria

AGUTTER, JENNY
Films:
East of Sudan (1964; British)............................Asua
A Man could Get Killed (1966).........Linda Frazier
Gates to Paradise (1968; British/German).......Maud
Star! (1968)... Pamela
I Started Counting (1970; British) ....Wynne
Walkabout (1971; Australia/U.S.)....................Girl
  (I can't locate this video tape.)
  Nude several times.
The Railway Children (1971; British) ....Bobbie
The Eagle Has Landed (1976; British)....Molly Prior

Logan's Run (1976)..Jessica
1:05 - Very brief topless and buns changing into fur coats in ice cave with Michael York. *
Equus (1977)... Jill Mason
2:00 - Nude in loft above the horses in orange light, then making love with "Alan." ***
The Man in the Iron Mask (1977)............................
Dominique is Dead (1978; British)...... Miss Ballard
China 9, Liberty 37 (1978; Italian)..........Catherine
(I can't locate this video tape either.)
Sweet William (1980; British).......................... Ann
0:27 - Buns, standing on balcony with Sam Waterston.
0:28 - Topless sitting on edge of the bed eating and talking with Waterston. **
0:44 - Brief left breast when Waterston takes her blouse off in the living room. *
Survivor (1980) .... Hobbs
An American Werewolf in London (1981)
.... Alex Price
0:41 - Brief right breast in bed with David Naughton. Dark, hard to see. *
Amy (1981).................................... Amy Medford
Riddle of the Sands (1984; British)... Clara Dollman
Secret Places (1984; British).................Miss Lowrie
Dark Tower (1987)..................... Carolyn Page
0:05 - In black teddy in her office while a window washer watches from outside.
Made for BBC TV:
Silas Marner (1985)....................... Nancy Lammeter

ALBERT, LAURA
Films:
Angel III: The Final Chapter (1988)
....Nude Dancer
0:00 - Brief topless dancing in a casino. *
0:06 - Side view of left breast and buns yelling at "Molly" for taking her picture. *
Glitch (1988).. Topless
0:35 - Brief topless auditioning for two guys by taking off her top. *
The Jigsaw Murders (1988)...........Blonde Stripper
0:19 - Topless and buns in black G-string, stripping during bachelor party in front of a group of policemen. ***
Bloodstone (1988)...................................... Kim Chi
0:05 - Very brief side view of left breast turning around in pool to look at a guy. *
The Unnameable (1988)................. Wendy Barnes
0:46 - Left breast while lying on floor kissing "John" then brief buns when he pulls her panties down. **
Dr. Alien (1989)............................. Rocker Chick #3
0:21 - Topless in black outfit during dream sequence with two other rocker chicks. ***
Roadhouse (1989)............................ Strip Joint Girl
0:45 - Topless dancing at the club. **

Made for HBO:
Tales From The Crypt: The Man Who was Death (1989)................................. Go-Go Dancer
0:20 - Brief topless a couple of times dancing in a cage in a nightclub. *
Dream On: The First Episode (1990)
....Whipped Cream Girl
0:22 - Laura covered with whipped cream in bed with "Martin."
Magazines:
Playboy (Nov 1989)............. "Sex in Cinema 1989" Page 136: Right breast in still from "Roadhouse." **

ALEXANDER, JANE
Films:
A Gunfight (1971) .... Nora Tenneray
The New Centurions (1972).....................Dorothy
The Betsy (1978) .... Alicia Hardeman
Kramer vs. Kramer (1979).............. Margaret Phelps
Brubaker (1980)....................................Lillian
Night Crossing (1982) ....Doris Strelzyks
Testament (1983).............................Carol Wetherly
City Heat (1984)....................................Addy
Sweet Country (1985)................................ Anna
1:39 - Brief side view of left breast after getting out of bed. *
Square Dance (1987) ....
Made for TV Movies:
Playing for Time (1984)..........................Alma Rose

ALHANTI, IRIS
Films:
Kramer vs. Kramer (1979).......................................
Partners (1982)...Jogger
0:21 - Topless in the shower when Ryan O'Neil opens the shower curtain. **

ALISE, ESTHER
Other:
a.k.a. Esther Elise.
Films:
Deathrow Game Show (1988)....................Groupie
0:08 - Topless in bed with "Chuck." **
Vampire at Midnight (1988).......... Lucia Giannini
1:00 - In black lingerie, then topless taking off clothes in bed to wish "Roger" a happy birthday. **
Hollywood Chainsaw Hookers (1988)............ Lisa
0:25 - Topless playing with a baseball bat while a "John" photographs her. ***

ALLEN, GINGER LYNN

Other:
Former adult film actress.
Films:
Vice Academy (1988).......................................Holly
Cleo/Leo (1988)..Karen
  0:39 - Full frontal nudity getting out of the shower
  and getting dried with a towel by Jane
  Hamilton, then in nightgown. ***
  0:57 - Full frontal nudity getting out of the shower
  and dried off again. ***
Wildman (1988)..
Dr. Alien (1989).......................... Rocker Chick #1
  0:21 - Topless in red panties during dream
  sequence with two other rocker chicks. ***
Magazines:
Playboy (Jul 1989)....................."B-Movie Bimbos"
  Page 137: Full frontal nudity standing in a car.
  ***

ALLEN, KAREN

Films:
National Lampoon's Animal House (1978)
....Katherine "Katy" Fuller
  1:21 - Brief buns putting on shirt when "Boone"
  visits her at her house.
Manhattan (1979)....................................TV Actor
The Wanderers (1979)...............................Nina
Cruising (1980)...Nancy
A Small Circle of Friends (1980).................Jessica
  0:47 - Brief topless in bathroom with Brad Davis.
  Don't see her face. *
  0:48 - Very brief topless, pushing Davis off her. *
  0:48 - Very, very brief half of left breast turning
  around to walk to the mirror.
Raiders of the Lost Ark (1981)..Marion Ravenwood
Shoot the Moon (1982)....................................Sandy
Split Image (1982).....................................Rebecca
Until September (1984).................... Mo Alexander
  0:41 - Topless in bed making love with Thierry
  Lhermitte. **
  1:13 - Topless and buns walking from bed to
  Lhermitte. **
  1:25 - Brief topless jumping out of bathtub. *
Starman (1984)....................................Jenny Hayden
The Glass Menagerie (1987) ....
Scrooged (1988)...............................Claire Phillips
Backfire...Mara
  0:48 - Lots of buns, then brief topless with Keith
  Carradine in the bedroom. *
  1:00 - Brief topless in the shower. *
Made for Cable Movies:
Secret Weapon (1990) ....Ruth
  1:12 - In black slip in room with Griffin Dunne. *
  1:27 - In black slip again in another room. *
  1:28 - Putting on white slip in bathroom.
Made for TV Movies:
Challenger (1990)........................ Christa McAuliffe
TV:
East of Eden (1981)...Abra

ALLEN, NANCY

Films:
The Last Detail (1973)....................................Nancy
Forced Entry (1975)..............................Hitchhiker
  0:44 - Topless and buns tied up by "Carl" on the
  beach. *
Carrie (1976)...............................Chris Hargenson
  0:01 - Nude in slow motion in girls locker room
  scene behind Amy Irving. **
I Wanna Hold Your Hand (1978).......................Pam
1941 (1979)...Donna
  0:17 - Wearing red bra in cockpit of airplane with
  Tim Matheson.
  1:12 - In red bra again with Matheson, but this
  time the airplane is in the air.
Dressed to Kill (1980)............................. Liz Blake
  1:21 - In black bra, panties and stockings in
  Michael Caine's office.
  1:36 - Topless (from above), buns and brief right
  breast in shower. *
Home Movies (1980) .... Kristina
Blow Out (1981)...Sally
  0:58 - Brief upper half of right breast with the
  sheet pulled up in B&W photograph that John
  Travolta examines. *
Strange Invaders (1983).......................Betty Walker
The Buddy System (1984) .... Carrie
Not for Publication (1984)............. Lois Thorndyke
The Philadelphia Experiment (1984)............ Allison
Terror in the Aisles (1984)...........................
Robocop (1987)................................... Ann Lewis
Sweet Revenge (1987) ....Jillian Grey
Poltergeist III (1988)......................Patricia Gardner
Robocop II (1990)...................................... Ann Lewis

ALLEY, KIRSTIE

Other:
Wife of actor Parker Stevenson.
Films:
Star Trek II: The Wrath of Kahn (1982)..Lt. Saavik
Blind Date (1982)............................. Claire Parker
  (<u>NOT</u> the same 1987 "Blind Date" with Bruce
  Willis.)
  0:12 - Brief topless making love in bed with
  Joseph Bottoms. Dark, hard to see anything. *
Runaway (1984)...Jackie
  1:04 - Briefly in white bra getting scanned at the
  police station for bugging devices.
Summer School (1987)....................Robin Bishop
Shoot to Kill (1988) ....Sarah
Loverboy (1989)................................Joyce Palmer
Look Who's Talking (1989).............................Molie
Made for HBO:
The Hitchhiker: Out of the Night................Angelica
Miniseries:
North and South (1985).................... Virgilia Hazard
Made for TV Movies:
The Prince of Bel Air (1986) ....
Stark: Mirror Images (1986) ....Maggie

TV:
    Masquerade (1983-84)..........................Casey Collins
    Cheers (1987-)..................................Rebecca Howe

ALMGREN, SUSAN
    Separate Vacations (1985)...............Helene Gilbert
        1:05 - Topless and buns in bed with David
        Naughton. **
    Shades of Love: Lilac Dream (1987).....................

ALONSO, MARIA CONCHITA
Other:
    a.k.a. Maria Conchita.
    Miss Teen World 1981.
    Miss Venezuela 1975.
Films:
    Fear City (1984)................................. Silver Chavez
    Moscow on the Hudson (1984).... Lucia Lombardo
        1:17 - Topless in bathtub with Robin Williams. **
    Touch and Go (1984)..............................Denise
    A Fine Mess (1986)..............................Claudia Pazzo
    Extreme Prejudice (1987)...............Sarita Cisneros
        0:27 - Brief topless in the shower while Nick
        Nolte is in the bathroom talking to her. **
    The Running Man (1987)................. Amber Mendez
    Colors (1988)....................................Louisa Gomez
        0:48 - Topless making love in bed with Sean Penn.
        ***
    Vampire's Kiss (1989)....................... Alva
        0:47 - In white bra, ironing her clothes in her
        living room.
        0:59 - In white bra getting attacked by Nicholas
        Cage.
Made for Showtime:
    Blood Ties (1986)..........................Caterina

ALPHEN, CORINNE
Other:
    Also see Corinne Wahl.
Films:
    Hot T-shirts (1980).. Judy
        0:55 - In braless T-shirt as a car hop.
        1:10 - In yellow outfit dancing in wet T-shirt
        contest. Brief flashes of topless flashing her
        breasts at the crowd. *
    C.O.D. (1983)..............................Cheryl Westwood
        0:21 - Brief topless changing clothes in dressing
        room while talking to "Zacks." *
        1:25 - Brief topless taking off her top in dressing
        room scene. *
        1:26 - In green bra talking to "Albert."
        1:28 - In green bra during fashion show.
    Spring Break (1983)..........................Joan
        0:32 - Taking a shower in a two piece bathing suit
        in an outdoor shower at the beach.
    Brainwaves (1983)..............................Lelia

New York Nights (1983)..................The Debutante
    0:10 - Topless, making love in the back seat of a
    limousine with the rock star. **
    1:38 - Topless dancing in the bedroom while the
    Financier watches from the bed. ***
Screwball Hotel (1988).....................Cherry Amour
    0:46 - Buns in black outfit on bed with "Norman."
Magazines:
    Penthouse (Jun 1978)...Pet
        Pages 99-111
    Penthouse (Aug 1981).. Pet
        Pages 83-101
    Penthouse (Nov 1982).....................Pet of the Year
        Pages 123-139

AMORE, GIANNA
Films:
    Screwball Hotel (1988)...........................Mary Beth
Magazines:
    Playboy (Aug 1989)..................................Playmate

ANDERSON, MELODY
Films:
    Flash Gordon (1980)..............................Dale Arden
    Dead and Buried (1981)..................................Janet
    Firewalker (1986)..........................Patricia Goodwyn
    The Boy in Blue (1986; Canadian)................Dulcie
        0:07 - Brief cleavage making love with Nicholas
        Cage, then very brief top half of right breast
        when a policeman scares her.
Made for TV Movies:
    Elvis - The Movie (1979)..............................
    Policewoman Centerfold (1983).....................
    Ladies of the Night (1986)..........................Claudia
TV:
    Manimal (1983)..........................Brooke McKenzie

ANDERSSON, BIBI
Films:
    The Seventh Seal (1956; Sweden/B&W)...........Mia
    Wild Strawberries (1957; Swedish/B&W).........Sara
    Brink of Life (1957; Sweden/B&W).............Hjordis
    The Magician (1959; B&W)..............................Sara
    The Devil's Eye (1960) .... Britt-Marie
    Persona (1966; Sweden/B&W).............Nurse Alma
    Duel at Diablo (1966)........................ Ellen Grange
    The Touch (1971; U.S./Swedish) ... Karen Vergerus
        0:31 - Topless in bed with Elliott Gould. *
        0:56 - Topless kissing Gould. ***
        1:13 - Very, very brief right breast washing
        Gould's hair in the sink.
    Scenes from a Marriage (1973; Sweden).....Katarina
    Twice a Woman................................Laura
        0:05 - Topless taking off her bra and putting a
        blouse on. *
        0:06 - Brief side view of left breast, getting into
        bed, brief left breast lying back in bed. *
    I Never Promised You a Rose Garden (1977)
        ....Dr. Fried

5

Quintet (1979)...Ambrosia
Exposed (1983)...Margaret
Babette's Feast (1987).................................

ANDREEFF, STARR

Films:

Dance of the Damned (1988)..........................Jodi
   0:03 - Topless dancing in black bikini bottoms on stage in a club. **
   1:06 - In black bra, panties, garter belt and stockings dancing in bar just for the vampire.
   1:08 - Topless in the bar with the vampire. **
The Terror Within...Sue
Ghoulies II (1988)...
Out of the Dark (1988)..............................Camille
Streets (1989)...................... Policewoman on Horse

ANDRESS, URSULA

Films:

Dr. No (1962; British)....................................Honey
Fun in Acapulco (1963)...........Margarita Douphine
Four for Texas (1963).......................Maxine Richter
Nightmare in the Sun (1964)...........Marsha Wilson
She (1965; British)......................................Ayesha
The Tenth Victim (1965; French/Italian)
   .... Caroline Meredith
What's New, Pussycat? (1965; U.S./French)......Rita
Up to His Ears (1966; French/Italian)...Alexandrine
The Blue Max (1966)....................... Countess Kasti
Casino Royale (1967; British).............. Vesper Lynd
Anyone Can Play (1968; Italian)....................Norma
The Southern Star (1969; French/British)
   ....Erica Kramer
Perfect Friday (1970; British).... Lady Britt Dorsett
   Nude a lot.
Red Sun (1972; French/Italian/Spanish).......Cristina
   1:12 - Almost side view of right breast, then left breast changing tops in room while Charles Bronson watches.
Loaded Guns (1975).....................................Laura
   0:15 - In stockings, white bra and panties while changing clothes in room.
   0:19 - In same outfit again in mirror.
   0:32 - Buns, lying in bed with a guy.
   0:33 - Topless and buns getting out of bed. Full frontal nudity in elevator. ***
   0:40 - Nude getting out of bed and putting dress on. **
   0:48 - Nude getting into bathtub, topless in tub, nude getting out and drying herself off. ***
   1:00 - Buns while getting undressed and hopping in to bed.
   1:02 - Brief side view of right breast while getting dressed. *
Stateline Motel (1975; Italian)....... Michelle Nolton
   a.k.a. Last Chance for a Born Loser
   0:34 - Left breast, then topless on bed with "Oleg." ***
The Loves and Times of Scaramouche (1976; Italian)....................................Josephine

Behind the Iron Mask (1978)
   ....Madame de la Valliere
The Fifth Musketeer (1979)..Madame de la Valliere
Slave of the Cannibal God (1979; Italian).............
   0:33 - Topless taking off shirt and putting on a T-shirt. **
   1:07 - Nude getting tied to a pole by the Cannibal Peoples and covered with red paint. ***
   1:20 - Brief peek at buns under her skirt when running away from the Cannibal People.
The Sensuous Nurse (1979).......................... Anna
   0:16 - Topless and buns in bed after making love. **
   0:22 - Nude swimming in pool. **
   0:50 - Nude slowly stripping and getting in bed with young boy. ***
   1:10 - Nude getting into bed. ***
Tigers in Lipstick (1979)
   .... "The Stroller" and "The Widow" segments
   0:02 - In black bra, panties and garter belt and stockings opening her fur coat to cause an accident.
   0:48 - In slip posing for photographer.
   0:50 - Very brief topless when top of slip accidentally falls down. *
   0:51 - More topless with the photographer. *
Clash of the Titans (1981)...................... Aphrodite
Mexico in Flames (1981; U.S.S.R./Mexico/Italian)
   .... Maybel Dodge
Famous T & A (1982)................................. herself
   0:15 - Full frontal nudity scenes from "Slave of the Cannibal God." ***
Made for TV Movies:
Man Against the Mob: The Chinatown Murders (1989)....................................Betty Starr
Magazines:
Playboy (Nov 1973).............................."Encore"
   Pages 102-109: Topless and buns.
Playboy (Apr 1976)............ "Incomparably Ursula"
   Pages 91-95: Photos from the film "The Loves and Times of Scaramouche." Full frontal nudity. ***
Playboy (Jan 1979)................. "25 Beautiful Years"
   Page 158: Topless in a stream. **
Playboy (Sep 1987)....................................
   Page 124
Playboy (Jan 1989)............ "Women of the Sixties"
   Pages 163: Topless running her fingers through her hair sitting by a pond. ***

ANDREWS, JULIE

Films:

Americanization of Emily (1964)................... Emily
Mary Poppins (1964).........................Mary Poppins
   (Academy Award for Best Actress.)
The Sound of Music (1965).............................Maria
Hawaii (1966)...............................Jerusha Bromley
Torn Curtain (1966).........................Sarah Sherman
The Singing Princess (1967; Italian)...Princess Zeila
Thoroughly Modern Millie (1967)
   ....Millie Dillmount
Star! (1968)........................ Gertrude Lawrence

Darling Lili (1970)....................................Lili Smith
The Tamarind Seed (1974)..................Judith Farrow
10 (1979) ....Sam
Little Miss Marker (1980) ....Amanda
S.O.B. (1981)... Sally Miles
    1:19 - Topless pulling the top off her red dress
    during the filming of a movie. **
Victor/Victoria (1982)...................... Victor/Victoria
The Man Who Loved Women (1983)........Marianna
That's Life! (1986)......................... Gillian Fairchild
Duet for One (1987).................Stephanie Anderson
    0:28 - Very brief left breast in gaping blouse in
    bathroom splashing water on her face because
    she feels sick, then wet T-shirt. *
    1:06 - Topless stretching, lying in bed. ***
    1:10 - Very brief right breast rolling over off the
    side of the bed. *
    1:30 - In wet white blouse from perspiring after
    taking an overdose of pills.
TV:
    The Julie Andrews Hour (1972-73)................hostess

ANNEN, GLORY
Films:
    Felicity (1978; Australia)............................. Felicity
    0:02 - Topless taking off leotard in girl's shower
    room, then nude taking a shower. **
    0:05 - Buns, then left breast, then right breast
    undressing to go skinny dipping. *
    0:10 - Topless and buns at night at the girl's
    dormitory. **
    0:15 - Topless undressing in room with
    "Christine." **
    0:16 - Left breast touching herself in bed. *
    0:20 - Lots of lower frontal nudity trying clothes
    on at "Adrian's." Lots of panty and bra shots.
    Brief topless. ***
    0:25 - Buns and topless taking a bath. Full frontal
    nudity when "Steve" peeks in at her. ***
    0:31 - Brief full frontal nudity losing her virginity
    on car with "Andrew." *
    0:38 - Full frontal nudity in bath with "Mei Ling"
    and two other girls. Long scene. Hot! ***
    0:58 - Full frontal nudity in bed with "Miles." ***
    1:13 - Full frontal nudity with "Mei Ling" making
    love on bed. Long scene. ***
    1:20 - Left breast making love standing up. *
    1:21 - Topless and buns making love with
    "Miles." **
    1:27 - Nude making love again with "Miles." **
    1:29 - Buns in the water with "Miles."
    Spaced Out (1980; British)..............................Cosia
    0:23 - Topless talking to the other two space
    women. Long scene. ***
    0:31 - Very brief topless changing clothes. *
    0:43 - Topless in bed with "Willy." **
    1:08 - Topless lying down. ***
    The Lonely Lady (1983)............................. Marion
    0:07 - Brief left breast in back seat of car with
    "Joe." Dark, hard to see. *
    Alien Prey (1984; British)..
    Supergirl (1984)........................... Midvale Protestor

ANNIS, FRANCESCA
Films:
    Macbeth (1972)...............................Lady Macbeth
    1:41 - Buns, walking around after the bad guys
    have attacked and looted the castle. Side view
    of left breast, hard to see because it's covered by
    her hair.
    Dune (1984).. Lady Jessica
    Under the Cherry Moon (1986)................................
Miniseries:
    Lily...Lily Langtree
Made for TV Movies:
    Coming Out of the Ice (1987)................................
    The Richest Man in theWorld: The Story of
    Aristotle Onassis (1988)
    ....Jacqueline Kennedy Onassis
Magazines:
    Playboy (Feb 1972)
    ...."The Making of 'Macbeth'" pictorial essay
    Page 80
    Playboy (Nov 1972)............. "Sex in Cinema 1972"
    Page 167: Right breast sticking out of hair.
    Photo from "MacBeth." *

ANN-MARGRET
Films:
    Pocketful of Miracles (1961).......................Louise
    State Fair (1962)................................... Emily Porter
    Bye Bye Birdie (1963).......................... Kim McAfee
    Kitten with a Whip (1964)...................Jody Dvorak
    The Pleasure Seekers (1964) ....Fran Hobson
    Viva Las Vegas (1964)...................... Rusty Martin
    Bus Riley's Back in Town (1965) ....Laurel
    The Cincinnati Kid (1965)........................... Melba
    Once a Thief (1965)...........................Kristine Pedak
    Murderer's Row (1966).........................Suzie Solaris
    Stagecoach (1966) .... Dallas
    The Swinger (1966) ....Kelly Olsson
    Tiger and the Pussycat (1967; U.S./Italian).Carolina
    Rebus (1969; German/Italian/Spanish/Argentina)....
    C.C. & Company (1970)...................................Ann
    R.P.M. (Revolutions Per Minute) (1970)...Rhoda
    0:07 - Brief left breast and buns getting out of bed
    talking with Anthony Quinn. **
    0:30 - In fishnet top.
    Carnal Knowledge (1971)............................ Bobbie
    0:48 - Topless and buns making love in bed with
    Jack Nicholson, then getting out of bed and into
    shower with Jack. **
    1:07 - Brief side view of left breast putting a bra
    on in the bedroom. *
    The Train Robbers (1973) ....Mrs. Lowe
    The Outside Man (1973; U.S./French)...........Nancy
    Tommy (1975)................................... Nora Walker
    The Prophet (1976)...
    Twist (1976)...
    Joseph Andrews (1977) ....Lady Boaby
    The Last Remake of Beau Geste (1977)
    ....Lady Flavia Geste
    The Cheap Detective (1978)............. Jezebel Desire

Magic (1978)................................ Peggy Ann Snow
   0:44 - Right breast, lying on her side in bed
   talking to Anthony Hopkins. ***
The Villan (1979).............................Charming Jones
Middle Age Crazy (1980; Canadian)..........Sue Ann
I Ought to be in Pictures (1982)................Stephanie
Lookin' to Get Out (1982).................... Patti Warner
Return of the Soldier (1985; British)..............Jenny
Twice in a Lifetime (1985)...........................Audrey
0:52 Pick-Up (1986)...................... Barbara Mitchell
A New Life (1988).......................................Jackie
A Tiger's Tale (1988)................................. Rose
   0:45 - Side view of left breast in bra, then topless
   jumping up after fire ants start biting her. Brief
   buns running along a hill. Long shot, probably
   a body double. *
Magazines:
   Playboy (Feb 1981)..................... "The Year in Sex"
   Page 146: Left breast in still from "Magic." **

ANSPACH, SUSAN
Films:
   Five Easy Pieces (1970).............Catherine Van Oost
   The Landlord (1970).. Susan
   Play It Again Sam (1972)................................. Nancy
   Blume in Love (1973)............................. Nina Blume
   Mad Bull (1977)...
   The Big Fix (1978)...Lila
   Running (1979).............................. Janet Andropolis
   The Devil and Max Devlin (1981).......... Penny Hart
   Gas (1981; Canadian)....................... Jane Beardsley
   Montenegro (1981; British/Swedish)
   ....Marilyn Jordan
   1:08 - Full frontal nudity taking a shower. **
   1:28 - Right breast making love with
   "Montenegro." *
   Misunderstood (1984)..Lilly
   Into the Fire (1988)..................... Rosalind Winfield
   0:31 - Topless in bedroom standing up with
   "Wade." *
   Blood Red (1988)...Widow
Made for HBO:
   The Hitchhiker: Dead Man's Curve ....Claudia
   (Available on The Hitchhiker, Volume II.)
   0:14 - Buns (probably a body double) in a hotel
   room with a guy. *
Made for Disney Cable:
   Gone Are the Days (1984).............................
Made for TV Movies:
   Dead Encounter (1982)..................................
TV:
   The Yellow Rose (1983)................ Grace McKenzie

ANTHONY, LYSETTE
Films:
   Krull (1983) ....Lyssa
   Looking for Eileen (1988; Dutch) ....
   (Not available on video tape yet.)
   Topless.
   Without a Clue (1988) ....Fake Leslie

Made for Cable Movies:
   A Ghost in Monte Carlo (1990) ....
Made for TV Movies:
   Jack the Ripper (1988) ....Mary Jane Kelly
   The Lady and the Highwayman (1989)
   ....Lady Panthea Vyne
Magazines:
   Playboy (Dec 1988)............................."Lysette"
   Pages 166-173: Topless B&W photos. *

ANTONELLI, LAURA
Films:
   Dr. Goldfoot and the Girl Bombs (1966; Italian)
   .... Rosanna
   Man Called Sledge (1971; Italian)......................Ria
   Docteur Popaul (1972; French)....................Martine
   Without Apparent Motive (1972; French)
   ....Juliette Vaudreuil
   How Funny Can Sex Be? (1973)
   ....Miscellaneous Personalities
   0:01 - Brief topless taking off swimsuit. *
   0:04 - Brief topless in bathtub covered with
   bubbles. *
   0:13 - Lying in bed in sheer nightgown.
   0:18 - Lying in bed again.
   0:26 - Topless getting into bed. *
   0:36 - Topless making love in elevator behind
   frosted glass. Shot at fast speed. *
   1:08 - In sheer white "nun's" outfit during fantasy
   sequence. Brief topless and buns. Nice slow
   motion. *
   1:16 - In black nightie.
   1:24 - In black bra and panties, then topless while
   changing clothes. *
   Malicious (1974; Italian)............................ Angela
   1:14 - Topless after undressing while two boys
   watch from above. *
   1:27 - Topless, undressing under flashlight. Hard
   to see because the light is moving around a lot.
   **
   1:29 - Topless and buns running around the house.
   *
   Till Marriage Do Us Part (1974; Italian)... Eugenia
   0:58 - Topless in the barn lying on hay after guy
   takes off her clothes. **
   1:02 - Full frontal nudity standing up in bathtub
   while maid washes her. **
   1:07 - Right breast with chauffeur in barn. **
   1:36 - Topless surrounded by feathers on the bed
   while priest is talking. **
   The Innocent (1976; Italian)..................... Julianna
   0:41 - Laura topless in bed with her husband. ***
   0:53 - Full frontal nudity in bed when her husband
   lifts her dress up. ***
   Chaste and Pure (1977)....................................
   The Divine Nymph (1977; Italian)
   ....Manoela Roderighi
   0:10 - Full frontal nudity reclining in chair and
   then smoking. **
   0:18 - Right breast in open blouse sitting in bed.
   Pubic hair while getting up. *

Wifemistress (1977; Italian)...... Antonia De Angelis
  0:50 - In lacy nightgown in her bedroom.
  1:22 - Brief upper half of left breast in bed with
    "Clara" and her husband.
  1:25 - In sheer lacy nightgown leaning out the
    window.
  1:29 - Almost right breast making love with a guy
    in bed.
Tigers in Lipstick (1979).... "The Pick Up" Segment
  0:24 - In brown lingerie lying in bed, then getting
    dressed.
  0:34 - In same lingerie, getting undressed, then in
    bed.
High Heels (1980) ....
Secret Fantasy (1981)................. Costanza Vivaldi
  (Topless a lot. Only ** and *** are listed.)
  0:16 - In black bra in Doctor's office, then left
    breast, then topless getting examined. ***
  0:18 - In black bra and panties in another Doctor's
    office. Topless and buns. **
  0:19 - Topless getting X-rayed. Brief topless
    lying down. **
  0:32 - Topless and buns when "Nicolo" drugs her
    and takes Polaroid photos of her. **
  0:49 - Topless and buns posing around the house
    for "Nicolo" while he takes Polaroid photos. **
  0:53 - Topless and buns during "Nicolo's" dream.
    **
  1:12 - Topless in Doctor's office. ***
  1:14 - Topless and buns in room with another guy.
    **
  1:16 - Topless on train while workers
    "accidentally" see her. **
  1:20 - Topless on bed after being carried from
    bathtub. **
  1:25 - Topless dropping dress during opera. **
  1:27 - More topless scenes from 0:49. **
Passion D'Amore (Passion of Love)
  (1982; Italian/French).................................... Clara
The Swashbuckler (1984)..
La Venexiana (1986)..Angela
Collector's Item (1988).................... Marie Colbert
  0:18 - In white lingerie with Tony Musante.
  0:20 - Lower frontal nudity, then right breast
    making love with Musante. Dark. *
  0:37 - In black bra, garter belt and stockings in
    open robe undressing for Musante.
  0:41 - In the same lingerie again dropping robe
    and getting dressed.
Magazines:
  Playboy (Nov 1980).............. "Sex in Cinema 1980"
    Page 179: Full frontal nudity. ***
  Playboy (Nov 1979)................. "Sex Stars of 1979"
    Page 250: Topless. ***

APOLLONIA
See Kotero, Apollonia.

APPLEGATE, COLLEEN
Other:
  a.k.a. Adult film actress Shauna Grant.
Films:
  Penthouse Love Stories (1986)
    .... "Service Station" segment
    0:10 - Nude, making love in a bedroom. Long
      scene. ***

APPLEGATE, CHRISTINA
Films:
  Streets (1989)..Dawn
    1:09 - Very, very brief almost side view of left
      breast kissing her boyfriend. His hand is over
      her breast. I don't think this is really a nude
      scene, but I'm including it beause some people
      might consider it and send this in.
TV:
  Married ...with Children ....Kelly Bundy

ARMSTRONG, BESS
Films:
  Four Seasons (1981)......................... Ginny Newley
    0:26 - In two piece swimsuit on boat putting lotion
      on herself.
    0:38 - Brief buns twice skinny dipping in the
      water with "Nick." *
    0:40 - In one piece swimsuit.
  Jekyll and Hyde... Together Again (1982) ......Mary
  Jaws 3 (1983)................................Kathryn Morgan
  High Road to China (1983)................................ Eve
  The House of God (1984)..............Dr. Worthington
    (Not available on video tape yet.)
    Topless.
  Nothing in Common (1986)..Donna Mildred Martin
  Second Sight (1989).......................................
TV:
  On Our Own (1977-78) ....Julia Peters
  All Is Forgiven (1986) ....Paula Russell
  Married People (1990-).............. Elizabeth Meyers

ARONSON, JUDIE
Films:
  Friday the 13th, Part IV-The Final Chapter
    (1984)...Samantha
    0:26 - Brief topless and very brief buns taking
      clothes off to go skinny dipping. *
    0:39 - Topless and brief buns taking off her T-shirt
      to go skinny dipping at night. **
  American Ninja (1985)................................. Patricia
  Weird Science (1985)....................................... Hilly
  The Sleeping Car (1990)................................. Kim
    0:42 - Brief topless on top of David Naughton
      making love. Brief topless three times after he
      hallucinates. **

ARQUETTE, ROSANNA

Films:

The Dark Secret of Harvest Home (1978)...............

More American Graffiti (1979)............................

Gorp (1980) ....Judy

S.O.B. (1981) ....Babs

    0:21 - Brief topless taking off white T-shirt on the deck of the house. Long shot, hard to see. *

The Executioner's Song (1982; European version)

.... Nicole Baker

    0:30 - Brief topless in bed, then getting out of bed. Nude from the back walking to kitchen. ***

    0:41 - Topless in bed with Tommy Lee Jones. ***

    0:48 - Topless on top of Jones making love. ***

    1:36 - Right breast and buns standing up getting strip searched before visiting Jones in prison. **

Off the Wall (1982) ....Pam

Baby, It's You (1983)...Jill

    1:17 - Left breast, making love in bed with Vincent Spano. **

After Hours (1984)..Marcy

    0:48 - In bed, dead, in panties. Arm covers breasts

The Aviator (1984)............................. Tilly Hansen

Desperately Seeking Susan (1985)... Roberta Glass

    0:24 - Almost topless in bathtub.

    0:46 - Topless getting dressed when Aidan Quinn sees her through the fish tank. Long shot, hard to see. *

Silverado (1985)..Hannah

8 Million Ways to Die (1986).........................Sarah

    1:00 - In a bra in Jeff Bridges' apartment.

Nobody's Fool (1986)...................................Cassie

Amazon Women on the Moon (1987)............Karen

The Big Blue (1988)....................................Johana

    1:00 - Brief right breast in bra in water when "Jacques" helps her out of the dolphin tank and her sweater gets pulled up

New York Stories (1989)............................Paulette

...Almost (1990; Australia)...........................Wendy

    0:07 - In slip in bed taking off her panty hose under the sheets.

Made for Cable TV:

Sweet Revenge (1990)...

Made for TV Movies:

Promised a Miracle (1988)..................................

Magazines:

Playboy (Sep 1990)............................. "Rosanna"

    Pages 126-137: B&W and color photos nude in the surf. Some are out of focus. ***

ASHLEY, JENNIFER

Films:

Your Three Minutes Are Up (1973)......................

The Centerfold Girls (1974)....................... Charly

    0:34 - Topless taking off top while changing clothes. *

    0:49 - Topless and buns posing for photographer outside with "Glory." **

The Pom Pom Girls (1976)...........................Laurie

Tintorera (1977) ....

Horror Planet (1980; British) ....Holly

Partners (1982)..Secretary

The Man Who Loved Women (1983)

....David's Mother

Magazines:

Playboy (Nov 1978).............. "Sex in Cinema 1978"

    Page 187: Topless above the water. *

ASTLEY, PAT

Films:

Playbirds (1978; British).............. Doreen Hamilton

    0:00 - Topless posing for photo session. **

Don't Open Till Christmas (1984; British)....Sharon

AUSTIN, TERI

Films:

Terminal Choice (1984)......................... Lylah Crane

    0:14 - Full frontal nudity, covered with blood on operating table. Long shot.

    0:21 - Right breast, on table being examined by Ellen Barkin. Dead, covered with dried blood.

    0:26 - Very brief left breast under plastic on table, hard to see.

The Vindicator (1984)....................Lauren Lehman

a.k.a. Frankenstein '88

    0:30 - Very brief left breast and buns in mirror getting out of the bubble bath covered with bubbles. Long shot, hard to see anything. *

Dangerous Love (1988) .... Dominique

Made for TV Movies:

Laura Lansing Slept Here (1988)

....Melody Gomphers

TV:

Knots Landing (1985-).........................Jill Bennett

AXELROD, NINA

Films:

Roller Boogie (1979) .... Bobby's Friend

Motel Hell (1980).. Terry

    0:58 - In wet white T-shirt tubin' with "Ida."

    1:01 - Topless sitting up in bed to kiss "Vincent." **

    1:04 - Very brief topless in tub when "Bruce" breaks the door down, then getting out of tub. *

Time Walker (1982)......................................Susie

Cross Country (1983)..............................Lois Hayes

    0:28 - Brief buns and sort of topless getting breasts fondled by "Richard."

    1:05 - Very, very brief topless fighting outside the motel in the rain with "Johnny."

Cobra (1985).. Waitress

AYER, LOIS

Films:
In Search of the Perfect 10 (1986).. Perfect Girl #2
(Shot on video tape.)
0:08 - In swimsuit, then topless exercising by the
pool. ***
Tougher Than Leather (1988) ....Charlotte

AYRES-HAMILTON, LEAH

Other:
a.k.a. Leah Ayres.
Films:
All That Jazz (1979)................... Nurse Capobianco
The Burning (1981).......................................Michelle
Eddie Macon's Run (1983) .... Chris
Hot Child in the City (1987)........................Rachel
0:38 - In braless white T-shirt walking out by the
pool and inside her sister's house.
1:12 - Very brief topless in the shower with a guy.
Long shot, hard to see anything. *
Bloodsport (1987) ....Janice
TV:
9 to 5 (1983).................................... Linda Bowman

B

BACH, BARBARA

Other:
Wife of singer/former "Beatles" drummer Ringo
Starr.
Films:
Black Belly of the Tarantula (1972; Italian) ....Jenny
Stateline Motel (1975; Italian)..........................Emily
a.k.a. Last Chance for a Born Loser
The Anonymous Avenger (1976; Italian) ....
The Spy Who Loved Me (1977; British)
.... Major Anya Amosova
Force Ten from Navarone (1978).............. Maritza
0:32 - Brief topless taking a bath in the German
officer's room. *
Screamers (1978; Italian) ....Amanda
a.k.a. The Island of the Fishmen
a.k.a. Something Waits in the Dark
Wolf Larsen (1978; Italian).....................................
The Humanoid (1979; Italian)..................................
Jaguar Lives (1979).. Anna
Great Alligator (1980; Italian)..................................
Caveman (1981)... Lana
Street Law (1981)..
The Unseen (1981).......................................Jennifer
Up the Academy (1981)......................................Bliss
Give My Regards to Broad Street (1984; British)
....Journalist
Miniseries:
Princess Daisy (1983)..

Magazines:
Playboy (Jun 1977) ...."Bonded Barbara"
Pages 106-109: In lingerie, partial buns and
topless. **
Playboy (Jan 1981).........................."Barbara Bach"
Pages 120-127: Full frontal nudity. ***
Playboy (Sep 1987)........"25 Years of James Bond"
Page 130: Left breast. **
Playboy (Jan 1989).........."Women of the Seventies"
Page 212-213: Buns.

BAGDASARIAN, CAROL

Films:
The Strawberry Statement (1970)..... Telephone Girl
Charge of the Model T's (1979)...............................
The Octagon (1980)...Aura
1:18 - Brief side view of right breast sitting on bed
next to Chuck Norris taking her top off. *
The Aurora Encounter (1985)...........................Alain

BAKER, CARROLL

Films:
Baby Doll (1956; B&W) ....Baby Doll
Giant (1956)......................................Luz Benedict II
The Big Country (1958)....................Patricia Terrill
How the West was Won (1963)............ Eve Prescott
Cheyenne Autumn (1964)............... Deborah Wright
The Carpetbaggers (1964) ....Rina
Harlow (1965)...................................... Jean Harlow
Sylvia (1965) .... Sylvia West
Orgasmo (1968)...
The Sweet Body of Deborah (1968)......... Deborah
(Not available on video tape yet.)
Topless.
Andy Warhol's Bad (1977; Italian) ....
The World is Full of Married Men (1979)
.... Linda Cooper
0:19 - Brief left breast sitting up in bathtub
covered with bubbles. *
My Father's Wife (1981; Italian).....................Lara
0:03 - Right breast making love in bed with her
husband, "Antonio." *
0:06 - Topless standing in front of bed talking to
"Antonio." **
0:18 - Topless kneeling in bed, then getting out
and putting a robe on while wearing beige
panties. ***
The Watcher in the Woods (1981)........ Helen Curtis
Star 80 (1983)...............................Dorothy's Mother
The Secret Diary of Sigmund Freud (1984)
....Mama Freud
Ironweed (1987)...............................Annie Phelan
Magazines:
Playboy (Jun 1980) ....Grapevine
Page 300: Left breast in bathtub in B&W still
from "The World is Full of Married Men." *

BAKER, CYNTHIA

Films:
Sector 13 (1982)..
Risky Business (1983) ....Test Teacher
Blood Diner (1987) .... Cindy
  0:44 - Nude outside by fire with her boyfriend,
  then fighting a guy with an axe. ***
Galactic Gigolo (1989)..

BAKER, LEEANNE

Films:
Breeder (1987)..
Necropolis (1987)... Eva
  0:04 - Right breast, dancing in skimpy black outfit
  during vampire ceremony. *
  0:38 - Brief topless in front of three evil things.
  (Before she has special make up to make it look
  like she has six breasts). *

BAKER, PENNY

Films:
Real Genius (1985)......................Ick's Girl at Party
The Men's Club (1986)................................. Lake
  1:13 - Topless in bed with Treat Williams. **
Million Dollar Mystery (1987)..............................
Video Tapes:
Playboy Video Magazine, Volume 4.......Playmate
Magazines:
Playboy (Jan 1984)...................................Playmate
Playboy (Nov 1986)......................"Sex in Cinema"
  Page 128: Topless in bed with Treat Williams. *
Playboy (Jan 1989)........... "Women of the Eighties"
  Page 253: Full frontal nudity. ***

BALASKI, BELINDA

Films:
Cannonball (1976; U.S./Hong Kong)....... Maryanne
Food of the Gods (1976)...................................Rita
Bobbie Jo and the Outlaw (1976).Essie Beaumont
  0:29 - Topless in pond with Marjoe Gortner and
  Lynda Carter. *
Piranha (1978) ....Betsy
Till Death (1978) ....
The Howling (1981)..........................Terry Fisher
Amazon Women on the Moon (1987)
  ....Bernice Pitnik
Made for TV Movies:
Deadly Care (1987)...................................Terry

BALDWIN, JANIT

Other:
a.k.a. Janet Baldwin.
Films:
Prime Cut (1972)................................. Violet
  0:25 - Very brief nude getting swung around when
  Gene Hackman lifts her up to show to Lee
  Marvin. *
  0:41 - Brief topless putting on a red dress. *

'Gator Bait (1972)..
  0:27 - Topless and buns walking into a pond, then
  getting out and getting dressed. **
  0:35 - Very brief right breast twice popping out of
  her dress when the bad guys hold her. *
  0:40 - Brief left breast struggling against two guys
  on the bed. *
Ruby (1977) ....
Where the Buffalo Roam (1980)...........................
Humongous (1982; Canadian) ....Donna Blake

BALDWIN, JUDY

Films:
Evel Knievel (1971)............................Sorority Girl
The Seven Minutes (1971).......Fremont's Girlfriend
No Small Affair (1984)...................... Stephanie
  0:36 - In white bra, panties and garter belt, then
  topless in Jon Cryer's bedroom trying to seduce
  him. ***
Made in the U.S.A. (1987)................................

BARBEAU, ADRIENNE

Films:
The Fog (1980)...............................Stevie Wayne
The Cannonball Run (1981)...........................Marcie
Escape from New York (1981).....................Maggie
Swamp Thing (1981)...........................Alice Cable
  1:03 - Side view of left breast washing herself off
  in the swamp. Long shot. *
Creepshow (1982)...........................Wilma Northrup
The Next One (1983) ....Andrea Johnson
Back to School (1986)...............................Vanessa
Open House (1988)....................Lisa Grant
  0:27 - In black lace lingerie, then very brief half of
  left breast making love with Joseph Bottoms on
  the floor. *
  1:15 - Brief side view of right breast getting out of
  bed at night to look at something in her
  briefcase. **
  1:16 - Brief topless taking off bathrobe and getting
  back into bed. Kind of dark. ***
Cannibal Women in the Avocado Jungle of Death
  (1988)..............................Dr. Kurtz
Made for TV Movies:
Red Alert (1977)...
Terror at London Bridge (1985).............................
TV:
Maude (1972-78).. Carol

BARBER, GLYNNIS

Film:
Terror (1979; British)....................................Carol
Yesterday's Hero (1979; British).....................Susan
The Hound of the Baskervilles (1983; British).........
The Wicked Lady (1983; British)............. Caroline
  0:58 - Topless and buns making love with "Kitt
  Larksby" in the living room. Possible body
  double. ***
The Edge of Sanity (1988)...............Elisabeth Jekyll

Dempsey and Makepeace (1984-86)
.... Detective Sergeant Harriet Makepeace

BARDOT, BRIGITTE

Films:

Doctor at Sea (1955; British).............Helene Colbert
...and God created woman (1957; French)..Juliette
  0:40 - Very brief side view of right breast getting
  out of bed. *
A Very Private Affair (1962; French/Italian).......Jill
Contempt (1963; French/Italian)........ Camille Javal
  0:04 - Buns.
  0:52 - Almost buns walking through door after
  bath.
  0:54 - Buns, while lying on rug.
  1:30 - Buns, while lying on beach. Long shot.
Dear Brigitte (1965).................................... Herself
Shalako (1968; British) .... Countess Irini Lazaar
Ms. Don Juan (1973)..................................... Joan
  0:19 - Left breast in bathtub. *
  1:19 - Topless through fish tank. Buns and left
  breast, then brief topless in mirror with "Paul."
  **
Famous T & A (1982)................................. herself
  0:25 - Buns, then brief topless in scene from "Ms.
  Don Juan." *

BARKIN, ELLEN

Other:

Wife of actor Gabriel Byrne.

Films:

Diner (1982).......................................Beth
Eddie and the Cruisers (1983)......................Maggie
Tender Mercies (1983)............................ Sue Anne
Harry and Son (1984)...................................... Katie
The Princess Who Had Never Laughed (1984).........
Terminal Choice (1984)................. Mary O'Connor
The Adventures of Buckaroo Banzai (1984)
.... Penny Priddy
Act of Vengeance (1985)...................................
Desert Bloom (1986).. Starr
Down by Law (1986)....................................Bobbie
The Big Easy (1987) ....Anne Osborne
  0:21 - White panties in lifted up dress in bed with
  Dennis Quaid.
  0:32 - Brief buns jumping up in kitchen after
  pinching a guy who she thinks is Quaid.
Made in Heaven (1987)...
Siesta (1987)... Diane
  0:03 - Brief full frontal nudity long shot taking off
  red dress, topless, brief buns standing up, then
  full frontal nudity lying down. ***
  1:23 - Right nipple sticking out of dress making
  love and getting raped by taxi driver. Lower
  frontal nudity then brief buns, dark, hard to see.
  1:28 - Very brief side view of right breast putting
  on dress in bed just before Isabella Rossellini
  comes into the bedroom to attack her. Long
  distance shot.

Johnny Handsome (1989)......................Sunny Boyd
Sea of Love (1989)..............................Helen Cruger
  0:56 - Side view of left breast of body double,
  then buns standing up making out with Al
  Pacino in his apartment.
  0:59 - Back view wearing panties, putting top on
  in bathroom.
  1:13 - Brief upper half of buns, lying in bed with
  Pacino.

BARNES, PRISCILLA

Films:

Tintorera (1977)...
  1:12 - Very brief topless dropping her beer into
  the water. *
  1:14 - Topless, on the beach after the shark attack
  (on the left). *
Texas Detour (1977).......................Claudia Hunter
  1:03 - Topless, changing clothes and walking
  around in bedroom. Wearing white panties.
  This is her best topless scene. ***
  1:11 - Topless sitting up in bed with Patrick
  Wayne. *
Delta Fox (1977)... Karen
  0:36 - Left breast undressing in room for "David
  Fox." Very dark, hard to see.
  0:38 - Very brief topless struggling with a bad guy
  and getting slammed against the wall. *
  0:39 - Very brief blurry left breast running in front
  of the fireplace.
  0:40 - Topless sneaking out of house. Brief
  topless getting into Porsche. *
  0:49 - Brief right breast reclining onto bed with
  "David." Side view of left breast several times
  while making love. *
  1:29 - Very brief side view of left breast in
  "David's" flashback.
Seniors (1978).. Sylvia
  0:18 - Topless at the top of the stairs while
  "Arnold" climbs up the stairs while the rest of
  the guys watch. **
The Last Married Couple in America (1980)
.... Helena Dryden
Sunday Lovers (1980; Italian/French)............Donna
Traxx (1988)...................... Mayor Alexandria Cray
License to Kill (1989)......................Della Churchill
Lords of the Deep (1989)................................Claire

TV:

The American Girls (1978)........... Rebecca Tomkins
Three's Company (1981-84)................... Terri Alden

Magazines:

Penthouse (Mar 1976)... Pet
  (Used the name Joann Witty.)
  Pages 77-89

BARRAULT, MARIE-CHRISTINE
Films:

My Night at Maud's (1970; French).......... Francoise
Chloe in the Afternoon (1972; French) ....
Cousin, Cousine (1975; French)................... Marthe
  1:05 - Topless in bed with her lover cutting his
    nails. **
  1:07 - Brief side view of right breast giving him a
    bath. *
  1:16 - Topless with penciled tattoos all over her
    body. ***
  1:33 - Braless in see-through white blouse saying
    "good bye" to everybody.
The Daydreamer (1975; French) ....Lisa
The Medusa Touch (1978; British).............. Patricia
Stardust Memories (1980) .... Isabel
Table for Five (1983)................................Marie
A Love in Germany (1984; French/German)
....Maria Wyler
Swann in Love (1985; French/German)
....Madame Verdunn

BARRETT, NITCHIE
Films:

Preppies (1984)................................ Roxanne
  0:11 - Brief topless changing into waitress
    costumes with her two friends. *
She-Devil (1989) ....Bob's Secretary

BARRETT, VICTORIA
Films:

Hot Resort (1984)................................Jane
Hot Chili (1985)........................ Victoria Stevenson
  0:55 - Very brief close up shot of right breast
    when it pops out of her dress. *
Three Kinds of Heat (1987)................................

BARRY, WENDY
Films:

Knights of the City (1986)......................Jasmine
Young Lady Chatterley II (1986)
................................Sybil "Maid in Hot House"
  0:12 - Topless in hot house with the Gardener. *
3:15 - The Moment of Truth (1987)................. Lora

BASINGER, KIM
Films:

Killjoy (1981)................................
Hard Country (1981)................... Jodie Lynn Palmer
Motherlode (1982)..........................Andrea Spalding
Never Say Never Again (1983) ....Domino Vitale
The Man Who Loved Women (1983)
....Louise "Lulu"
The Natural (1984)........................Memo Paris
Fool For Love (1985)................................ May

9 1/2 Weeks (1986)................................Elizabeth
  0:27 - Blindfolded while Mickey Rourke plays
    with an ice cube on her. Brief right breast. *
  0:36 - Masturbating while watching slides of art
  0:41 - Playing with food at the refrigerator with
    Rourke. Messy, but erotic.
  0:54 - Very brief left breast rolling over in bed. *
  0:58 - Making love with Rourke in clock tower.
  1:11 - In wet lingerie, then topless making love in
    a wet stairwell with Rourke. ***
  1:19 - Doing a sexy dance for Rourke in a white
    slip.
  1:22 - Buns, showing off to Rourke on building.
No Mercy (1986)................................Michel Duval
Blind Date (1987)................................ Nadia Gates
Nadine (1987)........................... Nadine Hightower
My Stepmother Is An Alien (1988) .. Celeste Martin
  0:40 - Dancing very seductively in a white slip in
    front of Dan Ackroyd while he lies in bed. No
    nudity, but still *very* exciting.
Batman (1989)................................Vicki Vale
Made for TV Movies:
Katie: Portrait of a Centerfold (1978)....................
Miniseries:
From Here to Eternity (1978)............ Lorene Rogers
TV:
Dog and Cat (1977)....................... Officer J.Z. Kane
From Here to Eternity (1979-80) ...... Lorene Rogers
Magazines:
Playboy (Feb 1983) ...."Betting on Kim"
  Pages 82-89: Nude. ***
Playboy (Dec 1983) .... "Sex Stars of 1983"
  Page 211: Topless. **
Playboy (Dec 1984) .... "Sex Stars of 1984"
  Page 208: Topless walking in water. ***
Playboy (Sep 1987)....... "25 Years of James Bond"
  Page 130: Topless. **
Playboy (Jan 1988)................................"Kim"
  Pages 78-85: Topless and buns from Feb 1983.
    ***
Playboy (Jan 1989)..........."Women of the Eighties"
  Page 256: Buns.

BATES, JO ANNE
Films:

Perfect Timing (1984)................................ Karen
  0:21 - Nude, getting ready to get her picture taken.
    ***
Heavenly Bodies (1986)................................
Immediate Family (1989)....................Home Buyer

BAUER, BELINDA
Films:

And Now the Screaming Starts (1973)....................
Winter Kills (1979)........................ Yvette Malone
  0:46 - Topless making love in bed with Jeff
    Bridges, then getting out of bed. **
  1:25 - Topless, dead as a corpse when sheet
    uncovers her body. *
The American Success Company (1980)......... Sarah

Flashdance (1983) .... Katie Hurley
Timerider (1983) ....Clair Cygne
The Rosary Murders (1987).....................Pat Lennon
Made for TV Movies:
The Sins of Dorian Gray (1983)..............................
Starcrossed (1985)... Mary
Made for HBO:
The Hitchhiker: Love Sounds..Veronica Hoffman
0:15 - Brief topless, making love in the house with
"Kerry." *
0:22 - Topless, making love in the boat. **

BAUER, JAIME LYN

Films:
The Centerfold Girls (1974)..........................Jackie
0:04 - Topless getting out of bed and walking
around the house. **
0:14 - Topless getting undressed in the bathroom.
***
0:15 - Brief topless and buns putting on robe and
getting out of bed, three times. **
Young Doctors in Love (1982) ....Cameo
TV:
Bare Essence (1983)........................... Barbara Fisher
Soap Operas:
The Young and the Restless (1973-82) ....
...........................Lauralee (Laurie) Brooks Prentiss
The Young and the Restless (1984)..........................
...........................Lauralee (Laurie) Brooks Prentiss

BAUER, MICHELLE

Other:
Also see Michelle McClellan.
Films:
Cave Girl (1985)....................Locker Room Student
0:05 - Topless with the other girls running around
in the girl's locker room. *
Screen Test (1985).......................Dancer/Ninja Girl
0:05 - Topless on stage. *
0:42 - Full frontal nudity (with Monique
Gabrielle) making love in a boy's dream. ***
Reform School Girls (1986)...................uncredited
0:25 - Topless, then nude in the shower. **
In Search of the Perfect 10 (1986)
.... Perfect Girl #10
(Shot on video tape.)
0:53 - In yellow outfit stripping in office. Topless
and buns in G-string bottom. ***
Penthouse Love Stories (1986)
.... "The Therapist" segment
0:45 - Nude making love in Therapist's office.
(she's the brunette). ***
Armed Response (1987)............................Stripper
0:41 - Topless, dancing on stage. *
Roller Blade (1987)...
The Tomb (1987)....................................Nefratis
Nightmare Sisters (1987)..

Phantom Empire (1987)......................Cave Bunny
0:32 - Running around in the cave a lot in two
piece loincloth swimsuit.
1:13 - Finally topless after losing her top during a
fight, stays topless until "Andrew" puts his
jacket on her. **
Sorority Babes in the Slimeball Bowl-O-Rama
(1988)..Lisa
0:12 - Topless, then full frontal nudity in shower.
***
0:41 - Topless, then nude making love. Long
scene. ***
The Jigsaw Murders (1988)............Cindy Jakulski
0:20 - Brief buns on cover of puzzle box during
bachelor party.
0:21 - Brief topless in puzzle on underside of glass
table after the policemen put the puzzle
together. *
0:29 - Very brief topless when the police officers
show the photographer the puzzle picture. *
0:43 - Very brief topless long shots in some
pictures that the photographer is watching on a
screen. *
Wildman (1988)...
Dr. Alien (1989)................................ Coed #1
a.k.a. I Was a Teenage Sex Mutant
0:53 - Topless taking off her top in the women's
locker room after another coed takes her's off in
front of "Wesley." ***
Beverly Hills Vamp (1989).......................Kristina
0:12 - Buns and brief side view of right breast in
bed biting a guy. *
0:33 - In red slip with "Kyle."
0:38 - Topless trying to get into "Kyle's" pants.
**
1:09 - In black lingerie attacking "Russell" in bed
with Debra Lamb and Jillian Kesner.
1:19 - In black lingerie enticing "Mr. Pendleton"
into bedroom.
1:22 - In black lingerie getting killed as a vampire
by "Kyle."
Magazines:
Playboy (Jul 1989).................... "B-Movie Bimbos"
Page 138: Topless and buns lying in a car that
looks like a shark. **

BEACHAM, STEPHANIE

Films:
The Games (1970) ....Angela Simmonds
The Nightcomers (1971; British) .... Miss Jessel
0:13 - Brief left breast lying in bed having her
breasts felt. *
0:30 - Topless in bed with Marlon Brando while a
little boy watches through the window. ***
0:55 - Topless in bed pulling the sheets down. **
Dracula A.D. 1972 (1972; British)
.... Jessica Van Helsing
The Devil's Widow (1972; British)................Janet
And Now the Screaming Starts (1973; British)
.... Catherine Fengrifen
The Confessional (1977; British)................. Vanessa
Mafia Junction (1977)..

Schizo (1977; British)................................. Beth
   a.k.a. Amok
   a.k.a. Blood of the Undead
Horror Planet (1980; British)............................ Kate
   a.k.a. Inseminoid
Troop Beverly Hill$ (1989)................. Vicki Sprantz
Miniseries:
Napolean and Josephine (1987)............................
TV:
The Colby's (1985-89).................Sable Scott Colby
Sister Kate (1989-90)........Sister Katherine Lambert
Magazines:
Playboy (Nov 1972)............. "Sex in Cinema 1972"
   Page 160: Right breast, B&W photo from "The
   Nightcomers." **
Playboy (Feb 1987).......................................
   Pages 112-121: Color photos taken in 1972. **

BEAL, CINDY
Films:
Slavegirls from Beyond Infinity (1987).......... Tisa
   Wearing skimpy outfits during most of the movie.
   0:25 - Talking around in white bra and panties.
   0:36 - Topless on beach wearing white panties.
   ***
   1:05 - Left breast leaning back on table while
   getting attacked by "Zed." *
My Chauffeur (1987).................................... Beebop

BEALL, SANDRA
Film:
A Night in Heaven (1983)............................. Slick
   1:09 - Brief close up of left breast in shower with
   Christopher Atkins. *
Birdy (1985)... Shirley
The Cotton Club (1984).......................... Myrtle Ray
Key Exchange (1985)............................... Marcy
   1:14 - Topless on bed taking off clothes and
   talking to Daniel Stern. ***
Loverboy (1989)... Robin

BEALS, JENNIFER
Films:
Flashdance (1983)... Alex
The Bride (1985)... Eva
   0:21 - Lower frontal nudity and buns coming
   down stairs and to kneel down and talk to Sting.
   Probably a body double.
   0:53 - Standing in wet white nightgown in the rain
   talking to Sting.
Split Decisions (1988) .... Barbara Uribe
Vampire's Kiss (1989).................................... Rachel
   0:14 - Almost topless in bed with Nicholas Cage.
   Squished left breast against Cage while she bites
   him. In one shot, you can see the beige pastie
   she put over her left nipple.
   0:27 - In bed again with Cage.
   0:41 - In black lingerie taking her dress off for
   Cage.

BÉART, EMMANUELLE
Films:
Manon of the Spring (1987; French).......... Manon
   0:11 - Brief nude dancing around a spring playing
   a harmonica. *
Date with an Angel (1987)............................. Angel

BECK, KIMBERLY
Films:
Your, Mine, and Ours (1968)............................
Massacre at Central High (1976)...............Theresa
   0:32 - Nude romping in the ocean with "David."
   Long shot, dark, hard to see anything. *
   0:42 - Topless on the beach making love with
   Andrew Stevens after a hang glider crash. **
Roller Boogie (1979) .... Lana
Friday the 13th Part IV - The Final Chapter (1984)
....Trish
Maid to Order (1987)...................................... Kim
Miniseries:
Rich Man, Poor Man-Book II (1976-77)
....Diane Porter
TV:
Peyton Place (1965) .... Kim Schuster
Lucas Tanner (1974-75)...................Terry Klitsner
General Hospital (1975).............Samantha Chandler
Capitol (1982-83)..................................Julie Clegg

BECKER, DESIREE
Films:
Good Morning, Babylon (1987)...................Mabel
   1:06 - Brief topless in the woods making love. *
Made for HBO:
The Hitchhiker: Out of the Night............... Kathy
   0:12 - Brief topless lying in the steam room
   talking to "Peter," then close up topless. **

BEDELIA, BONNIE
Films:
Lovers and Other Strangers (1970)
.... Susan Henderson
The Big Fix (1978)...............................Suzanne
Heart Like a Wheel (1983)........ Shirley Muldowney
The Stranger (1986)...................... Alice Kildee
   0:15 - Brief right breast sticking up from behind
   her lover's arm making love in bed during
   flashback sequence (B&W). *
   0:19 - Brief left breast turning over in hospital bed
   when a guy walks in. Long shot, hard to see. *
   0:38 - Right breast again making love (B&W).
   **
Violets Are Blue (1986).......................Ruth Squires
The Boy Who Could Fly (1987).................Charlene
The Prince of Pennsylvania (1988)...Pam Marshetta
   0:12 - In black bra in open blouse in kitchen.
   Long scene.
Die Hard (1988) ....Holly McClane
Fat Man and Little Boy (1989)... Kitty Oppenheimer

Die Hard 2: Die Harder (1990)........ Holly McClane
Presumed Innocent (1990)...
Made for TV Movies:
  Memorial Day (1983)...
TV:
  The New Land (1974) .... Anna Larsen

BELLER, KATHLEEN
Films:
  The Betsy (1978)........................... Betsy Hardeman
    0:12 - Brief nude getting into swimming pool.
    ***
    1:14 - Topless in bed with Tommy Lee Jones. **
  Movie Movie (1978) .... Angie Popchik
  Promises in the Dark (1979)................Buffy Koenig
  Surfacing (1980).. Kate
    0:22 - Very brief buns, pulling down pants to
      change. Dark, hard to see.
    0:23 - Very brief right breast undressing. Dark,
      hard to see.
    0:24 - Very, very brief topless turning over in bed.
      *
    0:25 - Buns, standing next to bed.
    1:23 - Topless washing herself in the water. One
      long shot, one side view of right breast. ***
  Fort Apache, The Bronx (1981).................... Theresa
  The Sword and the Sorcerer (1982)..............Alana
    Buns, getting oiled while lying down.
  Touched (1982) ....Jennifer
  Cloud Waltzing (1986)...
  Time Trackers (1989)...............................R. J. Craig
Miniseries:
  Blue and the Gray (1982)................ Kathy Reynolds
Made for TV Movies:
  Mary White (1977)...
TV:
  Search for Tomorrow (1971-74)...........Liza Walton
  Dynasty (1982-84)...............................Kirby Anders
  Bronx Zoo (1988-89)...............................Callahan

BELLI, AGOSTINA
Films:
  Bluebeard (1972)....................................... Caroline
    1:31 - Brief left breast lying on grass getting a tan.
      *
    1:32 - Topless taking off clothes and lying on the
      couch. **
  Blood in the Streets (1974)...............................Maria
  The Seduction of Mimi (1974)................................
  The Purple Taxi (1977) .... Anne Taubelman
  Holocaust 2000 (1978)........................... Sara Golen
    Topless.

BELLWOOD, PAMELA
Films:
  Two Minute Warning (1976).............Peggy Ramsay
  Airport '77 (1977)..Lisa
  Hanger 18 (1980)...Sarah
  Serial (1980)..Carol
  The Incredible Shrinking Woman (1981)
    ....Sandra Dyson
  Cellar Dweller (1987)................................. Amanda
Made for TV Movies:
  Cocaine: One Man's Seduction (1983)...............
  Double Standard (1988)......................................Joan
TV:
  W.E.B. (1978)............................. Ellen Cunningham
  Dynasty (1981-86)..........................Claudia Blaisdel
Magazines:
  Playboy (Apr 1983)........................."Going Native"
    Covered with mud and body paint. *

BENSON, VICKIE
Films:
  Private Resort (1985)...........................Bikini Girl
    0:28 - In blue two piece swimsuit, showing her
      buns, then brief topless with "Reeves." *
    1:11 - Buns, in locker room trying to slap
      "Reeves."
  Las Vegas Weekend (1986)....................................
  My Chauffeur (1987)............. One of the Party Girls
  The Wraith (1987) ....
  Blue Movies (1989)..
  Bloddy Pom Poms (1989)......................................

BENTON, BARBI
Films:
  For the Love of It (1980).......................................
  Hospital Massacre (1982)................. Susan Jeremy
    0:29 - Undressing behind a curtain while the
      Doctor watches her silhouette.
    0:31 - Topless getting examined by the Doctor.
      First sitting up, then lying down. ***
    0:34 - Great close up shot of breasts while the
      Doctor uses stethoscope on her. ***
  And the Wall Came Tumbling Down (1984)...........
  Deathstalker (1983; Argentina/U.S.).......... Codille
    0:39 - Topless struggling while chained up and
      everybody is fighting. **
    0:47 - Right breast, struggling on the bed with
      "Deathstalker." *
Video Tapes:
  Playboy Video Magazine: Volume 9.......Playmate
TV:
  Hee Haw (1971-76)......................................Regular
  Sugar Time! (1977-78).................................. Maxx
Magazines:
  Playboy (Dec 1973)........................."Barbi's Back"
    Page 143-149: Nude. ***
  Playboy (Jan 1989)........."Women of the Seventies"
    Page 210: Topless. ***

BENTON, SUZANNE

Other:
a.k.a. Susanne Benton.
Films:
That Cold Day in the Park (1969)................. Nina
0:38 - Side view of left breast putting top on.
Long shot. *
1:05 - Topless taking off her clothes and getting
into the bathtub. Another long shot. *
Catch-22 (1970)...............................Dreedle's WAC
A Boy and His Dog (1975).................... Quilla June
0:29 - Nude, getting dressed while Don Johnson
watches. **
0:45 - Right breast lying down with Johnson after
making love with him. *

BENTZEN, JANE

Other:
a.k.a. Jayne Bentzen.
Films:
Nightmare at Shadow Woods............................Julie
0:38 - In red lingerie, black stockings and garter
belt in her apartment with "Phil."
Made for HBO:
A Breed Apart (1984)...............................Reporter
0:55 - Left breast in bed with Powers Booth, then
full frontal nudity getting out of bed and putting
her clothes on. ***

BENZ, DONNA KEI

Films:
Stir Crazy (1980) .... Nancy
Looker (1981)... Ellen
The Challenge (1982).................................... Akiko
1:23 - Topless making love with Scott Glenn in
motel room. Could be a body double. Dark,
hard to see anything. *
Pray for Death (1985)......................................
Moon in Scorpio (1987).................... Nurse Mitchell
Magazines:
Playboy (Nov 1982)......................."Sex in Cinema"
Page 161: Topless. *

BERENSON, MARISA

Films:
Cabaret (1972) ....Natalia Landauer
Death in Venice (1971; Italian/French)
....Frau Von Aschenbach
Barry Lyndon (1973; British)............Lady Lyndon
Topless in bathtub.
Killer Fish (1979; Italian/Brazilian)....................Ann
Some Like It Cool
(1979; German/French/Italian/Austrian)...............
a.k.a. Sex on the Run
a.k.a. Casanova and Co.
1:23 - Almost right breast in bed with Tony Curtis
when she rolls over him.

S.O.B. (1981)...Mavis
1:20 - Topless in bed with Robert Vaughn. **
Playing for Time (1984)..................................
The Secret Diary of Sigmund Freud (1984)
.... Emma Herrmann
Miniseries:
Sins..Helene Junot
Magazines:
Playboy (Dec 1973)..................."Sex Stars of 1973"
Page 210: Right breast. *
Playboy (Nov 1976).............."Sex in Cinema 1976"
Page 114: Left breast in a shot that wasn't used in
"Barry Lyndon." *

BERGEN, CANDICE

Other:
Wife of French director Louis Malle.
Films:
The Group (1966)....................Lakey Eastlake
Getting Straight (1970)...........................Jan
Soldier Blue (1970).................Cresta Marybelle Lee
T. R. Baskin (1971)..
The Hunting Party (1971; British) .....Melissa Ruger
Carnal Knowledge (1971)............................Susan
11 Harrowhouse (1974; British).............................
Bite the Bullet (1975)..........................Miss Jones
The Wind and the Lion (1975).........Eden Pedecaris
Oliver's Story (1978)......................Marcie Bonwit
A Night Full of Rain (1978; Italian)..............Lizzy
(Not available on video tape.)
Topless.
Starting Over (1979)........................Jessica Potter
1:01 - In a sheer blouse sitting on couch talking to
Burt Reynolds.
1:29 - Very, very brief left breast in bed with
Reynolds when he undoes her top. You see her
breast just before the scene dissolves into the
next one. Long shot, hard to see. *
Rich and Famous (1981)............. Merry Noel Blake
Gandhi (1982)....................Margaret Bourke-White
Made for TV Movies:
Mayflower Madam (1987)..Sydney Biddle Barrows
TV:
Murphy Brown (1988-)...................Murphy Brown

BERGER, SOPHIE

Films:
Love Circles Around the World (1984).... Dagmar
0:38 - Topless in women's restroom in casino
making love with a guy in a tuxedo. ***
0:43 - Topless in steam room wearing a towel
around her waist, then making love. ***
Emmanuelle IV (1984)................................ Maria
0:46 - Full frontal nudity putting on robe. **
0:49 - Buns, taking off robe in front of Mia
Nygren.

BERGMAN, SANDAHL

Films:
All That Jazz (1979).....................................Sandra
   0:52 - Topless dancing on scaffolding during a
   dance routine. **
Xanadu (1980)... A Muse
Conan The Barbarian (1982)......................Valeria
   0:49 - Brief left breast making love with Arnold
   Schwarzenegger. **
Airplane II: The Sequel (1982)......................Officer
She (1983)... She
   0:22 - Topless getting into a pool of water to clean
   her wounds after sword fight. **
Red Sonja (1985)...............................Queen Gedren
Stewardess School (1987)...............Wanda Polanski
Kandyland (1987)............................. Harlow Divine
Programmed to Kill (1987).........................Samira
   a.k.a. The Retaliator
   0:11 - Brief side view of right breast taking off T-
   shirt and leaning over to kiss a guy. Don't see
   her face. *
Hell Comes to Frogtown (1987).............................
Made for TV Movies:
Getting Physical (1984)...
Magazines:
Playboy (Mar 1980)........................"All That Fosse"
   Pages 174-175: Topless stills from "All That
   Jazz." **
Playboy (Dec 1981)................... "Sex Stars of 1981"
   Page 239: Topless. **

BERLIN, JEANNIE

Films:
The Baby Maker (1970)..............................Charlotte
Housewife (1972).......................................
   Bottomless in bed.
The Heartbreak Kid (1972) ....Lila Kolodny
Portnoy's Complaint (1972)............ Bubbles Girardi
Sheila Levine is Dead and Living in New York
   (1975)..Sheila Levine

BERRIDGE, ELIZABETH

Films:
The Funhouse (1981).. Amy
   0:03 - Brief topless taking off robe to get into the
   shower, then very brief topless getting out to
   chase "Joey." **
Amadeus (1984)....................................... Constanze
Five Corners (1988)......................................Melanie

BESCH, BIBI

Films:
The Long Dark Night (1977)........................... Marge
Hardcore (1979)... Mary
The Beast Within (1982)........ Caroline MacCleary
   0:06 - Topless, getting her blouse torn off by the
   beast while she is unconscious. Dark, hard to
   see her face. **

Star Trek II: The Wrath of Kahn (1982)
   .... Dr. Carol Marcus
The Lonely Lady (1983)............................. Veronica
Who's That Girl (1987)...
Kill Me Again (1989)..................... Jack's Secretary
Steel Magnolias (1989).................Belle Marmillion
Tremors (1989)............. Megan - The Doctor's Wife
TV:
Secrets of Midland Heights (1980-81)
   ....Dorothy Wheeler
The Hamptons (1983)... Adrienne Duncan Mortimer

BESWICK, MARTINE

Films:
From Russia with Love (1963; British).............Zora
Thunderball (1965; British)............... Paula Caplan
One Million Years B.C. (1966; U.S./British)
   ....Nupondi
Dr. Jekyll and Sister Hyde (1971) ....Sister Hyde
The Happy Hooker Goes Hollywood (1980)
   ....Xaviera Hollander
   0:05 - Brief topless in bedroom with Policeman.
   **
   0:22 - Brief buns, jumping into the swimming
   pool, then topless next to the pool with Adam
   West. ***
   0:27 - Topless in bed with West, then topless
   waking up. *
Melvin and Howard (1980) ....Real Estate Woman
The Offspring (1986).....................Katherine White
TV:
Aspen (1977) ....Joan Carolinian

BINOCHE, JULIETTE

Films:
Hail Mary (1985)..Juliette
The Unbearable Lightness of Being (1988)
   ....Tereza
   0:22 - In white bra in "Tomas'" apartment.
   1:33 - Brief topless jumping onto couch. *
   1:36 - Buns, sitting in front of fire being
   photographed, then running around, trying to
   hide.
   2:18 - Left breast in "The Engineer's" apartment.
   *
Magazines:
Playboy (Nov 1987)............. "Sex in Cinema 1987"
   Page 143: Side view of right breast from
   "Rendez-vous." *

BIRD, MINAH

Films:
Oh, Alfie! (1975; British)............................... Gloria
The Stud (1978; British)................................Molly
   0:26 - Topless in bed when "Tony" is talking on
   the telephone. **

BIRKIN, JANE

Films:
Blow-Up (1966)..
  Nude
Ms. Don Juan (1973).....................................Clara
  0:58 - Lower frontal nudity lying in bed with
    Brigitte Bardot.
  1:00 - Brief topless in bed with Bardot. Long
    shot.
  1:01 - Full frontal nudity getting dressed. Brief
    topless in open blouse. **
Private Projection (1973)..............................
I Am as Happy as Pleasure (1974)....................
Dark Places (1974; British) ....Alta
I Love You More than I Love Myself (1975)........
Catherine & Co. (1975)...........................Catherine
  0:07 - Topless, standing up in the bathtub to open
    the door for another woman. *
  0:09 - Side view of left breast taking off her top in
    bed. **
  0:10 - Topless, sitting up and turning the light on,
    smoking a cigarette. ***
  0:17 - Right breast making love in bed. **
  0:24 - Topless taking off her dress, then buns
    jumping into bed. **
  0:36 - Buns and left breast posing for a painter. **
  0:45 - Topless taking off her dress and walking
    around the house, left breast inviting the
    neighbor in . *
Kung Fu Master (1989) ....Mary-Jane
Le Petit Amour (1989)..................................

BISIGNANO, JEANNINE

Films:
  Body Rock (1984)................................Girl
  My Chauffeur (1985).............One of the Party Girls
  Ruthless People (1986).....................Hooker in Car
    0:17 - Topless, hanging out of the car. Long, long
      shot, don't see anything.
    0:40 - Topless in the same scene three times on
      TV while Danny De Vito watches. *
    0:49 - Left breast hanging out of the car when the
      Chief of Police watches on TV. Closest shot. *
    1:15 - Same scene again in department store TV's.
      Long shot, hard to see.
  Stripped to Kill II (1988)...........................Sonny
    0:06 - Buns, in black bra in dressing room.
    0:38 - Topless and buns during strip dance routine
      in white lingerie. ***
  License to Kill (1989)...............................Stripper
Magazines:
  Playboy (Nov 1986)............. "Sex in Cinema 1986"
    Page 131: Topless in a photo from "Ruthless
    People" leaning out of the car. **

BISSET, JACQUELINE

Films:
  The Knack (1965; British) ....
  Cul-de-sac (1966)................................Jacqueline
  Two for the Road (1967; British)..................Jackie

Capetown Affair (1967; U.S./S. Africa)..................
Casino Royale (1967; British)........Miss Goodthighs
The Detective (1968) ....Norma McIver
Bullitt (1968)..Cathy
The Sweet Ride (1968) ....Vicki Cartwright
  (Not available on video tape yet.)
  Topless.
The First Time (1969)............................Anna
The Secret World (1969; French)..................Wendy
Airport (1970) ....Gwen Meighen
The Grasshopper (1970)................Christine Adams
  0:21 - In flesh colored Las Vegas style showgirl
    costume. Dark, hard to see.
  0:27 - More showgirl shots.
  1:14 - In black two piece swimsuit.
  1:16 - Almost left breast while squished against
    "Jay" in the shower.
Believe in Me (1971) ....Pamela
The Mephisto Waltz (1971)............Paula Clarkson
  0:48 - Very brief right and side view of left breast
    in bed with Alan Alda. *
  1:36 - Sort of left breast getting undressed for
    witchcraft ceremony. Long shot side views of
    right breast, but you can't see her face.
  1:45 - Very brief topless twice under bloody water
    in blood covered bathtub, dead. Discovered by
    Kathleen Widdoes. **
Secrets (1971)...................................... Jenny
  0:49 - Very brief lower frontal nudity putting
    panties on wearing a black dress.
  1:02 - Brief buns and a lot of topless on bed
    making love with "Raoul." ***
The Life and Times of Judge Roy Bean (1972)
  ....Rose Bean
Stand Up and Be Counted (1972). Sheila Hammond
Day for Night (1973)...............................Julie
The Thief Who Came to Dinner (1973)...........Laura
Murder on the Orient Express (1974; British)
  ....Countess Andrenyi
The Magnificent One (1974; French/Italian)
  .... Tatiana/Christine
The Spiral Staircase (1975; British).................Helen
St. Ives (1976)...........................Janet Whistler
The Deep (1977)...............................Gail Berke
  Swimming under water in a wet T-shirt. One of
    the best wet T-shirt scenes I've ever seen.
The Greek Tycoon (1978).....................Liz Cassidy
Who is Killing the Great Chefs of Europe?
  (1978 U.S./German)........................ Natasha
Together (1979)..
When Time Ran Out! (1980) ....Kay Kirby
Inchon (1981)..........................Barbara Hallsworth
Rich and Famous (1981)....................Liz Hamilton
Famous T & A (1982)...............................herself
  0:31 - Topless scene from "Secrets." ***
Class (1983) ....Ellen
Under the Volcano (1984)................Yvonne Firmin
High Season (1988).....................Katherine Shaw
  0:56 - Brief topless doing the backstroke in the
    water with "Rick," then left breast lying down.
    Hard to see, everything is lit with blue light. *
Scenes from the Class Struggle in Beverly Hills
  (1989)..Clare

Wild Orchid (1990)..
Made for Cable TV Movies:
Forbidden (1985)...........................Nina von Halder
0:25 - In bra and slip in villa with her Jewish lover.
0:47 - Squished breasts against Jurgen Prochnow in bed making love.
Miniseries:
Anna Karenina (1985).......................Anna Karenina
Napolean and Josephine (1987)
....Josephine Beauharnais
Lots of cleavage.

BLACK, KAREN
Films:
You're a Big Boy Now (1966).................................
Easy Rider (1969)..Karen
Five Easy Pieces (1970).................. Rayette Dipesto
0:48 - In sheer black nightie in bathroom, then walking to bedroom with Jack Nicholson.
Cisco Pike (1971).. Sue
Little Laura and Big John (1972)....................Laura
Drive, He Said (1972)...............................Olive
1:05 - Brief topless screaming in the bathtub when she gets scared when a bird flies in. *
1:19 - Brief lower frontal nudity running out of the house in her bathrobe.
Portnoy's Complaint (1972)................. The Monkey
Rhinoceros (1973)..Daisy
The Outfit (1973)............................. Bett Jarrow
The Great Gatsby (1974)....................Myrtle Wilson
Airport 1975 (1975).. Nancy
The Day of the Locust (1975) ....Faye
Nashville (1975)...................................Connie White
Burnt Offerings (1976)................................ Marion
Family Plot (1976)..Fran
In Praise of Older Women (1978; Canadian)
.... Maya
0:35 - Topless in bed with Tom Berenger. **
Capricorn One (1978)..................... Judy Drinkwater
Mr. Horn (1979)...
Separate Ways (1979)................... Valentine Colby
0:04 - Topless and in panties changing while her husband talks on the phone, then in bra. Long shot. *
0:18 - Topless in bed making love with Tony Lo Bianco. **
0:36 - Topless taking a shower, then getting out. **
Chanel Solitaire (1981) ....Emilienne D'Alencon
Killing Heat (1981)............................. Mary Turner
0:41 - Full frontal nudity giving herself a shower in the bedroom. **
Come Back to the Five and Dime, Jimmy Dean, Jimmy Dean (1982) ....Joanne
Can She Bake a Cherry Pie? (1983).....................
0:40 - Sort of left breast squished against a guy kissing him in bed.
1:02 - Very brief upper half of left breast in bed when she reaches up to touch her hair. *

Little Mermaid (1984) ....
Cut and Run (1985) ....Karin
Invaders from Mars (1986).........................Linda
Eternal Evil (1987)...
Miss Right (1987)... Amy
0:47 - Brief topless jumping out of bed and running to get a bucket of water to put out a fire. *
The Invisible Kid (1988) ....Mom
Out of the Dark (1988)..................................Ruth
Bad Manners (1989).......................Mrs. Fitzpatrick
Made for TV Movies:
Trilogy of Terror (1974)..
Made for HBO:
The Hitchhiker: Hired Help.............Mrs. Kay Mason
(Available on The Hitchhiker, Volume 1)
TV:
The Second Hundred Years (1967-68)
.... Marcia Garroway
Magazines:
Playboy (Dec 1973)....................."Sex Stars of 1973"
Page 207: Peak at left breast. *
Playboy (Dec 1976)....................."Sex Stars of 1976"
Page 185: In pink see-through night gown. **

BLACKBURN, GRETA
Films:
Time Walker (1982)...Sherri
48 Hours (1982)...Lisa
0:13 - Topless and buns in bathroom in hotel room with James Remar. **
Yellowbeard (1983)...
Party Line (1989)...

BLACKMAN, JOAN
Films:
Vengeance of Virgo (1972) ....
Pets (1974).......................................Geraldine Mills
0:46 - Brief side view of left breast getting out of bed after making love with "Bonnie." *
Macon County Line (1974) ....Carol Morgan
Moonrunners (1975).. Reba
One Man (1979; Canadian) ....
Return to Waterloo (1986).....................................

BLACKWOOD, NINA
Films:
Vice Squad (1982)...Ginger
TV:
Music Television................................Video Jockey
Entertainment Tonight............. Music Correspondent
Magazines:
Playboy (Aug 1978).......... "The Girls in the Office"
Page 142: Full frontal nudity (with brunette hair). ***

BLAKE, STEPHANIE

Films:
The Big Bet (1985)............................. Mrs. Roberts
   0:04 - Topless sitting on bed with "Chris." ***
   0:37 - Nude on bed with "Chris." **
   0:59 - Full frontal nudity in bed again. ***
Ferris Bueller's Day Off (1986)..........Singing Nurse

BLAIR, LINDA

Films:
Way We Live Now (1970)................. Sara Aldridge
The Sporting Club (1971)..................................Barby
The Exorcist (1973)......................................Regan
Airport 1975 (1974)........................... Janice Abbott
Exorcist II: The Heretic (1977).....................Regan
Roller Boogie (1979)..........................Terry Barkley
Wild Horse Hank (1979; Canadian). Hank Bradford
Summer of Fear (1980)..
Hell Night (1981)......................................Marti
Chained Heat (1983; U.S./German)................Carol
   0:30 - Topless in the shower. ***
   0:56 - Topless in the Warden's office when he
      rapes her. **
Ruckus (1984)...
Night Patrol (1985).......................................Sue
   1:19 - Brief left breast in bed. *
Savage Streets (1985).................................. Brenda
   1:05 - Topless sitting in the bathtub thinking. ***
Savage Island (1985) ....Daly
Night Force (1986)...
Red Heat (1987; U.S./German).......... Chris Carlson
   0:09 - In blue nightgown in the bedroom with her
      boyfriend, almost topless.
   0:56 - Topless in shower room scene. ***
   1:01 - Brief topless getting raped by Sylvia Kristel
      while the male guard watches. ***
Grotesque (1987) ....Lisa
Silent Assassins (1988)................................Sara
   0:48 - Very brief, wearing light blue bra struggling
      on couch with a masked attacker.
Witchery (1988)....................................Jane Brooks
Up Your Alley (1988).................... Vickie Adderly
Bedroom Eyes II (1989)................. Sophie Stevens
   0:31 - Buns in bed with Wings Hauser.
   0:33 - Brief left breast under bubbles in the
      bathtub. Don't see her face. *
Made for TV Movies:
Born Innocent (1974)..
Sarah T.: Portrait of a Teenage Alcoholic (1975)
....Sarah
Magazines:
Playboy (Dec 1983)................."Sex Stars of 1983"
   Page 209: Topless. ***
Playboy (Dec 1984)................."Sex Stars of 1984"
   Page 207: Topless in the water up to her breasts.
   ***

BLAISDELL, DEBORAH

Other:
   a.k.a. Adult film actress Tracey Adams.
Films:
The Lost Empire (1983).........................Girl Recruit
Screen Test (1987)................................. Stripper
   0:04 - Topless dancing on stage. *
Wimps (1987)........................... Roxanne Chandless
   1:22 - Brief topless and buns taking off clothes
      and getting into bed with "Francis" in bedroom.
      *
Student Affairs (1987)................................. Kelly
   0:26 - Topless sitting up in bed talking to a guy.
   ***

BLAKELY, SUSAN

Films:
Savages (1972)..Cecily
Way We Were (1973).................................Judianne
The Lords of Flatbush (1974)............Jane Bradshaw
The Towering Inferno (1974)............Patty Simmons
Capone (1975)................................. Iris Crawford
   (Not available on video tape yet.)
   Topless.
Report to the Commissioner (1975).......Patty Butler
The Concorde - Airport '79 (1979)............... Maggie
Over the Top (1987).........................Christine Hawk
Made for HBO:
The Hitchhiker: Remembering Melody....Melody
   0:17 - Right breast in shower with "Ted" and brief
      topless in the bathtub. ***
TV Miniseries:
Rich Man, Poor Man - Book I (1976)
   ....Julie Prescott Abbott Jordache
Made for TV Movies:
Broken Angel (1988) ....Catherine Coburn
Magazines:
Playboy (Mar 1972)............................... "Savages"
   Pages 142 & 145: Topless. *

BLANCHARD, VANESSA

Films:
Witchfire (1986)..Liz
   0:52 - Brief topless in bed and then the shower.
   **
Uphill All the Way (1987) ....Velma

BLEE, DEBRA

Films:
The Beach Girls (1982)................................ Sarah
   1:22 - Brief topless opening her swimsuit top on
      the beach. ***
Sloane (1984)..............................Cynthia Thursby
   0:15 - Very brief topless during attempted rape *
Savage Streets (1985)................................Rachel
   0:20 - In a bra in the girls locker room.
The Malibu Bikini Shop (1985)........................Jane
Hamburger - The Motion Picture (1986)..Mia Vunk
   0:25 - Briefly in wet dress in the swimming pool.

BLOOM, CLAIRE
Films:
Three into Two Won't Go (1969; British)
....Frances Howard
The Illustrated Man (1969) ....Felicia
A Severed Head (1971; British).......... Honor Klein
   1:10 - Topless leaning up then right beast while
   sitting up in bed with Richard Attenborough. *
A Doll's House (1973)........................Nora Helmer
Islands in the Stream (1977).........................Audrey
Deja Vu (1986)..

BLOOM, LINDSAY
Films:
Cover Girl Models (1975)......................................
Six Pack Annie (1975)...................................Annie
Texas Detour (1977)...................... Sugar McCarthy
French Quarter (1978)....... Big Butt/Policewoman
Hughes and Harlow: Angels in Hell (1978).............
The Main Event (1979) ....Girl in Bed
H.O.T.S. (1979).......................... Melody Ragmore
   0:28 - Very brief right breast on balcony. *
   1:34 - Brief topless during football game throwing
   football as quarterback. *
The Happy Hooker Goes Hollywood (1980)... Chris
TV:
Dallas (1982)...............................Bonnie Robertson
Mike Hammer (1984-1987)..............................Velda

BLOUNT, LISA
Films:
Sam's Song (1971)..
9/30/55 (1977)...Billie Jean
Dead and Buried (1981)............. Girl on the Beach
   0:06 - Brief topless on the beach getting her
   picture taken by a photographer. *
An Officer and a Gentleman (1982)
....Lynette Pomeroy
   1:25 - In a red bra and tap pants in a motel room
   with David Keith.
Radioactive Dreams (1984).......................................
Cease Fire (1985) ....Paula Murphy
Cut and Run (1985).............................Fran Hudson
Nightflyers (1987)..
South of Reno (1987)...........................Anette Clark
   1:02 - In black bra getting top torn open while
   lying down.
Prince of Darkness (1988)...
Made For HBO:
The Hitchhiker: One Last Prayer..................Miranda
   0:06 - Briefly in a black bra putting a new
   homemade outfit on.
Made For TV Movies:
Unholy Matrimony (1988)............. Karen Stockwell
TV:
Sons and Daughters (1990-)..................Mary Ruth

BOHRER, CORINNE
Films:
I, the Jury (1982).......................Soap Opera Actress
The Beach Girls (1982) ....Champagne Girl
My Favorite Year (1982).......................................
Zapped! (1982)..Cindy
Joysticks (1983).....................................Patsy Rutter
Surf II (1984) ....
Stewardess School (1987).................. Cindy Adams
Police Academy 4: Citizens on Patrol (1987)
....Laura
Vice Versa (1988)...Sam
Made for HBO:
Dead Solid Perfect (1988).................. Janie Rimmer
   0:31 - Nude, getting out of bed to get some ice for
   Randy Quaid. ***
TV:
E/R (1984-85)......................Nurse Cory Smith
Free Spirit (1989-90) ....Winnie Goodwin

BOLLING, TIFFANY
Films:
The Marriage of a Young Stockbroker (1967)
....Girl in the Rain
Tony Rome (1967)....................................Photo Girl
Triangle (1971)...
Bonnie's Kids (1973).. Ellie
   0:21 - Topless, modeling in office. **
   1:16 - Brief right breast making love in bed. *
Candy Snatch (1973)...
Wicked, Wicked (1973)......................Lisa James
The Centerfold Girls (1974)........................... Vera
   1:02 - Brief topless in photograph. *
   1:12 - Topless in the shower. ***
   1:21 - Brief topless in motel bed getting raped by
   two guys after they drug her beer. *
The Wild Party (1975).......................................Kate
Kingdom of the Spiders (1977)...........Diane Ashley
The Vals (1982).............Valley Attorney and Parent
Love Scenes (1984).. Val
   0:01 - Side view of left breast in bed with "Peter."
   **
   0:06 - Topless getting photographed by Britt
   Ekland in the house. ***
   0:09 - Brief topless opening her bathrobe to show
   "Peter." *
   0:12 - Topless in bathtub with "Peter." *
   0:19 - Topless lying in bed talking with "Peter,"
   then making love. ***
   0:43 - Topless acting in a movie when "Rick"
   opens her blouse. **
   0:57 - Nude behind shower door, then topless
   getting out and talking to "Peter." **
   0:59 - Topless making love tied up on bed with
   "Rick" during filming of movie. **
   1:07 - Topless, then full frontal nudity acting with
   "Elizabeth" during filming of movie. **
   1:17 - Full frontal nudity getting out of pool. **
   1:26 - Topless with "Peter" on the bed. **
Open House (1988)...............................Judy Roberts

Made for TV Movies:
Key West (1973)..Ruth
TV:
The New People (1969-70)................ Susan Bradley
Magazines:
Playboy (Apr 1972)................... "Tiffany's A Gem"
Pages 153-159:. ***
Playboy (Dec 1972)...................."Sex Stars of 1972"
Page 210: Topless. ***
Playboy (Nov 1973)...................."Sex in Cinema"
Page 152: Left breast in red light. *
Playboy (Dec 1973)................... "Sex Stars of 1973"
Page 208: Left breast. *

BONET, LISA
Films:
Angel Heart (1986)................. Epiphany Proudfoot
1:27 - Topless in bed with Mickey Rourke. It gets
kind of bloody. ***
1:32 - Topless in bathtub. *
1:48 - Topless in bed, dead. *
TV:
The Cosby Show (1984-1987)........Denise Huxtable
A Different World (1987-89)..........Denise Huxtable
The Cosby Show (1989-)..............Denise Huxtable

BONET, NAI
Films:
The Greatest (1977; U.S./British)........ Suzie Gomez
Fairytales (1979).................................. Sheherazade
0:29 - Buns and very brief left breast doing a belly
dance and rubbing oil on herself. *
Nocturna (1979)...Nocturna

BOORMAN, KATRINE
Films:
Excalibur (1981)..Igrayne
0:14 - Right breast, then topless in front of the fire
when "Uther" tricks her into thinking that he is
her husband and makes love to her. *
Dream One (1984; British/French)
....Duchka/Nemo's Mother
Marche A L'Hombre (1984; French)............Katrina

BOTSFORD, SARA
Films:
By Design (1982; Canadian) ....Angie
0:23 - Full frontal nudity in the ocean. Long shot,
hard to see anything. *
1:08 - Brief side view of left breast making love in
bed while talking on the phone. *
Deadly Eyes (1982) .... Kelly Leonard
Still of the Night (1982)........................ Gail Phillips

BOUCHE, SUGAR
Films:
Heavenly Bodies (1985).............................. Stripper
0:16 - Topless doing stripper-gram for "Steve." *
Graveyard Shift (1987)............... Fabulous Frannie
0:12 - Topless doing a stripper routine on stage
***
0:24 - Brief topless in the shower. *

BOUCHET, BARBARA
Films:
A Global Affair (1964)......................................Girl
Good Neighbor Sam (1964)................... Receptionist
John Goldfarb, Please Come Home (1964)
....Astrid Porche
Sex and the Single Girl (1964)....................Frannie
What a Way to Go (1964) ....Girl on Plane
In Harm's Way (1965; B&W)......... Liz Eddington
0:05 - Very, very brief right breast waving to a
guy from the water. *
Agent for H.A.R.M. (1966).....................Ava Vestak
Casino Royale (1967; British)............. Moneypenny
Danger Route (1968; British)........................... Mari
Sweet Charity (1969) ....Ursula
Hot Bed of Sex (1971)......................................
The Black Belly of the Tarantula (1972; Italian)
.... Maria Zani
The Syndicate (1972)..
The Deadly Game (1974).....................................
Down the Ancient Staircase (1975; Italian)......Carla
Surabaya Conspiracy (1975)...............................
Blood Feast (1976; Italian)..................................
Duck in Orange Sauce (1976; Italian)...............Patty
The Rogue (1976)..
Sex with a Smile (1976; Italian)
.................................."One for the Money" segment
0:50 - Topless sitting up in bed with a guy in bed,
then lying down, wearing glasses. ***
Death Race (1978; Italian) ....
Maniac Mansion (1978; Italian)..........................
The Cauldron of Death (1979; Italian)..................
I Am Photogenic (1980)..................................
Magazines:
Playboy (Nov 1972)....................."Sex in Cinema"
Page 161: Buns. *

BOULTING, INGRID
Films:
The Last Tycoon (1976)................. Kathleen Moore
Deadly Passion (1985)............. Martha Greenwood
0:46 - Brief buns taking off clothes and jumping
into pool. Long shot. *
0:47 - Topless getting out of pool and kissing
Brent Huff. Right breast in bed. **
0:54 - Topless in whirlpool bath with Huff. *
1:02 - Topless, wearing white panties and
massaging herself in front of a mirror. ***
1:31 - Topless taking off clothes and jumping into
bed with Huff. **

BOUQUET, CAROLE

Other:
Model for Chanel cosmetics.
Films:
That Obscure Object of Desire
(1977; French/Spanish)............................ Conchita
0:53 - Topless in bedroom. ***
1:01 - Topless in bed with Fernando Rey. ***
For Your Eyes Only (1981)........... Melina Havelock
Bingo Bongo (1983)..Laura
Dream One (1984; British/French) ....Rals-Akrai
Too Beautiful for You (1990; French)........ Florence

BOUSHEL, JOY

Films:
Terror Train (1980; Canadian)........................... Pet
0:49 - Topless wearing panties in sleeper room on
train with "Mo." **
Humongous (1982; Canadian)........ Carla Simmonds
Quest for Fire (1982; French/Canadian) ....
The Fly (1986).. Tawny
0:54 - Very brief topless viewed from below when
Jeff Goldblum pulls her by the arm to get her
out of bed. *
Keeping Track (1988) ....Judy
Look Who's Talking (1989)......................... Melissa

BOWSER, SUE

Films:
Stripes (1981)......................................Mud Wrestler
Doctor Detroit (1983)..............................Dream Girl
Into the Night (1985)........................... Girl on Boat
0:24 - Topless taking off blouse with "Jake" on his
boat after Michelle Pfeiffer leaves. **

BOYD, TANYA

Films:
Black Shampoo (1976)...................................Brenda
Wholly Moses (1980)....................................Princess
The Happy Hooker Goes Hollywood (1980)
....Sylvie
0:39 - Brief topless in jungle room when an older
customer accidentally comes in. *
Jo Jo Dancer, Your Life Is Calling (1986)...... Alicia

BRACCI, TEDA

Films:
R.P.M. (1970)...
C. C. and Company (1971)..
The Big Bird Cage (1972)........................ Bull Jones
The Centerfold Girls (1974)............................ Rita
0:18 - Topless taking off her clothes in the living
room in front of everybody. *
The Trial of Billy Jack (1974)........................ Teda
The World's Greatest Lover (1977).........................

BRAGA, SONIA

Films:
Dona Flor and Her Two Husbands
(1978; Brazilian)...Flor
0:13 - Buns and brief topless with her husband. *
0:15 - Topless lying on the bed. **
0:17 - Buns, getting out of bed
0:54 - Topless making love on the bed with her
husband. ***
0:57 - Topless lying on the bed. **
1:41 - Topless kissing her first husband. ***
Lady on the Bus (1978)...
0:11 - Brief left breast. *
0:12 - Topless, then buns, then full frontal nudity
in bed getting her slip torn off by her newlywed
husband. Long struggle scene. ***
0:39 - Right breast standing with half open dress,
then topless lying in bed, then getting into the
pool. **
0:48 - Topless and buns on the beach after picking
up a guy on the bus. ***
0:54 - Brief topless in bed dreaming. *
1:02 - Brief topless in waterfall with bus driver. *
1:05 - Topless in cemetery after picking up
another guy on the bus. **
1:13 - Topless on the ground with another guy
from a bus. *
1:16 - Left breast sitting on sofa while her
husband talks. *
I Love You (1982; Brazilian)......................... Maria
0:34 - Full frontal nudity making love with
"Paulo." ***
0:36 - Topless sitting on the edge of the bed. **
0:49 - Topless running around the house teasing
"Paulo." *
0:50 - Brief nude in strobe light. Don't see her
face. **
0:53 - Topless eating fruit with "Paulo." *
0:54 - Topless wearing white panties in front of
windows with "Paulo." Long scene. ***
1:03 - Left breast standing talking to "Paulo." *
1:10 - Left breast talking to "Paulo." *
1:23 - Topless with "Paulo" during an argument.
Dark, but long scene. ***
1:28 - Topless walking around "Paulo's" place
with a gun. Dark. **
1:33 - Various topless scenes. **
Gabriela (1984; Brazilian)........................ Gabriela
0:26 - Topless leaning back out the window
making love on a table with Marcello
Mastroianni. **
0:27 - Nude, taking a shower outside and cleaning
herself up. ***
0:32 - Right breast in bed. *
0:38 - Nude, making love with Mastroianni on the
kitchen table. **
0:45 - Nude, getting in bed with Mastroianni. **
1:13 - Full frontal nudity on bed with another man,
then getting beat up by Mastroianni
1:17 - Nude, changing clothes in the bedroom.
***
1:32 - Topless and buns making love outside with
Mastroianni. Lots of passion! **

Kiss of the Spider Woman (1985)
....Leni/Marta/Spider Woman
The Milagro Beanfield War (1988) . Ruby Archuleta
Moon Over Parador (1988)...........Madonna Mendez
   In black lace body suit.
HBO Film:
The Man Who Broke 1000 Chains (1987)...............
Magazines:
Playboy (May 1979).................."Foreign Sex Stars"
   Pages 165: Topless. **
Playboy (Nov 1983)............. "Sex in Cinema 1983"
   Page 149: Topless. ***
Playboy (Oct 1984)............ "The Girls from Brazil"
   Page 86-91: Nude. ***
Playboy (Dec 1984)..................."Sex Stars of 1984"
   Page 205: Full frontal nudity leaning against bed.
   ***
Playboy (Dec 1987)..................."Sex Stars of 1987"
   Page 153: Full frontal nudity. ***
Playboy (Dec 1988)..................."Sex Stars of 1988"
   Page 183: Full frontal nudity leaning against bed.
   ***

BRANDT, BRANDI
Films:
Wedding Band (1989)....... Serena (Gypsy Wedding)
Video Tapes:
Playboy Video Calendar 1989...................Playmate
Magazines:
Playboy (Oct 1987)................................. Playmate

BREMMER, LESLEE
Other:
a.k.a. Leslee Bremer or Leslie Bremmer.
Films:
Hardbodies (1984)..........Photo Session Hardbodies
   0:40 - Topless with a bunch of other girls posing
      topless getting pictures taken by "Rounder." **
School Spirit (1985)..Sandy
My Chauffeur (1987)............. One of the Party Girls
Another Chance (1989)
   .... Girl in Womanizer's Meeting

BRENNAN, EILEEN
Films:
The Last Picture Show (1971).................Genevieve
Scarecrow (1973).......................................Darlene
   0:27 - Brief topless in bed when Gene Hackman
      takes off her bra and grabs her breasts. *
The Sting (1973)...Billie
Daisy Miller (1974) .... Mrs. Walker
Hustle (1975) .... Paula Hollinger
Murder by Death (1976)............... Tess Skeffington
The Cheap Detective (1978)...............Betty DeBoop
FM (1978)...Mother
The Great Smokey Roadblock (1978)........Penelope
Private Benjamin (1980).......Captain Doreen Lewis
Clue (1986)...Mrs. Peacock

BRESEE, BOBBIE
Films:
Mausoleum (1983)............................ Susan Farrell
   0:25 - Topless and buns wrapping a towel around
      herself in her bedroom. ***
   0:26 - Topless on the balcony showing herself to
      the gardener. **
   0:29 - Topless in the garage with the gardener.
      Brief, dark, hard to see. *
   0:32 - Brief left breast kissing Marjoe Gortner. *
   1:10 - Topless in the bathtub talking to Gortner.
      Long shot. *
Surf Nazis Must Die (1986)................ Smeg's Mom
Star Slammer - The Escape (1986)..................Marai
Evil Spawn (1987)..............................Lynn Roman
   0:14 - Very brief half of right breast in bed with a
      guy.
   0:26 - In red one piece swimsuit.
   0:36 - Topless in bathroom looking at herself in
      the mirror, then taking a shower. ***
Magazines:
Playboy (Jul 1989)................... "B-Movie Bimbos"
   Page 133: Full frontal nudity leaning on a car.
   ***

BRIMHALL, CYNTHIA
Films:
Hard Ticket to Hawaii (1987)......................... Edy
   0:47 - Topless changing out of a dress into a
      blouse and pants. **
   1:33 - Topless during closing credits. **
Picasso Trigger (1989)................................... Edy
   0:59 - Topless in weight room with a guy. **
Video Tapes:
Playboy Video Magazine, Volume 10...... Playmate
Playboy Video Calendar 1987.................Playmate
Magazines:
Playboy (Oct 1985)................................. Playmate

BRISEBOIS, DANIELLE
Films:
The Premonition (1976).....................................Janie
If I Ever See You Again (1978)...............................
King of the Gypsies (1978)..................... Young Tita
Big Bad Mama II (1987)..... Billy Jean McClatchie
   0:12 - Topless with Julie McCullough playing in a
      pond underneath a waterfall. *
   0:36 - In a white slip standing at the door talking
      to McCullough, then talking to Angie
      Dickinson.
TV:
All In the Family (1978-83).............Stephanie Mills
Knots Landing (1983-84).....Mary-Frances Summer

BRITTANY, TALLY

Films:
Sex Appeal (1986)..Corinne
    1:22 - Brief topless at the door of "Tony's"
    apartment when he opens the door fantasizing
    about her. *
Slammer Girls (1987)............................Candy Treat
    0:57 - Doing a dance routine wearing feathery
    pasties and a swimsuit bottom for the Governor
    in the hospital.

BROADY, ELOISE

Films:
Dangerous Love (1988)...................................Bree
    0:06 - Topless changing into lingerie in the mirror.
    ***
To Die For (1988) ....Girl at Party
Troop Beverly Hills (1989)...............Starlet at Party
Video Tapes:
Playboy Video Calendar 1989 ....Playmate
Magazines:
Playboy (Apr 1988)......................................Playmate
    Page 92

BROOKE, SANDY

Films:
Bits and Pieces (1985)...........................Mrs. Talbot
    1:03 - Topless in bathtub washing herself before
    the killer drowns her. Very brief right breast
    when struggling. ***
    1:09 - Brief topless under water in bathtub, dead.
    *
Star Slammer - The Escape (1986)................Taura
    0:21 - Topless in jail putting a new top on. In
    braless white T-shirt for most of the rest of the
    film. ***
    1:09 - Topless changing into a clean top. **
The Terror on Alcatraz (1986)......................Mona
    0:05 - Right breast on bed getting burned with a
    cigarette by "Frank." *
Deep Space (1988) .... Woman in House

BROOKS, ELIZABETH

Films:
The Howling (1981).....................................Marsha
    0:46 - Full frontal nudity taking off her robe in
    front of a campfire. **
    0:48 - Topless sitting on "Bill" by the fire. *
The Forgotten One (1989)...............................Carla
TV:
Doctors' Hospital (1975-76)
    ....Nurse Connie Kimbrough
Magazines:
Playboy (Nov 1980)......................."Sex in Cinema"
    Page 174: Full frontal nudity. ***

BROOKS, RANDI

Films:
Looker (1981).....................................Girl in Bikini
Deal of the Century (1983)...............Ms. Della Rosa
The Man with Two Brains (1983)...................Fran
    1:11 - Brief topless showing Steve Martin her
    breasts in front of the hotel. Buns, changing in
    the hotel room, then wearing black see-through
    negligee. **
Tightrope (1984)...................................Jamie Cory
    0:20 - Topless taking off robe and getting into the
    Jacuzzi. ***
    0:24 - Buns, dead in the Jacuzzi while Clint
    Eastwood looks at her.
Hamburger: The Motion Picture (1986)
    ....Mrs. Vunk
    0:52 - Brief topless in helicopter with boy. **
The Monster Squad (1987)......................................
Assassination (1987)..
Cop (1988).......................................Jeanie Pratt
    0:32 - In a bra making love in her kitchen with
    James Woods.
TV:
Wizards and Warriors (1983).............. Witch Bethel
The Last Precinct (1986) ....Officer Mel Brubaker
Magazines:
Playboy (Nov 1983)............. "Sex in Cinema 1983"
    Page 150: See-through negligee. *
Playboy (Dec 1983).................."Sex Stars of 1983"
    Page 210: Side view of right breast and buns. *

BROWN, BLAIR

Films:
The Choirboys (1977)...........................Mrs. Lyles
Altered States (1980).........................Emily Jessup
    0:10 - Brief left breast making love with William
    Hurt in red light from an electric heater. *
    0:34 - Topless lying on her stomach during Hurt's
    mushroom induced hallucination. **
    1:39 - Buns, sitting in hallway with Hurt after the
    transformations go away.
One Trick Pony (1980)..................................Marion
Continental Divide (1981)...................................Nell
A Flash of Green (1984)....Catherine "Kat" Hubble
    1:30 - Very brief right breast moving around in
    bed with Ed Harris. *
Miniseries:
Space (1986)...
Made for TV Movies:
The Child Stealer (1979) ....
Hands of a Stranger (1987)................. Diane Benton
Made for Lifetime:
Days and Nights of Molly Dodd (1988-)
    ....Molly Dodd
TV:
Captains and the Kings (1976)
    ....Elizabeth Healey Hennessey
Wheels (1978)................................ Barbara Lipton
Days and Nights of Molly Dodd (1987-88)
    ....Molly Dodd

BROWN, JULIE

Other:
Comedienne.
Singer - "The Homecoming Queen's Got a Gun."
Not to be confused with the MTV Video Jockey with
   the same name.
Films:
Bloody Birthday (1980)...............................Beverly
   0:13 - Dancing in red bra, then topless while two
      boys peek through hole in the wall, then buns.
      Nice, long scene. ***
   0:48 - In bedroom wearing red bra.
   1:03 - In bedroom again in the red bra.
Any Which Way You Can (1980) ....
Earth Girls are Easy (1989) ....Candy

BRYANT, PAMELA JEAN

Films:
H.O.T.S. (1979)............................... Teri Lynn
   1:33 - Topless during football game.
Separate Ways (1979)...................Cocktail Waitress
Don't Answer the Phone (1980)...........................Sue
Lunch Wagon (1981).....................................Marcy
   0:00 - In white lingerie.
   0:04 - Topless changing tops in room in gas
      station with Rosanne Katon while a guy watches
      through key hole. **
   0:22 - In white bra in kitchen.
   0:55 - Left breast in van with "Bif" several times.
      *
   1:04 - In sheer blue teddy talking on the phone.
Private Lessons (1981)...................................Joyce
   0:03 - Very brief right breast, changing in the
      house while "Billy" and his friend peep from
      outside. *
Looker (1981)..Reston Girl
Made for TV Movies:
B.J. and the Bear (1978)...........................
Magazines:
Playboy (Sep 1977)..............."Girls of the Big Ten"
   Page: 148: Topless. **
Playboy (Apr 1978)....................... Playmate
   Page 118

BUCKMAN, TARA

Films:
Rollercoaster (1977)......................Coaster Attendant
Hooper (1978)............................... Debbie
The Cannonball Run (1981)...................................Jill
Silent Night, Deadly Night (1984)....Mother (Ellie)
   0:12 - Brief right breast twice when the killer
      dressed as Santa Claus, rips her blouse open.
      Topless lying dead with slit throat. *
   0:18 - Very, very brief topless during "Billy's"
      flashback. *
   0:43 - Brief topless a couple of times again in
      another of "Billy's" flashbacks. *
Never too Young to Die (1987)...............................

BUJOLD, GENEVIEVE

Films:
King of Hearts (1966; French/Italian)..... Colombine
La Guerre est Finie (1967; French/Swedish)
   .... Nadine Sallanches
The Thief of Paris (1967; French/Italian)..Charlotte
Anne of the Thousand Days (1969; British)
   ....Anne Boleyn
The Trojan Women (1972).......................Cassandra
Kamouraska (1973; Canadian/French).....Elisabeth
   Fully nude in long shot.
Earthquake (1974)... Denise
Obsession (1976)
   ....Elizabeth Courtland/Sandra Portinari
Coma (1978)..............................Dr. Susan Wheeler
   0:03 - Nude behind frosted glass shower door, so
      you can't see anything.
Murder by Decree (1979).....................Annie Crook
Last Flight of Noah's Ark (1980)
   .... Bernadette Lafleur
Final Assignment (1981).................Nicole Thomson
Monsignor (1982)... Clara
   1:05 - Topless getting undressed and climbing into
      bed while talking to Christopher Reeve. ***
Tightrope (1984)......................... Beryl Thibodeaux
Choose Me (1984).............................Dr. Love
Trouble in Mind (1986)...............................Wanda
The Moderns (1988).......................Libby Valentin
Dead Ringers (1988).........................Claire Niveau
   0:49 - Very brief right breast in bed with Jeremy
      Irons, then brief topless reaching for pills and
      water. Dark, hard to see. **
Made for TV Movies:
Red Earth, White Earth (1989)...................Madeline

BURGER, MICHELLE

Films:
Payback (1988)... Laura
   0:08 - Brief topless sitting up in bed just before
      getting shot, then brief topless twice, dead in
      bed. *
Road House (1989)........................... Strip Joint Girl

BURKETT, LAURA

Films:
Avenging Angel (1986) ....
Daddy's Boys (1988)..................................Christie
   0:17 - Topless in room with "Jimmy." ***
   0:20 - Left breast making love with "Jimmy" in
      bed again. **
   0:21 - Brief topless during "Jimmy's" nightmare.
      *
   0:43 - Brief topless in bed again, then getting
      dressed. *
   0:53 - Brief topless in bed consoling "Jimmy." *
   1:11 - Left breast in bed with "Jimmy." *

BURNS, BOBBI

Films:
I, the Jury (1982) .... Sheila Kyle
Q (1982) .... Sunbather
  Topless sunbathing on roof of building.
New York Nights (1983) .... The Authoress
  0:16 - Topless on the couch outside with the rock
  star, then topless in bed. **

BURSTYN, ELLEN

Films:
The Last Picture Show (1971; B&W) .... Lois
The Exorcist (1973) .... Chris
Harry and Tonto (1974) .... Shirley
Alice Doesn't Live Here Anymore (1975)
.... Alice Hyatt
Providence (1977) .... Sonia Langham
A Dream of Passion (1978) .... Brenda
Same Time Next Year (1978) .... Doris
Resurrection (1980) .... Edna McCauley
Silence of the North (1981) .... Olive Fredrickson
The Ambassador (1984) .... Alex Hacker
  0:06 - Topless opening her robe to greet her lover.
  ***
  0:07 - Brief topless making love in bed. ***
  0:29 - Topless in a movie while her husband,
  Robert Mitchum, watches. ***
Twice in a Lifetime (1985) .... Kate
Made for TV Movies:
Thursday's Game (1974) ....
Pack of Lies (1987) ....
TV:
The Iron Horse (1967-68) .... Julie Parsons
The Ellen Burstyn Show (1986-88) ...... Ellen Brewer

BYRD-NETHERY, MIRIAM

Films:
Lies (1984; British) ....
The Offspring (1986) .... Eileen Burnside
  0:26 - Topless in bathtub filled with ice while he
  tries to kill her with an ice pick. *
  0:29 - Very brief right breast, dead in bathtub
  while her husband is downstairs.
The Raven Red Kiss-Off (1990) ...... Motel Manager
TV:
Mr. T and Tina (1976) .... Miss Llewellyn

BYRNE, PATTI T.

Films:
Night Call Nurses (1972) .... Barbara
  0:59 - Topless several times in bed with the
  Doctor. **
Fuzz (1972) .... Abigail

C

CADELL, AVA

Films:
Happy Housewives (British) .... Schoolgirl
  0:39 - Buns, getting caught by the Squire and
  getting spanked.
Spaced Out (1980; British) .... Partha
  0:41 - Left breast making love on bed with "Cliff."
  **
  0:42 - Nude wrestling on bed with "Cliff." **
  0:43 - Brief left breast lying in bed alone. *
  1:08 - Topless sitting on bed **
Smokey and the Bandit - Part 3 (1983) .... Blond
Jungle Warriors (1985) .... Didi Belair
  0:50 - Brief topless getting yellow top ripped open
  by a bad guy. *
Not of This Earth (1988) .... Second Hooker
  0:41 - Topless in cellar with "Paul Johnson" just
  before getting killed with two other hookers.
  Wearing a gold dress. **
The Playboy Channel:
Pillow Previews .... Hostess
Magazines:
Playboy (Jun 1989) .... Grapevine
  Page 187: Buns, on bearskin rug in B&W photo.

CAFFARO, CHERI

Films:
Ginger (1970) .... Ginger
The Abductors (1971) .... Ginger
A Place Called Today (1972) ...... Cindy Cartwright
  0:14 - Full frontal nudity covered with oil or
  something writhing around on the bed. **
  1:21 - Brief side view of right breast undressing in
  the bathroom. *
  1:23 - Brief full frontal nudity getting kidnapped
  by two guys. *
  1:30 - Nude when they take off the blanket. **
  1:35 - Brief topless just before getting killed. *
Girls Are For Loving (1973) .... Ginger
Too Hot To Handle (1975) .... Samantha Fox
  0:06 - Topless wearing a black push-up bra and
  buns in black G-string. **
  0:13 - Full frontal nudity lying on boat. *
  0:39 - Topless making love in bed with
  "Dominco." ***
  0:55 - Full frontal nudity taking off clothes and
  lying in bed. ***
  1:06 - Brief left breast in bed with "Dominco." *
Magazines:
Playboy (Nov 1972) .... "Sex in Cinema 1972"
  Page 168: Left breast in red lighting in a photo
  from "A Place Called Today." *
Playboy (Dec 1972) .... "Sex Stars of 1972"
  Page 216: Frontal nudity. ***
Playboy (Nov 1973) .... "Sex in Cinema"
  Page 156: Left breast. *

CAIN, SHARON
Other:
a.k.a. Adult film actress Sharon Kane.
Films:
Slammer Girls (1987)......................................Rita
0:23 - Brief topless changing clothes under table in the prison cafeteria. *
1:02 - Topless walking around an electric chair trying to distract a prison guard. **

CALABRESE, GINA
Other:
a.k.a. Gina Calabrase.
Films:
Goin' All the Way (1981)....................................
0:12 - Left breast in the girl's locker room shower. Standing on the left. **
The Vals (1982).......................................Annie
0:04 - Topless changing clothes in bedroom with three of her friends. Long shot, hard to see. *
0:15 - Right breast making love with a guy at a party. *
0:32 - In black bra with her friends in a store dressing room.

CAMP, COLLEEN
Films:
The Swinging Cheerleaders (1974).....................
Smile (1974).................................Connie Thompson
0:47 - Side profile of right breast and buns in dressing room while "Little Bob" is outside taking pictures.
Fox Fire (1976)...
Death Game, The Seducers (1977)..............Donna
a.k.a. Mrs. Manning's Weekend
0:16 - Buns, in Jacuzzi with Sondra Locke trying to get "George" in with them.
0:47 - Brief topless jumping up and down on the bed while "George" is tied up. *
1:16 - Topless behind stained glass door taunting "George." Hard to see. **
Ebony, Ivory and Jade (1977)...............................
Love and the Midnight Auto Supply (1978)
....Billie Jean
Cat in the Cage (1978).......................Gilda Riener
0:36 - Very brief left breast twice making love in bed with "Bruce." *
Apocalypse Now (1979)............................Playmate
The Game of Death (1979)...................Anne Morris
Cloud Dancer (1980) ....Cindy
1:02 - In bra, driving a convertible car while Joseph Bottoms flies a plane over her.
They All Laughed (1981)....................Christy Miller
The Seduction (1982)...............................Robin
Smokey and the Bandit - Part 3 (1983)
....Dusty Trails
Valley Girl (1983)........................... Sarah Richman
Doin' Time (1984)...................................Catlett
The City Girl (1984).................................Rose
The Joy of Sex (1984).........................Liz Sampson

The Rosebud Beach Hotel (1985)....................Tracy
0:07 - In white lingerie in hotel room with Peter Scolari.
0:28 - In black one piece swimsuit on lounge chair, then walking on the beach.
D.A.R.Y.L. (1985) ....Elaine
Police Academy II: Their First Assignment (1985)
....Kirkland
Police Academy 4: Citizens on Patrol (1987)
.............................Mrs. Kirkland-Tackleberry
Illegally Yours (1988)...................Molly Gilbert
Track 29 (1988)................................. Arlanda
Wicked Stepmother (1989)..............................Jenny
Made for TV Movies:
Addicted to his Love (1988)................ Ellie Snyder
Magazines:
Playboy (Oct 1979)............. "'Apocalypse' Finally" Pages 118-119: Topless. ***
Playboy (Nov 1979).............."Sex in Cinema 1979" Page 175: Side view of right breast. *

CANNON, DYAN
Films:
Such Good Friends.........................Julie Messinger
(Not available on video tape)

CAPRI, AHNA
Films:
Company of Killers (1970) .... Mary Jane Smythe
Darker than Amber (1970)................................. Del
Payday (1972)................................ Mayleen
0:20 - Left breast in bed sleeping, then right breast with Rip Torn. *
0:21 - Topless sitting up in bed smoking a cigarette and talking to Torn. Long scene. ***
Enter the Dragon (1973)............................... Tania
0:47 - Very brief left breast three times in open blouse in bed with John Saxon. *
The Specialist (1975) ....Londa

CARA, IRENE
Films:
Aaron Loves Angela (1975)...........................Angela
Sparkle (1976)...
Fame (1980)..................................... Coco
1:16 - In leotard dancing and talking to "Hillary."
1:57 - Brief topless during "audition" on a black and white TV monitor. *
D.C. Cab (1983)...
City Heat (1984)...............................Ginny Lee
Certain Fury (1985)................................ Tracy
0:32 - Getting undressed to take a shower.
0:36 - Topless behind shower door while "Sniffer" comes into the bathroom. Brief topless in quick cuts when he tries to rape her. *
Killing 'Em Softly (1985)..................................
Miniseries:
Roots: The Next Generation (1979)
..............................Bertha Palmer Haley

CARL, KITTY
Films:
Your Three Minutes are Up (1973).........................
The Centerfold Girls (1974)...........................Sandi
  0:45 - Topless taking off her top while sitting on
  the bed with "Perry." **
  0:51 - Topless on the beach, dead. Long shot,
  hard to see.
Kitty Can't Help It (1975)...
Carhops (1980)...

CARLISI, OLIMPIA
Films:
Catch-22 (1970)...Luciana
  1:04 - Topless lying in bed talking with Alan
  Arkin. *
Casanova (1976; Italian) ....Isabella

CARLISLE, ANNE
Films:
Liquid Sky (1984) ....Margaret/Jimmy
Perfect Strangers (1984)...
Desperately Seeking Susan (1985)...............Victoria
Magazines:
Playboy (Sep 1984).............................."Cult Queen"
  Pages 80-85: Nude. **
Playboy (Dec 1984).................."Sex Stars of 1984"
  Page 203: Right breast and lower frontal nudity,
  standing in bra, garter belt and stockings. *

CARLSON, KAREN
Films:
Shame, Shame, Everybody Knows Her Name
  (1969)....................................Susan Barton
The Student Nurses (1970)...........................Phred
  0:08 - Topless in bed with the wrong guy. *
  0:19 - In bra on sofa with "Dr. Jim Casper."
  0:50 - In bed with "Jim," topless and buns getting
  out, then topless sitting in chair. Long scene.
  ***
  1:02 - Brief topless in bed. *
The Candidate (1972)........................Nancy McKay
Black Oak Conspiracy (1977)...........................Lucy
Matilda (1978)..................................Kathleen Smith
The Octagon (1980)......................................Justine
Fleshburn (1984) ....Shirley Pinter

CARLTON, HOPE MARIE
Films:
Hard Ticket to Hawaii (1987)......................Taryn
  0:07 - Topless taking a shower outside while
  talking to Dona Speir.
  0:23 - Topless in the Jacuzzi with Speir looking at
  diamonds they found. ***
  0:40 - Topless and buns on the beach making love
  with her boyfriend "Jimmy John." ***
  1:33 - Topless during closing credits. **

Slaughterhouse Rock (1988)..........Krista Halpern
  0:09 - Brief right breast, taking off her top in
  bedroom with her boyfriend. *
  0:49 - Topless, getting raped by "Richard" as he
  turns into a monster. **
Nightmare on Elm Street 4: The Dream Master
  (1988)....................................Pin-Up Girl
  0:21 - Brief topless swimming in a waterbed. *
Terminal Exposure (1988).........................Christie
  1:11 - Topless in bathtub licking ice cream off a
  guy. ***
Picasso Trigger (1989)................................Taryn
  0:17 - In white lingerie on boat with Dona Speir.
  0:56 - Topless and buns in Jacuzzi with a guy.
  ***
Savage Beach (1989).....................................Taryn
  0:09 - In two piece swimsuit by the pool.
  0:32 - Topless changing clothes in airplane with
  Dona Speir. *
  0:48 - Nude, going for a swim on the beach with
  Speir. **
Video Tapes:
Playboy Video Magazine Volume 9..........Playmate
Playmate Playoffs.......................................Playmate
Magazines:
Playboy (Jul 1985)................................. Playmate
  Page 96

CAROL, JEAN
Other:
  a.k.a. Jeannie Daly.
Films:
Payback (1988)................................Donna Nathan
  0:24 - Topless opening her pink robe for "Jason"
  while reclining on couch. ***
TV:
The Guiding Light.............................Nadine Cooper

CAROL, LINDA
Films:
School Spirit (1985).....................................Hogette
Reform School Girls (1986)........Jennifer Williams
  0:05 - Nude in the shower. **
  0:56 - Topless in the back of a truck with
  "Norton." *
  1:13 - Topless getting hosed down by "Edna." **
Future Hunters (1987)..

CARPENTER, LINDA
Films:
A Different Story (1977)..........................Chastity
  1:33 - Very brief topless in shower, shutting the
  door when Meg Foster discovers her with Perry
  King. *
Apocalypse Now (1979)............................Playmate

CARRERA, BARBARA

Films:
Embryo (1976).. Victoria
  0:36 - Almost topless meeting Rock Hudson for
    the first time. Hair covers breasts.
  1:09 - In see through top in bedroom with Hudson.
  1:10 - Brief buns and topless in the mirror after
    making love with Hudson. **
  1:11 - Left breast sticking out of bathrobe. *
The Island of Dr. Moreau (1977)..................... Maria
When Time Ran Out! (1980)........................... Iolani
Condorman (1981).. Natalia
I, The Jury (1982)................ Dr. Charolette Bennett
  1:02 - Nude on bed making love with Armand
    Asante. Very sexy. ***
  1:46 - Brief topless in hallway kissing Asante. *
Lone Wolf McQuade (1983) .... Lola
Never Say Never Again (1983) .... Fatima Blush
Wild Geese II (1985) .... Kathy
The Underachievers (1987) .... Katherine
Love at Stake (1988)...
Wicked Stepmother (1989)......................... Priscilla
Loverboy (1989)................................... Alex Barnett
Miniseries:
Masada (1981) .... Sheva
TV:
Centennial (1978-79).............................. Clay Basket
Dallas (1985-89)............................... Angelica Nero
Video Tapes:
Playboy Video Magazine, Volume 1........................
Magazines:
Playboy (Jul 1977)....................... "Acting Beastly"
  Pages 93-97: Topless. ***
Playboy (Mar 1982)....................... "Aye, Barbara"
  Pages 148-155: Nude, also photos from "I, the
  Jury." ***
Playboy (Sep 1987)........ "25 Years of James Bond"
  Page 129: Topless. **

CARRICO, MONICA

Films:
Lucky 13 (1984)....................................... Charlene
a.k.a. Running Hot
  0:09 - Lying on bed in white bra and open dress
    top.
  0:18 - Walking around in panties and a blouse.
  0:49 - Topless sitting on a rock after skinny
    dipping with Eric Stolz. **
  0:51 - Topless and buns after getting out of water
    and picking up clothes. **
  1:03 - Topless in bed making love with Stolz. **
  1:15 - Topless lying in bed with Stolz. ***
Highway to Hell (1984) ....

CARRILLO, ELPIDIA

Films:
Beyond the Limit (1976)............................... Clara
  0:31 - Topless making love with Richard Gere.
    Long scene. **
  1:08 - Topless talking to Gere. Another long
    scene. **
The Border (1982).. Maria
  Right breast in shack with Jack Nicholson.
Under Fire (1983)........................ Sandanista (Leon)
Salvador (1986).. Maria
  0:21 - Very brief right breast, lying in a hammock
    with James Woods. *
Let's Get Harry (1986)................................ Veronica
Predator (1987)... Anna
The Assassin (1989)... Elena
Made for TV Movies:
Dangerous Passion (1990) .... Angela

CARROLL, JILL

Films:
The Man Who Loved Women (1983)
  .... Sue the Baby Sitter
The Vals (1983) .... Sam
The Unholy (1988).. Millie
  1:10 - Very brief upper half of left breast talking
    in the courtyard with Ben Cross. *
Made for TV Movies:
American Harvest (1987)................ Calla Bergstrom

CARROLL, REGINA

Films:
Brain of Blood (1971; Philippines)...........................
Blazing Stewardesses (1975) ....
Jessi's Girls (1976).. Claire
  0:58 - Topless and buns in hay with Indian guy.
    Don't see her face. **

CARTER, HELENA BONHAM

Films:
A Room with a View (1986)....... Lucy Honeychurch
Lady Jane (1987)........................... Lady Jane Grey
  1:19 - Topless kneeling on the bed with
    "Guilford." *
  2:09 - Side view of right breast and very, very
    brief topless sitting by fire with "Guilford." *
Getting It Right (1989)............... Minerva Munday
  0:18 - Topless a couple of times in bed talking to
    "Gavin." It's hard to recognize her because she
    has lots of makeup on her face. **
Made for TV Movies:
A Hazard of Hearts (1987).....................................

CARTER, LYNDA
Other:
   Miss World U.S.A. 1973.
Films:
   Bobbie Jo and the Outlaw (1976)
   .... Bobbie Jo Baker
      0:17 - Brief left breast making love with Marjoe
         Gortner. **
      0:27 - Brief left breast making love with Gortner
         again. **
      0:29 - Very brief breasts in pond with Gortner
         experimenting with mushrooms. *
Made for TV Movies:
   Rita Hayworth: The Love Goddess (1983)
   .... Rita Hayworth
   Mickey Spillane's Mike Hammer: Murder Takes
      All (1989)........................ Helen Durant
TV:
   Wonder Woman (1976-79)
   .... Yeoman Diana Prince/Wonder Woman
   Partners in Crime (1984)................ Carole Stanwyck

CARTWRIGHT, VERONICA
Films:
   Inserts (1976)................................ Harlene
      0:16 - Topless sitting on bed with Richard
         Dreyfus. **
      0:31 - Nude on bed with Stephen Davies making a
         porno movie for Dreyfus. Long scene. ***
   Bernice Bobs Her Hair (1977; B&W)......................
   Goin' South (1978)................................ Hermine
   Invasion of the Body Snatchers (1978)
   .... Nancy Bellicec
   Alien (1979)................................ Lambert
   Nightmares (1983)................................ Claire
   The Right Stuff (1983)...................... Betty Grissom
   My Man Adam (1986).......................... Elaine Swit
      1:09 - Side view of right breast lying on tanning
         table when "Adam" steals her card keys. Long
         shot, hard to see. *
   Flight of the Navigator (1986).......... Helen Freeman
   Wisdom (1987)...................... Samantha Wisdom
   The Witches of Eastwick (1987)......... Felicia Alden
TV:
   Daniel Boone (1964-66)...................... Jenima Boone

CASH, ROSALIND
Films:
   Klute (1971)................................ Pat
   The Omega Man (1971).................................. Lisa
      1:09 - Side view of left breast and upper half of
         buns getting out of bed. Buns and topless sitting
         in bed. **
      1:21 - Side view topless in beige underwear while
         trying on clothes. *
   Hickey and Boggs (1972).............................. Nyona
   The New Centurions (1972)............................ Lorrie
   Uptown Saturday Night (1974).......... Sarah Jackson
   Wrong is Right (1982)...................... Mrs. Ford

The Adventures of Buckaroo Banzai (1984)
.... John Emdall
Go Tell It On the Mountain (1984)..... Aunt Florence

CASSIDY, JOANNA
Films:
   The Laughing Policeman (1973).................. Monica
   The Outfit (1973)................................ Rita
   Bank Shot (1974)................................ El
   Night Child (1975; British/Italian)...........................
   The Stepford Wives (1975) ....
   Stay Hungry (1976) .... Joe Mason
   The Late Show (1977) .... Laura Birdwell
   Stunts (1977)........................ Patti Johnson
   Our Winning Season (1978)...................... Sheila
   The Glove (1980)...................... Sheila Michaels
   Night Games (1980) .... Julie Miller
      0:44 - Buns, skinny dipping in the pool with Cindy
         Pickett.
      0:45 - Brief full frontal nudity sitting up. **
   Bladerunner (1982)........................ Zhora
      0:54 - Topless getting dressed after taking a
         shower while talking with Harrison Ford **
   Under Fire (1983)........................ Claire
   Club Paradise (1986) .... Terry Hamlin
   The Fourth Protocol (1987).................. Vassilieva
      1:39 - Brief left breast. She's lying dead in Pierce
         Brosnan's bathtub. *
      1:49 - Same thing, different angle. *
   1969 (1988).. Ev
   Who Framed Roger Rabbit (1988).............. Dolores
Miniseries:
   Hollywood Wives (1988).................... Maralee Gray
Made for Cable TV:
   Wheels of Terror (1990)................................ Laura
Made for TV Movies:
   Pleasures (1986)..
   Nightmare at Bitter Creek (1988)..........................
TV:
   Shields and Yarnell (1977)........................ Regular
   The Roller Girls (1978) .... Selma "Books" Cassidy
   0:240 Robert (1979-80)
   .... Deputy Morgan Wainwright
   The Family Tree (1983)................ Elizabeth Nichols
   Falcon Crest (1983) .... Katherine Demery
   Buffalo Bill (1983-84)........................ JoJo White
   Codename: Foxfire (1985)
   .... Elizabeth "Foxfire" Towne

CATES, PHOEBE
Films:
   Paradise (1981)................................ Sarah
      0:23 - Buns and topless taking a shower in a cave
         while Willie Aames watches. **
      0:36 - In wet white dress in a pond with Aames.
      0:40 - Very brief left breast caressing herself while
         looking at her reflection in the water. *
      0:43 - Buns, getting out of bed to check out
         Aames' body while he sleeps.
      0:46 - Buns, washing herself in a pond at night.

0:55 - Side view of her silhouette at the beach at night. Nude swimming in the water, viewed from below. **
1:11 - Topless making love with Aames. ***
1:12 - Full frontal nudity swimming under water with Aames. ***
1:16 - Topless making love with Aames again. ***

Fast Times at Ridgemont High (1982)
....Linda Barrett
0:50 - Topless getting out of swimming pool during Judge Reinhold's fantasy. ***
Private School (1983)..............................Christine
1:21 - Brief buns lying in sand with Mathew Modine.
1:24 - Upper half of buns flashing with the rest of the girls during graduation ceremony.
Gremlins (1984)....................................Kate
Date With an Angel (1987)................Patty Winston
Bright Lights, Big City (1988)....................Amanda
Shag (1989)..........................Carson McBride
Gremlins 2: The New Batch (1990)................Kate
Miniseries:
Lace..Lili
Lace II (1985)......................................Lili

CATTRALL, KIM
Films:
Rosebud (1975)...............................Joyce
Deadly Harvest (1976)............................
Tribute (1980; Canadian).....................Sally Haines
Porky's (1981).............................Honeywell
Brief buns, the very brief lower frontal nudity after removing skirt to make love in the boy's locker room.
Ticket to Heaven (1981)..............................Ruthie
City Limits (1984)...................................Wickings
1:02 - Right breast sitting up in bed with a piece of paper stuck to her. **
Police Academy (1984)................Karen Thompson
Turk 182 (1985)..........................Danny Boudreau
Big Trouble in Little China (1986)........Gracie Law
Mannequin (1987)..Emmy
Masquerade (1988)............. Mrs. Brooke Morrison
0:04 - Topless in bed with Rob Lowe. ***
0:47 - In white teddy after having sex with Lowe.
Midnight Crossing (1988)..................Alexa Schubb
0:29 - Brief left breast making love on small boat with her "husband" is a body double, Crisstyn Dante.
0:39 - In wet white blouse arguing in the water with her "husband."
TV:
Scruples (1980)...............................Melanie Adams
Magazines:
Playboy (Nov 1987)............. "Sex in Cinema 1987"
Page 138: Left breast lying in bed with Rob Lowe. *

CAYER, KIM
Films:
Screwballs (1983)..................Brunette Cheerleader
Loose Screws (1986)...........................Pig Pen Girl
Graveyard Shift (1987)................................Suzy
0:06 - In black bra, then brief left breast when vampire rips the bra off. **
0:53 - Brief topless in junk yard with garter belt, black panties and stockings. *

CAYTON, ELIZABETH
See Kaitan, Elizabeth.

CELLIER, CAROLINE
Films:
Life Love Death (1969; French/Italian)...................
This Man Must Die (1970)...............Helene Lawson
Petit Con (1986; French).................Annie Choupon
L'Annee Des Meduses (1987; French)
....Chris' Mother
0:02 - Topless taking off top at the beach. **
0:56 - Topless on boat at night with "Romain." **
1:06 - Topless on the beach with Valerie Kaprisky. **
1:14 - Left breast, lying on beach with "Romain" at night. *

CHADWICK, JUNE
Films:
The Golden Lady (1979; British).....................Lucy
Forbidden World (1982)...........Dr. Barbara Glaser
0:29 - Topless in bed making love with Jesse Vint. **
0:54 - Topless taking a shower with Dawn Dunlap **
The Last Horror Film (1984)......................Reporter
This is Spinal Tap (1984)..............Jeanine Pettibone
Distortions (1987)...
Quiet Thunder (1988)..
TV:
V (1984-85)...Lydia
Riptide (1986)...............................Lt. Joanna Parisi

CHAMBERS, MARILYN
Other:
Former adult film actress.
Films:
Rabid (1977)...................................... Rose
0:14 - Topless in bed. **
1:04 - Topless in closet selecting clothes. **
1:16 - Topless in white panties getting out of bed. **
My Therapist (1983)........................ Kelly Carson
(Shot on video tape.)
0:01 - Topless in sex therapy class. **
0:07 - Topless, then full frontal nudity undressing for "Rip." Long scene. **

0:10 - Topless undressing at home, then full frontal nudity making love on couch. Long scene. Nice. Then brief side view of right breast in shower. ***

0:18 - Topless on sofa with "Mike." *

0:21 - Topless taking off and putting red blouse on at home. **

0:26 - Nude in bedroom by herself masturbating on bed. ***

0:32 - Topless exercising on the floor, buns in bed with "Mike," topless in bed getting covered with whipped cream. ***

0:41 - Left breast and lower frontal nudity fighting with "Don" while he rips off her clothes. **

1:08 - Topless and brief buns in bed. **

1:12 - In braless pink T-shirt at the beach.

Angel of H.E.A.T. (1982)............... Angel Harmony

0:15 - Full frontal nudity making love with an intruder on the bed. **

0:17 - Topless in a bathtub. *

0:40 - Topless in a hotel room with a short guy. **

0:52 - Topless getting out of a wet suit. *

1:01 - Topless sitting on floor with some robots. **

1:29 - Topless in bed with "Mark." *

Up 'N' Coming (1987)................................. Cassie

(R-rated version reviewed here, there is an X-rated version available.)

0:01 - Nude, getting out of bed and taking a shower. ***

0:08 - Topless making love in bed with the record producer. **

0:30 - Brief topless in bed with two guys. *

0:47 - Full frontal nudity getting suntan lotion rubbed on her by another woman. **

0:55 - Topless taking off her top at radio station. **

Party Incorporated (1989)........... Marilyn Sanders

0:56 - In lingerie, then topless in bedroom with "Ronald Weston." Nice! ***

1:11 - Brief topless on the beach when "Peter" takes her swimsuit top off. *

Magazines:

Playboy (Aug 1973)........................... "Porno Chic"
Page 141: Full frontal nudity

Playboy (Jan 1989)........ "Women of the Seventies"
Page 214: Topless. ***

Playboy (Nov 1989)............. "Sex in Cinema 1989"
Page 134: Topless still from "Party Incorporated." ***

CHANEL, TALLY

Films:

Bits and Pieces (1985).....................................Jennifer
0:58 - In the woods with the killer, seen briefly in bra and panties before and after being killed.

Warrior Queen (1986)................................. Vespa
0:09 - Topless hanging on a rope, being auctioned. ***

0:20 - Topless and buns with black slave girl. ***

0:37 - Nude, before attempted rape by Goliath. **
0:57 - Topless during rape by Goliath. **

The Nightstalker (1987)............................Brenda
0:54 - Brief frontal nudity lying dead in bed covered with paint. Long shot, hard to see anything. *

Free Ride (1987)...Candy
0:57 - Brief topless in bedroom with "Dan." *

Hollywood Hot Tubs 2 - Educating Crystal (1989)
....Mindy Wright

Magazines:

Penthouse (May 1990)....................... "Dry as Dust"
Pages 40-49

CHAPLIN, GERALDINE

Other:

Daughter of actor Charlie Chaplin.
Granddaughter of Eugene O'Neill.

Films:

Dr. Zhivago (1965).. Tonya
Nashville (1975)...Opal
Buffalo Bill and the Indians (1976).... Annie Oakley
Roseland (1977)...Marilyn
Welcome to L.A. (1977).................... Karen Hood
1:28 - Full frontal nudity standing in Keith Carradine's living room. **

A Wedding (1978)..........................Rita Billingsley
The Moderns (1988)...................... Nathalie de Ville
White Mischief (1988)..Nina

CHARBONNEAU, PATRICIA

Films:

Manhunter (1986)...............................Mrs. Sherman
Desert Hearts (1986)..........................Cay Rivvers
1:09 - Brief topless making love in bed with Helen Shaver. ***

Call Me (1988).. Anna
1:18 - Brief left breast making love in bed with a guy, then topless putting blouse on and getting out of bed. **

Shakedown (1988)............................ Susan Cantrell

CHEN, JOAN

Films:

The Nightstalker (1987)..........................Mai Wong
Tai-Pan (1987)..................................... May May
0:55 - In sheer top sitting on bed talking to Bryan Brown.

0:56 - Brief left breast washing herself, hard to see anything. *

1:14 - Sheer top again.

1:30 - Sheer top again.

The Last Emperor (1987)........................ Wan Jung
The Blood of Heroes (1989)...........................Kidda

TV:

Twin Peaks (1990-)...................... Jocelyn Packard

CHILES, LOIS
Films:
The Way We Were (1973)........................Carol Ann
Coma (1978)................................... Nancy Greenly
Moonraker (1979)..............Dr. Holly Goodhead
Raw Courage (1983)...Ruth
Sweet Liberty (1986).....................................Leslie
Creepshow 2 (1987)........................ Annie Lansing
    0:59 - Brief topless getting out of boyfriend's bed,
    then getting dressed. **
Broadcast News (1987)......................Jennifer Mack
TV:
Dallas (1982-84)...............................Holly Harwood

CHONG, RAE DAWN
Other:
Daughter of comedian/actor Tommy Chong.
Films:
Quest For Fire (1982)................................Ika
    Nude but body paint all over.
Beat Street (1984)................................ Tracy
City Limits (1984).................................Yogi
Fear City (1984) .... Leila
    0:26 - Topless and buns, dancing on stage. ***
    0:50 - Brief topless in the hospital getting a shock
    to get her heart started. *
American Flyers (1985)..............................Sarah
The Color Purple (1985)................................Squeak
Commando (1986)..
Soul Man (1986)...Sarah
The Squeeze (1987).............................Rachel Dobs
Running Out of Luck (1987)...........................
    0:42 - Left breast hugging Mick Jagger, then a
    nicer left breast shot lying in bed with him. **
    1:12 - Left breast painting some kind of drug laced
    solution on herself. **
    1:14 - Right breast in prison offering her breast to
    the warden. **
    1:21 - Buns and left breast in bed with Jagger in
    flashback. *
The Borrower (1989) ....
Tales from the Darkside, The Movie (1990) ....
Magazines:
Playboy (Apr 1982)...................... "Quest For Fire"

CHRISTIAN, CLAUDIA
Films:
The Hidden (1987)..................................Brenda Lee
Never on Tuesday (1988).........................Tuesday
    0:43 - Brief side view of right breast in the shower
    with "Eddie" during his fantasy. *
    Note: There are a lot of braless T-shirt shots of
    her throughout the film.
TV:
Berrengers (1985)...........................Melody Hughes

CHRISTIE, JULIE
Films:
Billy Liar (1963)..Liz
Darling (1965)........................ Diana Scott
Doctor Zhivago (1965)...............................Lara
Fahrenheit 451 (1967)....................Linda/Clarisse
Petulia (1968)....................... Petulia Danner
McCabe and Mrs. Miller (1972)..............Mrs. Miller
Don't Look Now (1973)....................... Laura Baxter
    0:27 - Brief topless in bathroom with Donald
    Sutherland. *
    0:30 - Topless making love with Donald in bed.
    **
Shampoo (1975).. Jackie
Demon Seed (1977)............................Susan Harris
    0:25 - Side view of left breast getting out of bed.
    *
    0:30 - Topless and buns getting out of the shower
    while the computer watches with it's camera.
    **
Heaven Can Wait (1978)....................... Betty Logan
Heat and Dust (1982)..................................Anne
Separate Tables (1983).....................................
The Return of the Soldier (1985) ....
Power (1986)..............................Ellen Freeman
Miss Mary (1987)....................Miss Mary Mulligan
Made for TV Movies:
Dadah is Death (1988) ....Barbara

CLARK, CANDY
Films:
Fat City (1972).. Faye
American Graffiti (1973) ....Debbie
James Dean - A legend in His Own Time (1976).....
The Man Who Fell to Earth (1976)........Mary-Lou
    (Uncensored version)
    0:42 - Topless in the bathtub, washing her hair and
    talking to David Bowie. **
    0:55 - Topless sitting on bed and blowing out a
    candle. **
    0:56 - Topless in bed with Bowie. ***
    1:26 - Full frontal nudity climbing into bed with
    Bowie after he reveals his true alien self. ***
    1:56 - Nude with Bowie making love and shooting
    a gun.
Citizen's Band (1977)...........................Electra/Pam
The Big Sleep (1978)................. Camilla Sternwood
    0:18, 0:30, 0:39 and 1:04.
When Ya Comin' Back Red Ryder (1979). Cheryl
    (Not available on video tape yet.)
Rodeo Girl (1980)...
Q (1982)...Joan
Blue Thunder (1983).......................................Kate
Hambone and Hillie (1984)..........................Nancy
Cat's Eye (1985).....................................Sally Ann
At Close Range (1986)............................. Mary Sue
The Blob (1988).................................Fran Hewitt
Faerie Tale Theatre:
Tale of the Frog Prince (1982)................................

Magazines:
Playboy (Jan 1973)................."The Ziegfeld Girls"
Page 75: Right breast. **
Playboy (Nov 1978)............."Sex in Cinema 1978"
Page 181: Topless. *

CLARK, DAWN
Films:
The Happy Hooker Goes to Washington (1977)
.... Candy
1:18 - Topless, covered with spaghetti in a
restaurant. *
Stripes (1981)..

CLARK, SUSAN
Films:
Coogan's Bluff (1968)..Julie
Tell Them Willie Boy is Here (1969) ....Liz
0:21 - Very brief buns when Robert Redford turns
her over in bed.
0:57 - In slip, after taking off dress for Redford.
Skin Game (1971) ....Ginger
The Apple Dumpling Gang (1975)
.... Magnolia Dusty Clydesdale
Night Moves (1975)...................................... Ellen
Deadly Companion (1979)................... Paula West
0:19 - Brief left breast consoling Michael Sarrazin
in bed, then brief side view of left breast. *
0:20 - Brief topless sitting up in bed. *
The North Avenue Irregulars (1979)................ Anne
Promises in the Dark (1979)................Fran Koenig
Nobody's Perfekt (1981)...................................Carol
Porky's (1981)........................... Cherry Forever
Made for TV Movies:
Babe (1975)..................... Babe Didrickson Zaharias
(Emmy Award for Best Actress in a Special.)
Amelia Earhart (1976)...
TV:
Webster (1983-89)
.... Katherine Calder Young Papadapolis

CLARKSON, LANA
Films:
Blind Date (1982)..Rachel
(NOT the same 1987 "Blind Date" with Bruce
Willis.)
0:52 - Brief topless rolling over in bed when
Joseph Bottoms sneaks in. Dark, hard to see. *
1:11 - In two piece swimsuit on modeling
assignment.
1:18 - In two piece swimsuit by pool.
Fast Times at Ridgemont High (1982).. Mrs. Vargas
Scarface (1983) .... Woman at the Babylon Club
Deathstalker (1983; Argentina/U.S.)..............Kaira
0:26 - Topless when her cape opens talking to
"Deathstalker" and "Oghris." **
0:29 - Topless lying down by the fire when
"Deathstalker" comes to make love with her.
***

0:49 - Brief topless with gaping cape sword
fighting with a guard. *
Barbarian Queen (1985)..........................Amethea
0:38 - Brief topless during attempted rape. **
0:48 - Topless being tortured with metal hand then
raped by torturer ***
Amazon Women on the Moon (1987).... Alpha Beta

CLAYBURGH, JILL
Films:
Portnoy's Complaint (1972)...........................Naomi
The Thief Who Came to Dinner (1973)..........Jackie
The Terminal Man (1974) .... Angela Black
Hustling (1975)...
Silver Streak (1976)...............................Hilly Burns
Semi-Tough (1977)............. Barbara Jane Bookman
An Unmarried Woman (1978)...................... Erica
0:05 - Dancing around the apartment in white long
sleeve T-shirt and white panties.
0:12 - Brief topless getting dressed for bed, kind
of dark and hard to see. **
1:10 - In bra and panties in guy's apartment, then
brief topless lying on bed. **
Starting Over (1979)................ Marilyn Holmberg
0:45 - Very brief upper half of breasts taking a
shower while Burt Reynolds waits outside. *
Luna (1979)................................... Caterina Silveri
It's My Turn (1980) .... Kate Gunzinger
1:10 - Brief upper half of left breast in bed with
Michael Douglas after making love. *
I'm Dancing as Fast as I Can (1981)
....Barbara Gordon
First Monday in October (1981)...........Ruth Loomis
Hanna K. (1984)..
Where are the Children? (1986)..... Nancy Eldgridge
Shy People (1988).. Diana
Made for TV Movies:
Hustling (1975).. Wanda
Female Instinct (1985)............................... Mary
Who Gets the Friends? (1988)..............................

CLERY, CORRINE
Films:
Kleinhoff Hotel (1973)..
The Story of "O" (1975; French)........................ O
0:09 - Topless in bedroom with two women. **
0:12 - Topless being made love to. **
0:20 - Frontal nudity making love with two men.
**
0:29 - Topless taking a bath while a man watches.
**
0:42 - Buns, on a sofa while her boyfriend lifts her
dress up, then topless while another man plays
with her, then nude except for white stockings.
***
0:51 - Brief topless chained by wrists and gagged.
**
1:22 - Nude making love with a young guy. ***
Covert Action (1978)...
Moonraker (1979)........................... Corinne Dufour

I Hate Blondes (1981)................................Angelica
Yor: The Hunter from the Future (1983)......Ka-Laa
Magazines:
Playboy (Sep 1987)........"25 Years of James Bond"
Page 131: Topless. **

CLOSE, GLENN
Films:
World According to Garp (1982).......... Jenny Fields
The Big Chill (1983)..Sara
0:27 - Topless sitting down in the shower crying.
*

The Natural (1984)....................................Iris Gaines
The Stone Boy (1984).......................Ruth Hillerman
Maxie (1985) ....Jan/Maxie
The Jagged Edge (1986)..................... Teddy Barnes
0:46 - Side view of left breast, making love in bed
with Jeff Bridges.
1:38 - Very brief side view of right breast running
down the hall taking off her blouse. Back is
toward camera. Blurry shot.
Fatal Attraction (1987)....................... Alex Forrest
0:17 - Left breast when she opens her top to let
Michael Douglas kiss her. Then very brief
buns, falling into bed with him. **
0:20 - Brief left breast in freight elevator with
Douglas. *
0:32 - Topless in bed talking to Douglas. ***
Dangerous Liaisons (1988)..... Marquise de Merteuil
Immediate Family (1989)...................Linda Spector

COCHRELL, ELIZABETH
Other:
a.k.a. Liza Cochrell.
Films:
The Big Bet (1985)..................... Sister in Stag Film
1:05 - Topless and buns in a video tape that
"Chris" rents. ***
1:08 - Topless again from video tape watching it
at home. **
Sunset Strip (1986)......................................Stripper

COLLINGS, JEANNIE
Other:
a.k.a. Jeanie Collings.
Films:
Confessions of a Window Cleaner (1974; British)...
Happy Housewives (British).................. Mrs. Wain
0:16 - Very, very brief right breast with the
"Newsagent's Daughter" and "Bob" in the
bathtub.
Emily (1976; British)............................... Rosalind
1:05 - Brief topless on the couch with "Gerald"
while "Richard" watches. *
Carry on England (1976; British)... Private Edwards

COLLINS, ALANA
Other:
a.k.a. Alana Collins, Alana Hamilton or Alana
Stewart.
Wife of singer Rod Stewart.
Ex-wife of actor George Hamilton.
Films:
Night Call Nurses (1972)................................ Janis
0:12 - Topless in bed with "Zach." **
0:24 - In white two piece swimsuit on boat.
0:28 - Topless and buns on bed with "Kyle." **
0:52 - Brief right breast twice in shower with
"Kyle." *
The Ravagers (1979)................................. Miriam
Evel Knievel (1979).......................................Nurse
Swing Shift (1984)...........................Frankie Parker
Where the Boys Are '84 (1984)....................Maggie

COLLINS, CANDACE
Films:
Class (1983) ....Buxom Girl
Smokey and the Bandit - Part 3 (1983).............Maid
Magazines:
Playboy (Dec 1979)..................................Playmate
Page 198

COLLINS, JOAN
Films:
Decameron Nights (1953)................................Maria
Stopover Tokyo (1957).....................................Tina
Subterfuge (1969)................................Anne Langley
The Executioner (1970) .... Sarah Booth
Quest for Love (1971).....................................Ottilie
Fear in the Night (1972)..............Molly Charmichael
Also released as "Dynasty of Fear"
Tales from the Crypt (1972)..............Joanne Clayton
Dark Places (1973)..Sarah
Oh, Alfie! (1975; British)................................. Fay
a.k.a. Alfie Darling
0:28 - In white bra and panties running to answer
the phone and talking to "Alfie."
1:00 - Topless lying in bed after "Alfie" rolls off
her. ***
Bawdy Adventures of Tom Jones (1976)
.... Black Bess
Empire of the Ants (1977) ....Marilyn Fryser
The Bitch (1977)........................... Fontaine Khaled
0:01 - In long slip getting out of bed and putting a
bathrobe on.
0:03 - Brief topless in the shower with a guy. *
0:24 - Brief topless taking black corset off for the
chauffeur in the bedroom, then buns getting out
of bed and walking to the bathroom. **
0:39 - Making love in bed wearing a blue slip.
1:01 - Left breast after making love in bed. *
The Stud (1978)......................................Fontaine
0:10 - Brief left breast making love with "Tony"
in the elevator. *
0:27 - Brief buns in panties, stockings and garter
belt in "Tony's" apartment.

0:58 - Brief black bra and panties under fur coat in back of limousine with "Tony."
1:03 - Brief topless taking off dress to get in pool. *
1:04 - Nude in the pool with "Tony." *
Fearless (1978).. Bridgitte
0:01 - In bra and panties, then brief right breast during opening credits. *
0:41 - Topless after doing a strip tease routine on stage. **
1:17 - Undressing in front of "Wally" in white bra and panties, then right breast. *
1:20 - Brief right breast lying dead on couch. *
Sunburn (1979)................................... Nera
Homework (1982)...........................Diana
Body double used for Joan's nude scene.
Made for Cable:
Hansel & Gretel...
Miniseries:
Sins.....................................Helene Junot
Made For TV movies:
Paper Dolls (1982)..
Her Life as a Man (1984)............................
The Cartier Affair (1985)..............................
Monte Carlo (1986)........................Katrina Petrovna
TV:
Dynasty (1981-89).............Alexis Carrington Colby
Magazines:
Playboy (Nov 1978).............."Sex in Cinema 1978"
Page 185: Left breast and lower frontal nudity. *
Playboy (Dec 1983)..................................
Playboy (Dec 1984).................. "Sex Stars of 1984"
Page 209: Topless in bed. ***
Playboy (Jan 1989).......... "Women of the Eighties"
Page 250: Buns and side view of right breast in B&W photo. **

COLLINS, PAMELA

Films:
Sweet Sugar (1972)..................................... Dolores
0:26 - Brief topless when doctor tears her bra off. *
0:50 - Topless in the shower with Phyllis Davis. ***
So Long, Blue Boy (1973)...............................Cathy

COLLINS, PAULINE

Films:
Secrets of a Windmill Girl (1966; British)...............
Shirley Valentine (1989).............Shirley Valentine
(If you like older women, check this out.)
0:13 - Brief left breast giving "Joe" a shampoo in the bathtub. *
1:17 - Topless jumping from the boat into the water in slow motion. Very brief topless in the water. **
1:19 - Buns, hugging Tom Conti, left breast several times kissing him. **

COLLINS, ROBERTA

Films:
The Big Bird Cage (1972)......................................
Unholy Rollers (1972)...............................Jennifer
Caged Heat (1974).. Belle
a.k.a. Renegade Girls
1:01 - Topless while the prison doctor has her drugged so he can take pictures of her. ***
Death Race 2000 (1975)................ Matilda the Hun
0:27 - Topless being interviewed and arguing with "Calamity Jane." **
Hardbodies (1984)..Lana
School Spirit (1985)......................Helen Grimshaw
Vendetta (1986) .... Miss Dice

COLLINS, RUTH CORRINE

Films:
Firehouse (1987)..Bubbles
Doom Asylum (1987)....................................... Tina
Alexa (1988).. Marshall
0:01 - Topless a couple of times taking blue dress off and putting it on again. Long shot. *
New York's Finest (1988)................. Joy Sugarman
0:04 - Brief topless with a bunch of hookers. *
0:36 - Topless with her two friends doing push ups on the floor. *
1:02 - Topless making love on top of a guy talking about diamonds. **
Cleo/Leo (1989).. Sally
0:08 - Topless getting dress pulled off by "Leo." ***
Party Incorporated (1989)............................Betty
0:07 - Topless on desk with "Dickie." Long shot. *
1:08 - Topless in bed with "Ron Weston" when Marilyn comes in. **

COLLINSON, MADELEINE

Other:
Identical twin sister of Mary Collinson.
Films:
Come Back Peter (1971; British)............................
Twins of Evil (1971)........................ Freida Gelhorn
1:07 - Right breast, then brief topless undoing dress, then full frontal nudity after turning into a vampire in bedroom. **
Love Machine (1971)..................................... Sandy
1:22 - Topless in shower with "Robin" when Dyan Cannon discovers them all together. Can't tell who is who. **
Magazines:
Playboy (Oct 1970).................................... Playmate
Playboy (Dec 1972)................... "Sex Stars of 1972"
Page 211: Topless. **
Playboy (Jan 1979)................. "25 Beautiful Years"
Page 161: Topless lying on bed. ***

COLLINSON, MARY

Other:
Identical twin sister of Madeleine Collinson.
Films:
Come Back Peter (1971; British)...........................
Twins of Evil (1971)....................Maria Gelhorn
Love Machine (1971)................................. Debbie
    1:22 - Topless in shower with "Robin" when Dyan
    Cannon discovers them all together. Can't tell
    who is who. **
Magazines:
Playboy (Oct 1970)................................. Playmate
Playboy (Dec 1972)..................."Sex Stars of 1972"
    Page 211: Topless. **
Playboy (Jan 1979)................."25 Beautiful Years"
    Page 161: Topless lying on bed. ***

COLPITTS, CISSY

Films:
Billy Jack (1971)............................... Miss Eyelashes
The Happy Hooker Goes to Washington (1977)
....Miss Goodbody
    0:29 - Very brief topless when her top pops open
    during the senate hearing. *
TV:
The Ted Knight Show (1978).....................Graziella

CONGIE, TERRY

Films:
Malibu Hot Summer (1981)................. Dit McCoy
    a.k.a. Sizzle Beach
    0:02 - Side view of right breast on floor during
    opening credits. *
Shadows Run Black (1986).................Lee Faulkner

COOKE, JENNIFER

Films:
Gimme an "F" (1981)....................... Pam Bethlehem
    1:10 - Wearing United States flag pasties
    frolicking with "Dr. Spirit". Nice bouncing
    action.
    1:38 - Still of pasties scene during end credits.
Friday the 13th Part VI: Jason Lives (1986)..Megan
Made for HBO:
The Hitchhiker: Man's Best Friend............Elanor
    0:19 - Brief side view topless getting undressed to
    take a shower. *
TV:
The Guiding Light (1981-83)...........Morgan Nelson
V (1984-85) ....Elizabeth

COOLIDGE, RITA

Other:
Singer.
Films:
Pat Garrett and Billy the Kid (1973)........... Maria
    1:34 - Brief right breast getting undress to get into
    bed with Kris Kristofferson. *

COOPER, JEANNE

Films:
There Was a Crooked Man (1970).........Prostitute
    0:18 - Brief left breast trying to seduce the sheriff,
    Henry Fonda, in a room. *
TV:
Bracken's World (1970)................... Grace Douglas
The Young and the Restless
.... Kay Chancellor Sterling

COPLEY, TERI

Films:
New Year's Evil (1981)....................... Teenage Girl
    0:48 - Brief right breast in the back of the car with
    her boyfriend at a drive-in movie. Breast is half
    sticking out of her white bra. Dark, hard to see
    anything. *
Down the Drain (1989)...
Transylvania Twist (1990) ....
Made for TV Movies:
I Married a Centerfold (1984)...........................
In the Line of Duty: The F.B.I. Murders (1988)
....Vickie
TV:
We Got It Made (1983-84).......... Mickey McKenzie
I Had Three Wives (1985)......................... Samantha
Magazines:
Playboy (Nov 1990)........................... "Teri Copley"
    Pages 90-99: Nude - very nice! ***

COSTA, SARA

Films:
Weekend Pass (1984).............. Tuesday Del Mundo
    0:07 - Buns in G-string, then topless during strip
    dance routine on stage. ***
Stripper (1985).. Herself
    0:16 - Topless doing strip dance routine. ***
    0:46 - Topless and buns dancing on stage in a G-
    string. ***
    1:12 - Topless doing another strip routine. ***

COX, ASHLEY

Films:
Drive-In (1976).................................... Mary-Louise
King of the Mountain (1981) ....Elaine
Looker (1981)..Candy
Night Shift (1982)..............................Jenny Lynn
Magazines:
Playboy (Dec 1977)................................. Playmate

CRAMPTON, BARBARA

Films:
Body Double (1984)........................... Carol Sculley
    0:04 - Brief right breast making love in bed with
    another man when her husband walks in. **

Fraternity Vacation (1985) ....Chrissie
   0:16 - Topless and buns in bedroom with two guys
     taking off her swimsuit. ***
Re-Animator (1985)........................ Megan Halsey
   (unrated version)
   0:10 - Brief buns putting panties on, then topless,
     putting bra on after making love with "Dan." **
   1:09 - Full frontal nudity, lying unconscious on
     table getting strapped down. **
   1:10 - Topless getting her breasts felt by a
     headless body. *
   1:19 - Topless on the table. *
Kidnapped (1986).. Bonnie
   0:35 - In white bra and panties in hotel room.
   0:37 - Topless getting tormented by a bad guy in
     bed. ***
   1:12 - Topless opening her pajamas for David
     Naughton. **
   1:14 - Topless in white panties getting dressed. **
From Beyond (1986)..... Dr. Katherine McMichaels
   0:44 - Brief topless after getting blouse torn off by
     the creature in the laboratory. **
   0:51 - Buns getting on top of Jeffrey Combs in
     black leather outfit.
Chopping Mall (1987)...................................Suzie
   0:22 - Brief topless taking off top in furniture store
     in front of her boyfriend on the couch. **
Puppetmaster (1989) ....Woman at Carnival
TV:
   Days of Our Lives (1983)......................Trista Evans
   The Young and the Restless
    .... Leanna Randolph Newman
Magazines:
   Playboy (Dec 1986)..
     Pages 174-179: ***

CRAWFORD, CINDY
Other:
   Model and pin-up calendar girl.
Magazines:
   Playboy (Jul 1988)................................ "Skin Suits"
     Topless B&W photos. **

CROCKETT, KARLENE
Films:
   Charlie Chan & the Curse of the Dragon Queen
    (1981).. Brenda Lupowitz
   Eyes of Fire (1983)...Leah
   0:44 - Brief topless sitting up in the water and
     scaring "Mr. Dalton." *
   1:16 - Topless talking to "Dalton" who is trapped
     in a tree. Brief topless again when he pull the
     creature out of the tree. *
   Massive Retaliation (1984) .... Marianne Briscoe

CROSBY, CATHY LEE
Films:
   The Laughing Policeman (1974).............Kay Butler
   The Dark (1979)..Zoe
   Coach (1983)...Randy
   0:31 - Very brief side view of left breast when
     Michael Biehn opens the door while she's
     putting on her top. *
   0:52 - In wet white T-shirt at the beach and in her
     house with Biehn.
   1:11 - Very, very brief topless in shower room
     with Biehn. Blurry, hard to see anything.
Made for TV Movies:
   World War III (1982)..
TV:
   That's Incredible (1980-84)................................host

CROSBY, DENISE
Other:
   Granddaughter of actor Bing Crosby.
Films:
   The Trail of the Pink Panther (1982).......................
   48 Hours (1982).. Sally
   0:47 - Very, very brief side view of half of left
     breast swinging a baseball bat at Eddie Murphy.
   1:24 - Very brief side view of right breast when
     James Remar pushes her onto bed. *
   1:25 - Very brief topless then very brief side view
     of right breast attacking Nick Nolte. *
   Curse of the Pink Panther (1983).........Bruno's Moll
   The Man Who Loved Women (1983) ....Enid
   Eliminators (1986)............................... Nora Hunter
   0:47 - In wet white tank top inside an airplane
     cockpit that has crashed in the water.
   0:50 - Wet tank top getting out of the plane.
   Desert Hearts (1986)..Pat
   Arizona Heat (1988)........................... Jill Andrews
   1:13 - Brief upper half of left breast in shower
     with "Larry." *
   Skin Deep (1989)................................... Angie Smith
   Pet Sematary (1989)............................Rachel Creed
   Miracle Mile (1989)...Landa
TV:
   Star Trek: The Next Generation (1987- 88)
    .... Lt. Tasha Yar
Magazines:
   Playboy (Mar 1979). "A Different Kind of Crosby"
     Pages 99-103: Full frontal nudity. ***
   Playboy (Jun 1988) .... "Star Treat"
     Pages 74-79: Nude, photos from the 1979
     pictorial. ***

CROSBY, KATJA
Films:
   A Return to Salem's Lot (1988)....................Cathy
   0:36 - Topless making love in bed with "Joey."
     **
   0:48 - Side view of right breast kissing "Joey"
     outside next to a stream. *
   It's Alive III: Island of the Alive (1988)..................

CROSBY, LUCINDA
Films:
Blue Thunder (1983).........................Bel-Air Woman
The Naked Cage (1985)..............................Rhonda
Blue Movies (1987)............................. Randy Moon
0:10 - Topless in hot tub. *
0:11 - Topless shooting porno movie. **
0:30 - Topless auditioning for "Buzz." ***
0:59 - Topless on desk in porno movie. *

CRUIKSHANK, LAURA
Films:
Ruthless People (1986)...............................
Buying Time (1988)..........................Jessica
0:52 - Topless several times making love with
"Ron" on pool table. **

CSER, NANCY
Films:
Joy (1983; French/Canadian)...............................
Perfect Timing (1984)........................Lacy
0:54 - In white lingerie, taking off clothes for
"Harry" and posing.
0:56 - Topless getting photographed by "Harry."
***
0:58 - Topless, making love with "Harry." *
1:01 - Topless. *
Head Office (1986)....................Dantley's Secretary
Separate Vacations (1986).......................Stewardess

CUMMINS, JULIETTE
Films:
Friday the 13th, Part V - A New Beginning
(1986)..Robin
1:01 - Topless, wearing panties getting undressed
in her room and climbing into bed just before
getting killed. ***
1:05 - Very brief topless, covered with blood
when "Reggie" discovers her dead.
Psycho III (1986)............................. Red
0:39 - Topless making love with "Duke" in his
motel room, then getting thrown out. ***
Slumber Party Massacre II (1987)...............Sheila
0:24 - In black bra, then topless in living room
during a party with her girlfriends. **
Magazines:
Playboy (Nov 1986)............. "Sex in Cinema 1986"
Page 129: Topless in a photo from "Psycho III."
**

CURRIE, CHERIE
Other:
Singer.
Twin sister of singer/actress Marie Currie Lukather.
Films:
Foxes (1980)....................................Annie
Wavelength (1982)..............................Iris Longacre

0:09 - Brief side view of right breast and buns
getting out of bed. Dark, don't really see
anything.
Rosebud Beach Hotel (1985).........................Cherie
1:13 - Singing with her twin sister in braless pink
T-shirt on the beach.

CURRIE, SONDRA
Films:
Policewoman (1974)...............................
The Last Married Couple in America (1980)
....Lainy
1:32 - Topless taking off her clothes in bedroom
with Natalie Wood, George Segal and her
"husband." **
Jessi's Girls (1981).....................................Jessica
0:02 - Nude in water cleaning up, then brief left
breast getting dressed. *
0:07 - Topless getting raped by four guys. Fairly
long scene. *
0:37 - Topless kissing "Clay" under a tree. Hard
to see because of the shadows. *
The Concrete Jungle (1982).....................Katherine
Street Justice (1988)......................................Mandy
Magazines:
Playboy (Nov 1980).............."Sex in Cinema 1980"
Page 174: Side view of right breast. *

CURTIN, JANE
Films:
How to Beat the High Cost of Living (1980)..Elaine
1:28 - In pink bra, distracting everybody in the
mall so her friends can steal money.
1:29 - Close up topless, taking off her bra.
Probably a body double. *
O.C. and Stiggs (1987)...............................
Suspicion (1987)......................................
Made for TV Movies:
Common Ground (1990)....................Alice McGoff
TV:
Saturday Night Live (1975-80)
.............................Not Ready For Primetime Player
Kate and Allie (1984-90) ....Allie Lowell
Working It Out (1990-)..................Sarah Marshall

CURTIS, ALLEGRA
Other:
Daughter of actor Tony Curtis and his second wife,
actress Christine Kaufmann.
Films:
Midnight Cop (1988; German).......Monika Carstens
Magazines:
Playboy (Apr 1990)....................."Brava, Allegra!"
Pages 92-97: Full frontal nudity. ***

CURTIS, JAMIE LEE

Other:
Daughter of actor Tony Curtis and actress Janet Leigh.

Films:
Halloween (1978)...Laurie
The Fog (1979)..............................Elizabeth Solley
Prom Night (1980)..Kim
Terror Train (1980; Canadian).........................Alena
Halloween II (1981)...Laurie
Road Games (1981)...........................Hitch/Pamela
Student Bodies (1981)...
Trading Places (1983)............................... Ophelia
  1:00 - Topless in black panties after taking red dress off in bathroom while Dan Akroyd watches. ***
  1:09 - Topless and black panties taking off halter top and pants getting into bed with a sick Akroyd. ***
Grandview USA (1984)......Michelle "Mike" Cody
  1:00 - Left breast, lying in bed with C. Thomas Howell. ***
Love Letters (1984)......................... Anna Winter
  0:31 - Topless in bathtub reading a letter, then topless in bed making love with James Keach. ***
  0:36 - Brief topless in lifeguard station with Keach. *
  0:44 - Brief topless admiring a picture taken of her by Keach. ***
  0:46 - Topless and buns in bedroom undressing with Keach. ***
  0:49 - Topless in black and white Polaroid photographs that Keach is taking. *
  1:02 - In white slip in her house with Keach
  1:07 - Right breast sticking out of slip with Keach, then right breast, sleeping in bed. *
Terror in The Aisles (1984)...........................Hostess
Perfect (1986)......................................Jessie Wilson
  0:14 - No nudity, but doing aerobics in leotards.
  0:26 - More aerobics in leotards.
  0:40 - More aerobics, mentally making love with John Travolta while leading the class.
  1:19 - More aerobics when photographer is shooting pictures.
  1:32 - In red leotard after the article comes out in *Rolling Stone*.
A Man in Love (1987)............................Susan Elliot
Amazing Grace and Chuck (1987)...........................
Dominick & Eugene (1988)........................Jennifer
A Fish Called Wanda (1988).........................Wanda
  0:21 - In black bra and panties changing in the bedroom talking to Kevin Kline.
  0:35 - In black bra sitting on bed getting undressed.
Blue Steel (1989)...............................Megan Turner
  1:27 - Very, very brief buns twice when rolling out of bed, trying to get her gun. Dark.

Made for Cable:
Tall Tales and Legends: Annie Oakley (1985)
....Annie Oakley

Made for TV Movies:
Death of a Centerfold (1981).................................

She's in the Army Now (1981)...............................

TV:
Operation Petticoat (1977-78).....Lt. Barbara Duran
Anything but Love (1989-).............. Hannah Miller

Magazines:
Playboy (Nov 1983)............. "Sex in Cinema 1983"
  Page 151: Topless and right breast photo from the film "Trading Places." ***

D

D'ABO, MARYAM

Other:
Cousin of actress Olivia d'Abo.

Films:
Xtro (1982).. Analise
  0:25 - Topless making love with her boyfriend on the floor in her bedroom. ***
  0:56 - Brief topless with her boyfriend again. **
Until September (1984) ....Nathalie
White Nights (1985)....................French Girl Friend
The Living Daylights (1987)................Kara Milovy

Miniseries:
Master of the Game (1984)......................Dominique
Something Is Out There (1988)........................Ta'ra

Magazines:
Playboy (Sep 1987)....................................."D'Abo"
  Pages 132-139:. ***
Playboy (Dec 1987)..................."Sex Stars of 1987"
  Page 154: Right breast, sitting behind cello. ***

D'ABO, OLIVIA

Other:
Cousin of actress Maryam d'Abo.

Films:
Bolero (1984)..Paloma
  0:38 - Nude covered with bubbles taking a bath. *
  1:05 - Brief topless in the steam room with Bo. *
  1:32 - Topless in the steam room talking with Bo. Hard to see because it's so steamy. *
Conan the Destroyer (1984).............Princess Jehnna
Bullies (1985)....................................Becky Cullen
  0:39 - In wet white T-shirt swimming in river while "Matt" watches. **
Dream to Believe (1985; Canadian)...... Robin Crew
  0:29 - Working out in training room wearing a sexy cotton tank top.
Into the Fire (1988)......................................Liette
  0:07 - Very, very brief silhouette of left breast in bed with "Wade."
  0:32 - Topless on bed with "Wade." A little bit dark and hard to see. **
  1:10 - Topless in the bathtub. (Note her panties when she gets up.) **

TV:
The Wonder Years (1987-)......................................

DAHMS, GAIL

Films:

The Silent Partner (1978)............................ Louise
    0:31 - Right breast in bathroom with another guy
    when Elliott Gould surprises them. *
The Tomorrow Man (1979) ....

DAILY, ELIZABETH

Other:
    a.k.a. E. G. Daily.
Films:
    The Escape Artist (1982) ....Sandra
    Street Music (1982) ....Sadie
    Funny Money (1983; British)...............................
    One Dark Night (1983)...................................Leslie
    Valley Girl (1983).. Loryn
        0:16 - In bra through open jumpsuit, then brief
        topless on bed with "Tommy." **
    Wacko (1983)..Bambi
    No Small Affair (1984)...................................Susan
    Streets of Fire (1984) ....Baby Doll
    Pee-Wee's Big Adventure (1985)...................Dottie
    Loverboy (1989).. Linda
Magazines:
    Playboy (Nov 1983)............. "Sex in Cinema 1983"
    Page 146: Topless. **

DALE, CYNTHIA

Films:
    My Bloody Valentine (1981; Canadian).......... Patty
    Heavenly Bodies (1985)...................Samantha Blair
        0:30 - Brief topless fantasizing about making love
        with "Steve" while doing aerobic exercises. *
    The Boy in Blue (1986; Canadian)...........Margaret
        1:15 - Topless standing in a loft kissing Nicholas
        Cage in front of his bed. ***
    Moonstruck (1987).......................................Sheila
Made for TV Movies:
    Sadie and Son (1987)...........................Paula Melvin
Made for Disney TV Movies:
    The Liberators (1987)................ Elizabeth Giddings

DALE, JENNIFER

Films:
    Suzanne (1980) .... Suzanne
        0:29 - Topless when boyfriend lifts her sweatshirt
        up when she's sitting on couch doing
        homework. **
        0:53 - Topless with "Nicky" on the floor. **
    Your Ticket is No Longer Valid (1982)....... Laura
        0:27 - In black panties, then topless when her
        husband fantasizes, then makes love with her.
        **
        1:23 - Left breast in bed with "Montoya," then
        sitting, waiting for Richard Harris.
    Of Unknown Origin (1983) ....Lorrie

---

Separate Vacations (1985)................. Sarah Moore
    0:17 - Brief right breast in bed with her husband
    after son accidentally comes into their bedroom.
    *
    0:20 - In a bra and slip showing the baby sitter the
    house before leaving.
    1:14 - Topless on the cabin floor with "Jeff" after
    having a fight with her husband. **
    1:19 - Brief right breast, in bed with her husband.
    *

Magazines:
    Playboy (Nov 1980)............."Sex in Cinema 1980"
    Page 181: Right breast. *

DALLE, BÉATRICE

Films:
    Betty Blue (1986; French)............................... Betty
        0:01 - Topless making love in bed with "Zorg."
        Long sequence. ***
        0:30 - Nude on bed having sex with boyfriend.
        ***
        1:03 - Nude trying to sleep in living room. ***
        1:21 - Topless in white tap pants in hallway. ***
        1:29 - Topless lying down with "Zorg." ***
        1:39 - Topless sitting on bathtub crying & talking.
        ***

    On a Vole Charlie Spencer! (1987)......... Movie Star
Magazines:
    Playboy (Nov 1987)............."Sex in Cinema 1987"
    Page 141: Topless in blue light from "Betty
    Blue." **

DALY, TYNE

Other:
    Daughter of actor James Daly.
    Married to Actor Georg Stanford Brown since 1966.
Films:
    John and Mary (1969).....................................Hilary
    The Adultress (1973)..................................... Inez
        0:21 - Brief side view of right breast in room with
        "Carl." Brief out of focus topless in bed. *
        0:51 - Topless outside with "Hank." **
        0:53 - Topless on a horse with "Hank." ***
    The Enforcer (1976).............................Kate Moore
    Telefon (1977)...........................Dorothy Putterman
    Zoot Suit (1981)...Alice
    The Aviator (1985).............................Evelyn Stiller
    Movers and Shakers (1985) ....Nancy Derman
Made for TV Movies:
    In Search of America (1971)...............................
    Heat of Anger (1972) ....
    The Entertainer (1976).....................................
    Intimate Strangers (1977)..................................
    The Women's Room (1980).................................
    Your Place or Mine (1983).................................
    Kids Like These (1987).....................................
TV:
    Cagney & Lacey (1982-88).......... Mary Beth Lacey
    (Won four Emmy Awards.)

D'ANGELO, BEVERLY

Films:

Annie Hall (1977)........... Actress in Rob's TV Show

First Love (1977)... Shelley

    0:05 - Very, very brief half of left breast when her jacket opens up while talking to William Katt.

    0:11 - In white bra and black panties in Katt's bedroom.

    1:10 - Brief topless taking off her top in bedroom with Katt. *

The Sentinel (1977)...................................... Sandra

    0:26 - Masturbating in red leotard and tights on couch in front of Cristina Raines.

    0:33 - Brief topless playing cymbals during Raines' nightmare (in B&W). *

Hair (1979).. Sheila

    0:59 - In white bra and panties, then topless on rock near pond. Medium long shot. *

    1:01 - Topless and in panties getting out of the pond. ***

    1:38 - Side view of right breast changing clothes in car with "George." *

Coal Miner's Daughter (1980)................ Patsy Cline

Honky Tonk Freeway (1981)....................... Carmen

Paternity (1981)..Maggie

Faerie Tale Theatre: Sleeping Beauty (1983)...........

Finders Keepers (1983)................ Standish Logan

National Lampoon's Vacation (1983)

....Ellen Griswold

    0:18 - Brief topless taking a shower in the motel. **

    1:19 - Brief topless taking off shirt and jumping into the swimming pool. *

Highpoint (1984)............................... Lise Hatcher

National Lampoon's European Vacation (1985)

....Ellen Griswold

Big Trouble (1986)............................ Blanche Ricky

Every Which Way But Loose (1987)........................

In the Mood (1987) ....

Maid to Order (1987).. Stella

Aria (1988).. Gilda

High Spirits (1988)..Sharon

National Lampoon's Christmas Vacation (1989)

....Ellen Griswold

Made for TV Movies:

    A Streetcar Named Desire (1984)............................

    Hands of a Stranger (1987) ....

TV:

    Captains and the Kings (1976)...............Miss Emmy

DANNER, BLYTHE

Films:

To Kill a Clown (1971)....................... Lily Frischer

    1:10 - Side view of left breast sitting on bed talking to Alan Alda. Hair covers breast, hard to see. Buns, getting up and running out of the house. *

1776 (1972) ....Martha Jefferson

Lovin' Molly (1974)..

Hearts of the West (1975) .... Miss Trout

Futureworld (1976) ....Tracy Ballard

The Great Santini (1980) ....Lillian Meechum

Brighton Beach Memoirs (1986)....................... Kate

Man, Woman and Child (1983)...... Sheila Beckwith

Another Woman (1988)...................................Lydia

Made for TV Movies:

    Money, Power, Murder (1989)....................Jeannie

TV:

    Adam's Rib (1973)......................... Amanda Bonner

DANNING, SYBIL

Other:

a.k.a. Sybille Danninger.

Films:

Bluebeard (1972)............................... The Prostitute

    1:08 - Brief topless kissing Nathalie Delon showing her how to make love to her husband. *

    1:09 - Brief left breast, lying on the floor with Delon just before Richard Burton kills both of them. *

Naughty Nymphs (1982; German)............Elizabeth

    0:21 - Nude taking a bath while yelling at her two sisters. ***

    0:30 - Topless and buns throwing "Nicholas" out of her bedroom. *

    0:38 - Full frontal nudity running away from "Burt." **

The Loves of a French Pussycat (1976)...... Andrea

    0:18 - Topless dancing with her boss, then in bed. ***

    0:24 - Topless and buns in swimming pool. **

    0:40 - In sheer white bra and panties doing things around the house. Long sequence.

    0:46 - Topless in bathtub with a guy. *

    1:03 - Left breast sticking out of bra, then topless. *

Twist (1976).. Secretary

    1:24 - Brief topless sitting next to Bruce Dern. *

Albino... Sally

    0:19 - Topless, then full frontal nudity getting raped by the Albino and his buddies. *

God's Gun... Jenny

    1:09 - Right breast popping out of dress with a guy in the barn during flashback. *

Kill Castro (1978)....................................... Veronica

Cat in the Cage (1978) .... Susan Khan

    0:24 - Brief topless getting slapped around by "Ralph." *

    0:25 - Brief left breast several times smoking and talking to "Ralph," brief left breast getting up. *

    0:30 - Full frontal nudity getting out of the pool. **

    0:52 - Black bra and panties undressing and getting into bed with "Ralph." Brief left breast and buns. *

    1:02 - In white lingerie in bedroom.

    1:10 - In white slip looking out window.

    1:15 - In black slip.

    1:18 - Very brief right breast several times struggling with an attacker on the floor. *

Separate Ways (1979)... Mary

Battle Beyond the Stars (1980)................ St. Exmin

The Man with Bogart's Face (1980)............Cynthia
How to Beat the High Cost of Living (1980)
....Charlotte
The Day of the Cobra (1980)......................Brenda
    0:41 - Buns and side view of right breast getting
    out of bed and putting robe on with "Lou."
    Long shot. *
Nightkill (1981)..................................Monika Childs
S.A.S. San Salvador (1982)..... Countess Alexandra
    0:07 - Brief left breast kissing "Malko" while
    lying on the couch. *
Chained Heat (1983)......................................Erika
    0:30 - Topless in the shower with Linda Blair.
    ***
Hercules (1983) ....Arianna
Howling II (1984)...Stirba
    0:35 - Left breast, then topless with "Mariana" in
    bedroom about to have sex with a guy. *
    1:20 - Very brief topless during short clips during
    the end credits. Same shot repeated about 10
    times. *
The Seven Magnificent Gladiators (1984)...............
They're Playing with Fire (1984).....Diane Stevens
    0:04 - In two piece swimsuit on boat. Long scene.
    0:08 - Topless and buns making love on top of
    "Jay" in bed on boat. Nice! ***
    0:10 - Topless and buns getting out of shower,
    then brief side view of right breast. **
    0:43 - In black bra and slip in boat with "Jay."
    0:47 - In black bra and slip at home with
    "Michael," then panties, then topless and buns
    getting into shower. **
    1:12 - In white bra and panties in room with "Jay"
    then topless. ***
Malibu Express (1984)................Countess Luciana
    0:13 - Brief topless making love in bed with
    "Cody." *
Jungle Warriors (1985)..................................Angel
    0:53 - Buns, getting a massage while lying face
    down.
Private Passions (1985)..................................
    Nude.
Reform School Girls (1986)............................Sutter
Warrior Queen (1986)................................ Berenice
Young Lady Chatterley II (1986) ....
    1:02 - Topless in the hut on the table with the
    Gardener. ***
Amazon Women on the Moon (1987)....Queen Lara
Phantom Empire (1987)................. The Alien Queen
Made for HBO:
    The Hitchhiker: Face to Face .... Gloria Loring
    (Available on video tape in The Hitchhiker,
    Volume 4.)
    0:10 - In red bra and panties, then right breast
    making love with Robert Vaughn. **
Magazines:
    Playboy (Aug 1983)......................................
    Playboy (Nov 1983)............. "Sex in Cinema 1983"
    Page 145: Topless. **
    Playboy (Dec 1983)................... "Sex Stars of 1983"
    Page 210: Full frontal nudity. ***

Playboy (Dec 1984).................. "Sex Stars of 1984"
    Page 202: Half of right breast and lower frontal
    nudity. *
Playboy (Dec 1986)..................... "Sex Stars of 86"
    Page 158

D'ARBANVILLE, PATTI
Other:
    Has a son, Jesse, fathered by Don Johnson.
Films:
    Flesh (1968) ....
    L'Amour (1973)...
    Rancho Deluxe (1975)......................... Betty Fargo
    Big Wednesday (1978)..................................Sally
    The Fifth Floor (1978) ....Cathy Burke
    The Main Event (1979)...................................Donna
    Time After Time (1979; British)...................Shirley
    Hog Wild (1980; Canadian)............................ Angie
    Modern Problems (1981) .... Darcy
    Bilitis (1982; French)................................. Bilitis
        0:25 - Topless copying "Melissa" undressing. ***
        0:27 - Topless on tree. **
        0:31 - Full frontal nudity taking off swimsuit with
        "Melissa." ***
        0:36 min - Buns, cleaning herself in the
        bathroom.
        0:59 - Topless and buns making love with
        "Melissa." **
    The Boys Next Door (1985)........................... Angie
    Real Genius (1985)...............................Sherry Nugil
    Call Me (1988) .... Coni
    Fresh Horses (1988)......................................Jean
TV:
    Wiseguy (1989-90)........................... Amber Twine
Magazines:
    Playboy (May 1977)........ "Our Lady D'Arbanville"
    Full frontal nudity in Bilitis photos taken by David
    Hamilton. ***

DARNELL, VICKI
Films:
    Senior Week (1987).........Everett's Dream Teacher
    0:03 - Topless during classroom fantasy. **
    Brain Damage (1988)................Blonde in Hell Club

DAS, ALISHA
Films:
    The Slugger's Wife (1985)................................Lola
    Nightwish (1988)... Kim
    1:09 - Brief topless, then left breast in open dress
    caressing herself on the ground. **
    1:10 - Braless under see-through purple dress. *
    Danger Zone II: Reaper's Revenge (1989)
    .... Francine

DAVID, LOLITA
See Davidovich, Lolita

DAVIDOVICH, LOLITA

Other:
  a.k.a. Lolita David.
Films:
  Class (1983)..................... 1st Girl (motel)
  Recruits (1986)................................
  Big Town (1987)........... Black Lace Stripper
  A New Life (1988)............................
  Blindside (1988; Canada)................Adele
    0:32 - Topless dancing on stage. **
    0:39 - Sort of buns bending over and pointing a
      gun through her legs in front of mirror.
  Blaze (1989).......................... Blaze Starr
    0:09 - In bra doing her first strip routine. Very
      brief side views of left breast under hat.
    0:15 - Strip tease routine in front of Paul Newman.
      At the end, she takes off bra to reveal pasties.
    0:42 - In black bra and panties with Newman.
    0:48 - Topless on top of Newman, then side view
      of left breast. **

DAVIDSON, EILEEN

Films:
  Goin' All the Way (1981)................................BJ
    0:12 - Topless in the girl's locker room shower.
      Standing next to "Monica." ***
    0:22 - Exercising in her bedroom win braless pink
      T-shirt, then topless talking on the phone to
      "Monica." ***
  House on Sorority Row (1983)....................... Vicki
    0:16 - Topless and buns in room making love with
      her boyfriend. **
    0:19 - In white bikini top by the pool.
  Easy Wheels (1989)................................She Wolf
TV:
  The Young and the Restless................Ashley Abbott

DAVIS, CAROL

Other:
  a.k.a. Carole Davis.
Films:
  Piranha II: The Spawning (1981; Netherlands)........
  C.O.D. (1983)............................ Contessa Bazzini
    1:25 - Brief topless in dressing room scene in
      black panties, garter belt and stockings when
      she takes off her robe. *
    1:29 - In black top during fashion show.

DAVIS, GEENA

Films:
  Tootsie (1983) .... April
    0:34 - In white bra and panties in dressing room
      with Dustin Hoffman.
    0:44 - In white bra and panties exercising in
      dressing room while Hoffman reads his script.
  Transylvania 6-5000 (1985)................................
  The Fly (1986)........................... Veronica Quaife
    0:40 - Brief almost side view of left breast getting
      out of bed.

Beetlejuice (1988)........................ Barbara
The Accidental Tourist (1988)..............Muriel
  (Academy Award for Best Supporting Actress.)
Earth Girls are Easy (1989) ....Valerie
  0:11 - In yellow two piece swimsuit during song
    and dance number in beauty salon.
  0:12 - In frilly pink lingerie waiting at home for
    her fiance to return.
  0:22 - In pink two piece swimsuit doing a lot of
    different things for a long time. This is easily
    the greatest swimsuit scene in a PG movie!
Quick Change (1990)................................

DAVIS, JUDY

Films:
  High Rolling (1977).........................Lynn
  My Brilliant Career (1979)...............Syblla Melvyn
  Winter of Our Dreams (1981)..........................Lou
    0:19 - Brief left breast sticking out of yellow robe
      in bed with "Pete." *
    0:26 - Very brief side view of left breast taking off
      top to change. Long shot. *
    0:48 - Topless taking off top and getting into bed
      with Bryan Brown, then brief right breast lying
      down with him. **
  The Final Option (1982)............................... Frankie
  Heatwave (1983)............................ Kate
  A Passage to India (1984)................Adela Quested
  Kangaroo (1986).............................. Harriet Somers
  High Tide (1988) Lilli
Made for TV Movie:
  A Woman Called Golda (1982)................................

DAVIS, PHYLLIS

Films:
  The Last of the Secret Agents? (1966)
    .... Beautiful Girl
  Live a Little, Love a Little (1968)...... 2nd Secretary
  Sweet Sugar (1972).. Sugar
    (with brown hair)
    0:34 - Topless in bed with a guard. ***
    0:50 - Topless in the shower with Dolores. ***
    0:57 - Brief topless in the bathroom. **
  The Day of the Dolphin (1973) ....Secretary
  Terminal Island (1973)...........................Joy Lange
    0:39 - Topless and buns in a pond, then putting
      blouse on while some guy watches. ***
  Train Ride to Hollywood (1975) ....
  The Choirboys (1977)............................ Foxy/Gina
  Famous T & A (1982)................................ herself
    0:02 - Nude in lots of great out takes from
      "Terminal Island." Check this out if you are a
      Phyllis Davis fan! ***
    0:51 - Topless in scenes from "Sweet Sugar."
      Includes more out takes. ***
    1:04 - More out takes from "Sweet Sugar." ***
TV:
  Love, American Style (1970-74)... Repertory Player
  Vega$ (1978-81)...............................Beatrice Travis

DAVIS, SAMMI

Other:
Definitely *not* related to the late entertainer Sammy Davis, Jr.

Films:
A Prayer for the Dying (1987).......................... Anna
Hope and Glory (1987; British)...............................
The Lair of the White Worm (1988)....... Mary Trent
Consuming Passions (1988)........... .... Felicity
The Rainbow (1989)........................ Winifred Inger
  0:21 - Topless and buns with Amanda Donohoe undressing, running outside in the rain, jumping into the water, then talking by the fireplace. ***
  0:30 - Topless and buns posing for a painter. **
  1:33 - Brief right breast and buns getting out of bed. *
  1:44 - Nude running outside with Donohoe. ***

DAY, ALEXANDRA

Films:
Young Lady Chatterley (1976)
  ....Jenny "Maid in Hut"
  0:06 - Topless in hut on the bed with the Gardener. ***
  0:28 - Topless taking bath with Harlee McBride. ***
Erotic Images (1983)................. Logan's Girlfriend
  0:37 - Topless getting out of bed while "Logan" talks on the phone to Britt Ekland. **
Body Double (1984)................. Girl in Bathroom #1
Boarding House (1984)................. Girl in Bathroom

DEAN, FELICITY

Films:
Crossed Swords (1978)............................ Lady Jane
Success is the Best Revenge (1984; British)............
Steaming (1984)... Dawn
  1:12 - Topless painting on herself. **
The Whistle Blower (1987; British)........................

DeBELL, KRISTINE

Adult films:
Alice in Wonderland (1977)........................... Alice
Films:
Emmanuelle Around the World..........................
  Nude on dock.
Meatballs (1979; Canadian)............................... A.L.
The Big Brawl (1980).................................... Nancy
T.A.G.: The Assassination Game (1982)....... Nancy
Magazines:
Playboy (Nov 1976)............. "Sex in Cinema 1976"
  Page 152: Left breast. *

DE LA CROIX, RAVEN

Films:
Up (1976)..
  Topless.
The Lost Empire (1983)...................... White Star
  1:05 - Topless with a snake after being drugged by the bad guy. ***
  1:07 - Topless lying on a table. **
Screwballs (1983).................... Miss Anna Tomical
  1:08 - Topless during strip routine in nightclub. ***
Magazines:
Playboy (Nov 1976)............. "Sex in Cinema 1976"
  Page 153: Topless. **

DELANEY, KIM

Films:
That Was Then... This Is Now (1985)
  .... Cathy Carlson
Campus Man (1987)......................................
Hunter's Blood (1987) .... Melanie
The Drifter (1988)........................... Julia Robbins
  0:11 - Brief topless making love with Miles O'Keeffe on motel floor. *
  0:21 - Topless in bed talking with Timothy Bottoms. **
Made for TV Movies:
First Affair (1983)......................................
Cracked Up (1987)... Jackie
TV:
All My Children..Jenny
Tour of Duty (1988-89)........................Alex Devilin

DE LEEUW, LISA

Other:
Adult film actress.
Films:
Up 'N' Coming (1987)............... Altheah Anderson
  0:33 - Very brief topless by the pool when her robe opens. *
  0:48 - Brief topless walking around the house when her robe open. *
  0:49 - Left breast talking with a guy, then topless walking into the bedroom. **

DE LISO, DEBRA

Films:
The Slumber Party Massacre (1982)............. Kim
  0:08 - Very brief topless getting soap from "Trish" in the shower. *
  0:29 - In beige bra and panties, then topless putting on a U.S.A. shirt while changing with the other girls. **
Iced (1988)..Trina
  0:11 - In a bra, then brief nude making love with "Cory" in hotel room. *

DELON, NATHALIE

Films:
When Eight Bells Toll (1971; British)....... Charlotte
The Godson (1972; Italian/French)......Jan Lagrange
Eyes Behind the Stars (1972).....................................
Bluebeard (1972).. Erika
   1:03 - Topless in bed, showing Richard Burton her
    breasts. *
   1:09 - Brief right breast lying on the floor with
    Sybil Danning just before Richard Burton kills
    both of them. *
The Romantic Englishwoman
   (1975; British/French)................................Miranda

DELORA, JENNIFER

Films:
Deranged (1987)...
New York's Finest (1988)........... Loretta Michaels
   0:02 - Brief topless pretending to be a black
    hooker. *
   0:04 - Brief topless with a bunch of hookers. *
   0:36 - Topless with her two friends doing push ups
    on the floor. *
Sensations (1988) ....Della Randall
   0:11 - Brief topless talking to "Jenny" to wake her
    up. *
   0:13 - Brief topless a couple of times in open robe.
    *
   0:38 - Topless making love with a guy on bed. **
Cleo/Leo (1989)... Bernice
Bedroom Eyes II (1989)...................... Gwendolyn
   0:04 - Undressing in hotel room with "Vinnie."
    Topless, then making love. **

DE MORNAY, REBECCA

Films:
Risky Business (1983)...................................... Lana
   0:28 - Brief nude standing by the window with
    Tom Cruise. *
Runaway Train (1985).. Sara
The Slugger's Wife (1985)................. Debby Palmer
The Trip to Bountiful (1986)........................Thelma
And God Created Woman (1988)................. Robin
   (Unrated version.)
   0:06 - Brief Left breast and buns in gymnasium
    with Vincent Spano. Brief right breast making
    love. **
   0:53 - Brief buns and topless in the shower when
    Spano sees her. *
   1:01 - Wearing white panties making love on pool
    table with Frank Langella.
   1:02 - Brief left breast with Langella on the floor.
    **
   1:12 - Topless making love with Spano in a
    museum. ***
Feds (1988)...................................Elizabeth De Witt
Dealers (1989) .... Anna Schuman
   0:59 - In black bra making love with "Daniel."
Made for Cable Movies:
By Dawn's Early Light (1990)...........Cindy Moreau

DE MOSS, DARCY

Films:
Gimme an "F" (1981)................One of the "Ducks"
Hardbodies (1984)..Dede
   0:55 - Topless in the back seat of the limousine
    with "Rounder." ***
Friday the 13th Part VI: Jason Lives (1987)....Nikki
Reform School Girls (1987)..............................Knox
Return to Horror High (1987)...........Sheri Haines
   0:21 - Very brief left breast when her sweater gets
    lifted up while she's on some guy's back. *

DENEUVE, CATHERINE

Films:
The Umbrellas of Cherbourg (1964)
   ....Genevieve Emery
Repulsion (1965; B&W)................................Carol
The April Fools (1969)................Catherine Gunther
Skin Donkey (1971; French) ....
A Slightly Pregnant Man (1973; French).................
La Grande Bourgeoise (1974; Italian)...Linda Murri
Lovers Like Us (1977).......................................
   1:06 - Brief left upper half of left breast in bed
    with Yves Montand. Dark. *
   1:09 - Topless sitting up in bed. ***
The Last Metro (1980)...................................Marion
Je Vous Aime (I Love You All) (1981)...........Alice
A Choice of Arms (1983; French).................Nicole
The Hunger (1983)..................................... Miriam
   0:08 - Brief topless taking a shower with David
    Bowie. Probably a body double, you don't see
    her face. *
Love Songs (Paroles et Musique) (1985)....Margaux
Scene of the Crime (1987; French).....................Lili
Magazines:
Playboy (Sep 1963)......."Europe's New Sex Sirens"
Playboy (Oct 1965)......."France's Deneuve Wave"
Playboy (Jan 1989)............. "Women of the Sixties"
   Page 159: Topless sitting by the window. *

DE PRUME, CATHRYN

Films:
Deadtime Stories (1987)...........................Goldi-lox
   1:08 - Topless taking a shower, quick cuts. **
Five Corners (1988)...Brita

DEREK, BO

Films:
Fantasies (1976).. Anastasia
Orca, The Killer Whale (1977)........................Annie
10 (1979).. Jennifer Hanley
   1:18 - In yellow swimsuit running in slow motion
    towards Dudley Moore in his daydream.
   1:27 - Brief buns and topless taking off towel and
    putting on robe when Moore visits her. Long
    shot, hard to see. *
   1:34 - Brief topless taking off dress trying to
    seduce Moore. Dark, hard to see. *

1:35 - Topless, lying in bed. Dark, hard to see. *

1:39 - Topless, going to fix the skipping record. Long shot, hard to see. **

A Change of Seasons (1980)..... Lindsey Routledge

0:00 - Topless in hot tub during the opening credits. **

0:25 - Side view of left breast in the shower talking to Anthony Hopkins. *

Tarzan, The Ape Man (1981)......................... Jane

0:43 - Nude taking a bath in the ocean, then in a wet white dress. ***

1:35 - Brief topless painted all white. *

1:45 - Topless washing all the white paint off in the river with Tarzan. *

1:47 - Topless during the ending credits playing with Tarzan and the orangutan. ** (When I saw this film in a movie theater, everybody in the audience actually stayed to watch the credits!)

Bolero (1984)................................Ayre McGillvary

0:19 - Topless making love with Arabian guy covered with honey, messy. ***

0:58 - Topless making love in bed with the bullfighter. ***

1:38 - Topless during fantasy love making session with bullfighter in fog. ***

Video Tapes:

Playboy Video Magazine, Volume 1........................

Magazines:

Playboy (Mar 1980)... "Bo"
Pages 146-157: Nude. ***

Playboy (Aug 1980)........................... "Bo Is Back"
Pages 108-119: Nude in Japanese bath. ***

Playboy (Sep 1981)..................................."Tarzan"

Playboy (Dec 1984)................... "Sex Stars of 1984"
Page 209: Topless lying in water. ***

Playboy (Jan 1989).......... "Women of the Eighties"
Page 255: Full frontal nudity. ***

Playboy (Nov 1989)............. "Sex in Cinema 1989"
Page 133: Topless in still from "Ghosts Can't Do It." ***

DERVAL, LAMYA

Films:

The Lonely Guy (1983)
............................One of "The Seven Deadly Sins"

Hellhole (1984)..................................Jacuzzi Girl

1:08 - Topless sniffing glue in closet with another woman (she's on the right). ***

1:12 - Full frontal nudity in Jacuzzi room with Mary Woronov. ***

Howling IV, The Original Nightmare (1988)
....Elanor

0:32 - Brief left breast, then topless making love with "Richard." Nice silhouette on the wall. **

DERNIER, LYDIE

Films:

The Nightstalker (1987)..................... First Victim

0:03 - Topless making love with big guy. ***

Bulletproof (1988)... Tracy

0:14 - Topless in Gary Busey's bathtub. **

0:20 - Brief buns, putting on shirt after getting out of bed. Very, very brief side view of left breast.

Paramedics (1988)...Liette

Blood Relations (1989)................................. Marie

0:07 - Left breast making love with "Thomas" on stairway. **

0:44 - Brief left breast in bed with "Thomas'" father "Andrewas". Very brief cuts of her topless in B&W. *

0:47 - Getting out of swimming pool in a one piece swimsuit.

0:54 - Full frontal nudity undressing for the Grandfather. ***

DE ROSSI, BARBARA

Films:

Hearts and Armour (1983)................. Bradamante

1:05 - Topless while sleeping with "Ruggero." **

La Cicala (The Cricket) (1983; Italian)...... Saveria

0:39 - Nude swimming under waterfall with Clio Goldsmith. **

0:43 - Topless undressing in room with Goldsmith. **

0:57 - Brief right breast changing into dress in room. *

1:05 - In wet white lingerie in waterfall with a guy, then in a wet dress. *

1:26 - Very brief buns in bed with Anthony Franciosa.

1:28 - Topless in bathroom with Franciosa. **

1:36 - Brief right breast making love with trucker. *

Made for HBO:

Mussolini and I (1985)..

Made for Showtime:

Blood Ties (1986)...Luisa

DES BARRES, PAMELA

Other:

Author of the book "I'm with the Band: Confessions of a Groupie."

Magazines:

Playboy (Dec 1988).................. "Sex Stars of 1988"
Page 184: Topless. **

Playboy (Feb 1989).................... "The Year in Sex"
Page 139: Topless. **

Playboy (Mar 1989)............. "She's with the Band"
Pages 74-79: Full frontal nudity. ***

DESMOND, DONNA

Other:
a.k.a. Dona Desmond.
Films:
Tender Loving Care (1974)..
The Black Gestapo (1975)..................White Whore
Fugitive Girls (1975)..
The Naughty Stewardesses (1978).............. Margie
0:12 - Topless leaning out of the shower. **

DETMERS, MARUSCHKA

Films:
Devil in the Flesh (1986; French/Italian)
....Giulia Dozza
0:20 - Very brief side view of left breast and buns
going past open door way to get a robe. *
0:27 - Nude, talking to "Andrea's" dad in his
office. ***
0:55 - Topless putting a robe on. Dark. *
0:57 - Topless and buns in bedroom with
"Andrea." **
1:09 - Topless in hallway with "Andrea." **
1:19 - Performing fellatio on "Andrea." Dark,
hard to see.
1:22 - Full frontal nudity holding keys for
"Andrea" to see, brief buns. ***
1:42 - Lower frontal nudity dancing in living room
in red robe.
Hanna's War (1988)........................... Hanna Senesh
Magazines:
Playboy (Nov 1986).............. "Sex in Cinema 1986"
Page 128: Topless in a photo from "Devil in the
Flesh" with Federico Pitzalis. ***

DE VASQUEZ, DEVIN

Films:
House II: The Second Story (1987)........ The Virgin
Can't Buy Me Love (1987)......................................
TV:
Star Search Winner 1986 - Spokesmodel
Video Tapes:
Playboy Video Magazine, Volume 8....... Playmate
Playboy Video Calendar 1988..................Playmate
Magazines:
Playboy (Oct 1981)
..... "Girls of the Southeastern Conference, Part II"
Page 144: Topless. She was attending Louisiana
State University.
Playboy (Jun 1985)...................................Playmate
Playboy (Nov 1986)......................."Revvin' Devin"
Pages 80-87: Nude. ***

DEVINE, LORETTA

Films:
Little Nikita (1988)................... Verna McLaughlin
1:03 - Very brief left breast in bed after Sidney
Poitier jumps out of bed when River Phoenix
bursts into their bedroom. *
Sticky Fingers (1988).....................................Diane

DEY, SUSAN

Films:
Skyjacked (1972)............................... Elly Brewster
First Love (1977)...........................Caroline Hedges
0:31 - Topless making love in bed with William
Katt. Long scene. ***
0:51 - Topless taking off her top in her bedroom
with Katt. *
The Comeback Kid (1980)......................................
Looker (1981) ....Cindy
0:28 - In white one piece swimsuit shooting a
commercial at the beach.
0:36 - Buns, then brief topless in computer
imaging device. Topless in computer monitor.
*
Echo Park (1986)........................ Meg "May" Greer
1:17 - Brief glimpse of right breast doing a strip
tease at a party. *
Made for TV Movies:
The Gift of Life...............................Jolee Sutton
Love Leads the Way (1984)......................................
TV:
The Partridge Family (1970-1974). Laurie Partridge
Loves Me, Loves Me Not (1977)......................Jane
Emerald Point N.A.S. (1983-84)
.... Celia Mallory Warren
L.A. Law (1986-)........Dep. D.A. Grace Van Owen
Magazines:
Playboy (Dec 1977)................... "Sex Stars of 1977"
Page 213: Left breast under sheer white gown in a
photo from "First Love." *

DICKINSON, ANGIE

Films:
Rio Bravo (1959)...Feathers
Ocean's Eleven (1960).....................Beatrice Ocean
Cast a Giant Shadow (1966).............. Emma Marcus
The Chase (1966)................................... Ruby Calder
Point Blank (1967) ....Chris
0:46 - In white slip when John Vernon opens her
dress.
0:51 - Topless in background putting dress on.
Kind of a long shot. *
Pistolero of Red River (1967)................Lisa Denton
The Resurrection of Zachary Wheeler (1971)
.... Dr. Johnson
Pretty Maids All in a Row (1971).......... Miss Smith
Buns.
Big Bad Mama (1974)............... Wilma McClatchie
0:38 - Buns, making love in bed with Tom
Skerritt.
0:48 - Topless in bed with William Shatner. ***
1:18 - Topless and brief full frontal nudity putting
a shawl and then a dress on. ***
Dressed To Kill (1980)........................... Kate Miller
0:01 - Brief side view behind shower door. Long
shot, hard to see. *
0:02 - Frontal nudity in the shower is a body
double (Penthouse Pet Victoria Lynn Johnson).
0:24 - Brief buns getting out of bed after coming
home from museum with a stranger.

Charlie Chan and the curse of the Dragon Queen
(1981)................................. Dragon Queen
Death Hunt (1981).. Vanessa
Big Bad Mama II (1987)............. Wilma McClatchie
0:52 - Topless (probably a body double) in bed
with Robert Culp. You don't see her face with
the body. **
Miniseries:
Hollywood Wives (1988).....................Sadie La Salle
Made for TV Movies:
Once Upon a Texas Train (1988)................. Maggie
TV:
Police Woman (1974-78)
.............................Sgt. Suzanne "Pepper" Anderson
Pearl (1978) ....Midge
Cassie and Company (1982)............. Cassie Holland

DICKINSON, JANICE
Other:
Model.
Magazines:
Playboy (Mar 1988).... "Going Wild with a Model"
Pages 70-77: Full frontal nudity. ***

DIETRICH, CINDI
Films:
The Man Who Loved Women (1983) ....
Out of Control (1984)....................................Robin
0:29 - Topless taking off her red top. Long shot.
*
St. Elmo's Fire (1984) ....Flirt

DIGARD, USCHI
Other:
a.k.a Uschi Digart or Ursula Digard.
Films:
The Beauties and the Beast............................ Mary
Nude by lake.
Blood Hunger...
The Scavengers (1969).......................................
Truck Stop Women (1974)...... Truck Stop Women
0:18 - Topless getting arrested in the parking lot
by the police officer, then buns and topless
getting frisked in a room. **
Fantasm (1976; Australian)................................
Kentucky Fried Movie (1977).. Woman in Shower
0:09 - Topless getting breasts massaged in the
shower, then breasts getting squished against the
shower door. **
Superchick (1978)....................................Mayday
0:42 - Buns and topless getting whipped acting
during the making of a film, then talking to
three people. ***
Famous T & A (1982)............................. herself
0:44 - Topless scenes from "Harry, Cherry &
Raquel" and "Truck Stop Women." **

DI'LAZZARO, DALILA
Films:
Andy Warhol's Frankenstein
(1974; Italian/German/French)............................
The Last Romantic Lover (1978)............................
Creepers (1985; Italian) ....
Miss Right (1987)..
Magazines:
Playboy (Jan 1990)..
Page 104: Polaroid collage taken by Andy
Worhol. ***

DILLON, MELINDA
Films:
Bound for Glory (1977) .... Mary Guthrie
Close Encounters of the Third Kind (1977)
....Jillian Guiler
Slapshot (1977).. Suzanne
0:30 - Right breast, lying in bed with Paul
Newman, then topless sitting up and talking.
Nice, long scene. ***
F.I.S.T. (1978)................................ Anna Zerinkas
Absence of Malice (1981)............................Teresa
A Christmas Story (1983)...................... Mrs. Parker
Songwriter (1984)...............................Honey Carder
Harry and the Hendersons (1987)...................Nancy
Made for TV Movies:
Right of Way (1983) ....

DOMBASLE, ARIELLE
Films:
Tess (1980; French/British) .... Mercy Chant
The Story of "O" Continues..................................
Nude in bed with Klaus Kinski.
Le Beau Mariage (1982; French)................. Clarisse
Pauline at the Beach (1983; French).......... Marion
0:24 - Brief topless lying in bed with a guy when
her cousin looks in the window. *
0:43 - Brief topless in house kissing "Henri,"
while he takes her white dress off. **
0:59 - Topless walking down the stairs in a white
bikini bottom while putting a white blouse on.
**
The Boss' Wife (1986)......... Mrs. Louise Roalvang
1:01 - Brief topless getting a massage by the
swimming pool. *
1:07 - Topless seducing "Smokey" at her place.
***
1:14 - Brief topless in "Smokey's" Shower. **
Twisted Obsession (1989)................. Marion Derain
Miniseries:
Lace II (1985)..Maxine
Magazines:
Playboy (Dec 1983)................. "Sex Stars of 1983"
Page 209: Topless. **

DONNELLY, PATRICE

Films:

Personal Best (1982)..........................Tory Skinner
    0:16 - Full frontal nudity after making love with
      Mariel Hemingway. **
    0:30 - Full frontal nudity in steam room. **
    1:06 - Topless in shower
American Anthem (1987)............................Danielle

DONOHOE, AMANDA

Films:

Castaway (1986)................................... Lucy Irvine
    (Topless a lot, only the best are listed)
    0:32 - Nude on beach after helicopter leaves. **
    0:48 - Full frontal nudity lying on her back on the
      rocks at the beach. **
    0:51 - Topless on rock when Reed takes a blue
      sheet off her, then catching a shark. ***
    0:54 - Nude yelling at Reed at the campsite, then
      walking around looking for him. ***
    1:01 - Topless getting seafood out of a tide pool.
      ***
    1:03 - Topless lying down at night talking with
      Reed in the moonlight. **
    1:18 - Topless taking off bathing suit top after the
      visitors leave, then arguing with Reed. ***
    1:22 - Topless talking to Reed. ***
Foreign Body (1986; British)..........................Susan
    0:37 - Undressing in her bedroom down to
      lingerie. Very brief side view of right breast,
      then brief left breast putting blouse on.
    0:40 - Topless opening her blouse for "Ram." **
The Lair of the White Worm (1988)
    .... Lady Sylvia Marsh
    (Wears short black hair in this film.)
    0:52 - Nude, opening a tanning table and turning
      over. *
    0:57 - Brief left breast licking the blood off some
      phallic looking thing. *
    1:19 - Brief topless jumping out to attack
      "Angus," then walking around her underground
      lair (her body is painted for the rest of the film).
      *
    1:22 - Topless walking up steps with a large
      phallic thing strapped to her body. *
The Rainbow (1989)......................... Winifred Inger
    0:21 - Nude with Sammi Davis undressing,
      running outside in the rain, jumping into the
      water, then talking by the fireplace. ***
    0:43 - Full frontal nudity taking off nightgown and
      getting into bed with Davis, then long right
      breast shot. ***
    1:44 - Nude running outside with Davis. ***
Magazines:
Playboy (Nov 1987).............."Sex in Cinema 1987"
    Pages 144-145: Full frontal nudity from
    "Castaway." **

DOODY, ALISON

Films:

A Prayer for the Dying (1987)....................Siobhan
Taffin (1988).. Charlotte
    0:14 - Very, very brief side view of right breast
      when Pierce Brosnan rips her blouse open.
      Long shot, hard to see. *
Indiana Jones and the Last Crusade (1989)
    .... Dr. Elsa Schneider

DOSS, TERRI LYNN

Films:

Lethal Weapon (1987).................Girl in Shower #2
Die Hard (1988)..................................Girl at Airport
Video Tapes:
Playboy Video Calendar 1989...................Playmate
Magazines:
Playboy (Jul 1988)................................... Playmate
    Page 102

DOUGLASS, ROBYN

Films:

The Clone Master (1978)................................
Breaking Away (1979)..............................Katherine
Conquest of the Earth (1980)...................................
Partners (1982)...Jill
    1:00 - Brief topless taking off her top and getting
      into bed with Ryan O'Neil. **
The Lonely Guy (1983)............................. Danielle
    0:05 - Upper half of right breast in sheer
      nightgown in bed with "Raoul" while talking to
      Steve Martin. Great nightgown! *
    0:33 - In sheer beige negligee lying on couch
      talking to Martin on the phone.
    1:03 - Very,very brief peek at left nipple when she
      flashes it for Martin so he'll let her into his
      party. *
Romantic Comedy (1983)................................. Kate
Made for TV Movies:
The Clone Master (1978)..
Her Life As A Man (1984).......................................
TV:
Battlestar Galactica (1980).............. Jamie Hamilton
Houston Knights .... Lt. Joanne Beaumont
Magazines:
Playboy (Dec 1974)...............................Cover Girl
    Half of left breast. *
Playboy (Jul 1975)............ "A Long Look At Legs"
Playboy (Jan 1980).................. "World of Playboy"
    Page 11: Right breast wearing corset and white
    stockings. Small photo. *

DOWN, LESLEY-ANNE

Films:
From Beyond the Grave (1973).... Rosemary Seaton
The Pink Panther Strikes Again (1976).............Olga
The Betsy (1978)........................Lady Bobby Ayres
   0:38 - Brief left breast with Tommy Lee Jones. *
   0:57 - Very brief left breast in bed with Jones. *
A Little Night Music (1978)............. Anne Egerman
The Great Train Robbery (1979)..................Miriam
Hanover Street (1979).............. Margaret Sallinger
   0:22 - In bra and slip, then brief topless in
   bedroom with Harrison Ford. *
Rough Cut (1980).............................Gillian Bramley
Sphinx (1981)..................................Erica Baron
Nomads (1986)....................................Flax
Scenes from the Goldmine (1987).................Herself
Miniseries:
North and South (1985) ....Madeline Fabray
North and South: Book II (1986).. Madeline Fabray
The Last Days of Pompeii.......................................
TV:
Upstairs, Downstairs (1970's) ....
Magazines:
Playboy (Dec 1979)...................."Sex Stars of 1979"
   Page 254: Topless. **
Playboy (May 1985)................................Grapevine
   Page 217; B&W.

DRAKE, GABRIELLE

Films:
The Man Outside (1968; British)............B.E.A. Girl
There's a Girl in My Soup (1970)
   ....Julia Halford-Smythe
   0:09 - In beige bra with Peter Sellers, brief left
   breast in bed with him. Might be a body double.
   *
Connecting Rooms (1971; British).....................Jean
Commuter Husbands (1974)....................................
TV:
UFO (1970)...............................Lieutenant Gay Ellis

DRAKE, MARCIEE

Films:
Jackson County Jail (1976)
   ....Candy (David's Girlfriend)
   0:04 - Brief topless wrapping towel around herself
   with Howard Hessman. Long shot. *
The Toolbox Murders (1978).........................Victim

DRAKE, MICHELE

Films:
American Gigolo (1980)........... 1st Girl on Balcony
   0:03 - Topless on the balcony while Richard Gere
   and Lauren Hutton talk. *
History of the World, Part I (1981) ....
Magazines:
Playboy (May 1979)..................................Playmate

DREW, LINZI

Films:
Emmanuelle in Soho (1981)......................Showgirl
   Topless on stage.
An American Werewolf in London (1981)
   .... Brenda Bristols
   1:26 - Side view of left breast in porno movie
   while David Naughton talks to his friend "Jack."
   *
   1:27 - Brief topless in movie talking on the phone.
   *
Salome's Last Dance (1987)..................... 1st Slave
   (Appears with 2 other slaves - can't tell who is
   who)
   0:08 - Topless in black costumes around a cage.
   **
   0:52 - Topless during dance number. **
Aria (1988).. Girl
   1:09 - Topless on operating table after car
   accident. Hair is all covered with bandages. *
   1:10 - Topless getting shocked to start her heart.
   **
The Lair of the White Worm (1988).........Maid/Nun

DUFFEK, PATTY

Films:
Hard Ticket to Hawaii (1987)...............Patticakes
   0:48 - Topless talking to "Michelle" after
   swimming. **
Picasso Trigger (1989)...........................Patticakes
   1:04 - Topless taking a Jacuzzi bath. **
Savage Beach (1989).............................Patticakes
   0:06 - Topless in Jacuzzi with Lisa London, Dona
   Speir and Hope Marie Carlton. *
   0:50 - Topless changing clothes. **
Magazines:
Playboy (May 1984)................................ Playmate

DUFFY, JULIA

Films:
Battle Beyond the Stars (1980)...........................Mol
Cutter's Way (1981)................................Young Girl
   a.k.a. Cutter and Bone
Night Warning (1982)........................Julie Linden
   0:44 - Upper half of left breast.
   0:46 - Brief topless when he pulls the sheets down.
   *
   0:47 - Brief topless when Susan Tyrrell opens the
   bedroom door. **
Wacko (1983)....................................Mary Graves
Miniseries:
The Blue and the Gray (1982).................Mary Hale
TV:
Wizards and Warriors (1983).............Princess Ariel
Newhart (1983-90)..............Stephanie Vanderkellen

DUKE, PATTY

Other:
a.k.a. Patty Duke Astin.
Films:
The Goddess (1958; B&W)...
4D Man (1959).............................Marjorie Sullivan
The Miracle Worker (1962; B&W)...... Helen Keller
The Daydreamer (1966).........................Thumbelina
Valley of the Dolls (1967)................... Neely O'Hara
The Babysitter (1980)...
By Design (1982; Canadian)............................Helen
   0:49 - Left breast, lying in bed. **
   1:05 - Brief left breast sitting on bed. **
   1:06 - Brief left breast, then brief right breast lying
    in bed with the photographer. *
Something Special (1987).......................................
Miniseries:
Captains and the Kings (1976)
   .... Bernadette Hennessey Armagh
Made for TV Movies:
My Sweet Charlie (1970)..
A Family Upside Down (1978)...............................
The Miracle Worker (1979)................ Anne Sullivan
Everybody's Baby: The Rescue of Jessica McClure
   (1989)...
TV:
The Patty Duke Show (1963-66)
   .... Patty & Cathy Lane
It Takes Two (1982-83)....................... Molly Quinn
Hail to the Chief (1985).... President Julia Mansfield

DUNAWAY, FAYE

Films:
The Happening (1967).......................................Sandy
Bonnie and Clyde (1967)................... Bonnie Parker
Hurry Sundown (1967)..................... Lou McDowell
The Thomas Crown Affair (1968)...Vicky Anderson
The Arrangement (1969)...................................Gwen
   0:25 - Brief buns in various scenes at the beach
    with Kirk Douglas.
Little Big Man (1970) ....Mrs. Pendrake
Oklahoma Crude (1973)........................ Lena Doyle
The Three Musketeers (1973) ....Milady
Chinatown (1974)..Evelyn
   1:19 - Brief side view of right breast getting out of
    bed with Jack Nicholson after making love. *
The Towering Inferno (1974)............Susan Franklin
Three Days of the Condor (1975) ....Kathy Hale
The Four Musketeers (1975).........................Milady
Network (1976)...........................Diana Christensen
   (Academy Award for Best Actress)
   1:10 - Brief left breast twice, taking off clothes in
    room with William Holden. *
Voyage of the Damned (1976).........Denise Kreisler
Eyes of Laura Mars (1978)..................... Laura Mars
The Champ (1979)..Annie
The First Deadly Sin (1980)........... Barbara Delaney
Mommie Dearest (1981) ....Joan Crawford
The Wicked Lady (1983; British) ... Barbara Skelton

Supergirl (1984)...Selena
Ordeal by Innocence (1984).............. Rachel Argyle
Barfly (1987)....................................Wanda Wilcox
   0:58 - Brief upper half of breasts in bathtub
    talking to Mickey Rourke. *
Midnight Crossing (1988)................... Helen Barton
A Handmaid's Tale (1990)..................... Serena Joy
Miniseries:
Ellis Island (1984)...
Made for TV Movies:
Agatha Christie's "Thirteen at Dinner" (1985) ....
TV:
Ladies of the Night (1986).........................Lil Hutton

DUNLAP, DAWN

Films:
Laura (1979)...Laura
   0:20 - Brief side view of left breast and buns
    talking to Maud Adams, then brief side view of
    right breast putting on robe. *
   0:23 - Nude, dancing while being photographed.
    ***
   1:15 - Nude, letting "Paul" feel her so he can
    sculpt her, then making love with him. ***
   1:22 - Buns, putting on panties talking to Maud
    Adams.
Night Shift (1982).. Maxine
Forbidden World (1982)....................Tracy Baxter
   0:27 - Brief topless getting ready for bed. *
   0:37 - Nude in steam bath. ***
   0:54 - Topless in shower with June Chadwick. **
Heartbreaker (1983)..Kim
Barbarian Queen (1985)........................... Taramis
   0:00 - Topless, in the woods getting raped. *

DUSENBERRY, ANN

Films:
Desperate Women (1978).......................................
Goodbye Franklin High (1978) ....
Jaws II (1978)...................................... Tina Wilcox
Heart Beat (1979)... Stevie
   0:41 - Full frontal nudity frolicking in bathtub
    with Nick Nolte. **
Cutter's Way (1981)......................... Valerie Duran
   a.k.a. Cutter and Bone
Basic Training (1984)....................Melinda Griffin
   1:13 - Topless in Russian guy's bedroom. ***
Lies (1984; British)......................................Robyn
   Topless in the shower.
The Men's Club (1986)................................. Page
   1:05 - Topless lying in bed after making love with
    Roy Scheider. **
TV:
Little Women (1979) .... Amy March Laurence
The Family Tree (1983)......... Molly Nichols Tanner
Life with Lucy (1986-87).............Margo McGibbon

DUVALL, SHELLEY
Films:
Brewster McCloud (1970) .... Suzanne
McCabe and Mrs. Miller (1971) .... Ida Coyle
Thieves Like Us (1974) .... Keechie
Nashville (1975) .... L.A. Jane
Annie Hall (1977) .... Pam
Three Women (1977) .... Millie
Buffalo Bill and the Indians or Sitting Bull's History
Lesson (1980) .... Mrs. Cleveland
Popeye (1980) .... Olive Oyl
The Shining (1980) .... Wendy Torrance
Time Bandits (1981; British) .... Pansy
Roxanne (1987) .... Dixie
Magazines:
Playboy (Nov 1975) .... "Sex in Cinema 1975"
Page 188: Topless photo. ***

E

EASTERBROOK, LESLIE
Films:
Just Tell Me What You Want (1980)
.... Hospital Nurse
Police Academy (1984) .... Callahan
Private Resort (1985) .... Bobbie Sue
0:14 - Very brief buns taking off swimsuit, then
topless under sheer white nightgown. **
Police Academy II: Their First Assignment (1985)
.... Callahan
Police Academy III: Back in Training (1986)
.... Callahan
Police Academy 4: Citizens on Patrol (1987)
.... Callahan
0:35 - In wet T-shirt in swimming pool pretending
to be a drowning victim for the class.
Police Academy 5: Assignment Miami Beach
(1988) .... Callahan
Police Academy 6: City Under Siege (1989)
.... Callahan
TV:
Laverne and Shirley (1980-83) .... Rhonda Lee
Made for TV Movies:
The Taking of Flight 847: The Uli Derickson Story
(1988) .... Audrey

EASTON, JACKIE
Other:
a.k.a. Jacki Easton.
Films:
Hardbodies (1984) .... Girl in dressing room
0:27 - Topless taking off dress to try on swimsuit.
**
School Spirit (1985) .... Hogette

EDWARDS, BARBARA
Films:
Malibu Express (1984) .... May
0:10 - Topless taking a shower with Kimberly
McArthur on the boat. **
1:05 - Topless serving "Cody" coffee while he
talks on the telephone. **
Terminal Entry (1987) .... Lady Electric
0:05 - Topless taking a shower and getting a towel
during "video game" scene. ***
Another Chance (1989) .... Diana the Temptress
0:38 - Topless in trailer with "Johnny." ***
Video Tapes:
Playmate Review 3 (1985) .... Playmate
Playboy Video Magazine, Volume 4 .... Playmate
Playboy Video Calendar 1987 .... Playmate
Playmates of the Year - The '80's .... Playmate
Magazines:
Playboy (Sep 1983) .... Playmate

EDWARDS, ELLA
Films:
For Pete's Sake! (1966) ....
Nobody's Perfect (1968) ....
Sweet Sugar (1972) .... Simone
0:58 - Topless in bed with "Mojo." *
Detroit 9000 (1973) .... Helen
Mr. Ricco (1975) .... Sally

EGE, JULIE
Films:
On Her Majesty's Secret Sevice (1969; British)
.... Scandanavian Girl
Creatures the World Forgot (1971) .... Girl
Very brief topless.
The Mutations (1973) .... Hedi
Topless in bathtub.

EGGAR, SAMANTHA
Films:
The Collector (1965) .... Miranda Grey
A Name for Evil (1973) .... John Blake
0:42 - Very brief topless turning over in bed with
Robert Culp. Dark, hard to see. *
The Brood (1979) .... Nola Carveth
Curtains (1983) .... Samantha Sherwood
Made for Cable Movies:
A Ghost in Monte Carlo (1990) ....
TV:
Anna and the King (1972) .... Anna Owens

EICHHORN, LISA
Films:
The Europeans (1979; British) . Gertrude Wentworth
Yanks (1979) .... Jean Moreton
Brief topless.
Why Would I Lie (1980) .... Kay

Cutter's Way (1981)..............Maureen "Mo" Cutter
a.k.a. Cutter and Bone
1:07 - Brief right breast, wearing bathrobe, lying on lounge chair while Jeff Bridges looks at her. *

The Weather in the Streets (1983; British)...... Olivia
Wild Rose (1984)....................................June Lorich
Opposing Force (1986)................ Lieutenant Casey
a.k.a. Hell Camp
0:17 - Wet T-shirt after going through river *
0:33 - Topless getting sprayed with water and dusted with white powder. ***
1:03 - Topless after getting raped by Anthony Zerbe in his office, while another officer watches. **

EILBER, JANET
Films:
Whose Life Is It, Anyway? (1981)................. Patty
0:30 - Nude during B&W dream sequence dancing ballet. **
1:13 - Very brief side view of left breast when her back is turned while changing when Christine Lahti visits. *
Romantic Comedy (1983)............................ Allison
Hard to Hold (1984)..........................Diana Lawson
TV:
Two Marriages (1983-84) .... Nancy Armstrong
The Best Times (1985)............... Joanne Braithwaite

EKBERG, ANITA
Films:
Back from Eternity (1956; B&W)....................Rena
Hollywood or Bust (1956)............................Herself
War and Peace (1956; U.S./Italian)................Helene
Paris Holiday (1957) ....Zara
La Dolce Vita (1960; Italian, B&W)...............Sylvia
Boccaccio '70 (1962; Italian)........................... Anita
Four for Texas (1963) .... Elya Carlson
Woman Times Seven (1967)....................... Claudie
Northeast of Seoul (1972) ....
Made for TV Movies:
S.H.E. (1979)..
Magazines:
Playboy (Jan 1989)............. "Women of the Fifties"
Page 118: B&W photo sitting on the floor. **

EKLAND, BRITT
Films:
After the Fox (1966)........................Gina Romantiea
The Bobo (1967) ....Olimpia Segura
The Night they Raided Minsky's (1968)
.... Rachel Schpitendavel
Topless.
Stiletto (1969)... Illeana
The Cannibals (1969)............................... Antigone
What the Peeper Saw (1972)...............................
Topless.

The Man with the Golden Gun (1974)
....Mary Goodnight
The Wickerman (1973)............................... Willow
0:58 - Topless in bed knocking on the wall, then more topless and buns getting up and walking around the bedroom. Long scene. ***
Endless Night (1977)....................................Greta
1:21 - Brief topless several times with "Michael." *

Slavers (1977) ....Anna
Topless.
Some Like It Cool
(1979; German/French/Italian/Austrian)
.... Countess Trivulsi
a.k.a. Sex on the Run
a.k.a. Casanova and Co.
0:44 - Left breast while making love in bed with Tony Curtis (don't see her face). *
The Monster Club (1981).............. Lintom's Mother
Erotic Images (1983)............................ Julie Todd
0:16 - Brief side view of left breast in bed with "Glenn." *
0:29 - In bra, then topless in bed with "Glenn." ***
0:33 - In bra, in open robe looking at herself in the mirror.
1:27 - In black bra talking to "Sonny."
Love Scenes (1984) ....Annie
Moon in Scorpio (1987)...................................Linda
Scandal (1989)............................Mariella Novotny
(unrated version)
0:31 - Topless lying on table with John Hurt. **
0:51 - Right breast talking with Hurt and "Christine." *
Beverly Hills Vamp (1989) ....Madam Cassandra
Made for TV Movie:
The Great Wallendas (1978)....................................
Magazines:
Playboy (May 1989)................................ "Scandal"
Pages 87 & 88: Left and right breasts. *

ELENIAK, ERIKA
Films:
E.T. The Extraterrestrial (1982)................Pretty Girl
The Blob (1988)..................................Vicki De Soto
Video Tapes:
Playboy Video Centerfold: Fawna MacLaren
....Playmate
Made for TV Movies:
Baywatch (1989)..Shauni
TV:
Charles in Charge (1988)........................Stephanie
Baywatch (1989-90)..................................Shauni
Magazines:
Playboy (Jul 1989)............................... Playmate
Page 98
Playboy (Dec 1989)........ "Holy Sex Stars of 1989!"
Page 181: Topless, reclining. ***
Playboy (Aug 1990)............. "Beauty on the Beach"
Pages 68-75: Nude. ***

ELIAN, YONA

Films:
The Jerusalem File (1972; U.S./Israel)......... Raschel
The Last Winter (1983) ....Maya
0:48 - Topless taking off her robe to get into pool.
**
0:49 - Buns, lying on marble slab with Kathleen Quinlan.

ELISE, ESTHER

See Alise, Esther.

ELVIRA

Other:
Real name is Cassandra Peterson.
Films:
The Working Girls (1974)............................ Katya
0:18 - Dancing in a G-string on stage in a club
0:20 - Topless, dancing on stage. ***
Famous T & A (1982)................................ herself
0:28 - Topless scene from "Working Girls." ***
Stroker Ace (1983)........................Woman with Lugs
Uncensored (1984)..
Pee Wee's Big Adventure (1985)......... Biker Mama
Echo Park (1986)...................................Sheri
Allan Quartermain and the Lost City of Gold
(1987)..Sorais
Elvira, Mistress of the Dark (1988)................Elvira
0:31 - Getting undressed into black lingerie in her bedroom while being watched from outside the window.
1:31 - Very skillfully twirling two tassels on the tips of her bra.

EVANS, LINDA

Films:
Beach Blanket Bingo (1965) ....Sugar Kane
Those Calloways (1965)......................Bridie Mellot
The Avalanche Express (1979)................ Elsa Lang
Tom Horn (1980)......................Glendoline Kimmel
Made for TV Movies:
North and South, Book II (1986).........Rose Sinclair
TV:
Big Valley (1965-69)........................Audra Barkley
Hunter (1977)...................................Marty Shaw
Dynasty (1981-89).......Krystle Jennings Carrington
Magazines:
Playboy (Jul 1971)................... "Blooming Beauty"
Playboy (Dec 1981)................... "Sex Stars of 1981"
Page 241: Topless. ***
Playboy (Jan 1989)......... "Women of the Seventies"
Page 216: Topless sitting in water. ***

EVENSON, KIM

Films:
The Big Bet (1985).. Beth
0:36 - Right breast, sitting on couch with "Chris."
**
0:45 - Brief topless twice taking off swimsuit top.
***
0:54 - Brief topless three times in elevator when "Chris" pulls her sweater up. **
1:06 - Nude when "Chris" fantasizes about her. Long shot. **
1:19 - In white bra and panties, then nude while undressing for "Chris." ***
Kidnapped (1986)....................................... Debbie
0:25 - Right breast in bed talking on the phone. Long shot, hard to see. *
0:30 - In blue nightgown in room.
1:28 - Topless getting arm prepared for a drug injection. Long scene. ***
1:30 - Topless acting in a movie. Long shot, then close up. Wearing a G-string. ***
Porky's Revenge (1987).................................. Inga
0:02 - Right breast opening her graduation gown during "Pee Wee's" dream. **
1:27 - Topless showing "Pee Wee" that she doesn't have any clothes under her graduation gown. **
Kandyland (1987).. Joni
0:26 - In purple bra and white panties practicing dancing on stage.
0:31 - Topless doing first dance routine. ***
0:45 - Brief topless during another routine with bubbles floating around. **
Magazines:
Playboy (Sep 1984) .... Playmate

F

FABIAN, AVA

Films:
Dragnet (1987)..Baitmate
Terminal Exposure (1988) .... Bruce's Girl
To Die For (1988)......................................Franny
Video Tapes:
Playboy Video Magazine Volume 12 .... Playmate
Playmate Playoffs..................................... Playmate
Magazines:
Playboy (Aug 1986)................................... Playmate
Page 86

FAIRCHILD, JUNE
Films:
Pretty Maids All In a Row (1971)
.... Sonya "Sonny" Swingle
Drive, He Said (1972).................................. Sylvie
   0:16 - Buns and brief topless walking around in
   the dark while "Gabriel" shines a flashlight on
   her. *
   1:01 - Topless, then brief nude getting dressed
   while "Gabriel" goes crazy and starts trashing a
   house. *
Top of the Heap (1972)................. Balloon Thrower
Detroit 9000 (1973)..................................... Barbara
Thunderbolt and Lightfoot (1974).............. Gloria
   0:20 - Very brief right breast getting dressed in the
   bathroom after making love with Clint
   Eastwood. *
Your Three Minutes are Up (1973)................. Sandi

FAIRCHILD, MORGAN
Films:
The Seduction (1982)..................................... Jamie
   0:02 - Brief topless under water, swimming in
   pool. *
   0:05 - Very brief left breast, getting out of the pool
   to answer the telephone. *
   0:13 - In white bra changing clothes while
   listening to telephone answering machine.
   0:50 - In white lingerie in her bathroom while
   Andrew Stevens watches from inside the closet.
   0:51 - Topless pinning her hair up for her bath,
   then brief left breast in bathtub covered with
   bubbles. **
   1:21 - Topless getting into bed. Kind of dark, hard
   to see anything. *
Pee Wee's Big Adventure (1985)................."Dottie"
The Red-Headed Stranger (1986) ....
Deadly Illusion (1987)..Jane Mallory/Sharon Burton
Campus Man (1987)...
Midnight Cop (1988; German)........................... Lisa
   0:23 - In white panties with her dress pulled up in
   restroom with "Alex."
Miniseries:
79 Park Avenue (1977) ....
North and South (1985)...
North and South: Book II (1986) ....
Made for USA Network:
The Haunting of Sarah Hardy (1989)......................
Made for TV Movies:
Initiation of Sarah (1978)......................................
Honeyboy (1982)...
How to Murder a Millionaire (1990).............Loretta
TV:
Search for Tomorrow (1971)....................................
Dallas (1978)..Jenna Wade
Flamingo Road (1981-82)
.... Constance Weldon Carlyle
Paper Dolls (1984)...Racine
North and South (1985)................ Burdetta Halloran
Falcon Crest (1985-86)......................Jordan Roberts

Magazines:
   Playboy (Apr 1982)................................Grapevine
   Page 254: B&W photo of her in bathtub. Upper
   half of right breast. *

FAITHFUL, MARIANNE
Other:
Singer.
Former girlfriend of "Rolling Stones" singer Mick
Jagger.
Films:
Girl on a Motorcycle (1968)...................... Rebecca
   0:05 - Nude, getting out of bed and walking to the
   door. **
   0:38 - Brief side view of left breast putting
   nightgown on. *
   1:23 - Brief topless lying and talking with Alain
   Delon. *
   1:30 - Very brief right breast a couple of times
   making love with Delon. *
Hamlet (1969; British).................................Ophelia
Assault on Agathon (1976).............Helen Rochefort

FALANA, LOLA
Other:
Singer.
Films:
The Liberation of L. B. Jones (1970)....Emma Jones
   0:19 - Very brief topless walking by the doorway
   in the bathroom. Very long shot, don't really
   see anything.
Lady Cocoa (1974)...Coco
   0:45 - Left breast lying on bed, pulling up yellow
   towel. Long shot, hard to see. *
   1:23 - Topless on boat with a guy. ***
TV:
The New Bill Cosby Show (1972-73)........... regular
Ben Vereen... Comin' At Ya (1975)............. regular

FARROW, MIA
Other:
Sister of actress Tisa Farrow.
Daughter of actress Maureen O'Sullivan.
Films:
Rosemary's Baby (1968)..... Rosemary Woodhouse
   0:10 - Brief left breast in room in new apartment
   on floor with John Cassavetes. Hard to see
   anything. *
   0:43 - Brief close up of her breasts while she's
   sitting on a boat during a nightmare. *
   0:44 - Buns walking on boat, then breasts during
   impregnation scene with the devil. **
Secret Ceremony (1968)................................. Cenci
A Dandy in Aspic (1968)...........................Caroline
See No Evil (1971)..Sarah
The Great Gatsby (1974) .... Daisy Buchanan
Fingers (1977)..Carol
Avalanche (1978)............................. Caroline Brace
Death on the Nile (1978) ......Jacqueline de Bellefort

A Wedding (1978).............................Buffy Brenner
  1:10 - Topless posing in front of a painting in a
    wedding veil in front of a movie camera. ***
Hurricane (1979).......................Charlotte Bruckner
  0:39 - Brief left breast in open dress top while
    crawling under bushes at the beach. *
High Heels (1980)...
A Midsummer Night's Sex Comedy (1982)..... Ariel
Broadway Danny Rose (1984)................. Tina Vitale
Supergirl (1984).......................................Alura
Zelig (1984)...Dr. Fletcher
The Purple Rose of Cairo (1985)...................Cecelia
Hannah and Her Sisters (1986)....................Hannah
Radio Days (1987)..............................Sally White
New York Stories (1989)...................................Lisa
TV:
Peyton Place (1964-66)
  ....Allison MacKenzie/Harrington

FARROW, TISA
Other:
  Sister of actress Mia Farrow.
  Daughter of actress Maureen O'Sullivan.
Films:
Some Call It Loving (1972).......................Jennifer
  1:17 - Topless in bed with "Troy." ***
Fingers (1978)....................................Carol
Winter Kills (1979)..............................Nurse Two
Zombie (1980)..............................Anne Bolles
Search and Destroy (1981)..............................Kate
Magazines:
Playboy (Jul 1973)................................"Tisa"
  Page 87: Topless. **

FAVIER, SOPHIE
Films:
Frank and I (1983)...Maud
  0:16 - Nude, undressing then topless lying in bed
    with "Charles." *
  0:40 - Brief topless in bed with "Charles." *
Cheech and Chong's The Corsican Brothers (1984)
  ....Lovely

FAWCETT, FARRAH
Films:
Myra Breckinridge (1970)......................................
Logan's Run (1976)..............................Holly
Sunburn (1979)................................... Ellie
Saturn 3 (1980).................................... Alex
  0:17 - Brief right breast taking off towel and
    running to Kirk Douglas after taking a shower.
    **
Cannonball Run (1981)...........................Pamela
Murder in Texas (1983).......................................
Extremities (1986)............................... Marjorie
  0:37 - Brief side view of right breast when "Joe"
    pulls down her top in the kitchen. Can't see her
    face. *

See You in the Morning (1989)..........Jo Livingston
Double Exposure: The Story of Margaret Bourke-
  White ....Margaret Bourke-White
Made for TV Movies:
Murder on Flight 502 (1975) ....
The Red Light Sting (1984) ....
The Burning Bed (1986)......................................
Between Two Women (1986)................................
Poor Little Rich Girl: The Barbara Hutton Story
  (1987)..............................Barbara Hutton
Small Sacrifices (1989)....................... Diane Downs
Miniseries:
Poor Little Rich Girl (1987)..............................
TV:
Harry-O (1974-76).....................Next door neighbor
Charlie's Angels (1976-77)....................Jill Munroe

FENECH, EDWIGE
Films:
Sex with a Smile (1976).......................Dream Girl
  0:03 - Topless tied to bed with two holes cut in her
    red dress top. **
  0:09 - Buns, in jail cell in court when the guy pulls
    her panties down with his sword.
  0:13 - Brief topless in bed with "Dracula" taking
    off her top and hugging him. **
  0:16 - Topless in bathtub. Long shot. *
Phantom of Death (1988)......................................

FENN, SHERILYN
Films:
Out of Control (1984).............................Katie
  0:19 - In wet white T-shirt in pond with the other
    girls.
The Wild Life (1984) ....Penny Hallin
The Wraith (1986)................................ Keri
Just One of the Guys (1986)...........................Sandy
Thrashin' (1986)................................Velvet
Zombie High (1987)................................Suzi
Two Moon Junction (1988)............................April
  (Blonde hair throughout the film.)
  0:07 - Topless taking a shower in the country club
    shower room. ***
  0:27 - Brief topless on the floor kissing "Perry."
    **
  0:42 - Topless in gas station restroom changing
    camisole tops with Kristy McNichol. **
  0:54 - Brief topless making love with "Perry" in a
    motel room. *
  1:24 - Nude at "Two Moon Junction" making love
    with "Perry." Very hot! ***
  1:40 - Brief left breast and buns in the shower with
    "Perry." *
Crime Zone (1989)....................................... Helen
  0:16 - In black lingerie and stockings in bedroom.
  0:23 - Topless wearing black panties making love
    with "Bone." Dark, long shot. **

Meridian (1989).. Catherine
   0:23 - White bra and panties, getting clothes taken
      off by "Lawrence." Then topless. **
   0:28 - Topless in bed with "Oliver." ***
   0:51 - Topless getting her blouse ripped open
      lying in bed. **
   1:11 - Briefly in white panties and bra putting red
      dress on.
True Blood (1989)............................ Jennifer Scott
   1:22 - Very brief right breast in closet trying to
      stab "Spider" with a piece of mirror. *
TV:
   Twin Peaks (1990-) .... Audrey Horne

FERGUSON, KATE
Films:
   Break of Day (1977; Australian)........................Jean
   Spaced Out (1980; British).......................... Skipper
      1:07 - Brief topless making love with "Willy" in
         bed. Lit with red light. *
   The Pirate Movie (1982; Australian)................ Edith

FERRARE, CRISTINA
Other:
   Former Fashion Model.
   Ex-wife of ex-car maker John De Lorean.
   Spokeswoman for Ultra Slim-Fast.
Films:
   Mary, Mary, Bloody Mary (1975)................. Mary
      0:07 - Brief topless making love with some guy on
         the couch just before she kills him. **
      0:41 - Topless when "Greta" helps pull down
         Cristina's top to take a bath. ***
      1:12 - Bun and brief silhouette of left breast
         getting out of bed and getting dressed.
TV:
   Incredible Sunday (1988-89)........................ co-host

FERRATI, REBECCA
Films:
   Silent Assassins (1988) .... Miss Amy
Magazines:
   Playboy.. Playmate

FIEDLER, BEA
Films:
   Island of 1000 Delights (German)................... Julia
      0:25 - Full frontal nudity washing herself in
         bathtub, then nude taking off her towel for
         "Michael." **
      0:27 - Topless lying on floor after making love,
         then buns walking to chair. **
      0:46 - Full frontal nudity taking off her dress and
         kissing "Howard." **
      0:50 - Topless in white bikini bottoms coming out
         of the water to great "Howard." **
      1:06 - Topless sitting in the sand near the beach,
         then nude talking with "Sylvia." ***

   1:17 - Right breast (great close up) making love
      with "Sylvia." ***
   1:18 - Topless above "Sylvia." ***
Hot Chili (1985)........................ The Music Teacher
   0:08 - Topless playing the cello while being
      fondled by "Ricky." **
   0:29 - Buns, playing the violin.
   0:34 - Nude during fight in restaurant with "Chi
      Chi." Hard to see because of the flashing light.
      **
   0:36 - Topless lying on inflatable lounge in pool,
      playing a flute. ***
   0:43 - Left breast playing a tuba. ***
   1:01 - Topless and buns dancing in front of "Mr.
      Lieberman." ***
   1:07 - Buns, then right breast dancing with
      "Stanley." *

FIELD, SALLY
Films:
   Stay Hungry (1976)............. Mary Kay Farnsworth
      0:27 - Buns, then very, very brief side view of left
         breast jumping back into bed. Very fast,
         everything is a blur, hard to see anything.
   Heroes (1977)......................................Carol
   Smokey and the Bandit (1977)........................Carrie
   The End (1978).. Mary Ellen
   Hooper (1978)... Gwen
   Beyond the Poseidon Adventure (1979)
      ....Celeste Whitman
   Norma Rae (1979) .... Norma Rae
      (Academy Award for Best Actress.)
      0:11 - In white bra in motel room with "George."
   Back Roads (1981).................................Amy Post
   Absence of Malice (1982) .... Megan Carter
   Kiss Me Goodbye (1982)....................Kay Villano
   Places in the Heart (1984)................. Edna Spalding
      (Academy Award for Best Actress.)
   Murphy's Romance (1985)............. Emma Moriarity
   Surrender (1988)................................Daisy Morgan
      0:06 - In black slip getting up out of bed and
         washing up in the bathroom.
   Punchline (1988)............................... Lilah Krytsick
   Steel Magnolias (1989)................ M'Lynn Eatenton
Made for TV Movies:
   Sybil (1976) ....Sybil
      (Emmy Award for Best Actress in a Drama
         Special.)
TV:
   Gidget (1965-66) .... Francine "Gidget" Lawrence
   The Flying Nun (1967-70)................. Sister Bertrille
   Alias Smith and Jones (1971-73)....Clementine Hale
   Girl with Something Extra (1973-74)... Sally Burton

FIORENTINO, LINDA
Films:
   Visionquest (1985)..Carla
   Gotcha! (1985)... Sasha
      Brief topless.

After Hours (1985)............................ Kiki
  0:11 - In black bra and skirt doing paper maché
  0:19 - Topless taking off bra in doorway while
     Griffin Dunne watches. **
The Moderns (1988)...........................Rachel Stone
  0:40 - Topless sitting in bathtub while John Lone
     shaves her armpits. *
  0:41 - Right breast while turning over onto
     stomach in bathtub. *
  1:18 - Topless getting out of tub while covered
     with bubble to kiss Keith Carradine. **
Wildfire (1989)...
Made for Cable Movies:
  The Neon Empire (1989)................................. Lucy

FLANAGAN, FIONNULA

Films:
  Ulysses (1967; U.S./British).........Gerty MacDowell
  Sinful Davey (1969; British) ....Penelope
  Crossover (1980; Canadian)...................... Abadaba
     a.k.a. Mr. Patman
     0:27 - Brief topless opening her robe and flashing
        James Coburn. *
  P.K. and the Kid (1982).............................
  James Joyce's Women (1983)...........Molly Bloom
     0:48 - Brief topless getting out of bed. *
     0:56 - Topless getting back into bed. ***
     1:02 - Full frontal nudity masturbating in bed
        talking to herself. Very long scene - 9 minutes!
        ***
  Reflections (1984; British)............Charlotte Lawless
  Youngblood (1986)................................ Miss McGill
Miniseries:
  Rich Man, Poor Man - Book I (1976).........Clothilde
Made for TV Movies:
  Mary White (1977)....................................
  The Ewok Adventure (1984)...................... Catarine
  A Winner Never Quits (1986)...........Mrs. Wyshner
TV:
  How the West was Won (1978-79)
     ....Aunt Molly Culhane

FLUEGEL, DARLANNE

Films:
  Eyes of Laura Mars (1978)............................. Lulu
  Battle Beyond the Stars (1980)....................... Sador
  The Last Fight (1983)...................................... Sally
  Once Upon a Time in America (1984).............. Eve
  To Live and Die in L.A. (1985)........... Ruth Lanier
     0:44 - Brief topless sitting up in bed and buns
        when William L. Petersen comes home **
     1:29 - In stockings on couch with Petersen
     1:50 - Very brief topless on bed with Petersen in a
        flashback. *
  Running Scared (1986).....................Anna Costanzo
  Tough Guys (1986)...............................Skye Foster
  Bulletproof (1988) ....Devon Shepard

Freeway (1988)...................... Sarah "Sunny" Harper
  0:27 - In bra in bathroom taking a pill, then very,
     very brief right breast, getting into bed. *
  0:28 - Brief left breast putting on robe and getting
     out of bed. *
Border Heat (1988)..............................Peggy Martin
  0:23 - In black bra straddling "Ryan" in the
     bedroom.
Lock Up (1989)..Melissa
TV:
  Crime Story (1986-89)..........................Julie Torello
  Hunter (1990-)..............................Joanne Malinski
Magazines:
  Playboy (Aug 1978)........................"'Eyes' Has It"
     Page 96: Left breast. **
     Page 99: Topless in bed. *

FONDA, BRIDGET

Other:
  Daughter of actor Peter Fonda.
  Granddaughter of actor Henry Fonda.
Films:
  You Can't Hurry Love (1984) .... Peggy
  Aria (1988)...Girl Lover
     0:59 - Brief right breast, then topless lying down
        on bed in hotel room in Las Vegas. **
     1:02 - Topless in the bathtub with her boyfriend.
        **
  Scandal (1989)...........................Mandy Rice-Davis
     (Unrated version)
     0:20 - Brief topless dressed as an Indian dancing
        while "Christine" tries to upstage her. *
     0:54 - In white lingerie, then lower frontal nudity
        in sheer nightgown in room with a guy.
     1:05 - Brief buns walking back into bedroom.
        Long shot.
  Shag (1989).......................................Melaina Buller

FONDA, JANE

Other:
  Daughter of actor Henry Fonda.
  Sister of actor Peter Fonda.
Films:
  Period of Adjustment (1962)......... Isabel Haverstick
  Joy House (1964) ....Melinda
  Cat Ballou (1965)...............................Cat Ballou
  The Game is Over (1966)............... Renee Saccard
  The Chase (1966)................................. Anna Reeves
  Barefoot in the Park (1967)................Corrie Bratter
  Hurry Sundown (1967).............Julie Ann Warren
  Barbarella (1968; French/Italian)...........Barbarella
     0:04 - Topless getting out of space suit during
        opening credits in zero gravity. Hard to see
        because the frame is squeezed so the lettering
        will fit. **
  They Shoot Horses, Don't They? (1969)........Gloria
  Klute (1971) .... Bree Daniel
     (Academy Award for Best Actress.)
     0:27 - Side view of left and right breasts stripping
        in old man's office. *

A Doll's House (1973)....................................Nora
Steelyard Blues (1973)............................ Iris Caine
The Blue Bird (1976).................................Night
Fun with Dick and Jane (1977).............Jane Harper
Julia (1977)......................................Lillian Hellman
California Suite (1978)....................Hannah Warren
Comes a Horseman (1978)............................... Ella
Coming Home (1978)............................ Sally Hyde
    (Academy Award for Best Actress.)
    0:41 - Buns and brief left breast in bed making
      love with Jon Voight is a body double.
The Electric Horseman (1978)....................... Hallie
The China Syndrome (1979)........... Kimberly Wells
9 to 5 (1980)...Judy Bernly
On Golden Pond (1981)........Chelsea Thayer Wayne
Rollover (1981) ....Lee Winters
Agnes of God (1985).............Dr. Martha Livingston
The Morning After (1986)...........Alex Sternbergen
    1:08 - Brief topless making love with Jeff Bridges.
    *
Old Gringo (1989)......................... Harriet Winslow
Video Tapes:
    Lots of exercise video tapes.
Made for TV Movies:
    The Dollmaker (1984)...
    (Emmy Award for Best Actress.)

FORD, ANITRA
Films:
    The Big Bird Cage (1972)...............................Terry
    Invasion of the Bee Girls (1973).. Dr. Susan Harris
      0:47 - Topless and buns undressing in front of a
        guy in front of a fire. ***
    Stacey (1973)..Tish
      0:13 - Topless in bed making love with "Frank."
      **
    The Longest Yard (1974)............................ Melissa
      0:01 - Topless under see-though red nightgown
        with Burt Reynolds.
    Dead People (1974)..

FORD, MARIA
Films:
    Dance of the Damned (1988).....................Teacher
      0:11 - Brief topless during dance routine in club
        wearing black panties, garter belt and stockings.
      *
    Stripped to Kill II (1988)............................Shady
      0:21 - Topless, dancing on table in front of the
        detective. Buns, walking away. **
      0:40 - Brief upper half of left breast in the alley
        with the detective. *
      0:52 - Topless and buns during dance routine. **
Magazines:
    Playboy (Nov 1988)............. "Sex in Cinema 1988"
    Page 137: Full frontal nudity standing in front of
    a pole. ***

FOREMAN, DEBORAH
Other:
    a.k.a. Debby Lynn Foreman.
Films:
    I'm Dancing as Fast as I Can (1981)...............Cindy
    Valley Girl (1983)...Julie
    Real Genius (1985).......................................Susan
    April Fool's Day (1986).......................Muffy/Buffy
    3:15 - The Moment of Truth (1986)
        .... Sherry Havilland
      0:26 - Very brief blurry buns and side view of left
        breast jumping out of bed when her parents
        come home. Long shot, hard to see anything.
    Destroyer (1988)................................Susan Malone
    Waxwork (1988)...Sarah

FORTE, VALENTINA
Films:
    Cut and Run (1985) ....Ana
      0:29 - Brief left breast being made love to in bed.
        Then topless sitting up in bed and left side view
        and buns taking a shower. ***
    Inferno in Diretta (1985).................................

FOSTER, JODIE
Films:
    Kansas City Bomber (1972)...............................Rita
    Napolean and Samantha (1972)...............Samantha
    One Little Indian (1973)............................... Martha
    Tom Sawyer (1973)......................... Becky Thatcher
    Alice Doesn't Live Here Anymore (1975).... Audrey
    Echoes of Summer (1976)................Deirdre Striden
    Bugsy Malone (1976)................................ Tallulah
    Taxi Driver (1976)......................Iris Steensman
    Candleshoe (1977)..Casey
    Freaky Friday (1977)...................Annabel Andrews
    Carny (1980)... Donna
    Foxes (1980)..Jeanie
    The Hotel New Hampshire (1984)................ Franny
    Siesta (1987)...Nancy
      0:47 - In a black slip combing Ellen Barkin's hair.
      0:50 - In a slip again in bedroom with Barkin.
    Five Corners (1988)..Linda
    The Accused (1988)........................... Sarah Tobias
      (Academy Award for Best Actress.)
      1:27 - Brief topless a few times during rape scene
        on pinball machine by "Dan" and "Bob." *
    Backtrack (1989) ....
Made for HBO:
    The Blood of Others (1984)...............................
Made for TV Movies:
    The Little Girl Who Lives Down the Lane
      (1976; Canadian)..
    O'Hara's Wife (1982)..
    Svengali (1983)..
TV:
    Bob & Carol & Ted & Alice (1973)
      .... Elizabeth Henderson
    Paper Moon (1974-75)........................... Addie Pray

FOSTER, LISA RAINES

Other:
  a.k.a. Lisa Foster or Lisa Raines.
Films:
  Fanny Hill (1981; British)..................... Fanny Hill
    0:09 - Nude, getting into bathtub, then drying
      herself off. **
    0:10 - Full frontal nudity getting into bed. *
    0:12 - Full frontal nudity making love with
      "Phoebe" in bed. ***
    0:30 - Nude, making love in bed with "Charles."
      ***
    0:49 - Topless, whipping her lover, "Mr. H." in
      bed. **
    0:53 - Nude getting into bed with "William" while
      "Hannah" watches through the keyhole. **
    1:26 - Nude, getting out of bed, then running
      down the stairs to open the door for "Charles."
  Spring Fever (1983; Canadian)........................... Lena
  Ator, the Invincible (1984)..............................
  The Blademaster (1984)..................................
    a.k.a. Ator, The Invincible
Made for HBO:
  The Hitchhiker: Killer .... Patty
    0:02 - Very brief topless standing in the bathtub
      just before getting shot. *
    0:23 - Very brief topless again in Jenny
      Seagrove's flashback. *
Magazines:
  Playboy (Nov 1983)............. "Sex in Cinema 1983"
    Page 145: Topless. **

FOSTER, MEG

Films:
  Thumb Tripping (1972)................................. Shay
    1:19 - Very, very brief topless leaning back in
      field with Jack. Long shot. *
    1:20 - Topless at night. Face is turned away from
      the camera.
  Welcome to Arrow Beach (1973)... Robbin Stanley
    0:12 - Buns and brief side view of right breast
      getting undressed to skinny dip in the ocean.
      Don't see her face.
    0:40 - Topless getting out of bed. **
  A Different Story (1977)............................... Stella
    0:12 - In white bra and panties exercising and
      changing clothes in her bedroom.
    0:53 - Topless sitting on Perry King, rubbing cake
      all over each other on bed. **
    0:59 - Brief buns and side view of right breast
      getting into bed with King. *
  Carny (1980)... Greta
  Ticket to Heaven (1981; Canadian)................. Ingrid
  The Emerald Forest (1985)................. Jean Markham
  Masters of the Universe (1987) ....
  The Wind (1987)..
  They Live (1988).. Holly
  Leviathan (1989)... Martin
  Stepfather 2 (1989).......................... Carol Grayland

  Relentless (1989).................................... Carol Dietz
  Tripwire (1989).. Julia
Made for HBO:
  The Hitchhiker: The Martyr ....
TV:
  Sunshine (1975) .... Nora
  Cagney and Lacey (1982) .... Chris Cagney

FOX, SAMANTHA

Other:
  Former British "Page 3 Girl."
  Singer - "Touch Me."
  Not to be confused with the adult film actress with
    the same name.
Films:
  Playboy (Dec 1988)................. "Sex Stars of 1988"
    Page 185: Topless. ***
  Playboy (Feb 1989) .... "The Year in Sex"
    Page 142: Topless. ***

FOX, SAMANTHA

Other:
  Adult film actress not to be confused with the British
    singer with the same name.
Films:
  Babylon Pink (1979)...
  In Love (1983) ....
  Simply Irresistible (1983)................. Arlene Brooks
    1:20 - In see-through white nightgown, then brief
      peeks at right breast when nightgown gapes
      open. *
  Delivery Boys (1984)................... Woman in Tuxedo
  Streetwalkin' (1985)......................... Topless Dancer

FRANCE, MARIE

Films:
  Love Circles Around the World (1984)......... Suzy
    0:07 - Dancing in sheer black body stocking, then
      topless stripping it off, then topless and buns
      making love with "Jack." ***
  Under the Cherry Moon (1986) ....

FRANKLIN, DIANE

Films:
  The Last American Virgin (1982)................ Karen
    1:06 - Topless in room above the bleachers with
      "Jason." ***
    1:17 - Topless and almost lower frontal nudity
      taking off her panties in the clinic. **
  Amityville II, The Possession (1982)
    .... Patricia Montelli
    Brief topless in bed.
  Better Off Dead (1985)..................... Monique Junet
  Second Time Lucky (1986)............................... Eve
    0:07 - In white bra and panties in frat house
      bedroom taking her dress off because it's wet.
    0:13 - Topless a lot during first sequence in the
      Garden of Eden with "Adam." **

0:28 - Brief full frontal nudity running to "Adam" after trying an apple. ***

0:41 - Left breast taking top of dress down. *

1:01 - Topless, opening blouse in defiance in front of a firing squad. ***

Terrorvision (1986) ....Suzy Putterman

Bill & Ted's Excellent Adventure (1989)
.....................................Princess Joanna

FRAZIER, SHEILA

Films:

Superfly (1972)...Georgia

0:40 - Topless and buns in the bathtub with "Superfly" making love. **

California Suite (1978)......................Bettina Panama

Two of a Kind (1983)................................. Reporter

Made for TV Movies:

The Lazarus Syndrome (1976).........Gloria St. Clair

Three the Hard Way (1974)..................Wendy Kane

FREDERICK, VICKI

Films:

All That Jazz (1979).........................Menage Partner

...All the Marbles (1981)....................................Iris
a.k.a. The California Dolls

1:03 - Brief side view of left breast crying in the shower after fighting with Peter Falk. *

Body Rock (1984)..Claire

A Chorus Line (1985) ....Sheila

Stewardess School (1987)................Miss Grummet

G

GABRIELLE, MONIQUE

Films:

Night Shift (1982)... Tessie

0:56 - Brief topless on college guy's shoulders during party in the morgue. *

Black Venus (1983).............................. Ingrid

0:03 - Nude in Sailor Room at the bordello. ***

1:01 - Topless and buns, taking off clothes for "Madame Lilli's" customers. ***

Chained Heat (1983; U.S./German).............Debbie

0:08 - Nude after stripping for the Warden, then in the Jacuzzi with him. ***

Bachelor Party (1984)................................. Tracey

1:11 - Full frontal nudity in the hotel bedroom with Tom Hanks as his bachelor party "present." **

Hard to Hold (1984)................................... Wife #1

Love Scenes (1984)................................ Uncredited

1:11 - Full frontal nudity making love with "Rick" on bed. ***

The Big Bet (1985)............ Fantasy Girl in Elevator

0:51 - In purple bra, then eventually nude in elevator with "Chris." ***

Hot Moves (1985).. Babs

0:29 - Nude on the nude beach. *

1:07 - Topless on and behind the sofa with "Barry" trying to get her top off. **

The Rosebud Beach Hotel (1985).................... Lisa

0:22 - Topless and buns undressing in hotel room with two other girls. She's on the right. **

0:44 - Topless taking off her red top in basement with two other girls and two guys. **

0:56 - In black see-through nightie in hotel room with Peter Scolari. *

Screen Test (1985).................................... Roxanne

0:06 - Topless taking off clothes in back room in front of a young boy. **

0:42 - Nude, with another topless woman, seducing a boy in his day dream. ***

1:21 - Topless in bar. *

Young Lady Chatterley II (1986).............. Eunice

0:15 - Topless in the woods with the Gardener. **

0:43 - Topless in bed with "Virgil." ***

Weekend Warriors (1986)......... Showgirl on plane

0:51 - Brief topless taking off top with other showgirls. **

Penthouse Love Stories (1986)
.... "Monique" and "AC/DC" segments

0:01 - Nude in bedroom entertaining herself. A must for Monique fans! ***

0:18 - Nude making love with another woman. ***

Deathstalker II (1987)
...............................Reena the Seer/Princess Evie

0:57 - Brief topless getting dress torn off by guards. *

1:01 - Topless making love with Deathstalker. ***

1:24 - Topless, laughing during the blooper scenes during the closing credits. *

Up 'N' Coming (1987)........................ Boat Girl #1

0:39 - Topless wearing white shorts on boat. Long shot. *

0:40 - More brief nude shots on the boat. *

Amazon Women on the Moon (1987)
.... Taryn Steele

0:05 - Nude during "Penthouse Video" sketch. Long sequence of her nude in unlikely places. ***

Silk 2 (1989).........................Jenny "Silk" Sleighton

0:27 - Topless, then full frontal nudity taking a shower while killer stalks around outside. ***

0:28 - Very, very brief blurry right breast in open robe when she's on the sofa during fight. **

0:29 - Brief topless doing a round house kick on the bad buy. Right breast several times during the fight. *

0:55 - Topless taking off her blouse and making love on bed. Too much diffusion! ***

Made for HBO:

Dream On: 555-HELL (1990)............ Scuba Lady

0:07 - Topless wearing a scuba mask and bikini bottom when she opens the door. **

Magazines:

Penthouse (Dec 1982).. Pet
Pages 105-123

Playboy (Nov 1982)............. "Sex in Cinema 1982"
 Page 163: Topless still from "Night Shift." **
Playboy (Jul 1989).................... "B-Movie Bimbos"
 Page 131: Full frontal nudity sitting on a
 car/helicopter. ***

GALIK, DENISE
Films:
 The Happy Hooker (1975)............................Cynthia
 California Suite (1978)....................................Bunny
 Humanoids from the Deep (1980).........Linda Beale
 Melvin and Howard (1980) ....Lucy
 Partners (1982)..Clara
 Get Crazy (1983) ....
 Eye of the Tiger (1987)................................Christie
Made for HBO:
 The Hitchhiker: Dead Heat...........................Arielle
  0:20 - Topless taking off blouse and standing up
  with "Cal" in the barn, then right breast lying
  down in the hay with him. **

GANNES, GAYLE
Films:
 The Prey (1980)..Gail
  0:36 - Brief topless putting T-shirt on before the
  creature attacks her. *
 Hot Moves (1985)...Jamie
  1:09 - Topless in bed with Joey. **

GANZEL, TERESA
Films:
 The Toy (1982)......................................Fancy Bates
 C.O.D. (1983)... Lisa Foster
  0:46 - Right breast hanging out of dress while
  dancing at disco with "Zack." *
  1:25 - Brief side view of left breast taking off
  purple robe in dressing room scene. Then in
  white bra talking to "Albert." *
  1:29 - In white bra during fashion show.
Made for TV Movies:
 Rest In Peace, Mrs. Columbo (1990)... Dede Perkins

GARBER, TERRI
Films:
 Toy Soldiers (1983)...................................... Amy
  0:18 - Brief right breast taking off her tank top
  when the army guys force her. Her head is
  down. *
Miniseries:
 North and South (1985) ....Ashton Main
 North and South: Book II (1986).........Ashton Main
TV:
 Mr. Smith (1983) ....Dr. Judy Tyson
 Dynasty...Leslie

GARR, TERI
Films:
 Head (1968)..Testy True
 Young Frankenstein (1974; B&W)................... Inga
 The Conversation (1974) .... Amy
 Won Ton Ton, The Dog Who Saved Hollywood
  (1976)..Fluffy Peters
 Close Encounters of the Third Kind (1977)
  ....Ronnie Neary
 Oh God! (1977)...........................Bobbie Landers
 The Black Stallion (1979)..................Alec's Mother
 Mr. Mike's Mondo Video (1979)...........................
 Honky Tonk Freeway (1981).......................Ericka
 The Escape Artist (1982) ....Arlene
 The Black Stallion Returns (1983).....Alec's Mother
 Mr. Mom (1983)....................................Caroline
 One From the Heart (1983) ....Frannie
  0:09 - Brief topless getting out of the shower. **
  0:10 - In a bra, getting dressed in bedroom.
  0:40 - Side view of right breast changing in.
  bedroom while Frederic Forrest watches. **
  1:20 - Brief topless in bed when standing up after
  Forrest drops in though the roof while she's in
  bed with Raul Julia. ***
 The Sting II (1983)...............................Veronica
 Tootsie (1983)...................................... Sandy
 Firstborn (1984) ....
 After Hours (1985)...................................Julie
 Miracles (1986)...
 Full Moon in Blue Water (1988)...................Louise
  0:50 - Walking around in Gene Hackman's bar in
  a bra while changing blouses and talking to him.
 Out Cold (1988) ....Sunny Cannald
 Let It Ride (1989)...................................... Pam
Faerie Tale Theatre:
 Tale of the Frog Prince (1982)................................
Made for TV Movies:
 To Catch a King (1983) ....
 Fresno (1986) ....Talon Kensington
TV:
 The Ken Berry "Wow" Show (1972)............regular
 Burns and Schreiber Comedy Hour (1973)....regular
 Girl with Something Extra (1973-74)............ Amber
 The Sonny and Cher Comedy Hour (1973-74)
  ....regular
 The Sonny Comedy Revue (1974).................regular

GAVIN, ERICA
Films:
 Vixen (1968)..
 Caged Heat (1974)......................Jacqueline Wilson
 a.k.a. Renegade Girls
  0:08 - Buns, getting strip searched before entering
  prison. *
  0:25 - Topless in shower scene. **
  0:30 - Brief side view of left breast in another
  shower scene. *

GAVIN, MARY

Films:
Fantasm (1976; Australian)..
Superchick (1978)............................. Lady on Boat
   0:08 - Topless in bed with "Johnny" on boat. ***

GAYBIS, ANNE

Other:
   a.k.a. Annie Gaybis.
Films:
Fairytales (1979).................................. Snow White
   0:21 - Nude in room with the seven little dwarfs
   singing and dancing. ***
10 Violent Women (1982)............................... Vickie
The Lost Empire (1985)...
Hollywood Zap! (1986)...............................Debbie

GEESON, JUDY

Films:
To Sir, with Love (1967; British)......... Pamela Dare
Berserk (1967; British)....................... Angela Rivers
The Executioner (1970; British)........... Polly Bendel
10 Rillington Place (1971; British) .... Beryl Evans
Fear in the Night (1972; British)..........Peggy Heller
Brannigan (1975; British)..............Jennifer Thatcher
Carry on England (1976; British).............................
Horror Planet (1980; British)....................... Sandy
   a.k.a. Inseminoid
   0:31 - Brief topless on the operating table. **
   0:37 - Same scene during brief flashback. *
Here We Go Round the Mulberry Bush
   .... Mary Gloucester
   Nude, swimming.

GEFFNER, DEBORAH

Films:
All That Jazz (1979)................................... Victoria
   0:17 - Brief topless taking off her blouse and
   walking up the stairs while Roy Scheider
   watches. A little out of focus. *
Star 80 (1983)... Billie
Exterminator 2 (1984) .... Caroline
Magazines:
Playboy (Mar 1980)...................... "All That Fosse"
   Page 177: Topless sitting on couch. **

GEMSER, LAURA

Other:
   a.k.a. Moira Chen.
Films:
Black Emmanuelle (1976).................. Emmanuelle
   0:00 - Brief topless daydreaming on airplane. *
   0:19 - Left breast in car kissing a guy at night. *
   0:27 - Topless in shower with a guy. **
   0:30 - Full frontal nudity making love with a guy
   in bed. ***

   0:37 - Topless taking pictures with Karin
   Schubert. ***
   0:41 - Full frontal nudity lying on bed dreaming
   about the day's events while masturbating, then
   full frontal nudity walking around . **
   0:49 - Topless in studio with "Johnny." **
   0:52 - Brief right breast making love on the side of
   the road. *
   0:52 - Full frontal nudity by the pool kissing
   "Gloria." ***
   1:00 - Nude, taking a shower, then answering the
   phone. **
   1:04 - Topless on boat after almost drowning. **
   1:08 - Full frontal nudity dancing with African
   tribe, then making love with the leader. **
   1:14 - Full frontal nudity taking off clothes by
   waterfall with "Johnny." **
   1:23 - Topless making love with the field hockey
   team on a train. **
Emmanuelle's Amazon Adventure (1977)
   .... Emmanuelle
   0:17 - Brief left breast in flashback sequence in
   bed with a man. *
   0:21 - Brief topless making love in bed. *
   0:25 - Brief topless in the water with a blonde
   woman. *
   1:10 - Full frontal nudity painting her body. **
   1:11 - Brief topless in boat. *
   1:13 - Nude walking out of the water trying to
   save "Isabelle." *
   1:14 - Brief topless getting into the boat with
   "Isabelle." *
Emmanuelle in Bangkok (1977) .... Emmanuelle
   0:07 - Topless making love with a guy. **
   0:12 - Full frontal nudity changing in her hotel
   room. **
   0:17 - Full frontal nudity getting a bath, then
   massaged by another woman. ***
   0:35 - Topless during orgy sequence. **
   0:53 - Topless in room with a woman, then taking
   a shower. **
   1:01 - Topless in tent with a guy and woman. **
   1:08 - Full frontal nudity dancing in a group of
   guys. **
   1:16 - Full frontal nudity taking a bath with a
   woman. **
   1:18 - Topless on bed making love with a guy. **
Two Super Cops (1978; Italian)................. Susy Lee
Emmanuelle the Seductress (1979; Greek)
   .... Emmanuelle
   0:01 - Full frontal nudity lying in bed with
   "Mario." *
   0:02 - Brief topless riding horse on the beach. *
   0:42 - Topless making love then full frontal nudity
   getting dressed with "Tommy." **
   0:48 - Topless undressing in bedroom, then in
   white panties, then nude talking to "Alona."
   ***
   0:54 - Topless walking around in a skirt. **
   1:02 - Topless outside taking a shower, then on
   lounge chair making love with "Tommy." **

Bushido Blade (1979; British/U.S.)............. Tomoe
   1:08 - Brief right breast taking off her top in
     bedroom with "Captain Hawk." *
Famous T & A (1982)................................. herself
   0:55 - Topless scenes from "Emmanuelle Around
     the World." ***
Absurd - Antrophagous 2 (1982).........................
Ator: The Fighting Eagle (1983) ....
Caged Women (1984; French/Italian)
   ....Emmanuelle/Laura
a.k.a. Women's Prison Massacre
Endgame (1983)... Lilith
   1:10 - Brief topless a couple of times getting
     blouse ripped open by a gross looking guy. *
Magazines:
Playboy (May 1979)................. "Foreign Sex Stars"
   Page 170-171: Nude. **

GEORGE, SUSAN

Films:
The Looking Glass War (1970; British).......... Susan
Straw Dogs (1972)..Amy
   0:32 - Topless taking off sweater, tossing it down
     to Dustin Hoffman, then looking out the door at
     the workers. **
   1:00 - Topless on couch getting raped by one of
     the construction workers. ***
Die Screaming Marianne (1972) .... Marianne
Dirty Mary, Crazy Larry (1974)....................... Mary
Out of Season (1975).....................................
Mandingo (1975)...................................... Blanche
   1:36 - Brief topless in bed with Ken Norton. *
Small Town in Texas (1976) ....Mary Lee
Tintorera (1977)...................................... Gabriella
   0:42 - Very brief topless waking up "Steve." *
Enter the Ninja (1981) ....Mary-Ann Landers
Venom (1982)..Louise
Summer Heat (1983).....................................
The Jigsaw Man (1984) ....Penny
House Where Evil Dwells (1985)...................Laura
   0:21 - Topless in bed making love with Edward
     Albert. ***
   0:59 - Topless making love again. **
Lightning, The White Stallion (1986)
   .... Madame Rene
Made for TV Movies:
Jack the Ripper (1988).............................. Catherine
Magazines:
Playboy (Nov 1972)............. "Sex in Cinema 1972"
   Page 160: Topless on couch from "The Straw
     Dogs." **
Playboy (Dec 1972)................... "Sex Stars of 1972"
   Page 208 - Topless. **

GERSHON, GINA

Films:
Sweet Revenge (1987).....................................K.C. *
   0:41 - Brief topless in water under a waterfall with
     "Lee." *
   3:15 - The Moment of Truth (1987)
   ....One of the Cobrettes
Red Heat (1988)....................................Cat Manzetti
Cocktail (1988)..................................... Coral
   0:31 - Very, very brief right breast romping
     around in bed with Tom Cruise. *

GIBB, CYNTHIA

Films:
Salvador (1986)...................................Cathy Moore
Youngblood (1986)....................Jessie Chadwick
   0:50 - Brief topless and buns making love with
     Rob Lowe in his room. *
Modern Girls (1986)... Cece
Malone (1987)..Jo
Jack's Back (1987).............................Chris Moscari
   1:00 - Getting undressed in white camisole and
     panties while someone watches her from
     outside.
   1:30 - Running around the house in a white slip
     trying to get away from the killer.
Short Circuit 2 (1988) ....Sandy Banatoni
Made for TV Movies:
When We Were Young (1989).........................Ellen
The Karen Carpenter Story (1989)..Karen Carpenter
TV:
Search for Tomorrow (1981-83). Suzi Wyatt Martin
Fame (1983-86)...............................Holly Laird

GIBLIN, BELINDA

Films:
Jock Petersen (1975; Australian).......Moira Winton
   0:21 - Left breast several times, under a cover with
     "Jock," then buns when cover is removed. **
End Play (1975; Australian)............ Margret Gifford
Demolition (1977)...
The Empty Beach (1985)...................Marion Singer

GIFTOS, ELAINE

Films:
Gas-s-s! (1970)..
On a Clear Day You Can See Forever (1970)..........
The Student Nurses (1970)........................ Sharon
   1:14 - Brief topless undressing and getting into
     bed with terminally ill boy. Dark, hard to see. *
Everything You Wanted to Know About Sex, But
   We're Afraid to Ask (1972) ....Mrs. Ross
The Wrestler (1974)..Debbie
Paternity (1981)................................ Woman in Bar
Angel (1984)......................................Patricia Allen

GILBERT, MELISSA

Other:
Older sister of actress Sara Gilbert.
Films:
Sylvester (1985).. Charlie
   0:23 - Very, very brief topless struggling with a
     guy in truck cab. Seen through a dirty
     windshield. *
   0:24 - Very brief left breast after Richard
     Farnsworth runs down the stairs to help her.
     Seen from the open door of the truck. **
Ice House (1988) .... Kay
   0:51 - Making love with another guy while her
     real-life husband watches while he's tied up.
Made for TV Movies:
The Miracle Worker (1979) .... Helen Keller
The Diary of Anne Frank (1980) .... Anne Frank
Killer's Instinct (1989) ....
Forbidden Nights (1990) ....
TV:
Little House on the Prairie (1974-83)
   ....Laura Ingalls Wilder

GILBERT, PAMELA

Films:
Evil Spawn (1987) .... Elaine Talbot
   0:46 - Nude taking off black lingerie and going
     swimming in pool. Hubba, hubba! ***
   0:49 - Topless in the pool, then full frontal nudity
     getting out. ***
Demonwrap (1988) .... Carrie

GILDERSLEEVE, LINDA

Films:
Cinderella (1977) .... Farm Girl (redhead)
   0:21 - Topless and buns with her brunette "sister"
     in their house making love with the guy who is
     looking for "Cinderella." ***
   1:24 - Full frontal nudity with her sister again
     when the Prince goes around to try and find
     "Cinderella." **
The Happy Hooker Goes Hollywood (1977)
   .... Honeymoon Couple
   0:35 - Brief topless in a diner during the filming of
     a commercial. *
Beach Bunnies (1977) ....

GLAZOWSKI, LIZ

Films:
The Happy Hooker Goes Hollywood (1980) .... Liz
Magazines:
Playboy (Apr 1980) .... Playmate

GOLDSMITH, CLIO

Films:
Honey (1981) .... Annie
   0:05 - Nude kneeling in a room. **
   0:20 - Nude getting into the bathtub. **
   0:42 - Nude getting changed. **
   0:44 - Topless hiding under the bed. ***
   0:58 - Nude getting disciplined , taking off
     clothes, then kneeling. **
Plein Sud (The Heat of Desire) (1982) .... Carol
The Gift (1982; French) .... Barbara
   0:39 - Brief topless several times in the bathroom,
     then right breast in bathtub. **
   0:49 - Topless lying in bed sleeping. *
   0:51 - Very brief left breast turning over in bed.
   0:52 - Brief right breast then buns, reaching for
     phone while lying in bed. *
   1:16 - Very brief left breast getting out of bed.
     Dark, hard to see.
La Cicala (The Cricket) (1983; Italian) .... Cicala
   0:26 - Nude when "Wilma" brings her in to get
     Anthony Franciosa excited again. **
   0:39 - Nude swimming under waterfall with
     Barbara de Rossi. **
   0:43 - Full frontal nudity undressing in room with
     de Rossi. ***

GOLINO, VALERIA

Films:
Blind Date (1982) .... Girl in Bikini
   (<u>NOT</u> the same 1987 "Blind Date" with Bruce
     Willis.)
Detective School Dropouts (1986) .... Caterina
Rain Man (1988) .... Suzanna
   0:35 - Very brief left breast four times and very,
     very brief right breast once with open blouse
     fighting with Tom Cruise after getting out of the
     bathtub. *
Big Top Pee Wee (1988) .... Gina Piccolapupula

GOODFELLOW, JOAN

Films:
Lolly-Madonna XXX (1973) .... Sister Gutshall
Buster and Billie (1974) .... Billie
   0:33 - Brief topless in truck with Jan-Michael
     Vincent. Dark, hard to see.
   1:06 - Buns, then brief topless in the woods with
     Vincent. *
   1:25 - Brief left breast getting raped by jerks. *
Sunburn (1979) ....
A Flash of Green (1984) .... Mitchie

GRANT, FAYE

Films:
Internal Affairs (1990)................................. Penny
    0:50 - Right breast straddling Richard Gere while
    talking on the telephone. *
Miniseries:
    V: The Final Battle (1984)............. Dr. Julie Parrish
Movies:
    V (1983)... Dr. Julie Parrish
TV:
    Greatest American Hero (1981-83) .... Rhonda Blake
    V (1984-85) .... Dr. Julie Parrish

GRANT, LEE

Other:
    Mother of actress Dinah Manoff.
Films:
    Valley of the Dolls (1967) ....Miriam
    In the Heat of the Night (1967).. Mrs. Leslie Colbert
    Marooned (1969) ....Celia Pruett
    There Was a Crooked Man (1970)........Mrs. Bullard
    Plaza Suite (1971)..............................Norma Hubley
    Portnoy's Complaint (1972)............. Sophie Portnoy
    Shampoo (1975)................................Felicia
    0:03 - Brief topless in bed sitting up and putting
    bra on talking to Warren Beatty. Long shot,
    hard to see. *
    Airport '77 (1977)..............................Karen Wallace
    Damien, Omen II (1978)......................... Ann Thorn
    The Mafu Cage (1978).....................................Ellen
    a.k.a. My Sister, My Love
    When Ya Comin' Back Red Ryder (1979)
    ....Clarisse Ethridge
    (Not available on video tape yet.)
    Little Miss Marker (1980) .... The Judge
    Charlie Chan and the Curse of the Dragon Queen
    (1981)..............................Mrs. Lupowitz
    Visiting Hours (1982; Canadian)......Deborah Ballin
    Teachers (1984) ....Dr. Burke
    The Big Town (1987)....................................
Made for TV Movies:
    The Neon Ceiling (1971) ....
Miniseries:
    Backstairs at the White House (1979)
    .... Grace Coolidge
TV:
    Peyton Place (1965-66)......................Stella Chernak
    Fay (1975-76).......................................Fay Stewart

GRAY, JULIE

Films:
    Stryker (1983; Philippines)...........................Laurenz
    School Spirit (1985).....................................Kendall
    Dr. Alien (1989)... Karla
    0:44 - In white bra, then topless in Janitor's room
    with "Wesley." ***

GRIER, PAM

Other:
    Cousin of actor/former football player Rosey Grier.
Films:
    The Big Doll House (1971)............................. Grear
    The Big Bird Cage (1972).........................Blossom
    Cool Breeze (1972)..
    Topless.
    Twilight People (1972)............ The Panther Woman
    Naked Warriors (1973)............................Mamawi
    a.k.a. The Arena
    0:08 - Brief left breast, then lower frontal nudity
    and side view of right breast getting washed
    down in court yard. **
    0:52 - Topless getting oiled up for a battle. Wow!
    ***
    Coffy (1973).. Coffy
    0:05 - Upper half of right breast in bed with a guy.
    *
    0:19 - Buns, walking past the fireplace, seen
    through a fish tank
    0:25 - Topless in open dress getting attacked by
    two masked burglars. **
    0:38 - Buns and topless undressing in bedroom.
    Wow! ***
    0:42 - Brief right breast when breast pops out of
    dress while she's leaning over. Dark, hard to
    see. *
    0:49 - In black bra and panties in open dress with
    a guy in the bedroom.
    Scream, Blacula, Scream (1973)............Lisa Fortier
    Foxy Brown (1974)....................... Foxy Brown
    Bucktown (1975).. Aretha
    Friday Foster (1975)...........................Friday Foster
    Sheba, Baby (1975)......................Sheba Shayne
    Drum (1976)... Regine
    0:58 - Very brief topless getting undressed and
    into bed with "Maxwell." *
    Greased Lightning (1977)......................Mary Jones
    Fort Apache, The Bronx (1981).................Charlotte
    Something Wicked this Way Comes (1983)
    ....Dust Witch
    Tough Enough (1983)......................................Mura
    Stand Alone (1985).................................Catherine
    On the Edge (1985)... Cora
    (Unrated version - <u>not</u> the R rated version.)
    0:18 - In leotards, leading an aerobics dance class.
    0:42 - Topless in the mirror, then full frontal
    nudity making lvoe with Bruce Dern standing
    up. Then brief left breast. A little dark. **
    Vindicator (1986).. Hunter
    The All Nighter (1987)....................................
    Above the Law (1988) ....Delores "Jacks" Jackson
    Class of 1999 (1990)....................................
Made for TV Movies:
    Badge of the Assassin (1985)..............................
Magazines:
    Playboy (Nov 1972)............. "Sex in Cinema 1972"
    Page 162: Topless, sitting on Thalmus Rasulala.
    **

Playboy (Nov 1973).............."Sex in Cinema 1973"
Page 154: Topless and buns. **
Playboy (Dec 1973)................. "Sex Stars of 1973"
Page 205: Left breast. *

GRIFFETH, SIMONE

Films:
Death Race 2000 (1975)..................... Annie Smith
0:32 - Side view of left breast holding David
Carradine. Dark, hard to see. *
0:56 - Topless and buns getting undressed and
lying on bed with Carradine. ***
Fighting Back (1980)..
Hot Target (1985)........................ Christine Webber
0:09 - Topless taking off top for shower, then
topless and brief frontal nudity taking shower.
**
0:19 - Topless in bed after making love with Steve
Marachuck. ***
0:21 - Buns, getting out of bed and walking to
bathroom. **
0:23 - Topless in bed with Marachuck again. **
0:34 - Topless in the woods with Marachuck while
cricket match goes on. *
The Patriot (1986)... Sean
0:46 - Brief topless lying in bed, making love with
"Ryder." **

TV:
Ladies' Man (1980-81).............................. Gretchen
Bret Maverick (1982)......................Jasmine DuBois
Amanda's (1983)..........................Arlene Cartwright

GRIFFITH, MELANIE

Other:
Daughter of actress Tippi Hedren.
Films:
Smile (1974)... Karen Love
0:07 - Brief glimpse at panties, bending over to
pick up dropped box.
0:34 - Very, very brief side view of right breast in
dressing room, just before passing behind a rack
of clothes. *
0:47 - Very brief side view of right breast, then
side view of left breast when "Little Bob" is
outside taking pictures. *
0:48 - Very brief topless as Polaroid photograph
that "Little Bob" took develops. *
1:51 - Topless in the same Polaroid in the
policeman's sunvisor. *
Night Moves (1975)........................ Delly Grastner
0:42 - Brief topless changing tops outside while
talking with Gene Hackman. *
0:46 - Nude, saying "hi" from under water beneath
a glass bottom boat. *
0:47 - Brief side view of right breast getting out of
the water. *
The Drowning Pool (1975) ...... Schuuler Devereaux
One on One (1977).................................Hitchhiker

The Garden (1977)...
Joyride (1977)..Susie
0:05 - Topless in back of station wagon with
Robert Carradine, hard to see anything. *
0:59 - Brief topless in Jacuzzi with everybody. **
1:11 - Brief topless in shower with Desi Arnaz, Jr.
*
Underground Aces (1980) ....
Roar (1981)......................................Melanie
Body Double (1984)............................Holly Body
0:21 - Topless dancing around in bedroom while
Craig Wasson watches through a telescope. **
0:28 - Topless in bedroom again while Wasson
and the "Indian" welding on the satellite dish
watch. *
1:12 - Topless and buns on TV.
1:25 - In lingerie in house with Wasson.
Fear City (1984)................................... Loretta
0:04 - Buns, in blue G-string, dancing on stage.
0:07 - Topless, dancing on stage. **
0:23 - Topless dancing on stage wearing a red G-
string. ***
Something Wild (1986)......."Lulu"/Audrey Hankel
0:16 - Topless in bed with Jeff Daniels. ***
0:25 - Topless and buns standing in the window.
*
The Milagro Beanfield War (1988)...Flossie Devine
Stormy Monday (1988)..................................... Kate
Cherry 2000 (1988)................................. E. Johnson
0:19 - Topless in a shadow on the wall while
changing clothes.
Working Girl (1989)........................... Tess McGill
0:08 - In bra, panties, garter belt and stockings in
front of a mirror.
0:32 - In black bra, garter belt and stockings trying
on clothes.
0:43 - In black bra, garter belt and stockings
getting out of bed.
1:15 - In white bra, taking off her blouse with
Harrison Ford.
1:18 - Very, very brief right breast turning over in
bed with Ford. *
1:20 - Topless, vacuuming. Long shot seen from
the other end of the hall. *
Made for HBO:
Women & Men: Stories of Seduction (1990)
....Hadley
Made for TV Movies:
She's in the Army Now (1981)...............................
TV:
Once an Eagle (1976-77)..............Jinny Massengale
Carter Country (1978-79).................... Tracy Quinn
Magazines:
Playboy (Oct 1976)..........................."Fast Starter"
Pages 100-103: Nude. **
Playboy (Jan 1986)..........................."Double Take"
Page 94-103: Topless in buns in photos with Don
Johnson in photos that were taken in 1976. **

GRIFFITH, TRACY
Films:
Fear City (1984)......................................
The Good Mother (1988)........................ Babe
  0:06 - Brief topless opening her blouse to show a
  young "Anna" what it's like being pregnant. *
Fast Food (1989)................................Samantha
Sleepaway Camp 3: Teenage Wasteland (1989).....

GRUBEL, ILONA
Films:
Jonathan (1973; German)...........................Eleanore
Target (1985).....................................Carla
  1:12 - Brief topless in bed with Matt Dillon. *

GUERRA, BLANCA
Films:
Falcon's Gold (1982)..................................
Robbers of the Sacred Mountain (1982)...................
Erendira (1984; Mexican/French/German)
  ....Ulysses' Mother
Separate Vacations (1985)........................... Alicia
  0:56 - Topless on the bed with David Naughton
  when she turns out to be a hooker. *
Walker (1988)................................Yrena

GUERRERO, EVELYN
Films:
Wild Wheels (1969)..Sissy
Trackdown (1976) .... Social Worker
The Toolbox Murders (1978)........................... Butch
Fairytales (1979)................................S & M Dancer
  0:38 - Topless wearing masks with 2 other blonde
  S & M Dancers. **
  0:56 - Full frontal nudity dancing with the other S
  & M Dancers again. **
Cheech & Chong's Next Movie (1980)
  .... Welfare Office Worker
Cheech & Chong's Nice Dreams (1981)......Donna
  0:43 - Brief left breast sticking out of her spandex
  outfit, sitting down at table in restaurant. *
  0:56 - In burgundy lingerie in her apartment with
  Cheech Marin.
Things are Tough all Over (1982).................Donna
Magazines:
Playboy (Sep 1980)......... "Lights, Camera, Chaos!"
  Page 103: Nude. ***

GUNDEN, SCARLETT
Films:
Island of 1000 Delights (German)............. Francine
  0:02 - Topless on beach dancing with "Ching."
  Upper half of buns sitting down. ***
  0:20 - Dancing braless in sheer brown dress.
  0:44 - Full frontal nudity getting tortured by
  "Ming." **
  1:16 - Topless on beach after "Ching" rescues her.
  *

Melody in Love (1978) ....Angela
  0:17 - Full frontal nudity taking off dress and
  dancing in front of statue. ***
  0:50 - Nude with a guy on a boat. ***
  0:53 - Topless on another boat with "Octavio." **
  0:59 - Buns and topless in bed talking to "Rachel."
  **
  1:12 - Full frontal nudity getting a tan on boat with
  "Rachel." **
  1:14 - Topless making love in bed with "Rachel"
  and "Octavio." *

GUTHRIE, LYNNE
Films:
Night Call Nurses (1972)...........................Cynthia
  0:00 - Topless on hospital roof taking off robe and
  standing on edge just before jumping off. *
The Working Girls (1974)................................Jill
  0:43 - Topless, dancing on stage at club. ***
  0:48 - Topless in swimming pool with "Nick." **
Tears of Happiness (1974)......................................

GUTTERIDGE, LUCY
Films:
Top Secret (1984)...............................Hillary
The Trouble with Spies (1984).............. Mona Smith
Tusks (1990).. Micah Hill
  0:23 - Topless in tub taking a bath. **
Made for HBO:
The Hitchhiker: In the Name of Love .... Jackie
  0:08 - Topless on bed talking to herself about
  "Billy" after unzipping and opening the top of
  her dress. *
  0:17 - Topless making love with Greg Evigan. **
  0:21 - Topless in black and white photos that
  accidentally fall out of envelope.
Miniseries:
Little Gloria...Happy At Last! (1982) ....
Till We Meet Again (1989)................................ Eve
Made for TV Movies:
The Woman He Loved (1988) ....Thelma

H

HACKETT, JOAN
Films:
The Group (1966).............................Dottie Renfrew
Will Penny (1968)...........................Catherine Allen
Support Your Local Sheriff! (1969)....Prudy Perkins
The Terminal Man (1974)..................Dr. Janet Ross
One Trick Pony (1980)........................Lonnie Fox
  1:21 - Nude getting out of bed and getting dressed
  while talking to Paul Simon. ***
Only When I Laugh (1981)..............................Toby
The Escape Artist (1982) ....Aunt Sybil
Flicks (1985) ....
Reflections of Murder (1987)................................

Made for TV Movies:
Paper Dolls (1982)...
TV:
The Defenders (1961-62).........................Joan Miller
Another Day (1978)............................Ginny Gardner

HADDON, DAYLE
Films:
The World's Greatest Athlete (1973).................Jane
The Cheaters (1976; Italian)......................................
Spermula (1976).......................................Spermula
Sex with a Smile (1976)............................The Girl
    0:23 - Topless, covered with bubbles in the
      bathtub. **
    0:43 - Buns, taking off robe to take a shower, then
      brief topless with Marty Feldman. *
The Last Romantic Lover (1978)...........................
    0:56 - Topless.
The French Woman (1979)......................Elizabeth
    0:15 - Very, very brief topless in dressing room. *
    0:49 - Topless on bed with "Madame Claude." **
    0:55 - Topless kissing "Pierre", then buns while
      lying on the floor. *
    1:10 - In two piece swimsuit on sailboat.
    1:11 - Left breast, then buns on beach with
      "Frederick." *
North Dallas Forty (1979)..........................Charlotte
Cyborg (1989)....................................Pearl Prophet
Made for HBO:
Bedroom Eyes (1985).......................................Alixe
    1:06 - Getting undressed in tap pants and white
      camisole top while "Harry" watches in the
      mirror.
The Hitchhiker: Ghost Writer ....Debby Hunt
    (Available on video tape in Hitchhiker III.)
    0:05 - In black slip kissing Barry Bostwick.
    0:14 - Topless and buns, getting into hot tub with
      Willem DaFoe before trying to drown him. *
Magazines:
Playboy (Apr 1973)................ "Disney's Latest Hit"
    Pages 147-153: Topless and buns. ***
Playboy (Dec 1973).................. "Sex Stars of 1973"
    Page 209: Topless. **

HAHN, GISELA
Films:
They Call Me Trinity (1971; Italian)................Sarah
Julia (1974; German)...................................Miriam
    0:12 - Topless tanning herself outside. **
    1:14 - Brief topless sitting in the rain. *

HAHN, JESSICA
Other:
The woman in the TV evangelist Jim Bakker
    scandal.
Music Videos:
"Wild Thing" by comedian Sam Kinison.

Magazines:
Playboy (Nov 1987). "Jessica, On Her Own Terms"
    Pages 90-99: Topless. ***
Playboy (Dec 1987)................... "Sex Stars of 1987"
    Page 157: Topless. ***
Playboy (Feb 1988)...................... "The Year in Sex"
    Page 128: Topless wearing a hat. ***
Playboy (Sep 1988).................................. "Jessica"
    Pages 118-127: Nude. ***
Playboy (Dec 1988)................... "Sex Stars of 1988"
    Page 188: Topless. ***
Playboy (Jan 1989).......... "Women of the Eighties"
    Page 257: Full frontal nudity. ***
Playboy (Feb 1989)...................... "The Year in Sex"
    Page 137: Left breast.

HAJEK, GWENDOLYN
Films:
Traxx (1988)...Playmate
Magazines:
Playboy (Sep 1987)..................................Playmate
    Page 98

HALLIGAN, ERIN
Films:
I'm Dancing as Fast as I Can (1982) ....Denise
Joysticks (1983)...Sandy
    1:08 - Right breast, then topless in bed with
      "Jefferson" surrounded by candles. **

HAMILTON, JANE
Other:
a.k.a. Adult film actress Veronica Hart.
Films:
Delivery Boys (1984)..................................Art Snob
Sex Appeal (1986)..Monica
    0:58 - Topless dancing on the bed with "Tony" in
      his apartment. ***
Slammer Girls (1987)..
Wimps (1987)..Tracy
    0:40 - Lifting up her sweater and shaking her
      breasts in the back of the car with "Francis."
      Too dark to see anything. *
    0:44 - Topless and buns taking off sweater in a
      restaurant. **
Student Affairs (1987).............................Veronica
    0:48 - Topless changing in dressing room,
      showing herself off to a guy. **
    0:51 - Brief topless in a school room during a
      movie. *
    0:56 - In black lingerie outfit, then topless in
      bedroom while she tape records everything. **
New York's Finest (1988)............................Bunny
Sensations (1988)..Tippy

Cleo/Leo (1989).................................... Cleo Clock
  0:13 - Nude undressing in front of three guys. **
  0:21 - Topless changing in dressing room. *
  0:22 - Topless changing in dressing room with the "Store Clerk." ***
  0:40 - In bra and panties.
  1:07 - Left breast and lower frontal nudity making love with "Bob" on bed. **
Bedroom Eyes II (1989)...............JoBeth McKenna
  0:50 - Topless knifing Linda Blair then fighting with Wings Hauser. *

HAMILTON, LINDA
Films:
  Children of the Corn (1984)................. Vicky Baxter
  The Terminator (1984)..................... Sarah Connor
    1:18 - Brief topless about four times making love on top of Michael Biehn in motel room. **
  Black Moon Rising (1986)..............................Nina
    0:50 - Brief left breast, making love in bed with Tommy Lee Jones. *
  King Kong Lives! (1986)................... Amy Franklin
    0:47 - Very, very brief right breast getting out of sleeping bag after camping out near King Kong. *
Made for TV Movies:
  Rape and Marriage: The Rideout Case (1980).......
  Secrets of a Mother and Daughter (1983).................
  Secret Weapons (1985)...
  Club Med (1986)...Kate
  Go Toward the Light (1988)............. Claire Madison
TV:
  Secrets of Midland Heights (1980-81)...Lisa Rogers
  King's Crossing (1982)................... Lauren Hollister
  Beauty and the Beast (1987-90)................. Catherine

HAMILTON, SUZANNA
Films:
  Brimstone and Treacle (1982).......... Patricia Bates
    0:47 - Topless in bed when Sting open her top and fondles her. **
    1:18 - Topless in bed when Sting fondles her again. **
    1:20 - Brief lower frontal nudity writhing around on the bed after Denholm Elliott comes downstairs. *
  1984 (1984)...................................... Julia
    0:38 - Full frontal nudity taking off her clothes in the woods with John Hurt. **
    0:52 - Nude in secret room standing and drinking and talking to Hurt. Long scene. ***
    1:11 - Side view of left breast kneeling down. *
    1:12 - Topless after picture falls off the view screen on the wall. **
  Wetherby (1985)...............................Karen Creasy
    0:42 - In white lingerie top and bottom.
    1:03 - In white lingerie getting into bed and lying down.
    1:06 - In white lingerie fighting with "John."

HANNAH, DARYL
Films:
  The Final Terror (1981) ....Wendy
  Bladerunner (1982)...Pris
  Summer Lovers (1982)............. Cathy Featherstone
    0:07 - Very brief topless getting out of bed. *
    0:17 - In a two piece swimsuit.
    0:54 - Buns, lying on rock with Valerie Quennessen watching "Michael" dive off a rock.
    0:56 - In a swimsuit again.
    1:03 - Brief right breast sweeping the balcony. *
  The Pope of Greenwich Village (1984)...........Diane
  Reckless (1984).............................. Tracey Prescott
    0:48 - In a white bra fighting in gymnasium with "Johnny" then in pool area in bra and panties.
    0:52 - Topless in furnace room of school making love with "Johnny." Lit with red light. ***
  Splash (1984) .... Madison
    Buns, walking around the Statue of Liberty.
    Topless, but her hair is taped over nipples.
  Clan of the Cave Bear (1985)........................... Ayla
  Legal Eagles (1986) ....Chelsea Deardon
  Roxanne (1987)..........................Roxanne Kowalski
  Wall Street (1987)...........................Darian Taylor
  High Spirits (1988)........................... Mary Plunkett
  Steel Magnolias (1989)........ Annelle Dupuy Desoto
Made for TV Movies:
  Paper Dolls (1982) .... Taryn Blake
Music Videos:
  Jackson Browne/Tender is the Night

HANSON, KRISTINE
TV:
  Channel 3, KCRA in Sacramento, California
  ....Weatherperson
  Channel 7, KGO in San Francisco, California
  ....Weatherperson
Magazines:
  Playboy (Sep 1974).................................. Playmate

HANSON, MARCY
Films:
  10 (1979)...
TV:
  The Roller Girls (1978)................Honey Bee Novak
Magazines:
  Playboy (Oct 1978).................................. Playmate

HARGITAY, MARISKA
Films:
  Welcome to 18 (1986).................................... Joey
    0:26 - Buns, taking a shower when video camera is taping her. *
    0:43 - Watching herself on the videotape playback.
  Jocks (1986) ....Nicole

HARPER, JESSICA

Films:
Love and Death (1975)................................Natasha
Inserts (1976)......................................Cathy Cake
   1:15 - Topless in garter belt and stockings, lying in
   bed for Richard Dreyfus. Long scene . ***
Suspiria (1977; Italian)........................Susy Banyon
The Evictors (1979)..Ruth
Pennies from Heaven (1981)........................Joan
   0:43 - Brief topless opening her nightgown for
   Steve Martin. *
My Favorite Year (1982)....................K.C. Downing
Phantom of the Paradise (1974)..................Phoenix
Shock Treatment (1981).......................Janet Majors
Stardust Memories (1980; B&W)...............Violinist
The Imagemaker (1986)...........................Cynthia
The Blue Iguana (1988)..............................Cora
TV:
Aspen (1977)....................................Kit Pepe
Little Women (1979)..................................Jo March
Studs Logan (1979)..................................Loretta

HARRIS, LEE ANNE

Other:
a.k.a. Leigh Harris.
Twin sister of actress Lynette Harris.
Films:
I, the Jury (1982).. 1st twin
   0:48 - Topless on bed talking to Armand Asante.
   ***
   0:52 - Full frontal nudity on bed wearing red wig,
   talking to the maniac. *
Sorceress (1982)..................................... Mira
Magazines:
Playboy (Mar 1981).............. "My Sister, My Self"
   Pages 152-155: Topless and buns. ***
Playboy (Mar 1982)........................ "Aye, Barbara"
   Pages 152 - Topless in small photos from "I, the
   Jury." *

HARRIS, LYNETTE

Other:
Twin sister of actress Lee Anne Harris.
Films:
I, the Jury (1982)..................................... 2nd twin
   0:48 - Topless on bed talking to Armand Asante.
   ***
   0:52 - Full frontal nudity on bed wearing red wig,
   talking to the maniac. *
Sorceress (1982)..................................... Mara
Magazines:
Playboy (Mar 1981).............. "My Sister, My Self"
   Pages 152-155: Topless and buns. ***
Playboy (Mar 1982)........................ "Aye, Barbara"
   Pages 152 - Topless in small photos from "I, the
   Jury." *

HARRIS, MOIRA

Films:
The Fanatasist (1986; Irish)..........Patricia Teeling
   1:24 - Brief topless and buns climbing onto couch
   for the weirdo photographer. *
   1:28 - Brief right breast leaning over to kiss the
   photographer. *
   1:31 - Very brief side view of left breast in
   bathtub. *
One More Saturday Night (1986)....................Peggy

HARROLD, KATHRYN

Films:
Nightwing (1979)...................................Anne Dillon
Bogie (1980)..
The Hunter (1980)..................................Dotty
Heartbreakers (1981).................................Cyd
   0:02 - In black bra and panties changing clothes in
   Peter Coyote's studio.
Modern Romance (1981)..................Mary Harvard
   0:46 - Very brief topless and buns taking off robe
   and getting into bed with Albert Brooks. *
   1:05 - In pink lingerie opening her blouse to undo
   her skirt while talking to Brooks.
The Sender (1982)................................Gail Farmer
Yes, Giorgio (1982)........................Pamela Taylor
Pursuit of D.B. Cooper (1981)....................Hannah
Into the Night (1985)....................................Christie
Raw Deal (1986)......................................Monique
Made for HBO:
Dead Solid Perfect (1988)............... Beverly T. Lee
Made for TV Movies:
Man Against the Mob (1988)............Marilyn Butler
TV:
McGruder and Loud (1985)..Jenny Loud McGruder
Capital News (1990)..............................Mary Ward

HARRY, DEBORAH

Other:
Lead singer of the rock group "Blondie."
a.k.a. Debbie Harry.
Films:
Mr. Mike's Mondo Video (1979)............................
Union City (1980)..Lillian
Videodrome (1983)............................ Nicki Brand
   0:16 - Topless rolling over on the floor when
   James Woods is piercing her ear with a pin. **
   0:22 - In black bra, sitting on couch with James
   Woods.
Forever Lulu (1987)..Lulu
Hairspray (1988)..Velma
Satisfaction (1988)..Tina
Tales from the Darkside, The Movie (1990)...........

HART, LA GENA

Films:
Weekend Warriors (1986) ....Debbie (car hop)
Born to Race (1988)..Jenny
Made for HBO:
The Hitchhiker: Last Scene............................Leda
0:01 - Topless making love with a guy in bed. **

HART, ROXANNE

Films:
The Bell Jar (1979)......................................
The Verdict (1982).............................Sally Doneghy
Oh God, You Devil! (1984)...............Wendy Shelton
Old Enough (1984) .... Carla
The Tender Age (1984) ....Sara
1:01 - In bed in a camisole and tap pants talking to
John Savage.
Highlander (1986)............................ Brenda Wyatt
1:30 - Brief topless making love with Christopher
Lambert. Dark, hard to see. *
The Pulse (1989)..
Made for HBO:
The Last Innocent Man (1987)............................
1:06 - Topless in bed making love, then sitting up
and arguing with Ed Harris in his apartment.
***

HART, VERONICA

See Hamilton, Jane

HARTMAN, LISA

Films:
Deadly Blessing (1981) .... Faith
1:31 - Brief left breast after getting hit with a rock
by Maren Jensen. (It doesn't look like a real
chest, there is probably something covering her
breasts.)
Where the Boys Are '84 (1984)...................... Jennie
Made for TV Movies:
Just Tell Me You Love Me (1978).........................
Full Exposure: The Sex Tapes (1989) Sarah Dutton
TV:
Tabitha (1977-78)..........................Tabitha Stephens
Knots Landing (1982-83).........................Ciji Dunne
High Performance (1983)................... Kate Flannery
Knots Landing (1983-86)..................... Cathy Geary

HASSETT, MARILYN

Films:
The Other Side of the Mountain (1975)
.... Jill Kinmont
Two-Minute Warning (1976)............................ Lucy
The Other Side of the Mountain, Part II (1978)
.... Jill Kinmont

HAWN, GOLDIE

The Bell Jar (1979).................... Esther Greenwood
0:10 - In bra, then brief topless in bed with
"Buddy." Dark, hard to see. *
1:09 - Topless taking off her clothes and throwing
them out the window while yelling. **
Massive Retaliation (1984)............ Louis Fredericks
Messenger of Death (1988)....................... Josephine
Made for HBO:
The Hitchhiker: Man of Her Dreams .. Jill McGinnis

HAWN, GOLDIE

Films:
The One and Only, Genuine, Original Family Band
(1967)...Giggly Girl
Cactus Flower (1969)....................... Toni Simmons
(Academy Award for Best Supporting Actress.)
There's a Girl in My Soup (1970).............. Marion
0:37 - Buns and very brief right side view of her
body getting out of bed and walking to a closet
to get a robe. Long shot. *
Butterflies Are Free (1972)................................. Jill
Dollars (1972).......................................Dawn Divine
The Girl from Petrovka (1974)............... Oktyabrina
1:30 - Very, very brief topless in bed with Hal
Holbrook. Don't really see anything - it lasts
for about one frame.
The Sugarland Express (1974)........ Lou Jean Poplin
Shampoo (1975)...Jill
The Dutchess and the Dirtwater Fox (1976).........
Foul Play (1978)................................Gloria Mundy
Lovers and Liars (1979)................................. Anita
Private Benjamin (1980)................... Judy Benjamin
Seems Like Old Times (1980) ....Glenda
Best Friends (1982)....................... Paula McCullen
0:18 - Very, very brief side view of right breast
getting into the shower with Burt Reynolds. *
1:14 - Upper half of left breast in the shower,
twice. *
Protocol (1984)...Sunny
Wildcats (1986)..................................... Molly
0:30 - Brief topless in bathtub. *
Overboard (1987)............................Joanna/Annie
0:07 - Buns, wearing a revealing swimsuit that
shows most of her derriere on boat with Kurt
Russell.
Bird on a Wire (1990)...
TV:
Good Morning, World (1967-68).......Sandy Kramer
Rowan And Martin's Laugh-In (1968-70)....Regular

HAY, ALEXANDRA

Films:
Guess Who's Coming to Dinner? (1967).... Car Hop
How Sweet It Is (1968)................................Gloria
Skidoo (1968)............................... Darlene Banks
The Model Shop (1969) ....Gloria
1,000 Convicts and a Woman (1971; British)
.... Angela Thorne

The Love Machine (1971)............... Tina St. Claire
0:34 - Brief topless in bed with "Robin Stone." *
0:38 - Brief topless coming around the corner
putting blue bathrobe on. *
How to Seduce a Woman (1973)..... Nell Brinkman
1:05 - Brief right breast in mirror taking off black
dress. *
1:06 - Topless posing for pictures. Long scene.
***
1:47 - Topless during flashback. Lots of diffusion.
*

How Come Nobody's on our Side? (1976)...Brigitte
One Man Jury (1978)......................................Tessie

HAYDEN, JANE
Films:
Confessions of a Pop Performer (1975; British).......
Emily (1976; British)....................................Rachel
1:09 - Topless in bed with "Billy." **

HAYNES, LINDA
Films:
The Drowning Pool (1976) .... Gretchen
Rolling Thunder (1977)...................... Linda Forchet
Brubaker (1980)...Carol
1:03 - Topless getting dressed with "Huey" in
bedroom with Robert Redford comes in. *
Human Experiments (1980)................ Rachel Foster

HEATHERTON, JOEY
Other:
Singer.
Films:
Bluebeard (1972).. Anne
0:25 - Topless under black see-through nightie
while Richard Burton photographs her. Very
brief right breast. *
1:46 - Brief topless opening her dress top to taunt
Richard Burton. ***
The Happy Hooker Goes to Washington (1977)
.... Xaviera Hollander
TV:
Dean Martin Presents the Golddiggers (1968)
....regular
Joey & Dad (1975)....................................... co-host
Magazines:
Playboy (Dec 1972).................. "Sex Stars of 1972"
Page 214 - Topless. **

HELMCAMP, CHARLOTTE J.
Other:
Also see Kemp, Charlotte.
Films:
Posed for Murder (1988).......................Laura Shea
0:00 - Topless in photos during opening credits. *
0:22 - Posing for photos in sheer green teddy, then
topless in sailor's cap, then great topless shots
wearing just a G-string. ***

0:31 - Very brief right breast in photo on desk.
0:44 - In black one piece swimsuit.
0:52 - Topless in bed making love with her
boyfriend. ***
Frankenhooker (1990) ....

HEMINGWAY, MARGAUX
Other:
Model.
Older sister of actress Mariel Hemingway.
Granddaughter of writer Ernest Hemingway.
Films:
Lipstick (1976)............................Chris McCormick
0:10 - Brief topless opening the shower door to
answer the telephone. **
0:19 - Brief topless during rape attempt including
close up of side view of left breast. **
0:24 - Buns, lying on bed while rapist runs a knife
up her leg and back while she's tied to the bed
0:25 - Brief topless getting out of bed. **
Killer Fish (1979; Italian/Brazilian)...........Gabrielle
Over the Brooklyn Bridge (1983)...............Elizabeth
They Call Me Bruce? (1982) ....Karmen
Magazines:
Playboy (May 1990)............................"Papa's Girl"
Pages 126-135: Nude. ***

HEMINGWAY, MARIEL
Other:
Younger sister of actress Margaux Hemingway.
Granddaughter of writer Ernest Hemingway.
Films:
Lipstick (1976)........................... Kathy McCormick
Manhattan (1979)... Tracy
Personal Best (1982)............................Chris Cahill
(Before breast enlargement.)
0:16 - Brief lower frontal nudity getting examined
by Patrice Donnelly, then topless after making
love with her. **
0:30 - Topless in the steam room talking with
other the women. **
Star 80 (1983)...............................Dorothy Stratten
(After breast enlargement.)
Topless a lot. ***
Creator (1985).. Meli
0:38 - Brief topless cooling herself off by pulling
up T-shirt and letting a fan blow air.
1:10 - Brief topless flashing David Ogden Stiers
during football game to distract him. *
The Mean Season (1985).......... Christine Connelly
0:15 - Topless taking a shower. **
Superman IV: The Quest for Peace (1987)
....Lacy Warfield
Sunset (1988)...Cheryl King
Suicide Club (1988).........................Sasha Michaels
Made for HBO:
Steal the Sky (1988)............................Helen Mason
Topless, but too dark to see anything.

Magazines:
> **Playboy** (Apr 1982)........................"Personal Best"
> Pages: 104-109: Topless in stills from the film, buns doing the splits. *
> **Playboy** (Jan 1984)....................................."Star 80"
> **Playboy** (Jan 1989)..........."Women of the Eighties"
> Page 248: Topless. ***

HENDRY, GLORIA
Films:
> Live and Let Die (1973)....................................Rosie
> Black Cauldron (1973)..
> Black Belt Jones (1974)................................Sidney
> Savage Sisters (1974)..
> Bare Knuckles (1984)......................Barbara Darrow
Magazines:
> **Playboy** (Jul 1973).........................."Sainted Bond"
> Pages 147-149: Topless and buns. *
> Playboy (Nov 1973)......................."Sex in Cinema"
> Page 154: Nothing
> **Playboy** (Dec 1973)................. "Sex Stars of 1973"
> Page 204: Full frontal nudity. **

HENNER, MARILU
Films:
> Between the Lines (1977)........................... Danielle
> 0:27 - Dancing on stage wearing pasties.
> Saturday Night Fever (1977)....................................
> 0:20 - I heard she's the topless dancer in the bar (R version), but it doesn't look like her to me.
> Bloodbrothers (1978)..................................Annette
> Hammett (1982)................Kit Conger/Sue Alabama
> **The Man Who Loved Women** (1983)
> ....Agnes Chapman
> 0:18 - Brief topless in bed with Burt Reynolds. **
> Cannonball Run II (1984)................................Betty
> Johnny Dangerously (1984)...............................Lil
> Perfect (1985)....................................... Sally
> 0:13 - Working out on exercise machine.
> Rustler's Rhapsody (1985)..................... Miss Tracy
Made for Showtime:
> Love with a Perfect Stranger (1986)........................
TV:
> Taxi (1978-83)...................................Elaine Nardo

HENRY, LAURA
Films:
> Heavenly Bodies (1985)............................. Debbie
> 0:46 - Brief topless making love while her boyfriend "Jack" watches TV. *
> Separate Vacations (1987)..............................Nancy

HENSLEY, PAMELA
Films:
> **There was a Crooked Man** (1970).............Edwina
> 0:12 - Very brief left breast lying on pool table with a guy. *
> Doc Savage: The Man of Bronze (1975)........Mona
> Rollerball (1975)... Mackie
> Buck Rogers in the 25th Century (1979)
> ....Princess Ardala
> Double Exposure (1983)................Sergeant Fontain
TV:
> Marcus Welby, M.D. (1975-76).............Janet Blake
> Kingston: Confidential (1977)................Beth Kelly
> Buck Rogers (1979-80).................Princess Ardala
> 240-Robert (1981)................. Deputy Sandy Harper
> Matt Houston (1982-85).......................C. J. Parsons

HERRED, BRANDY
Films:
> **Some Call It Loving** (1972)................. Cheerleader
> 1:12 - Nude dancing in the club doing a strip tease dance in a cheerleader outfit. ***
> The Arousers (1973)..

HERRIN, KYMBERLY
Films:
> Romancing the Stone (1981)......................Angelina
> 0:00 - In wet white blouse in Western setting as Kathleen Turner types her story.
> Ghostbusters (1984).............................Dream Ghost
> Roadhouse (1989)..................................... Party Girl
Magazines:
> **Playboy**...Playmate

HERSHEY, BARBARA
Other:
> a.k.a. Barbara Seagull.
Films:
> **Last Summer** (1969)..................................... Sandy
> Topless in boat.
> Topless during rape.
> The Liberation of L. B. Jones (1970)
> ....Nella Mundine
> **The Baby Maker** (1970)................................. Tish
> 0:14 - Side view of left breast taking off dress and diving into the pool. Long shot and dark. Buns in water. *
> 0:23 - Left breast (out of focus) under sheet in bed.
> Boxcar Bertha (1972)................ Bertha Thompson
> 0:10 - Topless making love with David Carradine in a railroad boxcar, then brief buns walking around when the train starts moving. **
> 0:52 - Nude, side view in house with David Carradine. *
> 0:54 - Buns, putting on dress after hearing a gun shot.
> Diamonds (1975)..Sally
> Flood! (1977)..

The Stunt Man (1980) .... Nina
    1:29 - Buns and side view of left breast in bed in a
    movie within a movie while everybody is
    watching in a screening room. *
Americana (1981).. Girl
Take This Job and Shove It (1981) ....J. M. Halstead
The Entity (1983)................................ Carla Moran
    0:33 - Topless and buns getting undressed before
    taking a bath. Don't see her face. *
    0:59 - "Topless" during special effect where The
    Entity fondles her breasts with invisible fingers
    while she sleeps.
    1:32 - "Topless" again getting raped by The Entity
    while Alex Rocco watches helplessly. *
The Nightingale (1983)..
The Right Stuff (1983)..................... Glennis Yeager
The Natural (1984)................................Harriet Bird
Hannah and Her Sisters (1986) .... Lee
Tin Men (1986).. Nora
Shy People (1988).. Ruth
A World Apart (1988)............................Diana Roth
The Last Temptation of Christ (1988)
    .... Mary Magdelene
    0:16 - Brief buns behind curtain. Brief right breast
    making love, then brief topless *
    0:17 - Buns, sleeping
    0:20 - Topless, tempting "Jesus." **
Beaches (1988)..................... Hillary Whitney Essex
Made for TV Movies:
    A Killing in a Small Town (1990)...Candy Morrison
TV:
    The Monroes (1966-67)..................... Kathy Monroe
    From Here to Eternity (1980)............. Karen Holmes
Magazines:
    Playboy (Aug 1972)........................ "Boxcar Bertha"
    Pages 82-85: Nude with David Carradine. **
    Playboy (Nov 1972).............. "Sex in Cinema 1972"
    Page 161: Buns.
    Playboy (Dec 1972)................. "Sex Stars of 1972"
    Page 208: Topless. ***

HETRICK, JENNIFER
Other:
    a.k.a. Jenni Hetrick.
Films:
    Squeeze Play (1979)................................ Samantha
    0:00 - Topless in bed after making love. **
    0:26 - Right breast, brief topless with "Wes" on
    the floor. *
    0:37 - In bra in bedroom with "Wes."
TV:
    UNSUB (1989)..

HEY, VIRGINIA
Films:
    The Road Warrior (1981)............... Warrior Woman
    Norman Loves Rose (1982; Australian)..................
    The Living Daylights (1987)
    .... Rubavitch (Colonel Pushkin's girlfriend)
    1:10 - Brief side view of left breast when James
    Bond uses her to distract bodyguard. *
    Castaway (1986)... Janice
    Obsession: A Taste For Fear (1987)........... Diane
    0:04 - Buns and very brief side view of right
    breast dropping towel to take a shower. *
    0:14 - Brief right breast in bed when sheet falls
    down. **
    0:38 - Topless lying down wearing a mask talking
    to a girl. *
    1:03 - Topless waking up in bed. ***
    1:17 - Topless in hallway with "Valerie." ***
    1:19 - Brief lower frontal nudity and right breast
    in bed with "Valerie", then buns in bed. *
    1:20 - Topless getting dressed, walking and
    running around the house when "Valerie" gets
    killed. ***
    1:26 - Topless in chair all tied up while "Paul"
    torments her. *
Magazines:
    Playboy (Sep 1982)..................... "Warrior Women"
    Pages 162-63: Nude

HICKS, CATHERINE
Films:
    Death Valley (1982)... Sally
    Better Late Than Never (1983)....................... Sable
    The Razor's Edge (1984)................................ Isabel
    Garbo Talks (1984)... Jane
    Fever Pitch (1985)... Flo
    0:11 - Brief left breast, sitting on bed in hotel
    room talking with Ryan O'Neal. *
    Star Trek IV: The Voyage Home (1986)
    .... Gillian Taylor
    Peggy Sue Got Married (1986)............. Carol Heath
    Like Father, Like Son (1987)...........Dr. Amy Larkin
    Child's Play (1988)........................... Karen Barclay
    Souvenir (1988)...................................... Tina Boyer
    Daddy's Little Girl (1989)..
Made for HBO:
    Laguna Heat (1987)..................... Jane Algernon
    0:50 - Topless and buns, running around the beach
    with Harry Hamlin. **
    1:05 - Brief topless in bed making love with Harry
    Hamlin, having her head hit the headboard. **
Made for TV Movies:
    Happy Endings (1983)..
TV:
    The Bad News Bears (1979-80).. Dr. Emily Rappant
    Tucker's Witch (1982-83) .... Amanda Tucker

HIGGINS, CLARE

Films:

1919 (1984)...

Hellraiser (1987)..............................Julia
   0:17 - Very, very brief left breast and buns making love with "Frank." *
   1:10 - In white bra in bedroom putting necklace on.

Hellraiser II - Hellbound (1988).....................Julia
   0:20 - Very, very brief right breast lying in bed with "Frank." Scene from "Hellraiser."

HILL, MARIANA

Films:

Paradise, Hawaiian Style (1966)........................ Lani

Medium Cool (1969).. Ruth
   0:18 - Close-up of breast in bed with "John." *
   0:36 - Nude, running around the house frolicking with "John." **

El Condor (1971) ....Claudine

Thumb Tripping (1972)..................................Lynn
   1:14 - In black bra, then very, very brief left breast when "Jack" comes to cover her up. *
   1:19 - Topless frolicking in the water with "Gary." *
   1:20 - In white swimsuit, dancing in bar.

High Plains Drifter (1973).................Callie Travers

The Godfather, Part II (1974)...................... Deanna

The Last Porno Flick (1974)....................................

Schizoid (1980)...Julie
   0:58 - Left breast, making love in bed with Klaus Kinski. Dark, hard to see.

Blood Beach (1981)...................................Catherine

HOLCOMB, SARAH

Films:

National Lampoon's Animal House (1978)
   .... Clorette DePasto
   0:56 - Brief topless lying on bed after passing out in Tom Hulce's bed during toga party. **

Walk Proud (1979)...........................Sarah Lassiter

Caddyshack (1980).................. Maggie O'Hooligan

Happy Birthday, Gemini (1980).......Judith Hastings

HOLLOMAN, BRIDGET

Films:

Slumber Party '57 (1976)................... Bonnie May
   0:10 - Topless with her five girl friends during swimming pool scene. Hard to tell who is who. *
   0:26 - Left breast in truck with her cousin "Cal." *

Evils of the Night (1985)....................................

HORN, LINDA

Films:

American Gigolo (1980)..........2nd Girl on Balcony
   0:03 - Topless on the balcony while Richard Gere and Lauren Hutton talk. *

The Great Muppet Caper (1981)...............................

HOWELL, MARGARET

Films:

Tightrope (1984) .... Judy Harper
   0:44 - Brief left breast viewed from above in a room with Clint Eastwood. *

Girls Just Want to Have Fun (1985).....................

HUBLEY, SEASON

Other:

Ex-wife of actor Kurt Russell.

Films:

Hardcore (1979)................................ Niki
   0:27 - Topless acting in a porno movie. *
   1:05 - Full frontal nudity talking to George C. Scott in a booth. Panties mysteriously appear later on. ***

Vice Squad (1982) ....Princess
   0:34 - In black bra in "Ramrod's" apartment.
   0:57 - Buns, getting out of bed after making love with a John.
   1:25 - In black bra tied up by "Ramrod."

Prettykill (1987) ....Heather Todd

Made for HBO:

The Hitchhiker: Cabin Fever.......................Miranda
   0:12 - In a white bra under cabin with "Rick."

Made for TV Movies:

Elvis - The Movie (1979)...............................

Shakedown on Sunset Strip (1988)
   .... Officer Audre Davis

Child in the Night (1990)............... Valerie Winfield

TV:

Kung Fu (1974-75)...........................Margit McLean

Family (1976-77) .... Salina Magee

HUGHES, SHARON

Films:

Chained Heat (1983; U.S./German)................. Val
   0:30 - Brief topless in the shower with Linda Blair. **
   1:04 - Topless in the Jacuzzi with the Warden. **

The Man Who Loved Women (1983).............Nurse

Hard to Hold (1984)...

The Last Horror Film (1984) ....

American Justice (1986).....................................

A Fine Mess (1986)...

Grotesque (1988)...

HUGHES, WENDY

Films:

Jock Peterson (1975; Australian)........Patricia Kent
0:12 - Topless in her office with "Tony." ***
0:13 - Topless making love with "Tony" on the floor. *
0:44 - Nude running around the beach with "Tony." **
0:50 - Nude in bed making love with "Tony." **
1:24 - Full frontal nudity when "Tony" rapes her in her office. *
Newsfront (1978; Australian)......... Amy McKenzie
My Brilliant Career (1979; Australian).. Aunt Helen
Lonely Hearts (1981)................................. Patricia
1:05 - Brief topless getting out of bed and putting a dress on. Dark, hard to see. *
Careful, He Might Hear You (1984; Australian)
.... Vanessa
An Indecent Obsession (1985)...... Honour Langtry
0:32 - Possibly Wendy topless, could be "Sue" because "Luce" is fantasizing about Wendy while making love with "Sue." Dark, long shot, hard to see.
1:10 - Left breast, making love in bed with "Wilson." **
My First Wife (1985)..................... Helen
1:00 - Brief topless and lower frontal nudity under water during "husband's" dream. Could be anybody.
1:08 - In bra, then topless on the floor with her "Husband." **
1:10 - Topless in bed lying down, then fighting with her "husband." A little dark. **
Happy New Year (1987).............................
Warm Nights on a Slow Moving Train (1987)
.... The Girl
1:23 - Very, very brief silhouette of right breast getting back into bed after killing a man.
Echoes of Paradise (1989)...............................Maria
Made for HBO:
The Heist (1989)......................... Susan
0:52 - Very brief side view of right breast making love in bed with Pierce Brosnan *

HULL, DIANNE

Films:

The Arrangement (1969)................................. Ellen
The Magic Garden of Stanley Sweetheart (1970).....
Man on a Swing (1974)...................Maggie Dawson
Aloha, Bobby and Rose (1975)........................Rose
The Fifth Floor (1978)................... Kelly McIntyre
0:29 - Topless and buns in shower while "Carl" watches, then brief full frontal nudity running out of the shower. **
1:09 - Topless in whirlpool bath getting visited by "Carl" again, then raped. **
You Better Watch Out (1980)..........Jackie Stadling
The New Adventures of Pippi Longstocking (1988)
....

HUNT, MARSHA A.

Films:

The Sender (1982) .... Nurse Jo
The Howling II (1984) .... Mariana
0:33 - Topless in bedroom with Sybil Danning and a guy. **

HUNTER, KAKI

Films:

Roadie (1980)................................ Lola Bouiliabase
Just the Way You Are (1980)...........................Lisa
Willie and Phil (1980) ....Patti Sutherland
Whose Life Is It, Anyway? (1981).............. Mary Jo
Porky's (1981)... Wendy
1:02 - Brief full frontal nudity, then brief topless in the shower scene. *
Porky's II: The Next Day (1983)................... Wendy
Porky's Revenge (1985)............................... Wendy
1:22 - In white bra and panties taking off her clothes to jump off a bridge.

HUNTER, RACHEL

Other:

Sports Illustrated swimsuit model.

Video Tapes:

Sports Illustrated's 25th Anniversary Swimsuit Video (1989)... Herself
(The version shown on HBO left out two music video segments at the end. If you like buns, definitely watch this tape!)
0:03 - Right breast in see-through black swimsuit with white stars on it. *
Sports Illustrated Super Shape-Up Program: Body Sculpting with Rachel Hunter (1990).........Herself

HUNTLY, LESLIE

Films:

The Naked Cage (1985)...............................Peaches
Back to School (1987) ....Coed #1
Demon of Paradise (1987) ....Gobby
0:51 - Topless taking off her top on a boat, then swimming in the ocean. **
Stewardess School (1987)............ Alison Hanover
0:46 - Topless, doing a strip tease on a table at a party at her house. **

HUPPERT, ISABELLE

Films:

Going Places (1974)................................Jacqueline
The Lacemaker (1977)............................... Beatrice
Loulou (1977).. Nelly
Heaven's Gate (1980)...................................... Ella
1:10 - Nude running around the house and in bed with Kris Kristofferson. **
1:18 - Nude, taking a bath in the river and getting out. ***
2:24 - Very brief left breast getting raped by three guys. *

Clean Slate (1981) ....

Le Femme du Mon Ami (My Best Friend's Girl)
(1984; French) .... Vivian Arthund
0:40 - Brief left breast peeking out of bathrobe
walking around in living room. *
1:00 - Buns, making love with Thierry Lhermitte
while his friend watches.

La Truite (The Trout) (1982; French)... Frederique

Entre Nous (Between Us) (1983; French)....... Lena
Topless.

The Bedroom Window (1986)... Sylvia Wentworth
0:06 - Brief topless and bottomless looking out the
window at attempted rape. **

Sincerely Charlotte (1986; French).........Charlotte
0:20 - Brief topless in bathtub. Long shot, out of
focus.
1:07 - Very brief left breast changing into red
dress in the back seat of the car.
1:15 - Topless in bed with "Mathieu." Kind of
dark. **

HURLEY, ELIZABETH
Films:
Aria (1988)................................... Marietta
0:46 - Brief topless, turning around while singing
to a guy. *
0:47 - Buns.
Rowing with the Wind (1988)......... Clair Clairmont

HUSSEY, OLIVIA
Films:
Romeo and Juliet (1968)................................Juliet
1:37 - Very brief topless rolling over and getting
out of bed with "Romeo." *
Escape 2000 (1981) ....Chris
The Man with Bogart's Face (1980)....... Elsa Borsht
Virus (1980; Japanese)....................................Marit
Made for TV Movies:
Ivanhoe (1982)............................. Rebecca

HUSTON, ANJELICA
Other:
Daughter of actor/director John Huston.
Films:
Hamlet (1969; British)............................ Court Lady
A Walk with Love and Death (1969)...Lady Claudia
The Last Tycoon (1976)......................... Edna
Swashbuckler (1976)......... Woman of Dark Visage
The Postman Always Rings Twice (1981).. Madge
1:30 - Brief side view left breast sitting in trailer
with Jack Nicholson. *
Frances (1982)..Hospital Sequence: Mental Patient
Ice Pirates (1984).. Maida
This is Spinal Tap (1984)....................Polly Deutsch
Prizzi's Honor (1985)...................... Maerose Prizzi
(Academy Award)
Gardens of Stone (1987)................. Samantha Davis
The Dead (1987)..............................Gretta Conroy
Enemies, A Love Story (1989)..................... Tamara

The Witches (1990)...
Miniseries:
Lonesome Dove (1989)..........................Clara Allen

HUTCHINSON, TRACEY E.
Films:
Master Blaster ....
Topless in the shower.
The Wild Life (1984)......................... Poker Girl #2
1:23 - Brief topless in a room full of guys and girls
playing strip poker when Lea Thompson looks
in. *
Amazon Women on the Moon (1987)........ Floozie
1:18 - Brief right breast hitting balloon while
Carrie Fisher talks to a guy. This sketch is in
B&W and appears after the first batch of credits.

HUTTON, LAUREN
Films:
The Gambler (1974).......................................Billie
Gator (1976).................................... Aggie Maybank
Welcome to L.A. (1977)....................... Nora Bruce
0:56 - Very brief, obscured glimpse of left breast
under red light in photo darkroom. *
Viva Knievel (1977)............................Kate Morgan
A Wedding (1978) ....Florence Farmer
American Gigolo (1980)......................Michelle
0:37 - Left breast, making love with Richard Gere
in bed in his apartment. *
Paternity (1981)...................................Jenny Lufton
Zorro, The Gay Blade (1981)....................Charlotte
Starflight One (1982)......................................
The Cradle Will Fall (1983)......................................
Snow Queen (1983) ....
Lassiter (1984)............................ Kari Von Fursten
0:18 - Brief topless over the shoulder shot making
love with a guy on the bed just before killing
him. *
Once Bitten (1985)............................Countess
Malone (1987)...Jamie
Scandalous (1988).......................................
TV:
The Rhinemann Exchange (1977)
.... Leslie Hawkewood
Paper Dolls (1984) ....Colette Ferrier
Magazines:
Penthouse (Sep 1986)
...................."The Secret Nudes of Lauren Hutton"
Pages 158-169: 1962 B&W photos.

HYSER, JOYCE
Other:
Girlfriend of singer Bruce Springsteen for a couple
of years.
Films:
They All Laughed (1981)................................Sylvia
Staying Alive (1983)..Linda
Valley Girl (1983).. Joyce
This is Spinal Tap (1984)..............................Belinda

Just One of the Guys (1986)............. Terry Griffith
  0:10 - In two piece swimsuit by the pool with her boyfriend.
  1:27 - Brief topless opening her blouse to prove that she is really a girl. **
Wedding Band (1989)................... Karla Thompson

I

IMAN
Other:
  Model.
Films:
  The Human Factor (1979).............................. Sarah
  Out of Africa (1985).............................. Mariammo
  No Way Out (1987)................................. Nina Beka
  Surrender (1988) .... Hedy
Magazines:
  Playboy (Jan 1986)............ "Beauty and the Beasts"
  Pages 146-155: Topless. ***

INCH, JENNIFER
Films:
  Frank and I (1983)........................... Frank/Frances
  0:10 - Brief buns, getting pants pulled down for a spanking.
  0:22 - Nude getting undressed and walking to the bed. ***
  0:24 - Brief nude when "Charles" pulls the sheets off her. *
  0:32 - Brief buns, getting spanked by two older women.
  0:38 - Full frontal nudity getting out of bed and walking to "Charles" at the piano. ***
  0:45 - Full frontal nudity lying on her side by the fireplace. Dark, hard to see. **
  1:09 - Brief topless making love with "Charles" on the floor. **
  1:11 - Nude taking off her clothes and walking toward "Charles" at the piano. ***
  Physical Evidence (1989)........................... Waitress
Made for Cable:
  Playboy Channel: Birds in Paradise....................
  Topless.

INNES, ALEXANDRA
Films:
  Perfect Timing (1984)................................. Salina
  1:06 - Right breast and buns, posing for "Harry." **
  Joshua Then and Now (1985)........................ Joanna

ISAACS, SUSAN
Films:
  Deadly Passion (1985)................................. Trixie
  0:02 - Topless sitting up in bed talking to Brent Huff. **
  Compromising Positions (1985)............................
  She's Out of Control (1989)................. Receptionist
  The War of the Roses (1989)
  .... Auctioneer's Assistant

J

JACKSON, GLENDA
Films:
  Women in Love (1971).............. Gudrun Brangwen
  1:20 - Topless taking off her blouse on the bed with Oliver Reed watching her, then making love. ***
  1:49 - Brief left breast making love with Reed in bed again. **
  Sunday, Bloody Sunday (1971)........ Alex Greville
  The Music Lovers (1971).............. Nina Milyukova
  Full frontal nudity after stripping in railway carriage.
  A Touch of Class (1972).................... Vicki Allessio
  The Romantic Englishwoman (1975)..... Elizabeth
  0:30 - Brief full frontal nudity outside, taking robe off with Michael Caine. *
  0:31 - Buns, walking back into the house. *
  1:08 - Side view of right breast sitting at edge of poll talking to "Thomas." *
  1:45 - Very, very brief topless in bed talking with "Thomas." *
  The Incredible Sarah (1976)........... Sarah Bernhardt
  Nasty Habits (1977)............................... Alexandra
  The Class of Miss MacMichael (1978)
  .... Conor MacMichael
  House Calls (1978)........................... Ann Atkinson
  Stevie (1978)....................................... Stevie Smith
  Lost and Found (1979)..................................... Tricia
  Hopscotch (1980)...................... Isobel von Schmidt
  Sakharov (1984)...
  The Return of the Soldier (1985)...........................
  Turtle Diary (1986)................... Naerea Duncan
  Beyond Therapy (1987)........................... Charlotte
  Salome's Last Dance (1987).... Herodias/Lady Alice
  Strange Interlude (1988)...............................
  The Rainbow (1989)..................... Anna Brangwen
Magazines:
  Playboy (Dec 1973)................... "Sex Stars of 1973"
  Page 206: Right breast in see-through blouse. *
  Playboy (Nov 1976)............. "Sex in Cinema 1976"
  Page 146: Topless sitting by the pool in a photo from "The Romantic Englishwoman." *

JACKSON, LA TOYA

Other:
Singer.
Member of the singing Jackson clan.
Magazines:
Playboy (Mar 1989)..............."Don't Tell Michael"
Pages 122-133: Topless and buns. *******
Playboy (Dec 1989)........ "Holy Sex Stars of 1989!"
Page 185: Topless in bed. *******

JACKSON, VICTORIA

Films:
Baby Boom (1987)..
Casual Sex? (1988)..Melissa
0:30 - Brief buns lying down with Lea Thompson
at a nude beach.
0:33 - Brief buns wrapping a towel around herself
just before getting a massage. Long shot, hard
to see.
1:06 - Brief buns getting out of bed.
UHF (1989)...Teri
Family Business (1989)...............................Christine
TV:
Saturday Night Live (1986-87).....................Regular

JACOBS, EMMA

Films:
The Stud (1979; British)..........................Alexandra
0:44 - In bra, then topless taking bra off in
bedroom. ******
0:48 - Close up of breasts making love with
"Tony" in his dark apartment. *****
1:14 - Topless in bed with "Tony", yelling at him.
*
Lifeforce (1985)................................. Crew Member

JAHAN, MARINE

Films:
Flashdance (1983)
..........Uncredited Dance Double for Jennifer Beals
Streets of Fire (1984)................ "Torchie's" Dancer
0:28 - Buns in G-string dancing in club.
0:34 - More dancing.
0:35 - Very brief right breast under body stocking,
then almost topless under stocking when taking
off T-shirt. *****
Video Tapes:
Freedanse With Marine Jahan..........................herself

JAMISON, SHELLY

Other:
Former newscaster at KTSP, Channel 10 in Phoenix,
Arizona.
Magazines:
Playboy (Jul 1989)
.... "Shelly Jamison: TV News Knockout"
Pages 74-81: Nude. *******

JANSSEN, MARLENE

Films:
School Spirit (1985)..................... Sleeping Princess
0:42 - Topless and buns, sleeping when old guy
goes invisible to peek at her. ******
Video Tapes:
Playmate Review 2 (1984).......................Playmate
Magazines:
Playboy (Nov 1982)...................................Playmate

JEMISON, ANNA

Other:
Also see Monticelli, Anna-Maria.
Films:
Smash Palace (1981; New Zealand)....Jacqui Shaw
0:21 - Silhouette of right breast changing while
sitting on the edge of the bed.
0:39 - Topless in bed after arguing, then making
up with Bruno Lawrence. *******
My First Wife (1985)....................................Hillary

JENNINGS, CLAUDIA

Films:
The Love Machine (1971)............................Darlene
The Unholy Rollers (1972)........................... Karen
Group Marriage (1972)..................................
'Gator Bait (1972)..
0:06 - Brief left and right breasts during boat
chase sequence. *****
40 Carats (1973)......................................Gabriella
Truck Stop Women (1974)............................ Rose
0:27 - Brief topless taking off blouse and getting
into bed. *****
0:48 - Brief side view of right breast in mirror,
getting dressed.
1:10 - Brief topless wrapping and unwrapping a
towel around herself. *****
The Great Texas Dynamite Chase (1977)
....Candy Morgan
Moonshine County Express (1977)... Betty Hammer
Impulsion (1978)..
Death Sport (1978) ....Deneer
Fast Company (1979; Canadian).............................
Famous T & A (1982)................................ herself
0:26 - Topless scenes from "Single Girls" and
"Truck Stop Women." ******
Magazines:
Playboy (Nov 1969)..............................Playmate
Playboy (Nov 1972)............. "Sex in Cinema 1972"
Page 166: Topless lying down. *****
Playboy (Dec 1972)............. "Sex Stars of 1972"
Page 211: Topless. ******
Playboy (Dec 1973)................. "Sex Stars of 1973"
Page 208: Full frontal nudity. ******
Playboy (Jan 1979)................. "25 Beautiful Years"
Page 162: Topless. *******
Playboy (Sep 1979)............... "Claudia Recaptured"
Pages 118-123: Topless. *******
Playboy (Jan 1989)......... "Women of the Seventies"
Page 217: Topless. *******

JENRETTE, RITA

Other:

Ex-wife of former U.S. Representative John Jenrette, who was convicted in 1980 in the FBI's Abscam probe.

Starting in 1990, she is using her maiden name of Rita Carpenter.

Films:

Zombie Island Massacre (1984).................. Sandy
0:01 - Topless taking a shower while "Joe" sneaks up on her. Topless in bed with "Joe." ***
0:10 - Brief right breast with open blouse, in boat with "Joe." Left breast with him on the couch. **

End of the Line (1987)................................. Sharon

Magazines:

Playboy...

JENSEN, CHRISTINA

Films:

Death Stop 395 ....

Magazines:

Playboy (Jul 1989)................... "B-Movie Bimbos"
Page 135: Full frontal nudity standing in a heart shaped hot tub in the back of a car. **

JENSEN, MAREN

Films:

Deadly Blessing (1981)................................ Martha
0:27 - Topless and buns changing into a nightgown while a creepy guy watches through the window. **
0:52 - Buns, getting into the bathtub. Kind of steamy and hard to see.
0:56 - Brief topless in bathtub with snake. (Notice that she gets into the tub naked, but is wearing black panties in the water). *

Beyond the Reef (1981)................................ Diana
(Not available on video tape)

TV:

Battlestar Galactica (1978-79)........................Athena

JILLSON, JOYCE

Other:

Astrologer.

Films:

Slumber Party '57 (1977)..............................Gladys

Superchick (1978)............ Tara B. True/Superchick
0:03 - Brief upper half of right breast leaning back in bathtub. *
0:06 - Topless in bed throwing cards up. **
0:16 - Brief topless under net on boat with "Johnny." *
0:29 - Brief right breast several times in airplane restroom with a Marine. *
1:12 - Buns, frolicking in the ocean with Johnny. Don't see her face. *
1:27 - Close up of breasts (probably body double) when sweater pops open. *

JOHARI, AZIZI

Films:

Body and Soul (1981)........................Pussy Willow
0:31 - Topless sitting on bed with Leon Isaac Kennedy, then left breast lying in bed. ***

Magazines:

Playboy (Jun 1975)....................................Playmate

JOHNSON, MICHELLE

Films:

Blame it on Rio (1983).................... Jennifer Lyons
0:19 - Topless on the beach greeting Michael Caine and Joseph Bologna with Demi Moore, then brief topless in the ocean. **
0:26 - Topless taking her clothes off for Caine on the beach. Dark, hard to see. *
0:27 - Topless seducing Caine. Dark, hard to see. **
0:56 - Full frontal nudity taking off robe and sitting on bed to take a Polaroid picture of herself. ***
0:57 - Very brief topless in the Polaroid photo showing it to Caine. *

Gung Ho (1985)...Heather

Beaks The Movie (1987)............................. Vanessa
0:26 - Brief topless covered with bubbles after taking a bath. Don't see her face. *
0:31 - Brief topless covered with bubbles after getting out of bathtub with Christopher Atkins. Don't see her face. *

Slipping into Darkness (1987)................................

The Jigsaw Murders (1988)............ Kathy DaVonzo
0:51 - Posing in leotards in dance studio for the photographer.
1:07 - Posing in lingerie on bed for another photographer.
1:20 - In light blue dance outfit with the photographer.
1:27 - In blue swimsuit posing for the photographer outside.

Waxwork (1988)... China

TV:

Werewolf (1987)..

JOHNSON, SANDY

Films:

Two-minute Warning (1976)..............Button's Wife

Gas Pump Girls (1978)..

H.O.T.S. (1979).. Stephanie
0:27 - Topless on balcony in red bikini bottoms. **
1:34 - Topless during football game during huddle with all the other girls. **

Halloween (1978)............................. Judith Meyers
0:06 - Very brief topless covered with blood on floor after "Michael" stabs her to death

JOHNSON, SUNNY
Films:
National Lampoon's Animal House (1978)
....Otter's Co-Ed
Dr. Heckyl and Mr. Hype (1980).........Coral Careen
Where the Buffalo Roam (1980) ....
The Night the Lights Went Out in Georgia (1981)
.... Wendy
Flashdance (1983)...............................Jennie Szabo
1:28 - Topless on stage with other strippers. *
Made for TV Movies:
The Red Light Sting (1984)....................................

JOHNSON, VICTORIA LYNN
Other:
Body double for Angie Dickinson's shower scene in
"Dressed to Kill."
Magazines:
Penthouse (Aug 1976).......................... Pet
Pages 91-103
Penthouse (Nov 1977)..................... Pet of the Year
Pages 75-90

JOI, MARILYN
Films:
Kentucky Fried Movie (1977).................. Cleopatra
1:11 - Topless in bed with "Schwartz." *
The Happy Hooker Goes to Washington (1977)
....Sheila
0:09 - Left breast on couch. *
0:47 - Brief topless during car demonstration. *
1:14 - Topless in military guy's office. **
Nurse Sherri (1978) ....
C.O.D. (1983)................................. Debbie Winter
1:16 - Topless during photo session. **
1:25 - Brief topless taking off robe wearing red
garter belt during dressing room scene. *
1:26 - In red bra while talking to "Albert."
1:30 - In red bra during fashion show.

JONES, CHARLENE
Films:
Unholy Rollers (1972)...................................Beverly
The Woman Hunt (1975; U.S./Philippines)..............
Hard to Hold (1984)......................................A Wife
Avenging Angel (1985) ....
Perfect (1988)... Shotsy
0:17 - Topless stripping on stage in a club. Buns
in G-string. *

JONES, GRACE
Films:
Conan the Destroyer (1984).........................Zula
Deadly Vengeance (1985) ....
A View to a Kill (1985) ....
Vamp (1986)..Katrina
Straight to Hell (1987) ....

Magazines:
Playboy (Jan 1985)..
Page 101: Small color photo.
Playboy (Jul 1985)..................... "Amazing Grace"
Page 82-87: Topless band buns in B&W photos
of her and Dolph Lundgren. *
Playboy (Apr 1979)..

JONES, JOSEPHINE JAQUELINE
Other:
a.k.a. J. J. Jones.
Former Miss Bahamas.
Films:
Black Venus (1983)..Venus
0:05 - Topless in Jungle Room. **
0:11 - Nude, posing for "Armand" sketching her
in a bedroom. ***
0:14 - Topless and buns making love with
"Armand" in bed. *
0:17 - Nude, posing for "Armand" while he
models her in clay, then kissing him on the bed.
**
0:21 - Brief nude getting dressed. *
0:38 - Nude, making love in bed with Karin
Schubert. ***
0:45 - Nude talking and then making love in bed
with "Louise."
0:50 - Topless when "Pierre" brings everybody in
to see her. **
0:57 - Topless in silhouette while "Armand"
fantasizes about his statue coming to life. **
1:04 - Nude. ***
1:07 - Nude with the two diplomats on the bed.
***
1:16 - Nude frolicking on the beach with
"Louise." ***
1:18 - Topless in bedroom getting out of wet
clothes with "Louise." ***
1:21 - Topless in bed with "Jacques." **
1:24 - Full frontal nudity getting out of bed. **
Love Circles Around the World (1984).......Brigid
0:18 - Topless, then nude running around her
apartment chasing after "Jack." **
0:30 - Topless, making love with "Count Crispa"
in his hotel room. *
Warrior Queen (1987)............................... Chloe
0:20 - Topless making love with "Vespa." ***

JONES, MARILYN
Films:
Support Your Local Sheriff (1969)......Bordello Girl
The Scenic Route (1978)................................. Lena
Meteor (1979)..Stunt
The Men's Club (1986)............................. Allison
1:21 - Topless wearing gold panties standing in
bedroom talking to Harvey Keitel. **
TV:
Secrets of Midland Heights (1980-81)
.... Holly Wheeler
King's Crossing (1982)....................Carey Hollister

JONES, RACHEL
Films:
Dracula's Widow (1988)................................. Jenny
    Brief left breast, then brief topless lying in the
    bathtub getting stabbed by Sylvia Kristel. *
Fresh Horses (1988)..

JONES, REBUNKAH
Films:
Frankenstein General Hospital (1988)
    ....Elizabeth Rice
    1:05 - Topless in the office letting Mark
    Blankfield examine her back. **
Hide and Go Shriek (1988) ....

JOURDAN, CATHERINE
Films:
The Girl on a Motorcycle (1968; French/British)
    ....Catherine
The Godson (1972; Italian/French).... Hatcheck Girl
Aphrodite (1982; German/French)............... Valerie
    0:34 - Brief upper half of breasts in bathtub. *

K
=================

KAITAN, ELIZABETH
Other:
    a.k.a. Elizabeth Cayton.
Films:
Slavegirls from Beyond Infinity (1987)........ Daria
    (Wearing skimpy two piece loincloth outfit during
    most of the movie.)
    0:38 - Topless undressing and jumping into bed
    with "Rik." ***
Friday the 13th Part VII - A New Blood (1988)
    .... Robin
    0:53 - Brief left breast in bed making love with a
    guy. *
    0:55 - Brief topless sitting up in bed after making
    love and the sheet falls down. *
    1:00 - Brief topless again sitting up in bed and
    putting a shirt on over her head. **
Assault of the Killer Bimbos (1988)............... Lulu
    0:41 - Brief topless during desert musical
    sequence, opening her blouse, then taking off
    her shorts, then putting on a light blue dress.
    Don't see her face. **
Twins (1988)..Secretary
Dr. Alien (1989).. Waitress
    a.k.a. I was a Teenage Sex Mutant
Nightwish (1988).. Donna
    0:04 - In wet T-shirt, then brief topless taking it
    off during experiment. Long shot. *
Under the Boardwalk (1989)........................ Donna

KALLIANIOTES, HELENA
Films:
Five Easy Pieces (1970)....................Palm Apodaca
The Baby Maker (1970)............................... Wanda
    1:30 - Brief topless when Barbara Hershey sees
    her in bed with "Tad." *
Kansas City Bomber (1972).............Jackie Burdette
Shanks (1974)..
The Drowning Pool (1975)................Elaine Reaves
The Passover Plot (1976)............. Visionary Woman
Stay Hungry (1976)..Anita

KAMINSKY, DANA
Films:
Hot Resort (1984)...................................... Melanie
    1:02 - Topless taking off her white dress in a boat.
    **
Irreconcilable Differences (1984)
    .... Woman in Dress Shop

KANE, CAROL
Films:
Carnal Knowledge (1971)............................Jennifer
Desperate Characters (1971).................. Young Girl
The Last Detail (1973) ....Young Whore
    1:02 - Brief topless sitting on bed talking with
    Randy Quaid. Her hair is in the way, hard to
    see. *
Dog Day Afternoon (1975)............................ Jenny
Hester Street (1975)...................................... Gitl
Annie Hall (1977)..Allison
The World's Greatest Lover (1977)................Annie
The Mafu Cage (1978)................................Cissy
    a.k.a. My Sister, My Love
    0:08 - Very brief tip of left breast in the bathtub.
The Muppet Movie (1979)..............................
When a Stranger Calls (1979)................Jill Johnson
Norman Loves Rose (1982)............................
Over the Brooklyn Bridge (1983)..................Cheryl
Racing with the Moon (1984)........................Annie
Transylvania 6-5000 (1985) ....Lupi
Jumpin' Jack Flash (1986)..........................Cynthia
The Princess Bride (1987) ....Valerie
Ishtar (1987)..Carol
Sticky Fingers (1988)................................ Kitty
License to Drive (1988)............................Mom
Scrooged (1988)......The Ghost of Christmas Present
The Lemon Sisters (1990) ....
TV:
Taxi (1981-83)...............................Simka Gravas
All Is Forgiven (1986)............... Nicolette Bingham
American Dreamer (1990-)........................Lillian

KARLATOS, OLGA

Films:
Wifemistress (1977)........ Miss Paula Pagano, M.D.
   0:42 - Topless undressing in room with Laura
      Antonelli. Right breast and part of left breast
      lying in bed with Marcello Mastroianni. **
   0:46 - Brief topless in bed with Mastroianni and
      "Clara." *
Zombie (1980).................................... Mrs. Menard
   0:40 - Topless and buns taking a shower. *

KARMAN, JANICE

Films:
Switchblade Sisters (1975).......................................
Slumber Party '57 (1976)..............................Hank
   1:06 - Topless, sitting watching "Smitty" and
      "David" make love in the stable. **

KAPRISKY, VALERIE

Films:
Aphrodite (1982; German/French).............. Pauline
   0:12 - Nude, washing herself off in front of a two-
      way mirror while a man on the other side
      watches. ***
Breathless (1983).......................... Monica Poiccard
   0:23 - Brief side view of left breast in her
      apartment. Long shot, hard to see anything.
   0:47 - Topless in her apartment with Richard Gere
      kissing. ***
   0:52 - Brief full frontal nudity standing in the
      shower when Gere opens the door, afterwards,
      buns in bed. **
   0:53 - Topless, holding up two dresses for Gere to
      pick from, then topless putting the black dress
      on. **
   1:23 - Topless behind a movie screen with Gere.
      Lit with red light. *
L'Annee Des Meduses (1987).......................... Chris
a.k.a. The Year of the Jellyfish
   0:06 - Topless pulling down swimsuit at the
      beach. **
   0:24 - Full frontal nudity taking off dress on sofa
      with older man. ***
   0:42 - Topless walking around the beach talking to
      everybody. ***
   0:46 - Topless on the beach taking a shower. **
   1:02 - Topless on the beach with her "mom." ***
   1:37 - Nude dancing on the boat for "Romain."
      ***
   1:42 - Topless walking from the beach to the bar.
      **
   1:43 - Topless in swimming pool. **
Magazines:
Playboy (Dec 1983)...................."Sex Stars of 1983"
   Page 209: Topless. **

KAPTURE, MITZI

Films:
Private Road (1987)........................ Helen Milshaw
   0:50 - Wearing a white bra during a strip-spin-the-
      bottle game.
   1:29 - Topless, making love in bed with Greg
      Evigan. **
Angel III: The Final Chapter (1988) Molly Stewart
Lethal Obsession (1988)..

KASDORF, LENORE

Films:
Fly Me (1973)..
Dark Horse (1984) ....Alice
Missing in Action (1984)..................................
   0:41 - Very brief topless when Chuck Norris
      sneaks back in room and jumps into bed with
      her. *
Mr. Bill's Real Life Adventures (1986)....................
Made for Cable:
Dinner At Eight (1989)....................................Lucy

KATON, ROSANNE

Films:
The Swinging Cheerleaders (1974)...........................
Chesty Anderson, U.S. Navy (1975)...............Cocoa
Fox Fire (1976)..
Motel Hell (1980)...Suzi
Lunch Wagon (1981)................................ Shannon
   0:01 - Brief topless getting dressed. *
   0:04 - Brief side view of left breast changing tops
      in room in gas station with Pamela Bryant while
      a guy watches through key hole. **
   0:10 - Topless changing again in gas station. **
Body and Soul (1981) ....Melody
   0:04 - Left breast several times making love in
      restroom with Leon Isaac Kennedy. *
Zapped! (1982)..Donna
Coach (1983) .... Sue
   0:10 - Very brief topless flashing her breasts along
      with three of her girlfriends for their four
      boyfriends. *
Bachelor Party (1984)........... Bridal Shower Hooker
Harem (1985)..Judy
Magazines:
Playboy (Sep 1978).............................Playmate
Playboy (Jul 1981).............. "Body and Soulmates"
   Page 148: Left breast. **

KAYE, CAREN

Films:
Checkmate (1973).. Alex
Lords of Flatbush (1974)................. Wedding Guest
Looking for Mr. Goodbar (1977)....................Rhoda
Kill Castro (1982)..Tracy
   a.k.a. Cuba Crossing.
Some Kind of Hero (1982)............................. Sheila

My Tutor (1984)................................. Terry Green
  0:25 - Topless walking into swimming pool. **
  0:52 - Topless in the pool with Matt Lattanzi. **
  0:55 - Right breast, lying in bed making love with
    Lattanzi. ***
TV:
  Blansky's Beauties (1977)..................Bambi Benton
  The Betty White Show (1977-78)....... Tracy Garrett
  Who's Watching the Kids? (1978)....... Stacy Turner
  Empire (1984) .... Meredith
  It's Your Move (1984-85)...................Eileen Burton

KEATON, DIANE
Films:
  Lovers and Other Strangers (1970) ....Joan
  The Godfather (1972)............................. Kay Adams
  Play It Again Sam (1972)...................Linda Christie
  Sleeper (1973) ....Luna
  The Godfather, Part II (1974)................. Kay Adams
  Love and Death (1975)..................................... Sonja
  Harry and Walter Go to New York (1976)
  .... Lissa Chestnut
  I Will, I Will...For Now (1976).........Katie Bingham
  Annie Hall (1977)................................. Annie Hall
  Looking for Mr. Goodbar (1977)............. Theresa
    0:11 - Right breast in bed making love with her
    teacher, "Martin," then putting blouse on. **
    0:31 - Brief left breast over the shoulder when the
    Doctor playfully kisses her breast. *
    1:04 - Brief topless smoking in bed in the
    morning, then more topless after Richard Gere
    leaves **
    1:17 - Topless making love with Gere after doing
    a lot of cocaine. ***
    1:31 - Brief topless in the bathtub when "James"
    brings her a glass of wine. *
    2:00 - Getting out of bed in a bra.
    2:02 - Topless during rape by Tom Berenger,
    before he kills her. Hard to see because of
    strobe lights. **
  Interiors (1978)... Renata
  Manhattan (1979; B&W)......................Mary Wilke
  Reds (1981) .... Louise Bryant
  Shoot the Moon (1982) .... Faith Dunlap
  Mrs. Soffel (1984)..
  The Little Drummer Girl (1984) ....
  Crimes of the Heart (1986).............. Lenny Magrath
  Baby Boom (1987)................................J.C. Wiatt
  The Good Mother (1988)................................. Anna
  The Lemon Sisters (1990).................................

KELLER, MARTHE
Films:
  And Now My Love (1974)................................
  Marathon Man (1976)......................................Elsa
    0:42 - Topless lying on the floor after Dustin
    Hoffman rolls off her. **
  Black Sunday (1977)............................... Dahlia

Bobby Deerfield (1977).............................Lillian
The Formula (1980)..................................Lisa
The Amateur (1982)............................Elisabeth
Wagner (1982) .... Mathilde Wesedonck
Femmes de Persone (1986)..............................
Dark Eyes (1987; Italian/Russian).................... Tina

KELLERMAN, SALLY
Films:
  The Boston Strangler (1968)............ Dianne Cluny
  The April Fool's (1969)..................Phyllis Brubaker
  Brewster McCloud (1970) .... Louise
    Topless in fountain.
  M*A*S*H (1970).... Margaret "Hot Lips" Houlihan
    0:42 - Very, very brief left breast opening her
    blouse for "Frank Burns" in her tent. *
    1:11 - Very, very brief buns and side view of right
    breast during shower prank. Long shot, hard to
    see. *
    1:54 - Very brief topless in a slightly different
    angle of the shower prank during the credits. *
  Venus (1971)..
  Last of the Red Hot Lovers (1972)...Elaine Navazio
  Reflection of Fear (1973)............................ Anne
  Rafferty and the Gold Dust Twins (1975)
  ....Mac Beachwood
  The Big Bus (1976) ....Sybil Crane
  Welcome to L.A. (1977)........................ Ann Goode
  It Rained All Night the Day I Left (1978)...............
  A Little Romance (1979)...........................Kay King
  Foxes (1980)....................................... Mary
  Serial (1980)....................................... Martha
    0:03 - Topless sitting on the floor with a guy. ***
  Dempsey (1983)..
  You Can't Hurry Love (1984)...............Kelly Bones
  Fatal Attraction (1985; Canadian)......................
    a.k.a. Head On
    Bare breast.
  Moving Violations (1985)..Judge Nedra Henderson
  Back to School (1986)........................... Diane
  Someone to Love (1986) ....
  That's Life (1986)............................... Holly Parrish
  Meatballs III (1987)......................................
  Three for the Road (1987) ....
  Paramedics (1988)..................... Dispatcher's Voice
  All's Fair (1989)......................................
Faerie Tale Theatre:
  Sleeping Beauty (1983) ....
Tall Tales and Legends:
  Ponce de Leon and the Fountain of Youth (1986)....
Miniseries:
  Centennial (1978-79)...................... Lise Bockweiss
Made for TV Movies:
  Secret Weapons (1985)................................
Magazines:
  Playboy (Dec 1980)..................."Sex Stars of 1980"
    Page 243: Topless. **

KELLEY, SHEILA

Films:
Some Girls (1988)........................ Irenka
    0:13 - Topless and buns getting something at the
    end of the hall while "Michael" watches. Long
    shot, hard to see. *
    1:01 - Topless in window while "Michael"
    watches from outside. Long shot, hard to see. *
    1:17 - In black slip seducing "Michael" after
    funeral.
Breaking In (1989).....................................
Staying Together (1989)...........................

KELLY, PAULA

Films:
The Andromeda Strain (1971) .... Nurse
Top of the Heap (1972).................................. Singer
Sweet Charity (1972)................................... Helene
Trouble Man (1973)............................... Cleo
Uptown Saturday Night (1974) .... Leggy Peggy
Jo Jo Dancer, Your Life Is Calling (1986)
.... Satin Doll
    0:26 - Doing a strip tease in the night club wearing
    gold pasties and a gold G-string.
Miniseries:
Chiefs (1983) ....Liz Watts
TV:
Night Court (1984)................................Liz Williams
Magazines:
Playboy (Aug 1969).......................... "Sweet Paula"
    Debut of pubic hair in Playboy magazine
Playboy (Jul 1972)............................... "Too Much"
    Pages 138, 140 & 141: Topless. ***
Playboy (Nov 1972)............. "Sex in Cinema 1972"
    Page 163: Topless in photo from "Top of the
    Heap." **
Playboy (Jan 1979)................."25 Beautiful Years"
    Pages 160-161: Topless strobe photo from Aug
    1969. **
Playboy (Jan 1989)............. "Women of the Sixties"
    Pages 160-161: Topless strobe photo from Aug
    1969. **

KELLY, SHARON

Other:
    a.k.a. Adult film actress Colleen Brennan.
Films:
Hustle (1975) ....Gloria Hollinger
Alice Goodbody (1974)..
Gosh (1974) ....
Carnal Madness (1975)..
The Beauties and the Beast....................................
    Nude, being carried into a cave by the beast.
Shampoo (1975)................................... Painted Lady
    1:17 - Brief topless covered with tattoos all over
    her body during party. Lit with strobe light. *

Slammer Girls (1987)..............................Professor
    0:23 - Brief topless changing clothes under table
    in the prison cafeteria. *
    0:35 - Topless squishing breasts against the
    window during prison visiting hours. **
    0:37 - Topless with an inflatable male doll. **

KEMP, CHARLOTTE

Other:
    Also see Helmcamp, Charlotte J.
Video Tapes:
Playmate Review 3 (1985)........................ Playmate
Playboy Video Magazine, Volume 3........ Playmate
Magazines:
Playboy (Dec 1982)................................... Playmate

KENNEDY, SHEILA

Films:
Spring Break (1983).. Carla
    0:49 - Topless during wet T-shirt contest. **
The First Turn-on! (1983)..................... Dreamgirl
    0:52 - In red two piece swimsuit, then topless
    when the top falls down during "Danny's"
    daydream. *
    0:59 - Right breast in bed with "Danny." *
Ellie (1984)... Ellie May
    0:29 - Full frontal nudity posing for "Billy" while
    he takes pictures of her just before he falls over
    a cliff. **
    0:38 - In white bra and panties in barn loft with
    "Frank."
    0:58 - In white bra and panties stuggling to get
    away from Edward Albert.
    1:16 - In bra and panties taking off dress with
    "Art." Topless taking off bra and throwing
    them on antlers. Brief topless many times while
    frolicking around. *
Magazines:
Penthouse (Dec 1981)... Pet
    Pages 97-133
Penthouse (Dec 1983)......................Pet of the Year
    Pages 115-129
Penthouse (Oct 1987)................. "Sheila Revisited"
    Pages 52-61

KENSIT, PATSY

Other:
    Singer in the group "Eighth Wonder."
Films:
Oh, Alfie! (1975; British)................................ Penny
    a.k.a. Alfie Darling
Hanover Street (1979)......................Sarah Sallinger
Absolute Beginners (1986)........................ Suzette
Lethal Weapon 2 (1989)......... Rika Van Den Haas
    1:15 - Right breast lying in bed with Mel Gibson.
    **
    1:19 - Topless in bed with Gibson. **

KERNOHAN, ROXANNE

Other:
a.k.a. Roxanne Kernahan.
Films:
Angel III: The Final Chapter (1988). White Hooker
Critters 2: The Main Course (1988)............... Lee
0:37 - Brief topless after transforming from an
alien into a Playboy Playmate. **
Phoenix the Warrior (1988)............................Meda
Not of This Earth (1988)....................Lead Hooker
0:41 - Topless in cellar with "Paul Johnson" just
before getting killed with two other hookers.
Wearing a blue top. ***
Tango & Cash (1989).............. Dressing Room Girl
1:06 - Brief topless in dressing room with three
other girls. She's the second one in the middle.
*
Magazines:
Playboy (Jul 1989)................... "B-Movie Bimbos"
Page 136: Topless straddling a car wearing an
open bathing suit. ***

KERRIDGE, LINDA

Films:
Fade to Black (1980)....................................Marilyn
0:44 - Topless in the shower. *
Strangers Kiss (1984).....................................Shirley
Surf II (1984)..Sparkle
Down Twisted (1987).................................. Soames
Alien from L.A. (1988) ... Roeyis Freki/Auntie Pearl
Magazines:
Playboy (Dec 1980)........................."Double Take"
Pages 218-227: Full frontal nudity. ***

KERSH, KATHY

Films:
The Americanization of Emily (1964).....................
Gemini Affair (1974)....................................Jessica
0:10 - In white bra and black panties changing in
front of Marta Kristen.
0:11 - Nude getting into bed with Marta. **
0:12 - Brief topless turning over onto her stomach
in bed. *
0:17 - Nude, standing up in bed and jumping off.
**
0:57 - Nude in bed with Kristen. ***
1:04 - Left breast sitting up in bed after Kristen
leaves. **

KERWIN, MAUREEN

Films:
The Destructors (1974; British).................Lucianne
Laura (1979).. Martine
0:03 - Brief full frontal nudity getting out of bed
and putting white bathrobe on. *

KESNER, JILLIAN

Films:
The Student Body (1976)..............................Carrie
Firecracker (1981)......................... Susanne Carter
Moon in Scorpio (1987)................................Claire
0:39 - Topless sitting on deck of boat with bathing
suit top down. **
Beverly Hills Vamp (1989) ....Claudia
0:06 - In white lingerie riding a guy like a horse.
0:33 - In white slip with "Brock."
0:42 - Almost topless in bed with "Brock." Too
dark to see anything.
1:09 - In white nightgown attacking "Russell" in
bed with Debra Lamb and Michelle Bauer.
1:17 - In white nightgown getting killed as a
vampire by "Kyle."
TV:
Co-ed Fever (1979).. Melba

KIDDER, MARGOT

Films:
Gaily Gaily (1969)...................................... Adeline
Quackser Fortune has a Cousin in the Bronx
(1970)..Zazel
1:03 - Topless undressing on a char, then brief
right, then breasts when Gene Wilder kisses her.
**
1:05 - Side view of left breast, then buns, getting
out of bed. *
Sisters (1973)................................Danielle Breton
Topless on couch.
Gravey Train (1974)................................. Margie
The Reincarnation of Peter Proud (1975)
.... Marcia Curtis
1:29 - Brief topless sitting in bathtub masturbating
while remembering getting raped by husband. *
Superman (1978) .... Lois Lane
The Amityville Horror (1979)............Kathleen Lutz
Superman II (1980)........................ Lois Lane
Willie and Phil (1980)..............Jeanette Sutherland
Heartaches (1981)....................................Rita Harris
Topless.
Some Kind of Hero (1982)............................... Toni
0:52 - In white corset making love with Richard
Pryor on the floor.
0:56 - In bra with robe standing outside the door
talking to Pryor.
Trenchcoat (1983)........................ Mickey Raymond
Little Treasure (1985)....................................Margo
0:53 - Stripping in bar, doesn't show anything.
1:13 - Nude dancing by swimming pool. Long
shot, don't see anything.
Keeping Track (1988)...................Mickey Tremaine
Made for HBO Movies:
Glitter Dome (1985).......................................Willie
1:04 - Topless on balcony after making love with
James Garner the night before. Long shot, hard
to see anything.

Made for HBO:

The Hitchhiker: Night Shift............ Jane Reynolds
(Available on The Hitchhiker, Volume II.)
0:13 - In a white corset, then brief left breast over
the shoulder shot. *

Made for TV Movies:

Body of Evidence (1988)..

TV:

Nichols (1971-72)..Ruth

Magazines:

Playboy (Mar 1975)................................. "Margot"
Pages 86-93: Full frontal nudity. ***

KIDMAN, NICOLE

Films:

BMX Bandits (1984; Australia)..........................Judy
Dead Calm (1989)..................................Rae Ingram
0:59 - Brief buns and topless with the attacker. *
Days of Thunder (1990)......................................

KIEL, SUE

Films:

Survivor (1987)..
Red Heat (1987; U.S./German).....................Hedda
0:56 - Brief topless in shower room scene (third
girl behind Linda Blair). Long shot, hard to see.
*

KIGER, SUSAN LYNN

Films:

H.O.T.S. (1979)................................ Honey Shayne
0:00 - Topless in shower room with the other girls.
*
0:33 - Topless in pool making love with Doug. **
1:33 - Topless in football game. *
Seven (1979)...................................... Jennie
Angels Brigade (1980)...............................
The Return (1980)...................................
The Happy Hooker Goes Hollywood (1980). Susie
0:42 - Topless, singing "Happy Birthday" to a guy
tied up on the bed. *
0:43 - Topless, wearing a red garter belt playing
pool with K.C. Winkler. ***
Death Screams (1982)...............................

Magazines:

Playboy (Jan 1977)...............................Playmate
Playboy (Dec 1979)..................."Sex Stars of 1979"
Page 258: Full frontal nudity. ***

KING, TRACEY ANN

Films:

Hammer (1972)................ The Black Magic Woman
The Naughty Stewardesses (1978)............. Barbara
0:56 - Topless dancing by the pool in front of
everybody. **

KINMONT, KATHLEEN

Films:

Hardbodies (1984)...............................Pretty Skater
Fraternity Vacation (1985).....................Marianne
0:16 - Topless and buns taking off her swimsuit in
bedroom with two guys. **
Winners Take All (1987) ....Party Girl #5
Phoenix the Warrior (1988) ....Phoenix
Halloween 4: The Return of Michael Meyers
(1988).. Kelly
0:51 - In bra and panties in front of fireplace with
"Brady."
Midnight (1989) ....Party

KINNAMAN, MELANIE

Films:

Friday the 13th, Part V: A New Beginning (1985)
....Pam Roberts
1:08 - In wet white blouse coming back into the
house from the rain.
Thunder Alley (1986)..................................... Star
0:52 - Brief topless under water in pool talking to
a guy. *
1:14 - Topless and buns making love on bed and
getting out. *

KINSKI, NASTASSJA

Films:

To the Devil, a Daughter (1976)
.................................Catherine Beddows
Full frontal nudity at the end of the film.
Virgin Campus (1976)...
Stay As You Are (1978)...
Tess (1980).............................. Tess Durbeyfield
Boarding School (1980; Italian)................ Deborah
1:32 - Topless making love with a guy. *
Cat People (1982)............................... Irena Gollier
1:03 - Nude at night walking around outside
chasing a rabbit. ***
1:35 - Topless taking off top and walking up the
stairs and getting into bed. **
1:38 - Topless getting out of bed and walking to
the bathroom. **
1:46 - Full frontal nudity at night in a cabin. **
One from the Heart (1982)..............................Leila
1:13 - Brief topless in open blouse when she leans
forward after walking on a ball. *
Exposed (1983)..........................Elizabeth Carlson
Moon in the Gutter (1983) ....Loretta
For Your Love Only (1979).................................
The Hotel New Hampshire (1984)..... Susie the Bear
Paris, Texas (1984)...
Unfaithfully Yours (1984) ....
Maria's Lovers (1985)......................... Maria Bosic
0:59 - In a black bra.
1:12 - Brief right breast looking at herself in the
mirror. *
Revolution (1985)..................... Daisy McConnahay

Harem (1985)................................... Diane
   0:14 - Topless getting into swimming pool. *
   1:04 - Topless in motel room with Ben Kingsley.
   **

KIRKLAND, SALLY

Films:
  Coming Apart (1969)...
  Going Home (1971)...
  The Way We Were (1973).......................................
  The Sting (1973)..
  Big Bad Mama (1974)............... Barney's Woman
   0:13 - Topless and buns waiting for "Barney" then
   throwing shoe at "Billy Jean." **
  Tracks (1974)..uncredited
  Crazy Mama (1975)............................... Ella Mae
  A Star is Born (1976)............................Photographer
  Private Benjamin (1980) ....
  Double Exposure (1983)............................ Hooker
   0:26 - Topless in alley getting killed. **
  Love Letters (1984)...Hippie
  Fatal Games (1984) ....
  Anna (1987).. Anna
   0:28 - Topless in the bathtub talking to "Daniel."
   **
  Cold Feet (1989)...................... Maureen Linoleum
   She appears in tight fitting spandex dresses
   throughout most of this film.
   0:56 - In black bra and panties taking off her dress
   in bedroom with Keith Carradine. Brief right
   breast pulling bra down. *
   0:58 - Brief side view of right breast sitting up in
   bed talking to Carradine. *
  High Stakes (1989)............. Melanie "Bambi" Rose
   0:01 - In two piece costume, doing a strip tease
   routine on stage. Buns in G-string, then very,
   very brief topless flashing her breasts. *
   1:11 - In black bra cutting her hair in front of a
   mirror.
  Paint It Black (1989) .... Marion Easton
   0:05 - Most of left breast sitting in bed talking to
   Rick Rossovich.
  Revenge (1990) .... Rock Star
  Best of the Best (1990)..

KITAEN, TAWNY

Other:
  Wife of singer David Cloverdale of the rock group
  "Whitesnake."
Films:
  Bachelor Party (1984) .... Debbie Thompson
  **The Perils of Gwendolyne in the Land of the Yik
  Yak** (1984; French)........................... Gwendoline
   0:37 - Topless in the rain in the forest. **
   1:01 - Topless in a bondage outfit. *
   1:19 - Topless making love with Willard. **

Crystal Heart (1987)......................... Alley Daniels
   0:46 - Topless and buns "making love" with Lee
   Curreri through the glass. **
   0:50 - Nude, crashing through glass and covered
   with blood having a nightmare. **
   1:14 - Brief topless making love with Curreri in
   and falling out of bed. *
Witchboard (1987)... Linda
   1:26 - Topless, nude, brief full frontal nudity stuck
   in the shower and breaking the glass doors to
   get out. *
Instant Justice (1987)............................... Virginia
Happy Hour (1987)...........................Misty Roberts
Made for HBO:
  The Glory Years (1987)..
Music Videos:
  Whitesnake videos.....................................The Girl
TV:
  Santa Barbara (1989-)......................................Lisa

KOSCINA, SYLVA

Films:
  Hercules (1959; Italian)...................................... Iole
  The Secret War of Harry Frigg (1969)
  ....Countess di Montefiore
  The Slasher (1975)................................Barbara
   0:17 - Left breast lying down getting a massage.
   **
   1:18 - Topless undressing and putting a robe on at
   her lover's house. Left breast after getting
   stabbed. **
  Some Like It Cool
  (1979; German/French/Italian/Austrian)
  ....Jelsamina
  a.k.a. Sex on the Run
  a.k.a. Casanova and Co.
   0:28 - Topless and brief buns dropping her top for
   Tony Curtis, then walking around with the
   "other" Tony Curtis. ***
   1:20 - Topless talking to her husband. **

KOTERO, APOLLONIA

Other:
  Singer.
Films:
  Heartbreaker (1983)...Rose
  Purple Rain (1984)................................. Apollonia
   0:20 - Brief topless taking off jacket before
   jumping into lake. **
   0:41 - In lingerie making love with Prince.
   1:06 - In black lingerie and stockings singing on
   stage.
TV:
  Falcon Crest (1985-86).............................Apollonia
Magazines:
  Playboy (January 1985)
  ...."The Girls of Rock 'n' Roll"
  Page 98 - In leather bikini, rated PG.

KOZAK, HEIDI
Films:
Slumber Party Massacre, Part II (1987)....................
Friday the 13th Part VII - The New Blood
(1988)...Sandra
0:36 - Buns taking off clothes to go skinny
dipping. Brief topless under water just before
getting killed by Jason. *

KRIGE, ALICE
Films:
Chariots of Fire (1981)........................Sybil Gordon
Ghost Story (1981)................................. Alma/Eva
0:41 - Brief topless making love in bedroom with
Craig Wasson. *
0:44 - Topless in bathtub with Wasson. **
0:46 - Topless sitting up in bed. **
0:49 - Buns, then topless standing on balcony
turning and walking to bedroom talking to
Wasson. ***
King David (1985)...................................Bathsheba
1:16 - Full frontal nudity getting a bath outside at
dusk while Richard Gere watches. **
Barfly (1987) ....Tully
Haunted Summer (1988)....................Mary Godwin
See You in the Morning (1989).........Beth Goodwin
Made for HBO Movies:
Baja Oklahoma (1988)............................Patsy Cline

KRISS, KATHERINE
Films:
Hot Chili (1985)................................Allison Baxter
0:56 - Topless getting out of the pool talking to
"Ricky." ***
1:09 - Buns and side view of left breast lying
down and kissing "Ricky." *
American Flyers (1985)...

KRISTEL, SYLVIA
Films:
Game of Seduction..
Frontal nudity.
Because of the Cats (1973)......................................
Emmanuelle (1974)............................ Emmanuelle
0:11 - Topless making love with her husband
under a mosquito net in bed. *
0:26 - Topless making love with a stranger on an
airplane. ***
0:35 - Topless with blonde woman in squash court
after playing squash. **
1:03 - Topless after taking off clothes in locker
room with another woman to get ready for
squash. **
Julia (1974; German).......................................Julia
0:23 - Brief topless in the lake.
0:25 - Topless on deck in the lake. **
0:28 - Brief topless changing inside her house at
night. Long shot. *

0:34 - Topless on boat with two boys. **
0:42 - Topless taking off her towel. **
1:12 - Topless on tennis court with "Patrick." *
Goodbye Emmanuelle (1977).............Emmanuelle
0:03 - Full frontal nudity in bath and getting out.
**
0:04 - Full frontal nudity taking off dress. **
0:06 - Full frontal nudity in bed with "Angelique."
***
0:26 - Topless with photographer in old house.
***
0:42 - Brief side view of right breast in bed with
"Jean."
1:03 - Full frontal nudity on beach with movie
director. ***
1:06 - Full frontal nudity lying on beach sleeping.
**
1:28 - Side view of left breast lying on beach with
"Gregory" while dreaming. **
The Concorde: Airport '79 (1979)...............Isabelle
Tigers in Lipstick (1979)....... "The Arab" Segment
0:04 - Topless in photograph on the sand.
0:06 - Braless in sheer nightgown lying in bed.
0:09 - Topless lying in bed with "The Arab." **
0:16 - Lying in bed in red lingerie, then left breast
for awhile. **
Goodbye Emmanuelle (1981)............... Emmanuelle
Lady Chatterley's Lover (1981)
....Constance Chatterley
0:25 - Nude in front of mirror. **
0:59 - Brief topless with the Gardener. *
1:04 - Brief topless. *
1:16 - Nude in bedroom with the Gardener. ***
Private Lessons (1981).............................. Mallow
0:20 - Very brief topless sitting up next to the pool
when the sprinklers go on. *
0:24 - Topless and buns, stripping for "Billy."
Some shots might be a body double. **
0:51 - Topless in bed when she "dies" with
Howard Hessman. **
1:28 - Topless making love with "Billy." Some
shots might be a body double. *
Private School (1983)..........................Ms. Copuletta
0:57 - In wet white dress after falling in the pool.
Emmanuelle 4 (1984)....................................Sylvia
0:00 - Topless in photos during opening credits.
**
Mata Hari (1985)....................................Mata Hari
0:11 - Topless making love with a guy on a train.
***
0:31 - Topless standing by window after making
love with the soldier. **
0:35 - Topless making love in empty house by the
fireplace. *
0:52 - Topless masturbating in bed wearing black
stockings. **
1:02 - Topless having a sword fight with another
topless woman. **
1:03 - Topless in bed smoking opium and making
love with two women. **

The Big Bet (1985).................................... Michelle
    0:07 - Left breast in open nightgown while
    "Chris" tries to fix her sink. *
    0:20 - Topless dressing while "Chris" watches
    through binoculars. **
    0:28 - Topless undressing while "Chris" watches
    through binoculars. **
    0:40 - Topless getting out of the shower and
    drying herself off. ***
    1:00 - Topless getting into bed while "Chris"
    watches through binoculars. *
    1:13 - Topless in bedroom with "Chris," then
    making love. ***
Red Heat (1987; U.S./German)....................... Sofia
    0:23 - In red lingerie.
    0:56 - Topless in shower room scene. **
    1:01 - Brief topless raping Linda Blair. *
Dracula's Widow (1988)..............................Vanessa
Magazines:
Playboy (Dec 1976)................... "Sex Stars of 1976"
    Page 187: Topless drinking from champagne
    bottle. **
Playboy (Dec 1977)................... "Sex Stars of 1977"
    Page 212: Topless with Jeff Bridges. **
Playboy (Dec 1984)................... "Sex Stars of 1984"
    Page 205: Left breast, lying on chair. *

KRISTEN, MARTA
Films:
Terminal Island (1973)...........................Lee Phillips
Gemini Affair (1974)..Julie
    0:32 - Topless wearing beige panties talking with
    "Jessica" in the bathroom. ***
    0:56 - Very, very brief left breast and lower frontal
    nudity standing next to bed with a guy. Very
    brief left breast in bed with him. *
    0:59 - Topless and buns making love in bed with
    "Jessica." Wowzers! ***
Battle Beyond the Stars (1980) .... Lux
TV:
Lost in Space (1965-68).................... Judy Robinson

L

LAINE, KAREN
Films:
Pretty in Pink (1986) .... Girl at Prom
Made for HBO Movies:
Baja Oklahoma (1988)................... Girl at Drive-In
    0:04 - Left breast, in truck with a jerk guy. Dark,
    hard to see anything. *

LAMARR, HEDY
Other:
    First instance of celebrity nudity in film.
Films:
Ecstasy (1932; B&W).............................. The Wife
    0:25 - Brief topless starting to run after a horse in
    a field. *
    0:26 - Long shot running through the woods, side
    view naked, then brief topless hiding behind a
    tree. *
Ziegfield Girl (1941; B&W).............. Sandra Kolter
Dishonored Lady (1947; B&W)
    ....Madeleine Damien
Samson and Delilah (1949; B&W)................Delilah

LAMB, DEBRA
Films:
Deathrow Game Show (1988).......Shanna Shallow
    0:23 - Topless dancing in white G-string and
    garter belt during the show. ***
Stripped to Kill II (1988)............................Mantra
    0:04 - Topless during strip dance routine. **
    0:42 - Topless in black lingerie during strip dance
    routine ***
B.O.R.N. (1988)..Sue
Beverly Hills Vamp (1989)........................ Jessica
    0:33 - In black slip with "Russell."
    0:36 - Topless and buns in red G-string posing for
    "Russell" while he photographs her. ***
    0:41 - More topless posing on bed. ***
    1:09 - In white nightgown attacking "Russell" in
    bed with Michelle Bauer and Jillian Kesner.
    1:19 - In white nightgown getting killed as a
    vampire by "Kyle."

LANDRY, KAREN
Films:
The Personals (1982)................................Adrienne
Patti Rocks (1988).. Patti
    0:48 - Very brief right breast in shower with
    "Billy." *
    0:48 - Buns, walking from bathroom to bedroom
    and shutting the door. Long shot.
    1:04 - Topless in bed with "Eddie" while "Billy"
    is out in the living room. **

LANDRY, TAMARA
Films:
R.S.V.P. (1984)...Vicky
    0:43 - Topless sitting in van taking top off. **
    0:48 - Topless making love in the van with two
    guys. **
Tango & Cash (1989)............................ Girl in Bar

LANDS, WENDY
Films:
One Night Only (1984; Canadian) ....Jane
0:36 - Topless taking a bath while "Jamie"
watches through keyhole. **
0:38 - Brief left breast in open robe. **
1:15 - Brief topless in bed with policeman. *
Busted Up (1986) ....Drayton's Date

LANE, DIANE
Other:
Wife of actor Christopher Lambert.
Films:
A Little Romance (1979) ....Lauren
Touched by Love (1980) ....Karen
The Outsiders (1981) ....Cherry Valance
Ladies and Gentlemen The Fabulous Stains
(1982) ....
(Not available on video tape yet.)
Six Pack (1982) .... Breezy
Rumble Fish (1983) .... Patty
The Cotton Club (1984) .... Vera Cicero
Streets of Fire (1984) ....Ellen Aim
Big Town (1987) ....Lorry Dane
0:51 - Doing a strip routine in the club wearing a
G-string and pasties while Matt Dillon watches.
1:17 - Topless making love on bed with Dillon in
hotel room. ***
1:27 - Brief left breast wearing pasties walking
into dressing room while Dillon plays craps.
Lady Beware (1987) ....Katya Yarno
0:10 - Walking around in her apartment in a red
silk teddy getting ready for bed.
0:14 - Lying down in white semi-transparent
pajamas after fantasizing.
0:24 - In black bra in apartment.
0:46 - Topless in apartment and in bed making
love with "Mack." ***
0:52 - Brief topless during "Jack's" flashback
when he is in the store. **
0:59 - Brief side view topless in bed with "Mack"
again during another of "Jack's" flashbacks. **
1:02 - Very brief topless in bed with "Mack." *
1:06 - Brief topless lying in bed behind thin
curtain in another of "Jack's" flashbacks. **
Miniseries:
Lonesome Dove (1989) ....Lorena Wood

LANE, KRISTA
Other:
Adult film actress.
Films:
In Search of the Perfect 10 (1986). Perfect Girl #6
(Shot on video tape.)
0:37 - Topless playing Twister with Iris Condon.
Buns in G-string. ***

LANE, NIKKI
Films:
Death of a Soldier (1985) .... Stripper in bar
0:49 - Topless and bottomless dancing on stage.
**
The Big Hurt (1987)...

LANGE, JESSICA
Films:
King Kong (1976) ....Dwan
1:20 - Almost topless when King Kong is playing
with her in his hand. Hand covers nipple of left
breast.
How to Beat the High Cost of Living (1980). Louise
All That Jazz (1980)...........................Angelique
The Postman Always Rings Twice (1981)
.... Cora Papadakis
0:17 - Making love with Jack Nicholson on the
kitchen table. No nudity, but still exciting.
Frances (1982).............................Frances Farmer
0:41 - Very brief upper half of left breast lying on
bed and throwing a newspaper. *
0:50 - Brief full frontal nudity covered with
bubbles standing up in bathtub and wrapping a
towel around herself. Long shot, hard to see. *
1:01 - Brief buns and right breast running into the
bathroom when the police bust in. Very, very
brief full frontal nudity, then buns closing the
bathroom door. It might be a body double, you
don't see her face. *
Tootsie (1983)..................................... Julie Nichols
(Academy Award for Best Supporting Actress.)
Country (1984)..
Sweet Dreams (1985)...................Patsy Kline
Crimes of the Heart (1986)................. Meg Magrath
Everybody's All-American (1988)................. Babs
0:32 - Brief topless in sheer nightgown in
bedroom with Dennis Quaid.
0:54 - Buns and very, very brief side view of left
breast by the campfire by the lake with Timothy
Hutton at night. Might be a body double. *
Far North (1988)......................................Kate
Made for HBO:
Cat on a Hot Tin Roof (1985)...............................

LANGENCAMP, HEATHER
Films:
Nickel Mountain (1985).............................. Callie
0:24 - Topless in bed lying with "Willard." ***
0:29 - In white panties, peeking out the window.
0:29 - Side view of left breast and brief topless
falling on bed with "Willard." *
A Nightmare on Elm Street (1985)
....Nancy Thompson
A Nightmare on Elm Street 3: Dream Warriors
(1987)...Nancy Thompson
TV:
Just the Ten of Us (1989-)............................Marie

LANGENFELD, SARAH
Films:
Blood Link (1983)..................................... Christine
   1:01 - Topless in bed taking off her top in bed
     with "Craig." **
   1:04 - Topless in bed with "Keith." *
The Act (1984)... Leslie

LANGLOIS, LISA
Films:
Happy Birthday to Me (1980) .... Amelia
Class of 1984 (1981) .... Patsy
The Man Who Wasn't There (1982). Cindy Worth
   0:58 - Nude running away from two policemen
     after turning visible. **
   1:08 - Topless in white panties dancing in her
     apartment with an invisible Steve Guttenberg.
     ***
   1:47 - Very, very brief upper half of left breast
     throwing bouquet at wedding.
The Nest (1987)............................Elizabeth Johnson
Mind Field (1990) .... Sarah Paradis

LANKFORD, KIM
Films:
Malibu Beach (1978) .... Dina
   0:32 - Buns, running into the ocean.
   0:34 - Brief right breast getting out of the ocean. *
   1:16 - Right breast on beach at night with
     boyfriend. *
   1:19 - Brief topless at top of the stairs. *
   1:20 - Brief topless when her parent's come home.
     **
   1:21 - Topless in bed with her boyfriend. *
The Octagon (1980)....................................... Nancy
Cameron's Closet (1989).....................Dory Lansing
TV:
The Waverly Wonders (1978)............Connie Rafkin
Knots Landing (1979-83)..................... Ginger Ward
Made for HBO:
The Hitchhiker: A Time for Rifles
   ....Rae Bridgeman
   0:03 - Topless on the pool table making love with
     a guy. ***

LAURE, CAROLE
Films:
Get Out Your Handkerchiefs (1978) ....Solange
   0:21 - Topless sitting in bed listening to her
     boyfriend talk. **
   0:31 - Topless sitting in bed knitting. **
   0:41 - Upper half of left breast in bed. *
   0:47 - Left breast sitting in bed while the three
     guys talk. **
   1:08 - Brief right breast when the little boy peeks
     at her while she sleeps. *

   1:10 - Lower frontal nudity while he looks at her
     some more.
   1:17 - Full frontal nudity taking off nightgown
     while sitting on bed for the little boy. ***
Victory (1981) ....Renee
Heartbreakers (1984)..................................Liliane
   0:56 - Brief topless making love in car with Nick
     Mancuso. Dark, hard to see. *
   1:25 - In sheer black dress, then brief right breast
     making love in art gallery with Peter Coyote. *
The Surrogate (1984; Canadian). Anouk Vanderlin
   0:48 - Very brief topless when "Frank" rips her
     blouse open in his apartment. *
Sweet Country (1985)....................................... Eva
   0:31 - Topless changing in apartment while Randy
     Quaid watches. **
   0:43 - Nude in auditorium with other women
     prisoners. *
   1:13 - Nude in bed with Quaid. ***
Magazines:
Playboy (Nov 1979)............. "Sex in Cinema 1979"
   Page 181: Topless. **

LAURIN, MARIE
Films:
The Lonely Guy (1983)
   ....One of "The Seven Deadly Sins"
Creature (1985).............................. Susan Delambre
   0:41 - Topless and brief buns with blood on her
     shoulders with "Jon" getting him to take his
     helmet off. **
Talking Walls (1987)..
Made for HBO:
The Hitchhiker: Petty Thieves...................... Pearl
   0:09 - Topless making love with Steve Railsback
     on the couch. **
   0:15 - Topless playing with a doll in the bathtub,
     then buns, standing up and wrapping herself
     with a towel. **
   0:18 - In black bra, then topless undressing in
     front of John Colicos.

LAW, BARBARA
Films:
The Surrogate (1984; Canadian).... Maggie Simpson
Bedroom Eyes (1985; Canadian)...................Jobeth
   0:02 - Topless taking off clothes while "Harry"
     watches through the window. *
   0:07 - Topless and buns, kissing a woman. **
   0:14 - Topless during "Harry's" flashback when
     he talks to the psychiatrist. *
   0:23 - Topless and buns dancing in bedroom. **
   0:57 - Topless with "Mary" kissing on floor. **
   1:17 - In beige bra, panties, garter belt and
     stockings in bed with "Harry."
   1:23 - Brief topless on top of "Harry." *

LAWRENCE, SUZANNE REMEY

Films:
Delivery Boys (1984)..Nurse
   0:34 - In bra and panties after doing a strip tease
   with another "nurse" while dancing in front of a
   boy who is lying on an operating table.
R.S.V.P. (1984)..Stripper
   0:56 - Topless dancing in a radio station in front of
   a D.J. **

LE BEAU, BECKY

Films:
Joysticks (1983)..Liza
School Spirit (1985)....................................Hogette
Hollywood Hot Tubs (1984).....................Veronica
   0:49 - Topless changing in the locker room with
   other girl soccer players while "Jeff" watches.
   **
   0:54 - Topless in hot tub with the other girls and
   "Shawn." *
Back to School (1986).........................Hot Tub Girl
The Underachievers (1987)..........Ginger Bronsky
   0:40 - Topless in swimming pool playing with an
   inflatable alligator after her exercise class has
   left. ***
Takin' It All Off (1987)................................ Becky
   0:16 - Topless and brief full frontal nudity getting
   introduced to "Allison." **
   0:23 - In black bra and panties, then nude doing a
   strip routine outside. ***
   0:35 - Brief full frontal nudity pushing "Elliot"
   into the pool. *
   0:36 - Brief left breast in dance studio with
   "Allison." *
   0:36 - Brief topless in studio with "Allison" again.
   *
   1:23 - Nude, dancing with all the other women on
   stage. **
Rock-a-die Baby..
Not of This Earth (1988).........Happy Birthday Girl
   0:47 - Topless after doing a stripping Happy
   Birthday gram for the old guy. ***
Magazines:
Playboy (Feb 1989)..................................Grapevine
   Page 166: Left breast sticking out from under T-
   shirt in B&W photo. *
Playboy (Jul 1989)....................."B-Movie Bimbos"
   Page 139: Full frontal nudity standing in a car
   filled with bubbles wearing pink stockings and a
   garter belt. ***

LE BROCK, KELLY

Other:
Spokeswoman for Pantene cosmetics.
Wife of actor Steven Seagal.
Films:
The Woman in Red (1984).......................Charlotte
   0:02 - Wearing the red dress, dancing over the air
   vent in the car garage while Gene Wilder
   watches.

1:13 - Brief right breast, getting into bed. Too far
   to see anything.
1:15 - Brief lower frontal nudity getting out of bed
   when her husband comes home. Very brief left
   breast, but it's blurry and hard to see.
Weird Science (1985)......................................Lisa
   0:12 - In blue underwear and white top baring her
   midriff for the two boys when she is first
   created.
   1:29 - In blue leotard and grey tube top gym
   clothes to teach boy's gym class.
Hard to Kill (1990)..............................Andy Stewart

LEE, CYNTHIA

Films:
New York Nights (1983)...................The Porn Star
   1:15 - Topless in the steam room talking to the
   prostitute. **
   1:26 - Topless in office with the financier making
   love on his desk. ***
Hot Resort (1984)... Alice
   1:08 - Topless in the bathtub. *

LEE, LUANN

Films:
Terminal Exposure (1988) ....Bruce's Girl
Magazines:
Playboy (Jan 1987)...................................Playmate

LEE, PAT

Films:
Porky's (1982)..Stripper
   0:33 - Brief topless dancing on stage at Porky's
   showing her breasts to "Pee Wee." *
Starman (1984)..
And God Created Woman (1988)..................Inmate
Young Guns (1988)..Janey

LEE, ROBIN

Other:
a.k.a. Robbie Lee.
Films:
Big Bad Mama (1974)...................................Polly
   0:09 - Brief left breast in open dress in car when
   cops try to pull her car over. *
   0:22 - Polly in see-through slip on stage with her
   sister and a stripper.
   0:32 - Brief topless running around the bedroom
   chasing her sister. *
Switchblade Sisters (1975)...

LEE-HSU, DIANA

Films:
Â Â License to Kill (1989) .... Loti
Video Tapes:
Â Â **Playboy Video Calendar 1989** .... Playmate
Magazines:
Â Â **Playboy** (May 1988) .... Playmate
Â Â Page 98
Â Â **Playboy** (Aug 1989) .... "License to Thrill"
Â Â Pages 126-131: Nude. ***

LÉGERÈ, PHOEBE

Other:
Â Â Singer.
Films:
Â Â Mondo New York (1988) ....
Â Â **The Toxic Avenger: Part II** (1988) .... Claire
Â Â 0:31 - Brief right breast caressing herself while
Â Â making out with the Toxic Avenger. *
Magazines:
Â Â **Playboy** (Jun 1988) .... "Mondo Phoebe"
Â Â Page 70-77: Nude. **
Â Â **Playboy** (Nov 1988) .... "Sex in Cinema 1988"
Â Â Page 138: Left breast, lying on bed getting a hug
Â Â from the Toxic Avenger. *
Â Â **Playboy** (Dec 1988) .... "Sex Stars of 1988"
Â Â Page 184: Right breast, popping out of top. *

LEIGH, BARBARA

Films:
Â Â **The Student Nurses** (1970) .... Priscilla
Â Â 0:43 - Topless on the beach with "Les." Long
Â Â scene. ***
Â Â The Christian Licorice Store (1971) .... Starlet
Â Â Pretty Maids All in a Row (1971) .... Jean McDrew
Â Â Frenzy (1972) .... Brenda Blaney
Â Â Junior Bonner (1972) .... Charmagne
Â Â **Terminal Island** (1973) .... Bunny Campbell
Â Â 0:22 - Topless and buns undressing in room while
Â Â "Bobbie" watches from the bed. ***
Â Â Boss Nigger (1974) .... Miss Pruitt
Â Â **Seven** (1979) .... Alexa
Â Â Mistress of the Apes (1981) ....
Â Â **Famous T & A** (1982) .... herself
Â Â 0:45 - Topless scene from "Terminal Island."
Â Â Includes additional takes that weren't used. ***
Miniseries:
Â Â The Search for the Nile (1972)
Â Â .... Isabel Arundel Burton
Magazines:
Â Â **Playboy** (May 1973) .... "Indian"
Â Â Pages 149-155: Topless. ***
Â Â **Playboy** (Jan 1977) .... "Natural Leigh"
Â Â Pages 85-91: B&W photos. Full frontal nudity.
Â Â ***

LEIGH, CARRIE

Other:
Â Â Former girlfriend of Playboy founder Hugh Hefner.
Films:
Â Â A Fine Mess (1986) .... Second Extra
Â Â Beverly Hills Cop II (1987) .... Herself
Â Â Blood Relations (1989) .... Thomas' Girlfriend
Magazines:
Â Â **Playboy** (Jul 1986) .... "Carrie Leigh"
Â Â Pages 114-125: Nude. ***
Â Â **Playboy** (Aug 1988) ... "The Great Palimony Caper"
Â Â Page 64: Left breast and lower frontal nudity,
Â Â B&W. **
Â Â **Playboy** (Dec 1988) .... "Sex Stars of 1988"
Â Â Page 188: Full frontal nudity. ***
Â Â **Playboy** (Feb 1989) .... "The Year in Sex"
Â Â Page 143: Topless in B&W photo. **

LEIGH, JENNIFER JASON

Films:
Â Â **Eyes of a Stranger** (1981) .... Tracy
Â Â 1:15 - Very brief topless lying in bed getting
Â Â attacked by rapist. *
Â Â 1:19 - Left breast, cleaning herself in bathroom.
Â Â **
Â Â **Fast Times at Ridgemont High** (1982)
Â Â .... Stacy Hamilton
Â Â 0:18 - Left breast making out with "Ron" in a
Â Â dugout. *
Â Â 1:00 - Topless in pool side changing room. ***
Â Â Wrong is Right (1982) .... Young Girl
Â Â Easy Money (1983) .... Allison Capuletti
Â Â Grandview USA (1984) .... Candy Webster
Â Â **Flesh + Blood** (1985) .... Agnes
Â Â 0:45 - Brief right breast being held down. *
Â Â 1:05 - Full frontal nudity getting into the bath with
Â Â Rutger Hauer and making love. **
Â Â 1:16 - Full frontal nudity getting out of bed with
Â Â Hauer and walking to the window. ***
Â Â 1:35 - Nude throwing clothes into the fire. **
Â Â The Hitcher (1986) .... Nash
Â Â Best Little Girl in the World (1986) ....
Â Â The Men's Club (1986) .... Teensy
Â Â **Sister Sister** (1987) .... Lucy Bonnard
Â Â 0:01 - Topless making love during a dream. **
Â Â 0:52 - In lingerie talking with Eric Stolz. *
Â Â 0:53 - Left breast, making love with Stolz in her
Â Â bedroom. **
Â Â 0:58 - Topless in bathtub surrounded by candles.
Â Â *
Â Â Under Cover (1987) .... Tanille Lareoux
Â Â **Heart of Midnight** (1988) .... Carol
Â Â 0:27 - Very brief side view of right breast reaching
Â Â for soap in the shower. *
Â Â Last Exit to Brooklyn (1990) ....
Â Â Miami Blues (1990) ....
Made for TV Movies:
Â Â Girls of the White Orchid (1983) ....
Â Â The Killing of Randy Webster (1985) ....

LEIGHTON, ROBERTA

Films:
Barracuda (1978) ....
Stripes (1981) .... Anita
   0:07 - Topless coming out of the bathroom in blue
   panties putting her shirt on while talking to Bill
   Murray. *
Covergirl (1984; Canadian) .... Dee
TV:
The Young and the Restless (1978-86)
.... Dr. Casey Reed

LEMMONS, KASI

Films:
School Daze (1988) ....
Vampire's Kiss (1989) .... Jackie
   0:05 - In black bra and panties, then topless in
   living room with Nicholas Cage. **

LENSKA, RULA

Films:
Oh, Alfie! (1975; British) .... Louise
   a.k.a. Alfie Darling
   0:12 - Topless, then left breast in bed after making
   love with "Alfie." **
Confessions of a Pop Performer (1975) ....
Undercovers Hero (1975) .... Grenier Girl
The Deadly Females (1976) .... Luisa

LENTINI, SUSAN

Films:
Action Jackson (1988) ....
Road House (1989) ....
Made for HBO:
Dream On: Sex and the Single Parent (1990)
.... Ms. Brodsky
   0:04 - In white bra and panties in front of class
   while "Jeremy" fantasizes about her.
   0:10 - Topless twice talking to "Martin" while he
   fantasizes about her. **

LENZ, KAY

Films:
Breezy (1974) .... Breezy
   Topless and nude.
The Passage (1979; British) .... Leah Bergson
   Topless.
White Line Fever (1975) .... Jerri Hummer
The Great Scout and Cathouse Thursday (1976)
.... Thursday
Moving Violation (1979) .... Cam Johnson
Fast Walking (1981) .... Moke
   0:26 - Brief topless shutting the door after pulling
   James Woods into the room. *
   0:42 - Caressing herself under her dress while in
   the prison visiting room talking to "George."

   1:27 - Topless getting hosed down and dried off
   outside by James Woods. ***
   1:32 - Brief left breast, making love with Woods.
   *
Prisoners of the Lost Universe (1983) ....
House (1986) .... Sandy Sinclair
Stripped to Kill (1987) .... Cody Sheehan
   0:23 - Topless dancing on stage. **
   0:47 - Topless dancing in white lingerie. ***
Death Wish 4: The Crackdown (1987)
.... Karen Sheldon
Smoke (1988) ....
Fear (1988) .... Sharon Haden
Physical Evidence (1989) .... Deborah Quinn
Streets (1989) .... Sergeant
Made for TV Movies:
The Initiation of Sarah (1978) ....
Sanctuary of Fear (1979) ....
The Seeding of Sarah Burns (1979) ....
Miniseries:
Rich Man, Poor Man - Book I (1976) . Kate Jordache
Rich Man, Poor Man - Book II (1976-77)
.... Kate Jordache
Magazines:
Playboy (Nov 1982) .... "Sex in Cinema 1982"
   Page 161: Topless photo from "Fast Walking."
   ***

LEO, MELISSA

Films:
Always (1984) ....
Streetwalkin' (1985) .... Cookie
   0:15 - Topless, stripping and taking off her top for
   a customer. **
   0:18 - Brief right breast, having sex with her pimp
   on the floor. *
Deadtime Stories (1987) .... Judith "Mama" Baer
A Time of Destiny (1988) .... Josie
TV:
Young Riders (1989-90) .... Emma

LESNIAK, EMILIA

Films:
Fear City (1984) .... Bibi
   0:16 - Topless, dancing at the Metropole club. **
   1:00 - Topless, dancing on the stage. **
9 Deaths of the Ninja (1985) ....
Hollywood Vice Squad (1986) ....

LEWIS, CHARLOTTE

Films:
Pirates (1986) ....
The Golden Child (1986) .... Kee Nang
Dial Help (1988) .... Jenny Cooper
   1:06 - Black panties and bare back dressing in
   black corset top and stockings. Yowza!
   1:09 - Brief right breast rolling while rolling
   around in the bathtub. **
Tripwire (1989) .... Trudy

LEWIS, FIONA

Films:
Dr. Phibes Rises Again (1972).........................Diana
Lisztomania (1975)... Marie
   0:00 - Topless in bed getting breasts kissed by
    Roger Daltrey to the beat of a metronome. **
   0:01 - Brief topless swinging a chandelier to
    Daltrey. *
   0:03 - Brief topless catching a candle on the bed.
    **
   0:04 - Left breast, sitting inside a piano with
    Daltrey. **
Drum (1976)................................. Augusta Chauvet
   0:57 - Topless taking a bath, getting out, then
    having Pam Grier dry her off. ***
Tintorera (1977)...Patricia
   0:20 - Side view of left breast in silhouette. Long
    shot, hard to see. Nude swimming under water
    just before getting eaten by a shark. Don't see
    her face.
The Fury (1978)............................Dr. Susan Charles
Dead Kids (1981) .... Gwen Parkinson
  a.k.a. Strange Behavior
Strange Invaders (1983)...........Waitress/Avon Lady
Innerspace (1987)....................Dr. Margaret Canker
Magazines:
Playboy (Dec 1976)................. "Sex Stars of 1976"
   Page 186: Full frontal nudity. ***

LINDELAND, LIV

Films:
Picasso Trigger (1989).......................................Inga
Magazines:
Playboy (Jan 1971)......................................Playmate
Playboy (1972)....................... Playmate of the Year
Playboy (Dec 1972)................... "Sex Stars of 1972"
   Page 216

LINDEN, JENNIE

Films:
Nightmare (1963; British)................................Janet
Dr. Who and the Daleks (1965; British) ...... Barbara
A Severed Head (1971; British)...... Georgie Hands
   0:02 - Buns, rolling over on the floor with Ian
    Holm.
Women in Love (1971)................. Ursula Bragwen
   0:38 - Brief topless skinny dipping in the river
    with Glenda Jackson. *
   1:11 - Brief topless in a field with Alan Bates. For
    some reason, the whole scene is shown
    sideways on the TV. *
Hedda (1975; British)........................... Mrs. Elvsted
Old Dracula (1975; British)............................Angela

LINDLEY, GISELE

Films:
Forbidden Zone (1980; B&W)........... The Princess
   0:21 - Topless in jail cell. ***
   0:39 - Topless turning a table around. ***
   0:45 - Topless bending over, making love with a
    frog. **
   0:51 - Topless in a cave. **
   0:53 - More topless scenes. **
   1:06 - Even more topless scenes. **
S.O.B. (1981)...

LITTLE, MICHELE

Films:
Out of the Blue (1982).....................................
Radioactive Dreams (1984)................................
Appointment with Fear (1987)...........................
My Demon Lover (1987)......................................
Sweet Revenge (1987) ....Lee
   0:41 - Brief topless in water under a waterfall with
    "K.C." *

LITTLEFEATHER, SACHEEN

Other:
At the 1973 Academy Awards, she announced
   Marlon Brando's rejection of Best Actor Award.
Films:
The Laughing Policeman (1974) ....
Freebie and the Bean (1974)....................................
The Trial of Billy Jack (1974) .... Patsy Littlejohn
Johnny Firecloud (1975)...
Shoot the Sun Down (1981)....................................
Magazines:
Playboy (Oct 1973)............................... "Sacheen"
   Pages 93-95: Nude. **

LIZER, KARI

Films:
Smokey Bites the Dust (1981).........................Cindy
Private School (1983).......................................Rita
   0:30 - Very brief left breast popping out of
    cheerleader's outfit along with the Coach. *
Gotcha! (1985)...

LLOYD, EMILY

Films:
Wish You Were Here (1987).......................Lynda
   0:43 - Buns, singing in the alley and lifting up her
    skirt to moon an older neighbor woman.
Cookie (1989)..
In Country (1989)......................Samantha Hughes

LLOYD, SUE

Films:
Happy Housewives (British).................. The Blonde
The Bitch (1977; British).................. Vanessa Grant
  1:12 - Side view of left breast and topless in the
    swimming pool. *
Revenge of the Pink Panther (1978)
  ....Claude Russo/Claudine Russo
The Stud (1979; British)............................ Vanessa
  1:04 - Topless in the swimming pool with Joan
    Collins and "Tony." *
Rough Cut (1980; British) ....

LOCKE, SONDRA

Films:
The Heart is a Lonely Hunter (1968).... Mick Kelley
Willard (1971) ....
Suzanne...
  0:27 - Topless sitting, looking at a guy. Brief left
    breast several times lying down. **
  0:29 - Topless lying down. ***
The Outlaw Josey Wales (1976)............ Laura Lee
  1:20 - Brief topless and bottomless in rape scene.
    **
The Gauntlet (1977)..............................Gus Mally
  1:10 - Brief right breast, then topless getting raped
    by two biker guys in a box car while Clint is
    tied up. **
Death Games, The Seducers (1977)........... Jackson
  0:16 - Buns and brief right breast in Jacuzzi with
    Colleen Camp trying to get "George" in with
    them
  0:48 - Brief topless running around the room
    trying to keep "George" away from the
    telephone. *
Every Which Way But Loose (1978)
  .... Lynn Halsey Taylor
Any Which Way You Can (1980) .... Lynne
Bronco Billy (1980)..................................Antoinette
Sudden Impact (1983)....................Jennifer Spencer
Ratboy (1986)..................................Nikki Morrison

LOCKHART, ANNE

Other:
Daughter of actress June Lockhart.
Films:
Joyride (1977)..Cindy
  0:59 - Brief topless in the Jacuzzi with everybody.
    **
  1:00 - Topless, standing in the kitchen kissing
    Desi Arnaz Jr. ***
The Young Warriors (1983; US/Canada)...... Lucy
  0:42 - Topless and buns making love with "Kevin"
    on the bed. Looks like a body double. **
Troll (1986)......................... Young Eunice St. Clair
Dark Tower (1987)... Elaine
Big Bad John (1989).................. Lady Police Officer

Made for TV Movies:
  Just Tell Me You Love Me (1978)...........................
TV:
  Battlestar Galactica (1979)...........................Sheeba

LOMBARDI, LEIGH

Films:
The Wild Life (1984)............................ Stewardess
Murphy's Law (1986)............................ Stewardess
Moontrap (1989)....................................Mera
  1:08 - Topless with Walter Koenig in moon tent.
    **
A Tiger's Tale (1988)..

LOMEZ, CÉLINE

Films:
The Far Shore (1976) ....Eulalia Turner
Plague (1978) ....
The Silent Partner (1978).............................Elaine
  1:05 - Side view of left breast, then topless, then
    buns with Elliott Gould. *
The Gemini Strain (1980)......................................
The Kiss (1988)..

LONDON, LISA

Films:
H.O.T.S. (1979)..................................Jennie O'Hara
  1:22 - Topless changing clothes by the closet
    while a crook watches her. *
  1:33 - Topless playing football. *
The Happy Hooker Goes Hollywood (1980)..Laurie
Sudden Impact (1983)..................... Young Hooker
  Topless in motel room.
Private Resort (1985) ....Alice
  0:51 - In beige bra and panties several times with
    "Ben" and "Jack" while she's drunk.
The Naked Cage (1985)................................Abbey
  0:22 - Topless in S & M costume with Angel
    Tompkins. **
  0:38 - Left breast making out in bed with Angel
    Tompkins. **
Savage Beach (1989)................................ Rocky
  0:06 - Topless in Jacuzzi with Patty Duffek, Dona
    Speir and Hope Marie Carlton. *
  0:50 - Topless changing clothes. **

LOPEZ, MARIA ISABEL

Films:
Silip (1985)...Tonya
Mission Manila (1989)................................. Jessie
  0:22 - Brief right breast several times in bed while
    "Harry" threatens her with knife. *

LORDS, TRACI

Other:
Infamous under age adult film actress.
Unfortunately, all of the adult films she was in before she was 18 years old are now illegal. The last legal adult film she did after she turned 18 is "Traci, I Love You."

Films:
Not of This Earth (1988) .... Nadine
0:25 - Buns and side view of left breast drying herself off with a towel while talking to "Jeremy." **
0:27 - In blue swimsuit by swimming pool.
0:42 - Topless in bed making love with "Harry." **
0:46 - walking around the house in white lingerie
Fast Food (1989) .... Dixie Love
1:20 - In black bra in back storage room with "Auggie."
Cry Baby (1990) ....
Video Tapes:
Warm Up with Traci Lords .... Exercise Video Tape
Magazines:
Penthouse (Sep 1984) .... Pet
Pages 97-115: Nude. ***

LOREN, SOPHIA

Films:
Two Nights with Cleopatra (1954; Italian; B&W)
.... Cleopatra/Nisca
0:16 - Nude, but under water so you don't see anything.
The Pride and the Passion (1957) .... Juana
Era Lui, Si, Si (It Was Him, Yes! Yes!)
(1957; Italian) ....
Desire Under the Elms (1958) .... Anna Cabot
Houseboat (1958) .... Cinzia Zaccardi
A Breath of Scandal (1960) .... Princess Olympia
Heller in Pink Tights (1960) .... Angela Rossini
Two Women (1960; Italian) .... Cesira
El Cid (1961) .... Chimene
Boccaccio 70 (1962) .... Zoe
The Fall of the Roman Empire (1964) .... Lucilla
Yesterday, Today and Tomorrow (1964; Italian) ......
Arabesque (1966) .... Yasmin Azir
Man of La Mancha (1972) .... Dulcinea/Aldonza
The Cassandra Crossing (1977) .... Jennifer
Angela (1977) .... Angela
A Special Day (1977) .... Antonietta
Brass Target (1978) .... Mara
Firepower (1979) .... Adele Tasca
Magazines:
Playboy (Jan 1989) .... "Women of the Fifties"
Page 120: B&W photo from "Era Lui, Si, Si." *

LORING, LISA

Films:
Iced (1988) .... Jeanette
0:46 - Brief left breast in bathtub. *
0:53 - Buns and brief right breast in bathtub with "Alex." *
1:05 - Brief lower frontal nudity and buns getting into hot tub. Topless in hot tub just before getting electrocuted. **
1:13 - Full frontal nudity lying dead in the hot tub. **
1:18 - Brief full frontal nudity lying dead in the hot tub again. *
TV:
The Addams Family (1964-66)
.... Wednesday Thursday Addams

LORRAINE, NITA

Films:
The Viking Queen (1967) .... Nubian Girl-Slave
All Neat in Black Stockings (1969) .... Jolasta
Happy Housewives (British) .... Jenny Elgin
0:31 - Brief side view of left breast and buns in barn chasing after "Bob." *
0:32 - Brief topless in open dress talking to policeman. *

LOUISE, HELLI

Films:
Confessions of a Pop Performer (1975) ....
Happy Housewives (British)
.... Newsagent's Daughter
0:16 - Topless with "Mrs. Wain" and "Bob" in the bathtub. **

LOVE, LUCRETIA

Films:
Naked Warriors (1973) .... Deidre
a.k.a. The Arena
0:07 - Brief topless getting clothes torn off by guards. *
0:08 - Brief nude getting washed down in court yard. **
1:08 - Brief buns, bent over riding a horse.
Battle of the Amazons (1973) .... Eraglia
The Tormented (1978) ....
Dr. Heckyl & Mr. Hype (1980) ....

LOVE, PATTI

Films:
Butley (1974; British) .... Female Student
That'll Be the Day (1974; British) ... Sandra's Friend
Terror (1979; British) ....
The Long Good Friday (1982; British) .... Carol
Steaming (1984) .... Josie
0:08 - Frontal nudity, getting undressed. *
0:45 - Brief topless. *
1:30 - Topless, jumping around in the pool. *

LOVE, SUZANNA

Films:
Cocaine Cowboys (1979)..............................Lucy
Topless.
Devonshire Terror (1983)...................................
Olivia (1983) ....Olivia
Nude in bed.

LOVELACE, LINDA

Adult Films:
Deep Throat (1972)....................................
Nude, etc.
Films:
Linda Lovelace for President (1975) ....
Magazines:
Playboy (Apr 1973)..............................."Say 'Ah!'"
Page 95: Topless. **
Playboy (Dec 1973)................... "Sex Stars of 1973"
Page 200: Topless. *
Playboy (Jan 1989)........ "Women of the Seventies"
Page 214: Topless. **

LOWRY, LYNN

Films:
Sugar Cookies (1973).............................. Alta/Julie
0:03 - Brief topless falling out of hammock, then
topless on couch with "Max," then nude. Long
scene. (Brunette wig as Alta.) ***
0:13 - Brief right breast in B & W photo.
0:14 - Left breast on autopsy table. *
0:20 - Topless in movie. **
0:52 - Topless taking off clothes for Mary
Woronov. Topless on bed. (Blonde as Julie.)
**
1:00 - Topless and buns with Woronov in
bedroom, nude while wrestling with her. ***
1:04 - Topless with Woronov in bath tub. *
1:06 - Nude in bed with Woronov. Long scene.
***
1:11 - Right breast outside displaying herself to
"Max." **
1:16 - Right breast, then topless making love with
Woronov. *
1:20 - Nude with Woronov and "Max." Long
scene. ***
They Came From Within (1975; Canadian)............
Cat People (1982)...Ruthie
0:16 - In black bra in Malcolm McDowell's hotel
room, then very brief topless when bra pops
open after crawling down the stairs to get away
from the cat. *

LUNGHI, CHERIE

Films:
Excalibur (1981)...................................Guenevere
1:25 - Brief topless in the forest kissing
"Lancelot." *
Letters to an Unknown Lover (1985)............ Helene
0:40 - In white slip in her bedroom.

The Mission (1986; British).........................Carlotta
To Kill a Priest (1988) ....Halina
Miniseries:
Master of the Game (1984)
....Margaret Van der Merwe

LUSSIER, SHEILA

Films:
Bits and Pieces (1985).................................. Tanya
0:07 - In bra, tied down by "Arthur", then brief
topless a couple of times as he cuts her bra off
before he kills her. Brief right breast several
times with blood on her. **
My Chauffeur (1987).............One of the Party Girls

LUU, TUY ANN

Other:
a.k.a. Thuy An Luu.
Films:
Diva (1982; French).......................................Alba
0:13 - Topless in B&W photos when record store
clerk asks to see her portfolio. *
0:15 - More of the B&W photos on the wall. *
1:27 - Very brief upper half of left breast taking
off top, seen through window. Long shot.
Off Limits (1988)...Lanh
0:48 - Topless dancing on stage in a nightclub. **

LYNCH, KELLY

Films:
Cocktail (1989)..................................Kerry Coughlin
0:45 - Buns, on beach wearing a two piece
swimsuit.
1:01 - Buns, in string bikini swimsuit on boat with
Tom Cruise and Bryan Brown.
Roadhouse (1989) ....Doc
1:04 - Topless and buns getting out of bed with a
sheet wrapped around her. **
Drugstore Cowboy (1989) ....Dianne Hughes
0:17 - In black bra and pants in living room with
Matt Dillon.
Warm Summer Rain (1989)............................Kate
0:03 - Brief topless and side view of buns in B&W
lying on floor during suicide attempt. Quick
cuts topless getting shocked to start her heart. *
0:23 - Full frontal nudity when "Guy" gets off her
in bed. **
0:24 - Side view of right breast in bed, then
topless. **
0:58 - Buns then topless, getting washed by "Guy"
on the table. ***
1:07 - Brief buns making love. Quick cuts full
frontal nudity spinning around. Side view of
left breast with "Guy." ***
1:09 - Nude picking up belongings and running
out of burning house with "Guy." ***

Made for HBO:

The Hitchhiker: The Joker...............Theresa/Melissa
0:11 - Very, very brief left breast in storage room with "Alan" when a masked Timothy Bottoms ties them together.

Magazines:

Playboy (Nov 1989).............."Sex in Cinema 1989" Page 137: Upper half of left breast from "Roadhouse." *

LYNLEY, CAROL

Films:

The Light in the Forest (1958)
.... Shenandoe Hastings
The Poseidon Adventure (1972)........... Nonny Parry
Son of Blob (1972)......................................
The Four Deuces (1975)................................Wendy
Flood! (1976)...
The Washington Affair (1977)..........................
The Cat and The Canary (1978)........ Anabelle West
Dark Tower (1987)............................... Tilly
Blackout (1989)................... Esther Boyle
1:01 - Brief topless leaning against the wall while someone touches her left breast (probably "Alan"). **

Made for TV Movie:

The Night Stalker (1971)..............................
Fantasy Island (1977)................................

TV:

The Immortal (1970-71)................................Sylvia

LYNN, REBECCA

Films:

Thrilled to Death (1988)................. Elaine Jackson
0:01 - Topless twice when "Baxter" opens her blouse. *
0:31 - Topless in locker room talking to "Nan." **

Sensations (1988) ....Jenny Hunter
0:11 - Topless, sleeping on couch. *
0:23 - Topless talking on the telephone. **
1:09 - Topless making love in bed with "Brian." **

LYONS, SUSAN

Films:

The Good Wife (1987)......................Mrs. Fielding
1:22 - Very brief topless coming in from the balcony. *
...Almost (1990; Australia).......................... Caroline

M

MacGRAW, ALI

Films:

Goodbye, Columbus (1969)........................ Brenda
0:50 - Very brief side view of left breast, taking off dress before running and jumping into a swimming pool. Brief right breast jumping into pool. *
1:11 - Very brief side view of right breast in bed with Richard Benjamin. Brief buns, getting out of bed and walking to the bathroom. *
Love Story (1970)............................. Jenny Cavilleri
The Getaway (1972)........................ Carol McCoy
0:16 - In wet white blouse after jumping in pond with Steve McQueen.
0:19 - Very brief left breast lying back in bed kissing McQueen. *
Convoy (1978)...Melissa
Players (1979).......................................Nicole
Just Tell Me What You Want (1980)
.... Bones Burton
0:16 - Topless getting dressed in her bedroom. **
1:26 - Brief topless in bathroom getting ready to take a shower. **
Murder Elite (1985).................................

MACKENZIE, PATCH

Films:

Goodbye, Norma Jean (1975)............. Ruth Latimer
Serial (1980)..................................... Stella
0:59 - Brief topless in mirror in swinger's club with Martin Mull. *
Graduation Day (1981)................... Anne Ramstead

MacLAINE, SHIRLEY

Other:

Author.
Sister of actor Warren Beatty.

Films:

The Trouble with Harry (1955) ....Jennifer Rogers
Around the World in 80 Days (1956)
....................................Princess Houda
Some Came Running (1958) .... Ginny Moorhead
Hot Spell (1958; B&W)................... Virginia Duval
The Apartment (1960; B&W)............. Fran Kubelik
Can-Can (1960) ....Simone Pistache
All In a Night's Work (1961)..............Katie Robbins
Irma La Douce (1963) .... Irma La Douce
Gambit (1966)......................................Nicole
Woman Times Seven (1967).......................Paulette
Sweet Charity (1969).......... Charity Hope Valentine
Two Mules for Sister Sara (1970) ....Sara
Desperate Characters (1971)...................... Sophie
(Not available on video tape yet.)
Topless in bed with Kenneth Mars.
The Turning Point (1977)............................DeeDee
Being There (1979)...................................Eve Rand

Loving Couples (1980)..................................Evelyn
A Change of Seasons (1980)................Karen Evans
Terms of Endearment (1983).....Aurora Greenway
  1:00 - Very, very brief right breast wrestling with
  Jack Nicholson in the ocean when she finally
  frees his hand from her breast. One frame.
  Hard to see, but for the sake of thoroughness...
Cannonball Run II (1984)...........................Veronica
Madame Sousatzka (1988).........Madame Sousatzka
Steel Magnolias (1989)................Ouiser Boudreaux
Video Tapes:
  Shirley MacLaine's Inner Workout (1989)...Herself
Magazines:
  Playboy (Nov 1972)........................"Sex in Cinema"
  Page 159 - Topless lying in bed with Kenneth
  Mars. Small photo, hard to tell it's her. *

MACPHERSON, ELLE

Other:
  Model.
  Sports Illustrated magazine swimsuit model. Cover
  girl in 1986, 1987 and 1988.
  Spokesmodel for Biotherm cosmetics.
Video Tapes:
  Sports Illustrated's 25th Anniversary Swimsuit
  Video (1989)... Herself
  (The version shown on HBO left out two music
  video segments at the end. If you like buns,
  definitely watch this tape!)
  0:22 - In wet yellow tank top and orange bikini
  bottoms at the beach.
  0:23 - Very, very brief lower topless readjusting
  the yellow tank top. *
  Sports Illustrated Super Shape-Up Program: Stretch
  and Strengthen with Elle MacPherson (1990)
  ....Herself

MADIGAN, AMY

Films:
  Love Child (1982)........................Terry Jean Moore
  0:08 - Brief side view of right breast and buns
  taking a shower in jail while the guards watch.
  *
  0:53 - Brief topless and buns, making love with
  Beau Bridges in a room at the women's prison.
  **
Love Letters (1984) ....Wendy
Streets of Fire (1984)......................................McCoy
Places in the Heart (1984)....................Viola Kelsey
Alamo Bay (1985)..Glory
  0:28 - Topless lying in motel bed with Ed Harris.
  **
  0:30 - Topless sitting up in the bed. **
  0:40 - Walking in parking lot in a wet T-shirt
Twice in a Lifetime (1985)..................Sunny Sobel
Nowhere to Hide (1987)..................Barbara Cutter
  1:04 - Brief side view of right breast taking off
  towel to get dressed in cabin. Long shot, hard to
  see. *

The Prince of Pennsylvania (1988). Carla Headlee
  0:37 - Left breast and buns getting out of bed with
  Keanu Reeves and putting on a robe. *
Field of Dreams (1989).....................................Annie
Uncle Buck (1989)..................Chanice Kobolowski
Made for TV Movies:
  The Day After (1983).......................................Alison
  Roe vs. Wade (1989)..................Sarah Weddington

MADONNA

Other:
  Full name is Madonna Louise Cicconi.
  Singer.
  Ex-wife of actor Sean Penn.
Films:
  A Certain Sacrifice (1981)............................Bruna
  (Very grainy film, done before she got famous.)
  0:22 - Topless during weird rape/love scene with
  one guy and two girls. ***
  0:40 - Brief right breast in open top lying on floor
  after getting attacked by guy in back of
  restaurant. *
  0:57 - Brief topless during love making scene,
  then getting smeared with blood. *
Visionquest (1985)..........................Nightclub singer
Desperately Seeking Susan (1985)...................Susan
  0:09 - Briefly in black bra taking off top in bus
  station restroom.
  1:16 - In black bra getting out of pool and lying
  down on lounge chair.
Shanghai Surprise (1986)...................Gloria Tatlock
Who's That Girl? (1987)...............................
Dick Tracy (1990).....................Breathless Mahoney
Music Videos:
  Papa Don't Preach (1987).......................... Herself
  Very brief glimpse of a breast after a jumping
  spin.
Magazines:
  Playboy (Sep 1985).......................................pictorial
  Pages 119-131: B&W photos, need to shave her
  armpits! *
  Penthouse (Sep 1985)................................ pictorial
  Pages 150-161: B&W photos, need to shave her
  armpits! *
  Playboy (Dec 1986)......................"Sex Stars of 86"
  Playboy (Jan 1989)..........."Women of the Eighties"
  Page 247: Topless B&W photo. **
  Vanity Fair (Apr 1990)....................."White Heat"
  Page 144: Left breast in B&W photo taken by
  Helmut Neston. She's standing on a table,
  opening her vest. **

MADSEN, VIRGINIA

Films:
  Class (1983)..Lisa
  0:20 - Brief left breast when Andrew McCarthy
  accidentally rips her blouse open at the girl's
  school. **
Dune (1984) ....Princess Irulan
Electric Dreams (1984)...........................Madeline

Creator (1985)... Barbara
　　0:53 - Walking on beach in a blue one piece
　　　　swimsuit.
　　0:58 - Nude in shower with Vincent Spano. ***
Fire With Fire (1986)..Lisa
Modern Girls (1986)..Kelly
Slam Dance (1987)...................... Yolanda Caldwell
Zombie High (1987)...................................... Andrea
Hot to Trot (1988) ....Allison Rowe
Made for HBO:
　The Hitchhiker: Perfect Order................ Christina
　　0:11 - In black lingerie being photographed by the
　　　　photographer in his studio.
　　0:14 - Brief topless changing clothes while
　　　　"Simon" watches her on video monitor. **
　　0:16 - Topless getting into water in "Simon's"
　　　　studio. She's covered in white makeup all over
　　　　her body.
　Long Gone (1987)............................Dixie Lee Boxx
　　0:05 - Buns, sleeping on bed face down in
　　　　bedroom with William L. Petersen and a young
　　　　kid.
　Third Degree Burn (1989)...................Anne Scholes
Made for Showtime:
　Gotham (1988)................................. Rachel Carlyle
　a.k.a. The Dead Can't Lie
　　0:50 - Brief topless in the shower when Tommy
　　　　Lee Jones comes over to her apartment, then
　　　　topless lying on the floor. *
　　1:12 - Topless, dead, in the freezer when Jones
　　　　comes back to her apartment, then brief topless
　　　　on bed. **
　　1:18 - Topless in the bathtub underwater. *
Made for HBO:
　Mussolini (1985) ....Claretta Petacci

MAGNUSON, ANN

Films:
　The Hunger (1983)....... Young Woman from Disco
　　0:05 - Brief topless in kitchen with David Bowie
　　　　just before he kills her. *
　Perfect Strangers (1984)..............................Feminist
　Desperately Seeking Susan (1985)......Cigarette Girl
　Making Mr. Right (1987)..
　A Night in the Life of Jimmy Reardon (1987)
　..Joyce Fickett
　　1:01 - Right leg in stocking and garter belt kissing
　　　　River Phoenix in the library of her house.
　Mondo New York (1988)..
　Tequila Sunrise (1988)............................... Shaleen
　Checking Out (1989)..........................Connie Hagen
TV:
　Anything but Love (1989-) .... Catherine Hughes

MALIN, KYM

Films:
　Joysticks (1983)..Lola
　　0:03 - Topless with "Alva" showing a nerd their
　　　　breasts by pulling their blouses open. *
　　0:18 - Topless during strip-video game with
　　　　"Jefferson," then in bed with him. ***
　　0:57 - Topless during fantasy sequence, lit with
　　　　red lights, hard to see anything. *
　　1:02 - Brief topless in slide show in courtroom. *
　Mike's Murder (1984) .... Beautiful Girl #1
　Weird Science (1984)................. Girl Playing Piano
　　0:55 - Brief topless several times as her clothes get
　　　　town off by the strong wind and she gets sucked
　　　　up and out of the chimney. *
　Die Hard (1988)..Hostage
　Roadhouse (1989)....................................Party Girl
　Picasso Trigger (1989)................................. Kym
　　1:04 - Topless taking a shower. **
Video Tapes:
　1st Annual Playmate Review (1983)....... Playmate
Magazines:
　Playboy (May 1982)................................ Playmate
　Playboy (Nov 1983)............. "Sex in Cinema 1983"
　　Page 147: Right breast in photo from "Joysticks."
　　*

MANDEL, SUZY

Other:
　a.k.a. Susie Mandel.
Films:
　Confessions of a Driving Instructor (1976; British).
　Playbirds (1978; British)..................................Lena
　　0:12 - Nude stripping in Playbird office. **
　Blonde Ambition (1980; British)..............................

MANI, KAREN

Other:
　a.k.a. Karin Mani.
Films:
　Alley Cat (1982)...Billie
　　0:01 - Brief topless in panties taking night gown
　　　　off during opening credits. *
　　0:17 - In two piece swimsuit sitting by the pool.
　　0:38 - Brief side view of right breast and buns
　　　　getting into the shower. Full frontal nudity in
　　　　the shower. ***
　　0:48 - Topless in women's prison shower room
　　　　scene. Long scene. ***
　Avenging Angel (1985)...................Janie Soon Lee
　　0:06 - Nude taking a shower, right breast in mirror
　　　　drying herself off, then in bra getting dressed.
　　　　***

MANION, CINDY
Films:
Blow Out (1981)..................................Dancing Coed
Preppies (1984)...Jo
 0:11 - Brief topless changing into waitress
  costumes with her two friends. *
 0:44 - Topless during party with the three guys. *
The Toxic Avenger (1985)...............................Julie
 0:14 - In white two piece swimsuit in locker room.

MANSFIELD, JAYNE
Films:
Pete Kelly's Blues (1955)...................Cigarette Girl
Underwater! (1955) ....
The Girl Can't Help It (1957).................Jerri Jordan
A Guide for the Married Man (1967)
 ....Technical Advisor
Promises, Promises (1963; B&W)....Sandy Brooks
 0:02 - Bubble bath scene.
 0:04 - Topless drying herself off with a towel.
  Same shot also at 48 min. ***
 0:06 - Topless in bed. Same shot also at 0:08,
  0:39 and 0:40. ***
 0:59 - Buns, kneeling next to bathtub, right breast
  in bathtub, then topless drying herself off. ***
The Wild, Wild World of Jayne Mansfield
 (1968; B&W)..
 Topless.
Video Tapes:
**Playboy Video Centerfold: Van Breeschooten
 Twins** (1989)...Herself
 0:39 - Topless in color and B&W shots from
  "Promises, Promises." ***
TV:
Down You Go (1956)........................regular panelist
Magazines:
Playboy (Feb 1955)....................................Playmate
Playboy (Jan 1979).................."25 Beautiful Years"
 Page 154: Topless lying on a pink bed. **
Playboy (Jan 1979)
 ...."The Illustrated History of Playboy"
 Page 268: Left breast in bed in a color clip from
  "Promises, Promises." **

MARGOLIN, JANET
Films:
David and Lisa (1962; B&W)...........................Lisa
Bus Riley's Back in Town (1965).....................Judy
Take the Money and Run (1969)....................Louise
The Last Embrace (1979)......... Ellie "Eva" Fabian
 1:10 - Brief topless in bathtub with "Bernie,"
  before strangling him. *
 1:14 min - Right breast, reaching for the phone in
  bed with Roy Scheider. **
 1:20 - Left breast in photo that Scheider is looking
  at (it's supposed to be her grandmother). *
 1:22 - Almost topless in the shower.
Ghostbusters II (1989)...................... The Prosecutor
TV:
Lanigan's Rabbi (1977)..................... Miriam Small

MARIE, JEANNE
Films:
If Looks Could Kill (1986)......................................
Wimps (1987).. Janice
 0:20 - Topless in bed taking off top with
  "Charles." **
Student Affairs (1987)........................ Robin Ready
 0:35 - Brief topless wearing black panties in bed
  trying to seduce a guy. *
 0:41 - Topless making love with another guy
  banging her back against the wall. ***
 0:44 - Very brief topless in VW with a nerd. *
 1:09 - Very brief topless falling out of a trailer
  home filled with water. *

MARKOV, MARGARET
Films:
The Hot Box (1972)............................ Lynn Forrest
 0:12 - Topless when bad guy cuts her swimsuit top
  open. *
 0:16 - Topless in stream consoling "Bunny." **
 0:21 - Topless in the furthest hammock from
  camera. Long shot. *
 0:45 - Topless bathing in stream with the other
  girls. ***
Black Mama, White Mama
 (1973; U.S./Philippines).................... Karen Brent
Naked Warriors (1973)...............................Bodicia
 a.k.a. The Arena
 0:07 - Brief topless getting clothes torn off by
  guards. *
 0:13 - Topless getting her dress ripped off, then
  raped during party. *
 0:19 - Brief left breast, on floor making love, then
  right breast and buns. *
 0:45 - In sheer white dress consoling "Septimus,"
  then walking around.
 0:52 - Brief topless sitting down, listening to
  "Cornelia" talk. *

MARSILLACH, BLANCA
Films:
Flesh + Blood (1985)..................................... Clara
 0:11 - Full frontal nudity on bed having
  convulsions after getting hit on the head with a
  sword. **
Collector's Item (1988)........................Jacqueline
 0:52 - In white bra cleaning up Tony Musante in
  bed, then topless. **
 1:04 - Lower frontal nudity while watching
  Musante and Laura Antonelli making love in
  bed.
 1:18 - Topless getting dressed. A little dark. *
 1:22 - Topless changing clothes in bedroom while
  Antonelli talks to her. **

MARSILLACH, CRISTINA
Films:
Every Time We Say Goodbye (1986)............Sarah
1:00 - In white slip in her bedroom.
1:03 - In white slip again.
1:09 - Right breast, then brief topless lying in bed
with Tom Hanks. **
Collector's Item (1988)......................Young Marie
0:12 - Right breast in elevator with Tony Musante.
**
0:36 - Topless in open blouse, then full frontal
nudity in hut with Musante. **

MARTIN, PAMELA SUE
Films:
Buster and Billie (1974)..
The Lady in Red (1979)....................Polly Franklin
0:07 - Right breast in bedroom with a guy
clutching her clothes. *
0:20 - Topless in jail with a group of women
prisoners waiting to be examined by a nurse.
***
Torchlight (1985)...
Flicks (1985) ....
Made for TV Movie:
The Girls of Huntington House (1973) ....
TV:
The Hardy Boys Mysteries (1977-78)...Nancy Drew
The Nancy Drew Mysteries (1977-78)..Nancy Drew
Dynasty (1981-84)..............Fallon Carrington Colby
Magazines:
Playboy (Jul 1978).......... "Nancy Drew Grows Up"
Pages 87-91: Sort of topless. **

MASON, MARSHA
Other:
Ex-wife of playwright Neil Simon.
Films:
Blume in Love (1973)....................................Arlene
0:22 - Side view of right breast, then brief topless
lying in bed with George Segal. *
0:35 - Very brief right breast reaching over the
bed *
0:54 - Brief topless twice, reaching over to get a
pillow while talking to Segal. **
Cinderella Liberty (1973)................. Maggie Paul
0:09 - Brief panties shot leaning over pool table
when James Caan watches.
0:17 - Side view of left breast in room with Caan.
Brief right breast sitting down on bed. **
0:38 - Topless sitting up in bed yelling at Caan.
***
0:54 - Very brief left breast turning over in bed
and sitting up. *
Audrey Rose (1977)......................Janice Templeton
The Goodbye Girl (1977)..............Paula McFadden
The Cheap Detective (1978) ....Georgia Merkle
Promises in the Dark (1979)....Dr. Alexandra Kenda
Chapter Two (1979)....................Jennie MacLaine
Only When I Laugh (1981).........................Georgia

Max Dugan Returns (1983)..............................Nora
Heartbreak Ridge (1986) ....Aggie
Made for Cable:
Dinner At Eight (1989)................... Millicent Jordan
The Image (1990) .... Jean Cromwell
0:08 - Two brief side views of left breast standing
in bathroom after Albert Finney gets out of the
shower. *

MASSEY, ANNA
Films:
Peeping Tom (1960; British)............Helen Stephens
Frenzy (1972; British)........................ Babs Milligan
0:45 - Topless getting out of bed and then buns,
walking to the bathroom. Most probably a body
double. **
Sweet William (1979)...................................... Edna
Five Days One Summer (1982).........Jennifer Pierce
Foreign Body (1986; British)..................Miss Furze

MASTRANTONIO, MARY ELIZABETH
Films:
Scarface (1983).. Gina
2:36 - (0:39 into tape 2) Very, very brief left
breast when she gets shot and her nightgown
opens up when she gets hit. *
The Color of Money (1986) ....Carmen
0:41 - Brief topless in bathroom mirror drying
herself off while Paul Newman talks to to Tom
Cruise. Long shot, hard to see. *
Slam Dance (1987)..............................Helen Drood
The January Man (1988).............Bernadette Flynn
0:40 - Topless in bed with Kevin Kline. Side view
of left breast squished against Kline. *
0:42 - Topless after Kline gets out of bed. Brief
shot, but very nice! ***
The Abyss (1989)........................ Lindsey Brigman
1:41 - Topless during C.P.R. scene. *
Made for HBO:
Mussolini (1985)....................Edda Mussolini Ciano

MATHIAS, DARIAN
Films:
Blue Movies (1987).. Kathy
0:35 - Very brief topless twice acting for the first
time in a porno film. *
My Chauffeur (1987)......................................

MATLIN, MARLEE
Films:
Children of a Lesser God (1986)..................... Sara
(Academy Award for Best Actress.)
0:44 - Brief buns under water in swimming pool.
Walker (1987)................................... Ellen Martin
Made for TV Movies:
Bridge to Silence (1988)..

109

MATTSON, ROBIN

Films:
Namu, The Killer Whale (1966)............... Lisa Rand
Bonnie's Kids (1973)..................................... Myra
   0:05 - Brief side view of right breast changing in
     bedroom while two men watch from outside. *
   0:07 - Topless washing herself in the bathroom.
     ***
Candy Stripe Nurses (1974)......................... Dianne
   0:22 - Nude in gym with the basketball player. **
   0:40 - Nude in bed with the basketball player. ***
Return to Macon County (1975)...................... Junell
Take Two (1988)..............................Susan Bentley
   0:21 - Exercising in yellow outfit while Frank
     Stallone plays music.
   0:25 - Brief topless taking a shower. **
   0:26 - Showing Grant Goodeve her new two piece
     swimsuit
   0:29 - Topless in bed with Goodeve. ***
   0:45 - Right breast in shower, then topless getting
     into bed. ***
   0:47 - Brief topless getting out of bed and putting
     an overcoat on. *
   0:51 - One piece swimsuit by the swimming pool.
   1:12 - In two piece swimsuit at the beach.
   1:28 - Topless taking a shower after shooting
     Goodeve in bed. ***
TV:
The Guiding Light (1976-77)................ Hope Bauer
General Hospital (1980-83)..Heather Grant Webber
Ryan's Hope (1984)................................. Delia Reid
Santa Barbara (1985-)...... Gina Capwell Timmons

MAY, MATHILDA

Other:
a.k.a. Mathilda May Haim.
Daughter of French playwright Victor Haim.
Films:
Dream One (1984; British/French).................. Alice
Lifeforce (1985)....................................... Space Girl
   0:08 - Full frontal nudity in glass case upside
     down. *
   0:13 - Topless, lying down in space shuttle. Blue
     light. *
   0:16 - Topless sitting up in lab to suck the life our
     of military guard. Brief full frontal nudity. ***
   0:17 - Topless again in the lab. **
   0:19 - Topless walking around, then buns. **
   0:20 - Topless walking down the stairs. Brief
     nude fighting with the guards. ***
   0:44 - Topless with Steve Railsback in red light
     during his nightmare. **
   1:10 - Brief topless in space shuttle with
     Railsback. *
Letters to an Unknown Lover (1985).......... Agnes
   0:43 - Upper half of breasts in bathtub when
     "Gervais" opens the door. *
   0:58 - Buns and topless taking off her robe in
     "Gervais'" room. ***

MAYNE, BELINDA

Films:
Krull (1983)..Vella
Don't Open 'Till Christmas (1984; British).......Kate
Lassiter (1984)........................... Helen Boardman
   0:06 - In bra then topless letting Tom Selleck
     undress her while her husband is in the other
     room. ***
Fatal Beauty (1987)...Traci

MAYO-CHANDLER, KAREN

Films:
Beverly Hills Cop (1984).......Maitland Receptionist
Hamburger: The Motion Picture (1986)
    .... Dr. Victoria Gotbottom
   0:03 - Brief topless in her office trying to help,
     then seduce "Russell." *
Explorers (1986)....................Starkiller's Girl Friend
Stripped to Kill (1988)........................... Cassandra
   0:06 - Black bra and panties in dressing room.
   0:18 - Topless taking off her top for a customer.
     **
Take Two (1988)...Dorothy
   1:17 - Brief topless on bed when her gold dress is
     pulled down a bit. **
Out of the Dark (1988)...............................Barbara
   0:16 - Brief topless pulling red dress down
     wearing black stocking in "Kevin's" studio. *
   0:17 - Topless and buns posing during photo
     shoot. ***
Magazines:
Playboy (Dec 1989)..............."The Joker Was Wild"
   Page 94-103: Nude. ***

MAYRON, MELANIE

Films:
Harry and Tonto (1974).............................. Ginger
   (She's a lot heavier than she is now on
     "thirtysomething".)
   0:57 - Very brief topless in motel room with Art
     Carney taking off her towel and putting on
     blouse. Long shot, hard to see. *
Car Wash (1976)... Marsha
Gable and Lombard (1976)............................. Dixie
You Light Up My Life (1977) .... Annie Gerrara
Girlfriends (1978)........................Susan Weinblatt
   (She's still a bit overweight.)
   0:14 - Buns, very brief lower frontal nudity and
     brief left breast getting dressed in bathroom. *
The Great Smokey Roadblock (1978) ....Lulu
Heartbeeps (1981)..Susan
Playing for Time (1984)......................................
   (Lost a lot of weight.)
   0:11 - Brief side view of left breast getting her hair
     cut. She's behind Vanessa Redgrave. You
     can't really see anything.
Missing (1982).....................................Terry Simon
The Boss' Wife (1987)........................Janet Keefer
Sticky Fingers (1988)..Lolly
Checking Out (1989)........................ Jenny Macklin

Made for TV Movies:
Hustling (1975) .... Dee Dee
TV:
thirtysomething (1987-) .... Melissa Steadman

McARTHUR, KIMBERLY
Films:
Young Doctors in Love (1982) .... Jyll Omato
0:58 - Topless in front of Dabney Coleman after
taking off her Santa Claus outfit in his study. **
Easy Money (1983) .... Ginger
Topless sunbathing.
Malibu Express (1984) .... Faye
0:10 - Topless taking a shower on the boat with
Barbara Edwards. **
Slumber Party Massacre II (1987) .... Amy
Video Tapes:
1st Annual Playmate Review (1983) .... Playmate
Soap Operas:
Santa Barbara (1988-) .... Kelly
Magazines:
Playboy (Jan 1982) .... Playmate

McBRIDE, HARLEE
Films:
Young Lady Chatterley (1976) .Cynthia Chatterley
0:19 - Nude masturbating in front of mirror. **
0:41 - Nude in bathtub while maid washes her.
***
0:52 - Nude in car while the chauffeur is driving.
***
1:03 - Nude in the garden with the sprinklers on
making love with the Gardener. ***
House Calls (1978) ....
Young Lady Chatterley II (1986)
.... Cynthia Chatterley
0:20 - Topless getting a massage with Elanor. **
0:28 - Topless taking a bath with Jenny. ***
0:35 - Topless in library seducing Virgil. ***
0:50 - Topless in back of the car with the Count.
***
0:58 - Topless in the garden with "Robert." ***
Magazines:
Playboy (Dec 1977) .... "Sex Stars of 1977"
Page 217 - Full frontal nudity lying on bed. ***

McCLELLAN, MICHELLE
Other:
Also see Bauer, Michelle.
Films:
Hollywood Chainsaw Hookers (1988) ... Mercedes
0:09 - Nude in motel room with a "John" just
before chainsawing him to pieces. ***
Sorority Babes in the Slime Ball Bowl-O-Rama
(1988) .... Lisa
0:07 - In panties getting spanked with Linnea
Quigley.

0:12 - Topless brushing herself in the front of
mirror while Quigley takes a shower. ***
0:14 - Brief full frontal nudity when the three
nerds fall into the bathroom. *
0:33 - In black bra, panties, garter belt and
stockings asking for "Keith."
0:35 - In the same setup as above on top of
"Keith" in the locker room.
0:40 - Topless taking off her bra. ***
0:43 - More topless undoing garter belt. ***
0:46 - More topless in locker room. **
0:47 - More topless taking off stockings. **
1:04 - Full frontal nudity sitting on the floor by
herself. *
1:05 - full frontal nudity getting up after the lights
go out. Kind of dark. **
Assault of the Party Nerds (1988) .... Muffin
0:16 - Side view of left breast kissing "Bud." *
0:20 - Topless lying in bed seen from "Bud's"
point of view, then by sitting up by herself. ***
1:15 - Brief right breast, then topless in bed with
"Scott." *

McCORMICK, MAUREEN
Films:
Take Down (1978) ....
The Idolmaker (1980) ....
Texas Lightning (1980) .... Fay
1:04 - Very brief upper half of right breast
popping out of slip while struggling on bed with
two jerks. Long shot, hard to see.
Return to Horror High (1987) ....
TV:
The Brady Bunch (1969-74) .... Marcia Brady

McCULLOUGH, JULIE
Films:
Big Bad Mama II (1987) .... Polly McClatchie
0:12 - Topless with Danielle Brisebois playing in a
pond underneath a waterfall. **
0:36 - In lingerie, then topless sitting on "Jordan
Crawford" who is tied up in bed. **
The Blob (1988) .... Susie
TV:
Growing Pains (1989-) .... Julie
Video Tapes:
Playboy Video Calendar 1987 .... Playmate
Playboy Video Calendar 1988 .... Playmate
Magazines:
Playboy (Feb 1986) .... Playmate
Page 84
Playboy (Oct 1989) .... "Julie McCullough"
Pages 74-79: Nude. ***
Playboy (Dec 1990) .... "Holy Sex Stars of 1989!"
Page 181: Left breast sitting on a chair. **

McCURRY, NATALIE
Films:
Dead-End Drive-In (1986)..........................Carmen
0:19 - Topless in red car with Ned Manning. **
Made for TV Movies:
Danger Down Under (1988)...Katherine Dillingham

McDANIEL, DONNA
Films:
Angel (1984)..................................... Crystal
0:19 - Brief topless, dead in bed when the killer pulls the covers down. *
Hollywood Hot Tubs (1984)............. Leslie Maynard

McDONOUGH, MARY
Films:
Mortuary (1981)...............................Christie Parson
(All scenes with nudity are probably a body double.)
0:45 - Buns and very brief topless making love with her boyfriend on the floor. Long shot, hard to see.
1:06 - Full frontal nudity on table in the morgue, dead.
TV:
The Waltons (1972-81)..........................Erin Walton

McENROE, ANNIE
Films:
Running Scared (1980)..
The Hand (1981).................................. Stella Roche
0:51 - Topless undressing for Michael Caine. **
Warlords of the 21st Century (1982)...............Carlie
a.k.a. Battlestruck
The Survivors (1983)...............................Doreen
Howling II...Your Sister is a Werewolf (1984)
.... Jenny
Purple Hearts (1984).............................. Hallaway
1:23 - Brief topless coming out of the bathroom surprising Ken Wahl and Cheryl Ladd. **
True Stories (1986)........................... Kay Culver
Wall Street (1987)..................... Muffie Livingston
Beetlejuice (1988)........................... Jane Butterfield
Cop (1988)....................................... Amy Cranfield
Magazines:
Playboy (Nov 1981)............. "Sex in Cinema 1981"
Page 172: Topless. **

McGAVIN, GRAEM
Films:
My Tutor (1983).. Sylvia
0:21 - In white bra, then topless in back seat of a car in a parking lot with Matt Lattanzi. ***
Angel (1984)... Lana
0:31 - Topless standing in hotel bathroom talking to her "John." **
Weekend Pass (1984)........................... Tawny Ryatt

McGILLIS, KELLY
Films:
Reuben, Reuben (1983).................Geneva Spofford
Witness (1985)..Rachel
1:18 - Topless taking off her top to take a bath while Harrison Ford watches. ***
Top Gun (1986)................................. Charlie
Made in Heaven (1987)
..............................Annie Packert/Ally Chandler
Unsettled Land (1987) ....Anda
The House on Carroll Street (1988)............. Emily
0:39 - Brief topless reclining into the water in the bathtub. *
The Accused (1988)......................Kathryn Murphy
Winter People (1989)..........................Collie Wright

McGOVERN, ELIZABETH
Films:
Ordinary People (1980)............................... Jeanine
Ragtime (1981)..................................Evelyn Nesbit
0:52 - Topless in living room sitting on couch and arguing with a lawyer. Very long scene. ***
Lovesick (1983) ....Chloe Allen
Faerie Tale Theatre: Snow White and the Seven Dwarfs (1983)................................ Snow White
Racing with the Moon (1984).........Caddie Winger
0:45 - Upper half of breast in pond with Sean Penn. *
Once Upon a Time in America (1984)..... Deborah
(Long version.)
3:34 - Brief glimpses of left breast when Robert De Niro tries to rape her in the back seat of a car. *
The Bedroom Window (1987)................................
1:25 - Topless silhouette on shower curtain when Steve Guttenberg peaks in the bathroom.
She's Having a Baby (1988)........................... Kristy
Johnny Handsome (1989)............. Donna McCarty
0:47 - Right breast in bed with Mickey Rourke. **
A Handmaid's Tale (1990)........................... Moira
A Shock to the System (1990) ....
Made for HBO:
Women & Men: Stories of Seduction (1990)
.... Vicki
0:18 - In white lingerie in train car with Beau Bridges.
0:22 - Topless when Bridges takes her top off when she lies back in bed. ***

McGREGOR, ANGELA PUNCH
Films:
The Island (1980).. Beth
0:45 - Topless taking off poncho to make love with Michael Caine in hut after rubbing stuff on him. **
0:50 - Braless under poncho walking towards Caine.
We of the Never Never (1983)...................................
A Test of Love (1984)...

McINTOSH, VALERIE
Films:
- **Weekend Pass** (1984).. Etta
- **The Naked Cage** (1985)................................. Ruby
  - 0:24 - Topless and buns in infirmary, then getting attacked by "Smiley." Brief lower frontal nudity. ***
  - 0:28 - Topless, hanging by rope dead. *
- Jo Jo Dancer, You're Life Is Calling (1986)
  .... Lady at Grandmother's House
- Quicksilver (1986)..Hooker
- Candy Mountain (1988)..

McISSAAC, MARIANNE
Films:
- **In Praise of Older Women** (1978; Canadian)
  ....Julika
  - 0:23 - Topless and buns, getting into bed with Tom Berenger. **
TV:
- The Baxters (1980-81)........................Allison Baxter

McNEIL, KATE
Other:
- a.k.a. Kathryn McNeil.
Films:
- The House on Sorority Row (1982).......... Katherine
- **Monkey Shines** (1988)..................... Melanie Parker
  - 1:07 - Brief upper half of right breast making love with "Allan." Dark, hard to see anything. *
TV:
- WIOU (1990-)................................ Taylor Young

McNICHOL, KRISTY
Films:
- The End (1978)....................................Julie Lawson
- Little Darlings (1980)...................................... Angel
- The Night the Lights Went Out in Georgia (1981)
  ....Amanda Child
- Only When I Laugh (1981)............................. Polly
- The Pirate Movie (1982) ....Mabel
- **White Dog** (1982)............................... Julie Sawyer
  - Brief topless when blouse gapes open.
- You Can't Hurry Love (1984)..................... Rhonda
- **Just the Way You Are** (1984)..................... Susan
  - 0:50 - Very brief left breast showing her friend that she's not too hot because there is nothing under her white coat. Medium long shot. *
- **Dream Lover** (1986)...................... Kathy Gardner
  - 0:17 - Very, very brief right breast getting out of bed, then walking around in a white top and underwear. *
  - 0:21 - Walking around in the white top again. Same scene used in flashbacks at 0:34, 0:46 and 0:54.
- **Two Moon Junction** (1988).....................Patti Jean
  - 0:42 - Topless in gas station restroom changing camisole tops with Sherilyn Fenn. **

The Forgotten One (1989)...............Barbara Stupple
- 0:06 - Jogging in braless pink top, then talking to Terry O'Quinn.
- 1:33 - In pink top lying in bed.
Made for TV Movies:
- My Old Man (1979)...
- Like Mom, Like Me..
- Summer of My German Soldier ....
TV:
- Apple's Way (1974-75)....................Patricia Apple
- Family (1976-80)...........Letitia "Buddy" Lawrence

McVEIGH, ROSE
Other:
- a.k.a. Rosemary McVeigh.
Films:
- A Night in Heaven (1983) ....Alison
- **Porky's Revenge** (1987).................... Miss Webster
  - 0:39 - In black bra, panties, garter belt and stockings then topless in her apartment with "Mr. Dobish" while Pee Wee and his friends secretly watch. ***

MEJIAS, ISABELLE
Films:
- **The Bay Boy** (1985)...........................Mary McNeil
  - 1:28 - Brief topless in her bedroom with Kiefer Sutherland, then brief topless in bed with him. **
- Meatballs III (1987)..
- Fall From Innocence (1988)...................................
Made for TV Movies:
- Special People (1984)...................................... Julie

MELATO, MARIANGELA
Films:
- Love and Anarchy (1974; Italian).................Salome
- The Seduction of Mimi (1974; Italian)....................
- The Nada Gang (1974; French/Italian).............Cash
- **Swept Away** (1975; Italian)..........Raffaela Lenzetti
  - a.k.a. Swept Away...by an unusual destiny in the blue sea of august
  - 1:10 - Topless on the sand when Giancarlo Giannini catches her and makes love with her. **
- Moses (1976; British/Italian)............ Princess Bithia
- Flash Gordon (1980).. Kala
- So Fine (1981)..Lira
- **Summer Night** (1987; Italian)...........Signora Bolk
  - 0:26 - Topless behind gauze net over bed making love with a German guy. **
  - 1:02 - Topless on the bed making love with the prisoner. **
  - 1:09 - Topless again. **
  - 1:13 - Buns, walking out of the ocean, then topless with wet hair. ***

MELL, MARISA

Film:
5 Sinners (1961)...............................Liliane
Ordered to Love (1963) ....
French Dressing (1964) ....Francoise Fayol
Casanova '70 (1965; Italian) ....Thelma
City of Fear (1965)...Ilona
Masquerade (1965)...Sophie
Objective 500 Million (1966).............................Yo
Secret Agent Super Dragon (1966)....Charity Farrell
Anyone Can Play (1968) ....Paola
Danger: Diabolik (1968)...........................Eva Kant
Mahogany (1975)..............................Carlotta Gavin
Some Like It Cool
(1979; German/French/Italian/Austrian)
....Francesca
a.k.a. Sex on the Run
a.k.a. Casanova and Co.
1:12 - Braless in white nightgown.
0:52 - Very, very brief left breast getting out of
bed with Tony Curtis. *
Magazines:
Playboy (Mar 1977)...... "Comeback for Casanova"
Page 89: Topless in water. **

MENZIES, HEATHER

Films:
The Sound of Music (1965)...........................Louisa
Hawaii (1966)...................................Mercy Bromley
How Sweet It Is (1968).............................Tour Girl
Hail, Hero! (1969) ....Molly Adams
Outside In (1972)..Chris
Ssssssss (1973)................................Kristine Stoner
a.k.a. Ssssnake
Piranha (1978) ....Maggie McKeown
Endangered Species (1982) ....
TV:
Logan's Run (1977-78)...............................Jessica
Magazines:
Playboy (Aug 1973)...................... "Tender Trapp"
Pages 81-85: Nude. ***

MEREDITH, LEE

Films:
The Producers (1968)...Ulla
Hello Down There (1969).........................Dr. Wells
Welcome to the Club (1971)........Betsie Wholecloth
The Stoolie (1972)...
Hail (1973)..................................Mrs. Maloney
Sunshine Boys (1975).....................Nurse in Sketch
Magazines:
Playboy (Sep 1973)...................... "A Star is Made"
Pages 105-111: Nude. **

MEREDITH, PENNY

Films:
The Flesh & Blood Show (1974) ....
Happy Housewives (British)................. Margaretta
0:02 - Brief right breast talking on the telephone
while "Bob" makes love with her. *
0:19 - Topless standing up in bathtub talking to
"Bob." **
0:34 - In sheer black lingerie. *
1:05 - Brief topless pulling her top down when
interrupted by the policeman at the window. *

MEYER, BESS

Films:
One More Saturday Night (1986).................. Tobi
1:02 - Brief topless in bed with Tom Davis. *
She's Out of Control (1989).....................................
TV:
Parenthood (1990-)..............................Julie

MICHAELS, LORRAINE

Films:
Malibu Express (1984).................Liza Chamberlin
0:23 - Topless in the shower making love with
"Shane," while camera photographs them. ***
B.O.R.N. (1988)...Dr. Black
Magazines:
Playboy (April 1981)..............................Playmate

MICULA, STACIA

Films:
C.O.D. (1983)...............................Female Reporter
Sex Appeal (1986).. Sheila
1:15 - In black lingerie, then topless with
"Rhonda." ***
Slammer Girls (1987).............................Mosquito
0:17 - Topless in the shower hassling "Melody"
with "Tank." **
Warrior Queen (1987).............................. Philomena

MILES, SARAH

Films:
The Servant (1963)............................. Vera
Those Magnificent Men in their Flying Machines
(1965).......................................Patricia Rawnsley
Blow Up (1966) ....Patricia
Ryan's Daughter (1970)...................... Rosy Ryan
The Man Who Loved Cat Dancing (1973)
....Catherine Crocker
Topless.
Lady Caroline Lamb (1973). Lady Caroline Lamb
The Sailor Who Fell From Grace with the Sea
(1976)..Anne Osborne
0:18 - Topless sitting at the vanity getting dressed
while her son watches through peephole. *
0:23 - Topless, fantasizing about her husband. **
0:42 - Nude, making love with Kris Kristofferson.
**

1:15 - Brief right breast, in bed with Kristofferson.
*

The Big Sleep (1978).............Charolette Sternwood
Venom (1982) ....Dr. Marion Stowe
Ordeal By Innocence (1984) ....Mary Durrant
Steaming (1986)..Sarah
   0:23 - Topless getting into pool with Vanessa
    Redgrave. **
   0:49 - Topless getting undressed. **
   1:31 - Nude lying down next to pool. **
Hope and Glory (1987) ....
White Mischief (1988)...................................... Alice
Made for Cable Movies:
A Ghost in Monte Carlo (1990)...............................
Magazines:
Playboy (Jul 1976).......................... "Kris and Sarah"
   Pages 122-127: Nude. ***
Playboy (Jul 1976)................... "The Soul of Sarah"
   Pages 128-129: Nude. ***
Playboy (Dec 1976)................. "Sex Stars of 1976"
   Page 181: Full frontal nudity standing on bed
   with Kris Kristofferson. ***
Playboy (Jan 1989)........ "Women of the Seventies"
   Page 213: Topless in bed with Kris Kristofferson.
   **

MILFORD, PENELOPE
Films:
Man on a Swing (1974).......................Evelyn Moore
Coming Home (1978).........................Viola Munson
The Last Word (1979)..........................Denise Travis
Endless Love (1981)..................................... Ingrid
Take This Job and Shove It (1981) ....Lenore Meade
The Golden Seal (1983)..............................Tania Lee
Blood Link (1983)............................... Julie Warren
   0:22 - Topless in bed with "Craig". Very brief left
    breast grabbing pillow. **
   1:24 - In black bra in greenhouse with "Keith",
    then topless, then brief right breast. **
   1:35 - Topless in bedroom with "Keith." ***
Heathers (1989)..............................Pauline Fleming
Made for TV Movies:
The Burning Bed (1984) ....
Made for HBO:
The Hitchhiker: Man at the Window
   ....Diane Hampton
   0:09 - Topless in white panties making love with
   her "husband" on the couch. **

MILHENCH, ANN
Films:
Blood Debts (1983)...Lisa
Sloane (1984)................................Janice Thursby
   0:02 - Topless and buns getting out of shower and
   being held by kidnappers. **

MILLER, SHERRIE
Other:
   a.k.a. Sherry Miller.
Films:
Goin' All the Way (1981)............................Candy
   0:47 - Brief right breast getting out of bubble bath.
   0:49 - Topless with "Artie" during his fantasy. **
Separate Vacations (1986).............................Sandy

MILLIAN, ANDRA
Films:
Stacy's Knights (1983)...................................Stacy
Nightfall (1988)..Anna
   0:12 - Very brief topless making love with David
    Birney. *
   0:41 - Very brief topless making love in front of a
    fire. *
   0:58 - Same scene in a flashback while the guy is
    talking to another woman.

MILLS, DONNA
Films:
Play Misty for Me (1971)............................. Tobie
   1:10 - Brief side view of right breast hugging Clint
    Eastwood in a pond near a waterfall. Long shot,
    hard to see. *
Murph the Surf (1975)..........................Ginny Eaton
Fire! (1977)...
Made for TV Movies:
Doctor's Private Lives (1978) ....
Superdome (1978) ....
Bunco (1985)..
TV:
The Good Life (1971-72).......................Jane Miller
Knots Landing (1980-89)
   ....Abby Ewing Sumner Cunningham
Magazines:
Playboy (Oct 1987)...
   Rated PG.
Playboy (Nov 1989).........................."Oh! Donna"
   Pages 82-87: Buns from photos taken around
   1966.

MILLS, HAYLEY
Other:
   Daughter of actor Sir John Mills.
   Sister of actress Juliet Mills.
Films:
Tiger Bay (1959; British/B&W)......................Gillie
Pollyanna (1960)....................................Pollyanna
Whistle Down the Wind (1961; British/B&W)........
In Search of the Castaways (1962)..........Mary grant
The Moon-Spinners (1964)................... Nikky Ferris
The Chalk Garden (1964).............................Laurel
The Parent Trap (1964)
   ....Sharon McKendirck/Susan Evers
That Darn Cat (1965)..........................Patti Randall
The Trouble with Angels (1966) ....Mary Clancy

Deadly Strangers (1974; British).....................Belle
  1:02 - Buns in bathtub when her uncle watches
  her.
  1:05 - In black bra, garter belt and panties while
  "Steven" fantasizes as he sees her through a
  keyhole.
  1:13 - In white bra and panties while "Steven"
  watches through keyhole, then topless taking off
  bra and reading a newspaper. ***
  1:15 - In white bra, getting dressed.
Endless Night (1977)..Ellie
Made for TV Movies:
  The Flame Trees of Thicka..
  The Parent Trap II (1986)..

MILLS, JULIET

Other:
  Daughter of actor Sir John Mills.
  Sister of actress Hayley Mills.
Films:
  The Rare Breed (1966)...........................Hilary Price
  Avanti! (1973)...................................Pamela Piggott
    (Not available on video tape yet - shows up on
    cable TV on The Arts and Entertainment
    channel periodically)
    Buns, climbing out of the water onto a rock.
    Side view of right breast lying on rock talking to
    Jack Lemmon. *
    Brief topless waving to fishermen on a passing
    boat. ***
    Brief buns putting something up in the closet in
    Jack Lemmon's hotel room.
  Beyond the Door (1975; Italian/U.S.)............Jessica
Miniseries:
  Till We Meet Again (1989).........................Vivianne
TV:
  Nanny and the Professor (1970-71) Phoebe Figalilly
Magazines:
  Playboy (Nov 1973)............. "Sex in Cinema 1973"
    Page 153: Topless in photo from "Avanti." **

MILLS, ROBIN

Films:
  End of August (1974)...
  Slumber Party '57 (1976)....................Fast Martha
    0:59 - Topless, standing with an open blouse
    starting a race between two cars. **

MIMIEUX, YVETTE

Films:
  The Time Machine (1980)............................Weena
  Where the Boys Are (1960).........................Melanie
  Diamond Head (1962) ....Sloan Howland
  Three in the Attic (1968) ....Tobey Clinton
  Jackson County Jail (1976)............. Dinah Hunter
    0:39 - Topless in jail cell getting raped by
    policeman. *

The Black Hole (1979)................Dr. Kate McGraw
Circle of Power (1984)..
Made for TV Movies:
  Perry Mason: The Case of the Desperate Deception
    (1990)...Danielle Altmann
TV:
  The Most Deadly Game (1970-71)... Vanessa Smith
  Berrengers (1985)..............................Shane Bradley

MIOU-MIOU

Films:
  Going Places (1974; French)................Marie-Ange
  The Genius (1976; Italian/French/German)......Lucy
  Jonah - Who Will be 25 in the Year 2000
    (1976; Switzerland)......................................Marie
  Bottleneck (1979)..
  Memories of a French Whore (1979).....................
  My Other Husband (1981; French)..........................
  Josepha (1982; French).......................................
  Entre Nous (Between Us) (1983; French)
    ....Madeline
    a.k.a. Coup de Foudre
    Topless.
  Dog Day (1984; French)..
  La Lectrice (1989; French)...........Constance/Marie
    a.k.a. The Reader
    1:06 - Making love with a guy while reading to
    him in bed.
    1:18 - Full frontal nudity lying in bed. Close up
    pan from lower frontal nudity, then left breast,
    then right breast. *
    1:20 - Very brief right breast, then lower from
    nudity getting dressed. *

MIRACLE, IRENE

Films:
  Midnight Express (1978; British)...................Susan
    1:39 - Topless in prison visiting booth showing
    her breasts to Brad Davis so he can masturbate.
    **
  Inferno (1980; Italian)............................ Rose Elliot
  In the Shadow of Kilimanjaro (1985)
    ....Lee Ringtree
    0:18 - Brief breasts in bed with Timothy Bottoms.
    Kind of hard to see anything because it's dark.
  The Last Days of Philip Banter (1987)
    ....Elizabeth Banter
  Puppetmaster (1989)...........................Dana Hadley
  Watchers II (1990).........................Sarah Ferguson
    0:28 - In pink leotard, going into aerobics studio.
    0:40 - Side view in black bra, then topless a few
    times in the bathtub. ***
Made for TV Movies:
  Shattered Dreams (1990) ....Elaine
Magazines:
  Playboy (Nov 1978)............."Sex in Cinema 1978"
    Page 183: Topless still from "Midnight Express."
    **

MIRREN, HELEN

Films:
A Midsummer Night's Dream (1968)...........Hermia
Age of Consent (1969; Australia)....................Cora
0:06, 0:48, 0:56 & 1:21.
Savage Messiah (1972; Britain). Gosh Smith-Boyle
0:40 & 1:13.
O Lucky Man! (1973; British).........Patricia Burgess
Caligula (1980)...
(R-rated version)
0:51 - Topless in bed calling for Caligula. **
The Fiendish Plot of Dr. Fu Manchu (1980)
.... Alice Rage
The Long Good Friday (1980)....................Victoria
Excalibur (1981)....................................... Morgana
1:31 - Side view of left breast under a fishnet
outfit climbing into bed. *
Faerie Tale Theatre: The Little Mermaid (1984).....
2010 (1984)...
Cal (1984)...................................... Marcella
1:18 - In a white bra and slip.
1:20 - Brief frontal nudity taking off clothes and
getting into bed with "Cal" in his cottage, then
right breast making love. **
White Knights (1985)................... Galina Ivanova
The Mosquito Coast (1987)....................................
Pascali's Island (1988).................... Lydia Neuman
1:00 - Left breast, lying in bed with Charles
Dance. Long shot. *
When the Whales Came (1989)..... Clemmie Jenkins
The Cook, The Thief, His Wife & Her Lover
(1990)..

MOFFAT, KITTY

Films:
The Beast Within (1982)................... Amanda Platt
0:06 - Topless, getting her dress torn off by the
beast while she is unconscious. Don't see her
face, could be a body double. **
TV:
Boone (1983-84) ....Susannah Sawyer

MOLINA, ANGELA

Films:
That Obscure Object of Desire
(1977; French/Spanish)............................ Conchita
0:53 - Brief topless in bathroom. *
1:20 - Nude dancing in front of a group of tourists.
**
1:29 - Brief topless behind a gate taunting
Fernando Rey. *
The Sabina (1979; Spanish/Swedish)............... Pepa
The Eyes, The Mouth (1983; Italian/French). Vanda
Demons in the Garden (1984; Spanish)....................
Camorra (1986).................................... Annunziata
Streets of Gold (1986)......................................Elena
Half of Heaven (1987)...

MONIQUE

See Gabrielle, Monique.

MONROE, MARILYN

Films:
Love Happy (1949).......................Grunion's Client
All About Eve (1950)......................... Miss Casswell
Gentlemen Prefer Blondes (1953) .... Lorelei
How to Marry a Millionaire (1953)....................Pola
There's no Business like Show Business (1954)
....Vicky
Bus Stop (1956)....................................Cherie
The Prince and the Showgirl (1957)..... Elsie Marina
The Seven Year Itch (1957)........................The Girl
Some Like It Hot (1959)............. Sugar Kane Kowa
The Misfits (1961)..............................Roslyn Taber
0:33 - Almost left breast twice stretching and
sitting up in bed.
0:39 - In two piece swimsuit running out of the
lake.
Magazines:
Playboy (Dec 1953)...........Sweetheart of the Month
Premiere issue of Playboy Magazine.
Playboy (Jan 1979).................."25 Beautiful Years"
Page 152: Topless in pose from premiere issue.
**
Playboy (Jan 1987)............. "Marilyn Remembered"
Pages 88-95
Playboy (Jan 1989)............. "Women of the Fifties"
Page 114: Topless in pose from premiere issue.
**

MONTGOMERY, JULIE

Films:
Girls Night Out (1984)...
a.k.a. Scared to Death
Revenge of the Nerds (1984)......................... Betty
0:49 - Frontal nudity getting ready for a shower.
**

1:10 - Topless in the pie pan. *
Up the Creek (1984)...................................Lisa
Stewardess School (1987)....................Pimmie Polk
The Kindred (1987) ....Cindy Russell
South of Reno (1987) .... Susan
1:22 - Brief topless kissing "Martin." Dark, hard
to see. *
1:25 - In motel room wearing black top and
panties, then pink spandex top with the panties.
Made for TV Movies:
Earth-Star Voyager (1988).............. Dr. Sally Arthur

MONTICELLI, ANNA-MARIA

Other:
Also see Jemison, Anna.
Films:
Heatwave (1983; Australian)........................Victoria
Nomads (1986)...Niki
0:57 - Left breast, making love in bed with Pierce
Brosnan. Dark, hard to see anything. *

MOORE, CANDY

Other:
a.k.a. Debra Kelly.
Films:
Tommy and the Champ (1961)................................
The Night of the Grizzly (1966)......................... Meg
Lunch Wagon (1981).................................. Diedra
0:17 - Washing and painting lunch wagon in braless top.
0:21 - Weight lifting in two piece swimsuit.
0:30 - In braless pink top behind the truck.
0:35 - In pink bra and panties.
0:42 - Getting dressed in black bra, garter belt, stockings and orange panties.
0:53 - Topless under sheer robe, then topless on couch with "Arnie." **
1:06 - In blue two piece swimsuit weight lifting on stage.

MOORE, CHRISTINE

Films:
Thrilled to Death (1988)..................... Nan Christie
0:31 - In bra in women's locker room.
0:38 - Topless in office with "Mr. Dance" just before killing him. ***
Alexa (1988)..................................... Alexa
0:04 - In red slip in bedroom.
0:06 - In black bra on bed with "Tommy."
0:11 - In black lingerie talking on phone in bed.
0:24 - Topless lying in bed with "Anthony" while reminiscing. **
1:08 - Topless in bed with "Anthony" again. **

MOORE, DEMI

Other:
Wife of actor Bruce Willis.
Films:
Choices (1981)...
Parasite (1982).. Patricia
Blame It On Rio (1984)...................... Nicole Hollis
0:19 - Very brief left breast turning around to greet Michael Caine and Joseph Bologna. *
No Small Affair (1984)................................. Laura
1:34 - Very, very brief side view of left breast in bed with Jon Cryer. *
St. Elmo's Fire (1985)...................................... Jules
About Last Night... (1986).......................... Debbie
0:32 - In white bra getting dressed.
0:34 - Brief upper half of right breast in the bathtub with Rob Lowe. *
0:35 - In white bra getting dressed.
0:50 - Side view of right breast, then very brief topless. *
0:51 - Buns and topless in bed with Lowe, arching her back, then lying in bed when he rolls off her. ***
0:52 - Topless and buns in kitchen with Lowe. **
One Crazy Summer (1986)...................... Cassandra
Wisdom (1987)..Karen
The Seventh Sign (1988)..................... Abby Quinn

1:03 - Brief topless, taking off bathrobe to take a bath. She's about 8 months pregnant, so she's pretty big. *
We're No Angels (1989)................................ Molly
0:18 - One long shot, then two brief side views of left breast when Robert De Niro watches from outside. Reflections in the window are a little distracting. *
Ghost (1990)..

MOORE, TERRY

Films:
Mighty Joe Young (1949; B&W)..............Jill Young
Come Back, Little Sheba (1952; B&W)
...................................Marie Buckholder
Daddy Long Legs (1955) ....Linda
Double Exposure (1983)................Married Woman
Hellhole (1984)...........................Sidnee Hammond
TV:
Empire (1962-63)......................... Constance Garret
Magazines:
Playboy (Aug 1984)................................
Playboy (Dec 1984)................. "Sex Stars of 1984"
Page 208: Topless. ***
Playboy (Jan 1989)........... "Women of the Eighties"
Page 254: Topless. ***

MORGAN, ALEXANDRA

Films:
The First Nudie Musical (1979).........Mary La Rue
0:54 - Topless, singing and dancing during dancing dildo routine. *
1:04 - Full frontal nudity in bed trying to do a take. ***
1:07 - Topless in bed with a guy with a continuous erection.
1:17 - Topless in bed in another scene. **
The Happy Hooker Goes Hollywood (1980)...........
Erotic Images (1983)....................... Emily Stewart
0:57 - In black lingerie with "Glenn," then topless on the living room floor. **
1:05 - Topless in bed, making love with "Glenn." *
1:12 - Topless in the kitchen with "Glenn." ***
1:21 - Right breast, on couch with "Glenn." **
Spellbinder (1988).. Pamela

MORGAN, CINDY

Films:
Caddyshack (1980)........................ Lacey Underall
0:50 - Very, very brief side view of left breast sliding into the swimming pool. Very blurry.
0:58 - Topless in bed with "Danny" three times. **
Tron (1982) .... Lora/Yori
TV:
Bring 'Em Back Alive (1982-83).... Gloria Marlowe

MORGAN, DEBBI
Films:
    Mandingo (1975)..............................Dite
      0:17 - Topless in bed talking to Perry King. *
Miniseries:
    Roots: The Next Generation (1979)
    .... Elizabeth Harvey
Made for TV Movies:
    The Jesse Owens Story (1984)...............................
TV:
    Behind the Screen (1981-82)..............Lynette Porter
    All My Children ....
    Generations (1990-).....................Chantal Marshall

MORGAN, JAYE P.
Other:
    Singer.
Films:
    Loose Shoes (1977)............................Stop-It Nurse
    The Gong Show Movie (1980)....................Herself
      (Not available on video tape)
      Topless.
    Night Patrol (1984)...Kate
TV:
    The Gong Show (1976-80)........................... panelist
    The Chuck Barris Rah Rah Show (1978).......regular

MORGAN, SHELLY TAYLOR
Films:
    The Sword and the Sorcerer (1982)..........................
    My Tutor (1983)...Louisa
    Scarface (1983) ....Woman at the Babylon Club
    Malibu Express (1984).............. Anita Chamberlain
      0:22 - Topless doing exercises on the floor. *
      0:26 - Topless making love with "Shane" in bed
      while being video taped. **
TV:
    General Hospital.................................Lorena Sharpe

MORGANNA
Other:
    a.k.a. The Kissing Bandit.
    Chest measurement is 60 inches.
Magazines:
    Playboy (Sep 1989)...................."Ode to Morganna"
      Pages 122-125: Topless. ***
    Playboy (Dec 1989)........"Holy Sex Stars of 1989!"
      Page 183: Topless in open jacket. ***

MORITZ, LOUISA
Films:
    One Flew Over the Cuckoo's Nest (1975)........ Rose
    Death Race 2000 (1975)................................ Myra
      0:28 - Topless and buns getting a massage and
      talking to David Carradine. *
    Loose Shoes (1977).......................................Margie
    The Happy Hooker Goes to Washington (1977)
    ....Natalie Naussbaum

    Lunch Wagon (1981)................................Sunshine
      0:34 - In black lingerie.
      0:37 - Topless in Jacuzzi. *
    The Last American Virgin (1982).............Carmela
      0:42 - Topless and buns in her bedroom with
      "Rick" after the three boys come over. ***
    Hot Chili (1985)...Chi Chi
      0:06 - Brief buns turning around in white apron
      after talking with the boys.
      0:34 - Nude during fight in restaurant with the
      Music Teacher. Hard to see because of the
      flashing light. **
    Jungle Warriors (1985)...................Laura McCashin

MORRIS, ANITA
Films:
    The Happy Hooker (1975).... Linda Jo/Mary Smith
      0:59 - Topless lying on table while a customer
      puts ice cream all over her. *
      1:24 - Topless covered with whipped cream
      getting it sprayed off with champagne by
      another customer. *
    So Fine (1981) ....So Fine Dancer
    The Hotel New Hampshire (1984)...........Ronda Ray
    Maria's Lovers (1985) ....Mrs. Wynic
    Absolute Beginners (1986).................. Dido Lament
    Blue City (1986)........................... Molvina Kerch
    Ruthless People (1986)......................................Carol
    Aria (1988)...Phoebe
    18 Again! (1988)..Madeline
TV:
    Berrengers (1985)............................Babs Berrenger

MULLEN, PATTY
Films:
    Doom Asylum (1987).........Judy LaRue/Kiki LaRue
      In red two piece swimsuit a lot.
    Frankenhooker (1990) ....
Magazines:
    Penthouse (Aug 1986)..................................... Pet
    Penthouse (Jan 1988)....................... Pet of the Year
      Pages 125-139

MÜLLER, LILLIAN
Other:
    a.k.a. Liliane Mueller or Yulis Ruvaal.
Films:
    Some Like It Cool
      (1979; German/French/Italian/Austrian)..... Angela
      a.k.a. Sex on the Run
      a.k.a. Casanova and Co.
      0:15 - Second woman (blonde) to take off her
      clothes with the other two women, nude. Long
      scene. ***
Magazines:
    Playboy (Aug 1975)....................................Playmate
    Playboy (Nov 1977)................ "Sex in Cinema 77"
      Page 166: Topless. **

MUNRO, CAROLINE

Films:

Captain Kronos, Vampire Hunter (1972; England)
....Carla
0:24 - "Nude" scene in the barn with "Kronos." Dark, strategically placed shadows hide everything.
0:51 - In barn again, but now she has strategically placed hair hiding everything.
The Golden Voyage of Sinbad (1974; British)
....Margiana
The Spy Who Loved Me (1977; British)........Naomi
Starcrash (1979; Italian)............................Stella Star
Slaughter High (1986) ....Carol
0:19 - Walking around her house in lingerie and a robe.

MUTI, ORNELLA

Films:

Summer Affair (1979)......................................Lisa
0:44 - Topless silhouette in cave by the water. *
1:00 - Brief topless getting chased around in the grass and by the beach. *
Flash Gordon (1980)........................... Princess Aura
Love and Money (1980).......... Catherine Stockheinz
0:31 - In bra and panties in bedroom with Ray Sharkey getting dressed.
Famous T & A (1982)..................... Herself
0:07 - Brief topless in scenes from "Summer Affair." *
Tales of Ordinary Madness (1983)..................... Cass
Swann In Love (1984)................... Odette de Crêcy
1:15 - Brief left breast, making love with Jeremy Irons. **
1:28 - Topless sitting on bed talking to Irons. ***
Made for HBO:
The Hitchhiker: True Believer................................
(Available on video tape in Hitchhiker III.)

N

NAPLES, TONI

Films:

Doctor Detroit (1983)............................ Dream Girl
Deathstalker II (1987)................................Sultana
0:55 - Brief topless in strobe lights making love with the bad guy. Hard to see because of blinking lights. Might be a body double, don't see her face. *

NASSAR, DEBORAH ANN

Other:

a.k.a. Debbie Nassar.

Films:

Stripped to Kill (1987)............................... Dazzle
0:07 - Topless wearing a G-string dancing on stage with a motorcycle. ***

Dance of the Damned (1988)................... La Donna
0:07 - Brief topless during dance routine in club.
*

NATIVIDAD, KITTEN

Other:

Vital statistics: 5' 3" tall, 116 pounds, 44-25-35.

Films:

Up! (1976)..
Beneath the Valley of the Ultravixens (1979)..........
The Woman in Red (1979)................... Uncredited
0:39 - Brief topless outside during party. *
Titillation (1982)...
My Tutor (1983) ....Anna Maria
0:10 - Topless in room with Matt Lattanzi, then lying in bed. ***
Doin' Time (1984) ....Tassle
Takin' It Off (1984)........................ Betty Bigones
0:01 - Topless dancing on stage. **
0:04 - Topless and buns dancing on stage. ***
0:29 - Topless in the Doctor's office. **
0:32 - Nude dancing in the Psychiatrists' office. ***
0:39 - Nude in bed with a guy during fantasy sequence playing with vegetables and fruits. ***
0:49 - Topless in bed covered with popcorn. **
0:51 - Nude doing a dance routine in the library. *
1:09 - Nude splashing around in a clear plastic bathtub on stage. ***
1:20 - Nude at a fat farm dancing. **
1:24 - Nude running in the woods in slow motion. **
The Wild Life (1984)............................ Stripper #2
0:50 - Topless doing strip routine in a bar just before a fight breaks out. ***
The Tomb (1987) ....
Takin' It All Off (1987)................... Betty Bigones
0:12 - Nude, washing herself in the shower. ***
0:39 - Nude, on stage in a giant glass, then topless backstage in her dressing room. **
0:42 - Topless in flashbacks from "Takin' It Off." **
0:46 - Topless in group in the studio.
0:53 - Nude, dancing on the deck outside. Some nice slow motion shots. ***
1:16 - Topless on stage in club. **
1:23 - Nude, dancing with all the other women on stage. ***
Magazines:
Playboy (Nov 1982)............."Sex in Cinema 1982"
Page 160: Topless. ***

NEAL, CHRISTY

Films:

Coming Together (1978)................. Vicky Hughes
0:12 - In bra and panties in bedroom with "Frank."
0:30 - Brief right breast in shower with "Angie."
*

0:37 - Topless and buns making love standing up in front of sliding glass door with "Frank." Quick cuts. *
0:49 - Brief topless again during flashbacks. *
0:57 - Topless with "Angie" and "Richard." **
1:05 - Topless on beach with "Angie." Long shot. *

Take Down (1979)..............................Suzette Smith
Matter of Love (1979)...

NEGODA, NATALYA
Films:
Little Vera (1988; U.S.S.R.)............................ Vera
0:15 - Very brief topless band buns getting dressed. Dark, hard to see.
0:50 - Topless making love with "Sergei." ***
1:05 - Topless taking off her dress in the kitchen. **
Films:
Playboy (May 1989)................"That Glasnost Girl" Pages 140-149: Topless. ***
Playboy (Nov 1989)............."Sex in Cinema 1989" Page 131: Topless in out-of-focus still from "Little Vera." **
Playboy (Dec 1989)........"Holy Sex Stars of 1989!" Page 184: Topless. ***

NELLIGAN, KATE
Films:
Therese Raguin..
The Romantic Englishwoman (1975) ....Isabel
Bethune (1979)..
Dracula (1979)...Lucy
Crossover (1980; Canadian).........................Peabody
Eye of the Needle (1981).................................Lucy
0:52 - Brief left breast drying herself off after giving her son a bath when Donald Sutherland accidentally sees her. **
1:15 - Top half of buns in bed making love with Sutherland.
1:26 - Topless in bed making love with Sutherland after he killed her husband. Dark, hard to see. *
Without a Trace (1983) ....Susan Selky
Eleni (1985)..
Crossover (1985)...
Made for HBO Movies:
Control (1987)..
Made for TV Movies:
Kojak: The Price of Justice (1987)..................Kitty

NEWMAR, JULIE
Films:
Mackenna's Gold (1969)...........................Hesh-ke
1:09 - Brief topless and buns under water. Long shots, hard to see anything. Not clear because of all the dirty water. Brief buns, getting out of the pond.
Love Scenes (1984).....................................Belinda
Streetwalkin' (1985)...............................Queen Bee

Deep Space (1988)................................Lady Elaine
TV:
Batman..The Catwoman

NICHOLS, NICHELLE
Films:
Truck Turner (1974)...............................Dorinda
(Not available on video tape yet.)
TV:
Star Trek (1966-69) ....Lieutenant Uhura

NIELSEN, BRIGITTE
Other:
Ex-wife of actor Sylvester Stallone.
Films:
Red Sonja (1985).....................................Red Sonja
Rocky IV (1985)..Ludmilla
Cobra (1985)...Ingrid
Beverly Hills Cop II (1987).......................Karla Fry
Domino (1989)... Domino
0:05 - Right breast, lying down next to swimming pool, topless getting out. *
1:04 - Right breast, caressing herself in a white lingerie body suit, wearing a black wig. ***
Made for TV Movies:
Murder by Moonlight (1989)....................................
Magazines:
Playboy (Aug 1986)................................."Brigitte" Pages 70-77: Topless, but nothing spectacular. **
Playboy (Dec 1987)....................."Gitte the Great" Pages 80-93: Nice. ***
Playboy (Feb 1988)....................."The Year in Sex" Page 129: Topless at the beach. ***
Playboy (Dec 1988)................."Sex Stars of 1988" Page 187: Buns and side view of right breast. *
Playboy (Jan 1989).........."Women of the Eighties" Page 251: Topless. **

NIEMI, LISA
Other;
Wife of actor Patrick Swayze.
Films:
Slam Dance (1987) ....Ms. Schell
0:54 - Nude in Tom Hulce's apartment. ***
1:00 - Topless, dead, lying on the floor. *
She's Having a Baby (1988)..........................Model
Steel Dawn (1988)..Kasha

NIRVANA, YANA
Films:
Cinderella (1977)....................................Drucella
0:02 - Topless taking off clothes with her sister "Maribella" to let "Cinderella" wash. *
0:06 - Brief topless sitting up in bed with "Maribella." *
He's My Girl (1987)..Olga
TV:
The Last Precinct (1986) ....Sgt. Martha Haggerty

NORTH, NOELLE

Films:
Slumber Party '57 (1976)............................ Angie
   0:37 - Buns, then topless in bed with a party guest
   of her parents. **
Sweater Girls (1978)...
Report to the Commissioner (1975)...........Samantha
Jekyll & Hyde...Together Again (1982)....... Student

NORTON-TAYLOR, JUDY

TV:
The Waltons (1972-1981)
   .... Mary Ellen Walton Willard
Video Tapes:
Playboy Video Magazine, Volume 10.......................
Magazines:
Playboy (August 1985).......... "The Punch in Judy"
   Pages 77-81: Frontal nudity. ***

NOVAK, LENKA

Films:
Kentucky Fried Movie (1977).......Linda Chambers
   0:09 - Topless sitting on a couch with 2 other
   girls. *
Vampire Hookers (1979).............................. Suzy
   0:22 - In sheer green dress getting into coffin.
   0:33 - In sheer green dress again.
   0:45 - In sheer green dress again.
   0:51 - Topless in bed during the orgy with the guy
   and the other two Vampire Hookers. **
Coach (1983)...Marilyn
   0:10 - Very brief topless flashing her breasts along
   with her girlfriends for their boyfriends. *
Terror on Tape...
   Topless scene from "Vampire Hookers."

NYGREN, MIA

Films:
Emmanuelle IV (1984)...................Emmanuelle IV
   0:13 - Buns, lying on table after plastic surgery.
   0:15 - Full frontal nudity walking around looking
   at her new self in the mirror. ***
   0:20 - Brief topless a couple of times making love
   on top of a guy getting coached by Sylvia
   Kristel in dream-like sequence. *
   0:22 - Full frontal nudity taking off blouse in front
   of "Dona." **
   0:25 - Almost making love with a guy in bar.
   0:30 - Nude undressing in front of "Maria." ***
   0:39 - Full frontal nudity taking her dress off and
   getting covered with a white sheet. **
   0:40 - Full frontal nudity lying down and then
   putting dress back on. ***
   0:45 - Full frontal nudity during levitation trick.
   **
   0:49 - Right bra cup reclining on bed.
   0:52 - Brief topless in stable. *
   0:54 - Topless taking off black dress in chair.
   Brief lower frontal nudity. ***

   0:57 - Brief lower frontal nudity putting on white
   panties.
   1:00 - Brief topless when "Susanna" takes her
   dress off. *
   1:03 - Brief right breast making love on ground
   with a boy. *
   1:07 - Topless walking on beach. ***
   1:09 - Topless with "Dona." Dark. *
Plaza Real (1988)...

O

O'BRIEN, MAUREEN

Films:
She'll Be Wearing Pink Pyjamas (1984)........ Joan
   0:46 - Brief topless making love in bed with
   "Tom". Dark. *
Zina (1985)...

O'CONNELL, TAAFFE

Films:
Galaxy of Terror (1981)............................Damelia
   0:42 - Topless getting raped by a giant space slug.
   A little slimy. **
   0:46 - Buns, covered with slime being discovered
   by her crew mates.
Caged Fury (1984)...................................... Honey
   0:17 - Topless on bed with a guard. Mostly left
   breast. **
   0:40 - Very, very brief tip of left breast peeking
   out between arms in shower.
   1:06 - Very brief topless getting blouse ripped
   open by a guard in the train. *
Hot Chili (1985)..Brigitte
   0:21 - Topless lying on the bed. Shot with lots of
   diffusion. ***
   0:30 - Brief topless playing the drums. *
   1:11 - Brief topless in bed making love with
   "Ernie" next to her drunk husband. *
Not of This Earth (1988)...........................Damelia
   0:04 - Brief topless and buns from "Galaxy of
   Terror" during the opening credits. *
TV:
Blansky's Beauties (1977)...........Hillary S. Prentiss

O'CONNOR, GLYNNIS

Films:
Ode to Billy Joe (1976)...............Bobby Lee Hartley
California Dreaming (1978)......................... Corky
   0:11 - Topless pulling her top over her head when
   "T.T." is using the bathroom. **
   1:12 - In white bra in bed with "T.T."
   1:14 - Topless in bed with "T.T." ***

Those Lips, Those Eyes (1980) ....Ramona
   0:37 - Left breast in car with Tom Hulce. Dark, hard to see. *
   1:12 - Topless and buns on bed with Tom Hulce. Dark. **
Melanie (1982)...Melanie
   0:08 - Very brief right breast turning over in bed next to Don Johnson. *
   0:09 - Topless, sitting up and putting on a T-shirt, then getting out of bed. **
Night Crossing (1982).......................... Petra Wetzel
Made for TV Movies:
The Boy in the Plastic Bubble (1976)............... Gina
Why Me? (1984) ....
TV:
Sons and Daughters (1974) .... Anita Cramer

O'GRADY, LANI
Films:
Massacre at Central High (1976) ....Jane
   1:09 - Topless walking out of a tent and getting back into it with Rainbeaux Smith and Robert Carradine. ***
TV:
The Headmaster (1970-71)...............................Judy
Eight is Enough (1977-81)................Mary Bradford

OHANA, CLAUDIA
Films:
Erendira ('1983; Brazil).............................. Erendira
   0:14 - Topless getting fondled by a guy against her will. *
   0:26 - Topless lying in bed sweating and crying after having to have sex with an army of men. **
   1:04 - Topless lying in bed sleeping. ***
   1:08 - Brief topless getting out of bed. Long shot, hard to see
   1:24 - Topless and buns on bed behind curtains with "Ulysses." **
Magazines:
Playboy (Oct 1984)........... "The Girls from Brazil" Page 88-89: Nude. **
Playboy (Dec 1984)................. "Sex Stars of 1984" Page 205: Left breast, leaning on table. **

OLIN, LENA
Films:
Fanny and Alexander
   (1983; Swedish/French/German)..........................
After the Rehearsal (1984; Swedish)........................
The Unbearable Lightness of Being (1987)
   .... Sabina
   0:03 - Topless in bed with "Tomas" looking at themselves in a mirror. **
   0:17 - In black bra and panties looking at herself in a mirror on the floor.
   1:21 - In black bra, panties, garter belt and stockings.

   1:29 - Topless and buns while "Tereza" photographs her. Long shots, hard to see. **
   1:43 - Very brief left breast in bed with "Tomas." *
   2:32 - Brief B&W photo found in a drawer by "Tomas."
Enemies, A Love Story (1989).....................Masha
   0:16 - In white bra, then brief topless several times in bed with Ron Silver. Topless again after making love and starting to make love again. **

OLIVER, LESLIE
Films:
The Student Teachers (1973).................................
Thunderbolt and Lightfoot (1974)......... Teenager
   1:16 - Brief topless in bed when robbers break in and George Kennedy watches her. **

OLIVER, PITA
Films:
Deadly Companion (1979)........................ Lorraine
   0:14 - Very brief left breast then very brief topless sitting up in bed during Michael Sarrazin's daydream. Dark. *
   1:32 - Brief full frontal nudity dead on bed when Susan Clark comes into the bedroom.
Prom Night (1980)..Vicki

O'NEAL, TATUM
Films:
Paper Moon (1973)............................ Addie Loggins
The Bad News Bears (1976)......... Manda Whurlizer
International Velvet (1978)..................Sarah Brown
Circle of Two (1980).........................Sarah Norton
   0:56 - Topless standing behind a chair in Richard Burton's studio talking to him. **
Little Darlings (1980)...................................... Ferris
Faerie Tale Theatre: Goldilocks and the Three Bears (1982)..
Certain Fury (1985) ....Scarlet
Magazines:
Playboy (Nov 1982)............. "Sex in Cinema 1982" Page 165: Topless photo from "Circle of Two." **

O'NEILL, REMY
Films:
The Protectors, Book I (1981) ....
Angel of H.E.A.T. (1982)........... Andrea Shockley
   0:43 - Topless, wearing a blue swimsuit, wrestling in the mud with Mary Woronov. **
Erotic Images (1983)..................... Vickie Coleman
   0:04 - Topless sitting in chaise lounge talking to Britt Ekland. Long scene. ***
   0:06 - Topless in bed with "Marvin." Brief lower frontal nudity. *
   0:07 - Brief left breast in Jacuzzi with TV repairman, then brief topless. **

Hollywood Hot Tubs (1984)...............Pam Landers
  1:00 - Brief right breast in hot tub with "Jeff." *
Return to Horror High (1987).........Esther Molvania
To Die For (1988)................................Jane
Hollywood Hot Tubs 2 - Educating Crystal (1989)
....Pam Landers
  0:57 - Swinging tassels on the tips of her belly
  dancing top.

ONO, YOKO
Other:
  Wife of singer John Lennon.
Films:
  Imagine: John Lennon (1988)....................Herself
    0:43 - Nude in B&W photos from John Lennon's
    White Album. *
    0:57 - Brief full frontal nudity from album cover
    again during an interview.
    1:27 - Almost topless in bed with Lennon.

O'SHEA, MISSY
Films:
  Blow Out (1981)................................Dancing Coed
    0:00 - Dancing in sheer nightgown while a campus
    guard watches from outside the window and
    gets stabbed with a knife.
  New York Nights (1983)....................... The Model
    0:30 - In white bra in restroom making love with
    the photographer.
    0:37 - in black bra, panties, garter belt and
    stockings then topless taking off bra and getting
    into bed. **
    0:40 - Topless on floor when the photographer
    throws her on the floor and rips her bra off. **
    0:41 - Full frontal nudity putting bathrobe on. ***
    0:44 - Topless standing in front of a mirror with
    short black hair and a moustache getting dressed
    to look like a guy. *

OTIS, CARRÉ
Other:
  Model.
Films:
  Wild Orchid (1990)..............................Emily Reed
Magazines:
  Playboy (Jun 1990).........................."Wild Orchid"
    Pages 83-87: Nude in photos from "Wild
    Orchid." ***

O'TOOLE, ANNETTE
Films:
  Smile (1974).....................................Doria Houston
    0:34 - In white bra and panties in dressing room.
    1:06 - In white bra and slip talking to Joan Prather
    in bedroom.
  King of the Gypsies (1978)........................... Sharon

One on One (1980)...................................Janet Hays
Foolin' Around (1980)....................................Susan
48 Hours (1982)..Elaine
Cat People (1982)............................... Alice Perrin
  1:29 - In a bra, then topless changing in locker
  room. Right breast, getting out of swimming
  pool. ***
Superman III (1983)............................Lana Lang
Cross My Heart (1987)................................. Kathy
  0:44 - In pink bra standing in bedroom with
  Martin Short.
  0:46 - Left breast, in bed with Short. **
  0:48 - Topless in bed when Short heads under the
  covers. **
  0:49 - Brief topless again getting her purse. **
  1:05 - Brief topless and buns, dressing after Short
  finds out about her daughter. *
Made for HBO:
  Best Legs in the 8th Grade (1984) ....
Miniseries:
  The Kennedys of Massachusetts (1990)
  ....Rose Fitzgerald
Made for TV Movies:
  Love for Rent (1979)....................................
  Stand by Your Man (1981)...............................
Magazines:
  Playboy (Nov 1982).............."Sex in Cinema 1982"
    Page 166 - Buns, in a photo from "48 Hours" - but
    scene is not on video tape.

P

PACULA, JOANNA
Films:
  Gorky Park (1983).. Irina
    1:20 - Brief topless in bed making love with
    William Hurt. **
  Not Quite Paradise... Gila
    a.k.a. Not Quite Jerusalem
    1:04 - Left breast, lying in bed with Sam Robards.
    *
  Death Before Dishonor (1987)............................ Elli
  Sweet Lies (1988)..
  The Kiss (1988).. Felice
    0:49 - Side view topless making love with a guy.
    Inter cut with Meredith Salenger seeing a model
    of a body spurt blood. **
    0:57 - Topless covered with body paint doing a
    ceremony in a hotel room. *
    1:24 - Brief right breast making love with a guy on
    bed while Salenger is asleep in the other room.
    **
Made for Cable:
  36 Hours (1989) ....
TV:
  E.A.R.T.H. Force (1990-)............... Diana Randall

PAI, SUE FRANCIS

Other:
a.k.a. Suzie Pai or Suzee Pai.
Films:
Big Trouble in Little China (1986) ....Miao Yin
Jakarta (1988).. Esha
   1:01 - Brief right breast making love in the
     courtyard with "Falco." *
   1:13 - Side view of right breast, then brief topless
     twice, making love under a mosquito net with
     "Falco." Might be a body double. **
   1:13 - Brief side view of right breast kissing
     "Falso."

PAINE, HEIDI

Films:
In Search of the Perfect 10 (1986).. Perfect Girl #8
   (Shot on video tape.)
   0:45 - Brief topless pulling down her top outside
     of car. ***
New York's Finest (1988)............... Carley Pointer
   0:04 - Brief topless with a bunch of hookers. *
   0:36 - Topless with her two friends doing push ups
     on the floor. *
Skin Deep (1989)..Tina
Road House (1989)..

PALLENBERG, ANITA

Films:
A Degree of Murder (1967)........................... Marie
Barbarella (1968)........................... The Black Queen
Candy (1968)......................................Nurse Bullock
Performance (1970)...................................... Pherber
   0:44 - Side view of left breast, in bed with Mick
     Jagger. *
   0:47 - Topless in bathtub with "Lucy" and Jagger.
     ***
   1:20 - Right breast, lying on the floor. **

PALLETT, LORI DEANN

Films:
Screwball Hotel (1988)................................. Candy
   0:26 - Topless in the shower while "Herbie" is
     accidentally in there with her. ***
Magazines:
Penthouse (Jun 1989)..
   Pages 45-51

PALMER, GRETCHEN

Films:
Crossroads (1986) ....Beautiful Girl/Dancer
Red Heat (1988)..Hooker
   1:20 - Topless and buns in hotel during shoot out.
     *
When Harry Met Sally... (1989)...............................

PALUZZI, LUCIANNA

Films:
Muscle Beach Party (1964) ....Julie
Thunderball (1965)..............................Fiona Volpe
39 Women (1969)..
Manhunt (1973).. Eva
   a.k.a. The Italian Connection.
Black Gunn (1975).. Toni
The Sensuous Nurse (1979)....................................
   0:20 - Topless in room with covered furniture
     reluctantly making love with a guy. **

PAPANICOLAS, TANYA

Films:
Vamp (1986)..Waitress
Blood Diner (1987)......................... Sheetar & Bitsy
   0:15 - Brief topless as photographer during topless
     aerobics photo shoot. *
   0:24 - Topless, dead on operating table, then dead,
     standing up. *

PARKINS, BARBARA

Films:
Mephisto Waltz (1971)............................. Roxanne
   1:26 - Left breast kissing Alan Alda during
     witchcraft sequence. *
Valley of the Dolls (1967)....................Anne Welles
Asylum (1972).. Bonnie
Christina (1974)..Christina
Shout at the Devil (1976; British)......................Rosa
Bear Island (1980; British/Canadian).. Judith Ruben
Made for Cable:
To Catch a King (1984)..
TV:
Peyton Place (1964-69)
   ....Betty Anderson/Harrington/Cord
The Captains and the Kings (1976).........Martinique
Magazines:
Playboy (Dec 1977)..................."Sex Stars of 1977"
   Page 215 - Left breast standing looking out the
     window. *

PASCAL, OLIVIA

Films:
Vanessa (1977)... Vanessa
   0:08 - Nude undressing, taking a bath and getting
     washed by "Jackie." Long scene. ***
   0:16 - Buns, then full frontal nudity getting a
     massage. ***
   0:26 - Topless getting fitted for new clothes. *
   0:47 - Full frontal nudity when "Adrian" rips her
     clothes off. *
   0:56 - Full frontal nudity on beach with "Jackie."
     ***
   1:05 - Nude making love with "Jackie" in bed.
     Nice close up of left breast. ***
   1:19 - Full frontal nudity lying on the table. **
   1:27 - Topless in white panties, garter belt and
     stockings shackled up by "Kenneth." **

Island of 1000 Delights (German)................. Peggy
  0:16 - Topless, tied up while being tortured by two
  guys. Upper half lower frontal nudity. **
  0:23 - Full frontal nudity lying in bed, then buns
  running out the door. Full frontal nudity
  running up stairs, nude hiding in bedroom. **
  0:33 - In braless black dress.
  0:57 - Nude, taking off her clothes in shower with
  "Michael." ***
  1:26 - Brief topless running on the beach with
  "Michael." *
Some Like It Cool
  (1979; German/French/Italian/Austrian)
  ....Convent Girl
  a.k.a. Sex on the Run.
  a.k.a. Casanova and Co.
  0:15 - First woman (brunette) to take off her
  clothes with the other two women, full frontal
  nudity. Long scene. ***
C.O.D. (1983)... Holly Fox
  1:30 - In white top during fashion show.
The Joy of Flying.............................. Maria
  0:39 - Topless in bedroom with "George" wearing
  panties, then nude. **
  0:46 - Nude with "George" in bathroom. **

PAUL, ALEXANDRA
Films:
  American Nightmare (1981)
  ....Isabelle Blake/Tanya Kelly
  0:02 - Left breast while smoking in bed. Topless
  before getting killed. Long scene. ***
  Christine (1983)...................................... Leigh
  Just the Way You Are (1984)...................... Bobbie
  American Flyers (1985)............................. Becky
  0:50 - Very brief right breast, then very brief half
  of left breast changing tops with David Grant.
  Brief side view of right breast. Dark. *
  1:13 - Brief topless in white panties getting into
  bed with David Grant. **
  8 Million Ways to Die (1986)....................... Sunny
  0:24 - Full frontal nudity, standing in bathroom
  while Jeff Bridges watches. **
  Dragnet (1987)....................................Connie Swail
  Harlequin Romance: Out of the Shadows (1988)
  ....Jan Lindsey
Made for TV Movies:
  Perry Mason: The Case of the All-Star Assassin
  (1989)..................................... Amy Hastings
  The Laker Girls (1990).......................... Heidi/Jenny
Made for HBO:
  The Hitchhiker: Minuteman..........................Julie
  0:04 - Brief left breast in car with husband, then
  brief topless flashing the couple on the
  motorcycle. **
Made for TV Movie:
  Paper Dolls (1982)..Laurie

PAUL, NANCY
Films:
  Sheena (1984).......................................Betsy Ames
  Gulag (1985).......................................Susan
  0:42 - Buns, then topless taking a shower while
  David Keith daydreams while he's on a train.
  **

PAUL, SUE
Films:
  All That Jazz (1979)....................................... Stacy
  1:18 - Brief right breast in bed with Roy Scheider
  at the hospital. *
Magazines:
  Playboy (Mar 1980)........ "All That Fosse" pictorial
  Page 176: Right breast, kneeling on all fours. *

PAYNE, JULIE
Films:
  Private School (1983) .... Coach Whelan
  0:30 - Very brief left breast popping out of
  cheerleader's outfit along with "Rita's." *
  The Lonely Guy (1983).......................Rental Agent
  Fraternity Vacation (1985)...................Naomi Tvedt
  Jumpin' Jack Flash (1986)
  ....Receptionist at Elizabeth Arden
  Just Between Friends (1986)........................... Karen

PEABODY, DIXIE LEE
Films:
  Night Call Nurses (1972)............................. Robin
  0:35 - Topless taking off clothes in encounter
  group. **
  0:39 - Brief topless in "Barbara's" flashback. *
  Bury Me an Angel (1972).......................................

PEAKE, TERI LYNN
Other:
  a.k.a. Terri Leneé Peake.
Films:
  Murphy's Law (1986)..
  In Search of the Perfect 10 (1986).. Perfect Girl #9
  (Shot on video tape.)
  0:47 - Buns and topless taking a shower. ***
Magazines:
  Penthouse (Oct 1987)............................ Pet
  Pages 77-93

PEARCE, ADRIENNE
Films:
  Purgatory (1988)................................Janine
  0:51 - Brief topless in shower scene with
  "Kirsten." **
  American Ninja 3: Blood Hunt (1989) ....

PEARCE, JACQUELINE
Films:
White Mischief (1988) ....Idina
  0:07 - Topless standing up in the bathtub while
    several men watch. **
How to get Ahead in Advertising (1988).........Maud

PECKINPAUGH, BARBARA
Films:
Erotic Images (1983)............................ Cheerleader
  0:07 - Topless dancing in an office with another
    cheerleader. *
Body Double (1984)
  .... Girl #2 (Holly Does Hollywood)
Basic Training (1985)...........................Salesgirl 1
  0:00 - Topless on desk with another salesgirl. *
Penthouse Love Stories (1986)
  ....“The Therapist” segment
  0:45 - Nude making love in Therapist's office.
    (She's the blonde). ***

PEÑA, ELIZABETH
Films:
Times Square (1980) .... Disco Hostess
Crossover Dreams (1985).............................Liz
Down and Out in Beverly Hills (1986) .... Carmen
La Bamba (1987)............................. Rosie Morales
  0:06 - Brief side view of right breast taking a
    shower outside when two young boys watch her
    from a water tower. Long shot, hard to see. *
*batteries not included (1987).......................Marisa
Blue Steel (1989)...................................Tracy Perez
Made for TV Movies:
Shannon's Deal (1989)...................................Lucy
TV:
Tough Cookies (1986)........... Officer Connie Rivera
I Married Dora (1987-88)................................ Dora

PERLE, REBECCA
Films:
Bachelor Party (1984) .... Screaming Woman
Tightrope (1984) .... Becky Jacklin
Savage Streets (1985)...........................Cindy Clark
  0:24 - In bra and panties fighting with “Brenda” in
    the locker room.
  0:53 - Brief topless in biology class getting her top
    torn off by Linda Blair. **
Stitches (1985)...............................Bambi Belinka
  0:34 - Topless during female medical student's
    class where they examine each other. **
Heartbreak Ridge (1987).......... Student in Shower
  1:48 - Very brief topless getting out of shower
    when the Marines rescue the students. *
Not of This Earth (1988)..........................Alien Girl
  0:53 - In black swimsuit wearing sunglasses.

PERRINE, VALERIE
Films:
Slaughterhouse Five (1972)......Montana Wildhack
  0:39 - Topless in Playboy magazine as a playmate.
    *
  0:43 - Topless getting into the bathtub. *
  1:27 - Topless in a dome with Michael Sacks. ***
The Last American Hero (1973)..................Marge
Steambath (1973) ....
Lenny (1974; B&W) .... Honey Bruce
  0:04 - Doing a strip tease on stage down to pasties
    and buns in a G-string. No nudity, but still nice.
  0:14 - Topless in bed when Dustin Hoffman pulls
    the sheet off her then makes love. ***
  0:17 - Topless sitting on the floor in a room full of
    flowers when Hoffman comes in. **
  0:24 - Left breast wearing pastie doing dance in
    flashback.
  0:43 - Right breast with Kathryn Witt. *
Mr. Billion (1977)..............................Rosi Jones
Superman (1978) .... Eve
The Electric Horseman (1979).........Charlotta Steele
The Magician of Lublin (1979)....................Zeftel
Can't Stop the Music (1980)....... Samantha Simpson
Agency (1981) .... Brenda Wilcox
The Border (1982).....................................Marcy
Faerie Tale Theatre: The Three Little Pigs (1984)..
Water (1986)....................................Pamela
Maid to Order (1987)..................Georgette Starkey
TV:
Leo and Liz in Beverly Hills (1986)......... Liz Green
Magazines:
Playboy (May 1972).............................. “Valerie”
  Pages 103-107: Nice. ***
Playboy (Dec 1972)..................“Sex Stars of 1972”
  Page 210: Topless. **
Playboy (Nov 1973).......................“Sex in Cinema”
  Page 151: Right breast. **
Playboy (Dec 1977)..................“Sex Stars of 1977”
  Page 211: Left breast. *
Playboy (Nov 1981)............. “Sex in Cinema 1981”
  Page 165: Topless. **
Playboy (Aug 1981)....................... “Viva Valerie!”
  Pages 152-159: Topless. **
Playboy (Jan 1989)......... “Women of the Eighties”
  Page 251: Topless. **

PESCIA, LISA
Films:
Tough Guys (1986)............................Customer #1
Body Chemistry (1990)................................Claire
  0:18 - Topless making love with Marc Singer
    standing up, then at foot of bed. ***
  0:35 - In purple bra in van with Singer.
  0:55 - Buns, standing in hallway. Long shot.

PETERS, LORRAINE
Films:
More Deadly than the Male (1961) ....Rita
The Wicker Man (1973)................... Girl on Grave
0:22 - Side view of right breast sitting on grave,
crying. Dark, long shot, hard to see. *
The Innocent (1985)..

PETERSON, CASSANDRA
See Elvira.

PETTET, JOANNA
Films:
The Group (1966).................................... Kay Strong
Casino Royale (1967; British) ....Mata Bond
The Night of the Generals (1967; British/French)
.... Ulrike von Seidlitz-Gaber
Robbery (1967; British).........................Kate Clifton
Blue (1968).................................... Joanne Morton
The Best House in London (1969; British)
.................................Josephine Pacefoot
Welcome to Arrow Beach (1973).........Grace Henry
The Evil (1977)..Caroline
Double Exposure (1983).............. Mindy Jordache
0:55 - Topless, making love in bed with "Adrian."
**
Sweet Country (1985)................................. Monica
Miniseries:
Captains and the Kings (1976)
.... Katherine Hennessey
TV:
Knots Landing (1983)........................... Janet Baines

PETTIJOHN, ANGELIQUE
Other:
a.k.a. Angelique Pettyjohn or Heaven St. John.
Adult Films:
Titillation (1982)................................ Brenda Weeks
Topless and more!
Body Talk (1982)..Cassie
Topless and more!
Films:
Clambake (1967) .... Gloria
Childish Things (1969)............................. Angelique
The Curious Female (1969)............................ Susan
Heaven with a Gun (1969)..............................Emily
The Mad Doctor of Blood Island
(1969; Philippines/U.S.).................. Sheila Willard
Tell Me That You Love Me, June Moon (1970)
....Melissa
Up Your Teddy Bear (1970).....................................
The G.I. Executioner (1971).....................................
The Lost Empire (1983).......................... Whiplash
0:29 - In a black leather outfit fighting in prison
with "Heather." Buns and breasts are half out of
the top

Repo Man (1984) ....
Bio-Hazard (1984)...............................Lisa Martyn
0:30 - Partial left breast on couch with "Mitchell."
In beige bra and panties talking on telephone,
breast almost falling out of bra. **
1:15 - Left breast on couch with "Mitchell" out
take scene during the credits. ***
1:16 - Upper half of left breast on couch again
during a different take. *
Takin' It Off (1984) ....Anita Little
TV:
Star Trek: The Gamesters of Triskelion........ Shahna

PFEIFFER, MICHELLE
Films:
Falling in Love Again (1980)........... Sue Wellington
The Hollywood Knights (1980) .... Suzi Q.
Charlie Chan and the Curse of the Dragon Queen
(1981)......................Cordella Farrington III
Grease 2 (1982) .... Stephanie Zinone
Scarface (1983) .... Elvira
Into the Night (1985).................................... Diana
0:27 - Buns and very brief side nudity in her
brother's apartment getting dressed. Long shot,
hard to see. *
Ladyhawke (1985) ....Isabeau
Sweet Liberty (1986) ....Faith Healey
The Witches of Eastwick (1987)... Sukie Ridgemont
Amazon Women on the Moon (1987)
..............................Brenda Landers
Married to the Mob (1988)........... Angela de Marco
Tequila Sunrise (1988)...................................Jo Ann
1:14 - Upside down reflection in water getting on
top of Mel Gibson. Can't tell it's her. Only see
silhouette. Probably wearing a body suit. Brief
buns, holding onto Gibson when he pulls a sheet
over their heads. Blurry.
Dangerous Liaisons (1988).......Madame de Tourvel
The Fabulous Baker Boys (1989)......Susie Diamond
Made for PBS films:
Natica Jackson....................................Natica Jackson
Made for TV Movies:
The Solitary Man (1979)..
B.A.D. Cats (1980)...
The Children Nobody Wanted (1980) ....Jennifer
Splendor in the Grass (1980) ....
Callie and Son (1981)...
TV:
Delta House (1979)................................. Bombshell

PHILLIPP, KAREN
Other:
Singer in "Sergio Mendes and Brazil '66."
TV:
M*A*S*H (1972)..............................Lt. Maggie Dish
Magazines:
Playboy (Sep 1972) .... "M*A*S*H Dish"
Pages 157-163: Nude. ***

PICKETT, CINDY

Films:
  Night Games (1979)....................... Valerie St. John
    0:05 - Brief topless getting scared by her husband
      in the shower. **
    0:45 - Buns and topless by and in the swimming
      pool with Joanna Cassidy. *
    0:46 - Topless in sheer blue dress during fantasy
      sequence with Cassidy.
    0:48 - Brief full frontal nudity getting out of the
      pool, then topless lying down with Cassidy. **
    1:03 - Dancing at night in a see through
      nightgown.
    1:14 - Full frontal nudity standing up in bathtub,
      then topless during fantasy with a guy in gold.
      ***
    1:18 - Topless getting out of pool at night. **
    1:24 - Topless sitting up in bed and stretching.
      ***
  Circle of Power (1984)..
  The Men's Club (1986)............................... Hannah
  Ferris Bueller's Day Off (1986)...........Katie Bueller
  Hot to Trot (1988) ....Victoria Peyton
  Deepstar Six (1989)............................. Diane Norris
Made for TV Movies:
  Into the Homeland (1987) ....
TV:
  The Guiding Light (1976-80).....Jackie Scott Marler
  Call To Glory (1984-85) ....Vanessa Sarnac
Magazines:
  Playboy (Nov 1979)............... "Sex in Cinema 1979"
    Page 175: Topless, small photo, hard to see. *
  Playboy (Dec 1980)................... "Sex Stars of 1980"
    Page 244: Topless. **

PISIER, MARIE-FRANCE

Films:
  Love at Twenty
    (1963; French/Italian/Japanese/Polish/German)
    ....Colette
  Trans-Europ-Express (1968; French)..................Eva
  Stolen Kisses (1969; French)...............Colette Tazzi
  Cousin, Cousine (1975; French)....................Karine
  Barocco (1976; French)....................................Nelly
  Other Side of Midnight (1977)........... Noëlle Page
    0:10 - Very brief topless in bed with "Lanchon."
      *
    0:28 - Buns, in bed with John Beck. Medium long
      shot.
    0:45 - In white bra in dressing room talking to
      "Henri Correger."
    0:50 - Topless in bathtub giving herself an
      abortion with a coat hanger. Painful to watch!
    1:11 - Topless wearing white slip in room getting
      dressed in front of "Henri." **
    1:17 - Full frontal nudity in front of fireplace with
      "Armand", rubbing herself with oil, then
      making love with ice cubes. Very nice! ***
    1:35 - Full frontal nudity taking off dress for
      "Constantin Demeris" in his room. *
  The Bronte Sisters (1979; French)............. Charlotte

French Postcards (1979)...............Madame Tessier
    0:16 - In white bra, then topless in dressing room
      while a guy watches without her knowing. **
  Love on the Run (1979)............................. Colette
  Chanel Solitaire (1981)................. Gabrielle Chanel
  Miss Right (1987).. Bebe
    0:07 - Topless in open top dress when the reporter
      discovers her in a dressing room behind a
      curtain. **
Miniseries:
  Scruples (1980)............................ Valentine O'Neill

PITT, INGRID

Films:
  Where Eagles Dare (1969)................................Heidi
  Vampire Lovers (1970)............... Marcilla/Carmilla
    0:32 - Topless and buns in the bathtub and her
      reflection in the mirror talking to "Emma." **
  The House That Dripped Blood (1970)............Carla
  The Wicker Man (1973)........................Librarian
    1:11 - Brief topless in bathtub seen by Edward
      Woodward. **
  Transmutations (1986)............................Pepperdine

PLATO, DANA

Films:
  Return to Bogey Creek (1977)................................
TV:
  Diff'rent Strokes (1978-84)....Kimberly Drummond
Magazines:
  Playboy (Jun 1989) ...."Diff'rent Dana"
    Pages 78-83: Bottomless and wearing a pink see-
      through bra. *

PODEWELL, CATHY

Films:
  Night of the Demons (1987)............................Judy
    0:06 - Brief buns, changing clothes while talking
      on the phone.
    0:07 - In white bra taking off her sweater.
TV:
  Dallas (1989-)...

POREMBA, JEAN

Other:
  a.k.a. Jean Poramba.
Films:
  You Can't Hurry Love (1984)........Model in Back
    0:05 - Topless posing in the backyard getting
      photographed. *
    0:45 - Nude in backyard again getting
      photographed. **
  Takin' It All Off (1987)............................. Allison
    0:36 - In pink bra and G-string.
    0:49 - In white lingerie, then topless, then nude
      dancing . ***
    1:07 - Nude on the deck outside. ***

0:58 - Topless, dancing outside when she hears the music. ***

0:59 - Nude dancing in a park. ***

1:01 - Nude dancing in a laundromat. **

1:03 - Nude dancing in a restaurant. ***

1:07 - Nude in shower with "Adam." ***

1:13 - Topless dancing for the music in a studio. **

1:23 - Nude dancing with all the other women on stage. ***

POTTER, MADELEINE

Films:

The Bostonians (1984)..................... Verena Tarrant
The Suicide Club (1988)...
Slaves of New York (1989)........................... Daria
   1:14 - Topless making love with "Stash" on chair. Mostly see left breast. Dark. *
Bloodhounds of Broadway (1989)...........................

POTTS, ANNIE

Films:

King of the Gypsies (1978).............................. Persa
Corvette Summer (1978) .... Vanessa
   0:51 - Silhouette of right breast in van with Mark Hamill. Out of focus topless washing herself in the van while talking to him. Don't really see anything. *
Heartaches (1981; Canadian)........... Bonnie Howard
Ghostbusters (1984)..........................Janine Melnitz
Crimes of Passion (1984).......................Amy Grady
Jumpin' Jack Flash (1986).....................Liz Carlson
Pretty in Pink (1986)..................................Iona
Pass the Ammo (1988)..........................Darla Potter
Ghostbusters II (1989)......................Janine Melnitz
Who's Harry Crumb? (1989)...........Helen Downing
   0:55 - In sheer black bra lying in bed with Jeffrey Jones.
   1:00 - More in the same bra in photograph that Jones is looking at.
TV:

Goodtime Girls (1980)..................Edith Bedelmeyer
Designing Women (1986-)...........Mary Jo Shively

POWER, DEBORAH

Films:

Emmanuelle IV (1984)................................... Maria
   1:09 - Buns, lying down getting a massage from Mia Nygren.
Glamour (1985) ....

POWERS, BEVERLY

Films:

Kissin' Cousins (1964)....................................Trudy
More Dead than Alive (1968)........................Sheree
Angel in My Pocket (1969) ....Charlene de Gaulle
J. W. Coop (1971)............................... Dora Mae
Like a Crow on a June Bug (1972).........................

Invasion of the Bee Girls (1973).. Harriet Williams
   1:14 - In white bra and panties, then right breast and buns taking off her clothes for her husband. *

POWERS, STEPHANIE

Films:

Crescendo (1972; British)............................. Susan
(Not available on video tape yet.)

POWER, TARYN

Other:

Daughter of actor Tyrone Power.

Films:

Tracks (1974).. Stephanie
   0:32 - Brief side view of right breast changing in her room on the train. Don't see her face. *
   1:15 - Brief left breast making love with Dennis Hopper in a field. *
Sinbad and the Eye of the Tiger (1977; U.S./British) .... Dione
Made for TV Movies:

The Count of Monte Cristo (1975)...........................

PRATHER, JOAN

Films:

Single Girls..
Big Bad Mama (1974)...................... Jane Kingston
   1:15 - Topless and buns in the bathroom with Tom Skerritt. **
Smile (1974).. Robin
   0:47 - Brief buns in dressing room taking off pants. while "Little Bob" is outside taking pictures. (Wearing a pink ribbon in her hair.)
Rabbit Test (1978) .... Segoynia
Famous T & A (1982)................................... herself
   0:49 - Brief topless in scene from "Single Girls." *
Made for TV Movies:

The Deerslayer (1978)..
TV:

Executive Suite (1976-77) ....Glory Dalessio
Eight is Enough (1979-81)...............Janet Bradford

PRENTISS, PAULA

Films:

Where the Boys Are (1960).......... Tuggle Carpenter
The World of Henry Orient (1964)................. Stella
Man's Favorite Sport? (1964)...............Abigail Page
What's New Pussycat? (1965)............................Liz
In Harm's Way (1965; B&W) ....Bev
Move (1970)... Dolly Jaffe
Catch-22 (1970)............................... Nurse Duckett
   0:22 - Full frontal nudity in water throwing her dress to Alan Arkin who is swimming in the water during his dream. Long shot, over exposed, hard to see anything. *
Last of the Red Hot Lovers (1972).... Bobbi Michele

The Parallax View (1974) ....Lee Carter
The Stepford Wives (1974) ....Bobby
The Black Marble (1980) .. Sgt. Natalie Zimmerman
Buddy Buddy (1981) ....Celia Clooney
Saturday the 14th (1981) ....Mary
TV:
He & She (1967-68) ....Paula Hollister

PRESTON, KELLY
Other:
a.k.a. Kelly Palzis.
Films:
10 to Midnight (1983) ....Doreen
Christine (1983)..............................Roseanne
Metalstorm: The Destruction of Jared-Syn (1983)
.... Dhyana
Mischief (1985)...........................Marilyn McCauley
0:56 - In a bra, then topless making love with
Doug McKeon in her bedroom. ***
Secret Admirer (1985).........Deborah Anne Fimple
0:53 - Brief topless in car with C. Thomas Howell.
**
1:17 - Very brief topless in and out of bed. *
0:52 **Pick-Up** (1986).....................................Cini
0:09 - Brief buns in film made by blackmailers. *
0:36 - Topless on video tape made by kidnappers.
*
Space Camp (1986) ....Tish
Amazon Women on the Moon (1987).............Violet
Love at Stake (1988) ....Sara Lee
Spellbinder (1988)............................ Miranda Reed
0:19 - Topless in bed making love with Timothy
Daly. ***
1:26 - Dancing around in a sheer white gown with
nothing underneath during cult ceremony at the
beach.
Twins (1988) ....Marnie Mason
A Tiger's Tale (1988).................................. Shirley
0:03 - Topless in the car opening her blouse for C.
Thomas Howell to examine. **
The Experts (1989)..Bonnie
Made for HBO:
Tales from the Crypt: The Switch (1990)........Linda
0:19 - In red, one piece swimsuit at the beach with
a young "Carlton."
TV:
For Love and Honor (1983)......................Mary Lee

PRINCIPAL, VICTORIA
Films:
The Life and Times of Judge Roy Bean (1972)
.... Marie Elena
The Naked Ape (1972)................................ Cathy
(Not available on video tape yet.)
Topless.
Earthquake (1974)..Rosa
I Will... I Will... For Now (1976)...... Jackie Martin
Vigilante Force (1976)....................................Linda
TV:
Dallas (1978-89)....................Pamela Barnes Ewing

Made for TV Movies:
Naked Lie (1989)............................Joanne Dawson
Magazines:
Playboy (Dec 1972)..................."Sex Stars of 1972"
Page 210 - Left breast. ***
Playboy (Sep 1973)....................."The Naked Ape"
Page 161: Topless.
Playboy (Sep 1973)............................ "'Ape' Girl"
Page 162-167: Topless and buns.
Playboy (Dec 1973)................. "Sex Stars of 1973"
Page 210: Right breast. *
Playboy (Dec 1976)................."Sex Stars of 1976"
Page 183: Topless and in black panties lying
down. ***

PROPHET, MELISSA
Films:
Players (1979)..Ann
Van Nuys Blvd. (1979)...............................Cameille
Looker (1981).....................Commercial Script Girl
Time Walker (1982)......................................Jennie
0:27 - Brief topless putting bra on while a guy
watches from outside the window. *
1:17 - Very, very brief right breast in shower when
the mummy comes to get the crystal.
Invasion U.S.A. (1985)...............................McGuirre
Action Jackson (1988)...........................Newscaster
Magazines:
Playboy (May 1987)
.... "Diary of a Hollywood Starlet"
Pages 86-93: Full frontal nudity. ***

PROPS, BABETTE
Films:
Weird Science (1985)...............One of The Weenies
Free Ride (1986)... Kathy
0:13 - Brief topless in the shower while "Dan"
watches. *

PULITZER, ROXANNE
Other:
Author of the book, "The Prize Pulitzer."
Films:
Playboy (Jun 1985) ....
Playboy (Jan 1989)........... "Women of the Eighties"
Page 253: Full frontal nudity. ***

PURL, LINDA
Films:
Crazy Mama (1975)......................................Cheryl
0:05 - In pink, two piece swimsuit at the beach.
0:52 - Very brief buns, then brief topless when
"Snake" and Donny Most keep opening the door
after she has taken a shower. Long shot, hard to
see. *
The High Country (1980)..............................Kathy
1:03 - Brief buns taking a shower in the waterfall.
Visiting Hours (1982; Canadian).......Sheila Munroe

Viper (1988).......................................Laura Macalla
Made for TV Movies:
Pleasures (1986)...
TV:
Happy Days (1974-75)..................................Gloria
Happy Days (1982-83)......................Ashley Pfister
Matlock (1986-89).......................Charlene Matlock

Q

QUENNESSEN, VALERIE

Films:
French Postcards (1979)................................. Toni
Like a Turtle on Its Back (1981; French)...Nietzsche
Conan the Barbarian (1982)..................The Princess
Summer Lovers (1982)..................................Lina
   0:12 - Topless on balcony. *
   0:19 - Nude on the beach with "Michael." ***
   0:23 - Brief topless in a cave with "Michael." *
   0:30 - Topless lying on the floor with "Michael."
     **
   0:54 - Buns, lying on a rock with Daryl Hannah
     watching "Michael" dive off a rock.
   1:03 - Left breast in bed. *
   1:05 - Topless dancing on the balcony. **
   1:09 - Topless on the beach.

QUIGLEY, LINNEA

Films:
Fairytales (1979)................................... Dream Girl
   1:07 - Topless waking up after being kissed by
     The Prince. **
Summer Camp (1979)..
Nightstalker (1979)..
Stone Cold Dead (1979)..
Cheech & Chong's Nice Dreams (1981)
   ....Blondie Group #2
Don't Go Near the Park (1981) ....
Graduation Day (1981)............................Dolores
   0:36 - Topless in classroom with "Mr. Roberts" by
     the piano undoing her blouse. **
The Young Warriors (1983)....................... Ginger
   0:05 - Nude in and getting out of bed in bedroom.
     *
The Black Room (1984)..................................Milly
Silent Night, Deadly Night (1984)................Denise
   0:52 - Topless on pool table with "Tommy," then
     putting on shorts and walking around the house.
     More topless impaled on antlers. ***
Savage Streets (1985)................................Heather
   0:28 - Topless getting raped by the jerks. *
Return of the Living Dead (1986)..................Trash
   0:05 - Topless and buns, strip tease and dancing in
     cemetery. (Lower frontal nudity is covered with
     some kind of appliance). ***
   1:08 - Topless, walking out of the cemetery to eat
     someone *

Silent Night, Deadly Night, Part II (1986)................
Creepozoids (1987)..
Nightmare Sisters (1987) ....
Night of the Demons (1987)..................... Suzanne
   0:52 - Topless twice, opening her dress top while
     acting weird. Pushes a tube of lipstick into her
     left breast (Don't try this at home kids!). **
   0:56 - Lower frontal nudity lifting her skirt up for
     "Jay."
Treasure of the Moon Goddess (1987)....................
Sorority Babes in the Slimeball Bowl-O-Rama
   (1988)...Spider
Hollywood Chainsaw Hookers (1988).... Samantha
   0:32 - Topless, dancing on stage. **
   1:02 - Topless, (but her body is painted) dancing
     in a ceremony. *
Assault of the Party Nerds (1988)............... Bambi
   0:25 - Topless straddling "Cliff" in bed. ***
**A Nightmare on Elm Street 4: The Dream
   Master** (1988)................Soul from Freddy's Chest
   1:23 - Brief topless twice trying to get out of
     Freddy's body. Don't see her face clearly. *
Vice Academy (1988)....................................... Didi
American Rampage (1988).......................................
Dangerous Embrace (1988)....................................
Dr. Alien (1989)...........................Rocker Chick #2
   0:21 - Topless in white outfit during dream
     sequence with two other rocker chicks. ***
Assault of the Party Nerds (1989)...........................
Witchtrap (1989)...........................Ginger O'Shey
   0:34 - Nude taking off robe and getting into the
     shower. ***
   0:36 - Topless just before getting killed when the
     shower head goes into her neck. **
Magazines:
Playboy (Jan 1985)...."The Girls of Rock and Roll"
Playboy (Nov 1988).............."Sex in Cinema 1988"
   Page 137: Topless with tattoos across her breasts
     holding a chainsaw. **
Playboy (Jul 1989)................... "B-Movie Bimbos"
   Page 134: Full frontal nudity leaning on a car
     wearing stockings and an orange garter belt.
     ***

QUINLAN, KATHLEEN

Films:
Lifeguard (1976)..Wendy
I Never Promised You a Rose Garden (1977)
   .... Deborah
   0:27 - Topless changing in a mental hospital room
     with the orderly. *
   0:52 - Brief topless riding a horse in a
     hallucination sequence. Blurry, hard to see.
     Then close up of left breast (could be anyone's).
     *
The Runner Stumbles (1979) ....Sister Rita
The Promise (1979)............................ Nancy/Marie
Hanky Panky (1982)..............................Janet Dunn
Twilight Zone - The Movie (1983).................Helen

The Last Winter (1983)..................................Joyce
   0:48 - Brief side view of left breast taking off her
     robe and diving into pool Very brief buns. **
   0:49 - Buns, lying on marble slab with "Maya."
   0:50 - Very brief right breast sitting up. Long
     shot, hard to see.
Warning Sign (1985)............................Joanie Morse
Man Outside (1986)....................................
Wild Thing (1987).......................................
Sunset (1988)............................Nancy Shoemaker
Clara's Heart (1988).............................Leona Hart
Man Outside (1987)........................ Grace Freemont
Made for Cable Movies:
   Blackout (1985)............................... Chris
   0:26 - Brief side view of left breast making love in
     bed. Dark, hard to see.
   Trapped (1989)...

R

RAE, TAIJA
Other:
   Adult film actress.
Films:
   Delivery Boys (1984).......................................Nurse
   0:34 - In bra and panties after doing a strip tease
     with another "nurse" while dancing in front of a
     boy who is lying on an operating table.
   Sex Appeal (1986).. Sheila
   1:15 - In black lingerie, then topless in black
     pushup teddy with "Sheila." **

RAINES, FRANCES
Films:
   The Mutilator (1983)...
   Topless by the pool.
   Breeders (1986)............................ Karinsa Marshall
   Nude, exercising in photo studio.

RAINES, LISA
See Foster, Lisa Raines

RAINS, GIANNA
Films:
   Firehouse (1987)............................. Barrett Hopkins
   0:33 - Topless taking a shower, then drying herself
     just before the fire alarm goes off. ***
   0:56 - Topless making love with the reporter on
     the roof of a building. **
   Homeboy (1989) ....

RAMPLING, CHARLOTTE
Films:
   Rotten to the Core (1965; British) ....Sara
   Knack... And How to Get It (1965; British)
   .... Water Skier
   Georgy Girl (1966; British/B&W)..............Meredith
   The Long Duel (1967; British)........... Jane Stafford
   Sardinia: Ransom (1968; British)...............Cristina
   Three (1969; British) ....Marty
   The Ski Bum (1971)...............................Samantha
   Asylum (1972; British)..............................Barbara
   Corky (1972)...............................Corky's Wife
   Henry VIII and His Six Wives (1972; British)
   .... Anne Boleyn
   'Tis a Pity She's a Whore (1972; Italian)
   .... Annabella
   Giordano Bruno (1973; Italian) ....Fosca
   Caravan to Vaccares (1974; British/French)....Lila
   Brief buns standing at window, then brief full
     frontal nudity getting back into bed.
   The Night Porter (1974; Italian/U.S.)............Lucia
   0:11 - Side nudity being filmed with a movie
     camera in the concentration camp line. **
   0:13 - Nude running around a room while a Nazi
     taunts with her by shooting his gun near her. *
   1:12 - Topless doing a song and dance number
     wearing pants, suspenders and a Nazi hat. Long
     scene. ***
   Zardoz (1974; British)..............................Consuella
   1:44 - Very brief right breast feeding her baby in
     time lapse scene at the end of the film. *
   Farewell My Lovely (1975)........................ Velma
   Foxtrot (1976; Mexican/Swiss)............... Julia
   Orca, The Killer Whale (1977)........ Rachel Bedford
   The Purple Taxi (1977; French/Italian/Ireland)
   .... Sharon
   Stardust Memories (1980) ....Dorrie
   Target: Harry (1980)...........................Ruth Carlyle
   The Verdict (1982)......................................Laura
   Angel Heart (1987)................. Margaret Krusemark
   1:10 - Brief left breast dead on the floor, covered
     with blood. *
   1:46 - Very brief left breast during flashback of
     the dead-on-the-floor-covered-with-blood scene.
     *
   Mascara (1987)..
   D.O.A. (1988)..............................Mrs. Fitzwaring
Made for TV Movies:
   Sherlock Holmes in New York (1976) ....
Magazines:
   Playboy (Nov 1972)............. "Sex in Cinema 1972"
   Page 167: Topless lying down in bed in a photo
     from "'Tis a Pity She's a Whore." *
   Playboy (Mar 1974)................................"Zardoz"
   Page 142 - Buns and side view of left breast. *
   Playboy (Dec 1977)..................."Sex Stars of 1977"
   Page 213: Right breast and half of lower frontal
     nudity standing against fireplace. **

RANDALL, ANNE

Films:
       The Split (1968).....................................Negli's Girl
       The Model Shop (1969)...........................2nd Model
       Hell's Bloody Devils (1970).......................Amanda
       The Christian Licorice Store (1971).........Texas Girl
       A Time for Dying (1971)..................Nellie Winters
       Get to Know Your Rabbit (1972)...........Stewardess
       Stacey (1973)..................................Stacey Hansen
           0:01 - Topless taking off her driving jump suit.
               ***
           0:12 - Topless changing clothes. ***
           0:39 - Topless in bed with "Bob Eastwood." ***
       Westworld (1973)..................................Servant Girl
TV:
       Hee Haw (1972-73).......................................regular
Magazines:
       Playboy (May 1967)................................. Playmate
       Playboy (Dec 1973).................. "Sex Stars of 1973"
           Page 208: Left breast. *

RATTRAY, HEATHER

Films:
       Across the Great Divide (1976)........................Holly
       The Further Adventures of the Wilderness Family -
           Part 2 (1978)...........................Jenny Robinson
       The Sea Gypsies (1978).............................Courtney
       Mountain Family Robinson (1979) ....Jenny
       Basket Case 2 (1989)....................................Susan
           1:20 - Brief right breast twice when white blouse
               gapes open in bedroom with "Duane." Special
               effect scar on her stomach makes it a little
               unappealing looking. *
TV:
       As the World Turns (1990-).....................Lily Walsh

RAY, OLA

Films:
       Body and Soul (1981)............................Hooker #1
           0:54 - Brief topless sitting on top of Leon Isaac
               Kennedy in bed with two other hookers. *
       Night Shift (1982).. Dawn
       48 Hours (1982)........................... Vroman's Dancers
       10 to Midnight (1983)..Ola
           1:27 - Buns, then topless in the shower. **
       Fear City (1984)................................Honey Powers
       The Nightstalker (1987)...........................Sable Fox
Music Videos:
       Thriller by Michael Jackson (1983)....His Girlfriend
Magazines:
       Playboy (Jun 1980).................................. Playmate
           Page 144
       Playboy (Jul 1981)............... "Body and Soulmates"
           Page 148: Right breast. *
       Playboy (Dec 1984)................... "Sex Stars of 1984"
           Page 206: Topless. ***

REDGRAVE, LYNN

Other:
       Daughter of actor Sir Michael Redgrave.
       Sister of actress Vanessa Redgrave.
       Spokeswoman for Weight Watchers products.
Films:
       Georgy Girl (1966; British/B&W)................ Georgy
       The Deadly Affair (1967)...............................Virgin
       The Virgin Soldiers (1969)...............Phillipa Raskin
       The Happy Hooker (1975).......... Xaviera Hollander
           (Before Weight Watchers.)
           0:43 - In black bra and panties doing a strip tease
               routine in a board room while Tom Poston
               watches.
       Morgan Stewart's Coming Home (1987)..................
       Getting It Right (1989)......................................Joan
           0:46 - Brief right breast, then brief topless on
               couch seducing "Gavin." Longer right breast
               shot when wrestling with him. **
       Midnight (1989) ....Midnight
TV:
       Centennial (1978-79)
               ....Charlotte Buckland Lloyd Seccombe
       House Calls (1979-81) ....Ann Anderson
       Teachers Only (1982-83) ....Diana Swanson
       Chicken Soup (1989) ....Maddie
Magazines:
       Playboy (Nov 1989)............. "Sex in Cinema 1989"
           Page 131: Right breast lying in sofa in a still from
               "Getting It Right." *

REDGRAVE, VANESSA

Other:
       Daughter of actor Sir Michael Redgrave.
       Sister of actress Lynn Redgrave.
Films:
       Blow-Up (1966; British/Italian)........................Jane
       Morgan: A Suitable Case for Treatment
           (1966; British/B&W)...........................Leonie Delt
       Camelot (1967)....................................Guenevere
       The Sea gull (1968).. Nina
       Isadora (1968; British)....................Isadora Duncan
           0:47 - Brief glimpses of topless and buns dancing
               around her boyfriend's house at night. Hard to
               see anything.
           2:19 - Very brief topless dancing on stage after
               coming back from Russia. *
       The Devils (1971; British) ....
       The Seven-Per-Cent Solution (1976) Lola Deveraux
       Julia (1977)...Julia
       Agatha (1979)....................................Agatha Christie
       Yanks (1979)...Helen
           Brief buns and side view of left breast.
       Bear Island (1980; British/Columbia)
               ....Hedi Lindquist
       Wagner (1982) ....Cosima
       The Bostonians (1984).....................................
       Wetherby (1985; British) ....Jean Travers
       Steaming (1986; British) .... Nancy
           1:32 - Buns and brief side view of right breast
               getting into pool. *

Prick Up Your Ears (1987; British)... Peggy Ramsay
Consuming Passions (1988; U.S./British)
.... Mrs. Garza
    0:40 - Almost side view of left breast making love
    with a guy on her bed.
Made for TV Movies:
    Playing for Time (1984)..................... Fania Fenelon
    0:11 - Very brief buns sitting down to get her hair
    cut

REDMAN, AMANDA
Films:
    Richard's Things (1980)................................. Josie
    0:51 - Topless, lying in bed talking to Liv Ullman.
    **
    Give My Regards to Broad Street (1984)
    ....Office Receptionist
    For Queen and Country (1989) ....

REED, TRACY
Films:
    ...All the Marbles (1981)...................................Diane
    Running Scared (1986)............................ Maryann
    0:18 - Brief buns. *
    1:30 - Very brief topless in bed with Gregory
    Hines. *
Made for TV Movies:
    Death of a Centerfold: The Dorothy Stratten Story
    (1981)..
TV:
    Love, American Style (1969-70)....Repertory Player
    Barefoot in the Park (1970-71)............. Corie Bratter
    Love, American Style (1972-74)....Repertory Player

REGARD, SUZANNE M.
Films:
    48 Hours (1982).............................. Cowgirl Dancer
    0:39 - Dancer in redneck bar wearing silver star
    pasties.
    Malibu Express (1984)........................... Sexy Sally
    0:50 - Brief topless talking on the telephone. *
    1:06 - Topless talking on the telephone. **

REIDY, GABRIELLE
Films:
    Educating Rita (1983) .... Barbara
    The Fanatasist (1986; Irish)...........Kathy O'Malley
    0:03 - Topless getting attacked in a room. *

RENET, SINITTA
Films:
    Shock Treatment (1981)..
    Foreign Body (1986).................. Lovely Indian Girl
    0:06 - Buns, then topless in bedroom. *

RIALSON, CANDICE
Films:
    Candy Stripe Nurses (1974)......................... Sandy
    0:05 - Topless in hospital linen closet with a guy.
    **
    0:08 - Topless smoking and writing in bathtub. **
    0:14 - Topless in hospital bed. *
    The Eiger Sanction (1975)..................... Art Student
    Hollywood Boulevard (1976)..... Candy Wednesday
    Pets (1974).. Bonnie
    0:26 - Topless dancing in field while "Dan" is tied
    up watching her. **
    0:33 - Topless making love on top of "Dan" while
    he's still tied up. ***
    0:35 - Running through woods in braless orange
    top.
    0:40 - Topless getting into bath at "Geraldine's"
    house. **
    0:45 - Topless posing for "Geraldine." *
    0:54 - In black and red lingerie outfit getting ready
    for bed.
    1:02 - Topless taking off lingerie in bed with
    "Ron" then making love with him. ***
    1:34 - Almost topless getting whipped by
    "Vincent."
    Chatterbox (1977)....................................... Penny
    0:01 - Left breast in bed with "Ted" then topless
    getting out of bed. **
    0:10 - In white bra wrestling on couch with
    another woman.
    0:15 - Side view of right breast then topless during
    demonstration on stage. ***
    0:26 - Topless in bed talking on phone. ***
    0:32 - In open dress letting her "chatterbox" sing
    during talk show. Something covers pubic area.
    0:35 - Topless during photo shoot. **
    0:38 - Topless again for more photos while
    opening a red coat. **
    0:43 - Topless in bed with "Ted." **
    0:55 - Topless taking off white dress, walking up
    the stairs and opening the door. ***
    1:09 - Topless opening her raincoat for "Ted." **
    Moonshine County Express (1977) ....Mayella
    Stunts (1977)..Judy Blake
    Summer School Teachers (1977)........... Conklin T
    Winter Kills (1979)................... Second Blonde Girl

RICHARDE, TESSA
Films:
    The Last American Virgin (1982).............. Brenda
    0:15 - Brief topless walking into the living room
    when "Gary's" parents come home. **
    Cat People (1982).. Billie
    1:00 - Topless in bed with Malcolm McDowell
    trying to get him excited. **
    The Beach Girls (1982) ....Doreen

RICHARDS, KIM

Films:
Escape to Witch Mountain (1975).......................Tia
Assault on Precinct 13 (1976)..........................Kathy
No Deposit, No Return (1976)..........................Tracy
Special Delivery (1976)................................Juliette
The Car (1977)....................................Lynn Marie
Return from Witch Mountain (1978)...................Tia
Meatballs, Part II (1984)...............................Cheryl
Tuff Turf (1984) .... Frankie Croyden
   1:07 - In black lingerie getting dressed.
   1:29 - Brief topless supposedly of a body double
   (Fiona Morris) in bedroom with James Spader
   but I have heard from a very reliable source that
   it really was her. *

TV:
Nanny and the Professor (1970-71)
   .... Prudence Everett
Here We Go Again (1973)...................................Jan
James at 15 (1977-78).........................Sandy Hunter
Hello, Larry (1979-80)............................Ruthie Adler

RICHARDSON, JOELY

Other:
Daughter of actress Vanessa Redgrave and director
   Tony Richardson.
Sister of actress Natasha Richardson.
Films:
The Hotel New Hampshire (1984)...............Waitress
Wetherby (1985)...................... Young Jean Travers
   1:10 - Topless in room with "Jim" when he takes
   off her coat. **
Drowning by Numbers (1988)................................

RICHARDSON, NATASHA

Other:
Daughter of actress Vanessa Redgrave and director
   Tony Richardson.
Sister of actress Joely Richardson.
Films:
Gothic (1986)....................................Mary
A Month in the Country (1988).............Alice Keach
Patty Hearst (1989)..........................Patricia Hearst
   0:13 - Topless, blindfolded in the bathtub while
   talking to a woman member of the S.L.A. **
A Handmaid's Tale (1990)............................. Kate
   0:30 - Topless twice at the window getting some
   fresh air. **
   0:59 - Topless making love with Aidan Quinn. *
   1:00 - Topless after Quinn rolls off her. ***

RICHARDSON, RICKEY

Other:
a.k.a. Ricki Richardson.
Films:
The Hot Box (1972)...................... Ellie St. George
   0:16 - Topless cleaning herself off in stream and
   getting out. **

0:21 - Topless sleeping in hammocks. (She's the
   second one from the front.) *
0:26 - Topless getting accosted by the People's
   Army guys. *
0:43 - Full frontal nudity making love with
   "Flavio." ***
0:45 - Topless in stream bathing with the other
   three girls. ***
1:01 - Topless taking off top in front of soldiers. *
Bloody Trail (1972)........................... Miriam
   1:01 - Peek at left breast in torn blouse.
   1:05 - Right breast while sleeping, dark, hard to
   see. *

RICHMOND, FIONA

Films:
The House on Straw Hill (1976)...............................
Fiona (1978; British).....................Fiona Richmond
   0:23 - Topless on boat with a blonde woman
   rubbing oil on her. **
   0:27 - In a bra, then frontal nudity stripping in a
   guy's office for an audition. **
   0:35 - Topless, then frontal nudity lying down
   during photo session. **
   0:51 - Topless walking around her apartment in
   boots. *
   1:00 - Topless with old guy ripping each other's
   clothes off. **
   1:08 - Frontal nudity taking off clothes for a
   shower. **
History of the World, Part 1 (1981)................Queen

RICHTER, DEBI

Other:
a.k.a. Deborah Richter.
Miss California 1975.
Films:
Hometown, U.S.A. (1979) ....Dolly
Swap Meet (1979)..............................Susan
Gorp (1980)....................................Barbara
Hot Moves (1985)................................. Heidi
   0:29 - Topless on nude beach. *
   1:09 - Topless in bed with Michael. ***
Winners Take All (1987) ....Cindy Wickes
   0:25 - In bra, in bed with motorcycle racer.
Square Dance (1987)...........................Gwen
   (Shown on TV as "Home is Where the Heart Is")
Promised Land (1988)................................ Pammie
Cyborg (1989) ....Nady Simmons
   0:28 - Buns, after taking off clothes and running
   into the ocean.
   0:30 - Brief left breast by the fire showing herself
   to Jean-Claude Van Damme. *
TV:
Aspen (1977)....................................Angela Morelli
All Is Forgiven (1986)......................... Sherry Levy

RICHWINE, MARIA

Films:

The Buddy Holly Story (1978).... Maria Elena Holly
Hamburger: The Motion Picture (1986)
.... Conchita
0:49 - Topless trying to seduce "Russell" in a
room. **

TV:

a.k.a. Pablo (1984).. Carmen

RIO, NICOLE

Films:

The Zero Boys (1985) ....
The Visitants (1987)...
Sorority House Massacre (1987)................... Tracy
0:20 - In a sheer bra changing clothes with two
other girls in a bedroom. **
0:49 - Topless in a tepee with her boyfriend
"Craig" just before getting killed. **
Terminal Exposure (1988)................... Hostage Girl

RIXON, CHERYL

Films:

Swap Meet (1979)... Annie
Used Cars (1980)...................................... Margaret
0:29 - Topless after getting her dress torn off
during a used car commercial. **

Magazines:

Penthouse (Dec 1977).. Pet
Pages 127-139
Penthouse (Nov 1979)..................... Pet of the Year
Pages 158-169

ROBERTS, LUANNE

Films:

The Dark Side of Tomorrow (1970)
.... Producer's Wife
Weekend with the Babysitter (1970)... Mona Carlton
Simon King of the Witches (1971) ....
Welcome Home, Soldier Boys (1972)........ Charlene
Thunderbolt and Lightfoot (1974)
.... Suburban Housewife
0:57 - Brief full frontal nudity standing behind a
sliding glass door tempting Jeff Bridges. *

ROBERTS, MARIWIN

Films:

Cinderella (1977) .... Trapper's Daughter
0:11 - Frontal nudity getting a bath outside by her
blonde sister. Long scene. ***
Fairytales (1979) .... Elevator Operator
0:20 - Brief full frontal nudity operating the
elevator. *
0:23 - Topless again, closer shot. **

ROBERTS, TANYA

Films:

Forced Entry (1975)........................... Nancy Ulman
0:57 - In white bra and panties walking around the
house.
The Yum-Yum Girls (1976).....................................
Fingers (1977)... Julie
0:33 - In red two piece swimsuit talking on a pay
phone while Harvey Keitel talks with her.
California Dreaming (1978)..................... Stephanie
Racquet (1979)... Bambi
The Tourist Trap (1979)............................ Becky
The Beastmaster (1982)..................................... Kiri
0:35 - Topless in a pond while Marc Singer
watches, then topless getting out of the water
when his pet ferrets steal her towel. ***
Hearts and Armour (1983)........................ Angelica
Sheena (1984)... Sheena
0:19 - Nude taking a shower under a waterfall.
***
0:54 - Nude taking a bath in a pond while Ted
Wass watches. ***
A View to a Kill (1985)....................... Stacey Sutton
Purgatory (1988)............................... Carly Arnold
0:29 - Nude, getting into the shower. *
0:43 - In white lingerie in whorehouse.
0:57 - Left breast, then brief topless in bed talking
to "Tommy." **
0:42 - Very brief topless in bed with the Warden.
*
Night Eyes (1990).. Nikki
0:18 - In white one piece swimsuit by the pool
0:20 - Side view of left breast getting dressed
while sitting on bed. *
0:25 - In white lingerie in bed making love with
"Michael Vincent."
0:30 - Repeat of last scene on TV when Andrew
Stevens brings the video tape home to watch.
0:55 - Making love with Stevens. Don't see
anything, but still steamy. Bubble covered left
breast in tub with Stevens.
1:09 - Topless giving Stevens a massage, then
making love. Nice! Buns and left breast in the
shower making love. ***
1:27 - Buns, making love with Stevens in a chair.

Made for HBO:

Body Slam (1989)..

Made for TV Movies:

Waikiki (1980)..

TV:

Charlie's Angels (1980-81) .... Julie Rogers

Magazines:

Playboy (Oct 1982)..
Nice. ***
Playboy (Nov 1982)............. "Sex in Cinema 1982"
Page 161: Topless from "The Beastmaster." ***
Playboy (Jan 1989).......... "Women of the Eighties"
Page 251: Topless. **

ROBERTS, TEAL

Films:
Fatal Games (1984)..............................
Hardbodies (1984)..............................Kristi Kelly
   0:03 - Topless in bed after making love with
     "Scotty," then putting her sweater on. **
   0:47 - Topless standing in front of closet mirrors
     talking about breasts with "Kimberly." ***
   0:56 - Topless making love with "Scotty" on the
     beach. ***
   1:22 - Topless on fancy car bed with "Scotty." **
Beverly Hills Cop II (1987)........................ Stripper
   0:45 - Topless and buns, wearing G-string at the
     385 North Club. **

ROBERTSON, KIMMY

Films:
The Last American Virgin (1982) ....Rose
Bad Manners (1989).................... Sarah Fitzpatrick
   0:38 - Topless and buns taking off robe and
     getting into the shower when "Mouse" takes a
     picture of her. **
   1:16 - In white bra when "Piper" rips her blouse
     open while she's tied up on the piano.
   1:18 - Briefly on piano again.
Trust Me (1989).......................................
Honey, I Shrunk the Kids (1989).............................
TV:
Twin Peaks (1990-)..

ROHMER, PATRICE

Films:
The Harrad Summer (1974)..........................Marcia
Hustle (1975) ....Linda, a Dancer
Jackson County Jail (1976)................... Cassie Anne
A Small Town in Texas (1976) ....Trudy
Revenge of the Cheerleaders (1976)..........Sesame
   0:28 - Brief topless and buns in the boys shower
     room. *

ROJO, HELENA

Films:
Aguirre: Wrath of God (1972)..........................Inez
Foxtrot (1975)..Alexandra
Mary, Mary, Bloody Mary (1975)................Greta
   0:42 - Buns and brief topless getting into bathtub
     with Cristina Ferrare. *

ROMANELLI, CARLA

The Lonely Lady (1983)............Carla Maria Peroni
   1:10 - Brief topless taking off her top to make love
     with Pia Zadora while a guy watches. **
A Very Moral Night (1985).................................

ROME, SYDNE

Films:
Sex with a Smile (1976; Italian)
   ...."A Dog's Day" segment
Twist (1976)..
Just a Gigolo (1979)...Cilly
Diary of Forbidden Dreams (1973; Italian)
   .... The Girl
   0:06 - Brief topless taking off torn T-shirt in a
     room, then topless sitting on edge of bed. ***
   0:09 - Nude getting out of shower, drying herself
     off and getting dressed. ***
   0:20 - Brief side view of right breast talking to
     Marcello Mastroianni in her room. *
   0:22 - Brief topless putting shirt on. **
   1:28 - Topless outside on stairs fighting for her
     shirt. **
   1:30 - Brief buns and topless climbing onto truck.
     *
Looping (1981)..
Ten Days that Shook the World (1982)................
Magazines:
Playboy (Nov 1980).............."Sex in Cinema 1980"
   Page 178: Topless. **

ROSE, JAMIE

Films:
Just Before Dawn (1980)............................. Megan
   0:33 - Topless in pond. Long shot.
   0:34 - Brief topless in pond, closer shot. *
   0:36 - Brief upper half of left breast, then brief
     topless several times splashing in the water. **
   0:37 - Topless getting out of the water. *
Heartbreakers (1981).................................... Libby
   0:09 - Topless in bed talking with Nick Mancuso
     and Peter Coyote. ***
Tightrope (1984)................... Melanie Silber
   0:07 - Buns, lying face down on bed, dead.
Rebel Love (1985) ....
Made for TV Movies:
Voices Within: The Lives of Truddi Chase (1990)
   ....Truddi's Mother
TV:
Falcon Crest (1981-83)........ Victoria Gioberti Hogan
Lady Blue (1985-86).........Detective Katy Mahoney
St. Elsewhere (1986-88)................... Dr. Susan Birch

ROSE, LAURIE

Films:
The Hot Box (1972).. Sue
   0:16 - Topless cleaning herself off in stream and
     getting out. **
   0:21 - Topless sleeping in hammocks. (She's the
     first one from the front.) **
   0:26 - Topless getting accosted by the People's
     Army guys. *
   0:45 - Topless in stream bathing with the other
     three girls. ***
   0:58 - Full frontal nudity getting raped by "Major
     Dubay." *

The Roommates (1973)......................................Brea
The Working Girls (1973)..............................Denise
Policewoman (1974) ....
The Woman Hunt (1975).................................
The Wizard of Speed & Time (1988).......................

ROSE, SHERRIE ANN
Films:
   Summer Job (1989)........................... Kathy Shields
      0:25 - In bed wearing white bra and panties
      talking to "Bruce." Long scene.
      0:52 - Buns, walking around in swimsuit and
      jacket.
      0:53 - Topless taking off swimsuit top kneeling by
      the phone, then brief buns standing up. **
      1:15 - In yellow two piece swimsuit walking on
      the beach.
      1:24 - Brief topless taking off her yellow top on
      the beach talking to "Bruce." **
Magazines:
   Playboy (Apr 1989)..... "The Girls of Spring Break"
      Page 74: Topless lying down, wearing a bikini
      bottom. ***

ROSS, ANNIE
Films:
   Straight on Till Morning (1974)......................Liza
   Oh, Alfie! (1975; British) ....Claire
      a.k.a. Alfie Darling
      1:34 - Topless on top of "Alfie" in open black
      dress while he's lying injured in bed. **
   Yanks (1979)..
   Funny Money (1983)..
   Superman III (1983)............................Vera Webster

ROSS, KATHERINE
Films:
   The Graduate (1967) ....
   Butch Cassidy and the Sundance Kid (1969)............
   Tell Them Willie Boy is Here (1969) ....Lola
      0:22 - Very, very brief breast sitting up with
      Robert Blake. So blurry, that I can't tell which
      one it is. Topless getting up when guy with rifle
      disturbs her and Blake. Buns, getting dress.
      Long shot, dark, hard to see.
   They Only Kill Their Masters (1972).............Kate
      (Not available on video tape yet.)
   The Betsy (1978)............................Sally Hardeman
   The Legacy (1979)..
   The Final Countdown (1980)...............................
   Wrong is Right (1982)......................................
Made for TV Movies:
   Secrets of a Mother and Daughter (1983)................

ROSSELLINI, ISABELLA
Other:
   Daughter of actress Ingrid Bergman.
   Model for Lancome cosmetics.
Films:
   A Matter of Time (1976) ....
   White Nights (1985)...................Darya Greenwood
   Blue Velvet (1986)....................................Dorothy
      1:08 - Brief topless in apartment. *
      1:40 - Nude, standing bruised on porch. *
   Tough Guys Don't Dance (1987)............Madeleine
   Siesta (1987)... Marie
   Cousins (1989)....................................Marie Hardy
   Wild at Heart (1990)..

ROUTLEDGE, ALISON
Films:
   The Quiet Earth (1985; New Zealand)........ Joanne
      0:49 - Brief buns after making breakfast for "Zac"
      1:24 - Topless in guard tower making love with
      "Api." **
   Bridge to Nowhere (1986; New Zealand) ....Lise

ROWAN, GAY
Films:
   Sudden Fury (1975) .... Janet
   The Girl in Blue (1978; Canada)................. Bonnie
      a.k.a. U-Turn
      0:06 - Left breast in bed with "Scott." *
      0:31 - Brief topless in bathtub. *
      0:48 - Right breast in shower talking to "Scott."
      Brief topless (long shot) on balcony throwing
      water at him. *
      1:21 - Brief right breast and buns getting out of
      bed and running out of the room. *
   S.O.B. (1981)...
   Second Thoughts (1983)...............................Annie

ROWE, MISTY
Films:
   The Hitchhikers (1971).............................. Maggie
      0:00 - Brief side view of left breast getting
      dressed. *
      0:17 - Very brief topless getting dress ripped open,
      then raped in van. *
      0:48 - Brief right breast while getting dressed. *
      1:09 - Left breast making love with "Benson." *
      1:10 - Brief topless taking a bath in tub. *
      1:13 - Very brief right breast in car with another
      victim. *
   Goodbye, Norma Jean (1975).. Norma Jean Baker
      0:02 - In white bra putting makeup on.
      0:08 - In white bra and panties, then topless. **
      0:14 - Brief topless in bed getting raped. *
      0:31 - Very, very brief silhouette of right breast in
      bed with "Rob."
      0:59 - Topless during shooting of stag film, then in
      B&W when some people watch the film. ***
      1:14 - In white bra and panties undressing.

Loose Shoes (1977) ....Louise
Meatballs, Part II (1979)...
The Man with Bogart's Face (1980)............ Duchess
National Lampoon's Class Reunion (1982)
....Cindy Shears
  0:37 - Very brief topless running around school
  stage in Hawaiian hula dance outfit. *
Double Exposure (1983)................................. Bambi
Made for TV Movie:
  When Things Were Rotten (1975).......Maid Marion
TV:
  Hee Haw (1972-) ....Regular
  Happy Days (1974-75)................................. Wendy
  When Things Were Rotten (1975).......Maid Marion
  Hee Haw Honeys (1978-79).................Misty Honey
  Joe's World (1979-80)..........................Judy Wilson
Magazines:
  Playboy (Nov 1976)......................................"Misty"
  Pages 104-107: Nude. ***

ROYCE, ROSELYN
Films:
  Cheech & Chong's Nice Dreams (1981)
  ....Beach Girl #3
  0:29 - Brief topless on the beach with two other
  girls. Long shot, unsteady, hard to see. *
  Malibu Hot Summer (1981)............. Cheryl Rielly
  a.k.a. Sizzle Beach
  0:15 - On exercise bike, then topless getting into
  bed. **
  0:16 - Topless sitting up in bed, buns going to
  closet to get dressed to go jogging. ***
  0:26 - In pink two piece swimsuit running to
  answer the phone.
  0:52 - Topless on boat with "Brent." **
  Off the Wall (1982)........................ Buxom Blonde
  0:35 - Left breast kissing prisoner in visiting room
  while the guards watch. *
  0:51 - Left breast again kissing prisoner through
  bars while the guards watch. **

RUBENS, MARY BETH
Films:
  Firebird 2015 AD (1981)...
  Perfect Timing (1984)...................................... Judy
  0:04 - In a bra, then topless in bedroom with
  "Joe." *
  0:05 - Nude, walking to kitchen, then talking with
  "Harry." **
  0:08 - Left breast seen through the camera's view
  finder. *
  0:10 - Nude, getting dressed in bedroom. *
  0:49 - In red bra and panties.
  0:50 - Nude in bed with "Joe." **
  1:00 - Nude, discovering "Joe's" hidden video
  camera, then going downstairs. ***

RUSSELL, BETSY
Films:
  Private School (1983)............. Jordan Leigh-Jensen
  (Blonde hair.)
  0:02 - Taking a shower behind a frosted door.
  0:04 - Very, very brief right breast and buns when
  "Bubba" takes her towel off through window. *
  0:19 - Topless riding a horse to after Kathleen
  Wilhoite steals her blouse. ***
  0:35 - In jogging outfit stripping down to black
  bra and panties, brief upper half of buns.
  1:15 - In room with "Bubba" in white bra and
  panties.
  1:24 - Upper half of buns flashing with the rest of
  the girls during graduation ceremony.
  Out of Control (1984)................................Chrissie
  (Brunette hair.)
  0:19 - In white corset and panties in the pond.
  0:29 - Topless taking off her top while playing
  Strip Spin the Bottle. **
  0:30 - Buns, taking off her panties.
  Tomboy (1985)............. Tomasina "Tommy" Boyd
  0:44 - In wet T-shirt, then brief topless after
  landing in the water with her motorcycle. **
  0:59 - Topless making love with the race car
  driver in an exercise room. **
  Avenging Angel (1985) .... Angel/Molly Stewart
  Cheerleader Camp (1988)........... Alison Wentworth
  a.k.a. Bloody Pom Poms.

RUSSELL, KAREN
Films:
  Dr. Alien (1989)... Coed #2
  a.k.a. I was a Teenage Sex Mutant
  0:53 - Topless taking off her top in the women's
  locker room before another coed takes her's off
  in front of "Wesley." ***
  Vice Academy (1989)...
  Easy Wheels (1989) ....
  Hell High (1989)...

RUSSELL, THERESA
Films:
  Straight Time (1978)....................... Jenny Mercer
  1:00 - Left breast in bed with Dustin Hoffman.
  Don't see her face. ***
  Bad Timing - A Sensual Obsession (1980)............
  (Not available on video tape yet.)
  Topless.
  Eureka (1983; British)....................................Tracy
  0:38 - In lingerie talking to Rutger Hauer.
  0:40 - Right breast, lying in bed with Hauer. *
  1:04 - Very brief left breast in bed with Hauer,
  then brief lover frontal nudity and brief buns
  when Gene Hackman bursts into the room. *
  1:09 - Topless on a boat with Hauer. **
  1:41 - Left breast peaking out from under black
  top while lying in bed. *
  1:59 - Full frontal nudity kicking off sheets in the
  bed. ***

The Razor's Edge (1984)................................Sophie
Insignificance (1985)......................................Actress
Black Widow (1986)................................ Catherine
   0:28 - Brief topless and bottomless making love in
   cabin. *
   1:18 - Nude in pool with "Paul." **
Aria (1988)...King Zog
Track 29 (1988).....................................Linda Henry
Smoke (1988)...
Physical Evidence (1989)................... Jenny Hudson
Impulse (1989).. Lottie
   0:37 - Left breast making love with "Stan" in bed.
   **

Magazines:
   Playboy (Nov 1980)..............."Sex in Cinema 1980"
      Page 181: Topless. *
   Playboy (Nov 1983)..............."Sex in Cinema 1983"
      Page 145: Topless. *

RYAN, MEG
Films:
   Rich and Famous (1981).............Debbie at 18 years
   Armed and Dangerous (1986)....Maggie Cavanaugh
   Top Gun (1986)................................ Carole
   Innerspace (1987)......................................
   The Presidio (1988).......................................Donna
   D.O.A. (1988)........................... Sydney Fuller
   Promised Land (1988)............................... Beverly
      0:22 - Very brief side view of left breast in bed
      with Kiefer Sutherland. *
   When Harry Met Sally... (1989)......... Sally Albright
   Joe versus the Volcano (1990)............................
Soap Operas:
   As the World Turns......................................
TV:
   One of the Boys (1982)......................................Jane
   Wildside (1985)... Cally Oaks

S

SÄGEBRECHT, MARIANNE
Films:
   Sugarbaby (1985; German)......................Sugarbaby
   The Bagdad Café (1988)..............................Jasmin
      (Check this tape out if you like your women a
      little on the plump side.)
      1:09 - Right breast slowly lowering her top,
      posing while Jack Palance paints her. **
      1:12 - Topless posing for Palance. **
   Moon Over Parador (1988) .... Magor
   War of the Roses (1989)................................Susan
   Rosalie Goes Shopping (1990)............................
Magazines:
   Playboy (Nov 1988).............."Sex in Cinema 1988"
      Page 136: Topless from "Bagdad Café." *

ST. JON, ASHLEY
Films:
   Takin' It Off (1984).. Latta
      0:22 - Topless and buns doing two dance routines.
      ***
   The Wild Life (1984)..................... Stripper #1
      0:47 - Topless and brief buns doing strip tease
      routine in front of Christopher Penn and his
      friends. ***
   Weekend Pass (1984).........................Xylene B-12
      0:13 - Topless dancing on stage. **

ST. PIERRE, MONIQUE
Films:
   Motel Hell (1980)..Debbie
Magazines:
   Playboy (Nov 1978)....................................Playmate

SANDA, DOMINIQUE
Films:
   First Love (1970; German/Swiss)................Sinaida
   The Conformist (1971; Italian/French)
      .... Anna Quadri
   The Garden of the Finzi-Continis
      (1971; Italian/German).................... Micol
      0:24 - In braless wet white T-shirt after getting
      caught in a rainstorm.
      1:12 - Topless sitting on a bed after turning a light
      on so the guy standing outside can see her. *
   A Gentle Creature (1971; French).......................She
   Without Apparent Motive (1972; French)
      .... Sandra Forest
   Impossible Object (1973; French)............. Nathalie
   a.k.a. Story of a Love Story
   The Makintosh Man (1973; British)........................
   Night of the Flowers (1973; Italian).......................
   Steppenwolf (1974) ....Hermine
   Conversation Piece (1976; Italian/French)....Mother
   1900 (1976; Italian) ....Ada
   Damnation Alley (1977)................................Janice
   The Inheritance (1978; Italian)...................... Irene
      0:18 - Full frontal nudity getting undressed and
      lying on the bed with her new husband. **
      0:37 - Full frontal nudity lying in bed with her
      lover. ***
      1:19 - Very brief right breast undoing top for
      Anthony Quinn. *
      1:22 - Left breast, lying in bed. Full frontal nudity
      jumping out of bed after realizing that Quinn is
      dead. ***
   Caboblanco (1982)..............Marie Claire Allesandri
   Beyond Good and Evil
      (1984; Italian/French/German)..............................
Magazines:
   Playboy (Mar 1972)........ "Magnifique Dominique"
      Pages 87-89: Nice. ***
   Playboy (Nov 1972)....................."Sex in Cinema"
      Page 159: Topless. *
   Playboy (Dec 1972)..................."Sex Stars of 1972"
      Page 207: Left breast. **

Playboy (Nov 1973)........................"Sex in Cinema"
   Page 158: Left breast. *
Playboy (Dec 1973)................... "Sex Stars of 1973"
   Page 211: Left breast. **
Playboy (Nov 1978)............. "Sex in Cinema 1978"
   Page 184: Right breast. *

SANDLUND, DEBRA
Films:
  Tough Guys Don't Dance (1987)......Patty Lareine
   1:24 - Topless ripping her blouse off to kiss the
   policeman after they have killed and buried
   another woman. **
  Murder by Numbers (1990).............................Leslie
TV:
  Full House (1990-)..Cindy

SANDS, PEGGY
Films:
  Into the Night (1985)................. Shameless Woman
   0:43 - Topless putting dress on after coming out of
   men's restroom stall after a man leaves the stall
   first. *
  Beverly Hills Cop II (1987)........................ Stripper
   0:48 - Very brief topless, dancing at the 385 North
   Club. *
  Phoenix the Warrior (1988)............................. Keela

SARA, MIA
Films:
  Legend (1985)...Lili
  Ferris Bueller's Day Off (1986).........Slone Peterson
  Apprentice to Murder (1987).........................Alice
   0:29 - Left side view topless making love with
   Chad Lowe. *
  Queenie (1987)............Queenie Kelly/Dawn Avalon
  Shadows in the Storm (1988).......................Melanie
   0:51 - Standing in bathtub all covered with
   bubbles talking to Ned Beatty.
Miniseries:
  Till We Meet Again (1989) ....Delphine

SARANDON, SUSAN
Films:
  Joe (1970)..................................... Melissa Compton
   0:02 - Topless and very brief lower frontal nudity
   taking off clothes and getting into bathtub with
   "Frank." *
  Lady Liberty (1972; Italian/French)................. Sally
  The Haunting of Rosalind (1973)...........................
  The Front Page (1974)......................................Peggy
  Lovin' Molly (1974)..Sarah
  The Great Waldo Pepper (1975).............. Mary Beth
  The Rocky Horror Picture Show (1975; British)
  .... Janet
  The Great Smokey Roadblock (1976).............Ginny
  One Summer Love (1976) ....Chloe

The Other Side of Midnight (1977)
  .... Catherine Douglas
  1:10 - Topless in bedroom with John Beck. Long
  shot, hard to see, then right breast while lying in
  bed. *
  2:18 - Naked under wet white nightgown running
  around outside.
King of the Gypsies (1978).............................Rose
  0:49 - Brief right breast during fight with Judd
  Hirsch. *
Pretty Baby (1978)...................................... Hattie
  0:12 - Breast feeding a baby with her left breast
  sitting by the window in the kitchen.
  0:24 - Brief side view, taking a bath. *
  0:39 - Topless on the couch when Keith Carradine
  photographs her. ***
Something Short of Paradise (1979)
  .... Madeleine Ross
Loving Couples (1980)............................. Stephanie
Atlantic City (1981; U.S./Canadian)................Sally
  0:50 - Left breast cleaning herself with lemon
  juice while Burt Lancaster watches through
  window. **
The Tempest (1982)...................................... Aretha
  0:58 - In braless white tank top washing clothes
  with Molly Ringwald in the ocean.
  1:53 - In wet white T-shirt on balcony during
  rainstorm with Jason Robards and Raul Julia.
  1:55 - In wet white T-shirt on the beach.
  1:57 - Brief right, then left breasts in open T-shirt
  saving someone in the water. *
The Hunger (1983).......................... Sarah Roberts
  0:59 - In a wine stained white T-shirt, then topless
  during love scene with Catherine Deneuve. ***
Faerie Tale Theatre: Beauty and the Beast (1983)...
The Buddy System (1984) .... Emily
Compromising Positions (1985)...........Judith Singer
Witches of Eastwick (1987)................Jane Spofford
Sweet Hearts Dance (1988)...................Sandra Boon
  1:23 - Almost a left breast in bathroom mirror
  changing clothes.
  1:25 - Very, very brief left breast under white
  bathrobe arguing with Don Johnson in the
  bathroom.
Bull Durham (1988)............................Annie Savoy
  1:39 - Brief right breast peeking out from under
  her dress after crawling on the kitchen floor to
  get a match.
The January Man (1988).............. Christine Starkey
Made for HBO Films:
  Mussolini and I (1985)....................................

SAUNDERS, PAMELA
Films:
  Alien Warrior (1985) ....
Video Tapes:
  Playboy Video Magazine, Volume 11...... Playmate
Magazines:
  Playboy (Nov 1985)...................................Playmate

SAVOY, THERESA ANN

Films:
La Bambina (1976; Italian) ....
Caligula (1980)...Drucilla
   0:02 - Nude, running around in the forest with
     Malcolm McDowell. **
   1:08 - Nude, dead as McDowell tries to revive her.
     *

SCACCHI, GRETA

Films:
Heat and Dust (1982)......................... Olivia Rivers
   1:25 - Buns lying in bed with "Douglas," then
     topless rolling over. They are both under a
     mosquito net. **
The Ebony Tower (1985)..............................Mouse
   0:38 - Topless having a picnic. *
   0:43 - Brief nude walking into the lake. *
The Coca Cola Kid (1985)............................... Terri
   0:49 - Nude taking a shower with her daughter.
     ***
   1:20 - Brief topless in bed wearing a Santa Claus
     outfit with Eric Roberts. **
A Man in Love (1987)...........................Jane Steiner
   0:31 - Topless with Peter Coyote. ***
   1:04 - Buns and left breast in bed with Coyote. **
   1:10 - Brief side view topless, putting black dress
     on.
   1:24 - Brief topless in bed. *
Good Morning, Babylon (1987; Italian/French) .....
   1:05 - Topless in the woods making love with
     Vincent Spano. **
White Mischief (1988)................. Diana Broughton
   0:16 - Topless taking a bath while an old man
     watches through a peephole in the wall. **
   0:24 - Brief topless in bedroom with her husband.
     **
   0:29 - Brief topless taking off bathing suit top in
     the ocean in front of Charles Dance. **
   0:30 - Topless lying in bed talking to Dance. **
Presumed Innocent (1990)...
Magazines:
Playboy (Nov 1988)..............."Sex in Cinema 1988"
   Page 141: Topless in bathtub in a photo from
     "White Mischief." **

SCARABELLI, MICHELE

Other:
a.k.a. Michelle Scarabelli.
Films:
Perfect Timing (1984)............................... Charlotte
   1:11 - Brief buns, then topless in bed with
     "Harry." **
   1:18 - Topless in bed with "Harry" during the
     music video. *
Made for HBO:
The Hitchhiker: Face to Face..............Dr. Ensman
   0:07 - Topless in Robert Vaughn's office. ***
TV:
Alien Nation (1989-90)..................Susan Francisco

SCARWID, DIANA

Films:
Pretty Baby (1978)...............................Frieda
Honeysuckle Rose (1980)...........................Jeanne
Inside Moves (1980)..Louise
Mommie Dearest (1981).............Christina Crawford
Rumble Fish (1983)...................................Cassandra
Silkwood (1983)................................... Angela
Strange Invaders (1983)............................Margaret
Psycho III (1986) .... Maureen
   0:30 - Brief topless and buns getting ready to take
     a shower is a body double.
Extremities (1986) ....Terry
The Ladies Club (1987)......................Lucy Bricker
Heat (1987)...Cassie
Made for TV Movies:
After the Promise (1987) .... Anna
TV:
Studs Lonigan (1979)..................Catherine Banahan

SCHNEIDER, MARIA

Films:
Last Tango In Paris (1972)...........................Jeanne
   Nude a lot.
La Baby Sitter (1975; French/Italian/German)
   ....Michele
The Passenger (1975; Italian)...........................Girl
A Woman Called Eva (1979)................................
Memories of a French Whore (1979)...................
Mamma Dracula (1980; Belgian/French)
   ....Nancy Hawaii
Magazines:
Playboy (Feb 1973)....................."Two to 'Tango'"
   Page 132-133: Nude. ***
Playboy (Feb 1973)....................................."Maria"
   Page 134-137: Nude. ***
Playboy (Nov 1973)............. "Sex in Cinema 1974"
   Page 159: Topless. **
Playboy (Dec 1973).................. "Sex Stars of 1973"
   Page 211: Half of right breast. **

SCHNEIDER, ROMY

Films:
Boccaccio '70 (1962; Italian)....."The Job" Segment
   1:18 - In white slip talking on the phone.
What's New Pussycat? (1965)...........Carole Werner
The Sinners (1968)...
Vengeance... One by One ....
   0:02 - In black slip getting dressed.
   0:28 - Very brief left breast when a soldier rips her
     bra open during struggle.
   1:14 - In black lingerie in her husband's flashback.
Dirty Hands (1975; French) ....Julie
   0:01 - Buns and right breast getting a tan, lying on
     the grass after a man's kite lands on her. *
   0:09 - Side view of right breast lying in bed with a
     man, then topless. **
   1:04 - Topless lying on floor, then brief topless
     sitting up and looking at something on the table.
     *

Bloodline (1979)................................. Helene Martin
Magazines:
Playboy (Dec 1976)................... "Sex Stars of 1976"
Page 186: Topless lying down, hard to recognize it's her. **

SCHOELEN, JILL
Films:
D.C. Cab (1983)... Claudette
Hot Moves (1984)...................................... Julie Ann
That Was Then... This Is Now (1985)
.... Angela Shepard
Thunder Alley (1986)...................................... Beth
The Stepfather (1987)................... Stephanie Drake
1:15 - Brief topless and buns taking a shower. **
Curse II: The Bite (1989)..
Phantom of the Opera (1989)...................... Christine
Made for TV Movies:
Shattered Spirits (1986)................................. Allison

SCHUBERT, KARIN
Other:
Claimed to be the Shah of Iran's lover.
Films:
Bluebeard (1972).. Greta
1:43 - Brief topless, spinning around, unwrapping herself from a red towel for Richard Burton. *
Till Marriage Do Us Part (1974; Italian)....... Evelyn
Black Emmanuelle (1976)................ Anne Danielli
0:06 - Brief topless adjusting a guy's tie. *
0:14 - Topless making love in a gas station with a gas station attendant. ***
0:37 - Nude, running in the jungle while Laura Gemser takes pictures of her. ***
0:40 - Topless, kissing Gemser. *
0:44 - Right breast making love with "Johnny" in bed. *
Black Venus (1983).. Marie
0:38 - Nude in bed with "Venus" making love. **

SCHYGULLA, HANNA
Films:
Wrong Move (1975; German) ....
The Marriage of Maria Braun (1979; German)
.... Maria Braun
Berlin Alexanderplatz (1983; German) ....
A Love in Germany (1984; German)
.... Paulina Kropp
The Delta Force (1986)................................... Ingrid
Forever Lulu (1987)...................................... Elaine
1:03 - Brief topless in and getting out of bubble bath. *

SCOGGINS, TRACY
Films:
Toy Soldiers (1983) .... Monique
In Dangerous Company (1988)...................... Evelyn
0:12 - In a white bra, lying on bed making love with a guy.
0:42 - Very, very brief half of left breast in bed with "Blake". Then, very, very brief left breast getting out of bed. Blurry, hard to see.
0:58 - Brief upper half of left breast taking a bath. Long shot, hard to see.
The Raven Red Kiss-Off (1990).......... Vala Vuvalle
Watchers II (1990)............................ Barbara White
The Gumshoe Kid (1990)................... Rita Benson
0:33 - In two piece white swimsuit. Nice bun shot while Jay Underwood hides in the closet.
1:10 - Side view of left breast in the shower with Underwood. Excellent slow motion topless shot while turning around. Brief side view of right breast in bed afterwards. ***
Video Tapes:
Tracy Scoggins' Tough Stuff Workout.....................
TV:
Renegades (1983).. Tracy
Hawaiian Heat (1984).......................... Irene Gorley
The Colbys (1985-1988)................... Monica Colby

SCOTT, DEBRA LEE
Films:
Dirty Harry (1971) .... Anne Murray Deacon
1:10 - Full frontal nudity, dead, being pulled up from a hole in the ground. Very long shot, hard to see.
TV:
Welcome Back, Kotter (1975-76)...... Rosalie Totzie
Mary Hartman, Mary Hartman (1976-78)
.... Cathy Shumway
Angie (1979-80)................................... Marie Falco

SEAGROVE, JENNY
Films:
Harlequin Romance: Magic Moments (1989)
.... Melanie James
The Guardian (1990)...
Topless.
Made for TV Movies:
In Like Flynn (1985)..

SENIT, LAURIE
Films:
Body and Soul (1981)............................ Hooker #3
0:54 - Brief topless lying next to Leon Isaac Kennedy in bed with two other hookers. *
Doctor Detroit (1983)............................ Dream Girl
R.S.V.P. (1984)................................. Sherry Worth
1:00 - Topless in the shower with Harry Reems. **
1:06 - Topless again. **

SENNET, SUSAN

Films:

Big Bad Mama (1974)............................. Billy Jean
0:49 - Topless and buns with Tom Skerritt. *
0:51 - Topless and buns in bed with Skerritt. **
Tidal Wave (1975; U.S./Japan)...............................
TV:
Ozzie's Girls (1973)......................... Susie Hamilton

SERNA, ASSUMPTA

Films:

Matador (1986; Spain).................... Maria Cardinal
0:03 - Topless taking off wrap and making love
with a guy just before she kills him. *
1:38 - Topless on floor with "Diego." Long shot,
hard to see. Topless in front of the fire. ***
1:41 - Brief topless making love with "Diego." *
1:43 - Topless lying on floor dead. *
Lola (1986)......................................Silvia
Wild Orchid (1990)..
Magazines:
Playboy (Jun 1990).......................... "Wild Orchid"
Page 84: Topless in photos from "Wild Orchid."
**

SEVERANCE, JOAN

Films:

No Holds Barred (1989)................Samantha Moore
See No Evil, Hear No Evil (1989)................... Eve
1:08 - Topless in and leaning out of the shower
while Gene Wilder tries to get her bag. **
TV:
Wiseguy (1989)................................... Susan Profitt
Magazines:
Playboy (Jan 1990)........................"Texas Twister"
Pages 84-95: Nude. ***

SEYMOUR, JANE

Films:

The Only Way (1970; Panama/Denmark/U.S.).........
Young Winston (1972; British)...... Pamela Plowden
Live and Let Die (1973; British).................Solitaire
Sinbad and the Eye of the Tiger
(1977; U.S./British)......................................Farah
Oh, Heavenly Dog! (1980)................ Jackie Howard
Somewhere in Time (1980)............. Elise McKenna
Jamaica Inn (1982)......................Mary Yellan
1:47 - (0:14 into volume 2) Braless under a wet
white dress changing clothes in a stagecoach.
The Haunting Passion (1983)................................
Lassiter (1984)..Sara
0:10 - Buns and brief side view of right breast
lying on stomach on bed with Tom Selleck.
Head Office (1986).......................................Jane
The Tunnel (1987).. Maria
0:29 - Very brief left breast in bed with Peter
Weller when the sheet is pulled down. *
0:44 - Brief right beast getting dressed, throwing
off her robe. **

Miniseries:

Captains and the Kings (1976).....Chisholm Armagh
Seventh Avenue (1977) .... Eva Meyers
East of Eden (1981) ....Cathy/Kate Ames
Crossings (1986)..
The Woman He Loved (1988)......... Wallis Simpson
War and Remembrance (1988).........Natalie Jastrow
Made for TV Movies:
The Dallas Cowboy Cheerleaders (1979)................
Frankenstein..
Battlestar Gallactica (1978) .... Serina
Obsessed with a Married Woman (1985)................
The Richest Man in the World: The Story of
Aristotle Onassis (1988)....................Maria Callas
Jack the Ripper (1988)...............................Emma
The Woman He Loved (1988)......... Wallis Simpson
Magazines:
Playboy (Jul 1973)............................"Sainted Bond"
Page 147: Nothing
Playboy (Dec 1973)................."Sex Stars of 1973"
Page 204: Wet T-shirt, nothing
Playboy (Jan 1987)..
Pages 138-145: Rated PG

SFERRAZZAS, LESLIE

Other:

Ex-wife of Reno, Nevada mayor Pete Sferrazzas.
Magazines:
Playboy (Sep 1989)................."Reno Confidential"
Pages 130-137: Nude. ***

SHAPIRO, HILARY

Other:

Also see Shepard, Hilary.
Films:
Soup for One (1982)..
Weekend Pass (1984) .... Cindy Hazard
1:05 - In red bra, then topless taking off bra. **
1:07 - Buns and topless getting into bathtub. *
Private Resort (1985)................................ Shirley
0:36 - Topless, then buns, taking off her dress in
front of "Ben." ***
Radioactive Dreams (1987)................................

SHARPE, CORNELIA

Films:

Kansas City Bomber (1972)...........Tammy O'Brien
Serpico (1973)....................................Leslie
0:41 - Topless in bathtub with Al Pacino. **
Busting (1974) ....Jackie
Open Season (1974; U.S./Spanish)................ Nancy
The Reincarnation of Peter Proud (1975)
....Nora Hayes
0:03 - Topless in bed with Michael Sarrazin, then
buns when getting out of bed. **
The Next Man (1976)........................ Nicole Scott
(Not available on video tape yet.)
Nude in the shower.
Venom (1982; British)........................ Ruth Hopkins

Made for TV Movies:
Cover Girls (1977)..
S.H.E. (1979) ....

SHATTUCK, SHARI
Films:
The Naked Cage (1985) ....Michelle
0:42 - Buns and topless in shower, then getting
slashed by "Rita" during a dream. **
1:00 - Left breast getting attacked by "Smiley" in
jail cell, then fighting back. **
1:28 - Panties during fight with "Rita."
Hot Child in the City (1987)..................................
Desert Warrior (1988)...
The Uninvited (1988)..
Made for TV Movies:
The Laker Girls (1990)..................................Libby

SHAVER, HELEN
Films:
Shoot (1976; Canadian)....................Paula Lissitzen
The Supreme Kid (1976; Canadian)..................Girl
Outrageous! (1977; Canadian)..............................Jo
High-Ballin' (1978) ....Pickup
In Praise of Older Women (1978; Canadian)
....Ann MacDonald
1:40 - Blue bra and panties, then topless with Tom
Berenger. ***
1:42 - Nude lying in bed with Berenger, then
getting out and getting dressed. ***
Starship Invasions (1978; Canadian)...............Betty
The Amityville Horror (1979) ....Carolyn
Who has Seen the Wind (1980; Canadian).............
Gas (1981; Canadian)................................Rhonda
Harry Tracy (1982; Canadian).................Catherine
The Osterman Weekend (1983)
....Virginia Tremayne
0:24 - Topless in an open blouse yelling at her
husband in the bedroom. *
0:41 - Topless in the swimming pool when
everyone watches on the TV. *
Best Defense (1984)............................Claire Lewis
Color of Money (1986)..............................Janelle
Desert Hearts (1986)........................... Vivian Bell
1:05 - Brief topless in bed in hotel room. *
1:09 - Topless in bed making love with Patricia
Charboneau. ***
The Believers (1987).......................Jessica Halliday
0:38 - Brief glimpse of right breast while lying in
bed with Martin Sheen. *
1:17 - Buns, getting out of bed.
Made for HBO:
The Park is Mine (1985)................ Valery Weaver
0:46 - Very brief topless undressing then very,
very brief left breast catching clothes from
Tommy Lee Jones. *
Made for TV Movies:
Mothers, Daughters and Lovers (1989)...................
Rest In Peace, Mrs. Columbo (1990).Vivian Dimitri

TV:
United States (1980)...........................Libby Chapin
Jessica Novak (1981).......................Jessica Novak
WIOU (1990-)..............................Kelby Robinson
Magazines:
Playboy (Oct 1978).... "Observing 'Older Women'"
Page 193-194: Topless and buns. **
Playboy (Nov 1978)............."Sex in Cinema 1978"
Page 185: Full frontal nudity on bed. **

SHAW, TINA
Films:
Salome's Last Dance (1987)....................2nd Slave
(Appears with 2 other slaves - can't tell who is
who)
0:08 - Topless in black costumes around a cage.
**
0:52 - Topless during dance number. **
Taffin (1988)...........................Lola the Stripper
1:04 - Topless doing routine in a club. **
The Lair of the White Worm (1988).........Maid/Nun

SHAYNE, LINDA
Films:
Humanoids from the Deep (1980).....Miss Salmon
1:06 - Topless after getting bathing suit ripped off
by a humanoid. *
Screwballs (1983)........................ Bootsie Goodhead
The Lost Empire (1983)......................Cindy Blake
Big Bad Mama II (1987)...................... Bank Teller
Daddy's Boys (1988) ....Nanette

SHEA, KATT
Other:
a.k.a. Kathleen Shea, Kathy Shea, Kathleen M. Shea
or Katt Shea Ruben.
Actress turned Director.
Films:
The Cannonball Run (1981)..................Starting Girl
My Tutor (1983) ....Mud Wrestler
0:48 - Brief topless when a guy rips her dress off.
*
Scarface (1983)........... Woman at the Babylon Club
Cannonball Run II (1984)......................................
Hollywood Hot Tubs (1984).....................Dee-Dee
0:21 - Topless with her boyfriend while "Shawn"
is working on the hot tub. *
Preppies (1984)...................................... Margot
0:20 - Topless teasing "Richard" through the glass
door of her house. ***
0:54 - In bra and panties with "Trini" practicing
sexual positions on the bed.
1:07 - Brief topless after taking off bra in bed. *
R.S.V.P. (1984)..............................Rhonda Rivers
0:31 - Side view of left breast making love in bed
with "Jonathan." *
Barbarian Queen (1985)........................... Estrild
0:31 - Brief topless getting top torn off by guards.
*

The Destroyers (1985).................................... Audrey
Psycho III (1986)... Patsy
The Devastator (1987)..

SHEAR, RHONDA
Films:
Basic Training (1984)....................................Debbie
0:07 - Topless making love with "Mark." **
0:15 - In bra making love on "Mark's" desk.
Doin' Time (1984)......................................Adrianne
Spaceballs (1987)........................... Woman in Diner

SHEEDY, ALLY
Films:
Wargames (1983)..Jennifer
Bad Boys (1983)................................J. C. Walenski
0:12 - Very, very brief left breast kneeling on floor
next to bed when Sean Penn leave. A little
blurry and a long shot. *
Blue City (1985)............................. Annie Rayford
0:44 - Very very brief left breast lying on bed
reaching her arm around Judd Nelson while
kissing him. Dark and blurry.
The Breakfast Club (1985)............ Allison Reynolds
St. Elmo's Fire (1985)......................................
Short Circuit (1986)..
Maid to Order (1987)..................Jessie Montgomery
0:40 - Buns, taking off dress and diving into the
pool. Long shot and dark. Don't see her face.
0:42 - Buns, walking with a towel around her hair.
Another long shot and you don't see her face.

SHEPARD, HILARY
Other:
Also see Shapiro, Hilary.
Films:
Hunk (1987)..Alexis Cash
Peace Maker (1990)............................Dori Caisson
1:08 - Brief upper half of buns taking off shirt
getting into shower. Brief side view of upper
half of left breast twice, making love with
"Townsend."
Made for HBO:
Dream On: The First Episode (1990)............ Date 2

SHEPARD, JEWEL
Films:
My Tutor (1983)......................Girl in Phone Booth
0:40 - Brief left breast in car when Matt Lattanzi
fantasizes about making love with her. *
Christina (1984).......................................Christina
Hollywood Hot Tubs (1984)...........Crystal Landers
Not topless, but bouncing around a lot in short
braless T-shirts.
The Return of the Living Dead (1985)............ Casey
Party Camp (1987)............................Dyanne Stein
0:57 - In white bra and panties, then topless
playing strip poker with the boys. ***

The Underachievers (1987)............ Sci-Fi Teacher
0:27 - Topless ripping off her Star Trek uniform
when someone enters her classroom. Dark, hard
to see. *
Scenes from the Goldmine (1987)....................Dana
Hollywood Hot Tubs 2 - Educating Crystal (1989)
.... Crystal Landers
0:38 - In white slip during "Gary's" fantasy.
1:12 - Brief left breast lying down, kissing "Gary."
*

SHEPHERD, CYBILL
Films:
The Last Picture Show (1971; B&W) Jacy Farrow
(Not available on video tape yet.)
Brief topless.
The Heartbreak Kid (1972).............. Kelly Corcoran
Daisy Miller (1974)...........Annie P. "Daisy" Miller
At Long Last Love (1975)...................Brooke Carter
Special Delivery (1976)...........................Mary Jane
Taxi Driver (1976)......................................Betsy
Silver Bears (1978)......................Debbie Luckman
The Lady Vanishes (1979; British).... Amanda Kelly
The Return (1980)...................................Daughter
Texasville (1990)................................Jacy Farrow
Made for TV Movies:
Secrets of a Married Man (1984)..........................
Moonlighting (1985)....................... Maddie Hayes
Seduced (1985)...
TV:
The Yellow Rose (1983-84)........ Colleen Champion
Moonlighting (1985-89)..................... Maddie Hayes
Magazines:
Playboy (Nov 1972)......................."Sex in Cinema"
Page 170 - B&W topless. *
Playboy (Dec 1972)..................."Sex Stars of 1972"
Page 208 - B&W topless. **

SHERIDAN, NICOLLETTE
Films:
Made for Showtime:
Deceptions (1990)...................... Adrienne Erickson
0:00 - Swimming underwater in black s piece
swimsuit.
0:04 - In white nightgown.
0:18 - In another two piece swimsuit.
0:34 - Side view of left breast taking off bathrobe
in bed with Harry Hamlin.
0:35 - Very, very brief silhouette of breasts
hugging Hamlin when camera tilts down from
her head to her buns. *
0:47 - Side view of right breast.
1:04 - In swimsuit again talking with Hamlin by
the pool.
TV:
Dallas (1990-)..

SHERMAN, GERALDINE

Films:
Dead Fall (1968)..
Interlude (1968)..Natalie
Poor Cow (1968)...Trixie
Take a Girl Like You (1970)............................Anna
There's a Girl in My Soup (1970)............ Caroline
   0:43 - Topless in bed, then getting out of bed
     when Goldie Hawn splashes water on her in
     bed. **
Get Carter (1971)....................................Girl in Cafe
Cry of the Penguins (1972)..............................Penny

SHIELDS, BROOKE

Films:
Alice, Sweet Alice (1977)...............................Karen
King of the Gypsies (1978).................................Tita
Pretty Baby (1978)...................................... Violet
   (She was only 13 years old at this time so there
     isn't really a whole lot to see here!)
   0:57 - Topless and buns taking a bath. *
   1:26 - Topless posing on couch for Keith
     Carradine. *
   1:28 - Buns, getting thrown out of the room, then
     trying to get back in. *
Tilt (1978)..Tilt
Just You and Me, Kid (1979)............................Kate
Wanda Nevada (1979)......................Wanda Nevada
Blue Lagoon (1980).................................Emmeline
   (Nudity is a body double, Kathy Trout.)
   0:27 - Nude swimming underwater after growing
     up from little children.
   0:43 - More underwater swimming.
   1:00 - Topless body double lying on a rock.
   1:09 - Right breast of body double in hammock.
   1:24 - Body double breast feeding the baby.
Endless Love (1981)...Jade
   0:37 - Body double side view of right breast in bed
     with "David."
   1:08 - Body double very brief left breast in bed
     with another guy during "David's" dream.
Sahara (1984)..Dale
   0:51 - In a wet T-shirt taking a shower under a
     wafer fall.
The Muppets Take Manhattan (1984) ....
Speed Zone (1989)...................................Stewardess

SHIRLEY, ALEISA

Films:
Sweet Sixteen (1984)..
Made for HBO:
The Hitchhiker: Shattered Vows...............Pamela
   0:08 - Topless and buns in bathroom with "Jeff."
     *
   0:12 - In bedroom wearing white lingerie.
   0:18 - In bed wearing black bra, panties, garter
     belt and stockings, then topless. **

SHOOP, PAMELA SUSAN

Films:
Empire of the Ants (1977) ....Coreen Bradford
One Man Jury (1978)....................................Wendy
Halloween II (1981)......................................Karen
   0:48 - Topless getting into the whirlpool bath with
     "Budd" in the hospital. ***
Made for TV Movies:
Dallas Cowboy Cheerleaders (1979) ....

SHOWER, KATHY

Films:
Double Exposure (1983).................Mudwrestler #1
Commando Squad (1987)......................Kat Withers
Frankenstein General Hospital (1988)
     ....Dr. Alice Singleton
   0:35 - In white lingerie outfit pacing around in her
     office.
   1:15 - Brief topless running out of her office after
     the monster, putting her lab coat on. *
The Further Adventures of Tennessee Buck
   (1987).....................................Barbara Manchester
   0:22 - In white lingerie in her hut getting dressed.
   0:57 - Topless getting rubbed with oil by the
     cannibal women. Nice close up shots. ***
   1:02 - Topless in a hut with the Chief of the tribe.
     **
Bedroom Eyes II (1989) ....Carolyn Ross
   0:22 - Topless in the artist's studio fighting with
     him while Wings Hauser watches through the
     window. **
   0:58 - In lingerie in bed with Hauser, then in
     bathroom.
Video Tapes:
Playboy Video Magazine, Volume 9........ Playmate
Playboy Video Calendar 1987.................. Playmate
Playmates of the Year - The '80's............ Playmate
TV:
Santa Barbara (1987-)...
Magazine:
Playboy (May 1985)................................ Playmate
   Playmate of the Year 1986.
Playboy (Dec 1986)...................... "Sex Stars of 86"
   Page 156
Playboy (May 1988)........"Kathy Goes Hollywood"
   Pages 130-137: Nude. ***
Playboy (Jan 1989)..........."Women of the Eighties"
   Page 254: Full frontal nudity. ***

SHUE, ELIZABETH

Films:
The Karate Kid (1984)... Ali
Link (1986).. Jane Chase
   0:50 - Brief right breast and buns side view
     standing in bathroom getting ready to take a
     bath while "Link" watches. (I have conflicting
     sources who tell me it was and wasn't really her
     nude here.) *
Adventures in Babysitting (1987)..............................

Cocktail (1988)...............................Jordan Mooney
    0:52 - Side view of left breast standing up in
      waterfall with Tom Cruise when she takes off
      her swimsuit top.
Back to the Future, Part II (1989) ....Jennifer
Made for TV Movies:
Call to Glory (1984)............................Jackie Sarnac
TV:
Call to Glory (1984-85).......................Jackie Sarnac

SILVER, CINDY
Films:
Gimme an "F" (1981)................ One of the "Ducks"
Hardbodies (1984) ....Kimberly
    0:07 - Brief topless on beach when a dog steals her
      bikini top. **
    0:47 - Topless standing in front of closet mirrors
      talking about breasts with "Kristi." ***
    0:56 - Topless making love with "Scotty" on the
      beach. ***
    1:22 - Topless on fancy car bed with "Scotty." **

SIMMONS, ALLENE
Films:
Porky's (1982)..Jackie
    1:02 - Topless in the shower scene. *
Time Walker (1982)...Nurse
R.S.V.P. (1984)............................Patty De Fois Gras
    0:13 - Topless taking off red top behind the bar
      with the bartender. **
    0:38 - Topless in bed with "Mr. Edwards," then
      buns running to hide in the closet. **
    0:41 - Frontal nudity in room with "Mr.
      Anderson." **
    0:51 - Topless talking to "Toby" in the hallway
      trying to get help for the Governor. ***

SINGER, LORI
Other:
Sister of actor Marc Singer.
Films:
Footloose (1984) ....Ariel
The Falcon and the Snowman (1985) ....Lana
The Man With One Red Shoe (1985)............Maddy
Trouble in Mind (1986).............................Georgia
    1:01 - Very brief left breast, in bed with Kris
      Kristofferson. *
Summer Heat (1987)..................................... Roxy
    0:36 - Topless in bed with "Jack." Kind of dark
      and hard to see. **
Made in the USA (1988)..............................Annie
    0:26 - Brief left breast and very brief lower frontal
      nudity in the back of a convertible with "Dar" at
      night. *
    0:44 - In white, braless tank top talking to a used
      car salesman.
TV:
Fame (1982-83) ....Julie Miller

SIRTIS, MARINA
Films:
Blind Date (1982)...................................... Hooker
    (NOT the same 1987 "Blind Date" with Bruce
    Willis.)
    0:21 - Topless walking to and lying in bed just
      before taxi driver kills her. ***
The Wicked Lady (1983; British).....Jackson's Girl
    1:06 - Full frontal nudity in and getting out of bed
      when Faye Dunaway discovers her in bed with
      Alan Bates. ***
    1:20 - Topless getting whipped by Dunaway
      during their fight during Bates' hanging. ***
Death Wish III (1985)...................................Maria
    0:42 - Topless getting blouse ripped open next to a
      car by the bad guys. *
    0:43 - More topless on mattress at the bad guy's
      hangout. *
TV:
Star Trek: The Next Generation (1987-)
    ....Counselor Deanna Troi

SKINNER, ANITA
Films:
Girlfriends (1978)............................ Anne Munroe
Sole Survivor (1982)......................Denise Watson
    0:29 - Very, very brief right breast in bed with
      "Dr. Richardson." Brief side view of right
      breast when he jumps out of bed. *
    1:13 - In bra, zipping up pants.

SKINNER, RAINEE
Films:
Rebel (1985)...................................Prostitute in bed
    0:37 - Brief topless sitting up in bed. *
Kiss the Night (1988)......................................
Pandemonium (1988)......................................

SKYE, IONE
Other:
a.k.a. Ione Skye Leitch.
Films:
River's Edge (1987)....................................Clarissa
Stranded (1987) .... Deirdre Clark
A Night in the Life of Jimmy Reardon (1988)
    ....Denise Hunter
Say Anything (1989)............................Diane Court
The Rachel Papers (1989).......................... Rachel
    0:58 - Topless getting undressed and getting into
      bed with "Charles." Long shot, then topless in
      bed. **
    1:03 - Brief topless in three scenes. From above
      in bathtub, in bed and in bathtub again. ***
    1:04 - Left breast making love sitting up with
      "Charles." **
    1:06 - Brief topless sitting up in bathtub. *
    1:08 - Brief topless long shot getting dressed in
      "Charles'" room. *

1:28 - Brief topless kissing "Charles" in bed
during his flashback. *
Made for HBO:
Nightmare Classics: Carmilla (1989) .... Marie

SLATER, HELEN

Films:
Supergirl (1984)........................ Linda Lee/Supergirl
The Legend of Billie Jean (1985)............. Billie Jean
0:06 - Brief wet T-shirt getting out of pond.
Ruthless People (1986)........................ Sandy Kessler
The Secret of My Success (1987)................. Christy
Sticky Fingers (1988)...
Happy Together (1988)...... Alexandra "Alex" Page
0:17 - Brief right breast changing clothes while
talking to Patrick Dempsey. Unfortunately,
she's got a goofy expression on her face. **
0:57 - In red lingerie tempting Dempsey. Later,
panties under panty hose when Dempsey pulls
her dress up while she's on roller skates.
1:07 - Very brief panties under panty hose again
straddling Dempsey in the hallway.
1:14 - Panties under white stockings while
changing in the closet.
TV:
Capital News (1990)........................ Anne McKenna

SLATER, SUZANNE

Other:
a.k.a. Suzee Slater.
Films:
Savage Streets (1985)............................. uncredited
0:09 - Topless being held by jerks when they yank
her tube top down. **
Chopping Mall (1986)................................. Leslie
0:28 - Brief topless in bed showing breasts to
"Mike." **
0:31 - Walking around the mall in panties and a
blouse.
Take Two (1988).. Sherrie
0:11 - Topless in office talking with Grant
Goodeve, wearing panties, garter belt and
stockings. **
1:00 - Topless undressing to get into hot tub
wearing black underwear bottom. *
Cartel (1990)... Nancy
0:28 - In red two piece swimsuit modeling on
motorcycle.
0:35 - Brief bra and panties on bed during
struggle.
0:36 - Topless during brutal rape/murder scene. *
Magazines:
Playboy (Jul 1989)................... "B-Movie Bimbos"
Page 137: Full frontal nudity lying on a car
wearing a girdle and stockings. **

SMITH, CHERYL

Other:
Also see Smith, Rainbeaux.
Films:
Cinderella (1977)................................... Cinderella
0:03 - Topless dancing and singing. **
0:30 - Frontal nudity getting "washed" by her
sisters for the ball. ***
0:34 - Topless in the forest during a dream. **
0:41 - Topless taking a bath. Frontal nudity
drying herself off. ***
1:16 - Brief topless with the Prince. *
1:30 - Brief left breast after making love with the
Prince to prove it was her. *
1:34 - Brief side view of left breast making love in
the Prince's carriage. *

SMITH, CRYSTAL

Films:
Hot Dog...The Movie (1984)................. Motel Clerk
0:10 - Nude getting out of Jacuzzi and going to the
front desk to sign people in. **
Magazines:
Playboy (Sep 1971)................................... Playmate

SMITH, JULIE KRISTEN

Films:
Pretty Smart (1986)........... Samantha Falconwright
0:26 - Topless in bed. **
0:40 - Topless in bed. *
0:52 - Topless sitting in lounge by the pool
Angel III: The Final Chapter (1988)....... Darlene
0:40 - Topless during caveman shoot with a
brunette girl. ***
0:44 - Topless again dancing in caveman shoot.
***

SMITH, LINDA

Films:
Hardcore (1979) .... Hope (Mistress Victoria)
The Beastmaster (1982)..................... Kiri's Friend
0:35 - Topless in a pond with Tanya Roberts. *

SMITH, MADELINE

Films:
Vampire Lovers (1970)............................... Emma
0:32 - Topless trying on a dress in the bedroom
after "Carmilla" has taken a bath. **
0:49 - Topless in bed when "Carmilla" pulls her
top down to make love to her. *
Live and Let Die (1973)....................... Miss Caruso
The Bawdy Adventures of Tom Jones (1976)
.... Sophia
TV:
Doctor in the House (1970-73)........................ Nurse

SMITH, MARTHA

Films:
National Lampoon's Animal House (1978)
.... Babs Jansen
Blood Link (1983)...................................... Hedwig
0:41 - Topless with black panties in bed with
"Keith." **
0:50 - Topless getting slapped around by "Keith."
*
0:51 - Topless sitting up in bed when "Craig" and
"Keith" meet each other for the first time. ***
1:13 - Topless, wearing red panties in bed with
"Keith." *
TV:
Scarecrow and Mrs. King (1983-88)
....Francine Desmond
Magazines:
Playboy (Jul 1973)..................................... Playmate

SMITH, RAINBEAUX

Other:
Also see Smith, Cheryl.
Films:
Caged Heat (1974)..................................... Lauelle
a.k.a. Renegade Girls
0:04 - Brief left breast, dreaming in her jail cell
that a guy is caressing her through the bars. *
0:11 - Very brief topless getting blouse ripped
open by "Juanita." *
0:25 - Topless in the shower scene. **
0:50 - Brief nude in the solitary cell. **
Farewell, My Lovely (1975)........................... Doris
0:56 - Frontal nudity in bedroom in a bordello
with another guy before getting beaten by the
madam. *
Drum (1976).................................. Sophie Maxwell
0:54 - Topless in the stable trying to get Yaphet
Kotto to make love with her. **
Massacre at Central High (1976).................. Mary
0:27 - Brief topless in a classroom getting attacked
by some guys. *
1:09 - Nude walking around on a mountain side
with Robert Carradine and Lani O'Grady. ***
Revenge of the Cheerleaders (1976)......... Heather
0:00 -Brief topless changing tops in back of car.
Blonde on the far right. *
0:28 - Buns in shower room scene.
0:36 - Full frontal nudity, but covered with
bubbles.
Slumber Party '57 (1976).............................. Sherry

SMITH, SAVANNAH

Films:
Five Days from Home (1978) ....Georgie Haskin
North Dallas Forty (1979)...........................Joanne
0:27 - Very brief topless in bed tossing around
with Nick Nolte. *
The Long Riders (1980)...................................... Zee

SNODGRESS, CARRIE

Films:
Diary of a Mad Housewife (1970)........ Tina Balser
0:01 - Topless taking off nightgown and getting
dressed, putting on white bra while Richard
Benjamin talks to her. ***
0:36 - Buns and brief side view of left breast
kissing Frank Langella.
0:41 - Very brief topless lying on floor when
Langella pulls the blanket up. *
0:54 - Topless lying in bed with Langella. *
1:03 - In white bra and panties getting dressed in
Langella's apartment.
1:10 - In white bra and panties in Langella's
apartment again.
1:21 - Topless in the shower with Langella, then
drying herself off. ***
The Fury (1978)...Hester
Homework (1982)................................Dr. Delingua
Trick or Treats (1982).......................................Joan
Murphy's Law (1983)..
A Night in Heaven (1983) ....Mrs. Johnson
Pale Rider (1985)...............................Sarah Wheeler
Rainy Day Friends (1985) ....
Blueberry Hill (1988)...

SOCAS, MARIA

Films:
The Warrior and the Sorceress (1984)...........Naja
(Topless in every scene she's in.)
0:15 - Topless wearing robe and bikini bottoms in
room with "Zeg." Sort of brief buns leaving the
room. ***
0:22 - Topless standing by a wagon at night. **
0:27 - Topless in room with David Carradine.
Dark. Most of buns when leaving the room. **
0:31 - Topless and buns climbing down wall. **
0:34 - Brief topless, then left breast with rope
around her neck at the well. *
0:44 - Topless when Carradine rescues her. *
0:47 - Topless walking around outside. *
0:57 - More topless outside. *
1:00 -Topless watching a guy pound a sword. *
1:05 - Topless under a tent after Carradine uses
the sword. Long shot. *
1:09 - Topless during big fight scene. *
1:14 - Topless next to well. Long shot. *
Deathstalker II (1987)...
0:50 - In see-through nightgown after telling
Deathstalker she is going to marry him.

SOLES, P.J.

Other:
P. J. stands for Pamela Jane.
Ex-wife of actor Dennis Quaid.
Films:
Carrie (1976).....................................Norma
Halloween (1978)........................... Lynda
1:04 - Brief right breast sitting up in bed after
making love in bed with "Bob." *
1:07 - Brief topless getting strangled by the bad
guy in the bedroom. *
Breaking Away (1979).....................................Suzy
Old Boyfriends (1979).....................................Sandy
Rock 'n' Roll High School (1979).........Riff Randell
Stripes (1981)....................................Stella
Sweet Dreams (1985)................................ Wanda
Saigon Commandos (1987) ....
B.O.R.N. (1988).......................................Liz
Magazines:
Playboy (Nov 1981)............. "Sex in Cinema 1981"
Page 166: Topless. **

SOMERS, KRISTI

Films:
Rumble Fish (1983) ....
Hardbodies (1984)....................................Michelle
0:53 - Nude, dancing on the beach while "Ashley"
plays the guitar and sings. **
Girls Just Want to Have Fun (1985)................Rikki
Mugsy's Girls (1985)...............................
Topless showering in van.
Savage Streets (1985)....................................Valerie
0:24 - In bra and panties in the locker room.
Tomboy (1985).................................Seville Ritz
0:14 - Topless taking a shower while talking to
Betsy Russell. **
0:53 - Brief topless stripping at a party. *
Return to Horror High (1987)............Ginny McCall

SOMERS, SUZANNE

Films:
American Graffiti (1973)...The Blonde in the T-bird
Magnum Force (1973)......................... Uncredited
0:26 - In blue swimsuit getting into a swimming
pool, brief topless a couple of times before
getting shot, brief topless floating dead. **
Yesterday's Hero (1979; British).......Cloudy Martin
Nothing Personal (1980; Canadian)............Abigail
1:07 - In wet T-shirt sitting with her feet in a pond
talking with Donald Sutherland.
Miniseries:
Hollywood Wives (1988).................Gina Germaine
TV:
Three's Company (1977-81).............. Chrissy Snow
She's the Sheriff (1987-90) ....Hildy

Magazines:
Playboy (Feb 1980)
........................"Suzanne Somers' Playmate Test"
Pages 136-145: Old photos taken before she was
famous. Nude. **
Playboy (Dec 1984)..............."Suzanne Take Two"
Pages 120-129: New photos. Topless and buns.
***

SOMMER, ELKE

Films:
Sweet Ecstasy (1962; B&W)........................... Elke
Nude.
A Shot in the Dark (1964)..............Maria Gambrelli
Boy, Did I Get a Wrong Number (1966)............ Didi
The Corrupt Ones (1966)....................................Lily
The Oscar (1966) ....Kay Bergdahl
The Torture Chamber of Baron Blood (1972) ....
Left for Dead...
Topless.
The House of Exorcism (1975)..............................
Topless.
Ten Little Indians (1975) .... Vera
The Prisoner of Zenda (1979)............. The Countess
Lily in Love (1985)......................................
Magazines:
Playboy (Sep 1970) ....
Playboy (Jan 1979)................. "25 Beautiful Years"
Page 159: Topless getting into a pool. **
Playboy (Jan 1989).........."Women of the Seventies"
Page 217: Topless getting into pool. **

SOMMERFIELD, DIANE

Films:
Blackjack (1978)..
Love in a Taxi (1980)....................................Carine
Back Roads (1981)..Liz
The Nightstalker (1987)................. Lonnie Roberts
0:35 - Side view of right breast lying dead in
morgue. *

SORENSON, HEIDI

Films:
Fright Night (1985)...................................... Hooker
Magazines:
Playboy (Jul 1981)....................................Playmate
Page 120

SOUTENDIJK, RENEÉ

Other:
a.k.a. Reneé Soutenduk.
Films:
Spetters (1980; Netherlands)........................Fientje
1:12 - Topless making love in trailer with "Jeff."
**
The Girl with the Red Hair (1983; Netherlands)
....Hannie

The Fourth Man (1984; Netherlands) ...... Christine
  0:27 - Full frontal nudity removing robe, brief
    buns in bed, side view left breast, then topless in
    bed with "Gerard." ***
  0:32 - Brief left breast in bed with "Gerard" after
    he hallucinates she cuts his penis off. *
  0:53 - Left breast, then right breast in red dress
    when "Gerard" opens her dress. ***
  1:11 - Topless making love with "Herman" while
    "Gerard" watches through keyhole. *
The Cold Room (1984) Lili
Made for HBO:
The Hitchhiker: Murderous Feelings Sara Kendal
  0:04 - In bra, then topless with stockings and a
    garter belt on couch with a guy. ***
  0:18 - Right breast when mysterious attacker
    surprises her from behind. *
Murderers Among Us: The Simon Wiesenthal Story
  (1989)..Cyla

SPACEK, SISSY
Films:
  Prime Cut (1972)... Poppy
    0:25 - Brief side view of left breast lying in hay,
      then buns when Gene Hackman lifts her up to
      show to Lee Marvin. *
    0:30 - Topless sitting in bed, then getting up to try
      on a dress while Marvin watches. ***
    0:32 - Close up of breasts though sheer black dress
      in a restaurant.
  Badlands (1973)..Holly
  Ginger in the Morning (1973) ....Ginger
  Carrie (1976)..................................... Carrie White
    0:02 - Nude, after having her first menstrual
      period in the girl's locker room. Hard to see, a
      lot of steam. *
  Three Women (1977)..............................Pinky Rose
  Welcome to L.A. (1977).................... Linda Murray
    0:51 - Brief topless after bringing presents into
      Keith Carradine's bedroom. **
  Heart Beat (1979)..........................Carolyn Cassady
  Coal Miner's Daughter (1980)............. Loretta Lynn
  Raggedy Man (1981)...Nita
    0:43 - Side view of left breast washing herself off
      while two guys peep from outside window.
      Long shot, don't really see anything.
  Missing (1982)....................................Beth Horman
  The River (1984).................................Mae Garvey
  Marie (1985)..............................Marie Ragghianti
  Violets Are Blue (1986)................... Gussie Sawyer
  'night Mother (1986)............................Jessie Cates

SPEIR, DONA L.
Films:
  Doin' Time (1984)................................ Card Holder
  Into the Night (1985)..

Hard Ticket to Hawaii (1987).....................Donna
  0:01 - Topless on boat kissing boyfriend
    "Rowdy." *
  0:23 - Topless in the Jacuzzi with Hope Marie
    Carlton looking at diamonds they found. ***
  1:04 - Topless and buns with "Rowdy" after
    watching a video tape. ***
  1:33 - Topless during closing credits. **
Dragnet (1987)....................................... Baitmate
Picasso Trigger (1989)...............................Donna
  0:17 - In white lingerie on boat with Hope Marie
    Carlton.
  0:49 - Topless and buns standing, then making
    love in bed. ***
Savage Beach (1989).................................Dona
  0:09 - In two piece swimsuit by the pool.
  0:32 - Topless changing clothes in airplane with
    Hope Marie Carlton. *
  0:48 - Nude, going for a swim on the beach with
    Carlton. **
Video Tapes:
  Playboy Video Calendar 1987..................Playmate
Magazines:
  Playboy (Mar 1984)................................. Playmate

SPELVIN, GEORGINA
Other:
  Adult flim actress.
Films:
  Police Academy III: Back in Training (1986)
  .... The Hooker

SPRADLING, CHARLIE
Other:
  a.k.a. Charlie.
Films:
  The Blob (1988)..Co-ed
  Twice Dead (1989)....................................... Tina
    1:11 - Topless taking off jacket next to bed. **
    1:14 - Topless making love with her boyfriend in
      bed. ***
    1:18 - Brief topless dead in bed. *
  Meridian (1989).. Gina
    0:22 - Topless getting her top torn off by
      "Lawrence" while lying on the table. **
    0:28 - Topless standing next to fireplace, then
      topless on the couch. ***

SPRINKLE, ANNIE
Other:
  Adult film actress.
Films:
  Wimps (1987)................................... Head Stripper
    1:12 - Topless on stage with two other strippers
      teasing "Francis." **

STALEY, LORA

Films:

American Nightmare (1981; Canadian)
....Louise Harmon
0:44 - Topless and buns in G-string dancing on stage. **
0:54 - Topless making love in bed with "Eric." ***
0:59 - Brief right breast, then topless auditioning in TV studio. *
Thief (1981)..Paula

STALLER, ILONA

Other:

a.k.a. adult film actress "Cicciolina."
Was elected to a seat on the Italian Parliament in 1987.

Films:

Inhibition (Italy)...Anna
0:08 - Nude taking a shower with "Carol." ***
0:43 - Brief full frontal nudity getting out of swimming pool. *
0:55 - Topless making love in the water with "Robert." ***
1:00 - Full frontal nudity getting disciplined by "Carol." ***

Magazines:

Playboy (Feb 1988)....................."The Year in Sex"
Page 134: Full frontal nudity. ***

STARK, KOO

Other:

Former girlfriend of Prince Andrew of England in 1982 before he met and married "Fergie."
Special Stills Photographer in the film "Aria."

Films:

The Rocky Horror Picture Show (1975; British)
....Bridesmaid
Emily (1976; British)..Emily
0:08 - Topless, lying in bed caressing herself fantasizing about "James." **
0:30 - Topless in studio posing for "Augustine," then kissing her. ***
0:42 - Buns and topless taking a shower after posing for "Augustine." ***
0:56 - Left breast under tree with "James." **
1:16 - Topless in the woods seducing "Rupert." *
Justine...Justine
0:09 - Topless getting fondled by a nun. **
0:16 - Topless getting attacked by a nun. *
0:57 - Topless in open dress getting attacked by old guy. *
1:00 - Topless getting bathed, then lower frontal nudity. ***
1:28 - Right breast and buns taking off clothes, then brief full frontal nudity getting dressed again. *
1:32 - Topless getting thrown in to the water. *
Cruel Passion (1978)...
Electric Dreams (1984)............... Girl in Soap Opera

STAVIN, MARY

Films:

Octopussy (1983)..............................Octopussy Girl
A View to a Kill (1985)................Kimberley Jones
Howling V (1989).. Anna
1:09 - Topless three times drying herself off while "Richard" watches in the mirror. Possible body double. **

STEENBURGEN, MARY

Other:

Wife of actor Malcolm McDowell.

Films:

Goin' South (1978)...................................Julia Tate
Time After Time (1979).....................Amy Robbins
Melvin and Howard (1980)............Lynda Dummar
0:31 - Topless and buns, ripping off barmaid outfit and walking out the door. **
Ragtime (1981)... Mother
A Midsummer Night's Sex Comedy (1982).. Adrian
Romantic Comedy (1983)............................ Phoebe
Cross Creek (1983)......... Marjorie Kinnan Rawlings
Faerie Tale Theatre: Little Red Riding Hood
(1983)..
Dead of Winter (1987)
......................Julie Rose/Katie McGovern/Evelyn
End of the Line (1987)...
Miss Firecracker (1989)..............................Elain
Parenthood (1989)...........................Karen Buckman
Back to the Future III (1990) ....
Made for TV Movies:
One Magic Christmas (1985; U.S./Canadian)
....Ginny Grainger
The Attic - The Hiding of Anne Frank (1988)
....Miep Gies

STEFANELLI, SIMONETTA

Films:

The Godfather (1972)............................ Apollonia
1:50 - Topless in bedroom on honeymoon night. **
Three Brothers (1982; Italian)
....Young Donato's Wife

Magazines:

Playboy (Nov 1972)............."Sex in Cinema 1972"
Page 161: Left breast, grainy photo from "The Godfather." *
Playboy (Mar 1974) "The Don's Daughter-In-Law"
Pages 97-99: Topless. ***

STEPHENSON, PAMELA

Films:

Stand Up Virgin Soldiers (1976)................. Nurse
Topless and brief buns after removing clothes and getting into bed.
The Secret Policeman's Other Ball (1982; British)..
Superman III (1983).....................Lorelei Ambrosia
Scandalous (1983)..................Fiona Maxwell Sayle

Bloodbath at the House of Death (1985; British)
....Barbara Coyle
  0:50 - Very brief topless getting clothes ripped off
  by an unseen being. *

TV:
  Saturday Night Live (1984-85) ....regular

STERN, ELLEN

Films:
  Jessi's Girls (1976).. Kana
    1:10 - Left breast, then topless in bed with a guy.
    ***
  The Duchess & the Dirtwater Fox (1976).................

STEVENS, BRINKE

Films:
  Slumber Party Massacre (1982)....................Linda
    0:07 - Buns, then topless taking a shower during
    girls locker room scene. **
  Sole Survivor (1982)................................Jennifer
    0:45 - In bra playing cards, then topless. **
  The Man Who Wasn't There (1982)....... Nymphet
    0:45 - Buns and brief right and left breasts when
    she gets shampoo from an invisible Steve
    Guttenberg. *
  Private School (1983)..........Uncredited School Girl
    0:42 - Brief topless and buns in shower room
    scene. She's the brunette wearing a pony tail
    who passes in front of the chalkboard. **
  Body Double (1984) .... Girl in Bathroom #3
    1:12 - Topless sitting in chair in porno film trailer
    that Craig Wasson watches on TV. *
  Slavegirls from Beyond Infinity (1987)........ Shala
    0:29 - Chained up wearing black lingerie.
    0:31 - Brief side view of left breast on table. Nice
    side view pan from her feet to her head. *
  Sorority Babes in the Slimeball Bowl-O-Rama
    (1988).. Taffy
    0:07 - In panties getting spanked with Michelle
    McClellan.
    0:12 - Nude showering off whipped cream in
    bathtub while talking to a topless Michelle
    McClellan. Excellent long scene! ***
  Grandmother's House (1988)...................... Woman
  The Jigsaw Murders (1988)................ Stripper #1
    0:28 - Very, very brief topless posing for
    photographer in white bra and panties when
    camera passes between her and the other
    stripper. *
  Warlords (1988)..

STEVENS, CONNIE

Films:
  Scorchy (1971).................................... Jackie Parker
    0:23 - Open blouse, revealing left bra cup while
    talking on the telephone. Brief topless
    swimming in the water after taking off bathing
    suit top. **
    0:52 - Side view left breast, taking a shower. **
    0:56 - Brief right breast making love in bed with
    Greg Evigan. Topless getting tied to the bed by
    the thieves. Kind of a long shot and a little dark
    and hard to see. ***
    1:00 - Brief topless getting covered with a sheet
    by the good guy. *
  Back to the Beach (1987)................................
  Tapeheads (1988)...................................June Tager
Miniseries:
  Scruples (1980)..........................Maggie McGregor
Made for TV Movies:
  The Littlest Angel (1969)................................
  Playmates (1972)..
  Love's Savage Fury (1979) ....
TV:
  Hawaiian Eye (1959-63).................... Cricket Blake
  Wendy and Me (1964-65)................ Wendy Conway

STEVENS, STELLA

Other:
  Mother of actor Andrew Stevens.
Films:
  Li'l Abner (1959)..............Appasionata von Climax
  Girls! Girls! Girls! (1962)..................Robin Gantner
  The Nutty Professor (1963) ....Stella Purdy
  The Ballad of Cable Hogue (1970)............... Hildy
    1:12 - Buns changing into nightgown in bedroom.
    1:14 - Brief top half of breasts in outdoor tub, then
    buns running into cabin when stagecoach
    arrives. *
  The Poseidon Adventure (1972)............Linda Rogo
  Arnold (1973)..Karen
  The Manitou (1977)...................... Amelia Crusoe
  Chained Heat (1983)................................. Taylor
  The History of White People in America
    (Volume II) (1986).....................................
  The Longshot (1986) ....Nicki
Made for TV Movies:
  Cruise into Terror (1977) ....
  No Man's Land (1984).....................................
  Man Against the Mob (1988)..................Joey Day
TV:
  Ben Casey (1965)............................. Jane Hancock
  Flamingo Road (1981-82)...........Lute-Mae Sanders
  Santa Barbara...................................... Phyllis Blake
Magazines:
  Playboy (Jan 1960)..............................Playmate
  Playboy (Dec 1973).................. "Sex Stars of 1973"
    Page 210: Topless behind plants. *
  Playboy (Jan 1989)............ "Women of the Sixties"
    Pages 161: Half of left breast behind pink
    material.

STEWART, ALEXANDRA

Films:
Goodbye Emmanuelle (1977).....................Dorothee
In Praise of Older Women (1978; Canadian)
....Paula
   1:09 - Left breast, then topless in bed with Tom
     Berenger. **
   1:22 - Topless in bed with Berenger. *
The Last Chase (1980)...................................Eudora
Agency (1981)...Mimi
Under the Cherry Moon (1986; B&W) .Mrs. Sharon
Made for HBO:
The Hitchhiker: Shattered Vows.. Jackie Winslow
   0:04 - In white bra and panties, then side view
     topless making love in bed with "Jeff." *
Magazines:
Playboy (Oct 1978)...."Observing 'Older Women'"
   Page 193-194: Topless. *

STEWART, SUSAN

Films:
Mantis in Lace (1968)..Lila
The First Nudie Musical (1979).................Joy Full
   0:19 - Full frontal nudity taking off dress and
     lying on floor auditioning for movie by faking
     an orgasm. **

STONE, DEE WALLACE

Films:
The Hills Have Eyes (1977)...................Lynne Wood
10 (1979).. Mary Lewis
The Howling (1981)..............................Karen White
   0:08 -
E.T. The Extraterrestrial (1982)..........................Mary
Cujo (1983)...Donna
Jimmy the Kid (1983)... May
Secret Admirer (1985)..........................Connie Ryan
Critters (1986)....................................... Helen Brown
Shadow Play (1986)......................... Morgan Hanna
   1:06 - Brief topless making love with Ron
     Kuhlman. Kind of dark and hard to see. *
Made for TV Movies:
The Sky's No Limit (1984)..
Addicted to his Love (1988).......Betty Ann Brennan
Sins of Innocence (1986)................... Vicki McGary
TV:
Together We Stand (1986)....................Lori Randall

STONE, SHARON

Films:
Irreconcilable Differences (1984). Blake Chandler
   0:56 - Topless lowering her blouse in front of
     Ryan O'Neal during film test. **
King Solomon's Mines (1985).......................Jessica
Cold Steel (1987)........................... Kathy Conners
   0:33 - Brief left breast making love in bed with
     Brad Davis. Dark, hard to see. Brief topless
     turning over after making love. *

Police Academy 4: Citizens on Patrol (1987)
....Claire Matson
Action Jackson (1987)...............Patrice Dellaplane
   0:34 - Topless in a steam room. Hard to see
     because of all the steam. **
   0:56 - Brief right breast, dead, on the bed when
     police view her body. *
Allan Quartermain and the Lost City of Gold
   (1987).......................................Jesse Huston
Above the Law (1988) ....Sara Toscani
Total Recall (1990)..Lori
Miniseries:
War and Remembrance (1988)............ Janice Henry
TV:
Bay City Blues (1983)......................Cathy St. Marie
Magazines:
Playboy (Jul 1990)............... "Dishing with Sharon"
   Pages 118-127: Topless in B&W photos. ***

STONER, SHERRI

Films:
Impulse (1984)..Young Girl
Lovelines (1984).. Suzy
Reform School Girls (1986)..........................Lisa
   1:03 - Very brief topless lying on stomach getting
     branded by bad girls on the restroom floor. *

STOWE, MADELINE

Films:
Stakeout (1987)................................ Maira McGuire
   0:43 - Buns and brief side view of right breast
     getting a towel after taking a shower while
     Richard Dreyfus watches her.
Tropical Snow (1989)................................. Marina
   0:05 - Very brief side view of left breast putting
     red dress on. *
   0:11 - Buns, lying in bed. Very brief right breast
     sitting up. (I wish they could have panned the
     camera to the right!) *
   0:24 - Topless in mirror putting red dress on. **
   0:32 - Nuns, lying on top of "Tavo" in bed.
   0:54 - Brief topless making love in the water with
     "Tavo." Then buns, lying on the beach (long
     shot.) *
   1:22 - Long shot side view of right breast in water
     with "Tavo."
Revenge (1990)...Miryea
   0:44 - Side view of buns when Kevin Costner
     pulls up her dress to make love with her.
   0:52 - In white slip talking to Costner in bedroom.
   1:00 - Buns, making love with Costner in jeep.
     Very brief topless coming out of the water. *
   1:07 - Very brief topless when Costner is getting
     beat up. *
TV:
The Gangster Chronicles (1981)........... Ruth Lasker

STRASBERG, SUSAN

Other:
Daughter of acting teacher Lee Strasberg.
Films:
The Trip (1967) .... Sally Groves
The Brotherhood (1968).................... Emma Ginetta
Psych-Out (1968)................................ Jennie Davis
The Manitou (1977)........................... Karen Tandy
    1:33 - Topless fighting the creature in bed. Really
    bad special effects. Too dark to see anything
Rollercoaster (1977)................................... Fran
In Praise of Older Women (1978; Canadian)
    .... Bobbie
    1:03 - Left breast making love in bed with Tom
    Berenger. **
    1:04 - Topless after Berenger rolls off her. ***
Bloody Birthday (1980).......................... Miss Davis
Sweet Sixteen (1983)...................................... Joanne
The Delta Force (1986) .... Debra Levine
TV:
The Marriage (1954) .... Emily Marriott
Toma (1973-74)................................... Patty Toma

STRATTEN, DOROTHY

Films:
Americathon (1979)..
Skatetown USA (1979) ....
Autumn Born (1979)..................................... Tara
    0:03 - In dressing room in beige bra, panties,
    garter belt and stockings changing clothes.
    Long, close-up lingering shots.
    0:16 - Unconscious in beige lingerie, then
    conscious, walking around the room.
    0:21 - In bra and panties getting her rear end
    whipped while tied to the bed.
    0:26 - Left breast taking bath, then right breast
    getting up, then topless dressing. **
    0:30 - Side view of left breast, then topless
    climbing back into bed. *
    0:35 - In beige bra and panties in the shower with
    her captor.
    0:43 - Quick cuts of various scenes.
    0:46 - In white bra and panties, side view of left
    breast and buns, then topless in bathtub. Long
    scene. ***
    0:50 - Side view of left breast and buns getting
    undressed. Nice buns shot. Right breast lying
    down in chair. *
    1:03 - Brief topless shots during flashbacks. *
Galaxina (1980)....................................... Galaxina
They All Laughed (1981)................. Dolores Martin
Playboy Video Tapes:
Dorothy Stratten, The Untold Story .... Herself
Playboy Video Magazine, Volume 4 .... Playmate
Playmates of the Year - The '80's .... Playmate
Magazines:
Playboy (Aug 1979)............................... Playmate
Playboy (Dec 1979)................. "Sex Stars of 1979"
    Page 258: Topless. ***

Playboy (June 1980)........... "Playmate of the Year"
    Pages 168-179: Nude. ***
Playboy (Jan 1989).......... "Women of the Eighties"
    Page 219: Full frontal nudity.

STREEP, MERYL

Films:
Julia (1977).. Anne Marie
The Deer Hunter (1978)................................... Linda
Kramer vs. Kramer (1979)............... Joanna Kramer
Manhattan (1979)... Jill
The Seduction of Joe Tynan (1979)... Karen Traynor
The French Lieutenant's Woman (1981)
    .... Sarah/Anna
Sophie's Choice (1982) .... Sophie
Still of the Night (1982)................. Brooke Reynolds
Falling In Love (1984)..................... Molly Gilmore
Silkwood (1984)............................ Karen Silkwood
    0:24 - Very brief glimpse of upper half of left
    breast when she flashes in nuclear reactor office.
    *
Out of Africa (1985)........................... Karen Blixen
Plenty (1985) .... Susan
Heartburn (1986) .... Rachel
Ironweed (1988)............................... Helen
A Cry in the Dark (1988)........... Lindy Chamberlain
    1:44 - Brief side view of right breast in jail being
    examined by two female guards. Don't see her
    face, probably a body double.
She-Devil (1989) .... Mary Fisher
Miniseries:
Holocaust (1978) .... Inga Helms Weiss

STROMEIR, TARA

Other:
a.k.a. Tara Strohmeier.
Films:
Hollywood Boulevard (1976)................ Jill McBain
    Topless.
Kentucky Fried Movie (1977).......................... Girl
    1:16 - In bra then topless making love on couch
    with her boyfriend while people on the TV news
    watch them. **
Malibu Beach (1978)............................. Glorianna
    0:08 - Topless kissing her boyfriend on the beach
    when someone steals her towel. *

STRUTHERS, SALLY

Films:
Five Easy Pieces (1970)................................. Betty
    0:15 - In a bra sitting on a couch in the living
    room with Jack Nicholson and another man and
    a woman.
    0:33 - Brief topless a couple of times making love
    with Nicholson. Lots of great moaning, but
    hard to see anything. *
The Getaway (1972)........................... Fran Clinton
    1:15 - In black bra getting out of bed and leaning
    over injured bad guy to get something.

Made for TV Movies:
    Aloha Means Goodbye (1974)...............................
    Hey, I'm Alive (1975)...
    Intimate Strangers (1977).......................................
TV:
    The Summer Smother's Show (1970)..........Regular
    The Tim Conway Comedy Hour (1970).......Regular
    All in the Family (1971-78).....Gloria Bunker Stivic
    Gloria (1982-83).......................Gloria Bunker Stivic
    9 to 5 (1986-88)...........................Marsha Shrimpton

STUART, CASSIE
Films:
    Ordeal by Innocence (1984)...........Maureen Clegg
    1:14 - Topless in bed talking to Donald
    Sutherland. **
    Slayground (1984; British)............................. Fran

STUBBS, IMOGEN
Films:
    A Summer Story (1988)....................Megan David
    0:36 - Left breast several times, then right breast
    making love with "Frank" in barn. **
    0:41 - Very, very brief buns, frolicking in pond at
    night with "Frank."
    1:03 - Very brief silhouette of left breast during
    "Frank's" flashback sequence.
    Deadline! (1988)........................ Lady Romy-Burton
Made for HBO:
    Fellow Traveller (1989) ....Sarah Aitchison
    0:54 - Topless in bed with "Asa". Very, very brief
    right breast when he rolls off her. *

SUKOWA, BARBARA
Films:
    The Sicilian (1987) ..... Camilia Duchess of Crotone
    0:05 - Buns and brief topless taking a bath. **
    0:08 - Very brief right breast when watching
    Christopher Lambert steal the horses.
Made for TV:
    Berlin Alexanderplatz (1983; West German)...........

SUTTON, LORI
Films:
    History of the World, Part I (1981) ....
    Looker (1981)..Reston Girl
    Fast Times at Ridgemont High (1982).......Playmate
    Up the Creek (1984)................................Cute Girl
    0:40 - Brief topless pulling up her T-shirt to get
    the crowd excited while cheerleading the crowd.
    *
    Malibu Express (1984)...............................Beverly
    0:54 - Topless and buns making love in bed with
    "Cody." ***
    Night Patrol (1985)............................Edith Hutton
    0:47 - Topless taking off bra in bedroom with the
    Police officer. *

SWANSON, JACKIE
Films:
    Lethal Weapon (1987)............Amanda Huntsacker
    0:01 - Brief topless standing on balcony rail
    getting ready to jump. **
    It's Alive III: Island of the Alive (1988)..................
    Perfect Victim (1988)..

SYKES, BRENDA
Films:
    The Baby Maker (1970)............................... Francis
    Getting Straight (1970)......................................Luan
    The Liberation of L. B. Jones (1970).................Jelly
    Honky (1971)...................................... Sheila Smith
    Pretty Maids All in a Row (1971).....Pamela Wilcox
    Skin Game (1971)..................................... Naomi
    Black Gunn (1972)....................................... Judith
    0:45 - Brief side view of right breast getting out of
    bed with Jim Brown. *
    Cleopatra Jones (1973)................................ Tiffany
    Mandingo (1975)... Ellen
    0:58 - Topless in bed with Perry King. *
    Drum (1976).. Calinda
    0:19 - Topless standing next to bed with Ken
    Norton. *
TV:
    Ozzie's Girls (1973)...Brenda (Jennifer) MacKenzie
    Executive Suite (1976-77) .... Summer Johnson
Magazines:
    Playboy (Oct 1972)....... "Brown, Black and White"
    Page 88: Almost topless. *
    Playboy (Nov 1972)............."Sex in Cinema 1972"
    Page 162: Left breast, in a photo from "Black
    Gunn." *

T

TALLMAN, PATRICIA
Films:
    Knightriders (1981)... Julie
    0:46 - Brief topless in the bushes in moonlight
    talking to her boyfriend while a truck driver
    watches. *
    Monkey Shines (1988)...
    Road House (1989)...

TAMERLIS, ZOE
Films:
    Ms. 45 (1980).. Thana
    Special Effects (1984)....................... Amelia/Elaine
    0:01 - Side view of right breast, wearing pasties
    during photo session.
    0:16 - Brief topless sitting by pool with Eric
    Bogozian. *
    0:19 - Topless getting into bed and in bed with
    Bogozian. **

0:22 - Topless, dead in Jacuzzi while Bogozian washes her off. *

0:44 - Brief topless in moviola that Bogozian watches.

1:12 - Topless making love with "Keefe." **

1:17 - Topless getting into bed during filming of movie. Brief topless during Bogozian's flashbacks. *

1:20 - More left breast shots on moviola getting strangled.

1:33 - Topless with Bogozian when he takes her dress off. ***

1:35 - Topless sitting on bed kissing Bogozian. More topless and more flashbacks. *

1:40 - Brief topless during struggle. Dark. *

TATE, SHARON

Other:
Wife of director Roman Polanski.
Victim of the Manson family murders in 1969.
Films:
Valley of the Dolls (1967)..................Jennifer North
The Fearless Vampire Killers (1967)... Sarah Shagal
Ciao Frederico! (1971)..
TV:
The Beverly Hillbillies (1963-65).......... Janet Trego
Magazines:
Playboy (Jan 1989).............."Women of the Sixties"
Page 160: Side view of right breast taking a bubble bath. *

TAYLOR, ELIZABETH

Films:
Psychotic (1975; Italian) ....
a.k.a. Driver's Seat
0:03 - In sheer beige bra in changing room.
0:34 - In sheer white slip walking around.

TAYLOR, KIMBERLY

Films:
Party Incorporated (1989)..........................Felicia
0:26 - Topless trying an outfit on. **
0:39 - Topless and buns in G-string in the bar with "the guys." ***
Cleo/Leo (1989)....................................Store Clerk
0:22 - Topless in white panties, changing in dressing room with Jane Hamilton. Very nice! ***

TAYLOR-YOUNG, LEIGH

Films:
I Love You, Alice B. Toklas (1968).............. Nancy
The Big Bounce (1969)......................Nancy Barker
(Not available on video tape yet.)
The Adventurers (1970) .... Amparo
The Buttercup Chain (1970)..........................Manny
The Gang that Couldn't Shoot Straight (1971)
.... Angela Palumbo

The Horsemen (1971)......................................Zereh
Soylent Green (1973)......................................Shirl
Looker (1981)................................... Jennifer Long
Jagged Edge (1985) .... Virginia Howell
Secret Admirer (1985)................... Elizabeth Fimple

TERASHITA, JILL

Films:
Terminal Entry (1986)..
Night of the Demons (1987)......................Frannie
0:57 - Topless making love with her boyfriend in coffin. **
Sleepaway Camp 3: Teenage Wasteland (1989).....

THACKRAY, GAIL

Films:
In Search of the Perfect 10 (1986). Perfect Girl #5
(Shot on video tape.)
0:31 - Topless and buns trying on all sorts of lingerie in dressing room. ***
Takin' It All Off (1987) ....
Party Favors (1987)....................................Nicole
(Shot on video tape.)
0:04 - Topless in dressing room with the other three girls changing into blue swimsuit. *
0:11 - Brief left breast in the swimsuit during dance practice. *
0:12 - Topless during dance practice. *
0:17 - More topless during dance practice. *
0:42 - Topless doing strip routine at anniversary party. Great buns in G-string shots. **
1:01 - Topless and buns in G-string after stripping from cheerleader outfit. Lots of bouncing breast shots. Mingling with the men afterwards. ***
1:16 - Nude by the swimming pool during the final credits. *

THEEL, LYNN

Films:
Fyre (1979)...
Humanoids from the Deep (1980).....Peggy Larsen
0:30 - Brief topless getting raped on the beach by a humanoid. *
0:51 - Brief topless, dead, lying on the beach all covered with seaweed. *
Without Warning (1980)..

THELEN, JODI

Films:
Four Friends (1981)................................. Georgia
0:17 - Left breast in open blouse three times with her three male friends. **
0:58 - In pink bra taking off her blouse.
The Black Stallion Returns (1983)................Tabari
Twilight Time (1983)....................................Lena
Made for TV Movies:
Follow Your Heart (1990) ....Cecile

THOMAS, BETTY

Films:
Tunnelvision (1976)......................................
Jackson County Jail (1976)........................Waitress
Loose Shoes (1977)........................Biker Chick #1
    0:02 - Brief right breast dancing on the table
    during the "Skateboarders from Hell" sketch. *
Used Cars (1980)...Bunny
    0:37 - Dancing on top of a car next to Kurt Russell
    wearing pasties to attract customers (wearing a
    brunette wig).
Homework (1982)...
Troop Beverly Hills (1989) ....Velda Plendor
TV:
Hill Street Blues (1981-87)..................... Lucy Bates

THOMAS, HEATHER

Films:
Zapped! (1982)..............................Jane Mitchell
    0:20 - Brief open sweater, wearing a bra when
    Scott Baio uses telekinesis to open it.
    1:28 - Very, very brief topless photo that Willie
    Aames gives to "Robby" is a body double.
    1:29 - Body double brief topless when Baio drops
    her dress during the dance.
Cyclone (1986)....................................Teri Marshall
Deathstone (1986)...
TV:
Co-ed Fever (1979)...Sandi
The Fall Guy (1981-86)...........................Jodi Banks
Magazines:
Playboy (Jan 1987).....................................
    Page 71: Covered with a towel, Rated PG.

THOMPSON, CYNTHIA ANN

Films:
Cave Girl (1985).. Eba
    1:04 - Topless making love with "Rex." **
Tomboy (1985).................................. Amanda
    0:23 - Brief right breast getting out of car in auto
    repair shop. *
    1:02 - Topless delivering drinks to two guys in the
    swimming pool. **
Not of This Earth (1988)
    .... Third Hooker (black dress)

THOMPSON, LEA

Films:
All The Right Moves (1983)............................ Lisa
    1:00 - Topless, getting undressed and into bed
    with Tom Cruise in his bedroom. ***
Jaws 3-D (1983)......................Kelly Ann Bukowski
Red Dawn (1984)..Erica
The Wild Life (1984)......................................Anita
    0:38 - In bra and panties putting body stocking on.
Back to the Future (1985)....Lorraine Baines-McFly
Howard the Duck (1986) ....Beverly Switzler

Space Camp (1986)......................................Kathryn
Some Kind of Wonderful (1987) ....
The Wizard of Loneliness (1988).....................Sybil
Casual Sex? (1988) .... Stacy
    0:27 - Buns, lying down at nude beach with
    Victoria Jackson.
    0:30 - Buns at the beach. Pan shot from her feet to
    her head.
Going Undercover (1988)...............................
Back to the Future, Part II (1989)
    .... Lorraine Baines-McFly
Back to the Future, Part III (1990)...........................
Made for HBO:
Tales From The Crypt: Only Sin Deep (1989)
    ....Sylvia

THOMPSON, VICTORIA

Films:
The Harrad Experiment (1973)......... Beth Hillyer
    0:08 - Buns, in the bathroom talking to "Harry."
    0:10 - Brief topless getting into bed. *
    0:21 - Topless in nude encounter group. **
    0:41 - Topless getting into the swimming pool
    with Don Johnson and Laurie Walters. *
    0:49 - Buns, getting dressed after making love
    with Johnson.
The Harrad Summer (1974).............. Beth Hillyer
    0:53 - Buns and brief topless running down the
    hallway. *
    0:59 - Buns on inflatable lounge in the pool.
    1:00 - Buns, lying face down on lounge chair.
Famous T & A (1982)................................. herself
    1:07 - Brief topless scene from "The Harrad
    Experiment." *

THORNTON, SIGRID

Films:
The Getting of Wisdom (1977)...............................
The Day After Halloween (1978; Australia)
    ....Angela
a.k.a. Snapshot
    0:04 - Very brief topless in ad photos on wall. *
    0:19 - Topless during photo modeling session at
    the beach. **
    0:21 - More topless at the beach. ***
    0:37 - Topless in magazine ad several times. **
    0:43 - Brief right breast in magazine ad. *
    0:46 - Topless in ad again. *
    1:18 - Entering room covered with the ad. *
    1:20 - In beige bra in room with weirdo guy.
The Man from Snowy River (1982; Australia)
    ....Jessica
Slate, Wyn & Me (1987; Australia).....Blanche/Max
Best Enemies ....Fennimore
The Lighthorsemen (1988)..
Return to Snowy River (1988)......................Jessica
TV:
Paradise (1989).. Amelia

THURMAN, UMA
Films:
Kiss Daddy Goodnight (1987)..........................Laura
Johnny Be Good (1988)....................Georgia Elkans
Dangerous Liaisons (1988).......Cécile de Volanges
   0:59 - Topless taking off her nightgown in her
   bedroom with John Malkovitch. ***
The Adventures of Baron Munchausen (1989)
   ....Venus/Rose
   1:14 - Brief upper half of right breast when the
   flying ladies wrap her with the flowing cloth.
Where the Heart Is (1990)....................................
   Topless, but her body is painted.

TICOTIN, RACHEL
Films:
Fort Apache, The Bronx (1981)................. Isabelle
   1:25 - Brief upper half of breasts in bathtub while
   Paul Newman pours bubble bath in. *
Critical Condition (1987)..............................Rachel
Total Recall (1990)..
Made for TV Movie:
Love, Mary (1985)...
Made for TV Movies:
Spies, Lies & Naked Thighs (1988)................Sonia
TV:
For Love and Honor (1983)..........Cpl. Grace Pavlik
Ohara (1987-1988)..

TILLY, MEG
Films:
Fame (1980)...................................Principal Dancer
Tex (1982)......................................Jamie Collins
Psycho II (1983)................................... Mary
   0:35 - Buns and very brief topless (don't see her
   face, probably a body double) getting out of the
   shower while Anthony Perkins watches through
   a peep hole. **
The Big Chill (1983) ....Chloé
One Dark Night (1983) ....Julie
Impulse (1984)...Jenny
   0:58 - In wet red swimsuit in photograph, then
   topless in B&W photograph (don't see her face)
   when Tim Matheson looks at photos.
Agnes of God (1985)...........................Sister Agnes
Off Beat (1986) ....Rachel Wareham
Masquerade (1988)........................ Olivia Lawrence
   0:55 - In pink nightgown in bedroom
The Girl in a Swing (1989)................ Karin Foster
   0:44 - In white bra, then topless and buns. **
   0:50 - Nude, swimming under water. **
   1:14 - Topless sitting on swing, making love. ***
   1:18 - In white bra, sitting in front of a mirror.
   1:44 - Topless at the beach. ***
Valmont (1989) .... Tourvel
Made for HBO:
Nightmare Classics: Carmilla (1989).........Carmilla
Made for TV Movies:
In the Best Interest of the Child (1990)
   .... Jennifer Colton

TIPPO, PATTI
Films:
10 to Midnight (1983)..............................Party Girl
   0:52 - Topless, making love in the laundry room at
   a party when Andrew Stevens surprises them at
   gunpoint. **
Omega Syndrome (1986)................................. Sally
Sid and Nancy (1986)..... Tanned and Sultry Blonde

TOLAN, KATHLEEN
Films:
Death Wish (1974)............................... Carol Toby
   0:09 - Brief topless and buns getting raped by
   three punks. *
The Line (1982)......................................
The Rosary Murders (1987)...........Sister Ann Vania

TOLO, MARILU
Films:
The Oldest Profession (1967)
   ...."Anticipation" sequence
   1:23 - Brief side view of left breast walking to the
   bathroom. Shown as a negative image, so it's
   hard to see.
Confessions of a Police Captain (1971)
   .... Serena Li Puma
Bluebeard (1972)....................................Brigitt
   1:25 - Topless in sheer blue blouse arguing with
   Richard Burton. *
   1:27 - Topless getting whipped by Burton. **
Beyond Fear (1975)......................................Nicole
The Greek Tycoon (1978) ....Sophia Matalas
Magazines:
Playboy (Nov 1978)............. "Sex in Cinema 1978"
   Page 184: Upper half of left breast. *

TOMASINO, JEANA
Films:
Looker (1981)......................................Suzy
The Beach Girls (1982)...............................Ducky
   0:12 - Topless and buns, lying on the beach with
   "Ginger" while a guy looks through a telescope.
   **
   0:54 - Topless on a sailboat with a guy. ***
   0:55 - Brief topless on the beach after being
   "saved" after falling off the boat. *
   1:12 - Topless in sauna with "Ginger" and an
   older guy. **
10 to Midnight (1983)......................................Karen
   0:26 - In white lingerie changing in bedroom
   while the killer watches from inside the closet.
Double Exposure (1983).............................. Renee
   0:20 - Very brief glimpse of left breast under
   water in swimming pool. *
Up the Creek (1984)...Molly
Magazines:
Playboy (Nov 1980)................................Playmate

TOMPKINS, ANGEL

Films:

Hang Your Hat on the Wind (1969)...... Fran Harper
I Love My Wife (1970).................Helene Donnelly
Prime Cut (1972)....................................Clarabelle
  1:03 - Very brief left breast sitting up in bed to talk to Lee Marvin. *
  1:04 - Very brief back side view of left breast jumping out of bed.
The Don is Dead (1973)....................................Ruby
Little Cigars (1973)...Cleo
How to Seduce a Woman (1973)..................Pamela
  1:28 - In bra and panties for a long time getting a massage in bedroom.
The Teacher (1974).........................Diane Marshall
  0:09 - Topless on a boat taking off her swimsuit. ***
  0:12 - More topless on the boat getting a suntan. ***
  0:36 - Topless taking off her top in bedroom, then buns and topless taking a shower. ***
  0:41 - Brief right breast lying back on bed. *
  0:43 - Brief topless opening her bathrobe for Jay North. **
  0:47 - Side view of right breast lying on bed, then right breast from above. **
  0:52 - Topless in boat after making love. **
Walking Tall, Part II (1975).......... Marganne Stilson
The Farmer (1977)...Betty
One Man Jury (1978).. Kitty
The Bees (1978)................................. Sandra Miller
Alligator (1980) ....News Reporter
The Naked Cage (1985).....................Diane Wallace
  0:22 - In lingerie, then topless with "Abbey." **
  0:38 - Brief right breast in bed with "Abbey." *
Murphy's Law (1986).. Jan
  0:19 - Topless doing a strip routine on stage while Charles Bronson watches. *
  0:27 - Brief topless doing another routine. *
Dangerously Close (1986) ....Mrs. Waters
Amazon Women on the Moon (1987)......First Lady
  1:00 - In white nightgown, then black bra, panties, garter belt and stockings.
A Tiger's Tale (1988)...............................La Vonne
Crack House (1989)..Mother
Relentless (1989) ....Carmen
Made for HBO:

The Hitchhiker: Homebodies................Janet O'Mell
TV:

Search (1972-73) .... Gloria Harding
Magazine:

Playboy (Feb 1972)....................................."Angel"
  Pages 87-91: Lots of photos of her in a river. ***
Playboy (Jun 1972) ...."Prime Cut"
  Page 123: Topless. ***
Playboy (Dec 1972)..................."Sex Stars of 1972"
  Page 210 - Full frontal nudity. ***
Playboy (Dec 1973)................. "Sex Stars of 1973"
  Page 209: Full frontal nudity. **

TOREK, DENISE

Films:

Sensations (1988)...............................Phone Girl #2
  0:23 - Topless talking on the phone sex line. *
New York's Finest (1988).......................................

TOWNSEND, K.C.

Films:

Husbands (1970)... Barmaid
All That Jazz (1979)..................................Stripper
  0:21 - Topless backstage getting "Joey" excited before he goes on stage. Lit by red light. *
Below the Belt (1980)..................................... Thalia

TRAVIS, NANCY

Films:

Three Men and a Baby (1987) ....Sylvia
Married to the Mob (1988)................Karen Lutnig
  0:15 - Buns and brief side view of right breast with "Tony" in hotel room. Then brief topless in the bathtub. *
Internal Affairs (1990)....................Kathleen Avila
  0:38 - Side view of left breast when "Raymond" opens the shower door to talk to her. *
Air America (1990)...

TREAS, TERRI

Films:

Headin' for Broadway (1980)..............................
The Nest (1987) .... Dr. Morgan Hubbard
Deathstalker III: The Warriors From Hell (1988)
  ....Camlearde
The Fabulous Baker Boys (1989)......... Girl in Bed
  0:00 - Brief upper half of right breast when sheet falls down when she leans over in bed. *
The Terror Within (1989)......................................
TV:

Seven Brides for Seven Brothers (1982-83)
  ....Hannah McFadden
Alien Nation (1989-90).......................Cathy Frankel

TRISTAN, DOROTHY

Films:

End of the Road (1969)..
Klute (1971) ....Arlyn Page
Scarecrow (1973)...Coley
Man on a Swing (1974)...................................Janet
California Dreaming (1978)............................ Fay
  0:05 - In braless white top, jogging on the beach with Glynnis O'Connor.
  0:20 - Brief topless changing in her bikini store while a group of boys peek through a hole in the wall. *

TWOMEY, ANNE

Films:
Refuge (1981)..
The Imagemaker (1985)..................Molly Grainger
   0:11 - Very, very brief topless reading newspaper
   in bedroom (wearing flesh colored tape over her
   nipples). Then in white bra and panties talking
   to a guy in bed.
   1:04 - In bra and skirt undressing in front of
   Michael Nouri.
Deadly Friend (1986)......................Jeannie Conway
Last Rites (1988).....................................

TURNER, KATHLEEN

Films:
Body Heat (1981)............................Maddy Walker
   0:22 - Brief side view of left breast in bed with
   William Hurt. *
   0:24 - Topless in a shack with Hurt. **
   0:32 - Buns, getting dressed. Long shot, hard to
   see.
   0:54 - Brief left breast in bathtub. Long shot, hard
   to see. *
The Man With Two Brains (1983)
   .... Dolores Benedict
   0:08 - Right breast when Steve Martin is operating
   on her in the operating room. *
   0:22 - In sheer lingerie in bedroom with Steve
   Martin, teasing him driving him crazy.
Romancing the Stone (1984)..................Joan Wilder
Crimes of Passion (1984)
   ....Joanna Crane/China Blue
   0:45 - Topless, lying in bed with "Donny" wearing
   black panties and stockings. ***
   1:00 - Right breast in back of a limousine with a
   rich couple. *
   1:22 - In blue bra and panties.
   1:27 - Right breast in bed with "Donny." *
The Jewel of the Nile (1984)..................Joan Wilder
Prizzi's Honor (1985).........................Irene Walker
   0:30 - Very brief left breast making love with Jack
   Nicholson on bed. *
Peggy Sue Got Married (1986) ....Peggy Sue
Julia and Julia (1987)....................................Julia
   (Note this "film" was shot using high-definition
   video tape and then transferred to film.)
   0:33 - Topless making love in bed with her
   husband. ***
   1:09 - Topless, then right breast making love in
   bed with Sting. ***
Switching Channels (1988)..........................Christy
The Accidental Tourist (1988)........................Sarah
The War of the Roses (1989)..............Barbara Rose
   0:06 - In braless white blouse walking around on
   the sidewalk with Michael Douglas.
Made for HBO:
A Breed Apart (1984)...................... Stella Clayton
   1:12 - Topless in bed with Rutger Hauer, then left
   breast. **

TWEED, SHANNON

Films:
Of Unknown Origin (1983; Canadian)...........Meg
   Topless in the shower.
Hot Dog...The Movie (1984).............. Sylvia Fonda
   0:42 - Topless getting undressed, then making
   love in bed and in hot tub with "Harkin." ***
The Surrogate (1984; Canadian)............. Lee Wake
   0:03 - Topless taking a Jacuzzi bath. ***
   0:42 - Brief topless changing in bedroom, then in
   bra getting dressed. Long shot. *
   1:02 - Topless in sauna talking with "Frank."
   Long scene. ***
Meatballs III (1986)..................................
Lethal Woman (1988).................................Tory
   1:04 - Topless at the beach with "Derek." Brief
   buns in white bikini bottom. ***
Cannibal Women in the Avocado Jungle of Death
   (1988)...........................Dr. Margot Hunt
Night Visitor (1989)....................................
Video Tapes:
1st Annual Playmate Review (1983)....... Playmate
Playboy Video Magazine, Volume 1.........Playmate
Playmates of the Year - The '80's ....Playmate
Made for HBO:
The Hitchhiker: Doctor's Orders..... Dr. Rita de Roy
   0:15 - In black bra, panties, garter belt and
   stockings.
TV:
Falcon Crest (1982-83).......................Diana Hunter
Magazines:
Playboy (Nov 1981).........................Playmate
Playboy (1982)...................... Playmate of the Year
Playboy (Nov 1983)............. "Sex in Cinema 1983"
   Page 146: Topless. **
Playboy (Jan 1989)........... "Women of the Eighties"
   Page 249: Full frontal nudity, lying in bed. B&W
   photo. *

TYRRELL, SUSAN

Other:
   Likes to only show one breast in nude scenes!
Films:
The Steagle (1971).. Louise
   0:48 - Brief left breast twice, lying on bed with
   Richard Benjamin. *
Fat City (1972)..Oma
The Killer Inside Me (1975)............Joyce Lakeland
Andy Warhol's Bad (1977) ....Mary Aiken
I Never Promised You a Rose Garden (1977).....Lee
Loose Shoes (1977) ....Boobies
Forbidden Zone (1980; B&W)........... Queen Doris
   0:19 - Left breast sticking out of dress, sitting on
   big dice with Herve Villechaize. **
   1:02 - Left breast sticking out of dress after
   fighting with the Ex-Queen. **
Fast Walking (1981).. Evie
Night Warning (1982).................... Cheryl Roberts
   0:17 - Left breast, sticking out of dress just before
   she stabs the TV repairman. *

Angel (1983)..Selly Mosler
Liar's Moon (1983)......................................
Avenging Angel (1985)........................Selly Mosler
Flesh + Blood (1985)....................................Agnes
   1:35 - Right breast sticking out of her dress when everybody throws their clothes into the fire. *
The Offspring (1986)........................Beth Chandler
The Underachievers (1987)....................Mrs. Grant
Big Top Pee Wee (1988)................Midge Montana
Far From Home (1989)......................Agnes Reed
   0:29 - Very, very brief right breast in bathtub getting electrocuted. *
Cry Baby (1990)..
Made for TV Movies:
Lady of the House (1978)..
TV:
Open All Night (1981-82).............Gretchen Feester

TYSON, CATHY
Films:
Mona Lisa (1987)...Simone
The Serpent and the Rainbow (1988)
  ....Dr. Marielle Duchamp
   0:41 - Brief topless making love with "Dennis." Probably a body double, don't see her face. *
Business as Usual (1988; British)............................

U

UDY, CLAUDIA
Films:
American Nightmare (1981)......................Andrea
   0:22 - Buns getting into bathtub. Topless during struggle with killer. *
Joy (1983; French/Canadian)...............................Joy
Savage Dawn (1984)..
Out of Control (1984)....................................Tina
   0:19 - In leopard skin pattern bra and panties.
   0:28 - In leopard bra and panties playing Strip Spin the Bottle, then very brief topless taking off her top. Long shot. *
   0:47 - Brief left breast getting raped by bad guy on the boat. *
   0:54 - Brief left breast, then right breast making love with "Cowboy." *
Night Force (1986)........................Christy Hanson
   0:07 - Topless making love in the stable with "Steve" during her engagement party**
   0:10 - Nude, fantasizing in the shower. ***
The Pink Chiquitas (1987)..
Dragonard (1988)....................................Arabella
   1:11 - Topless dressed as Cleopatra dancing a routine in front of a bunch of guys. **
Edge of Sanity (1988)..Liza

UDY, HELENE
Films:
My Bloody Valentine (1981)..........................Sylvia
Pick-Up Summer (1981)..............................
One Night Only (1984; Canadian)..............Suzanne
   0:50 - Buns and right breast in bed talking with a guy. *
   1:12 - Over the shoulder, brief left breast on top of a guy in bed. *

V

VACCARO, BRENDA
Films:
Midnight Cowboy (1969)............................Shirley
   1:28 - Brief topless in bed with Jon Voight. Might be a body double because you don't see her face. **
House by the Lake (1977; Canadian)............Diane
  Topless.
I Love My Wife (1970)........................Jody Burrows
Once is Not Enough (1975)............................Linda
Airport '77 (1977)...............................Eve Clayton
The First Deadly Sin (1980)..............Monica Gilbert
Zorro, The Gay Blade (1981)........................
Supergirl (1984)..Bianca
Water (1986; British)..
Heart of Midnight (1988)........................Betty
Made for TV Movies:
Paper Dolls (1984)....................Julia Blake
TV:
Sara (1976)..Sara Yarnell
Dear Detective (1979)
  ....Detective Sergeant Kate Hudson

VALEN, NANCY
Films:
The Heavenly Kid (1985)...........................Melissa
Porky's Revenge (1985)................................Ginger
Listen to Me (1989)..Mia
   0:06 - Very, very brief left breast in bed with "Garson" when Kirk Cameron first meets him. *
The Big Picture (1989)..
Loverboy (1989)..
TV:
Hull High (1990-)........................Donna Breedlove

VAN DE VEN, MONIQUE
Films:
Turkish Delight (1974; Holland)....................Olga
   0:24 - Topless when Rutger Hauer opens her blouse, then nude on the bed. **
   0:27 - Topless, waking up in bed. **
   0:33 - Topless on bed with Hauer, then nude getting up to fix flowers. ***
   0:42 - Buns, with Hauer at the beach

0:46 - Topless modeling for Hauer, then brief nude running around outside. **

0:54 - Topless in bed with open blouse with flowers. **

1:04 - In wet T-shirt in the rain with Hauer, then brief topless coming down the stairs. *

Katie's Passion (1978; Holland) .... Katy

0:38 - Brief buns when guy rips her panties off.

0:45 - Topless in hospital when a group of doctors examine her. **

0:50 - Left breast a couple of times talking to a doctor. Brief buns sitting down.

1:12 - Buns, getting into bed.

1:18 - Nude burning all her old clothes and getting into bathtub. ***

The Assault (1986; Holland)
.... Truus Coster/Saskia de Graaff

Amsterdamned (1988; Holland)........................Laura

Paint It Black (1989) ....Kyla Leif

VAN DOREN, MAMIE

Films:

Running Wild (1955)............................... Irma Bean

High School Confidential (1958; B&W)
....Gwen Dulaine

Teacher's Pet (1958; B&W).............. Peggy De Fore

Sex Kittens Go to College (1960)
.... Dr. Mathilda West

Three Nuts in Search of a Bolt (1964).Saxie Symbol

Free Ride (1986)........................... Debbie Stockwell

Magazines:

Playboy (Jan 1989).............."Women of the Sixties"
Page 156: Topless under sheer yellow dress in photo from 1964. *

VANITY

Other:

Singer.

a.k.a. D. D. Winters.

Films:

Tanya's Island (1980; Canadian)................... Tanya

0:04 - Very brief topless and buns covered with paint during B&W segment.

0:07 - Nude caressing herself and dancing during the opening credits. ***

0:09 - Nude making love on the beach. **

0:11 - Brief right breast talking to "Lobo."

0:19 - Brief topless on the beach with "Lobo" then more topless yelling at him. **

0:28 - Mostly topless in flimsy halter top exploring a cave. *

0:33 - Full frontal nudity undressing in tent. *

0:35 - Left breast sleeping. Dark, hard to see. *

0:37 - Buns while sleeping.

0:40 - Topless superimposed over another scene. *

0:48 - Brief buns swimming in the ocean.

0:51 - Full frontal nudity walking out of the ocean and getting dressed. **

0:53 - Brief topless in open blouse. *

1:08 - Topless in middle of compound when "Lobo" rapes her in front of "Blue." **

1:16 - Full frontal nudity running through the jungle in slow motion. Brief buns. *

Terror Train (1980; Canadian)........................Merry

Famous T & A (1982)................................. herself

1:02 - Topless scenes from "Tanya's Island." *

The Last Dragon (1985)..................................Laura

Never Too Young to Die (1986).......Donja Deering

0:25 - In white bra in the kitchen with John Stamos while he tends to her wounded arm.

1:04 - Wearing a bikini swimsuit, putting on suntan lotion. Brief topless in quick cuts making love with John in a cabin bedroom. *

52 Pickup (1986)... Doreen

0:50 - Topless, stripping in room while Roy Scheider takes Polaroid pictures. ***

Deadly Illusion (1987)...................................... Rina

Action Jackson (1988)........................ Sydney Ash

0:29 - Topless in bed with Craig T. Nelson. **

Magazines:

Playboy (Jan 1985)..... "The Girls of Rock 'n' Roll"
Page 106

Playboy (May 1985).......................................
Pages 83-87

Playboy (Sep 1986)....................."Playboy Gallery"
Page 129: Photo taken Jan 1981

Playboy (Apr 1988)................................."Vanity"
Page 68-79: Nude. ***

Playboy (Dec 1988)..................."Sex Stars of 1988"
Page 185: Topless. ***

Playboy (Jan 1989).........."Women of the Eighties"
Page 256: Right breast. **

Playboy (Oct 1989).............................Grapevine
Page 175: Upper half topless in B&W photo. *

VAN KAMP, MERETE

Films:

The Osterman Weekend (1983).... Zuna Brickman

0:01 - Topless in bed on a TV monitor, then topless getting injected by two intruders. **

0:35 - Brief topless on video again while Rutger Hauer watches in the kitchen on TV. *

1:30 - Topless again on video during TV show. *

You Can't Hurry Love (1984)....................Monique

Mission Kill (1985)..

Lethal Woman (1988)....................Diana Christine

1:26 - Almost topless getting out of bathtub.

Miniseries:

Princess Daisy (1983)..................................... Daisy

TV:

Dallas (1985-86).. Grace

VON PALLESKE, HEIDI
Films:
Dead Ringers (1988)............................Cary
  0:45 - Brief left breast sticking out of bathrobe
  talking to Jeremy Irons in the bathroom. *
Renegades (1989)..

VARGAS, VALENTINA
Films:
The Name of the Rose (1986)................... The Girl
  0:46 - Topless and buns making love with
  Christian Slater in the monastery kitchen. ***
The Big Blue (1988)..Bonita

VASQUEZ, ROBERTA
Films:
Picasso Trigger (1989)....................................Pantera
Magazines:
Playboy (Nov 1984)....................................Playmate

VEGA, ISELA
Films:
Bring Me the Head of Alfredo Garcia (1974)
  ....Elita
  0:25 - Brief right breast a couple of times, then
  brief topless in bed with Warren Oaks. *
  0:44 - Topless when Kris Kristofferson rips her
  top off. Long scene. ***
  0:52 - Topless sitting in shower with wet hair. **
  1:49 - Still from shower scene during credits. **
Drum (1976)..Marianna
  0:04 - Topless in bed with the maid, "Rachel" *
  0:22 - Brief topless standing next to the bed with
  "Maxwell." **
The Streets of L.A. (1979)....................................
Barbarosa (1982) ....Josephina
Magazines:
Playboy (Jul 1974)..............................."Viva Vega"
  Nude scenes from "Bring Me the Head of Alfredo
  Garcia."
Playboy (Nov 1976)............. "Sex in Cinema 1976"
  Page 155: Topless. **

VENORA, DIANE
Films:
Wolfen (1981)..
Terminal Choice (1984)................................. Anna
  0:44 - In lingerie talking to "Frank"
  0:48 - Brief left breast making love in bed with
  "Frank." Don't see her face. *
F/X (1986) ....Ellen
  0:37 - Walking around her apartment in a white
  slip.
Bird (1988)...

VENUS, BRENDA
Films:
The Eiger Sanction (1975) .... George
  0:50 - Very brief topless opening her blouse to get
  Clint Eastwood to climb up a hill. *
  1:06 - Topless taking off her clothes in
  Eastwood's room, just before she tries to kill
  him. Dark, hard to see. *
48 Hours (1982) .... Hooker
Magazines:
Playboy (Jul 1986)........................ "Henry's Venus"
  Page 72-79: B&W photos. Full frontal nudity
  with lots of diffusion. **

VERONICA, CHRISTINA
Other:
  a.k.a. Christina Veronique.
Films:
Thrilled to Death (1988)..................................Satin
  0:33 - Topless talking to "Cliff" during porno film
  shoot. **
Girlfriend from Hell (1989).........................Dancer
  1:17 - Topless dancing on stage in club. ***
Party Incorporated (1989)........................Christina
  0:52 - Buns and topless dancing in front of
  everybody at party. ***
Road House (1989)........................... Strip Joint Girl

VERUSCHKA
Other:
  Ballet dancer.
Films:
Blow-Up (1966; British/Italian)............... Veruschka
Magazines:
Playboy (Jan 1989)........."Women of the Seventies"
  Page 214: Topless wearing body paint. **

VETRI, VICTORIA
Other:
  a.k.a. Angela Dorian (Playmate of the Year 1968).
Films:
Group Marriage (1972)...
Invasion of the Bee Girls (1973).............Julie Zorn
  0:30 - Brief topless getting molested by jerks. *
  1:19 - Topless in the bee transformer, then brief
  buns getting rescued. ***
Made for TV Movies:
Night chase (1970)...
Magazines:
Playboy (Sep 1967) ....Playmate
  Used alternate name of Angela Dorian for the
  centerfold. Playmate of the Year 1968.
Playboy (Nov 1972)............. "Sex in Cinema 1972"
  Page 166: Topless in a photo from "Group
  Marriage". Small photo, hard to see anything.
  *

VICKERS, VICKI
Other:
a.k.a. Adult film actress Raven.
Films:
Penthouse Love Stories (1986)
.... "Snapshot" segment
0:37 - Nude, taking pictures of herself. ***

VOORHEES, DEBORAH
Other:
a.k.a. Debisue Voorhees.
Films:
Avenging Angel (1985)....................................Roxie
Friday the 13th, Part V: A New Beginning
(1985)..Tina
0:41 - Topless after making love with "Eddie,"
then lying down and relaxing just before getting
killed. ***
0:43 - Buns and brief left breast when "Eddie"
turns her over.
Appointment with Fear (1988).......................Ruth
0:21 - Very, very brief side view of left breast
taking off bra to go swimming, then very brief
topless getting out of the pool. *

VORGAN, GIGI
Films:
Hardcore (1979)...................................Teenage Girl
0:32 - Topless on sofa in Peter Boyle's apartment.
*
Red Heat (1980).. Audrey
Rain Man (1988) .... Voice-Over Actress

W
==

WAGNER, LINDSAY
Films:
Two People (1973)...................... Deidre McCluskey
(Not available on video tape yet.)

WAHL, CORINNE
Other:
Also see Alphen, Corinne.
Films:
Equalizer 2000 (1986)..
Amazon Women on the Moon (1987)........... Shari
1:13 - In black bra, then topless on TV while
"Ray" watches. ***

WALKER, ARNETIA
Films:
The Wizard of Speed & Time (1988).......................
Scenes from the Class Struggle in Beverly Hills
(1989).. To-Bel
0:37 - Topless making love with "Frank" on the
sofa. *
1:10 - Topless in bed waking up with "Howard."
**
1:23 - Topless making love on top of Ed Begley,
Jr. on the floor. ***

WALLACE, DEE
See Stone, Dee Wallace.

WALTER, JESSICA
Films:
Lilith (1964; B&W)...Laura
Grand Prix (1966)..Pat
The Group (1966).......................Libby MacAusland
Play Misty for Me (1971)............................Evelyn
0:13 - Very brief right breast in bed with Clint
Eastwood. Lit with blue light. Hard to see
anything. *
Spring Break (1983; Canadian) ....
The Flamingo Kid (1984)................... Phyllis Brody
Miniseries:
Wheels (1978)..Ursula
Bare Essence (1983)...........................Ava Marshall
TV:
For the People (1965)..........................Phyllis Koster
Amy Prentiss (1974-75).......................Amy Prentiss
All That Glitters (1977).......................Joan Hamlyn

WALTERS, JULIE
Films:
Educating Rita (1983; British)...........................Rita
She'll be Wearing Pink Pajamas (1985)........ Fran
0:07 - Full frontal nudity taking a shower with the
other women. Long scene. ***
0:58 - Nude, undressing and going skinny dipping
in mountain lake, then getting out. Nice bun
shot walking into the lake. **
Personal Services (1987)................. Cynthia Payne
0:21 - Very brief side view of left breast reaching
to turn off radio in the bathtub. Her face is
covered with cream. *
Prick Up Your Ears (1987)..................... Elise Orton
Buster (1988) ....June

WALTERS, LAURIE
Films:
The Harrad Experiment (1973)........ Sheila Grove
0:29 - Topless in white panties with Don Johnson.
*
0:40 - Nude taking off blue dress and getting into
the swimming pool with Johnson. *

The Harrad Summer (1974) ....Sheila Grove
    0:02 - Topless undressing in bathroom. Long
      shot, out of focus.
    1:00 - Topless lying face up getting a tan on
      lounge chair, then buns getting up and pushing
      "Harry" into the pool. **
Famous T & A (1982)................................. herself
    1:08 - Topless scene from "The Harrad
      Experiment." *
    1:11 - Full frontal nude scene from "The Harrad
      Experiment." *
Made for TV Movies:
    Eight is Enough: A Family Reunion (1987)
    ....Joannie Bradford
TV:
    Eight is Enough (1977-81).............Joannie Bradford

WALTRIP, KIM
Films:
    Pretty Smart (1986) .... Sara Gentry (the teacher)
    0:53 - Topless sunbathing with her students. **
    Nights in White Satin (1987)........... Stevie Hughes
    0:53 - Topless in bathtub with "Walker." Out of
      focus, hard to see. *
    0:37 - In white wig, bra, panties, garter belt and
      stocking during photo session.
    0:39 - Brief side view of left breast in black slip
      during photo session.

WARD, PAMELA
Films:
    School Spirit (1985).............. Girl in Sorority Room
    0:15 - Buns, then topless while "Billy" is invisible.
      More topless with other women in shower room.
      ***
    Hellhole (1985).. Tina

WARD, RACHEL
Films:
    Night School (1980)......................................Elanor
    0:24 - In sheer white bra and panties, taking off
      clothes to take a shower. Topless taking off bra.
      Hard to see because she's behind a shower
      curtain. *
    0:28 - Buns, when her boyfriend rubs red paint all
      over her in the shower.
    Terror Eyes (1981)...
    The Final Terror (1981)............................Margaret
    Sharky's Machine (1981)...........................Dominoe
    Dead Men Don't Wear Plaid (1982).....Juliet Forrest
    Against All Odds (1984)...................... Jessie Wyler
    0:49 - Very brief buns lying down with Jeff
      Bridges
    0:50 - Wet white dress in water. Long shot, don't
      see anything.
    1:01 - The sweaty temple scene. Erotic, but you
      don't really see anything.

The Good Wife (1987)...
Hotel Colonial (1988)...........................Irene Costa
How to Get Ahead in Advertising (1988)..........Julia
After Dark My Sweet (1990) ....
Made for HBO:
    Fortress (1985)....................................... Sally Jones
    0:38 - Swimming in a sheer bra underwater *
Miniseries:
    The Thorn Birds (1983) .... Meggie Cleary
Magazines:
    Playboy (Mar 1984)........................ "Roving Eye"
    Page 203: Topless in photos that weren't used in
      Night School. ***

WARREN, JENNIFER
Films:
    Night Moves (1975)..Paula
    0:56 - Topless in bed with Gene Hackman. **
    0:57 - Right breast after making love in bed with
      Hackman. *
    1:09 - Very brief right breast and very, very brief
      topless in bed with Hackman. Dark, hard to see.
      *
    Another Man, Another Chance (1977; U.S./French)
    ....Mary
    Slap Shot (1977)............................Francine Dunlop
    Ice Castles (1979).........................Deborah Macland
    The Swap (1980)..
    Mutant (1984)..
TV:
    Paper Dolls (1984) .... Dinah Caswell

WASA, MAXINE
Films:
    Savage Beach (1989)...........................Sexy Beauty
    0:08 - Side view of left breast in pool with
      "Shane," then topless getting out of pool. ***
    0:10 - Topless while "Shane" talks on the phone.
      ***
    L. A. Bounty (1989)..
Made for HBO:
    Dream On: The First Episode (1990). Andrea Kelly
Magazines:
    Playboy (Nov 1989)............. "Sex in Cinema 1989"
    Page 134: Side view of left breast from "Savage
      Beach" **

WATKINS, MICHELLE
Films:
    Terms of Endearment (1983) ....Woman
    The Outing (1987)......................................Faylene
    0:12 - Topless taking off her top, standing by the
      edge of the swimming pool, then running
      topless through the house with panties on. *

WATSON, ALBERTA

Films:

In Praise of Older Women (1978; Canadian) Mitzi
   0:51 - Topless sitting in chair talking with Tom
     Berenger, then more topless lying in bed. Long
     scene. **

Power Play (1978; Canada/England) .... Donna
   0:21 - Brief topless lying on table getting shocked
     through her nipples.

The Soldier (1982)...........................Susan Goodman

The Keep (1983)...................................... Eva Cuza
   0:59 - Very brief topless making love with Scott
     Glenn, then brief lower frontal nudity. *

Best Revenge (1984) ....

WAYNE, APRIL

Other:

Former Model for Ujena Swimwear (*Swimwear
   Illustrated* magazine).

Films:

Moon in Scorpio (1987)..................................Isabel
   0:32 - Brief right breast in bed with a guy. *
   0:35 - Brief topless putting bathing suit on in a
     bathroom on a boat when a guy opens the door.
     *

Party Camp (1987).............................Nurse Brenda

WAYNE, CAROL

Films:

Gunn (1967)...

The Party (1968)...................................June Warren

Scavenger Hunt (1979)....................................Nurse

Heartbreakers (1981)................................... Candy
   0:22 - In black wig and bra posing for Peter
     Coyote in his studio.
   0:41 - In white bra and panties, then brief topless
     in the mirror stripping in front of Coyote and
     Nick Mancuso. Then brief topless lying in bed
     with Coyote. ***

Savannah Smiles (1983).............................. Doreen

Surf II (1984).......................................Mrs. O'Finlay

TV:

The Tonight Show... Regular

Magazines:

Playboy (Feb 1984)......... "101 Nights with Johnny"
   Pages 56-61: Full frontal nudity. ***

WEATHERLY, SHAWN

Other:

Former Miss America.

Films:

Cannonball Run II (1984) .... Dean's Girl

Police Academy III: Back in Training (1986)
   ....Adams

Shadowzone (1989)...............................Dr. Kidwell

Thieves of Fortune (1990)......................................
   Topless.

TV:

Baywatch (1988-90)..

WEAVER, JACKI

Films:

Stork (1971)..

Jock Petersen (1974)...................... Susie Petersen
   0:01 - Full frontal nudity lying in bed with "Jock."
     ***

Picnic at Hanging Rock (1975)..................... Minnie

The Removalists (1975).....................Marilyn Carter

Caddie (1976)...Josie

Squizzy Taylor (1984) ....Dolly

WEAVER, SIGOURNEY

Films:

Annie Hall (1977)....... Alvy's Date Outside Theatre

Eyewitness (1981) ....Tony Sokolow

Alien (1979)..Ripley

Deal of the Century (1983)................. Mrs. De Voto

The Year of Living Dangerously (1983; Australian)
   ....Jill Bryant

Ghostbusters (1984)............................Dana Barrett

One Woman or Two (1986; French)........... Jessica
   (Une Femme Ou Deux)
   1:30 - In braless white blouse.
   1:31 - Very brief side view of left breast in bed
     with Gerard Depardieu. **

Half Moon Street (1986)............. Lauren Slaughter
   0:05 - Brief topless in the bathtub. *
   0:11 - Brief topless in the bathtub again. **
   0:18 - Brief buns and side view of right breast
     putting on makeup in front of the mirror.
     Wearing a black garter belt and stockings. *
   0:39 - Topless riding exercise bike while being
     photographed, then brief topless getting out of
     the shower. ***
   0:46 - Very, very brief topless wearing a sheer
     black blouse with no bra during daydream
     sequence.
   0:50 - Brief topless in bed with Michael Caine,
     then left breast. *
   1:16 - In braless, wet, white blouse in bathroom
     after knocking a guy out.

Aliens (1986)...Ripley

Gorillas in the Mist (1988)....................Dian Fossey

Working Girl (1989)..................... Katherine Parker
   1:22 - In white lingerie, sitting in bed, then talking
     to Harrison Ford.

Ghostbusters II (1989) ....Dana Barrett

WEBB, CHLOE

Films:

Sid & Nancy (1986).. Nancy
   0:21 - Left breast under "Sid's" arm in bed with
     him. Covered up, hard to see. *
   0:44 - Topless in bed after making love, then
     arguing with "Sid." **

Twins (1988)....................................... Linda Mason

TV:

Thicke of the Night (1983)........................... regular

China Beach (1989)......................................Laurette

WEIGEL, TERI

Films:

Cheerleader Camp (1988) .... Pam Bently
Topless sunbathing.
Return of the Killer Tomatoes (1988) ....
In bed in camisole and tap pants.
Glitch (1988) .... Lydia
0:41 - In pink bathing suit talking to blonde guy
0:54 - Very brief side view of right breast in
bathtub with dark haired guy. *
Far From Home (1989) .... Woman in Trailer
0:16 - Topless making love when Drew
Barrymore peeks in window. **
Savage Beach (1989) .... Anjelica
0:33 - Topless taking off black teddy and getting
into bed to make love. ***
0:47 - Topless making love in the back seat of car.
**

Video Tapes:

Playboy Video Calendar 1988 .... Playmate
Playboy Video Centerfold: Teri Weigel .. Playmate

Magazines:

Playboy (Apr 1986) .... Playmate

WEISS, ROBERTA

Films:

Autumn Born (1979) .... Melissa
0:07 - Rear end, wearing panties and bending over
desk to get whipped.
Cross Country (1983; Canadian) .... Alma Jean
0:59 - Topless on bed with two other people. **
Abducted (1987) ....

Made for HBO:

The Hitchhiker: And If We Dream
.... Rosanne Lucas
0:11 - Topless and buns in barn making love with
Stephen Collins. **
0:17 - Topless in dream classroom with Collins.
**
0:23 - Brief topless in bed after second dream with
Collins. *

WELCH, LISA

Films:

Revenge of the Nerds (1984) .... Suzy

Magazines:

Playboy (Sep 1980) .... Playmate
Page 118

WELCH, TAHNEE

Other:

Daughter of actress Raquel Welch.

Films:

Cocoon (1986) .... Kitty
0:61 - Buns walking into swimming pool.
Lethal Obsession (1987) .... Daniela Santini
0:14 - Buns, putting on robe after talking to
"John" on the phone.

0:15 - Half of left breast taking off coat to hug
"John" in the kitchen. *
0:16 - Sort of left breast in bed with "John." Too
dark to see anything.
1:16 - Buns, getting an injection.
Cocoon, The Return (1988) .... Kitty

TV:

Falcon Crest (1987-1989) .... Shannon

WELD, TUESDAY

Films:

Serial (1980) .... Kate
1:20 - Side view of right breast getting into
shower with Martin Mull.

WELLER, MARY LOUISE

Films:

The Evil (1977) .... Laurie Belden
National Lampoon's Animal House (1978)
.... Mandy Pepperidge
0:38 - In white bra, then topless in bedroom while
John Belushi watches on a ladder through the
window. ***
The Bell Jar (1979) .... Doreen
Forced Vengeance (1982) .... Claire Bonner
Blood Tide (1982) .... Sherry

WELLES, GWEN

Films:

A Safe Place (1971) .... Bari
Helle (1972) ....
Hit (1973) .... Sherry Nielson
California Split (1974) .... Susan Peters
Nashville (1975) .... Sueleen Gay
2:09 - In bra singing to a room full of men, then
topless doing a strip tease, buns walking up the
steps and out of the room. **
Between the Lines (1977) .... Laura
0:32 - Buns and topless drying off with a towel in
front of a mirror. **
Desert Hearts (1986) ....
The Men's Club (1986) .... Redhead

Magazines:

Playboy (Nov 1972)
.... "Variation of a Vadim Theme"
Page 111-115: Full frontal nudity. ***
Playboy (May 1975) .... "The Splendor of Gwen"
Pages 96-99: Full frontal nudity. ***

WELLES, TERRI

Films:

Looker (1981) .... Lisa
0:02 - Brief topless getting photographed for
operation. In black bra and panties in her
apartment a lot. *

Video Tapes:
  Playmates of the Year - The '80's............Playmate
Magazines:
  Playboy (Dec 1980)...................................Playmate

WELLS, JENNIFER

Other:
  a.k.a. Jennifer Welles.
Films:
  Sugar Cookies (1973)..................... Max's Secretary
    0:28 - Topless in red panties in "Max's" office
      while he talks on the phone, then lower frontal
      nudity. *
    0:56 - Full frontal nudity getting dressed. **
  The Groove Tube (1974).............. The Geritan Girl
    0:21 - dancing nude around her "husband", Chevy
      Chase. **

WELLS, VICTORIA

Films:
  Cheech & Chong's Nice Dreams (1981)
    .... Beach Girl #1
    0:29 - Brief topless on the beach with two other
      girls. Long shot, unsteady, hard to see. *
  Losin' It (1983) ....

WHITAKER, CHRISTINA

Films:
  The Naked Cage (1985).................................. Rita
    0:08 - Topless in bed with "Willy." ***
    0:55 - Brief topless in gaping sweatshirt during
      fight with "Sheila." *
    1:28 - Panties during fight with Shari Shattuck.
    1:29 - Sort of left breast in gaping dress.
  Assault of the Killer Bimbos (1987) ....
  Vampire at Midnight (1988) ....
  Stormquest (1988)..

WHITCRAFT, ELIZABETH

Films:
  Angel Heart (1987)....................................... Connie
    (Blonde hair.)
    0:33 - Topless in bed talking with Mickey Rourke
      while taking off her clothes. **
  Working Girl (1989).................... Doreen DiMucci
    (Brunette hair.)
    0:29 - Topless on bed on Alec Baldwin when
      Melanie Griffith opens the door and discovers
      them. **

WHITE, VANNA

Films:
  Gypsy Angels...
    (Unreleased film.)
  Looker (1981)....................................... Reston Girl
  Graduation Day (1981)..................................... Doris

Made for TV Movies:
  The Goddess of Love (1988).......................... Venus
TV:
  Wheel of Fortune (1982-)............................Hostess
Video Tapes:
  Vanna White - Get Slim, Stay Slim................Herself
Magazines:
  Playboy (May 1987)...................................."Vanna"
    Pages 134-143: In sheer lingerie from catalog she
      did before Wheel of Fortune. ***
  Playboy (Dec 1987)..................."Sex Stars of 1987"
    Page 150: In sheer black lingerie. ***
  Playboy (Dec 1988)..................."Sex Stars of 1988"
    Page 183: Right breast under lingerie. **

WHITLOW, JILL

Films:
  Porky's (1982)...Mindy
  Weird Science (1984)................... Perfume Salesgirl
  Night of the Creeps (1986)......Cynthia Cronenberg
    0:31 - In bra and panties taking off sweater.
    0:33 - Brief topless putting nightgown on over her
      head in her bedroom. *
  Thunder Run (1986)..Kim
  Twice Dead (1989)........................... Robin/Myrna
    0:27 - In white slip, getting ready for bed, then
      walking around the house.

WHITTON, MARGARET

Films:
  Love Child (1982)............................Jacki Steinberg
  9 1/2 Weeks (1986)......................................Molly
  The Best of Times (1986)................................Darla
  The Secret of My Success (1987).......Vera Prescott
    0:31 - Very brief topless taking off swimsuit top in
      swimming pool with Michael J. Fox. *
  Ironweed (1987)... Katrina
    1:19 - Full frontal nudity leaving the house and
      walking down steps while young "Francis"
      brushes a horse. **
  Major League (1989)..........................Rachel Phelps
  Little Monsters (1989)..
TV:
  Hometown (1985)........................ Barbara Donnelly
  Fine Romance (1989)....................................Louisa

WIDDOES, KATHLEEN

Films:
  The Group (1966)...........................Helena Davidson
  Petulia (1968; U.S./British) ....Wilma
  The Sea Gull (1968)......................................Masha
  The Mephisto Waltz (1971)................. Maggie West
  Savages (1972)...Leslie
  The End of August (1982)............................. Adele
  I'm Dancing as Fast as I Can (1982) ... Dr. Rawlings
  Without a Trace (1983)...
Magazines:
  Playboy (Mar 1972)................................."Savages"
    Pages 142 & 145: Topless. *

WIESMEIER, LYNDA

Films:

Private School (1983)...........................School Girl
   0:42 - Nude in shower room scene. First blonde in
   shower on the left. ***

Joysticks (1983)...Candy

Malibu Express (1984)...................June Khnockers
   0:04 - Topless in locker room taking jumpsuit off.
   **

   1:16 - Topless leaning out of racing car window
   while a helicopter chases her and "Cody." *

Preppies (1984)....................................Trini
   0:54 - In bra and panties practicing sexual
   positions on beds with "Margot."
   1:06 - Topless on bed with "Mark." ***

R.S.V.P. (1984) ....Jennifer Edwards
   0:11 - Topless diving into the pool while "Toby"
   fantasizes about her being nude. **
   0:19 - Topless in kitchen when "Toby" fantasizes
   about her again. *
   1:21 - Nude getting out of the pool and kissing
   "Toby," when she really is nude. ***

Wheels of Fire (1984)..
Avenging Angel (1985)..................................Debbie
Real Genius (1985).....................Chris' Girl at Party
Video Tapes:

1st Annual Playmate Review (1983)....... Playmate
Playboy Video Magazine, Volume 2........Playmate
Magazines:

Playboy (Jul 1982)................................. Playmate

WILCOX, TOYAH

Films:

The Ebony Tower (1985)..............................Freak
   0:41 - Buns lying down in grass next to lake.
Quadrophenia (1979; British).......................Monkey
The Tempest (1980; British)...................................

WILDSMITH, DAWN

Other:
   Wife of director Fred Olen Ray.
Films:

Surf Nazis Must Die (1986)...........................Eva
   0:25 - Topless betting fondled at the beach
   wearing a wet suit by "Adolf." Mostly right
   breast. *
Star Slammer - The Escape (1986)................ Muffin
Phantom Empire (1987)....................Eddy Colchilde
Deep Space (1988)....................................Janice
Hollywood Chainsaw Hookers (1988).......Samantha
B.O.R.N. (1988)...Singer
Warlords (1988)..Danny
Beverly Hills Vamp (1989) .....Sherry Santa Monica

WILKES, DONNA

Films:

Schizoid (1980)................................ Allison Foles
   0:12 - Topless taking off her bra in bathroom
   while Klaus Kinski watches. Buns, getting into
   the shower. Out of focus shots.
   0:13 - Side view topless getting into the shower.
   **
Angel (1984).......................................Angel/Molly
Grotesque (1987)...
TV:
Hello, Larry (1979) .... Diane Adler

WILKINSON, JUNE

Films:

Sno-Line (1984).. Audrey
Magazines:

Playboy (Jan 1989)............. "Women of the Fifties"
   Page 116: Topless, wearing a gold bikini bottom.
   ***

WILLIAMS, BARBARA

Films:

Thief of Hearts (1984)...................... Mickey Davis
   (Special home video version.)
   0:53 - Topless making love with Steven Bauer in
   his condo. ***
   0:46 - Right breast in bathtub when her husband
   comes in and tries to read her diary. *
Tell Me That You Love Me (1984) ....
Jo Jo Dancer, Your Life is Calling (1986).......Dawn
Watchers (1988)... Nora
Tiger Warsaw (1988) .... Karen

WILLIAMS, EDY

Films:

The Secret Life of an American Wife (1968)
   .... Susie Steinberg
   0:32 - In blonde wig wearing black bra and panties
   getting into bed.
   1:15 - In black bra and panties again coming out
   of bedroom into the hallway.
Dr. Minx (1975)..
   Topless.
Famous T & A (1982)................................ herself
   0:39 - Topless scenes from "Dr. Minx." **
Chained Heat (1983; U.S./German).............. Paula
   0:30 - Frontal nudity in the shower, soaping up
   with another woman. **
   0:36 - Topless in bed after another prisoner comes
   to Edy's bed at night. **
Hollywood Hot Tubs (1984).....................Desiree
   0:26 - Topless, trying to seduce "Shawn" while he
   works on a hot tub. ***
   1:26 - In black lingerie outfit in the hallway.
   1:30 - Partial topless with breasts sticking out of
   her bra while she sits by hot tub with "Jeff." *
   1:32 - Topless in hot tub room with "Shawn." **
   1:38 - Topless again in the hot tub lobby. *

Hellhole (1985) .... Vera
   0:22 - Topless on bed posing for "Silk." ***
   0:24 - Topless in white panties in shower, then
     fighting with another woman. ***
   1:03 - Topless in mud bath with another woman.
     Long scene. ***
Mankillers (1987) .... Sergeant Roberts
Rented Lips (1988) .... Heather Darling
   0:22 - Topless in bed, getting fondled by Robert
     Downey, Jr. during porno movie shoot. *
Dr. Alien (1989) .... Buckmeister
   0:54 - Topless taking off her top in the women's
     locker room in front of "Wesley." ***
Bad Manners (1989) .... Mrs. Slatt
Magazines:
  Playboy (Mar 1973) .... "All About Edy"
    Pages 135-141: Nude. ***
  Playboy (Jan 1978) .... "The Year in Sex"
    Page 201: Nude in swimming pool. **
  Playboy (Nov 1989) .... "Sex in Cinema 1989"
    Page 134: Topless still from "Bad Girls From
    Mars." ***

WILLIAMS, JO BETH

Films:
  Kramer vs. Kramer (1979) .... Phyllis Bernard
    0:45 - Buns and brief topless in the hallway
      meeting Dustin Hoffman's son. *
  The Dogs of War (1980; British) .... Jessie
  Stir Crazy (1980) .... Meredeth
  Poltergeist (1982) .... Diane Freeling
  Endangered Species (1982) .... Harriet Purdue
  The Big Chill (1983) .... Karen
  American Dreamer (1984) .... Cathy Palmer
  Teachers (1984) .... Lisa
    1:39 - Brief topless taking off clothes and running
      down school hallway yelling at Nick Nolte. *
  Desert Bloom (1986) .... Lily
  Poltergeist II: The Other Side (1986)
    .... Diane Freeling
  Memories of Me (1988) .... Lisa McConnell
Miniseries:
  Baby M (1988) .... Mary Beth Whitehead
Made for TV Movies:
  Adam (1983) ....
  The Day After (1983) .... Nancy
  Murder Ordained (1987) ....
  My Name is Bill W. (1989) .... Lois Wilson
  Child in the Night (1990) .... Dr. Jackie Hollis
Soap Operas:
  Somerset (1975-76) .... Carrie Wheeler
  The Guiding Light (1977-81) .... Brandy Shelooe

WILLIAMS, VANESSA

Other:
  Dethroned Miss America 1984.
  Singer.
Made for TV Movies:
  Full Exposure: The Sex Tapes (1989) .... Valentine

Magazines:
  Penthouse (Sep 1984)
    .... "Here She Comes, Miss America"
    Pages 66-75: B&W nude photos. ***
  Penthouse (Nov 1984) ..... "Tom Chiapel" interview
    Pages 85-89: More B&W nude photos. ***

WILLIAMS, WENDY O.

Other:
  Lead singer of "The Plasmatics."
Adult Films:
  Candy Goes to Hollywood ....
Films:
  Reform School Girls (1986) .... Charlie
    0:26 - Topless talking to two girls in the shower.
    **
Magazines:
  Playboy (Oct 1986) .... "Oh, Wendy O.!"
    Pages 70-75: Topless. **

WILSON, AJITA

Films:
  The Joy of Flying ....
  Love Lust and Ecstasy .... Sara
    0:02 - Nude taking a shower and getting into bed
      with an old guy. **
    0:04 - Nude making love with a young guy. **
    0:17 - Topless in bathtub, then making love on
      bed. **
    0:22 - Topless making love in a swimming pool,
      in a river, by a tree. **
    0:26 - Nude getting undressed and taking a
      shower. **
    0:35 - Full frontal nudity changing clothes. **
    0:54 - Full frontal nudity making love in bed. ***
  Savage Island (1985) ....

WILSON, ALISA

Films:
  The Terror on Alcatraz (1986) .... Clarissa
    1:14 - Brief topless opening her blouse to distract
      "Frank" so she can get away. *
  Loverboy (1989) ....

WILSON, CHERYL-ANN

Films:
  Terminal Choice (1984) .... Nurse Fields
  Cellar Dweller (1987) .... Lisa
    0:59 - Brief right breast, then topless taking a
      shower. **
Soap Operas:
  Days of Our Lives ....

WILSON, SHEREE J.
Films:
    Fraternity Vacation (1985)..................Ashley Taylor
      0:43 - In white leotard at aerobics class.
      0:47 - Topless and buns of her body double in the bedroom (Roberta Whitewood) when the guys photograph her with a telephoto lens. *
      1:01 - In white leotard exercising in living room with Leigh McCloskey.
    Crimewave (1986) ....
TV Miniseries:
    Kane and Abel......................................
TV:
    Our Family Honor (1985-86)..................Rita Danzig
    Dallas (1987-) .... April

WINDSOR, ROMY
Films:
    Thief of Hearts (1984)................... Nicole
    (Special home video version.)
      0:12 - Full frontal nudity with Steven Bauer getting dressed. ***
    Howling IV: The Original Nightmare (1988). Marie
    Big Bad John (1989)........................Marie Mitchelle

WINGER, DEBRA
Films:
    Slumber Party '57 (1976)............................Debbie
      0:10 - Topless during swimming pool scene with her five girl friends. Hard to tell who is who. *
      0:53 - Topless three times lying down making out "Bud Hanson." ***
    Thank God It's Friday (1978)......................Jennifer
    French Postcards (1979) ....Melanie
    Urban Cowboy (1980) ....Sissy
    An Officer and a Gentleman (1982)
    ....Paula Pokrifki
      1:05 - Brief side view of right breast, then topless making love with Richard Gere in a motel. ***
    Cannery Row (1982)....................................Suzy
    Terms of Endearment (1983)
    .... Emma Greenway Horton
    Mike's Murder (1984)................................... Betty
      0:26 - Brief left breast in bathtub. *
    Black Widow (1986)...............................Alexandra
    Legal Eagles (1986)..............................Laura Kelly
    Made in Heaven (1987) ....
    Betrayed (1988) ....Katie Phillips/Cathy Weaver
TV:
    Wonder Woman...................... Drusilla/Wonder Girl

WINKLER, K.C.
Films:
    H.O.T.S. (1979)..Cynthia
      0:27 - Topless in blue bikini bottom on balcony. *
      0:31 - Topless in van making love, then arguing with "John." **

The Happy Hooker Goes Hollywood (1980)
    .... Amber
      0:41 - Topless in cowboy outfit on bed with a guy. **
      0:43 - Topless, wearing a blue garter belt playing pool with Susan Kiger. ***
    Night Shift (1982).. Cheryl
    They Call Me Bruce? (1982) ....
    Armed and Dangerous (1986)......................... Vicki
TV:
    High Rollers............................ Game Show Hostess
Magazines:
    Playboy (Jan 1979)........"The Great Playmate Hunt"
    Page 190: Full frontal nudity. ***
    Playboy (Oct 1985)............................... Grapevine
    Page 241: In swimsuit. showing left breast B&W. *
    Playboy (Mar 1986)............................... Grapevine
    Page 176: In wet swimsuit. B&W. *
    Playboy (Sep 1989) ...."Body by Winkler"
    Page 82-87: Nude. ***

WINNINGHAM, MARE
Films:
    One Trick Pony (1980)...........McDeena Dandridge
      0:14 - Topless in the bathtub with Paul Simon, smoking a cigarette. Long scene. **
    Threshold (1983; Canadian).......... Carol Severance
      0:56 - Brief full frontal nudity, lying on operating table, then side view of left breast getting prepped for surgery. *
    St. Elmo's Fire (1985).............................Wendy
    Nobody's Fool (1986)................................ Pat
    Made in Heaven (1987).................. Brenda Carlucci
    Shy People (1988)..................................Candy
    Miracle Mile (1989).......................Julie Peters
    Turner & Hooch (1989) ....Emily Carson
Miniseries:
    The Thorn Birds (1983) ....Justine O'Neill
Made for TV Movies:
    Amber Waves (1980)...
    Helen Keller - The Miracle Continues......................
    A Winner Never Quits (1986)......................... Annie
    Eye on the Sparrow (1987).............................
    Love & Lies (1990)................................. Kim Paris
    Crossing to Freedom (1990)..........Nicole Rougeron
Magazines:
    Playboy (Nov 1981)............."Sex in Cinema 1981"
    Page 170: Topless in bathtub from "One Trick Pony." **

WINTERS, D. D.
See Vanity.

WITT, KATHRYN

Other:
a.k.a. Kathy Witt.
Films:
Lenny (1974; B&W)............................ Girl
    0:43 - Right breast with Valerie Perrine while
    Dustin Hoffman watches. *
Looker (1981)...................................... Tina Cassidy
    0:17 - In beige lingerie undressing in her room.
Star 80 (1983)................................... Robin
Cocaine Wars (1986)........................Janet
    0:36 - Brief topless and buns making love in bed
    with John Schneider. *
Demon of Paradise (1987)................. Annie
TV:
Flying High (1978-79)......................... Pam Bellagio

WITTER, KAREN

Films:
Dangerously Close (1986).................... Betsy
The Perfect Match (1987) .... Tammy
Hero and the Terror (1988) .... Ginger
Paramedics (1988)................................Danger Girl
    0:03 - In white bra and panties in bedroom with a
    heart attack victim while the paramedics try to
    save him.
    0:07 - In wet blouse after getting in a car crash
    with a guy in the fountain.
Silent Assassins (1988) .... Sushi Bar Girl
The Vineyard (1988) ....
Out of the Dark (1988)....................Jo Ann
Another Chance (1989) .... Nancy Burton
    0:44 - Brief side view of right breast and buns
    getting out of bed. *
    0:45 - In two piece swimsuit.
Midnight (1989) .... Missy Angel
    0:32 - In bed with "Mickey." Nice squished
    breasts against him, but only a very brief side
    view of left breast. *
    0:48 - In two piece swimsuit, going into the pool.
    0:58 - In nightgown, walking around with lots of
    makeup on her face.
Video Tapes:
1st Annual Playmate Review (1983).......Playmate
TV:
One Life to Live (1990-)............Tina Lord Roberts
Magazines:
Playboy (Mar 1982)............................. Playmate

WOOD, CYNDI

Other:
a.k.a. Cynthia Wood.
Films:
Apocalypse Now (1979)............................Playmate
Van Nuys Blvd. (1979) ....Moon
Magazines:
Playboy (Feb 1973)................................Playmate

WOOD, JANE

Films:
The Ragman's Daughter (1974)...............................
She'll Be Wearing Pink Pyjamas (1984)........ Jude
    0:07 - Nude shaving her legs in the women's
    shower room. *
Lassiter (1984)....................................Mary Becker
Blood Red Roses (1986)...

WOOD, JANET

Films:
Terror House (1972)..
The Centerfold Girls (1974).......................... Linda
    0:14 - Topless putting on robe and getting out of
    bed. **
Slumber Party '57 (1976)............................Smitty
    0:10 - Topless with her five girl friends during
    swimming pool scene. Hard to tell who is who.
    *
    1:06 - Left breast, then topless in stable with
    "David" while his sister watches. **

WOOD, LANA

Other:
Sister of actress Natalie Wood.
Films:
The Searchers (1956)....................Debbie as a Child
Diamonds are Forever (1971)...........Plenty O'Toole
A Place Called Today (1972)...... Carolyn Scheider
    0:40 - Side view of left breast, then topless lying
    down talking to "Ron." ***
Demon Rage (1981)..
    Topless in bed.
Dark Eyes (1987)...
TV:
The Long Hot Summer (1965-66).........Eula Harker
Peyton Place (1966-67)......................Sandy Webber
Capitol (1983)....................................... Fran Bruke
Magazines:
Playboy (Apr 1971)..
Playboy (Nov 1972)......................."Sex in Cinema"
    Page 159: Hard to see anything
Playboy (Sep 1987)........"25 Years of James Bond"
    Page 128: Topless. ***

WORONOV, MARY

Films:
Sugar Cookies (1973).............................. Camila
    0:10 - Topless in bathtub, then wearing white
    panties exercising topless on the floor. Long
    scene. ***
    1:04 - Topless with "Julie" in the bathtub. *
    1:07 - Brief topless making love with "Julie," then
    left breast. *
    1:17 - Brief right breast when Lynn Lowry yanks
    her dress up. *
Silent Night, Bloody Night (1974)................... Diane
Cover Girl Models (1975) ....

Death Race 2000 (1975)....................Calamity Jane
0:27 - Brief topless arguing with "Matilda the
Hun." *
Hollywood Boulevard (1976)..........Mary McQueen
Jackson County Jail (1976)............................Pearl
Mr. Billion (1977)..Actress
Rock 'n' Roll High School (1979).......Evelyn Togar
The Lady in Red (1979)............Woman Bankrobber
Heartbeeps (1981)......................Party House Owner
The Protectors, Book 1 (1981)................................
Eating Raoul (1982).........................Mary Bland
0:46 - Topless on the couch struggling with Ed
Begley, Jr. More topless while "Raoul" counts
money on her stomach. Long scene. ***
0:53 - Buns and side view of right breast in
hospital room whit "Raoul". A little dark. *
Angel of H.E.A.T. (1982)............Samantha Vitesse
0:11 - Frontal nudity changing clothes on a boat
dock after getting out of the lake. ***
0:43 - Topless wrestling in the mud after wearing
white bathing suit. **
Get Crazy (1983) ....
Hellhole (1984)..Dr. Fletcher
Night of the Comet (1984)..............................Carol
Nomads (1986)...
Chopping Mall (1987) ....
Scenes from the Class Struggle in Beverly Hills
(1989)...Lizabeth
1:06 - In black lingerie, then topless in bedroom
with "Juan," then in bed. ***
Watchers II (1990)...................................Dr. Glatman

WRIGHT, AMY
Films:
The Deer Hunter (1978)..
Girlfriends (1978)...Ceil
0:42 - Brief topless getting out of bed to talk to
Melanie Mayron. *
The Amityville Horror (1979) ....Jackie
Breaking Away (1979)....................................Nancy
Wise Blood (1979)................................Sabbath Lilly
Stardust Memories (1980) ....
Inside Moves (1980)..Ann
Heartland (1981)...Clara
The Telephone (1987)...
The Accidental Tourist (1988)................ Rose Leary

WRIGHT, JENNY
Films:
Pink Floyd The Wall (1982)......American Groupie
0:41 - Topless backstage in back of a truck doing a
strip tease dance in front of some people. ***
The World According to Garp (1982)........ Curbie
0:33 - Brief topless behind the bushes with Robin
Williams giving him "something to write
about." **
The Wild Life (1984).................................... Eileen
0:22 - In bra and panties, then topless changing in
her bedroom while Christopher Penn watches
from the window. **

Out of Bounds (1987)..
Near Dark (1987) ....Mae
The Chocolate War (1988)................................Lisa
A Shock to the System (1990) ....
TV:
Capital News (1990)........................Doreen Duncan

WRIGHT, SYLVIA
Films:
Terror on Tour (1980)....................................Carol
Malibu Hot Summer (1981)..........Actress at Party
a.k.a. Sizzle Beach
0:01 - Nude, standing up during opening credits.
**

1:07 - Topless fixing her hair in front of mirror,
then full frontal nudity talking to "Howard."
***

1:09 - Topless on top of "Howard." *
Bloody Birthday (1986) ....

WYSS, AMANDA
Films:
Fast Times at Ridgemont High (1982)...............Lisa
Nightmare on Elm Street (1984)...............Tina Gray
Better off Dead (1985)............................Beth Truss
Silverado (1985)..Phoebe
To Die For (1988)....................................Celia Kett
Powwow Highway (1988) ....
Deadly Innocents (1990)...................................
Topless.

Y

YATES, CASSIE
Films:
Rolling Thunder (1977) ....Candy
The Evil (1977)...Mary
F.I.S.T. (1978)..Molly
FM (1978)...Laura Coe
Convoy (1978)...Violet
0:21 - Very brief left breast in truck sleeper with
Kris Kristofferson. *
The Osterman Weekend (1983)...... Betty Cardone
0:48 - Topless getting into bed while Rutger Hauer
watches on TV. **
0:51 - Right breast, making love with Sarandon. *
Unfaithfully Yours (1984) ....Carla Robbins
Made for TV Movies:
Listen To Your Heart (1983) ....
Of Mice and Men (1981) ....
St. Helens (1981)...
TV:
Rich Man, Poor Man - Book II (1976-77)
....Annie Adams
Nobody's Perfect (1980)
.................................Detective Jennifer Dempsey
Detective in the House (1985) ....Diane Wyman

176

YORK, SUSANNAH

Films:

Tunes of Glory (1960)......................Morag Sinclair
Tom Jones (1963)...Sophie
A Man for All Seasons (1966)...........Margaret More
The Killing of Sister George (1968)
.... Alice McNaught
  0:19 - Topless under sheer blue nightgown.
  0:59 - In black bra and panties.
  1:45 - In black bra and panties getting undressed.
  2:07 - (0:09 into tape 2) Topless lying in bed with
    another woman. **
X, Y and Zee (1972)..................................... Stella
That Lucky Touch (1975) .... Julia Richardson
The Silent Partner (1978)............................. Julie
  0:38 - Very brief right breast pulling her dress
    back up with Elliott Gould. *
Superman (1978)..Lara
The Shout (1979).........................Rachel Fielding
  0:53 - Brief topless changing from a bathrobe to a
    blouse in bedroom. **
  1:02 - Brief nude in upstairs room getting ready to
    make love with Alan Bates. *
  1:05 - Brief buns, standing at end of hallway.
  1:09 - In white slip inside and outside house.
  1:11 - Topless in bathtub with John Hurt.
  1:18 - Brief topless getting up from bed with
    Bates. Long shot, hard to see anything. *
The Adventures of Eliza Fraser...........................
  1:15 & 1:34.
Images.. Cathryn
The Awakening (1980)..........................Jane Turner
Falling in Love Again (1980)................... Sue Lewis
Pretty Kill (1987)...Toni
A Summer Story (1988).............Mrs. Narracrombe
Made for TV Movies:
Jane Eyre (1970; British)...

YOUNG, KAREN

Films:

Handgun (1983; British)............. Kathleen Sullivan
  a.k.a. Deep in the Heart
  Brief buns and topless when rapist forces her to
  remove her clothes.
Almost You (1985).......................................
Birdy (1985)..................................Hannah Rourke
9 1/2 Weeks (1986) ....Sue
Heat (1987)..Holly
Jaws the Revenge (1987)...............................
Criminal Law (1988) ....Ellen Falkner
  1:21 - Very brief buns, then brief topless in bed
    with "Ben." *
Torch Song Trilogy (1988) ....Laurel
Night Game (1989)................................... Roxy
  0:02 - In white slip with Roy Scheider.
  0:06 - Right breast in bed with Scheider after he
    answers the phone. *

YOUNG, ROBBIN

Films:

For Your Eyes Only (1981)..........Flower Shop Girl
Night Shift (1982)..Nancy
Magazines:
Playboy (Jun 1981).............. "For Your Eyes Only"
  Pages 126-127 - Topless (won a contest to appear
  in the film and in Playboy magazine). ***
Playboy (Dec 1981)................. "Sex Stars of 1981"
  Page 244 - Frontal nudity. ***

YOUNG, SEAN

Films:

Jane Austen in Manhattan (1980)................Ariadne
Stripes (1981)....................................Louise Cooper
Bladerunner (1982)......................................Rachael
Young Doctors in Love (1982).Dr. Stephanie Brody
  0:48 - In white panties and camisole top in the
    surgery room with Michael McKean.
Dune (1984)..Chani
Baby...Secret of the Lost Legend (1985)
.... Susan Matthew-Loomis
No Way Out (1987)...........................Susan Atwell
  0:11 - In black stockings, garter belt & corset in
    love scene in back of limousine with Kevin
    Costner.
  0:13 - Side view of left breast, then brief right
    breast going into "Nina's" apartment with
    Costner. ***
  0:21 - In bed in pink lingerie and a robe talking on
    telephone when Costner is in Manila.
  0:31 - In corset and stockings with garter belt in
    bathroom talking to Costner.
Wall Street (1987)............................. Kate Gekko
Cousins (1989)...............................Tish Kozinski
The Boost (1989)...............................Linda Brown
  0:16 - Very, very brief topless jumping into the
    swimming pool with James Woods. Very, very
    brief side view of right breast getting out of the
    pool, sitting on edge, then getting pulled back
    in.
  0:17 - Left breast in pool talking to Woods. **
  0:48 - Brief topless under water in Jacuzzi with
    Woods.
Fire Birds (1990).......................................

Z

ZABOU

Films:

Perils of Gwendoline in the Land of the Yik Yak
  (1984; French)...Beth
  0:59 - Topless in torture chamber. *
  1:05 - Topless chained by the hands. *
One Woman or Two (1986; French)........Constance
  a.k.a. Une Femme Ou Deux
  0:28 - Brief topless pulling up her blouse for
    Gerard Depardieu. **

Etats D'Ame (1987; French) ....
Suivez Mon Regard (1987; French)..........................

ZADORA, PIA
Other:
Singer.
Films:
Santa Claus Conquers the Martians (1964) ... Girmar
Butterfly (1982)...Kady
   0:15 - Silhouette changing while Stacey Keach
    watches.
   0:33 - Topless and buns getting into the bath. **
   0:35 - Topless in bathtub when Stacey Keach is
    giving her a bath. This is supposed to be incest,
    but the tension is still exciting. ***
Fake Out (1982)..
The Lonely Lady (1983).................JeniLee Randall
   0:12 - Brief topless getting raped by "Joe" after
    getting out of the pool. *
   0:22 - Brief topless, then left breast making love
    with "Walter." **
   0:28 - Side view topless lying in bed with
    "Walter." **
   0:44 - Buns and side view of left breast taking a
    shower. **
   0:46 - Very brief right breast in bed with
    "George." *
   1:05 - Left breast, then brief topless making love
    with "Vinnie." **
Voyage of the Rock Aliens (1985)...............DeeDee
a.k.a. When the Rains Begin to Fall
Pajama Tops..
Hairspray (1988).......................... The Beatnik Chick
Magazines:
Penthouse (Oct 1983) ...."Pia"
   Pages 103-119
Playboy (Nov 1983)............. "Sex in Cinema 1983"
   Page 144: Frontal nudity. **

ZANE, LISA
Films:
Gross Anatomy (1989)..
Bad Influence (1990).................................... Claire
   0:39 - Brief topless on video tape seen on TV at
    party. *

ZANN, LENORE
Films:
Happy Birthday to Me (1980)....................... Maggie
American Nightmare (1981; Canadian).......... Tina
   0:25 - Topless and buns dancing on stage. ***
   1:05 - Topless and buns dancing on stage again.
    **
Visiting Hours (1982)..Lisa

One Night Only (1984; Canadian)..................Anne
   0:20 - Topless getting dressed in bedroom with
    "Jamie." **
   1:04 - Right breast in bedroom with "Jamie." *
   1:19 - Topless and buns making love with
    "Jamie." ***
Def-Con 4 (1985)..J. J.
The Hounds of Notre Dame.....................................

ZINSZER, PAMELA
Films:
The Happy Hooker Goes to Washington (1977)
   ....Linda
   1:19 - Brief topless in raincoat flashing in front of
    congressional panel. *
Magazines:
Playboy (Mar 1974)...................................Playmate

ZUCKER, MIRIAM
Films:
Sensations (1988)...........................Cookie Woman
   0:06 - Topless on couch making love with a guy
    while "Jenny" and "Brian" watch. *
New York's Finest (1988).......................................
A Woman Obsessed (1989) ....

ZUNIGA, DAPHNE
Films:
The Initiation (1984)...............................Kelly Terry
Visionquest (1985)............................Margie Epstein
The Sure Thing (1985)....................Alison Bradbury
Modern Girls (1986)...................................Margo
Spaceballs (1987)....................Princess Vespa
Last Rites (1989)...Angela
   0:04 - Very brief topless running into the
    bathroom to escape from being shot. Covered
    with blood, don't see her face. Very brief right
    breast reaching for a bathrobe. Don't really see
    anything. *
   0:40 - Buns, behind a shower door.
   0:50 - Buns, getting out of bed and standing in
    front of Tom Berenger.
The Fly II (1989)...Beth
Boys (1989)...
Gross Anatomy (1989).....................Laurie Rorbach

Actors

A

AAMES, WILLIE
Films:
Paradise (1981)...David
  0:42 - Buns, walking into the ocean with a fishing net. Dark, hard to see anything.
  1:12 - Frontal nudity swimming with Phoebe Cates under water. **
Zapped! (1982)..Peyton
TV:
We'll Get By (1975)..............................Kenny Platt
Swiss Family Robinson (1975-76).... Fred Robinson
Eight is Enough (1977-81)............Tommy Bradford
We're Movin' (1982).. host
Charles in Charge (1984-85).......... Buddy Lembeck

ABELE, JIM
Films:
Student Affairs (1987)............. Andrew Armstrong
  1:07 - Buns, when his friends play a practical joke on him in the shower. *
Wimps (1987)..

AGTENBERG, TOON
Films:
Spetters (1980)... Hans
  0:35 - Frontal nudity, measuring and comparing his manlihood with his friends in the auto shop. ***
  1:21 - Buns, getting gang raped by gay guy he has been stealing money from. *

ALBERT, EDWARD
Other:
Son of actor Eddie Albert.
Films:
Butterflies are Free (1972)..................................Don
Forty Carats (1973) ....Peter Latham
The Domino Principle (1977) ....Ross Pine
The Purple Taxi (1977; French/Italian/Irish).... Jerry
The Greek Tycoon (1978)..................Nico Tomasis
Galaxy of Terror (1981)...............................Cabren
Ellie (1984)..Tom
The House Where Evil Dwells (1985)............. Ted
  1:00 - Very brief, upper half of buns, making love with Susan George on the floor. *
Getting Even (1986).......................................Taggar
The Underachievers (1987)....................................
The Rescue (1988)...................Commander Merrill
Miniseries:
The Last Convertible (1979) .... Ron Dalrymple
TV:
The Yellow Rose (1983-84).......... Quisto Champion
Falcon Crest (1986-89)..................Jeff Wainwright

ALDEN, JOHN
Films:
The Young Warriors (1983; U.S./Canada)....Jorge
  0:16 - Dropping his pants in a room during pledge at fraternity. *

ALIN, JEFF
Films:
Coming Together (1978)..................Frank Hughes
  1:05 - Buns, putting pants on with "Richard." *

ANDERSON, MARC
Films:
Coming Together (1978).............. Richard Duncan
  0:13 - Buns kneeling and kissing "Angie," then more buns making love. **
  0:58 - Buns, making love with "Vicky." *
  1:05 - Buns, putting pants on with "Frank." *

ANGLADE, JEAN-HUGHES
Films:
Betty Blue (1986; French)................................ Zorg
  0:09 - Frontal nudity. ***
  1:03 - Nude trying to sleep in living room. **
  1:39 - Frontal nudity walking to the bathroom. **
  1:45 - Frontal nudity talking on the telephone. **

ANTIN, STEVE
Films:
The Last American Virgin (1982) ....Rick
The Goonies (1985)..Troy
Penitentiary III (1987) ....
The Accused (1988)...........................Bob Joiner
  1:29 - Buns, raping Jodi Foster on the pinball machine. *

ARKIN, ALAN
Films:
The Russians are Coming, The Russians are Coming (1966).. Rozanov
Wait Until Dark (1967)..................................... Boat
Woman Times Seven (1967) ....Fred
The Heart is a Lonely Hunter (1968)......John Singer
Catch-22 (1970).......................Captain Yossarian
  0:52 - Buns, standing in just his hat, talking to "Dreedle." Don't see his face. *
Last of the Red Hot Lovers (1972)
  .... Barneau Cashman
Freebie and the Bean (1974)........................... Bean
Hearts of the West (1975).............................Kessler
Rafferty and the Gold Dust Twins (1975)...Rafferty
The Seven-Per-Cent Solution (1976)
  ....Sigmund Freud
The In-Laws (1979) ....Sheldon Kornpett
Simon (1980) ....Simon Mendelssohn
Chu Chu and the Philly Flash (1981)................Flash
Improper Channels (1981; Canadian)............Jeffrey

Bad Medicine (1985).............................Dr. Madera
Joshua Then and Now (1985; Canadian)
....Reuben Shapiro
Big Trouble (1986).......................Leonard Hoffman

ATKINS, CHRISTOPHER
Films:
The Blue Lagoon (1980).............................Richard
    0:27 - Nude swimming underwater after growing
    up from little children. **
    0:29 - Buns, underwater. **
    1:03 - Nude swimming under water. **
    1:05 - Buns, kissing Brooke Shields. *
    1:09 - Very brief frontal nudity in water slide with
    Shields. **
The Pirate Movie (1982; Australian)...........Frederic
A Night in Heaven (1983)...............................Rick
    1:03 - Very brief frontal nudity when he pulls
    down his pants in hotel room with Leslie Ann
    Warren. *
    1:15 - Brief buns on boat with Leslie Ann
    Warren's husband. *
Beaks The Movie (1987) ....Peter
Listen to Me (1989) ....Bruce Arlington
TV:
Dallas (1983-84)..............................Peter Richards
Rock 'n' Roll Summer Action (1985)................host
Magazines:
Playboy (Nov 1980)............. "Sex in Cinema 1980"
    Page 183: Frontal nudity. **

B

BABB, ROGER
Films:
Working Girls (1987).......................................Paul
    1:18 - Frontal nudity with "Molly." *

BACON, KEVIN
Films:
Animal House (1978).............................Chip Diller
Friday the 13th (1980)......................................Jack
    0:39 - Close up of buns when "Marci" squeezes
    them. *
Diner (1982)..
Footloose (1984)...
Enormous Changes at the Last Minute (1985)
.... Dennis
Quicksilver (1986)....................................Jack Casey
White Water Summer (1987)..................................
End of the Line (1988).................................Everett
She's Having a Baby (1988)
....Jefferson "Jake" Briggs
Criminal Law (1989) ....Martin Thiel
Tremors (1989)........................... Valentine McKee
The Big Picture (1989)...................... Nick Chapman
Flatliners (1990)...

BAGGETTA, VINCENT
Films:
The Man Who Wasn't There (1983).............Riley
    0:23 - Buns, lying on the floor after fighting with
    the other guys. *
TV:
Chicago Story (1982)........................ Lou Pellegrino

BAHNER, BLAKE
Films:
Sensations (1988)................................. Brian Ingles
    0:10 - Very, very brief lower frontal nudity
    pushing the covers off the bed, then buns getting
    out of bed. **

BAKER, SCOTT
Films:
Cleo/Leo (1989)...............................Leo Blockman
    0:09 - Very brief buns after getting his butt kicked.
    *

BARRO, CESARE
Films:
My Father's Wife (1981)............................Claudio
    0:52 - Buns, bringing "Patricia" champagne. *

BATES, ALAN
Films:
Whistle Down the Wind (1962; B&W)
....Arthur Blakey, The Man
Zorba the Greek (1963; B&W)........................ Basil
Georgy Girl (1966; B&W)..................................Jos
King of Hearts (1966)...... Private Charles Plumpick
Women in Love (1971)...................................Rupert
    0:25 - Buns and brief frontal nudity walking
    around the woods rubbing himself with
    everything. *
    0:50 - Buns, making love with "Ursula" after a
    boy and girl drown in the river. *
    0:54 - Nude fighting with Oliver Reed in a room
    in front of a fireplace. Long scene. ***
An Unmarried Woman (1978)......................... Saul
The Rose (1979)..Rudge
The Shout (1979) ....Charles Crossly
Quartet (1981; British/French)..............H.J. Heidler
Separate Tables (1983)......................................
The Wicked Lady (1983; British)....... Jerry Jackson
The Return of the Soldier (1985) ....
Duet for One (1987)......................David Cornwallis
A Prayer for the Dying (1987)............Jack Meehan
We Think the World of You (1989)................Frank

182

BEATTY, WARREN
Other:
Brother of actress/author Shirley MacLaine.
Films:
Splendor in the Grass (1961)...............Bud Stamper
Lilith (1964; B&W)...........................Vincent Bruce
Bonnie and Clyde (1967)...............................Clyde
Dollars (1971) ....Joe Collins
McCabe & Mrs. Miller (1971)...........John McCabe
The Parallax View (1974) ....Joe
The Fortune (1975)................................... Nicky
Shampoo (1975)............................... George
   0:42 - Upper half of buns with pants a little bit
   down in the bathroom with Julie Christie. *
   1:24 - Buns, making love with Christie when
   Goldie Hawn discovers them. Long shot, hard
   to see. *
Heaven Can Wait (1978).....................Joe Pendleton
Reds (1981) ....John Reed
Ishtar (1987)...........................Lyle Rogers
Dick Tracy (1990) ....Dick Tracy
TV:
The Many Lives of Dobie Gillis (1959-60)
.... Milton Armitage

BEGHE, JASON
Films:
Compromising Positions (1985)................. Cupcake
Monkey Shines (1988) ....Allan Mann
   0:01 - Side view of buns on the floor, stretching to
   go running. *

BEGLEY, ED, JR.
Films:
Blue Collar (1978)....................................Bobby Joe
Hardcore (1979)...Soldier
Private Lessons (1981)....................Jack Travis
Eating Raoul (1982) ....Hippie
Cat People (1982)..........................Joe Creigh
Get Crazy (1983)...Colin
Protocol (1984)... Hassler
Streets of Fire (1984)................................Ben Gunn
Transylvania 6-5000 (1985).............Gil Turner
Amazon Women on the Moon (1987).........Griffin
   0:54 - Buns, walking around as the "Son of the
   Invisible Man." This section is in B&W. *
The Accidental Tourist (1988).....................Charles
Scenes from the Class Struggle in Beverly Hills
   (1989)..Peter
Faerie Tale Theatre:
Rip Van Winkle (1985)...
Made for TV Movies:
A Shining Season (1979)...
Spies, Lies & Naked Thighs (1988)........................
In the Best Interest of the Child (1990)
.... Howard Feldon
TV:
Roll Out (1973-74)............. Lt. Robert W. Chapman
St. Elsewhere (1982-88)................Dr. Victor Erlich
Parenthood (1990-)............................Gil Buckman

BELLE, EKKHARDT
Films:
Julia (1974; German).....................Patrick
   1:01 - Very brief buns in bed with "Terry." *

BELTRAN, ROBERT
Films:
Eating Raoul (1982)...........................Raoul
Lone Wolf McQuade (1983) ....Kayo
Night of the Comet (1984)...........................Hector
Gaby, A True Story (1987)...
Scenes from the Class Struggle in Beverly Hills
   (1989)... Juan
   1:34 - Brief buns when "Frank" pulls his shorts
   down. *

BENJAMIN, RICHARD
Films:
Goodbye, Columbus (1969)...........................Neil
   1:11 - Brief buns, walking into the bathroom.
   Very, very brief frontal nudity. Blurry, hard to
   see anything. *
Catch-22 (1970)...................................Major Danby
Diary of a Mad Housewife (1970)...Jonathan Balser
The Steagle (1971).............................Harold Weiss
Portnoy's Complaint (1972)....... Alexander Portnoy
The Last of Sheila (1973) ....Tom
Westworld (1973)............................... Peter Martin
The Sunshine Boys (1975)........................ Ben Clark
House Calls (1978)..................Dr. Norman Solomon
Love at First Bite (1979)............. Dr. Jeff Rosenberg
Scavenger Hunt (1979)............................... Stuart
How to Beat the High Cost of Living (1980). Albert
Witches' Brew (1980)..
First Family (1980).........Press Secretary Bunthorne
Saturday the 14th (1981) ....John
Packin' It In (1982)..
TV:
He & She (1967-68).............................Dick Hollister
Quark (1978).. Adam Quark

BERGER, HELMUT
Films:
The Damned (1969; Italian/German)........................
The Garden of the Finzi-Continis
   (1971; Italian/German)............................. Alberto
Conversation Piece (1977; Italian)................Konrad
The Greatest Battle (1979)..
The Romantic Englishwoman (1985; British)
....Thomas
   1:08 - Upper half of buns, sitting at edge of pool
   talking to Glenda Jackson. *
Code Name: Emerald (1985)................Ernst Ritter

BERENGER, TOM

Films:
Looking for Mr. Goodbar (1977)......................Gary
In Praise of Older Women (1978; Canadian)
....Andras Vayda
1:04 - Buns, rolling off Susan Strasberg. *
1:06 - Very brief lower frontal nudity three times, standing up and picking up Susan Strasberg. **
1:09 - Brief frontal nudity turning over in bed. ***
1:22 - Very, very brief blurry frontal nudity turning over in bed after getting mad at Alexandra Stewart. *
1:40 - Buns, undressing with Helen Shaver. Long scene. **
Butch and Sundance: The Early Days (1979)
.... Butch Cassidy
The Big Chill (1983)..Sam
Eddie and the Cruisers (1983) ....Frank
Fear City (1985)...
Rustler's Rhapsody (1985)...............Rex O'Herlihan
Platoon (1986) ....Barnes
Someone to Watch Over Me (1987)....Mike Keagan
Betrayed (1988)................................ Gary Simmons
Shoot to Kill (1988)........................Jonathan Knox
Last Rites (1989)...Michael
Major League (1989)..............................Jake Taylor
TV:
One Life to Live...

BERLING, PETER

Films:
Julia (1974; German).......................... Alex Lovener
0:12 - Brief buns, playing the piano outside on the dock.

BERNSEN, CORBIN

Other:
Husband of actress Amanda Pays.
Films:
Hello Again (1987)..
Major League (1989) ....Roger Dorn
0:58 - Brief buns running in locker room to cover himself with a towel when "Rachel" comes in to talk to the team. *
Bert Rigby, You're a Fool (1989).......... Jim Shirley
Disorganized Crime (1989) .... Frank Salazar
TV:
L.A. Law (1986-)............................... Arnie Becker

BIEHN, MICHAEL

Films:
Coach (1978)...Jack
0:71 - Upper half of buns in shower with Cathy Lee Crosby. *
The Fan (1981)...

The Terminator (1984).........................Kyle Reese
0:06 - Side view of buns after arriving from the future. Brief buns running down the alley. A little dark. *
Aliens (1986)....................................Corporal Hicks
The Seventh Sign (1988)....................Russell Quinn
In a Shallow Grave (1988).............Garnet Montrose
The Abyss (1989)........................Lieutenant Coffey

BLAKE, ROBERT

Films:
PT 109 (1963)..
This Property is Condemned (1966)........................
In Cold Blood (1967; B&W) ....
Tell Them Willie Boy is Here (1969)............ Willie
0:22 - Sort of buns when Katherine Ross lies down with him. Very, very brief lower frontal nudity seen through spread legs (one frame). More buns. Long shot, hard to see.
Electra Glide in Blue (1973)....................................
Coast to Coast (1980)...
Made for TV Movies:
Of Mice and Men (1981) ....
TV:
Baretta (1975-78)..................Detective Tony Baretta
Hell Town (1985)......................Father Noah Rivers

BOGOSIAN, ERIC

Films:
Special Effects (1984)................................ Neville
0:21 - Buns, while fighting with Zoe Tamerlis in bed. Medium long shot. *
Arena Brains (1988)..
Talk Radio (1989)..

BONANNO, LOUIS

Films:
Sex Appeal (1986)...Tony
Wimps (1987).. Francis
1:13 - Buns, running into a restaurant kitchen. *
Student Affairs (1987) ....Louie Balducci

BOND, STEVE

Films:
H.O.T.S. (1979).. John
0:32 - Buns, trapped in van with K. C. Winkler. *
The Prey (1983) ....Joel

BOORMAN, CHARLEY

Other:
Son of British director John Boorman.
Films:
The Emerald Forest (1985)....................... Tommy
  0:23 - Brief buns, running through camp. *
  0:24 - Brief buns running from waterfall and
    diving into pond. *
  0:30 - Buns, during ceremony. *
  0:45 - Buns, running away from the Fierce People
    with his dad. *
  1:02 - Buns running on the rocks, then bun in hut.
    *
  1:31 - Buns climbing up the building. **
  1:35 - Buns running down the hall to save
    "Kachiri." *

BORETSKI, PAUL

Films:
Perfect Timing (1984)...Joe
  0:11 - Brief frontal nudity and buns, rolling over
    on the bed. **
  0:29 - Frontal nudity on the roof in the snow with
    "Bonnie." *
  0:35 - Buns, on bed getting slapped on the behind.
    *
  0:50 - Buns, in bed with "Judy." *
  1:03 - Brief frontal nudity on TV with "Judy"
    while he and "Bonnie" watch. **

BOTTOMS, JOSEPH

Other:
Brother of actors Sam and Timothy Bottoms.
Films:
Crime and Passion (1976) ....Larry
The Black Hole (1979).......Lieutenant Charles Pizer
Surfacing (1980).. Joe
  0:23 - Buns, in bed with Kathleen Beller. *
Cloud Dancer (1980)........................... Tom Loomis
King of the Mountain (1981).......................... Buddy
Blind Date (1984)........................Jonathon Ratcliffe
Born to Race (1988)...............................Al Pagura
  0:55 - Brief buns taking off bathrobe on deck and
    jumping into the lake. *
Miniseries:
Holocaust (1978)................................... Rudi Weiss

BOTTOMS, TIMOTHY

Other:
Brother of actors Joseph and Sam Bottoms.
Films:
Johnny Got His Gun (1971)................. Joe Bonham
The Paper Chase (1973).................................. Hart
The White Dawn (1974)........................... Daggett
A Small Town in Texas (1976)........................ Poke
Rollercoaster (1977)............................Young Man
The Other Side of the Mountain, Part II (1978)
....John Boothe
Hurricane (1979) .... Jack Sanford

The High Country (1980; Canadian)................ Jim
  1:19 - Buns, walking into the pond with Linda
    Purl. *
  1:24 - Buns, pulling underwear on after getting out
    of sleeping bag. *
Hambone and Hillie (1984).........................Michael
Invaders from Mars (1986).............. George Gardner
Tin Man (1987)..
Return from the River Kwai (1988).....................
The Drifter (1988)................................... Arthur
Istanbul (1990).. Frank
Miniseries:
East of Eden (1981) ....Adam Trask

BOWIE, DAVID

Other:
Singer.
Films:
The Man Who Fell to Earth (1976; British)
....Thomas Jerome Newton
  (Uncensored version)
  0:58 - Brief buns, turning over in bed with Candy
    Clark.
  1:56 - Frontal nudity and brief buns in bed with
    Clark. Can't tell if a body double is used, don't
    see his face.
The Hunger (1983)..John
Merry Christmas, Mr. Lawrence
  (1983; British/Japanese)............................Celliers
Into the Night (1985) ....Colin Morris
Labyrinth (1986).. Jareth
Absolute Beginners (1986; British)
.... Vendice Partners
The Last Temptation of Christ (1988) Pontius Pilate

BRANAGH, KENNETH

Films:
High Season (1988; British) ....Rich Lamb
  0:56 - Buns, putting a wrap around Jacqueline
    Bisset after they fool around in the water. *
A Month in the Country (1988; British)...................

BRIDGES, JEFF

Other:
Son of actor Lloyd Bridges.
Brother of actor Beau Bridges.
Films:
Bad Company (1972)............................Jake Rumsey
Fat City (1972)...Ernie
The Last American Hero (1973)... Elroy Jackson, Jr.
  a.k.a. Hard Driver
Thunderbolt and Lightfoot (1974)..............Lightfoot
Hearts of the West (1975)........................ Lewis Tater
Rancho Deluxe (1975)........................Jack McKee
King Kong (1976)................................Jack Prescott
Stay Hungry (1976) .... Craig Blake
Winter Kills (1979).............................. Nick Kegan
  0:50 - Buns, getting dressed after making love
    with Belinda Bauer. **

Heaven's Gate (1980)..........................John
Cutter's Way (1981)...........................Richard Bone
a.k.a. Cutter and Bone
Kiss Me Goodbye (1982)...................Rupert Baines
Tron (1982)................................. Flynn/Clu
Against All Odds (1984).....................Terry Brogan
Starman (1984).. Starman
Jagged Edge (1985) ....Jack Forester
8 Million Ways to Die (1986)....... Matthew Scudder
The Morning After (1986)............................Turner
Nadine (1987)............................ Vernon Hightower
Tucker: The Man and His Dream (1988)
.... Preston Tucker
See You in the Morning (1989).......................Larry
The Fabulous Baker Boys (1989)............Jack Baker

BROSNAN, PIERCE
Films:
The Long Good Friday (1980)............First Irishman
Nomads (1986)...........................Pommier
0:56 - Buns, taking his pants off by the window.
Kind of dark, hard to see. *
The Fourth Protocol (1987; British)..........Petrofsky
The Deceivers (1988).......................William Savage
Taffin (1988; U.S./British).....................Mark Taffin
Made for HBO:
The Heist (1989)............................... Bobby Skinner
TV:
Remington Steele (1982-86)......... Remington Steele

BROWN, BYRAN
Other:
Husband of actress Rachel Ward.
Films:
Breaker Morant (1979)...........................
Winter of Our Dreams (1981)........................Reb
0:48 - Brief buns falling into bed with Judy Davis.
*
F/X (1985) ....Rollie Tyler
The Empty Beach (1985).......................Cliff Hardy
Parker (1985)...
Rebel (1985)..................................... Tiger Kelly
Tai-Pan (1986).......................................
The Good Wife (1987)..............................
Cocktail (1988)................................ Doug Coughlin
Gorillas in the Mist (1988)................. Bob Campbell
Miniseries:
The Thornbirds (1983)..............................

BROWN, CLANCY
Films:
Bad Boys (1983)...............................Viking Lofgren
Thunder Alley (1985)....................................Weasel
The Bride (1985)................................... Viktor
Highlander (1986)..Kuragan
Extreme Prejudice (1987)................................
Shoot to Kill (1988)...................................

Blue Steel (1989)...................................Nick Mann
1:27 - Upper half of buns lying on the bathroom
floor. Don't see his face, so it could be
anybody. *
Season of Fear (1989) ....Ward St. Clair

BROWN, WOODY
Films:
The Accused (1988)............................ Danny
1:28 - Buns, raping Jodi Foster on the pinball
machine. *
Off Limits (1988) ....Co-Pilot
TV:
Flamingo Road (1981-82)............... Skipper Weldon
The Facts of Live (1983-84).............................Cliff

BULLINGTON, PERRY
Films:
Chatterbox (1977)...............................Ted
0:02 - Buns, stumbling around the room. *

BURTON, JEFF
Films:
Planet of the Apes (1968)............................ Dodge
0:26 - Very brief buns taking off clothes to go
skinny dipping. (Guy on the right.) *

BUTCHER, GLENN
Films:
Young Einstein (1989; Australia)
....Ernest Rutherford
0:56 - Buns standing in front of sink when "Marie
Curie" comes to rescue "Einstein." (He's the
one on the left.) *

BYRNE, GABRIEL
Other:
Husband of actress Ellen Barkin.
Films:
The Keep (1983).....................................Kaempffer
Hanna K. (1984).......................................
Defense of the Realm (1986; British)... Nick Mullen
Gothic (1986; British).................................
Siesta (1987)... Augustine
1:28 - Brief buns and frontal nudity getting out of
bed. Long shot, hard to see anything
Hello Again (1987)...................................
Lionheart (1987).......................................
Julia and Julia (1988; Italian)...........................Paolo
A Soldier's Tale (1988; New Zealand)............. Saul
Made for HBO:
Mussolini (1985)......................... Vittorio Mussolini

C

CADMAN, JOSH
Films:
  Goin' All the Way (1981)................. Bronk
  1:05 - Buns, in the shower talking to "Boom
  Boom." *

CALI, JOSEPH
Films:
  Saturday Night Fever (1977)................Joey
  The Competition (1980)................Jerry Di Salvo
  The Lonely Lady (1983).............. Vincent Dacosta
  1:05 - Buns, near pool table and walking around
  the house with Pia Zadora. *
TV:
  Flatbush (1979) ....Presto Prestopopolos
  Today's F.B.I. (1981-82).....................Nick Frazier

CALLOW, SIMON
Films:
  A Room with a View (1986; British)
  .... The Reverend Mr. Beebe
  1:04 - Frontal nudity taking off clothes and
  jumping into pond. *
  1:05 - Nude running around with "Freddy" and
  "George Emerson" in the woods. Lots of
  frontal nudity. **
  The Good Father (1986)...................... Mark Varner
  Manifesto (1988).........................Police Chief Hunt

CARRADINE, DAVID
Other:
  Son of actor John Carradine.
  Brother of actors Robert and Keith Carradine.
Films:
  Macho Callahan (1970)... Colonel David Mountford
  Kung Fu (1971).......................... Kwai Chang Caine
  Boxcar Bertha (1972)..................... Big Bill Shelly
  0:54 - Buns, putting pants on after hearing a gun
  shot. *
  Mean Streets (1973)........................Drunk
  Death Race 2000 (1975)...................... Frankenstein
  Bound For Glory (1976)............... Woody Guthrie
  Cannonball (1976)..............."Cannonball" Buckman
  Gray Lady Down (1977)............... Captain Gates
  The Serpent's Egg (1977) .... Abel Rosenberg
  Thunder and Lightning (1977)........ Harley Thomas
  Death Sport (1978)................... Kaz Oshay
  Circle of Iron (1979)
  ....Chang-Sha/Blind Man/Monkey Man/Death
  Mr. Horn (1979).......................................
  Cloud Dancer (1980)......................Brad Randolph
  High Noon, Part Two (1980)...................................
  Americana (1981)............................Soldier
  Q (1982).......................Detective Shepard
  Lone Wolf McQuade (1983).......................Rawley

The Warrior and the Sorceress (1984)...............Kain
On the Line (1984; Spanish).........................Bryant
  0:11 - Buns, lying on a table, getting a massage by
  three women. *
Armed Response (1986)............................Jim Roth
P.O.W.: The Escape (1986)............ Colonel Cooper
Night Children (1989)............................
Tropical Snow (1989)............................Oskar
Crime Zone (1989)............................Jason
Bird on a Wire (1990)............................
Made for TV Movies:
  A Winner Never Quits (1986) ....Pete Gray
TV:
  Shane (1966)............................... Shane
  Kung Fu (1972-75).................... Kwai Chang Caine
  North and South (1985).................... Justin LaMotte

CARRADINE, KEITH
Other:
  Son of actor John Carradine.
  Brother of actors Robert and David Carradine.
Films:
  Kung Fu (1971)...............................
  McCabe and Mrs. Miller (1971)................. Cowboy
  Nashville (1975)................................... Tom Frank
  0:47 - Buns, sitting on floor after getting out of
  bed. *
  Lumiere (1976; French).......................David Foster
  The Duellists (1977)................................. D'Hubert
  Welcome to L.A. (1977).................... Carroll Barber
  Pretty Baby (1978)............................Bellocq
  An Almost Perfect Affair (1979)........................Hal
  Old Boyfriends (1979)............................ Wayne
  Southern Comfort (1981)............................Spencer
  Choose Me (1984) .... Mickey
  Maria's Lovers (1985) ....Clarence Butts
  Trouble in Mind (1986) ....Coop
  The Inquiry (1986)............................Titus Valerius
  The Moderns (1988)............................ Nick Hart
  1:17 - Buns, walking into bathroom with Linda
  Fiorentino. **
  Backfire (1988)................................. Clinton James
  Cold Feet (1989)................................ Monte
Miniseries:
  Chiefs (1983) ....Foxy Funderburke
Made for TV Movies:
  A Rumor of War (1980)...............................

CASEY, BERNIE
Other:
  Former football player.
Films:
  Boxcar Bertha (1972)......................Von Morton
  Cleopatra Jones (1973)...................... Reuben
  Big Mo (1973) ....
  The Man Who Fell to Earth (1976; British).Peters
  (Uncensored version)
  1:42 - Buns, getting out of swimming pool during
  a black and white dream sequence. *
  Sharkey's Machine (1981).............................Arch

Never Say Never Again (1983) .... Felix Leiter
Revenge of the Nerds (1984)............ U. N. Jefferson
Steele Justice (1987)..
Backfire (1988)................................... Clinton James
I'm Gonna Git You Sucka (1988) .... John Slade
Bill and Ted's Excellent Adventure (1989)
.... Mr. Ryan
Made for TV Movies:
  Brian's Song (1971)...
  Ring of Passion (1978)............................... Joe Louis
  Sophisticated Gents (1981)....................................
  Love is Not Enough (1978) ....
TV:
  Harris and Company (1979).................... Mike Harris
  Bay City Blues (1983)......................... Ozzie Peoples

CASEY, LAWRENCE
Films:
  The Student Nurses (1970)............. Dr. Jim Casper
    0:52 - Buns, walking to Karen Carlson to talk. **
TV:
  The Rat Patrol (1966-68).... Private Mark Hitchcock

CAZENOVE, CHRISTOPHER
Films:
  Eye of the Needle (1981)...
  Heat and Dust (1982)...................... Douglas Rivers
    1:25 - Buns lying in bed with Greta Scacchi under
    a mosquito net. **
  Until September (1984) ....
  Mata Hari (1985) .... Captain Karl Von Byerling
  Souvenir (1988) ....

CEINOS, JOSE ANTONIO
Films:
  Black Venus (1983)................................... Armand
    0:14 - Buns, making love with "Venus" in bed. *

CHAPMAN, GRAHAM
Films:
  And Now for Something Completely Different
    (1972)..
  Monty Python and the Holy Grail (1974)................
  Monty Python's Life of Brian (1979)
    .... Brian Called Brian
    1:03 - Buns before opening window, frontal nudity
    opening window and being surprised by his
    flock of followers, buns putting clothes on.
    Funniest full frontal nude scene. ***
  Monty Python's the Meaning of Life (1983)............
  The Secret Policemen's Other Ball (1982)..............
  Yellowbeard (1983)............................. Yellowbeard
  The Secret Policeman's Private Parts (1984)...........
TV:
  The Big Show (1980)................................... regular
  Monty Python's Flying Circus...................... regular

CLAY, NICHOLAS
Films:
  Love Spell (1979)...
  Lady Chatterley's Lover (1981; French/British)
    .... Oliver Mellors (The Gardener)
    0:21 - Frontal nudity washing himself while
    Sylvia Kristel watches from the trees. ***
  Excalibur (1981; British)........................... Lancelot
    1:13 - Buns, fighting with himself in a suit of
    armor. **
    1:31 - Brief buns, running into the woods after
    waking up. Long shot, hard to see. *
  Evil Under the Sun (1982) .... Patrick Redfern
  Adventures of Sherlock Holmes: The Resident
    Patient (1985) ....
  Lionheart (1987)..
Made for TV Movies:
  Poor Little Rich Girl: The Barbara Hutton Story
    (1987)................................. Prince Alexis Mdivani

COLEMAN, WARREN
Films:
  Young Einstein (1989; Australia)
    .... Lunatic Professor
    0:55 - Buns in Lunatic Asylum taking a shower. *
    0:56 - More buns standing in front of sink when
    "Marie Curie" comes to rescue "Einstein."
    (He's the one on the right.) *
    0:58 - Brief buns crowding into the shower stall
    with the other Asylum people. *

COLOMBY, SCOTT
Films:
  Porky's (1982; Canadian)................................. Brian
  Porky's Revenge (1985)............................... Brian
    0:16 - Buns, running around a swimming pool
    after the girls trick the boys into removing their
    swim suits. Hard to tell who is who. *
TV:
  Sons and Daughters (1974).............................. Stash
  Szysznyk (1977-78) .... Tony La Placa

CONLON, TIM
Films:
  Prom Night III (1989)................................... Alex
    0:15 - Brief buns and very brief balls when flag
    he's wearing falls off. *

CORBO, ROBERT
Films:
  Last Rites (1989).. Gino
    0:03 - Buns and frontal nudity in a room with
    Daphne Zuniga just before getting caught by
    another woman and shot. *

CORRI, NICK
Films:
Gotcha! (1985)...Manolo
Lawless Land (1988)......................................
Tropical Snow (1989)...................................Tavo
  0:11 - Buns in bed with Madeline Stowe. **
  0:44 - Buns, standing naked in police station. **
Slaves of New York (1989)...........Marley Mantello

COSTNER, KEVIN
Films:
Malibu Hot Summer (1981)..................John Logan
  a.k.a. Sizzle Beach.
Night Shift (1982) ....Frat Boy #1
American Flyers (1985)............................Marcus
Silverado (1985)....................................Jake
Fandango (1985) ....Gardner Barnes
Shadows Run Black (1986)...................Jimmy Scott
No Way Out (1987)..................................
The Untouchables (1987)...........................
Bull Durham (1988)...........................Crash Davis
Chasing Dreams (1989).............................
The Gunrunner (1989)........................Ted Beaubien
Field of Dreams (1989) ....Ray Kinsella
Revenge (1990)....................................Cochran
  1:14 - Brief buns getting out of bed and wrapping
  a sheet around himself. **

CRAMER, GRANT
Films:
New Year's Evil (1981)....................Derek Sullivan
Hardbodies (1984)...Scotty
  0:03 - Brief buns, getting out of bed after making
  love with "Kristi." *
Killer Klowns from Outer Space (1988)..........Mike

CRAWFORD, JOHNNY
Films:
Village of the Giants (1965)...........................Horsey
The Naked Ape (1972).......................................Lee
  (not available on video tape yet)
  Frontal nudity. **
The Great Texas Dynamite Chase (1976)..........Slim
Tilt (1979) ....Mickey
TV:
The Rifleman (1958-63)....................Mark McCain
Magazines:
Playboy (Dec 1973)..................."Sex Stars of 1973"
  Page 211: Frontal nudity.

CREW, CARL
Films:
Blood Diner (1987)........................George Tutman
  1:02 - Buns, mooning "Sheeba" through the
  passenger window of a van. *

CRUISE, TOM
Films:
Taps (1981)..David Shawn
Endless Love (1981)..Billy
Losin' It (1982)....................................Woody
The Outsiders (1983)..........................Steve Randle
All the Right Moves (1983)..............................Stef
  1:00 - Very brief frontal nudity getting undressed
  in his bedroom with Lea Thompson. **
Risky Business (1983).......................................Joel
Top Gun (1986) ....Maverick
Legend (1986).......................................Jack
The Color of Money (1986)........................Vincent
Cocktail (1988).........................Brian Hanagan
Rain Man (1988)............................Charlie Babbitt
Born on the Fourth of July (1989)..........Ron Kovic
Days of Thunder (1990).......................................

CULP, ROBERT
Films:
Sammy, The Way-Out Seal (1962) ....
Bob & Carol & Ted & Alice (1969)..................Bob
A Name for Evil (1973)........................ John Blake
  0:52 - Frontal nudity running through the woods
  with a woman. **
  1:07 - Buns, going skinny dipping. Lots of bun
  shots underwater. *
The Great Scout and Cathouse Thursday (1976)
  ....Jack Colby
Goldengirl (1979)..............................
Turk 182 (1985)......................... Mayor Tyler
Big Bad Mama II (1987)...................Daryl Pearson
Silent Night, Deadly Night III: Better Watch Out!
  (1989)...
TV:
I Spy (1965-68)..............................Kelly Robinson
The Greatest American Hero (1981-83)
  .... Bill Maxwell
Magazines:
Playboy (Mar 1973)......... "'Evil' Doings" pictorial
  Page 148: Side view naked.

CVETKOVIC, SVETOZAR
Films:
Montenegro (1981; British/Swedish)... Montenegro
  1:07 - Frontal nudity taking a shower while Susan
  Anspach watches. ***

D

DACUS, DON
Films:
Hair (1979).....................................Woof
  0:57 - Buns, taking off clothes and diving into
  pond with Treat Williams and "Woof." *

DALTREY, ROGER
Other:
Singer with "The Who" and on his own.
Films:
Tommy (1975; British)................................ Tommy
Lisztomania (1975; British).................. Franz Liszt
  0:01 - Brief buns standing on bed tying a sheet to
    make some pants. Dark, don't see his face. *
The Kids are Alright (1979; British) ....
McVicar (1980; British)...................... Tom McVicar

DANIELS, JEFF
Films:
Terms of Endearment (1983)................. Flap Horton
The Purple Rose of Cairo (1985)
    .... Tom Baxter/Gil Shepherd
Something Wild (1986)................... Charles Driggs
  0:16 - Buns, lying in bed after making love with
    Melanie Griffith. **
Heartburn (1986) .... Richard
Marie (1986)...................................... Eddie Sisk
The House on Carroll Street (1988)............ Cochran
Sweet Hearts Dance (1988)............... Sam Manners
Checking Out (1989) .... Ray Macklin

DAUGHTON, JAMES
Films:
Malibu Beach (1978)..................................... Bobby
  0:32 - Buns, running into the beach with his
    friends. *
The Beach Girls (1982)................................... Scott
  0:33 - Buns and very brief frontal nudity taking
    off clothes and running into the ocean. *
Blind Date (1984)...David
House of the Rising Sun (1987)..............................

DAVIES, STEPHEN
Films:
Inserts (1976)..Rex
  0:31 - Buns and balls making porno movie for
    Richard Dreyfus. **
Heart Beat (1979)................................ Bob Bendix
The Nest (1987) ....Homer
Made for HBO:
Philip Marlowe, Private Eye: Finger Man (1983)...

DAVIS, BRAD
Films:
Midnight Express (1978; British).........Billy Hayes
  0:12 - Buns, standing naked in front of guards
    after getting caught trying to smuggle drugs. *
A Small Circle of Friends (1980)....... Leo DaVinci
  1:22 - Brief buns, dropping his pants with several
    other guys for Army draft inspection. **
Querelle (1982)..Querella
Cold Steel (1987).......................Johnny Modine
Blood Ties (1987)..
Rosalie Goes Shopping (1990)................................

Miniseries:
Roots (1977).............................Ol' George Johnson
Chiefs (1983)...............................Chief Sonny Butts
Made for TV Movie:
A Rumor of War (1980)..

DAVIS, MAC
Other:
Singer.
Films:
North Dallas Forty (1979)........................Maxwell
  0:53 - Brief buns getting a can of Coke in the
    locker room. *
Cheaper to Keep Her (1980)................................
The Sting II (1983)..
TV:
The Mac Davis Show (1974-76).........................Host

DEMPSEY, PATRICK
Films:
Meatballs III (1987)..
In the Mood (1987)......................Sonny Wisecarver
Can't Buy Me Love (1987)................................
Some Girls (1988)..................................Michael
  0:34 - Brief frontal nudity, then buns running all
    around the house chasing Jennifer Connelly. *
Loverboy (1989)................................. Randy Bodek
Happy Together (1988)
    ....Christopher "Chris" Wooden
TV:
Fast Times (1986)............................. Mike Damone

DENNEY, DAVID
Films:
Under Cover (1987)............................ Hassie Pearl
  0:43 - Brief buns walking around boy's locker
    room wearing his jock strap. *

DEPP, JOHNNY
Films:
Private Resort (1985)...................................... Jack
  0:12 - Buns, in hotel room with Leslie
    Easterbrook. **
Platoon (1986)..Lerner
Cry Baby (1990)..
TV:
21 Jump Street (1987-).................. Tommy Hanson

DERN, BRUCE
Films:
Marnie (1964).......................................Sailor
Hush...Hush, Sweet Charlotte (1965; B&W)
    ....John Mayhew
The Wild Angels (1966).............Loser (Joey Kerns)
Rebel Rousers (1967)..............................J. J.
The St. Valentine's Day Massacre (1967) John May
The Trip (1967)..................................... John, Guru

Waterhole 3 (1967).. Deputy
Support Your Local Sheriff! (1969).........Joe Danby
Bloody Mama (1970)....................... Kevin Kirkman
Silent Running (1971) ....Lowell
The Cowboys (1972)............................... Long Hair
The Great Gatsby (1974).................. Tom Buchanan
The Laughing Policeman (1974)..............Leo Larsen
Twist (1972)... William
   0:45 - Buns, taking off his clothes and walking
   onto stage during a play. Long shot. *
Family Plot (1976).. Lumley
Black Sunday (1977)......................................Lander
The Driver (1978).............................. The Detective
Coming Home (1978)................. Captain Bob Hyde
   1:19 - Buns, taking off his clothes at the beach and
   running into the ocean. **
Tattoo (1981)... Karl Kinski
   1:36 - Buns, while making love with Maud Adams
   before she kills him. **
Harry Tracy (1982).............................. Harry Tracy
That Championship Season (1982)
   .... George Sitkoswki
On the Edge (1985)... Wes
   (Unrated version.)
   0:52 - Brief buns, seen from below while floating
   in a pond. *
1969 (1988) ....Cliff
The 'burbs (1989)...........................Mark Rumsfield
After Dark My Sweet (1990).....................................
Made for TV Movies:
   Toughlove (1987)...
TV:
   Stoney Burke (1962-63)........................E. J. Stocker

DIEHL, JOHN

Films:
   Angel (1984)................................. Crystal
      0:35 - Buns for a long time washing blood off
      himself. Dark, hard to see. *
   City Limits (1985).. Whitey
TV:
   Miami Vice (1984-89)..............Detective Larry Zito

DIMONE, JERRY

Films:
   Tomboy (1985)....................................... Randy Star
      0:59 - Buns, making love with Betsy Russell in the
      exercise room. **

DOUGLAS, KIRK

Other:
   Father of actor Michael Douglas.
Films:
   Out of the Past (1947; B&W).............. Whit Sterling
   Champion (1949; B&W)........................Midge Kelly
   A Letter to Three Wives (1949; B&W)
   .... George Phipps
   The Glass Menagerie (1950; B&W) ..Jim O'Connor
   Along the Great Divide (1951; B&W)..Len Merrick

Detective Story (1951; B&W).............. Jim McLeod
The Big Carnival (1951; B&W)........Charles Tatum
The Big Sky (1952; B&W).........................Deakins
20,000 Leagues Under the Sea (1954).......Ned Land
Man without a Star (1955)................. Dempsey Rae
Ulysses (1955; Italian)................................Ulysses
Gunfight at the O.K. Corral (1957)
   ....John H. "Doc" Holliday
Paths of Glory (1957; B&W)................ Colonel Dax
The Vikings (1958)..Einar
Last Train from Gun Hill (1959) ....Matt Morgan
Spartacus (1960)....................................... Spartacus
Seven Days in May (1964; B&W)
   .... Colonel Martin "Jiggs" Casey
In Harm's Way (1965; B&W)..........Paul Eddington
Cast a Giant Shadow (1966)
   ....Colonel Mickey Marcus
The Way West (1967)....Senator William J. Tadlock
The Brotherhood (1968)..................... Frank Ginetta
The Arrangement (1969) ....Eddie and Evangelos
There Was a Crooked Man (1970)
   .... Paris Pitman, Jr.
   0:11 - Brief upper half of buns leaving bedroom
   wearing only his gun belt. *
   1:09 - Brief buns and balls, jumping into a barrel
   to take a bath in prison. **
A Gunfight (1971) .... Will Tenneray
Once is Not Enough (1975).................Mike Wayne
The Fury (1978)...............................Peter Sandza
The Chosen (1978; Italian/British)................. Caine
The Villain (1979)..........................Cactus Jack
The Final Countdown (1980)
   ....Captain Matthew Yelland
Saturn 3 (1980)... Adam
   0:57 - Brief buns fighting with Harvey Keitel,
   more brief buns sitting down in bed with Farrah
   Fawcett. *
The Man from Snowy River (1982; Australian)
   ....Spur/Harrison
Eddie Macon's Run (1983).......................Marazack
Tough Guys (1986)............................. Archie Long
   Brief buns on top of railroad train mooning
   Charles Durning in a helicopter. Probably a
   body double. *
Made for TV Movies:
   Draw! (1984) ....

DOUGLAS, MICHAEL

Other:
   Son of actor Kirk Douglas.
Films:
   Napolean and Samantha (1972).....................Danny
   Coma (1978).................................Dr. Mark Bellows
   Running (1979)........................ Michael Andropolis
   The China Syndrome (1979) ....Richard Adams
   It's My Turn (1980)................................Ben Lewin
   The Star Chamber (1983)...................Steven Hardin
   Romancing the Stone (1984)..................Jack Colton
   A Chorus Line (1985)....................................Zack
   The Jewel of the Nile (1985) ....Jack Colton

Fatal Attraction (1987)................... Dan Gallagher
    0:16 - Brief buns pulling his pants down to make love with Glenn Close on the kitchen sink. **
    0:17 - Very brief buns falling into bed with Close. *
    0:22 - Brief buns, taking a shower. *
Wall Street (1987).............................Gordon Gekko
Black Rain (1989)...............................Nick Conklin
The War of the Roses (1989)................Oliver Rose
    1:36 - Almost buns, cleaning himself in the bidet.
TV:
The Streets of San Francisco (1972-76)
    ....Inspector Steve Keller

DOWNEY, JR., ROBERT
Films:
Firstborn (1984)..
Tuff Turf (1985)...............................Jimmy Parker
Weird Science (1985).................................Ian
Back to School (1986).....................................Derek
Less than Zero (1987)......................................Julian
    1:22 - Very brief blurry buns in bedroom with another guy when Andrew McCarthy discovers them.
Johnny Be Good (1988).......................Leo Wiggins
Rented Lips (1988)........................... Wolf Dangler
    0:01 - Buns, wearing fishnet shorts in S & M outfit during porno movie shoot. *
    0:22 - Buns, through shorts again during playback of the film. *
The Pick-Up Artist (1987).....................................
1969 (1988).. Ralph
Chances Are (1988)...............................Alex Finch
Air America (1990)......................................
TV:
Saturday Night Live (1985-86)..................... regular

DUKES, DAVID
Films:
The Wild Party (1975).....................James Morrison
A Little Romance (1979).............George De Marco
The First Deadly Sin (1980)...............Daniel Blank
Without a Trace (1983).......................Graham Selky
Cat on a Hot Tin Roof (1985)............................
The Men's Club (1986) ....Phillip
See You in the Morning (1989).......................Peter
Made for HBO:
The Hitchhiker: Remembering Melody......... Ted
    0:05 - Buns, taking a shower. *
Miniseries:
Beacon Hill (1975)...........................Robert Lassiter
79 Park Avenue (1977)......................Mike Koshko
The Winds of War (1983).......................Leslie Slote

DYE, CAMERON
Films:
Body Rock (1984).....................................
The Joy of Sex (1984)................................
Fraternity Vacation (1985)...................Joe Gillespie

Heated Vengeance (1987).......................................
Stranded (1987)..
Out of the Dark (1988)..............Kevin Silver/Bobo
    0:32 - Brief buns when "Kristi" yanks his underwear down while he is throwing a basketball. Don't see his face. *
Scenes From the Goldmine (1988)......Niles Dresden

E

EARHAR, KIRT
Films:
Summer Job (1988).. Tom
    0:30 - Buns in black G-string bikini when his swim trunks get ripped off. *
    0:43 - Buns in G-string underwear getting out of bed and going to the bathroom. *

EASTWOOD, CLINT
Other:
Former Mayor of Carmel, California.
Films:
For a Few Dollars More (1965; Italian)
    .... The Man With No Name
A Fistful of Dollars (1967; Italian)
    .... The Man With No Name
The Good, The Bad, and The Ugly
    (1967; Italian/Spanish).....................................Joe
Hang 'em High (1968) ....Jed Cooper
Coogan's Bluff (1968) ....Coogan
Where Eagles Dare (1968)
    ....Lieutenant Morris Schaffer
Kelly's Heroes (1970)...................................... Kelly
Two Mules for Sister Sara (1970)...................Hogan
The Beguiled (1971).......................... John McBurney
Play Misty for Me (1971)....................Dave Garland
Dirty Harry (1971) ....Harry Callahan
Joe Kidd (1972)...Joe Kidd
High Plains Drifter (1973) ....The Stranger
Magnum Force (1973) ....Harry Callahan
Thunderbolt and Lightfoot (1974)
    ....John "Thunderbolt" Doherty
The Eiger Sanction (1975).......... Jonathan Hemlock
The Outlaw Josey Wales (1976)...........Josey Wales
The Enforcer (1976)..........................Harry Callahan
The Gauntlet (1977).........................Ben Shockley
Every Which Way But Loose (1978).. Philo Beddoe
Escape from Alcatraz (1979)............ Frank Morris
    0:07 - Buns, walking down jail hallway with two guards, don't see his face, so probably a body double.
Any Which Way You Can (1980)....... Philo Beddoe
Bronco Billy (1980) ....Bronco Billy
Firefox (1982)....................................Mitchell Gant
Honkytonk Man (1982)..........................Red Stovall
Sudden Impact (1983)....................Harry Callahan
City Heat (1984).............................Lieutenant Speer

Tightrope (1984)....................................Wes Block
0:33 - Buns, on the bed on top of "Becky." Slow pan, red light, covered with sweat. *
Pale Rider (1985)..Preacher
Heartbreak Ridge (1986)............................Highway
The Dead Pool (1988) ....Harry Callahan
Pink Cadillac (1989)..........................Tommy Nowak
TV:
Rawhide (1959-66).............................. Rowdy Yates

ELWES, CARY
Films:
Another Country (1984; British)................Harcourt
The Bride (1985)..Josef
Lady Jane (1987; British)............. Guilford Dudley
1:19 - Brief buns, getting out of bed *
The Princess Bride (1987)...... Westley the Farmboy

ESTEVEZ, EMILIO
Other:
Son of actor Martin Sheen.
Brother of actor Charlie Sheen.
Films:
Tex (1982)...Johnny Collins
Nightmares (1983)...................................J. J.
The Outsiders (1983)...................Two-Bit Matthews
Repo Man (1984).......................................Otto
The Breakfast Club (1985)................ Andrew Clark
St. Elmo's Fire (1985)...................................Kirbo
That Was Then... This is Now (1985)
.... Mark Jennings
Maximum Overdrive (1986) ....Bill Robinson
Stakeout (1987)................................Bill Reimers
Wisdom (1986)...................................John Wisdom
Young Guns (1988)
.... William H. Booney (Billy the Kid)
1:19 - Brief buns standing up in the bathtub. *
Young Guns II (1990)
.... William H. Booney (Billy the Kid)
Men at Work (1990)..

F

FAHEY, JEFF
Films:
Psycho III (1986).. Duane
Backfire (1988)..Donnie
0:22 - Brief, partial buns taking a shower, then very brief, out of focus frontal nudity in shower when blood starts to gush out of the shower head. *
Split Decisions (1988)........................ Ray McGuinn
Impulse (1989)..Stan
True Blood (1989)....................Raymond Trueblood

FERRIS, LARRY
Films:
Penthouse Love Stories (1986)
................................"Ecstacize" segment
0:32 - Frontal nudity and buns with a woman in the shower. **

FIRTH, PETER
Films:
King Arthur, The Young Warlord (1975)................
Equus (1977).. Alan Strang
1:19 - Frontal nudity standing in a field with a horse. *
2:00 - Nude in loft above the horses in orange light with Jenny Agutter. Long scene. ***
Joseph Andrews (1977; British/French)
....Joseph Andrews
Tess (1979; British) .... Angel Clare
Lifeforce (1985)...Caine
Letter to Brezhnev (1986; British)...................Peter

FLETCHER, DEXTER
Films:
Revolution (1985)....................................Ned Dobb
Lionheart (1987)..
The Rachel Papers (1989).......... Charles Highway
0:58 - Very brief buns, jumping into bed with Ione Skye. *
Twisted Obsession (1989) ....Malcolm Greene

FORSTER, ROBERT
Films:
Justine (1969)..
Medium Cool (1969).. John
0:36 - Nude, running around the house frolicking with "Ruth." **
The Don is Dead (1973)..
The Death Squad (1974)..
Avalanche (1978)..
The Black Hole (1979)..
The Lady in Red (1979)..
Hollywood Harry (1985) ....Harry Petry
The Delta Force (1986)...............................Abdul
Walking the Edge (1986)..
Once a Hero (1988) ....
TV:
Banyon (1972-73)...........................Miles C. Banyon
Nakia (1974)...........................Deputy Nakia Parker

FREY, SAM
Films:
Nea (A Young Emmanuelle) (1978; French)...........
Little Drummer Girl (1984)............................Khalil
Black Widow (1986)..Paul
1:18 - Buns, walking into swimming pool. **
Miniseries:
War and Remembrance (1988)................ Rabinovitz

FRIELS, COLIN

Films:

Kangaroo (1986; Australian)......... Richard Somers
    1:08 - Buns, running into the ocean. **
    1:09 - Frontal nudity walking towards Judy Davis.
       Long shot, hard to see anything. *
Malcolm (1986; Australian).....................Malcolm
Warm Nights on a Slow Moving Train (1987)
....The Man
High Tide (1987; Australian)....................................
Ground Zero (1988; Australian).......Harvey Denton
Darkman (1990)..

G

GALLAGHER, PETER

Films:

The Idolmaker (1980).....................................Cesare
Summer Lovers (1982)..................Michael Pappas
    0:22 - Buns, running into the water after Valerie
       Quennessen. *
    0:54 - Frontal nudity getting ready to dive off a
       rock while Daryl Hannah and Quennessen
       watch. Long shot, hard to see anything. *
Dreamchild (1986; British).....................Jack Dolan
Made for TV Movies:
Skag (1980)..John Skagska

GANIOS, TONY

Films:

Continental Divide (1981)...........................Possum
Porky's (1981) .... Meat
Porky's II: The Next Day (1983).................... Meat
Porky's Revenge (1985)......................... Meat
    0:16 - Buns, running around a swimming pool
       after the girls trick the boys into removing their
       swim suits. Hard to tell who is who. *

GARCIA, ANDRES

Films:

Dance of Death (1971)...
Tintorera (1977)......................................Miguel
    0:41 - Very brief frontal nudity in boat kitchen
       with Susan George and "Steve." *
    0:42 - Nude, picking up George and throwing her
       overboard. **
Day of the Assassin (1979)..

GARRISON, BOB

Films:

Hollywood Hot Tubs 2 - Educating Crystal
    (1989)................................... Billy "Derrick" Dare
    0:53 - Buns, running up to hot dog stand. *

GERE, RICHARD

Films:

Strike Force (1975)...
Looking for Mr. Goodbar (1977)...................Tony
    1:00 - Buns, on Diane Keaton's floor doing
       pushups, then running around in his jock strap.
       **
Blood Brothers (1978) ....
Days of Heaven (1978).. Bill
American Gigolo (1980)............................Julian
    0:39 - Buns and frontal nudity, but a long shot, so
       it's hard to see anything. **
An Officer and a Gentleman (1982)........Zack Mayo
Beyond the Limit (1983)............ Dr. Eduardo Plarr
    0:21 - Buns. *
Breathless (1983)....................................Jesse
    0:11 - Frontal nudity dancing and singing in the
       shower. Kind of steamy and hard to see. **
    0:52 - Buns, taking his pants off to get into the
       shower with Valerie Kaprisky, then more buns
       in bed. Very brief frontal nudity. Dark, hard to
       see. **
    0:53 - Very, very brief top of lower frontal nudity
       popping up when Kaprisky gets out of bed. *
The Cotton Club (1984) ....Dixie Dwyer
King David (1985) .... David
Power (1986)...................................Pete St. John
No Mercy (1986).............................Eddie Jilletie
Miles From Home (1988).................Frank Roberts
Internal Affairs (1990) ....Dennis Peck
Pretty Woman (1990)........................Edward Lewis

GIBSON, MEL

Films:

Summer City (1976)...
Mad Max (1979)...Max
Tim (1979) ....Tim Melville
The Road Warrior (1981)...............................Max
Attack Force Z (1981)...
Gallipoli (1981) ....Frank Dunne
    1:18 - Buns, running into the water. (He's the guy
       on the left.) **
The Year of Living Dangerously (1983)
    .... Guy Hamilton
The Bounty (1984) ....Fletcher Christian
Mrs. Soffel (1984)..............................Ed Biddle
The River (1984).............................. Tom Garvey
Mad Max Beyond Thunderdome (1985) ....Max
Lethal Weapon (1986)................. Martin Riggs
    0:06 - Buns, getting out of bed and walking to the
       refrigerator. ***
Tequila Sunrise (1988)...........................McKussie
Lethal Weapon II (1989)......................Martin Riggs
Bird on a Wire (1990)...
Air America (1990)..

GLENN, SCOTT

Films:
The Baby Maker (1970)................................... Tad
   1:30 - Buns in bed with "Charlotte." *
Fighting Mad (1976) ....
Urban Cowboy (1980).......................................
The Challenge (1982)...................................Rich
Personal Best (1982) ....
The Keep (1983)..
The Right Stuff (1983)......................................
Wild Geese II (1985)..........................John Haddad
Silverado (1985).. Emmett
Man on Fire (1987) ....
Off Limits (1988)........... Colonel Dexter Armstrong
Verne Miller (1988)............................ Verne Miller
Miss Firecracker (1989).............................Mac Sam

GOLDAN, WOLF

Films:
Melody in Love (1978)............................... Octavio
   1:14 - Buns making love in bed with "Rachel" and
   "Angela." *

GOLDBLUM, JEFF

Films:
Death Wish (1974).......................................Freak 1
   0:10 - Brief buns standing with pants down in
   living room raping a woman with his two punk
   friends. *
Between the Lines (1977) ....Max
Invasion of the Body Snatchers (1978)
   ....Jack Bellicec
Thank God It's Friday (1978) .... Tony
Rehearsal for Murder (1982)............................
The Big Chill (1983) ....Michael
The Right Stuff (1983)............................ Recruiter
Threshold (1983; Canadian)................Aldo Gehring
The Adventures of Buckaroo Banzai (1984)
   .... New Jersey
Into the Night (1985)...................................Ed Okin
Silverado (1985).. Slick
Transylvania 6-5000 (1985)................Jack Harrison
The Fly (1986).....................................Seth Brundle
Beyond Therapy (1987).............................Bruce
Vibes (1988).....................................Nick Deezy
Earth Girls are Easy (1989)............................Mac
Twisted Obsession (1989)....................Daniel Gillis
Faerie Tale Theatre:
   The Three Little Pigs (1984) ....
TV:
   Tenspeed and Brown Shoe (1980)
   .... Lionel "Brown Shoe" Whitney

GONZALES, JOE

Films:
Brain Damage (1987)...................... Guy in Shower
   0:54 - Buns, taking a shower. *

GOODEVE, GRANT

Films:
Take Two (1988)........ Barry Griffith/Frank Bentley
   0:31 - Buns, in bed with Robin Mattson. *
   0:46 - Buns, getting into bed with Mattson again.
   ***
License to Drive (1988)...
TV:
Eight is Enough (1977-81)...............David Bradford
Dynasty (1983)....................................Chris Deegan
Northern Exposure (1990)................................Rick

GRANT, DAVID

Films:
American Flyers (1985)................................ David
   0:05 - Brief buns and very, very brief penis taking
   off shorts and walking to bathroom. *
Bat 21 (1988)...Ross Carver

GRANT, RICHARD E.

Films:
Withnail and I (1987)..
How to Get Ahead in Advertising (1988)... Bagley
   0:19 - Brief buns wearing apron in kitchen all
   covered with food. Brief buns again talking
   with Rachel Ward at top of stairs. *

GRAVES, RUPERT

Films:
A Room with a View (1986; British)
   ....Freddy Honeychurch
   1:05 - Nude running around with "Mr. Beebe" and
   "George Emerson" in the woods. Lots of
   frontal nudity. **
Maurice (1987)..
A Handful of Dust (1988)......................John Beaver

GREENQUIST, BRAD

Films:
The Bedroom Window (1987)...............Henderson
   0:35 - Buns, turning off the light while Steve
   Guttenberg spies on him. *

GREGORY, ANDRE

Films:
My Dinner with Andre (1981)........................Andre
Protocol (1984)............................ Nawaf Al Kabeer
The Mosquito Coast (1986)................Mr. Spellgood
Street Smart (1987)..
Some Girls (1988)................................. Mr. D'Arc
   1:24 - Buns, standing in the study looking at a
   book. Very brief frontal nudity when he turns
   around to sit at his desk. *
The Last Temptation of Christ (1988)
   ....John the Baptist

GUEST, CHRISTOPHER

Films:
Death Wish (1974)..........................Patrolman Reilly
Girlfriends (1978)...Eric
   1:04 - Buns, running after Melanie Mayron in her
   apartment, then hugging her. *
The Long Riders (1980)..
Heartbeeps (1981)..Calvin
This is Spinal Tap (1984)......................Nigel Tufnel
Little Shop of Horrors (1986)............... 1st Customer
Beyond Therapy (1987)...
Sticky Fingers (1988)..Sam
TV:
Saturday Night Live (1984-85)...................... regular

GUNNER, ROBERT

Films:
Planet of the Apes (1968)............................Landon
   0:26 - Very brief buns taking off clothes to go
   skinny dipping. (Guy on the left.) *

GUTTENBERG, STEVE

Films:
The Chicken Chronicles (1977)..........David Kessler
Can't Stop the Music (1980)..................Jack Morell
Diner (1982)...Eddie
The Man Who Wasn't There (1983)..Sam Cooper
   0:54 - Buns, dropping his pants in office with
   three other men. ***
   1:46 - Brief buns kissing "Cindy" during wedding
   ceremony. *
Police Academy (1984) ....Carey Mahoney
Police Academy II (1985)................Carey Mahoney
Cocoon (1985) ....Jack Bonner
Bad Medicine (1985)...................................Jeff Marx
Police Academy III (1986)...............Carey Mahoney
Short Circuit (1986).........................Newton Crosby
The Bedroom Window (1987).........Terry Lambert
   0:05 - Buns, getting out of bed and walking to the
   bathroom. **
Police Academy IV (1987)..............Carey Mahoney
Amazon Women on the Moon (1987)....Jerry Stone
Three Men and a Baby (1987).......................Michael
Surrender (1988)..Marty
Cocoon, The Return (1988)...................Jack Bonner
High Spirits (1988)...Jack
Made for TV Movies:
The Day After (1983)...............................Stephen
TV:
Billy (1979)...Billy Fisher
No Soap, Radio (1982)......................................Roger

H

HALL, MICHAEL KEYES

Films:
Blackout (1989).....................................Alan Boyle
   1:19 - Buns and balls viewed from the rear while
   stabbing "Richard Boyle" in bed. *

HAMLIN, HARRY

Films:
Blue Skies Again (1983).............................. Sandy
Clash of the Titans (1981).............................Perseus
King of the Mountain (1981) ....Steve
Making Love (1982).. Bart
Movie Movie (1978)............................Joey Popchik
Made for HBO:
Laguna Heat (1987)...................... Tom Shephard
   0:50 - Buns, walking into the ocean with
   Catherine Hicks. *
Made for Cable:
Dinner At Eight (1989)......................Larry Renault
Made for Showtime:
Deceptions (1990)............................... Nick Gentry
Miniseries:
Master of the Game (1984)............ Tony Blackwell
TV:
Studs Lonigan (1979)......................Studs Lonigan
L.A. Law (1986-) ....Michael Kuzak

HANEY, DARYL

Films:
Daddy's Boys (1988)..............................Jimmy
   0:17 - Buns, getting undressed in room with
   "Christie." *

HARRIS, ED

Films:
Knightriders (1981).............................. Billy Davis
   0:01 - Buns, kneeling in the woods. Long shot,
   hard to see. *
   1:51 - Upper half of buns, standing in a pond
   doing something with a stick. *
Borderline (1980).....................................Hotchkiss
The Right Stuff (1983)...........................John Glenn
Under Fire (1983)..Gates
Places in the Heart (1984)................. Wayne Lomax
A Flash of Green (1984).........................Jimmy Wing
Swing Shift (1984) ....Jack Walsh
Code Name: Emerald (1985)................... Gus Lang
Sweet Dreams (1985)........................Charlie Dick
Alamo Bay (1985).. Shang
Walker (1987) .... William Walker
To Kill a Priest (1988) ....Stefan
Jackknife (1989)...Dave
The Abyss (1989)................. Virgil "Bud" Brigman

HARRIS, JIM

Films:
Squeeze Play (1979)...Wes
   0:39 - Buns, tied up in a room while people
   walking by look in through open door. **
Waitress! (1982).. Jerry

HARRIS, RICHARD

Films:
The Bible (1966) ....Cain
Hawaii (1960)................................Rafer Hoxworth
Camelot (1967)......................................King Arthur
Cromwell (1970; British)..........................Cromwell
The Molly Maguires (1970)
   ....James McParlan/McKenna
A Man Called Horse (1970)........ Lord John Morgan
99 and 44/100% Dead (1974)..............Harry Crown
Juggernaut (1974; British)..............................Fallon
Return of a Man Called Horse (1976)..John Morgan
Robin and Marian (1976)................... King Richard
The Cassandra Crossing (1977; British)
   .... Chamberlain
Orca (1977) ....Captain Nolan
The Wild Geese (1978; British).......... Rafer Janders
The Last Word (1980)........................Danny Travis
Tarzan, The Ape Man (1981) .... Parker
Your Ticket is No Longer Valid (1982)........Jason
   1:19 - Buns, taking off robe and sitting on the
   floor. *
Triumphs of a Man Called Horse
   (1983; U.S./Mexican) ....Man Called Horse
Highpoint (1984; Canadian)................ Louis Kinney
Martin's Day (1985; Canadian)................................
Wetherby (1985) .... Sir Thomas

HARTMAN, BILLY

Films:
Slaughter High (1986).....................................Frank
   1:00 - Brief buns in bed with "Stella." *

HASSELHOFF, DAVID

Other:
Husband of actress Catherine Hickland.
Films:
Revenge of the Cheerleaders (1976)............. Boner
   0:28 - Buns in shower room scene. *
   0:30 - Frontal nudity in shower room scene while
   soaping "Gail." ***
Starcrash (1979)..
Made for TV Movies:
The Cartier Affair (1985) ....
TV:
The Young and the Restless.........................Snapper
Knightrider (1982-86) ....Michael Knight
Baywatch (1989-90)..

HAUER, RUTGER

Films:
Turkish Delight (1974; Holland) ....Erik
   0:01 - Brief nude walking around his apartment
   talking to a woman he has just picked up. ***
   0:04 - Buns, in bed (covered with a sheet), then
   very brief frontal nudity throwing another girl
   out. *
   0:36 - Frontal nudity getting up to answer the door
   with flowers. **
   1:12 - Frontal nudity lying in bed depressed. **
   1:16 - Buns, making love with "Olga" in bed. **
Katie's Passion (1978)..................................Dandy
   1:12 - Buns seen through torn pants while he is
   kneeling on the floor. *
   1:15 - Brief frontal nudity getting out of bed. **
Soldier of Orange (1979; Holland)....................Erik
Chanel Solitaire (1981)...............Etienne De Balsan
Nighthawks (1981)...................................... Wulfgar
Inside the Third Reich (1982)..................................
Blade Runner (1982).............................. Roy Batty
The Osterman Weekend (1983)............John Tanner
Eureka (1983; British) ......Claude Maillot Van Horn
A Breed Apart (1984)...........................Jim Malden
Ladyhawke (1985).....................Etienne of Navarre
Flesh + Blood (1985)...................................Martin
   1:35 - Buns, in a jock strap running up stairs after
   everybody throws their clothes into the fire. *
The Hitcher (1986)................................ John Ryder
Wanted: Dead or Alive (1987) ....Nick Randall
The Blood of Heroes (1989)...........................Sallow
Blind Fury (1990)...

HAYES, ALAN

Films:
Friday the 13th, Part IV-The Final Chapter
   (1984)...Paul
   0:26 - Brief buns, swinging on a rope jumping into
   the lake. *
Neon Maniacs (1985)...

HEARD, JOHN

Films:
First Love (1977)..David
Between the Lines (1977)..............................Harry
   1:17 - Buns, putting his pants on. **
Chilly Scenes of Winter (1979)................... Charles
Heat Beat (1979)..............................Jack Kerouac
Cutter's Way (1981)............................. Alex Cutter
Cat People (1982)............................... Oliver Yates
   1:50 - Buns, making love with Nastassja Kinski in
   bed in a cabin. *
C.H.U.D. (1984)..............................George Cooper
After Hours (1985)..............................Bartender
Heaven Help Us (1985) ....Brother Timothy
The Trip to Bountiful (1986)................Ludie Watts
The Milagro Beanfield War (1988)...Charlie Bloom
Beaches (1988).......................................John Pierce
Big (1988)...Paul

Made for TV Movies:
Necessity (1988)..Charlie
Cross of Fire (1989)...................... Steve Stephenson

HEHN, SASCHA
Films:
Melody in Love (1978)....................................Alain
1:08 - Buns with "Melody" outside. Very brief
erect penis under covers. **
1:16 - Buns, twice while making love with
"Melody" near an erupting volcano. *

HERRIER, MARK
Films:
Porky's II: The Next Day (1983; Canadian).... Billy
Porky's Revenge (1985)................................ Billy
0:16 - Buns, running around a swimming pool
after the girls trick the boys into removing their
swim suits. Hard to tell who is who. *

HESTON, CHARLTON
Films:
The Ten Commandments (1956).............................
Ben-Hur (1959)...
El Cid (1961)...
Planet of the Apes (1968)................. George Taylor
0:26 - Buns, seen through a waterfall and while
walking on rocks. Long shots. *
1:04 - Buns standing in middle of the room when
the apes tear his loin cloth off. *
The Omega Man (1971)...............................Neville
Three Musketeers (1973).....................................
Soylent Green (1973)...
Earthquake (1974) ....
Airport 1975 (1975)...
Midway (1976)..
Gray Lady Down (1977)......................................
Mother Lode (1982)...
TV:
The Colbys (1985-86)...........................Jason Colby

HEWITT, MARTIN
Films:
Endless Love (1981)....................................,. David
0:22 - Buns when seen in front of fireplace in
living room with Brooke Shields. Long shot. *
0:27 - Very brief buns in bedroom when Shields
closes the door. Another long shot. *
0:28 - Buns, jumping into bed with Shields. **
0:38 - Buns, lying on top of Shields in bed. *
Out of Control (1984).......................................Keith
Killer Party (1986).. Blake
Alien Predator (1987)...
TV:
The Family Tree (1983)......................Sam Benjamin

HINTON, DARBY
Films:
Malibu Express (1984)......................Cody Abilene
0:08 - Brief buns, taking a shower on his boat. *
TV:
Daniel Boone (1964-70).........................Israel Boone

HOFFMAN, DUSTIN
Films:
The Graduate (1967).......................... Ben Braddock
John and Mary (1969)......................................John
Midnight Cowboy (1969)...............................Ratso
Little Big Man (1970)............................ Jack Crabb
Straw Dogs (1972).......................... David
Papillon (1973)..............................Louis Dega
Lenny (1974; B&W)...........................Lenny Bruce
1:49 - Pubic hair (no penis) lying dead on the
floor.
All the President's Men (1976)..........Carl Bernstein
Marathon Man (1976).................................... Babe
1:09 - Buns, getting out of the bathtub and putting
some pajamas on while someone lurks outside
the bathroom. **
Straight Time (1978)...........................Max Dembo
0:38 - Very, very brief tip of penis in jail shower
scene after getting sprayed by guard. Don't
really see anything.
Agatha (1979)................................ Wally Stanton
Kramer vs. Kramer (1979).....................Ted Kramer
Tootsie (1982)................................. Michael
Ishtar (1987)................................Chuck Clarke
Rain Man (1988)......................Raymond Babbitt
Family Business (1989)....................................... Vito
Made for TV Movies:
Death of a Salesman (1985)....................................

HOFFMAN, THOM
Films:
The Fourth Man (1984)........................... Herman
1:00 - Frontal nudity on cross when "Gerard" pulls
his red trunks down. Long shot. *
1:10 - Nude in bathroom when "Gerard" comes in.
**
1:11 - Buns making love on bed with "Christine"
while "Gerard" watches through keyhole. ***
Shadowman (1988)..

HOLBROOK, HAL
Other:
Husband of actress Dixie Carter.
Films:
Wild in the Streets (1968).........Senator John Fergus
The People Next Door (1970)..........David Hoffman
Magnum Force (1973) ....Lieutenant Briggs
The Girl from Petrovka (1974) .... Joe
0:40 - Brief buns, getting out of bed, putting on a
robe and talking to Goldie Hawn. *
Midway (1976)..........Commander Joseph Rochefort
The Fog (1980)..Malone

The Kidnapping of the President (1980; Canadian)..
Creepshow (1982) ....Henry Northrup
The Star Chamber (1983)...........Benjamin Caulfield
Wall Street (1987) .... Lou Mannheim
The Unholy (1988).................... Archbishop Mosley
Miniseries:
The Blue and the Gray (1982)
.................................President Abraham Lincoln
Made for TV Movies:
A Killing in a Small Town (1990).......Dr. Beardsley
TV:
The Senator (1970-71).............Senator Hayes Stowe

HOPPER, DENNIS
Films:
Rebel Without a Cause (1955)..........................Goon
Giant (1956)...............................Jordan Benedict III
The Trip (1967)..Max
Easy Rider (1969)...Billy
Tracks (1976) ....Sgt. Jack Falen
0:58 - Frontal nudity running through the train.
Long scene. **
Mad Dog Morgan (1976)...................Daniel Morgan
The American Friend (1977)...........................Ripley
Wild Times (1980) ....
Let It Rock (1981)..
King of the Mountain (1981)..............................Cal
The Osterman Weekend (1983)...Richard Tremayne
Rumble Fish (1983; B&W).............................Father
My Science Project (1985)....................Bob Roberts
Blue Velvet (1986)................................Frank Booth
Hoosiers (1986)....................................... Shooter
The Texas Chainsaw Massacre 2 (1986)
.................................Lieutenant "Lefty" Enright
River's Edge (1987).. Feck
Running Out of Luck (1987).............Video Director
Straight to Hell (1987)..
Black Widow (1987) .... Ben
Colors (1988)...
Riders of the Storm (1988)........................... Captain
Backtrack (1989)...
Chattahoochee (1990) ....
Magazines:
Playboy (Dec 1976)........... "The Year in Sex 1976"
Page 141: Frontal nudity running through train

HOWARD, ADAM COLEMAN
Films:
Quiet Cool (1986)...............................Joshua Greer
Slaves of New York (1989)............................ Stash
1:15 - Buns, putting on his pants and silhouette of
penis. Dark, hard to see. *

HOWELL, C. THOMAS
Films:
The Outsiders (1983) ....Ponyboy Curtis
Red Dawn (1984)...Robert
Tank (1984) .... Billy
Grandview, U.S.A. (1984)................... Tim Pearson
Secret Admirer (1985) ....Michael Ryan
The Hitcher (1986)................................Jim Halsey
Soul Man (1986)................................Mark Watson
A Tiger's Tale (1988).....................Bubber Drumm
0:38 - Upper half of buns getting undressed in
bedroom while Ann-Margret changes in the
bathroom. *
Made for TV Movies:
Into the Homeland (1987)..
TV:
Two Marriages (1983-84)...................Scott Morgan

HOWES, DOUGIE
Films:
Salome's Last Dance (1987).......... Phoney Salome
1:05 - Very brief frontal nudity at the end of a
dance routine when you think he's a female
Salome. *

HUGHES, BRENDAN
Films:
Return to Horror High (1987)................................
Stranded (1987) ....
To Die For (1988)...............................Vlad Tepish
1:13 - Buns, making love with "Kate." *

HURT, JOHN
Films:
10 Rillington Place (1971)........Timothy John Evans
The Ghoul (1975)..................................... Tom
The Disappearance (1977).......................................
Midnight Express (1978)...................................Max
The Shout (1979)........................... Anthony Fielding
Alien (1979)..Kane
The Elephant Man (1980; B&W)........John Merrick
Heaven's Gate (1980)................................ Irvine
East of Elephant Rock (1981)..............................
Night Crossing (1981) .... Peter Strelzyks
Partners (1982)..Kerwin
The Osterman Weekend (1983). Lawrence Fassett
0:01 - Buns, getting out of bed and walking to the
shower. *
1984 (1984)........................... Winston Smith
1:11 - Buns, walking from the bed to the window
next to Suzanna Hamilton. *
Champions (1984) .... Bob Champion
The Hit (1984) ....Braddock
Jake Speed (1986)...................................... Sid
From the Hip (1987)..
Aria (1988)................................... The Actor
White Mischief (1988)...............................Colville
Scandal (1989)...................................Stephen Ward

HURT, WILLIAM

Films:

Altered States (1980)...........................Eddie Jessup
    0:46 - Brief pubic hair twice when Charles Haid
    and Bob Balaban help him out of isolation tank.
    0:54 - Very brief buns, standing in the shower
    when he starts transforming. More buns
    standing near door and walking to bed. *
Body Heat (1981)....................................Ned Racine
Eyewitness (1981) ....Daryll Deever
The Big Chill (1983)....................................Nick
Gorky Park (1983) ....Arkady Renko
Kiss of the Spider Woman (1985) ....Luis Molina
Children of a Lesser God (1986) ....James Leeds
Broadcast News (1987)........................ Tom Grunik
    0:59 - Brief buns getting up from bed after making
    love with "Jennifer." Shadow of semi-erect
    penis on the wall when she notices it. **
A Time of Destiny (1988)..............................Martin
The Accidental Tourist (1988).......................Macon

I

IPALÉ, AHARON

Films:

Too Hot to Handle (1975).....Dominco de la Torres
    0:39 - Buns, in bed with Cheri Caffaro. Dark,
    hard to see. *

IRONSIDE, MICHAEL

Films:

American Nightmare (1981)....................Sgt. Skylar
Visiting Hours (1982)....................................
Cross Country (1983)....................................
The Falcon and the Snowman (1985).......FBI Agent
Jo Jo Dancer, Your Life is Calling (1986)...............
Top Gun (1986) ....Dick Wetherly
Extreme Prejudice (1987)..................................
Hello Mary Lou: Prom Night II (1987)...................
Nowhere to Hide (1987)...................................
Watchers (1988)...
Office Party (1988).......................................
Destiny to Order (1989)...................................
Mind Field (1990)........................ Kellen O'Reilley
    0:40 - Buns, supposedly of his, but you never see
    his face. *

Miniseries:

V: The Final Battle (1984)..................... Ham Tyler

TV:

V (1984-85) .... Ham Tyler

J

JAGGER, MICK

Other:

    Singer with "The Rolling Stones."
    Husband of actress/model Jerry Hall.

Films:

Performance (1970)...
Burden of Dreams (1982)...................................
Running Out of Luck (1985)..................... Himself
    0:42 - Brief buns in mirror in room with Rae
    Dawn Chong lying in bed. Another buns long
    shot in bed on top of Chong. *
At Close Range (1986).....................................

JANSSEN, DAVID

Films:

To Hell and Back (1955)...................Lieutenant Lee
The Green Berets (1968).............George Beckworth
The Shoes of a Fisherman (1968)....... George Faber
Marooned (1969)............................Ted Dougherty
Macho Callahan (1970).....Diego "Macho" Callahan
Once is Not Enough (1975)......................Tom Colt
    1:22 - Buns, taking off clothes and walking to the
    bathroom. *
Two-Minute Warning (1976)..........................Steve
Golden Rendezvous (1977)............Charles Conway

TV:

Richard Diamond, Private Detective (1957-60)
    ....Richard Diamond
The Fugitive (1963-67)............. Dr. Richard Kimble
O'Hara, U.S. Treasury (1971-72)...........Jim O'Hara
Harry-O (1974-76) ....Harry Orwell
Centennial (1978-79) ....Paul Garrett

JENKINS, JOHN

Films:

Patti Rocks (1988) ....Eddie
    1:07 - Buns, making love with "Patti" in bed. *

JETER, MICHAEL

Films:

Hair (1979)................................Woodrow Sheldon
    1:06 - Buns in front of Army guys. *
The Money Pit (1986)...................................... Arnie
Dead Bang (1989)................................. Dr. Krantz
Tango & Cash (1989)...................................Skinner

JOHNSON, DON

Films:

The Harrad Experiment (1973)........ Stanley Cole
    0:18 - Brief frontal nudity after getting out of the
    shower while Laurie Walters watches. **
The Magic Garden of Stanley Sweetheart (1970)
    ....Stanley Sweetheart
Zachariah (1971).. Matthew

Return to Macon County (1975) .... Harley McKay
A Boy and His Dog (1976) Vic
Melanie (1982)... Carl
Miami Vice (1984)........................... Sonny Crockett
Cease Fire (1985)...................... Tim Murphy
Sweet Hearts Dance (1988).................... Wiley Boon
Dead Bang (1989) .... Detective Jerry Beck
Made for TV Movies:
First You Cry (1978)...................................
The Rebels (1979) ....
The Revenge of the Stepford Wives (1980).............
From Here to Eternity (1980)
.... Jefferson Davis Prewitt
Beulah Land (1980)...................................
The Long Hot Summer (1985)................................
TV:
Miami Vice (1984-89)...................... Sonny Crockett

JOHNSON, JOSEPH ALAN
Films:
Berserker (1987)..
Iced (1988).. Alex
0:46 - Brief buns in bathtub reminiscing about
making love with a girl. *

JONES, SAM J.
Films:
10 (1979)............................ David Hanley
Flash Gordon (1980) .... Flash Gordon
My Chauffeur (1986)........................ Battle
0:44 - Buns, running around the park naked. **
Jane and the Lost City (1987) .... "Jungle" Jack
Silent Assassins (1988) .... Sam Kettle
Driving Force (1990)........................ Steve
TV:
Code Red (1981-82)........................... Chris Rorchek
Highwayman (1987-88)...................... Highwayman

JONES, TOMMY LEE
Films:
Jackson County Jail (1976) .... Coley Blake
Rolling Thunder (1977)................... Johnny Vohden
The Betsy (1978)................................ Angelo Perino
The Eyes of Laura Mars (1978)............ John Neville
Coal Miner's Daughter (1980)
.... Doolittle "Mooney" Lynn
Back Roads (1981)................................ Elmore Pratt
The Executioner's Song (1982; European version)
.... Gary Gillmore
0:48 - Buns, walking to kitchen after hitting
Rosanna Arquette. **
Nate and Hayes (1983)............. Captain Bully Hayes
The River Rat (1984).. Billy
Cat on a Hot Tin Roof (1985) ....
Yuri Nosenko, KGB (1986)................................
Black Moon Rising (1986)................................ Quint
Stormy Monday (1988)................... Cosmo
Fire Birds (1990) ....

Made for HBO:
The Park Is Mine (1985)................................ Mitch
Made for Showtime:
Gotham (1988)................................ Eddie Mallard
0:50 - Buns, walking over to Virginia Madsen.
Dark, hard to see anything. *
Miniseries:
Lonesome Dove (1989) .... Woodrow F. Call
Made for TV Movies:
The Amazing Howard Hughes (1977).....................

JONES, TYRONNE GRANDERSON
Films:
Angel III: The Final Chapter (1988)....L.A. Pimp
0:32 - Buns, standing in alley after "Angel"
pushes him out of the car. **
Twins (1988)... Mover #2
Harlem Nights (1989).................................. Gambler

JULIA, RAUL
Films:
Panic in Needle Park (1971).......................... Marco
The Eyes of Laura Mars (1978)....... Michael Reisler
The Escape Artist (1982)..................... Stu Quinones
Tempest (1982)................................ Kalibanos
One From the Heart (1983)........................... Ray
1:20 - Very brief buns getting out of bed with Teri
Garr when Frederic Forrest crashes through the
ceiling. *
Compromising Positions (1985).......... David Suarez
Kiss of the Spider Woman (1985; U.S./Brazilian)
.... Valentin
The Morning After (1986)............... Joaquin Manero
Moon Over Parador (1988)....... Roberto Strausmann
Tequila Sunrise (1988)............................ Escalante
Trading Hearts (1988)............................ Vinnie
Presumed Innocent (1990)................................
Made for TV Movies:
Florida Straits (1986)................................

K

KANTOR, RICHARD
Films:
Out of Control (1984)..................................... Gary
0:29 - Buns, pulling his underwear down during a
game of strip spin the bottle. *
TV:
Finder of Lost Loves (1984-85)......... Brian Fletcher

KAY, NORMAN
Films:
Lonely Hearts (1981)..................................... Peter
   1:03 - Buns, getting out of bed. Very brief frontal
   nudity. *
Man of Flowers (1984)...
Frenchman's Farm (1986) ....

KEITEL, HARVEY
Films:
Mean Streets (1973)...Charlie
Alice Doesn't Live Here Anymore (1975).........Ben
Taxi Driver (1976)..Sport
The Duellists (1977)..Feraud
Welcome to L.A. (1977)...........................Ken Hood
Fingers (1977)..Julie
Blue Collar (1978)..Jerry
Death Watch (1980)..Roddy
Saturn 3 (1980) ....Benson
The Border (1982) ....Cat
Exposed (1983)..Rivas
Falling in Love (1984)...............................Ed Lasky
The Inquiry (1986)...................... Pontius Pilate
Off Beat (1986)............................ Bank Robber
Wise Guys (1986).................................. Bobby Dilea
The Men's Club (1986)................................... Sully
   1:22 - Buns, getting up off the bed to talk to
   "Allison."
Blindside (1988)... Gruber
The Last Temptation of Christ (1988).............Judas
The January Man (1988)..................... Frank Starkey

KEITH, DAVID
Films:
The Rose (1979)...............................~........Mal
The Great Santini (1979) .... Red Pettus
Brubaker (1980)...........................Larry Lee Bullen
Back Roads (1981)...Mason
Take This Job and Shove It (1981)...... Harry Meade
An Officer and a Gentleman (1982)....... Sid Worley
Independence Day (1983)......................Jack Parker
The Lords of Discipline (1983) ....Will
Firestarter (1984) ....Andrew McGee
Gulag (1985)..................................... Mickey Almon
   1:26 - Buns, standing outside with Malcolm
   McDowell in the snow being hassled by guards.
   **
White of the Eye (1988)............................Paul White
Heartbreak Hotel (1988)......................Elvis Presley
Made for TV Movies:
Are You in the House Alone? (1978)......................
Friendly Fire (1978)...
The Golden Moment (1980).............................
Guts & Glory (1989)...
TV:
Co-ed Fever (1979)... Tuck

KELLER, TODD
Films:
Penthouse Love Stories (1986)
   ...."Service Station" segment
   0:11 - Brief frontal nudity in bedroom with a
   woman. **

KERWIN, BRIAN
Films:
Nickel Mountain (1985)............................... George
Murphy's Romance (1985). Bobbie Jack Moriarity
   0:55 - Brief buns walking into the bathroom. **
King Kong Lives (1986)....................Hank Mitchell
Torch Song Trilogy (1988)................................Ed
Miniseries:
The Blue and the Gray (1982)............ Malachi Hale
TV:
The Chisholms (1979)...................Gideon Chisholm
Lobo (1979-81).............. Deputy Birdwell Hawkins

KIME, JEFFREY
Films:
Quartet (1981; British/French)...................... James
   0:49 - Nude, posing with two women for the
   pornographer. **

KING, PERRY
Films:
The Lords of Flatbush (1974)...........................Chico
Mandingo (1975)...................................Hammond
   0:17 - Frontal nudity walking to bed to make love
   with "Dite." **
The Wild Party (1975) ....Dale Sword
Lipstick (1976)...............................Steve Edison
Andy Warhol's Bad (1977)................................L-T
A Different Story (1979)................................Albert
   1:33 - Buns, through shower door, and then brief
   buns getting out of the shower to talk to Meg
   Foster. *
Search and Destroy (1981)..................... Kip Moore
Class of 1984 (1982)...................................... Andy
The Killing Hour (1984).......................................
Miniseries:
Captains and the Kings (1976)............Rory Armagh
Aspen (1977)....................................Lee Bishop
The Last Convertible (1979)................ Russ Currier
Made for TV Movies:
Cracker Factory (1979)....................................
Love's Savage Fury (1979).................................
Shakedown on Sunset Strip (1988).........................
TV:
The Quest (1982) ....Dan Underwood
Riptide (1984-86)....................................Cody Allen

KINGSLEY, BEN

Films:
Gandhi (1982) .... Mahatma Gandhi
(Academy Award for Best Actor.)
Betrayal (1983; British) .... Robert
Harem (1985; French) ....
Turtle Diary (1986; British) .... William Snow
Maurice (1987; British) .... Lasker Jones
Without a Clue (1988) .... Dr. Watson
Pascali's Island (1988; British) .... Basil Pascali
Made for HBO:
Murderers Among Us: The Simon Wiesenthal
Story (1989) .... Simon Wiesenthal
0:27 - Buns and brief frontal nudity standing in
and leaving a line in a concentration camp. **

KIRBY, BRUNO

Other:
a.k.a. B. Kirby, Jr.
Films:
The Harrad Experiment (1973) .... Harry Schacht
0:41 - Brief frontal nudity, getting into the
swimming pool with "Beth," Don Johnson and
Laurie Walters. *
Between the Lines (1977) .... David
Borderline (1980) .... Jimmy Fante
Where the Buffalo Roam (1980) .... Marty Lewis
Modern Romance (1981) .... Jay
Birdy (1985) .... Renaldi
When Harry Met Sally... (1989) .... Jess
Bert Rigby, You're a Fool (1989) ...... Kyle DeForest
We're No Angels (1989) .... Deputy
TV:
The Super (1972) .... Anthony Girelli

KNIGHT, WYATT

Films:
Porky's (1981) .... Tommy Turner
Porky's II: The Next Day (1983) .... Tommy Turner
Porky's Revenge (1985) .... Tommy Turner
0:16 - Buns, running around a swimming pool
after the girls trick the boys into removing their
swim suits. Hard to tell who is who. *
0:54 - Buns, getting his underwear pulled down
while trying to escape from a motel room from
"Balbricker." *

KOLOGIE, RON

Films:
Iced (1988) .... Carl
0:39 - Buns, in bathroom snorting cocaine. *

KOTTO, YAPHET

Films:
The Liberation of L. B. Jones (1970)
.... Sonny Boy Mosby
Man and Boy (1971) .... Nate Hodges
Across 110th Street (1972) .... Det. Lt. Pople
Live and Let Die (1973) .... Kananga
Shark's Treasure (1975) .... Ben
Drum (1976) .... Blaise
1:02 - Buns, getting hung upside down in barn and
spanked along with Ken Norton. *
Blue Collar (1978) .... Smokey
Alien (1979) .... Parker
Brubaker (1980) .... Dickie Coombes
Fighting Back (1982) ....
The Star Chamber (1983) .... Det. Harry Lowes
Warning Sign (1985) .... Major Connolly
Eye of the Tiger (1986) .... J. B. Deveraux
Pretty Kill (1987) .... Harris
The Jigsaw Murders (1988) .... Dr. Fillmore
Tripwire (1989) .... Lee Pitt
Made for HBO:
The Park Is Mine (1985) .... Eubanks
Made for TV Movies:
Raid on Entebbe (1977) ....
For Love and Honor (1983)
.... Platoon Sgt. James "China" Bell

KRABBÉ, JEROEN

Films:
The Fourth Man (1984) .... Gerard
0:03 - Frontal nudity getting out of bed and
walking down the stairs. ***
0:26 - Frontal nudity drying himself off and
getting into bed. **
0:33 - Buns, getting out of bed. *

KRISTOFFERSON, KRIS

Films:
Blume in Love (1973) .... Elmo
Pat Garrett and Billy the Kid (1973) . Billy the Kid
0:37 - Buns, getting into bed with a girl after
Harry Dean Stanton gets out. Long shot, hard to
see. *
Bring Me the Head of Alfredo Garcia (1974) ... Paco
Alice Doesn't Live Here Anymore (1975) ...... David
A Star is Born (1976) .... Johnny
The Man Who Fell From Grace with the Sea (1976)
.... Jim Cameron
Vigilante Force (1976) .... Aaron Arnold
Semi-Tough (1977) .... Shake Tiller
Convoy (1978) .... Rubber Duck
Heaven's Gate (1980) .... Averill
Rollover (1981) .... Hub Smith
Act of Passion (1984) ....
Flashpoint (1984) ....
Songwriter (1984) .... Blackie Buck
Trouble in Mind (1986) .... Hawk
Big Top Pee Wee (1988) .... Mace Montana
Millennium (1990) .... Bill Smith

Made for HBO:
    The Tracker (1988).............................Noble Adams
Magazines:
    Playboy (Jul 1976)........."Kris and Sarah" pictorial
    Pages 126: Buns, in pictorial with Sarah Miles for
    the film "The Man Who Fell From Grace with
    the Sea."

KUHLMAN, RON
Films:
    Omega Syndrome (1986)..
    Shadow Play (1986)..............................John Crown
    1:06 - Buns, standing and holding Dee Wallace in
    his arms. *
Made for TV Movies:
    The Brady Brides (1981).........Phillip Covington III

L

LACKEY, SKIP
Films:
    Once Bitten (1985)... Russ
    1:11 - Brief buns in the school showers trying to
    see if "Mark" got bitten by a vampire. *

LAMBERT, CHRISTOPHER
Other:
    Husband of actress Diane Lane.
Films:
    Greystoke: The Legend of Tarzan, Lord of the Apes
    (1984)...
    Subway (1985; French)....................................Fred
    Highlander (1986)......................Conner MacLeod
    1:30 - Buns making love with Roxanne Hart. *
    The Sicilian (1987).....................Salvatore Giullano

LANG, PERRY
Films:
    1941 (1979)...
    Alligator (1980)...Kelly
    The Hearse (1980)..Paul
    Body and Soul (1981)................... Charles Golphin
    O'Hara's Wife (1982)...........................Rob O'Hara
    T.A.G.: The Assassination Game (1982).................
    Spring Break (1983) .... Adam
    0:27 - Brief buns opening his towel in the shower,
    mooning his three friends. *
    Sahara (1984)..Andy
    Jocks (1986)..
TV:
    Bay City Blues (1983) ....Frenchy Nuckles

LATTANZI, MATT
Other:
    Husband of singer/actress Olivia Newton-John.
Films:
    My Tutor (1983)...............................Bobby Chrystal
    Rich and Famous (1981)................... The Boy, Jim
    1:10 - Buns, making love with Jacqueline Bisset.
    ***
    That's Life! (1986)...............................Larry Bartlet
    Roxanne (1987)...Trent
    Blueberry Hill (1988)...
    Catch Me If You Can (1989) ....

LAUGHLIN, JOHN
Films:
    Crimes of Passion (1984)............................... Grady
    0:58 - Buns, getting dressed after having sex with
    Kathleen Turner viewed through peep hole by
    Anthony Hopkins. *
    The Hills Have Eyes, Part II (1985)...................Hulk
    Space Rage (1987) ....
    Midnight Crossing (1988).................Jeffrey Schubb
TV:
    The White Shadow (1980-81)........... Paddy Falahey

LAWRENCE, BRUNO
Films:
    Smash Palace (1981; New Zealand).......... Al Shaw
    0:39 - Buns in bed after arguing, then making up
    with "Jacqui." ***
    Warlords of the 21st Century (1982) ....Willie
    The Quiet Earth (1985; New Zealand)
    ....Zac Hobson
    0:02 - Brief frontal nudity lying on the bed. **
    0:04 - Brief nude getting back into bed. **
    0:33 - Very brief frontal nudity jumping out of the
    ocean. Blurry, hard to see anything. *
    1:01 - Frontal nudity during flashback lying in
    bed. **
    An Indecent Obsession (1985)..............Matt Sawyer
    Rikky & Pete (1988; Australian) ....Sonny

LEE, MARK
Films:
    Gallipoli (1981) ....Archy Hamilton
    1:18 - Buns, running into the water with Mel
    Gibson. (Mark is the guy on the right.) **
    Emma's War (1986).........................John Davidson

LEIBMAN, RON
Films:
    Where's Poppa? (1970)...............Sidney Hocheiser
    0:45 - Buns running across the street, then in front
    of door in hall, then brief buns leaving George
    Segal's apartment. *
TV:
    Kaz (1978-79).....................Martin "Kaz" Kazinsky

LEMMON, JACK

Films:

It Should Happen to You (1954; B&W)
....Pete Sheppard
Mister Roberts (1955) ..Ens. Frank Thurlowe Pulver
Fire Down Below (1957)................................. Tony
Bell, Book and Candle (1959)...........Nicky Holroyd
Some Like it Hot (1959; B&W)...........Jerry/Daphne
The Apartment (1960; B&W) .... C. C. Baxter
The Wackiest Ship in the Army (1961)
....Lt. Rip Crandall
Days of Wine and Roses (1962; B&W)...............Joe
Irma La Douce (1963) .... Nestor
Good Neighbor Sam (1964) .... Sam Bissel
The Great Race (1965) ....Professor Fate
The Fortune Cookie (1966; B&W) ......Harry Hinkle
Luv (1967)................................Harry Berlin
The Odd Couple (1968)........................Felix Ungar
The April Fools (1969)................. Howard Brubaker
The Out of Towners (1970)......... George Kellerman
Avanti! (1972)..........................Wendell Armbruster
Buns, standing up in bathtub talking to Juliet
Mills. *
Save the Tiger (1973)........................... Harry Stoner
The Front Page (1974).......................Hildy Johnson
The Prisoner of Second Avenue (1975)............. Mel
Airport '77 (1977)............................Don Gallagher
The China Syndrome (1979).................Jack Godell
Buddy Buddy (1981)....................... Victor Clooney
Tribute (1981; Canadian)............Scottie Templeton
Missing (1982).. Ed Horman
Mass Appeal (1984)...
Macaroni (1985; Italian)....................Robert Traven
That's Life! (1986)........................Harvey Fairchild
TV:
That Wonderful Guy (1949-50).....................Harold
Toni Twin Time (1950)............................... host
Ad Libbers (1951)...regular
Heaven for Betsy (1952) .... Pete Bell

LENNON, JOHN

Other:
Singer with "The Beatles" and on his own.
Films:
How I Won the War (1967).....................................
Imagine: John Lennon (1988)...................Himself
0:43 - Nude in B&W photos from his White
Album. *
0:57 - Brief frontal nudity of album cover again
during interview.

LEWIS, DANIEL DAY

Films:
The Bounty (1984).. Fryer
My Beautiful Laundrette (1985) ....Johnny
A Room with a View (1986; British)...... Cecil Vyse
The Unbearable Lightness of Being (1988). Thomas

Stars and Bars (1988)...................Henderson Bores
1:21 - Brief buns, trying to open the window.
Very, very brief frontal nudity when he throws
the statue out the window. Blurry and dark.
More buns, climbing out the window and into a
trash dumpster. **

LHERMITTE, THIERRY

Films:
Next Year if All Goes Well (French; 1983). Maxime
My Best Friend's Girl (Le Femme du Mon Ami)
(1984; French)..............................Pascal Saulnier
Until September (1984)......... Xavier de la Pérouse
0:43 - Buns, after making love with Karen Allen.
**
0:53 - Almost frontal nudity getting out of
bathtub.

LINDON, VINCENT

Films:
Half Moon Street (1986).............................. Sonny
1:04 - Buns, getting out of bed with Sigourney
Weaver. *

LIPTON, ROBERT

Films:
Lethal Woman (1988)........... Major Derek Johnson
1:05 - Brief buns in the water on the beach with
Shannon Tweed. *
TV:
The Survivors (1969-70)..................................... Tom

LITHGOW, JOHN

Films:
Obsession (1976) ....Robert La Salle
The Big Fix (1978)...........................Sam Sebastian
All That Jazz (1979)........................Lucas Sergeant
Rich Kids (1979)................................. Paul Philips
Blow Out (1981)..Burke
The World According to Garp (1982) ....Roberta
Terms of Endearment (1983)...................Sam Burns
Twilight Zone - The Movie (1983)........................
The Adventures of Buckaroo Banzai, Across the 8th
Dimension (1984)..
Footloose (1984)...........................Reverend Moore
The Glitter Dome (1984) ....
2010 (1984)...Curnow
Santa Claus (1985)................................Bozo
The Manhattan Project (1987).......John Mathewson
Harry and the Henderson (1987) ....George
Distant Thunder (1988)...
Out Cold (1988)..
Made for HBO:
Traveling Man (1989)...
0:48 - Brief buns, trying to get the VCR away
from "Mona" in her living room. *
Miniseries:
The Day After (1983).......................................

LLOYD, CHRISTOPHER
Films:
Goin' South (1978).....................................Towfield
Schizoid (1980).. Gilbert
Mr. Mom (1983)..Larry
To Be or Not To Be (1983)................. Capt. Schultz
The Adventures of Buckaroo Banzai, Across the 8th
  Dimension (1984)......................................
Star Trek III: The Search for Spock (1984)....Kruge
Clue (1985)......................................Professor Plum
Back to the Future (1985)........... Dr. Emmett Brown
Miracles (1986)..
Walk Like a Man (1987)...............................
Track 29 (1988; British) ....Henry Henry
  0:34 - Very brief side view of his buns lying in the
    hospital getting spanked by Sandra Bernhard. *
Eight Men Out (1988)..............................Bill Burns
Who Framed Roger Rabbit (1988)....... Judge Doom
Back to the Future, Part II (1989)
  ....Dr. Emmett Brown
Back to the Future, Part III (1990)
  ....Dr. Emmett Brown
TV:
Taxi (1979-83)............."Reverend Jim" Ignatowski

LOWE, ROB
Films:
The Outsiders (1983)...................................Sodapop
Class (1983)... Skip
The Hotel New Hampshire (1984)....................John
Oxford Blues (1984)......................................
St. Elmo's Fire (1985) .... Billy
About Last Night... (1986)............................Danny
  0:52 - Buns and almost frontal nudity when he
    opens the refrigerator with Demi Moore. **
Youngblood (1986)....................Dean Youngblood
  0:16 - Buns, standing in hallway in jockstrap and
    walking around while Cindy Gibb watches. ***
Square Dance (1987) ....Rory
  a.k.a. Home is Where the Heart Is
Illegally Yours (1988)......................... Richard Dice
Masquerade (1988).............................. Tim Whalen
  0:04 - Buns, getting up from bed with Kim
    Cattrall. ***
  0:30 - Buns, making love with Meg Tilly in bed.
    **
Bad Influence (1990)......................................Alex
  1:27 - Buns, going into the bathroom. ***
Video Tapes:
Rob Lowe's Home Video (1989)................ himself
  Rob's video tape of his sexual tryst with two
    teenage girls can be purchased from Midnight
    Blue. The address is located at the end of this
    book.
TV:
A New Kind of Family (1979-80) .... Tony Flanagan

LUTHER, MICHAEL
Films:
Malibu Beach (1978)... Paul

0:32 - Buns, running into the ocean with his
  friends. *

LYNCH, JOHN
Films:
Cal (1984; Irish).. Cal
  1:20 - Buns, getting into bed with Helen Mirren. *

M

MacLACHLAN, KYLE
Films:
Dune (1984) ....Paul Atreides/Maudib
Blue Velvet (1986)..Jeffrey
  0:41 - Buns and very brief frontal nudity running
    to closet in Isabella Rossellini's apartment. **
The Hidden (1987)..........................Lloyd Gallagher
TV:
Twin Peaks (1990-)............................Dale Cooper

MADSEN, MICHAEL
Made for HBO:
The Hitchhiker: Man at the Window
  ....John Hampton
  0:09 - Buns, making love with his wife on the
    couch. **
TV:
Our Family Honor (1985-86).............. Augie Danzig

MAIDEN, TONY
Films:
Spaced Out (1980; British)............................ Willy
  0:38 - Buns, getting examined by "Cosia." *

MARGOTTA, MICHAEL
Films:
Drive, He Said (1972).................................. Gabriel
  1:21 - Running nude across the grass and up some
    stairs, then trashing a biology room at the
    university. **
Can She Bake a Cherry Pie? (1983)................Larry

MARINARO, ED
Films:
Dead Aim (1987)............Malcolm "Mace" Douglas
  0:52 - Buns in bed making love with "Amber."
    Dark, hard to see. *
TV:
Laverne & Shirley (1980-81)....... Sonny St. Jacques
Hill Street Blues (1981-87)......... Officer Joe Coffey

MARIN, RICHARD "CHEECH"
Films:
Up in Smoke (1978).........................Pedro De Pacas
Cheech & Chong's Next Movie (1980)........Himself
Cheech & Chong's Nice Dreams (1981)...Himself
   0:57 - Brief buns climbing over railing to escape
   "Donna's" husband, "Animal." *
Things Are Tough All Over (1982).....Mr. Slyman
   0:21 - Buns in the laundromat dryer. *
It Came from Hollywood (1982)............................
Still Smokin' (1983)...................................Himself
Yellowbeard (1983)................................El Segundo
The Corsican Brothers (1984)....................................
Get Out of My Room (1985).......................................
After Hours (1985)..Neil
Echo Park (1986)...Sid
The Shrimp on the Barbie (1990)............................

MARKLE, STEPHEN
Films:
Perfect Timing (1984)....................................Harry
   0:58 - Buns, making love with "Lacy." *

MARTINEZ, NACHO
Films:
Matador (1986; Spain)......................Diego Montes
   0:29 - Buns making love with "Eva" in bed. ***

MATHERS, JAMES
Films:
Aria (1988)..Boy Lover
   1:00 - Brief dark outline of frontal nudity in hotel
   room with his girlfriend. *
   1:02 - Frontal nudity under water in the bathtub
   with his girlfriend. *

MATHESON, TIM
Films:
Magnum Force (1973)....................................Sweet
Animal House (1978)..............Eric "Otter" Stratton
   0:08 - Buns, changing clothes in his bedroom
   while talking to "Boone." *
1941 (1979)..Birkhead
A Little Sex (1982)......................Michael Donovan
To Be or Not To Be (1983).......Lieutenant Sobinski
Impulse (1984)...Stuart
   0:17 - Buns, getting out of bed with Meg Tilly. *
Up the Creek (1984)..
Fletch (1985)....................................Alan Stanwyk
Speed Zone (1989)...Jack
Made for TV Movies:
Listen To Your Heart (1983)................................
Obsessed with a Married Woman (1985).................
Warm Hearts, Cold Feet (1987)..............................
TV:
Window on Main Street (1961-62).....Roddy Miller
Jonny Quest (1964-65)............Jonny Quest's voice
The Virginian (1969-70).....................Jim Horn

Bonanza (1972-73)....................................Griff King
The Quest (1976).........................Quentin Beaudine
Tucker's Witch (1982-83)....................Rick Tucker
Just in Time (1988)......................................

MAURY, DERREL
Films:
Massacre at Central High (1976)..................David
   0:32 - Buns, romping around in the ocean with
   Kimberly Beck. Dark, long shot. Hard to see
   anything. *
TV:
Apple Pie (1978)...........................Junior Hollyhock
Joanie Loves Chachi (1982-83)......................Mario

McCARTHY, ANDREW
Films:
Class (1983)...
Heaven Help Us (1985)....................Michael Dunn
   Brief buns by the swimming pool.
St. Elmo's Fire (1985)....................................Kevin
Pretty in Pink (1986)..................Blane McDonough
Less than Zero (1987).......................................Clay
   0:03 - Very brief buns getting out of bed to answer
   the phone. *
Mannequin (1987).......................................
Fresh Horses (1988)..............................Matt Larkin
Kansas (1988)..................................Wade Corey
Weekend at Bernie's (1989)................Larry Wilson

McDOWELL, MALCOLM
Other:
Husband of actress Mary Steenburgen.
Films:
If... (1969)..Mick Travers
Long Ago Tomorrow (1970)...........Bruce Pritchard
A Clockwork Orange (1971)..............................Alex
O Lucky Man! (1973)...........................Mick Travis
Voyage of the Damned (1976)..............Max Gunter
Time After Time (1979)................Herbert G. Wells
Caligula (1980)..Caligula
Cat People (1982)............................Paul Gollier
   1:06 - Buns lying on the bathroom floor. *
Blue Thunder (1983)................................Cochrane
Get Crazy (1983)..Reggie
Gulag (1985).....................................Englishman
   1:26 - Buns, standing outside with David Keith in
   the snow being hassled by guards. **
The Caller (1989)..
Class of 1999 (1990)....................................
Faerie Tale Theatre:
Little Red Riding Hood (1983)............................

McGANN, PAUL

Films:
Withnail and I (1987; British).................... Marwood
The Rainbow (1989)................. Anton Skrebensky
   1:30 - Buns, opening a bottle of wine in room with
   Sammi Davis. **
   1:44 - Very brief frontal nudity and buns running
   up a hill with Amanda Donohoe. *

McKEON, DOUG

Films:
On Golden Pond (1981)............................ Billy Ray
Night Crossing (1982) .... Frank Strelzyks
Mischief (1985).. Jonathan
   0:56 - Brief buns, putting on his underwear after
   making love with Kelly Preston. *
Turnaround .... Ben
TV:
Centennial (1978-79)........................ Philip Wendell
Big Shamus, Little Shamus (1979).......... Max Sutter

MEADOWS, STEPHEN

Films:
Night Eyes (1990) ....Michael Vincent
   0:27 - Buns and balls in bed with Tanya Roberts
   while Andrew Stevens watches on monitor. *

MITCHELL, MARK

Films:
The Outing (1987)...............................Mike Daley
   1:08 - Buns when his friend gets killed, then very
   brief frontal nudity sitting up. *

MODINE, MATTHEW

Films:
Streamers (1983)................................ Billy
Private School (1983)..............................Jim
Mrs. Soffel (1984) ....
Birdy (1985)... Birdy
   1:25 - Buns, squatting on the end of his bed,
   thinking he's a bird. *
   1:29 - Buns, sitting on the bed. Longer shot. *
   1:33 - Buns, walking around naked in his
   bedroom. **
   1:42 - Buns, waking up when Nicholas Cage
   comes into his bedroom. *
Baby It's You (1983)...Steve
The Hotel New Hampshire (1984)........... Chip Dove
Visionquest (1985)............................ Louden Swain
   1:29 - Very brief buns taking off underwear to get
   weighed for wrestling match. *
Full Metal Jacket (1987)......................Private Joker
Orphans (1987).. Treat
Married to the Mob (1988).................Mike Downey
Gross Anatomy (1989)............................Joe Slovac

MOIR, RICHARD

Films:
Heatwave (1983).. Steven
An Indecent Obsession (1985)..........Luce Daggett
   0:31 - Buns at the beach with his pals. Don't see
   his face. *

MONAHAN, DAN

Films:
Porky's (1981)...Pee Wee
Porky's II: The Next Day (1983)..............Pee Wee
Up the Creek (1984)..
Porky's Revenge (1985)..........................Pee Wee
   0:02 - Buns, when his graduation gown gets
   accidentally torn off during a dream. *
   0:16 - Buns, running around a swimming pool
   after the girls trick the boys into removing their
   swim suits. Hard to tell who is who. *
   1:27 - Buns, getting his graduation gown town off.
   *
The Prince of Pennsylvania (1988)
....Tommy Rutherford

MONTGOMERY, CHAD

Films:
Nightmare at Shadow Woods........................ Gregg
   0:52 - Brief buns, making love with "Andrea" on
   diving board just before getting killed. *

MOORE, DUDLEY

Films:
The Wrong Box (1966; British)..........John Finsbury
Bedazzled (1968; British)....................Stanley Moon
30 is a Dangerous Age, Cynthia (1968; British)
....Rupert Street
Foul Play (1978)............................... Stanley Tibbets
10 (1979).......................................George Webber
   0:47 - Buns, at neighbor's party just before Julie
   Andrews sees him through a telescope. *
Wholly Moses! (1980) ....Harvey/Herschel
Arthur (1981) .... Arthur Bach
Six Weeks (1982)........................... Patrick Dalton
Lovesick (1983) .... Saul Benjamin
Romantic Comedy (1983)................................ Jason
Best Defense (1984)..
Micki & Maude (1984)........................ Rob Salinger
Unfaithfully Yours (1984) ....
Santa Claus (1985)... Patch
Like Father, Like Son (1987).....Dr. Jack Hammond
Arthur 2 On the Rocks (1988)............... Arthur Bach

MOORE, KENNY

Films:

Personal Best (1982)............................ Denny Stiles
1:31 - Nude, getting out of bed and going to the bathroom. **

MOORE, MICHAEL J.

Films:

Border Heat (1988)................................ J. C. Ryan
0:14 - Buns, taking off his clothes and getting into Jacuzzi with Darlanne Fluegel. *

MORROW, ROB

Films:

Private Resort (1985).. Ben
0:36 - Brief buns standing with Hillary Shapiro worshiping Baba Rama. *
0:39 - Buns getting caught naked by "Mrs. Rawlins," then more buns, running through the halls. **

TV:

Northern Exposure (1990)............... Joel Fleischman

MOSES, MARK

Films:

Someone to Watch Over Me (1987) ..Win Hockings

Made for HBO:

The Tracker (1988)............................. Tom Adams
0:35 - Buns, getting out of the river after washing himself, then getting hassled by some bandits. **

MULKEY, CHRIS

Films:

Patti Rocks (1988)..Billy
0:24 - Nude in restroom with "Eddie," undressing and putting on underwear. **

Heartbreak Hotel (1988)........................Steve Ayres

N

NASSI, JOE

Films:

Sorority House Massacre (1987)................... Craig
0:50 - Buns, running away from the killer that has just killed his girlfriend "Tracy" in a tepee. *

NAUGHTON, DAVID

Films:

Separate Ways (1979) ....Jerry Lansing
Midnight Madness (1980)............................... Adam

An American Werewolf in London (1981)
....David Kessler
0:24 - Very brief buns running naked through the woods. *
0:58 - Buns, during his transformation into a werewolf. *
1:09 - Brief frontal nudity and buns waking up in wolf cage at the zoo. Long shot, hard to see anything. More buns, running around the zoo. **

Hot Dog... The Movie (1984)................................
Not for Publication (1984)................................
Separate Vacations (1986)................ Richard Moore
The Boy in Blue (1986) .... Bill
Kidnapped (1986)......................... Vince McCarthy
The Sleeping Car (1990)..................... Jason McCree

TV:

Makin' It (1979)................................Billy Manucci
At Ease (1983)......................... P.F.C. Tony Baker
My Sister Sam (1986-89).............................Jack

NICHOLSON, JACK

Films:

The Little Shop of Horrors (1960; B&W)
.... Wilbur Force
Studs Lonigan (1960; B&W)............... Weary Reilly
The Raven (1963)............................Rexford Bedlo
The Terror (1963)...................... Lt. Andre Duvalier
Ride in the Whirlwind (1965)...........................Wes
Rebel Rousers (1967)................................Bunny
Easy Rider (1969).............................George Hanson
Five Easy Pieces (1970)..................... Robert Dupea
On a Clear Day, You Can See Forever (1970)
....Tad Pringle
Carnal Knowledge (1971)........................... Jonathan
A Safe Place (1971)....................................... Mitch
The Last Detail (1973)............................ Buddusky
Chinatown (1974)..J.J.
1:21 - Brief buns, putting pants on getting out of bed after making love with Faye Dunaway. *
Tommy (1975)..Specialist
One Flew Over the Cuckoo's Next (1975)
.... R. P. McMurphy
The Passenger (1975; Italian)............... David Locke
The Last Tycoon (1976)............................. Brimmer
The Missouri Breaks (1976)................... Tom Logan
The Shooting (1976)......................... Billy Spear
Goin' South (1978)............................. Henry Moon
The Shining (1980)........................Jack Torrance
The Postman Always Rings Twice (1981)
.... Frank Chambers
Reds (1981)................................... Eugene O'Neill
The Border (1982) ....Charlie
Terms of Endearment (1983)........ Garrett Breedlove
Prizzi's Honor (1985)................... Charley Partanna
2:05 - Buns, sort of. Viewed from above while he takes a shower. Hard to see anything.
Heartburn (1986) ....Mark
Ironweed (1987)........................Francis Phelan
The Witches of Eastwick (1987) ...Daryl Van Horne
Batman (1989) ....Jack Napier/The Joker
The Two Jakes (1990) ....

NOCK, THOMAS
Films:
Alpine Fire (1985; Switzerland)........................Bob
0:08 - Brief buns, outside taking a bath. *

NOLAN, TOM
Films:
School Spirit (1985)............................. Billy Batson
0:17 - Buns in open hospital smock by car. More
buns while running up stairs. *
TV:
Jessie (1984).....................................Officer Hubbell

NOLTE, NICK
Films:
Return to Macon County (1975)...........Bo Hollinger
The Deep (1977)................................ David Sanders
Who'll Stop the Rain (1978)..............................Ray
North Dallas Forty (1979)...............Phillip Elliott
0:49 - Brief buns, pulling down underwear to get
into whirlpool bath in locker room. *
Heart Beat (1979)................................Neal Cassady
48 Hours (1982)..Jack Cates
Cannery Row (1982)...................................Doc
Under Fire (1983)...................................Russel Price
Teachers (1984) ....
Grace Quigley (1985)......................................
Down and Out in Beverly Hills (1986)
.... Jerry Baskin
0:28 - Buns, changing out of wet clothes on patio.
*
1:37 - Brief buns, changing out of Santa Claus
outfit. *
Weeds (1987)......................................Lee Umstetter
0:51 - Buns, getting out of bed and putting his
pants on. **
Three Fugitives (1989).........................Daniel Lucas
New York Stories (1989).....................Lionel Dobie
Another 48 Hrs. (1990)............................Jack Cates
Miniseries:
Rich Man, Poor Man - Book I (1979). Tom Jordache

NORTON, KEN
Other:
Former boxer.
Films:
Mandingo (1975)................................ Mede
1:36 - Buns, standing in bed with Susan George.
More buns making love with her. **
Drum (1976).................................... Drum
1:02 - Buns, getting hung upside down in barn and
spanked along with Yaphet Kotto. *
TV:
The Gong Show (1976-80)...........................Panelist

O

O., GEORGE
Films:
Summer Job (1988)...................................Herman
0:17 - Buns getting his underwear torn off by five
angry women then running back to his room. *

OCCHIPINTI, ANDREA
Films:
Bolero (1984).........................Angel the Bullfighter
0:57 - Buns, lying in bed with Bo Derek, then
making love with her. **

O'KEEFFE, MILES
Films:
Tarzan the Ape Man (1981)...........................Tarzan
Ator: The Fighting Eagles (1983).........................
The Blade Master (1984) ....
Sword of the Valiant (1984)................................
Lone Runner (1986)......................................
Campus Man (1987)......................................
Iron Warrior (1987)..
The Drifter (1988)................................Trey
0:11 - Brief upper half of buns on the motel floor
with Kim Delaney. *
Waxwork (1988)...............................Count Dracula

OLANDT, KEN
Films:
April Fool's Day (1986)...............................Rob
Summer School (1987)...................................Larry
0:48 - Brief buns wearing a red G-string in a male
stripper club. **
Made for TV Movies:
The Laker Girls (1990)..Rick

OLDMAN, GARY
Films:
Sid and Nancy (1986; British) ....Sid Vicious
Prick Up Your Ears (1987; British) .... Joe Orton
Track 29 (1988; British)................................ Martin
1:24 - Buns, holding onto Christopher Lloyd and
stabbing him. *
Criminal Law (1988)............................Ben Chase
1:21 - Very, very brief blurry frontal nudity in bed
with "Ellen." *
We Think the World of You (1988; British).............
Chattahoochee (1990)......................................

OLIVIERO, SILVIO
Films:
Nightstick (1987) ....Ismael
Graveyard Shift (1987)................. Stephen Tsepes
0:09 - Buns, climbing into his coffin. *
Psycho Girls (1987).......................................
The Understudy: Graveyard Shift II (1988)...Baisez

O'NEAL, RYAN
Films:
Love Story (1970) .... Oliver Barret IV
What's Up Doc? (1972)
..........................Professor Howard Bannister
Paper Moon (1973)................................ Moses Pray
The Thief Who Came to Dinner (1973)........Webster
Barry Lyndon (1975; British)............. Barry Lyndon
The Driver (1978)................................. The Driver
Oliver's Story (1978)...................... Oliver Barret IV
The Main Event (1979)
.... Eddie "Kid Natural" Scanlon
Green Ice (1981; British)................................ Wiley
So Fine (1981).. Bobby
Partners (1982).. Benson
0:48 - Buns, in Indian outfit for photo session with
Robyn Douglass. Don't see his face. **
Irreconcilable Differences (1984) .... Albert Brodsky
Fever Pitch (1985)..................................... Taggart
Tough Guys Don't Dance (1987)......... Tim Madden
Chances Are (1988)...............................Philip Train
TV:
Empire (1962-63)............................... Tal Garret
Peyton Place (1964-69)..............Rodney Harrington

ONTKEAN, MICHAEL
Films:
Slapshot (1977)....................................... Ned Braden
1:56 - Brief buns skating off the hockey rink
carrying a trophy wearing his jock strap. **
Voices (1979).................................. Drew Rothman
Willie and Phil (1980)...................................... Willie
Making Love (1982)... Zack
Just the Way You Are (1984)............................Peter
The Allnighter (1987)...
Maid to Order (1987)........................Nick McGuire
Clara's Heart (1988)..................................... Bill Hart
Street Justice (1988)...............................Curt Flynn
Made for TV Movies:
The Blood of Others (1984) ....
TV:
The Rookies (1972-74)............ Officer Willie Gillis
Twin Peaks (1990-) ....Harry S. Truman

O'QUINN, TERRY
Other:
a.k.a. Terrance O'Quinn.
Films:
Mischief (1985)...
Stephen King's Silver Bullet (1985)
.... Sheriff Joe Haller
Spacecamp (1986)......................Launch Director
Black Widow (1987)...
The Stepfather (1987)..
Young Guns (1988)......................... Alex McSween
The Forgotten One (1989)..................................
1:11 - Brief buns turning over in bed with
"Evelyn." *
Pin (1989)...................................Dr. Linden

PACKER, DAVID
Films:
You Can't Hurry Love (1984)......................Eddie
0:56 - Buns, in store taking his pants off while
people watch him from the sidewalk. *
Miniseries:
V: The Final Battle (1984)............Daniel Bernstein
TV:
The Best Times (1985).........Niel "Trout" Troutman
What's Alan Watching? (1989)..........................Jeff

PANKOW, JOHN
Films:
The Hunger (1983).............. 1st Phone Booth Youth
To Live and Die in L.A. (1985)...... John Vukovich
1:06 - Buns, changing in the locker room. *
The Secret of My Success (1987)...........................
*batteries not included (1987).....................Kovacs
Monkey Shines (1988).....................Geoffrey Fisher
Talk Radio (1988)... Dietz

PARKER, JAMESON
Films:
The Bell Jar (1979)....................................Buddy
0:09 - Frontal nudity silhouette standing in
bedroom with Marilyn Hassett, then buns.
Dark, hard to see. *
A Small Circle of Friends (1980)...........Nick Baxter
White Dog (1982)................................Roland Gray
American Justice (1986).................Dave Buchanon
Prince of Darkness (1987) ....
TV:
Simon & Simon (1981-89)
.... Andrew Jackson (A.J.) Simon

PASDAR, ADRIAN
Films:
Streets of Gold (1986) .... Timmy Boyle
Near Dark (1987)..
Made in the USA (1988)................................ Dar
0:12 - Buns, walking to sit down at the laundromat
when he washes all his clothes with Christopher
Penn. *

PATTERSON, JIMMY
Films:
The Young Warriors (1983; US/Canada)
......................................"Ice Test" Monty
0:14 - Buns, dropping pants and sitting on a block
of ice during pledge at fraternity. *

PATRICK, RANDAL

Made for HBO:
By Dawn's Early Light (1990)................ O'Toole
    0:14 - Brief buns in shower room getting dressed
    during read alert. *

PAXTON, BILL

Films:
Weird Science (1984)...................... Chet
    0:30 - Buns taking off towel to give to his younger
    brother in the kitchen. **
Impulse (1984)............................... Eddie
Streets of Fire (1984)....................... Clyde
The Terminator (1984)...................... Punk Leader
Commando (1985).......................... Intercept Officer
Aliens (1986)............................... Private Hudson
Near Dark (1987)...............................
Pass the Ammo (1988)...................... Jesse
Next of Kin (1989)............................ Gerald Gates

PECK, BRIAN

Films:
The Last American Virgin (1982)............ Victor
    0:20 - Buns, during penis measurement in boy's
    locker room. Don't see his face. *

PENN, CHRISTOPHER

Films:
The Wild Life (1984)...........................
Footloose (1984)..............................
Pale Rider (1985)............................. Josh LaHood
At Close Range (1986)............. Tommy Whitewood
Made in the USA (1988)..................... Tuck
    0:12 - Buns, walking to sit down at the laundromat
    when he washes all his clothes with Adrian
    Pasdar. *
Return from the River Kwai (1988)...........

PENN, SEAN

Other:
Ex-husband of singer/actress Madonna.
Films:
Bad Boys (1983)................. Mick O'Brien
    0:10 - Brief buns getting up off the floor with Ally
    Sheedy. *
    0:46 - Buns taking a shower. **
The Falcon and the Snowman (1985)....Daulton Lee
Shanghai Surprise (1986)................ Glendon Wasey
At Close Range (1986)............. Brad Whitewood, Jr.
Colors (1988).......................... Danny McGavin
Judgment in Berlin (1988)..................... Gunther X
Casualties of War (1989)............... Sergeant Meserve
We're No Angels (1989) .... Jim

PEPE, PAUL

Films:
Saturday Night Fever (1977)............... Double J.
    (R-rated version)
    0:22 - Buns making love in back seat of car with a
    girl. *

PETERSEN, WILLIAM L.

Films:
To Live and Die in L.A. (1985)..... Richard Chance
    0:44 - Brief frontal nudity, but hard to see
    anything because it's dark. *
Manhunter (1986)...................... Will Graham
Amazing Grace and Chuck (1987)...................
Cousins (1989)........................ Tom Hardy
Young Guns II (1990)...........................
HBO Movie:
Long Gone (1987)................... Cecil "Stud" Cantrell

PITZALIS, FREDRICO

Films:
Devil in the Flesh (1986; French/Italian)..... Andrea
    0:57 - Brief buns in bed with Maruschka Detmers.
    *
    1:19 - Frontal nudity when Detmers performs
    fellatio on him. *

PRESCOTT, ROBERT

Films:
The Lords of Discipline (1983)...............
Bachelor Party (1984)................... Richard Chance
    1:18 - Buns, after being hung out the window by
    sheets by Tom Hanks and his friends. *
Real Genius (1985)........................... Kent

PRICE, ALAN

Films:
O Lucky Man! (1973)...........................
Oh, Alfie! (1975; British)................ Alfie Elkins
    0:14 - Buns washing himself off in the kitchen
    while talking to "Louise's" husband. **

PRYOR, RICHARD

Other:
Comedian.
Films:
Lady Sings the Blues (1972).................... Piano Man
Some Call It Loving (1974) .... Jeff
Uptown Saturday Night (1974)
    .... Sharpe Eye Washington
Car Wash (1976)...................... Daddy Rich
Silver Streak (1976)..................... Grover Muldoon
Greased Lightning (1977).................. Wendell Scott
Which Way Is Up? (1977)
    .... Leroy Jones/Rufus Jones/Rev. Thomas
Blue Collar (1978) .... Zeke
The Wiz (1978)............................ The Wiz

The Muppet Movie (1979)..
Richard Pryor - Live in Concert (1979).......Himself
Stir Crazy (1980)...............................Harry Monroe
Wholly Moses! (1980)...............................Pharaoh
Bustin' Loose (1981)............................Joe Braxton
Richard Pryor Live on the Sunset Strip (1982)
....Himself
Some Kind of Hero (1982)...................Eddie Keller
The Toy (1982).....................................Jack Brown
Richard Pryor - Here and Now (1983).........Himself
Superman III (1983)..........................Gus Gorman
Brewster's Millions (1985)...Montgomery Brewster
Richard Pryor - Live and Smokin' (1985)....Himself
Jo Jo Dancer, Your Life is Calling (1986)
....Jo Jo Dancer/Alter Ego
0:06 - Buns, walking naked out of the hospital
waiting for the limousine. **
Moving (1988)...Arlo Pear
See No Evil, Hear No Evil (1989)..................Wally
Harlem Nights (1989)...........................Sugar Ray
TV:
The Richard Pryor Show (1977).........................Host

Q

QUAID, DENNIS
Other:
Brother of actor Randy Quaid.
Films:
The Seniors (1978).. Alan
Breaking Away (1979)......................................Mike
The Long Riders (1980).............................Ed Miller
The Night the Lights Went Out in Georgia (1981)
....Travis Child
Jaws 3 (1983)......................................Mike Brody
The Right Stuff (1983).....................Gordon Cooper
Tough Enough (1983)...............................Art Long
Dreamscape (1984)...
Enemy Mine (1985)...
Innerspace (1987)............................Tuck Pendleton
0:08 - Buns, standing naked in the street as taxi
drives off with his towel. Kind of a long shot.
**
Suspect (1987)..Eddie Sanger
The Big Easy (1987)......................Remy McSwain
0:24 - Brief buns when Ellen Barkin pulls his
underwear down in bed. *
0:51 - Buns, putting underwear on after getting out
of bed after talking on the telephone. ***
Everybody's All-American (1988)..................Gavin
D.O.A. (1988)...............................Dexter Cornell
Great Balls of Fire (1989)..............Jerry Lee Lewis
Made for TV Movies:
Bill (1981)..

QUINN, AIDAN
Reckless (1984)..............................Johnny Rourke
1:03 - Very brief frontal nudity and buns running
into Daryl Hannah's brother's room when her
parents come home early. *
1:12 - Side view nude, taking a shower. *
Desperately Seeking Susan (1985)....................Dez
The Mission (1986)..Felipe
Stakeout (1987)..........Richard "Stick" Montgomery
Crusoe (1989)...Crusoe
A Handmaid's Tale (1990)...............................Nick

R

RAILSBACK, STEVE
Films:
The Stunt Man (1979)...............................Cameron
Escape 2000 (1981)...Paul
The Golden Seal (1983)..............................Jim Lee
Lifeforce (1985)...Carlsen
1:26 - Buns, standing with Mathilda May after he
stabs her with the sword. Surrounded by special
effects. *
Torchlight (1985)...
Armed and Dangerous (1986)..............The Cowboy
The Blue Monkey (1987)...................................
Scenes from the Goldmine (1987)........Harry Spiros
The Wind (1987)..
The Assassin (1989)............................Hank Wright
Made for TV Movies:
Helter Skelter (1976).....................Charles Manson

RECKERT, WINSTON
Films:
Your Ticket is No Longer Valid (1982)
....Antonio Montoya
1:24 - Buns, in bed with Jennifer Dale. *

REED, MATHEW
Films:
Perfect (1985).. Roger
1:01 - Buns, dancing in a jock strap at
Chippendale's. *

REED, OLIVER
Films:
The Curse of the Werewolf (1961)...................Leon
Oliver (1968)...Bill Sikes
The Devils (1971)..
Women in Love (1971)........................Gerald Crich
0:54 - Nude, fighting with Alan Bates in a room in
front of a fireplace. Long scene. ***
The Three Musketeers (1973)........................Althos
Blood in the Streets (1974; French/Italian)
....Vito Cipriani
The Four Musketeers (1975)..........................Athos

Ten Little Indians (1975)..................................Hugh
Tommy (1975)......................................Frank Hobbs
Burnt Offerings (1976).......................................Ben
The Great Scout and Cathouse Thursday (1976)
....Joe Knox
The Big Sleep (1978)..................Eddie Mars
The Class of Miss MacMichael (1978)
....Terence Sutton
The Prince and the Pauper (1978)......Miles Hendon
a.k.a. Crossed Swords
The Brood (1979)..............................Dr. Raglan
Condorman (1981)..Krokov
Spasms (1982)..............................Suzanne Kincaid
Venom (1982)...Dave
The Sting II (1983)......................Doyle Lonnegan
Black Arrow (1984).................Sir Daniel Brackley
Castaway (1986)...........................Gerald Kingsland
Rage to Kill (1988)..
Dragonard (1988)........................Captain Shanks
Skeleton Coast (1989)...................Captain Simpson
The Return of the Musketeers (1989)..............Athos
Made for TV Movies:
The Lady and the Highwayman (1989)
....Sir Philip Gage

REVES, ROBBIE

Films:
Shadowzone (1989)...........................James
0:16 - Frontal nudity long shot.
0:26 - Frontal nudity lying under plastic bubble. *

REYNOLDS, BURT

Films:
Operation C.I.A. (1965; B&W)........Mark Andrews
Shark! (1969)...Caine
a.k.a. Maneaters!
Deliverance (1972)...Lewis
Fuzz (1972).........................Detective Steve Carella
The Man Who Loved Cat Dancing (1973)
....Jay Grobart
White Lightning (1973)................Gator McKlusky
The Longest Yard (1974)......................Paul Crewe
The Hustle (1975)................Lieutenant Phil Gaines
Gator (1976)..................................Gator McKlusky
Silent Movie (1976)..
Semi-Tough (1977)...................Billy Clyde Puckett
Smokey and the Bandit (1977)......................Bandit
The End (1978).................................Sonny Lawson
Hooper (1978)..............................Sonny Hooper
Starting Over (1979)................................Phil Potter
Rough Cut (1980)..............................Jack Rhodes
Smokey and the Bandit II (1980)...................Bandit
Cannonball Run (1981)....................J. J. McClure
Paternity (1981)....................................Buddy Evans
Sharky's Machine (1981)..............................Sharky
Best Friends (1982).......................Richard Babson
The Best Little Whorehouse in Texas (1982)
....Ed Earl

The Man Who Loved Women (1983)
....David Fowler
1:25 - Brief buns, chiseling a statue after making
love with Julie Andrews. **
Stroker Ace (1983)...........................Stroker Ace
Smokey and the Bandit III (1983)... The Real Bandit
Cannonball Run II (1984)....................J. J. McClure
City Heat (1984)................................Mike Murphy
Stick (1985).. Stick
Heat (1987)..Mex
Malone (1987)..
Smoke (1988)..
Rent-a-Cop (1988) .... Church
Physical Evidence (1989)...........................Joe Paris
Breaking In (1989) ....Ernie Mullins
TV:
Riverboat (1959-60)............................ Ben Frazer
Gunsmoke (1962-65) ....Quint Asper
Hawk (1966)............................... Lt. John Hawk
Dan August (1970-71) ....Det. Lt. Dan August
B. L. Stryker (1989-90)....................... B. L. Stryker
Evening Shade (1990-).....................Wood Newton
Magazines:
Cosmopolitan (Apr 1972) ....Centerfold

ROBBINS, TIM

Films:
Toy Soldiers (1983) ....Bean
No Small Affair (1984)................................Nelson
Fraternity Vacation (1985)...Larry "Mother" Tucker
The Sure Thing (1985).........................Gary Cooper
Howard the Duck (1986)................... Phil Blumburtt
Five Corners (1988) ....Harry
Bull Durham (1988)
..............................Ebby Calvin "Nuke" La Loosh
0:03 - Buns, in locker room making love with
"Millie" when the coach sees them. *
Tapeheads (1988).................................Josh Tager
Miss Firecracker (1989)............ Delmount Williams
Erik the Viking (1989).......................................Erik
Cadillac Man (1990)..

ROBINSON, DAVID

Films:
Revenge of the Cheerleaders (1976)........... Jordan
0:13 - Buns when "Tish" plays with him while
she's under the counter. *

ROSS, CHELCHIE

Films:
One More Saturday Night (1986)..... Dad Lundahl
0:39 - Buns, squished against the car window in
back seat with Moira Harris. *

ROSSI, LEO

Films:
  Halloween II (1981).. Budd
    0:48 - Buns, getting out of the whirlpool bath to
    check the water temperature. *
  Heart Like a Wheel (1983)............Jack Muldowney
  River's Edge (1987)..Jim
  Leonard, Part 6 (1988)....................................Chef
  The Accused (1989)...........Cliff "Scorpion" Albrect
  Relentless (1989)................................... Sam Dietz
TV:
  Partners in Crime (1984)................. Lt. Ed Vronsky
  Tour of Duty (1988-90)........................Jake Bridger

ROSSOVICH, RICK

Films:
  Streets of Fire (1984)........................Officer Cooley
  The Terminator (1984).....................................Matt
  Warning Sign (1985).......................................
  The Morning After (1986)...............................
  Top Gun (1986)...
  Roxanne (1987)...
  Spellbinder (1988).......................................
  Paint it Black (1989)....................Jonathan Dunbar
    0:48 - Upper half of buns getting out of bed with
    Julie Carmen. *
Made for HBO:
  Tales from the Crypt: The Switch (1990).... Hans
    0:23 - Buns standing in front of mirror after being
    transformed into a younger "Carlton." **
TV:
  MacGruder & Loud (1985) ....Geller
  Sons and Daughters (1990-)............. Spud Lincoln

ROWLATT, MICHAEL

Films:
  Spaced Out (1980; British)..............................Cliff
    0:42 - Buns, getting out of bed trying to get away
    from "Partha." *

RUBBO, JOE

Films:
  The Last American Virgin (1982)...............David
    0:45 - Buns, in bed making love with "Carmilla"
    while his buddies watch through the key hole. *
  Hot Chili... Arney
    0:24 - Brief buns getting whipped by "Brigitte." *

RUSSELL, KURT

Films:
  The Horse in the Gray Flannel Suit (1968)..............
  The Computer Who Wore Tennis Shoes (1969).......
  The Barefoot Executive (1971)............................
  Now You See Him, Now You Don't (1972)............
  Charley & the Angel (1973)...............................
  Superdad (1973)...

Used Cars (1980)..
    1:04 - Very brief buns putting on red underwear.
    *
Escape from New York (1981)...........Snake Pliskin
The Thing (1982)..
Silkwood (1984)...
Swingshift (1984)...
The Mean Season (1985)..................................
The Best of Times (1986).................................
Big Trouble in Little China (1986).....................
Tequila Sunrise (1988)....................................
Overboard (1988)..
The Winter People (1989) ....
Tango & Cash (1989)...............................Cash
    0:31 - Brief buns walking into the prison shower
    room with Sylvester Stallone. **

RUST, RICHARD

Films:
  The Student Nurses (1970)............................. Les
    0:43 - Buns, lying in sand with Barbara Leigh. *
  The Great Gundown (1976)...............................

S

SADOR, DANIEL

Films:
  Sugar Cookies (1973)..Gus
    0:37 - Buns in bed with "Dola," then running
    around.

SANDS, JULIAN

Films:
  The Killing Fields (1984)................................
  Oxford Blues (1984)......................................
  The Doctor and the Devils (1985) ....Dr. Murray
  Gothic (1987; British)....................................
  A Room with a View (1986; British)
    ....George Emerson
    1:05 - Nude running around with "Freddy" and
    "Mr. Beebe" in the woods. Lots of frontal
    nudity. **
  Siesta (1987)...Kit
  Vibes (1988)....................Dr. Harrison Steele
Magazines:
  Playboy (Nov 1986)............. "Sex in Cinema 1986"
    Page 128: Buns, in a photo from "A Room with a
    View." Kind of blurry

SARANDON, CHRIS
Films:
Lipstick (1976)............................Gordon Stuart
   0:50 - Buns, standing in his studio talking to
     Margaux Hemingway on the telephone. **
The Sentinel (1977) ....Michael Lerman
Cuba (1979)..Juan Polido
The Osterman Weekend (1983).......Joseph Cardone
Protocol (1984)..
Fright Night (1986)..........................Jerry Dandridge
The Princess Bride (1987).......Prince Humperdinck
Child's Play (1988)..............................Mike Norris
Slaves of New York (1989)................Victor Okrent
Made for TV Movies:
Mayflower Madam (1988).......................................

SCHOTT, BOB
Films:
The Working Girls (1974)............................ Roger
   0:07 - Buns, getting out of bed to meet "Honey."
   *

SCHNEIDER, JOHN
Films:
Eddie Macon's Run (1983)................ Eddie Macon
   0:15 - Brief left side view of buns when beginning
     to cross the stream. Dark, hard to see. *
Cocaine Wars (1986)...Cliff
Stagecoach (1986) ....
The Curse (1987) ....
Speed Zone (1989)..............................Cannonballer
Ministry of Vengeance (1989)..............David Miller
TV:
The Dukes of Hazzard (1979-85)............... Bo Duke

SCHWARZENEGGER, ARNOLD
Other:
Husband of Kennedy clan member/news reporter
   Maria Shriver.
Films:
Hercules in New York (1970)....................Hercules
   a.k.a. Hercules Goes Bananas
The Long Goodbye (1973).............................Hoods
Stay Hungry (1976) ....Joe Santo
Pumping Iron (1977)..
The Villain (1979) ....Handsome Stranger
Conan the Barbarian (1982)...........................Conan
Conan the Destroyer (1984)...........................Conan
The Terminator (1984)................. The Terminator
   0:03 - Buns, kneeling by garbage truck, walking to
     look at the city and walking toward the three
     punks at night. ***
Red Sonja (1985)...Kalidor
Commando (1986)..
Raw Deal (1986)........................... Mark Kaminsky

Predator (1987)......................Major Dutch Schaefer
The Running Man (1987)................... Ben Richards
Red Heat (1988)....................................Ivan Danko
   0:02 - Buns in the sauna and outside fighting in
     the snow. **
Twins (1988)...................................Julius Benedict
Total Recall (1990)..
Made for TV Movie:
The Jayne Mansfield Story (1980)..........................

SCUDDAMORE, SIMON
Films:
Slaughter High (1986)................................... Marty
   0:05 - Nude in girl's shower room when his
     classmates pull a prank on him. *

SELBY, DAVID
Films:
Up the Sandbox (1972)..
The Girl in Blue (1978; Canada).....................Scott
   0:10 - Brief buns getting out of bed and putting on
     pants. Dark. *
   0:44 - Left half of buns in shower.
   1:14 - Buns, walking into the bathroom. **
Raise the Titanic (1980)..
Rich and Famous (1981)...
TV:
Flamingo Road (1981-82)............... Michael Tyrone
Falcon Crest (1982-86).................Richard Channing

SELLECK, TOM
Films:
Terminal Island (1977)..............Dr. Norman Milford
The Washington Affair (1977)..............Jim Hawley
Coma (1978)... Sean
High Road to China (1983)........................O'Malley
Lassiter (1984)....................................... Lassiter
   1:00 - Buns, getting out of bed after making love
     with Lauren Hutton. *
Runaway (1984)..Ramsay
Three Men and a Baby (1987) ....Peter
Her Alibi (1989)............................ Phil Blackwood
Hard Rain (1989) ....
An Innocent Man (1989)...............Jimmy Rainwood
Miniseries:
The Sacketts (1979) ....
Made for TV Movies:
Bunco (1977)..
The Gypsy Warriors (1978)....................................
Boston and Kilbride (1979)....................................
TV:
The Rockford Files (1979-80)..............Lance White
Magnum P.I. (1980-1988)............. Thomas Magnum

SERNA, PEPE

Films:
    The Student Nurses (1970)................................Luis
    The Day of the Locust (1975)..................... Miguel
      2:01 - Buns on top of Karen Black, then buns
      jumping out of bed. *

SHANE, MICHAEL

Films:
    Savage Beach (1989)........................ Shane Abeline
      0:08 - Buns, getting out of pool. **

SHANNON, GEORGE

Films:
    Sugar Cookies (1973)..................................... Max
      0:14 - Buns, on top of Mary Woronov in bed. **

SHARKEY, RAY

Films:
    Stunts (1977)...Pauley
    Who'll Stop the Rain? (1978) .... Smitty
    Heart Beat (1979)..Ira
    The Idolmaker (1980).....................Vince Vacarddi
    Willie and Phil (1980).. Phil
    Some Kind of Hero (1982).............................. Vinnie
    Body Rock (1984)...
    Hellhole (1985) .... Silk
    Wise Guys (1986)... Marco
    Private Investigations (1987)............................
    Scenes from the Class Struggle in Beverly Hills
    (1989)...Frank
      1:10 - Brief buns sleeping in bed with "Zandra." *

SHEEN, MARTIN

Films:
    Rage (1972).....................................Major Holliford
    Badlands (1973)...Kit
    Catholics (1973)...
    The Little Girl Who Lives Down the Lane (1976)
    ....Frank Hallet
    The Cassandra Crossing (1977)....................Navarro
    Apocalypse Now (1979)................Captain Willard
      0:07 - Brief buns, in bedroom after opening door
      for military guys. *
    Enigma (1982)................................... Alex Holbeck
    The Final Countdown (1980)............. Warren Lasky
    Gandhi (1982) .... Walker
    That Championship Season (1982).........Tom Daley
    The Dead Zone (1983).........................Greg Stillson
    Man, Woman and Child (1983)..........Bob Beckwith
    Firestarter (1984)...
    The Guardian (1984) ....
    Wall Street (1987) ....Carl Fox
    The Believers (1987)...

SHELLEN, S

Films:
    Gimme an "F
      0:56 - Dancin
      shower room
      0:57 - Brief uppe
    Modern Girls (1986
    The Stepfather (1987
    Modern Girls (1987)...
    American Gothic (1988)
    Casual Sex? (1988)..........
    Murder One (1988; Canad
Made for HBO:
    The Hitchhiker: Love Soun
      0:15 - Brief buns, making lov
      Belinda Bauer. **
      0:22 - Buns, making love in the
      **
    Tales From the Crypt: Lover Com
    (1989)..
      0:10 - Buns, getting undressed with h
      wife in a strange house. *

SHIRIN, MOTI

Films:
    Little Drummer Girl (1984)...................... Mi
      1:07 - Nude, in a prison cell when Diane Keato
      looks at his scars. **
    Unsettled Land (1987)...............................Salim

SIBBIT, JOHN

Films:
    Love Circles Around the World (1984)......... Jack
      0:06 - Very brief frontal nudity pulling his
      underwear down and getting into bed. *
      0:19 - Buns, trying to run away from "Brigid"
      after she yanks his underwear off. **

SINGER, MARC

Other:
    Brother of actress Lori Singer.
Films:
    If You Could See What I Hear (1982).....................
    The Beastmaster (1982)......................................
    Born to Race (1988)........................Kenny Landruff
    Body Chemistry (1990)...................................
      0:18 - Buns, standing up in hallway holding
      "Claire" while making love. Long shot. *
    Watchers II (1990)............................Paul Ferguson
Miniseries:
    V: The Final Battle (1984)............... Mike Donovan
Made for TV Movies:
    V (1983).. Mike Donovan
TV:
    V (1984-85) .... Mike Donovan
    Dallas (1986-87)................................. Matt Cantrell

SKARSGA
Films:
    The Unl
    ....
    2:18
    ap

SLATE
Films:
    The
    Th

...RD, STELLAN

...earable Lightness of Being (1987)
....The Engineer
  Buns, making love with "Tereza" in his
  ...artment. *

...R, CHRISTIAN

Legend of Billie Jean (1985)......................Binx
...e Name of the Rose
...(1986; Italian/German/French)......... Adso of Melk
  0:48 - Buns, making love with "The Girl" in the
  monastery kitchen. *
...ucker: The Man and His Dreams (1988)......Junior
...Gleaming the Cube (1988).......................................
Heathers (1989) ....J.D.
The Wizard (1989)............................... Nick Woods
Young Guns II (1990)..
Pump Up the Volume (1990)....................................

SLOANE, LANCE

Films:
The Big Bet (1985)...Chris
  0:38 - Buns, taking off robe and getting into bed
  with "Angela Roberts." **
  0:52 - Buns, on elevator floor with Monique
  Gabrielle during his daydream. **
  1:07 - Buns, getting into tub with Kimberly
  Evenson. Long shot. *

SMITH, CHARLIE MARTIN

Films:
The Culpepper Cattle Co. (1972)..............Tim Slater
Fuzz (1972)... Baby
Pat Garrett and Billy the Kid (1973).............Bowdre
American Graffiti (1973)...................Terry the Toad
Rafferty and the Gold Dust Twins (1975).........Alan
The Buddy Holly Story (1978)................... Ray Bob
More American Graffiti (1979) ....Terry the Toad
Herbie Goes Bananas (1980).............................D. J.
Never Cry Wolf (1983)...................................Tyler
  0:32 - Buns warming himself and drying his
  clothes after falling through the ice. *
  1:18 - Very brief frontal nudity running and
  jumping off a rock into the pond. *
  1:20 - Buns running in meadow with the caribou.
  *
  1:23 - Brief silhouette of lower frontal nudity
  while scampering up a hill. More buns when
  chasing the caribou. *
Starman (1984).. Shermin
The Untouchables (1987)..............................Wallace

SPANJER, MAARTEN

Films:
Spetters (1980)... Jeff
  0:35 - Frontal nudity, measuring and comparing
  his manlihood with his friends in the auto shop.
  **
  1:12 - Buns climbing into bed in trailer with
  Reneé Soutendijk. *

SPANO, JOE

Films:
Terminal Choice (1984)....................... Frank Holt
  0:34 - Buns, taking off towel and getting dressed
  in locker room while talking to "Anna." ***
  0:49 - Buns, making love in bed with "Anna."
  Long shot, don't see his face. *
Made for TV Movies:
The Girl Who Came Between Them (1990)....... Jim
TV:
Hill Street Blues (1981-87)......... Henry Goldblume

SPANO, VINCENT

Films:
The Black Stallion Returns (1983).....................Raj
Rumble Fish (1983; B&W)............................ Steve
Alphabet City (1984) ....
Maria's Lovers (1985) .... Al Griselli
Creator (1985)...
  0:28 - Brief buns, in shower room with David
  Ogden Stiers after working out in a gym. *
  0:57 - Brief buns, before taking a shower. *
Blood Ties (1987)..
Good Morning, Babylon (1987)...............................

SPRINGFIELD, RICK

Other:
Singer.
Films:
Hard to Hold (1984) ....James Roberts
  0:06 - Buns, running down the hall getting chased
  by a bunch of young girls. *
  0:15 - Buns, lying in bed sleeping. **

STALLONE, SYLVESTER

Adult Films:
The Italian Stallion (1970).............................. Stud
  X-rated film that Stallone did before he got
  famous. Originally called "A Party at Kitty and
  Stud's." Re-titled and re-released in 1985. He
  has lots of nude scenes in this film.
Films:
The Lords of Flatbush (1974).........Stanley Rosiello
Capone (1975).. Frank Nitti
Death Race 2000 (1975)...Machine Gun Joe Viterbo
Farewell, My Lovely (1975; British)....Kelly/Jonnie
Rocky (1976)......................................Rocky Balboa
Paradise Alley (1978)....................Cosmo Carboni
F.I.S.T. (1978)................................Johnny Kouak

Rocky II (1979) .... Rocky Balboa
Nighthawks (1981).............................Deke De Silva
Victory (1981) ....Robert Hatch
First Blood (1982)...Rambo
Rocky III (1982)............................... Rocky Balboa
Rhinestone (1984) ....
Rambo: First Blood, Part II (1985)...............Rambo
Rocky IV (1985)............................... Rocky Balboa
Cobra (1986) .... Marion Cobretti
Over the Top (1987)..
Tango & Cash (1989)............................. Ray Tango
    0:31 - Brief buns walking into the prison shower
      room with Kurt Russell. **
Lock Up (1989) ....Frank

STERN, DANIEL

Films:
    Starting Over (1979).................................Student 2
    A Small Circle of Friends (1980).......... Crazy Kid
        1:22 - Brief buns, dropping his pants with several
          other guys for Army draft inspection. *
    Stardust Memories (1980; B&W) .... Actor
    Diner (1982)..Shrevie
    Blue Thunder (1983) ....Lymangood
    Get Crazy (1983)... Neil
    C.H.U.D. (1984)..
    Key Exchange (1985)................................... Michael
    The Boss' Wife (1986)...........................Joel Keefer
    The Milagro Beanfield War (1988)........Herbie Platt
    D.O.A. (1988)....................................Hal Petersham
TV:
    Hometown (1985) .... Joey Nathan

STEVENS, ANDREW

Other:
    Son of actress Stella Stevens.
Films:
    Massacre at Central High (1976)...................... Mark
    The Boys in Company C (1978) ....
    The Fury (1978)..
    Death Hunt (1981)..
    Forbidden Love (1982).....................................
    The Seduction (1982)......................................
    Ten to Midnight (1983)....................................
    Scared Stiff (1986)...
    The Terror Within (1989)..............................David
    Night Eyes (1990)...Will
        1:11 - Buns in the shower. ***
        1:26 - Side view of buns with Tanya Roberts seen
          through a window. ***
TV:
    Code Red (1981-82)............................ Ted Rorchek
    Emerald Point N.A.S. (1983-84)
      .... Lieutenant Glenn Matthews

STING

Other:
    Singer with "The Police" and on his own.
Films:
    Quadrophenia (1979; British)............. The Ace Face
    Brimstone and Treacle (1982; British)
    ....Martin Taylor
        1:19 - Buns, making love with Suzanna Hamilton
          on her bed. Dark, hard to see. *
    Dune (1984)...
    Plenty (1985) ....Mick
    The Bride (1985)..................................Frankenstein
    Stormy Monday (1988; British).....................Finney
    Julia and Julia (1988; Italian)........................Daniel

STOCKWELL, JOHN

Films:
    Christine (1983)..Dennis
    Losin' It (1983).. Spider
    My Science Project (1985)...............Michael Harlan
    City Limits (1985)..Lee
    Top Gun (1986) ....Cougar
    Radioactive Dreams (1987).............................
    Dangerously Close (1988)............. Randy McDevill
        0:33 - Brief buns in steamy locker room. *
Miniseries:
    North and South (1985) .... Billy Hazard

STOKES, BARRY

Films:
    Happy Housewives (British).............................Bob
        0:31 - Brief buns, running away from "Mrs. Elgin"
          and her daughter in the barn. *
    Spaced Out (1980; British)............................ Oliver
        0:54 - Buns, undressing to get in bed with
          "Prudence." *

STOLZ, ERIC

Films:
    Fast Times at Ridgemont High (1982).... Stoner Bud
    Surf II (1984)...
    The Wild Life (1984)......................................
    Code Name: Emerald (1985)........... Andy Wheeler
    The New Kids (1985)....................................Mark
    Mask (1985).....................................Rocky Dennis
    Lionheart (1987) ....
    Sister, Sister (1987) ....Matt Rutledge
    Some Kind of Wonderful (1987)......... Keith Nelson
    The Fly II (1988) ....Martin
    Haunted Summer (1988)................. Percy Shelley
        0:09 - Nude, under the waterfall and walking
          around in the river. Long scene. Too bad more
          actors aren't brave enough to do nude scenes
          like this. ***
    Say Anything (1989)....................................Vahlere
Made for TV Movies:
    Paper Dolls (1982)..Steve

STONE, CHRISTOPHER

Films:

The Grasshopper (1970)...................... Jay Rigney
   0:26 - Buns through shower door when Jacqueline
   Bisset comes in to join him.
   1:17 - Brief buns lying in bed talking to Bisset. *

The Howling (1981)........... R. William "Bill" Neill
   0:48 - Brief buns, rolling over while making love
   with Elizabeth Brooks in front of a campfire. *

Cujo (1983)...Steve
The Annihilators (1985)............................ Bill Esker

Miniseries:

The Blue and the Gray (1982).........Major Fairbairn

TV:

The Interns (1970-71)................... Dr. Pooch Hardin
Spencer's Pilots (1976)...........................Cass Garrett
Harper Valley P.T.A. (1981-82)....... Tom Meechum
Dallas (1984) .... Dave Stratton

STREET, ELLIOT

Films:

The Harrad Experiment (1973).................. Wilson
   0:44 - Frontal nudity taking off clothes and getting
   into the swimming pool. **

SUTHERLAND, DONALD

Films:

Dr. Terror's House of Horrors (1965) ....Bob Carroll
Die, Die, My Darling (1965) ....Joseph
The Dirty Dozen (1967)................... Vernon Pinkley
Kelly's Heroes (1970)..................................Oddball
M*A*S*H (1970)........................... Hawkeye Pierce
Start the Revolution Without Me (1970)
...................................Charles Coupe/Pierre De Sisi
Johnny Got His Gun (1971)...................Jesus Christ
Klute (1971)..John Klute
Don't Look Now (1973) ....John Baxter
   0:27 - Buns, in the bathroom with Julie Christie. *
Steelyard Blues (1973).........................Jesse Veldini
The Day of the Locust (1975)........................Homer
The Disappearance (1977)..................................Jay
The Eagle Has Landed (1977).............. Liam Devlin
Kentucky Fried Movie (1977) ....Clumsy
Invasion of the Body Snatchers (1978)
....Matthew Bennell
Animal House (1978) .... Dave Jennings
   1:22 - Buns, reaching up in kitchen to get
   something when his sweater goes up. Out of
   focus. *
The Great Train Robbery (1979)..................... Agan
A Man, A Woman and a Bank (1979)............. Reese
Murder by Decree (1979)..................... Robert Lees
Bear Island (1980) ....Frank Lansing
Nothing Personal (1980).......Professor Roger Keller
Ordinary People (1980) ....Calvin
Eye of the Needle (1981)...............................Faber

Gas (1981)...............................Nick the Noz
Threshold (1983; Canadian)......................Dr. Vrain
Max Dugan Returns (1983)............................. Brian
Crackers (1984)...
Ordeal by Innocence (1984)..............Arthur Calgary
Heaven Help Us (1985)...................Brother Thadeus
Revolution (1986)................... Sergeant Major Peasy
The Rosary Murders (1987)............. Father Koesler
Lost Angels (1989)........................Dr. Charles Loftis
Lock Up (1989)........................ Warden Drumgoole

SWAYZE, PATRICK

Other:

Husband of actress Lisa Niemi.

Films:

Skatetown U.S.A. (1979) ....Ace
The Outsiders (1983) ....Darrel
Uncommon Valor (1983)...............................Scott
Grandview, U.S.A. (1984) ....
Red Dawn (1984)..
Youngblood (1986)...........................Derek Sutton
Dirty Dancing (1987).....................Johnny Castle
Steel Dawn (1988) .... Nomad
Tiger Warsaw (1988) .... Chuck "Tiger" Warsaw
Roadhouse (1989) ....Dalton
   0:30 - Brief buns getting out of bed while
   Kathleen Wilhoite watches. ***
Next of Kin (1989)............................Truman Gates
Ghost (1990)..

Miniseries:

North and South (1985)............................ Orry Main
North and South: Book II (1986)........... Orry Main

TV:

Renegades (1983)..Bandit

T

TEPPER, WILLIAM

Films:

Drive, He Said (1972) .... Hector
Breathless (1983) .... Paul
Miss Right (1987)............................... Terry Bartell
   0:47 - Buns, jumping out of bed with Karen Black
   when the bed catches fire. *

TERRY, NIGEL

Films:

Excalibur (1981)................................... King Arthur
Deja Vu (1984)....................................Michel/Greg
   1:17 - Very brief buns, jumping out of bed when
   Jaclyn Smith tries to kill him with a knife. *
Sylvia (1985; New Zealand)................. Aden Morris

THOMPSON, JACK

Films:
Jock Petersen (1974)..........................Tony Petersen
   0:13 - Buns, making love with Wendy Hughes on
   the floor. ***
   0:20 - Frontal nudity under tarp with "Moira"
   during protest. ***
   0:22 - Buns in bed with "Suzy." *
   0:44 - Nude running around the beach with
   Hughes. **
   0:50 - Frontal nudity undressing, then buns lying
   in bed. **
Mad Dog Morgan (1976)......................................
Breaker Morant (1979; Australian).........................
The Earthling (1980) ....
The Man from Snowy River (1982).........................
Sunday Too Far Away (1983; Australian)...............
Flesh + Blood (1985)........................... Hawkwood
Burke and Wills (1987; Australian).........................
Ground Zero (1988).......................................

THOMSEN, KEVIN

Films:
Cleo/Leo (1989)..................................... Bob Miller
   1:07 - Brief frontal nudity, then buns making love
   with Jane Hamilton on bed. *

TORN, RIP

Films:
Baby Doll (1956).......................................
You're a Big Boy Now (1966)...............................
Payday (1972)..................................... Maury Dann
   1:21 - Brief buns getting up out of bed. *
Coma (1978)...
Heartland (1979) ....
The Seduction of Joe Tynan (1979) ....
One Trick Pony (1980)....................................
Beastmaster (1982)......................................
Cross Creek (1983).....................................
Flashpoint (1984)......................................
Summer Rental (1985)...................................Scully
Beer (1986)...................................Buzz Beckerman
Extreme Prejudice (1987)...............................
Made for HBO:
Laguna Heat (1987)......................................

TOVATT, PATRICK

Films:
Ellie (1984)... Art
   1:19 - Brief blurry buns while falling down the
   stairs. *

TUBB, BARRY

Films:
Mask (1985)...................................Dewey
The Legend of Billy Jean (1985)...................Hubie
Top Gun (1986)...........................Henry Ruth
Valentino Returns (1989)...................Wayne Gibbs

Warm Summer Rain (1989)...........................Guy
   0:23 - Lower frontal nudity getting off Kelly
   Lynch in bed. **
   0:25 - Side view of buns dreaming in bed.
   0:58 - Frontal nudity kneeling on floor and behind
   the table while washing Lynch. **
   1:00 - Buns while getting washed by Lynch. *
   1:07 - Brief buns making love with Lynch. Quick
   cuts. *
   1:09 - Nude picking up belongings and running
   out of burning house with Lynch. ***
TV:
Bay City Blues (1983) ....Mickey Wagner

TYSON, RICHARD

Films:
Three O'Clock High (1987)................................
Two Moon Junction (1988)...........................Perry
   0:58 - Very, very brief buns wrestling with
   "April" in a motel room. Dark, hard to see. *
TV:
Hardball (1989-90).......................................

U

UNDERWOOD, JAY

Films:
The Boy Who Could Fly (1986).......................Eric
The Invisible Kid (1988)...................Grover Dunn
   0:27 - Brief buns running around the school halls
   after becoming visible with his friend "Milton."
   *
Uncle Buck (1989)..................................Bug
The Gumshoe Kid (1990)...................Jeff Sherman

V

VALENTINE, SCOTT

Films:
Deadtime Stories (1987)................................ Peter
   0:19 - Buns, getting out of bath. *
My Demon Lover (1987).......................................
TV:
Family Ties (1985-89)..........................Nick Moore

VAN DAMME, JEAN CLAUDE

Films:
No Retreat, No Surrender (1986)....Ivan the Russian
Bloodsport (1988)...Frank
   0:50 - Brief buns putting underwear on after
   spending the night with "Janice." **
Black Eagle (1988)..
Cyborg (1989).........................Gibson Rickenbacker
Kick Boxer (1989)...............................Kurt Sloane

VAN HETENRYCK, KEVIN
Films:
Basket Case (1982)..Duane
Basket Case 2 (1989)....................................Duane
   0:34 - Buns standing in front of mirror looking at his large scar on the side of his body. *

VAN HOFFMAN, BRANT
Films:
The Further Adventures of Tennessee Buck
(1987)... Ken Manchester
   0:38 - Brief buns, behind a mosquito net making love with his disinterested wife. *

VAN TONGEREN, HANS
Films:
Spetters (1980)................................... Ron Hartman
   0:35 - Frontal nudity, measuring and comparing his manlihood with his friends in the auto shop. **

VENTURA, CLYDE
Films:
Terminal Island (1973)................................. Dillon
   0:42 - Buns, taking off pants with Phyllis Davis, then covered with honey and bees, then running to jump into a pond. **
Gator Bait (1973)...

VINCENT, JAN-MICHAEL
Films:
The Mechanic (1972).......................Steve McKenna
The World's Greatest Athlete (1973)...............Nanu
Buster and Billie (1974)....................Buster Lane
   1:06 - Frontal nudity taking off his underwear and walking to "Billie." Buns, in slow motion, swinging into the water. ***
Bite the Bullet (1975)....................................Carbo
White Line Fever (1975) ....Carrol Jo Hummer
Vigilante Force (1976)........................Ben Arnold
Damnation Alley (1977)..............................Tanner
Big Wednesday (1978) .... Matt
Hooper (1978).. Ski
Defiance (1980) ....Tommy
The Return (1980)..Deputy
Hard Country (1981)....................Kyle Richardson
Last Plane Out (1983).....................................
Born in East L.A. (1987) ....
Enemy Territory (1987).....................................
Miniseries:
The Winds of War (1983)....................Byron Henry
TV:
The Survivors (1969-70).................. Jeffrey Hastings
Airwolf (1984-86).................... Stringfellow Hawke

VOIGHT, JON
Films:
Midnight Cowboy (1969) .... Joe Buck
   0:20 - Very brief buns, walking into bedroom and jumping into bed with "Cass." *
   1:28 - Buns, in bed with Brenda Vaccaro. *
Deliverance (1972)...Ed
Conrack (1974)...................................Pat Conroy
The Odessa File (1974; British)............Peter Miller
Coming Home (1978)...................Luke Martin
The Champ (1979) ....Bill
Lookin' to Get Out (1982) ....Alex Kovac
Table for Five (1983)........................J. P. Tannen
Runaway Train (1985) ....Manny
Desert Bloom (1986)....................................... Jack

W

WALSH, M. EMMET
Films:
Slapshot (1977).....................................Dickie Dunn
Straight Time (1978) .... Earl Frank
   0:47 - Buns, handcuffed to fence in the middle of the road with his pants down. *
Fast Walking (1981).................. Sgt. George Sager
   0:59 - Frontal nudity standing in the doorway of "Evie's" mobile home yelling at James Woods after he interrupts Walsh making love with "Evie." *
Blade Runner (1982)...................................... Bryant
Scandalous (1983).........................Simon Reynolds
Blood Simple (1984)..................... Private Detective
Missing in Action (1984) ....Tuck
Fletch (1985)................................... Dr. Dolan
Back to School (1986)...................Coach Turnbull
The Best of Times (1986).......................... Charlie
Critters (1986).. Harv
Wildcats (1986).. Coes
Harry and the Hendersons (1987)..........George, Sr.
The Milagro Beanfield War (1988)...........Governor
Sunset (1988) ....Chief Dibner
Red Scorpion (1989).....................Dewey Ferguson
Chattahoochee (1990)..
Made for TV Miniseries:
The Right of the People (1986)......................Mayor
Brotherhood of the Rose (1989)..................... Hardy
Love & Lies (1990)...........................Clyde Wilson
TV:
The Sandy Duncan Show (1972) ...... Alex Lembeck
Dear Detective (1979)...................Capt. Gorcey
East of Eden (1981).............................Sheriff Quinn
UNSUB (1989)..Ned

WARD, WALLY

Films:
Weird Science (1984)................................A Weenie
Thunder Run (1986)..Paul
The Invisible Kid (1988)............... Milton McClane
   0:27 - Brief buns running around the school halls
   after becoming visible with his friend "Grover."
     *
The Chocolate War (1988)..............................Archie
TV:
Fast Times (1986).................................Mark Ratner

WARREN, MIKE

Films:
Drive, He Said (1972)..................... Easly Jefferson
   0:09 - Buns and very brief frontal nudity in the
   shower room with the other basketball players.
     *
Butterflies are Free (1972).................................. Roy
Fast Break (1979)..Preacher
TV:
Sierra (1974)...............................Ranger P.J. Lewis
Paris (1979-80)................................. Willie Miller
Hill Street Blues (1981-87)........ Officer Bobby Hill

WASSON, CRAIG

Films:
Go Tell the Spartans (1978)
   .... Corporal Stephen Courcey
Schizoid (1980) ....Doug
Four Friends (1981)........................... Danilo Prozor
Ghost Story (1981)................................. Don/David
   0:08 - Brief frontal nudity falling out the window,
   then buns, landing next to the pool. **
   0:41 - Buns, making love with Alice Krige in
   bedroom. *
Body Double (1984)...Jake
The Men's Club (1986).....................................Paul
Nightmare on Elm Street Part III: The Dream
   Warriors (1987) ....Dr. Neil Goldman
Made for TV Movies:
Skag (1980) ....David Skagska
Why Me? (1984) ....
TV:
Phyllis (1977).......................................Mark Valenti

WATERSTON, SAM

Films:
The Great Gatsby (1974)..................Nick Carraway
Rancho Deluxe (1975)........................ Cecil Colson
Capricorn One (1978)...........................Peter Willis
Interiors (1978)..Mike
Sweet William (1979)...................................William
   0:27 - Buns, seen through a window in the door,
   standing on balcony with Jenny Agutter. *
Heaven's Gate (1980)......................................Canton
Hopscotch (1980)..Cutter
The Killing Fields (1984)............ Sydney Schanberg
Warning Sign (1985)................................ Cal Morse

Just Between Friends (1986) .... Harry Crandall
September (1987)... Peter
Made for Cable Movies:
Finnegan Begin Again (1985) ....
Miniseries:
Q.E.D. (1982)............................Quentin E. Deverill
Made for TV Movies:
The Glass Menagerie (1973) ....

WEAVING, HUGO

Films:
For Love Alone (1985)...
The Right Hand Man (1987)...................................
...Almost (1990; Australia)................................Jake
   0:52 - Very brief out of focus buns when he drops
   his pants in front of Rosanna Arquette. Don't
   see his face. Note in the very next scene, he's
   wearing underwear!

WEHE, OLIVER

Films:
Erendira (1983; Brazil)...............................Ulysses
   1:24 - Buns, getting into bed with "Erendira." *

WELLER, PETER

Films:
Just Tell Me What You Want (1980)
   .... Steven Routledge
Shoot the Moon (1982).................Frank Henderson
Of Unknown Origin (1983) ....Bart
The Adventures of Buckaroo Banzai (1984)
   ....Buckaroo Banzai
First Born (1984) ....
Robocop (1987) .... Alex Murphy/Robocop
The Tunnel (1987)...................................Juan Pablo
Shakedown (1988)............................Roland Dalton
Leviathan (1989)............................. William Beck
Robocop 2 (1990)............... Alex Murphy/Robocop
Made for HBO:
Apology (1986)................................. Rad Hungare
   1:03 - Brief buns, putting pants on, getting out of
   bed to chase after intruder at night. *
Women & Men: Stories of Seduction (1990).Hobie
Faerie Tale Theatre:
The Dancing Princess (1984)...................................

WESTON, JACK

Films:
Gator (1976)..
Can't Stop the Music (1980)................................
Four Seasons (1981).....................Danny Zimmer
   0:48 - Brief buns in water while skinny dipping
   with Rita Moreno. *
High Road to China (1983).................................
Dirty Dancing (1987)..
Ishtar (1987)..
Short Circuit 2 (1988)......................Oscar Baldwin

WHITING, LEONARD
Films:
Romeo and Juliet (1968)................................Romeo
1:34 - Buns, in bed with "Juliet," then getting out
to stretch. Long scene. **

WILBY, JAMES
Films:
Maurice (1987)..
A Summer Story (1988).....................Frank Ashton
0:08 - Buns in creek with "Mr. Garten" while
skinny dipping. *
A Handful of Dust (1988)........................ Tony Last

WILDER, GENE
Films:
The Producers (1967)............................. Leo Bloom
Quackser Fortune has a Cousin in the Bronx
(1970; Irish)................................Quackser Fortune
Start the Revolution Without Me (1970)
.................................Claude Coupe/Philippe De Sisi
Willy Wonka and the Chocolate Factory (1971)
....Willy Wonka
Blazing Saddles (1974)...Jim
The Little Prince (1974; British)................. The Fox
Young Frankenstein (1974; B&W)
....Dr. Frankenstein
The Adventure of Sherlock Holmes' Smarter
Brother (1975)........................... Sigerson Holmes
Silver Streak (1976)....................... George Caldwell
The World's Greatest Lover (1977). Rudy Valentine
The Frisco Kid (1979) .... Avram Belinsky
Stir Crazy (1980) .... Skip Donahue
Hanky Panky (1982)........................Michael Jordon
The Woman in Red (1984)........... Theodore Pierce
1:15 - Side view of buns getting back into bed
with Kelly Le Brock after getting out to take his
underwear off the lamp. *
Haunted Honeymoon (1986) ....Larry Abbot
See No Evil, Hear No Evil (1989)....................Dave

WILLIAMS, TREAT
Films:
The Ritz (1976)..
Hair (1979)... Berger
0:57 - Buns, taking off clothes and diving into
pond with "Hud" and "Woof." *
1941 (1979)..
Prince of the City (1981) .... Daniel Ciello
The Pursuit of D. B. Cooper (1981)...............Meade
Flashpoint (1984)..
Smooth Talk (1985)............................ Arnold Friend
The Men's Club (1986) ....Terry
Dead Heat (1988)................................ Roger Mortis
Sweet Lies (1988)..

Made for HBO:
A Streetcar Named Desire (1984).............................
Third Degree Burn (1989).................Scott Weston
0:43 - Brief buns taking off his robe with Virginia
Madsen in his bedroom. *

WILSON, ROBERT BRIAN
Films:
Silent Night, Deadly Night (1984).........Billy at 18
0:30 - Sort of buns in bed with "Pamela." *

WILSON, ROGER
Films:
Porky's (1981)................................... Mickey
Porky's II: The Next Day (1983)................. Mickey
Second Time Lucky (1986)................Adam Smith
0:13 - Buns, in the Garden of Eden. **
0:30 - Buns, standing out in the rain. **
Thunder Alley (1986)....................................Richie
TV:
Seven Brides for Seven Brothers (1982-83)
....Daniel McFadden

WINN, DAVID
Films:
My Therapist (1983)............................ Mike Jenner
0:19 - Buns, making love with Marilyn Chambers
in bed. **

WOLTZ, RANDY
Films:
The Young Warriors (1983; U.S./Canada)
...."Brick Test" Frank
0:16 - Dropping his pants in a room during pledge
at fraternity. *

WOOD, TIMOTHY
Films:
Love Circles Around the World (1984).... Michael
1:29 - Frontal nudity, lying in bed with "Jill" after
making love while video taping it. **

WOODS, JAMES
Films:
Night Moves (1975)..................................... Quentin
The Onion Field (1979).................Gregory Powell
1:33 - Buns, taking a shower in the prison. **
The Black Marble (1980).........................Fiddler
Fast Walking (1981)............. Fast-Walking Miniver
Split Image (1982) ....Prattt
Videodrome (1983; Canadian)................Max Renn
Against All Odds (1984)..........................Jake Wise
Once Upon a Time in America (1984)..............Max
Cat's Eye (1985)....................................... Morrison
Joshua Then and Now (1985; Canadian)
....Joshua Shapiro

Salvador (1986)....................Richard Boyle
Best Seller (1988).............................Cleve
Cop (1988).........................Lloyd Hopkins
True Believer (1989).............Eddie Dodd
The Boost (1989)..................Lenny Brown
Immediate Family (1989)...............Michael Spector
Miniseries:
Holocaust (1978)......................Karl Weiss
Made for HBO:
Women & Men: Stories of Seduction (1990)
....Robert
Made for TV Movies:
My Name is Bill W. (1989)...................Bill Wilson

WOODS, MICHAEL
Films:
Lady Beware (1987)................Jack Price
0:43 - Buns, lying down in Diane Lane's bed. **
TV:
Bare Essence (1983)...........................Sean Benedict
Our Family Honor (1985-86).... Jerry Cole (Danzig)
Capital News (1990)..............................Clay Gibson

WRIGHT, DORSEY
Films:
Hair (1979)...Hud
0:57 - Buns, taking off clothes and diving into
    pond with Treat Williams and "Woof." *

Y

YOUNGS, JIM
Films:
Out of Control (1984)...................Cowboy
0:54 - Buns making love with Claudia Udy. *
Nobody's Fool (1986).......................Billy
Youngblood (1986).....................Kelly Youngblood
Hot Shot (1986)...
You Talkin' To Me (1987).......................................

YURASEK, JOHN
Films:
Less than Zero (1987)........................... Naked Man
1:22 - Brief buns standing up from bed when
    Andrew McCarthy discovers him with Robert
    Downey, Jr. *

Z

ZANE, BILLY
Films:
Back to the Future (1985)............................... Match
Critters (1986)...........................Steve Elliot
Dead Calm (1989)........................Hughie Warriner
1:01 - Buns, walking around on the boat. *
Back to the Future, Part II (1989)...................Match
Made for TV Movies:
The Case of the Hillside Stranglers (1989)
....Kenneth Bianchi

OTHER SOURCES

An excellent magazine that you should definitely check out is *Celebrity Sleuth*. In it, you'll find photographs of many celebrities that don't or won't do nudity for video tapes. People like Jackie Onassis, Karen Lynn Gorney, Deidre Hall, Carey Lowell and Caroline Munro are featured in various issues of *Celebrity Sleuth*. If you can't find it at your local newsstand or you need back issues, contact:

Celebrity Sleuth
P.O. Box 273
West Redding, CT 06896

If you can't find the video tapes listed in *The Bare Facts Video Guide* for rent at your local video tape rental stores, an excellent source for purchasing video tapes is *Movies Unlimited*. Their catalog costs $7.95 plus $2.00 shipping, but you get a $5.00 credit voucher to use on your order. The address is:

Movies Unlimited
6736 Castor Avenue
Philadelphia, PA 19149

Back issues of *Playboy* magazine can be purchased through *The Playboy Catalog*. Their catalog is free by calling 1-800-345-6066. They have a large assortment of *Playboy* magazine back issues from the 1960's to the present in addition to *Playboy Video Magazines* and other video tapes.

Another source for locating hard to find video tapes is *Critic's Choice*. Their catalog is free by calling 1-800-544-9852. They have over 2,300 video tapes for sale. They also have a Video Search Line that operates Monday through Friday, from 9 a.m. to 5 p.m. EST. Their phone number is 1-900-370-6500. The cost is $1 for the first minute and $.50 for each additional minute. They will research your request and call you back within 1 to 2 weeks. The decision to buy–or not to buy–is yours.

The book I use to help locate adult film stars is called, *The Blue Guide to Adult Film Stars*. It is published every January and is available for $19.95 (plus $2.55 for shipping and handling. New Jersey residents add 6% sales tax.) from:

> The Blue Guide
> Box 16
> Ogdensburg, NJ   07439
> (201)-729-3022

If you are interested in writing to your favorite actor or actress to get an autograph or ask a question, you might want to purchase the book *Celebrity Access - The Directory*. The cost is $19.95 (plus $1.75 for shipping and handling. California residents add 6.25% sales tax.) and is available from:

> Thomas Burford
> 20 Sunnyside Avenue, Suite A241
> Mill Valley, CA   94941
> (415) 389-8133

If you are interested in viewing the Rob Lowe video tape that he accidentally made in 1989, you can purchase it from Al Goldstein, publisher of *Screw* magazine. His New York cable TV show, *Midnight Blue*, showed some of the footage on show #672. The cost is $29.95, you need to specify VHS or Beta. Contact:

> Media Ranch, Inc.
> P.O. Box 432
> Old Chelsea Station
> New York, NY   10013

Since all of the descriptions in *The Bare Facts Video Guide* are listed by minutes, you should have a VCR that uses a real-time counter. VCR's made by Mistubishi and Sony do this as well as S-VHS models from most all the manufacturers.

REFERENCES

Books:

The Complete Directory to Prime Time Network TV Shows, 1946-Present
Tim Brooks and Earle Marsh
Ballantine, 1985

HBO's Guide to Movies on Videocassette and Cable TV 1990
Daniel Eagan
Harper & Ross, 1989

The Motion Picture Guide
Stanley Ralph Ross and Jay Robert Nash
CineBooks, Inc., 1984

Roger Ebert's Movie Home Companion 1990 Edition
Roger Ebert
Andrews and McMeel, 1989

Video Movie Guide 1990
Mick Martin and Marsha Porter
Ballantine, 1989

The Blue Guide to Adult Film Stars - 1990 Edition
FD Enterprises, 1990

MORE REFERENCES

Periodicals:

The Cable Guide magazine
Various issues from 1987-1990
TVSM, Inc., 309 Lakeside Drive, Horsham, PA 19044

Movies Unlimited catalog
Various catalogs from 1987-1990
Movies Unlimited, 6736 Castor Avenue, Philadelphia, PA 19149

Playboy magazine
Various issues from 1972-1990
919 North Michigan Avenue, Chicago, IL 60611

Penthouse magazine
Various issues from 1980-1990
1965 Broadway, New York, NY 10023-5965

Premiere magazine
Various issues from 1987-1990
Premiere Publishing, 2 Park Avenue, New York, New York 10016

The San Jose Mercury News newspaper
Various issues from 1987-1990
750 Ridder Park Drive, San Jose, CA 95190

TV Guide magazine
Various issues from 1987-1990
Triangle Publications, Inc., 100 Matsonford Road, Radnor, PA 19088

Movie Collector's World newsletter
Various issues from 1988-1989
P.O. Box 309 Fraser, MI 48026

ABOUT THE AUTHOR

Craig Hosoda is a Software Engineer. He grew up in Silicon Valley
California, then went to the University of California at Berkeley where he
graduated with a B.S. degree in Electrical Engineering and Computer
Science. After graduation, he worked at Hewlett-Packard for two years
before getting a programming job at Industrial Light and Magic, George
Lucas' special effects division of Lucasfilm Ltd.

While working at ILM, the seeds for *The Bare Facts Video Guide* were
planted during a casual conversation one day with his friend, Marty
Brenneis. While working on the film, *Howard the Duck*, Marty asked
Craig about Lea Thompson's film credits. When Marty didn't know about
her nude scene in *All the Right Moves*, Craig thought, "There should be a
book that lists all this important information in one place..."

After moving back to Silicon Valley in 1987 to start raising a family with
his wife, he began research for the book during the evenings while
working as a software engineer during the day. Unfortunately, it was
difficult to balance a full-time job, work on *The Bare Fact* and have time
for his family, so in July 1990, he quit his full-time job to devote his life to
uncovering the bare facts.